SEVENTH EDITION

EMPLOYEE BENEFITS

Burton T. Beam, Jr.
John J. McFadden

Dearborn™
Real Estate Education

This publication is designed to provide accurate and authoritative information in regard to the subject matter covered. It is sold with the understanding that the publisher is not engaged in rendering legal, accounting, or other professional service. If legal advice or other expert assistance is required, the services of a competent professional person should be sought.

President: Roy Lipner
Publisher: Evan M. Butterfield
Associate Publisher: Louise Benzer
Editorial Project Manager: Michael J. Scafuri
Managing Editor, Production: Daniel Frey
Quality Assurance Editor: David Shaw
Creative Director: Lucy Jenkins

Published by Dearborn™ Real Estate Education
a division of Dearborn Financial Publishing, Inc.®
30 South Wacker Drive
Suite 2500
Chicago, IL 60606-7481
(312) 836-4400
http://www.dearbornRE.com

Printed in the United States of America.

05   06   07   10 9 8 7 6 5 4 3 2 1

Library of Congress Cataloging-in-Publication Data

Beam, Burton T.
   Employee benefits / Burton T. Beam, Jr., John J. McFadden.—7th ed.
    p. cm.
   Includes bibliographical references and index.
   ISBN 0-7931-9174-2
   1. Employee fringe benefits--United States. 2. Compensation management--United States. I. McFadden, John J. II. Title.
   HD4928.N62U623 2005
   658.3'25--dc22   2004017110

To Betsy, Greg, Grant, Gretchen, and Claire
Burton T. Beam, Jr.

To Diane, Rhoda, and Susanna
John J. McFadden

CONTENTS

Over the last two decades, few fields have changed as dramatically as that of employee benefits. Employers are spending an ever-increasing portion of total compensation dollars on benefit plans. Some of this increased spending is a result of new or expanded benefits being offered. However, a significant portion of the increase arises because the cost of certain benefits, such as medical expense coverage, has risen at a faster rate than wages. This spiraling cost has made employers increasingly concerned with containing benefit costs.

Legislation has also had a significant effect on employee benefit plans, causing employers to continually monitor and often to revise their plans. For example, the impact of the Employee Retirement Income Security Act of 1974 (ERISA) and subsequent legislation continually alters the area of pensions. The Age Discrimination in Employment Act resulted in benefits being provided to persons who previously had coverages terminated at a certain age, such as 65, and the Health Insurance Portability and Accountability Act of 1996 has greatly changed the area of medical expense insurance. In addition, the states continue to mandate the types of benefits that employees must be provided.

The federal tax treatment of employee benefit plans also has had a particularly significant impact on employee benefit plans. Certain types of plans, such as medical expense plans and qualified retirement plans, owe their popularity in large part to federal tax advantages. Cafeteria plans, consumer-directed health plans, and Section 401(k) cash-or-deferred plans have become more widespread largely because of legislative clarification of their tax treatment. Since the tax benefits for employee benefit plans result in a substantial annual loss of federal tax revenues, Congress has imposed an elaborate and ever-changing scheme of regulation on these plans; in the last 15 years, there have been 14 major tax law changes. The information in this text reflects current law through mid-2004.

This changing environment and the resultant need for up-to-date materials was one reason for the first edition of this book and has remained a major consideration in the latest edition. Since the last edition of the book was prepared, there have been significant changes affecting employee benefits.

Nowhere have the changes occurred any faster than in the area of medical expense coverage. Managed care plans have, by far, become the dominant method of providing medical expense coverage to employees. However, this has led to a consumer backlash and concern over the quality of care. There has been considerable reaction to this backlash at the state level and through voluntary changes adopted by managed care plans. Debate on the issue continues at the federal level. Employers have also reacted by increasingly requiring accreditation of managed care plans that they offer to their employees.

Within the managed care arena, there have also been significant changes as plans continue to evolve. Concerns about restrictions on the ability of patients to select their own providers have led to the continued growth of preferred-provider arrangements and point-of-service plans at the expense of HMOs.

All types of medical expense plans are more likely to provide an increasing array of benefits for alternatives to traditional medicine. In addition, carve-outs for benefits, such as prescription drugs and disease management, continue to grow in use.

Finally, considerable interest is being shown in consumer-directed health plans by both employees and employers. Such plans, at least in theory, give employees an incentive to control medical care expenditures.

These changes are all reflected in a significant revision of the chapters on medical expense benefits.

Some of the other changes for this edition are explained below.

■ Key terms have been highlighted in each chapter and also listed at the end of each chapter.

■ Examples have been set off from the main text, and more examples have been added.

■ Links to Internet Web sites have been added.

■ A Glossary has been added to the book.

■ Statistics and indexed numbers have been changed throughout the book as needed.

■ Coverage on outsourcing of benefits has been expanded.

■ The chapter on Social Security and Medicare has been revised and expanded to include numerous changes, including Medicare Advantages plans and prescription drug coverage.

■ Increased emphasis has been given to voluntary benefit plans.

■ Coverage has been added on the Financial Services Modernization Act.

■ The section on group universal life insurance has been reorganized.

■ Coverage has been added on paid time off (PTO) programs.

■ The material on group dental insurance and group long-term care insurance has been rewritten to reflect the current market.

■ Material on the Uniformed Services Employment and Reemployment Rights Act (USERRA) has been added.

■ The retirement plan and IRA material has been revised to reflect the many significant changes resulting from recent tax law changes, including the Economic Growth and Tax Relief Reconciliation Act of 2001 (EGTRRA) and the Jobs and Growth Tax Relief Reconciliation Act of 2003 (JGTRRA).

■ Important changes in tax regulations are incorporated, such as the new regulations for minimum distributions from qualified plans and IRAs.

■ The chapters relating to qualified retirement plans have been revised and reorganized to reflect current practice in retirement plan design.

■ Coverage of defined benefit plans has been reduced from two chapters to one and reorganized to reflect the current role of defined benefit plans. Material that has become less relevant to current plan design has been de-emphasized.

We have continued to use four other major guidelines in preparing this book. First, the book covers the broad spectrum of employee benefits, from social insurance programs to executive benefits. Second, the book is applicable to all sizes of employer groups, from the small employer using a multiple-employer trust to the large employer relying on alternative funding methods, including self-insurance. Third, the book explains the decisions involved in designing an employee benefit plan; it doesn't just describe the products available. Finally, we have tried to write a book that can be used not only in courses given by colleges and professional organizations but also as a reference resource for practitioners.

We have also tried to write a book that can be flexible for classroom use. If students have had other insurance courses, perhaps the material on social insurance could be eliminated. Depending on the length of the course and student backgrounds, the detailed material on group insurance taxation and rate making might be skipped or covered superficially. In the retirement plan part, Chapters 26, 27, and possibly 28 could also be omitted. The material on retirement plans could also logically be taught before the material on group insurance and other welfare benefits.

It was difficult to decide where we should place the chapter on employee benefit planning and management. On the one hand, readers should be aware of the importance of planning and management issues before they pursue the material further. On the other hand, they will probably better understand the issues after they are familiar with the benefit environment and the products and services that exist in this environment. We recommend that the principles of the chapter not be ignored after an initial reading. This is an important chapter that should be reviewed again after the remainder of the book is read.

The changing nature of employee benefits makes it essential to remain up-to-date. For this reason, we have included a list of additional resources, including Web sites. We particularly urge readers to become familiar with the loose-leaf services, periodicals, and Web sites mentioned.

■ LEGAL REFERENCES IN THIS TEXT

In this text, legal authorities will be cited occasionally to help in finding further information about the subject, if the reader wishes. The term *the Code* will be used in referring to the Internal Revenue Code, and the Treasury Regulations will be cited as *the regulations*, with other citations given more fully. ERISA *Section 000* will be used to refer to the indicated section of the Employee Retirement Income Security Act of 1974.

No attempt is made to provide a complete citation of authorities for all of the propositions set forth. However, the general discussion in this text should be adequate to enable the interested reader to obtain citations of the necessary legal authorities from one of the loose-leaf qualified plan or tax services or one of the handbooks in the field of qualified plans. If accurate legal references are to be obtained, it is important to have thorough and up-to-date materials, because the legal authorities are voluminous and subject to very frequent change.

■ ACKNOWLEDGMENTS

As with any undertaking of this scope, we owe gratitude to the many persons who have been helpful in making this book a reality, from those persons who were immensely helpful in preparing the first edition to those who have offered valuable suggestions for its revisions.

We would like to thank the following reviewers for their contributions to the seventh edition: Thomas J. Atchison, Economic Research Institute; Nita Cahn, Amstar Group, LTD, and Keller Graduate School of Management; Michael J. McNamara, Washington State University; and Robert T. Trimper, Adjunct Professor, College of Business Administration, Northeastern University.

We owe a particular gratitude to Evelyn Rice for her hard work in helping us with the preparation of this manuscript.

Finally, we wish to acknowledge The American College, Bryn Mawr, Pennsylvania, for giving us permission to use the copyrighted material previously written by Burton T. Beam, Jr., and contained in *Group Benefits: Basic Concepts and Alternatives,* 10th edition (2004).

Burton T. Beam, Jr.
John J. McFadden

PART ONE

Introduction

CHAPTER 1

Introduction to Employee Benefits

OBJECTIVES

■ Explain the meaning of the term *employee benefits*.

■ Explain the significance of employee benefits in terms of both employer cost and benefits provided to employees.

■ Identify the factors that have influenced the growth of employee benefits and explain the significance of each factor.

■ Identify the employee benefit trends that are likely to occur in the near future.

■ Identify the job opportunities available in the field of employee benefits.

CHAPTER OUTLINE

In the early part of the 20th century, very few employees received any compensation from their employers other than direct wages for time actually worked. Employees or their families were responsible for meeting the needs of old age, poor health, and death. Vacations, if allowed at all, were usually without pay.

The 1940s and 1950s witnessed the increasing use and acceptance of employee benefits as a form of compensation in addition to direct wages. During the last two decades, this growth accelerated as new types of benefits were added and existing benefits expanded. Further, while employee benefits were once fairly standardized and free of government regulations, employers must now make more complex decisions regarding the benefits to be provided and the methods with which these benefits are funded.

■ DEFINITION OF EMPLOYEE BENEFITS

Before continuing, it is best to define exactly what is meant by **employee benefits**. The narrowest definition of employee benefits includes only employer-provided benefits for situations involving death, accident, sickness, retirement, or unemployment. Even this narrow interpretation produces disagreement over whether the definition should include benefits that are financed by employer contributions but are provided under social insurance programs, such as workers' compensation insurance, unemployment insurance, Social Security, and Medicare.[1]

On the other hand, the broadest definition of employee benefits includes all benefits and services, other than wages for time worked, that employees receive in whole or in part from their employers. This book uses a broad definition and defines employee benefits as including the following five categories[2]:

1. Legally required payments for government programs. These include employer contributions to such programs as the following:
   - Social Security
   - Medicare
   - Unemployment compensation insurance
   - Workers' compensation insurance
   - Temporary disability insurance

2. Payments for private insurance and retirement plans. These include the cost of establishing such plans, as well as contributions in the form of insurance premiums or payments through alternative funding arrangements. Benefits are provided under these plans for personal loss exposures, for example:
   - Old age
   - Death
   - Disability
   - Long-term care expenses
   - Medical expenses
   - Dental expenses
   - Legal expenses
   - Property and liability losses

3. Payments or other benefits for time not worked. These include the following:
   - Vacations
   - Holidays
   - Jury duty
   - Maternity/paternity leave
   - Reserve/National Guard duty
   - Military leave

4. Extra cash payments, other than wages and bonuses based on performance, to employees. Benefits in this category may include the following:
   - Educational assistance
   - Moving expenses
   - Suggestion awards
   - Christmas bonuses

5. Cost of services to employees, for example:
   - Subsidized cafeterias
   - Employee discounts
   - Wellness programs
   - Employee-assistance programs
   - Day care
   - Adoption assistance
   - Financial planning programs
   - Retirement counseling
   - Free parking

■ BOOK OVERVIEW

The first category previously mentioned is usually referred to as **social insurance**, and is covered in Part Two of this book. The remaining categories are commonly called **group benefits** and consist of group insurance, other nonretirement benefits, and retirement benefits. The legal term that is often applied to group insurance and other nonretirement benefits is **welfare benefits**. Group insurance benefits are discussed in Part Three and other nonretirement benefits are covered in Part Four. Part Five is devoted to a discussion of retirement benefits.

■ SIGNIFICANCE OF EMPLOYEE BENEFITS

Looking at some often quoted data of the U.S. Chamber of Commerce, LIMRA International, and the Bureau of Labor Statistics can best show the significance of employee benefits. These data come from surveys conducted by the three organizations and are periodically updated. It often takes a year or more to collect and tabulate these statistics, and the data shown are for the latest survey years available at the time this book was revised.

U.S. Chamber of Commerce

In a 2003 study of 372 companies that employed the full-time equivalent of over 506,578 employees, the U.S. Chamber of Commerce found that the average payment by employers for employee benefits was equal to 42.3 percent of payroll.[3] This figure has increased from 3 percent in 1929, 21.5 percent in 1965, and 30 percent in 1975. Of the 42.3 percent figure, 8.7 percent of payroll went for the employer's share of legally required social insurance payments, 6.2 percent for payments to private retirement and savings plans, and 15.2 percent for medical and medically related benefits. The remaining 12.2 percent was for all other types of benefits, with paid vacations being the single most costly item in this category. The study showed substantial variations among business firms, with one-tenth of employers having benefit costs less than 21.4 percent of payroll and another one-tenth having benefit costs in excess of 48.7 percent. Large variations were also shown by industry, with public utilities having the highest percentage (56.6) and rental, leasing, and real estate having the lowest (25.8). Within specific industries, benefit percentages tend to be higher for firms with 100 employees or more than for firms with fewer than 100 employees, and nonmanufacturing firms have slightly higher percentages than manufacturing firms. The percentages also vary by geographic region, from 34.0 in the Pacific states (Alaska, California, Hawaii, Oregon, and Washington) to 49.7 in the West South Central states (Arkansas, Louisiana, Oklahoma, and Texas). In addition, metropolitan areas have a higher percentage (43.0) than do nonmetropolitan areas (41.2).

The Chamber of Commerce study also shows that employees received an average of $18,000 in benefits. However, there was a significant range, with one-tenth of employees receiving more than $25,684 and one-tenth receiving $7,358 or less. These variations are the result of company, industry, geographic, and employee differences.

In addition to employer costs, employee payroll deductions for benefits averaged $6,749, equal to 15.3 percent of payroll. The majority of this amount was for Social Security and Medicare taxes and contributions to retirement and savings plans.

The complete Chamber of Commerce study can often be found in libraries or at local chambers of commerce. It can also be ordered on the U.S. Chamber of Commerce's Web site: *www.uschamber.com.*

LIMRA International

LIMRA International is a membership organization of life insurance and financial services organizations that provides marketing and distribution information and advice to its more than 800 members. The data it gathers and the reports it issues can be found on its Web site: *www.limra.com.* However, much of its data is proprietary and can be accessed by members only.

One 2003 LIMRA report is devoted to the changing group insurance marketplace, and one portion of that report contains statistics about the percentage of employers that provide certain group insurance benefits to at least some of their employees. This information, broken down by employer size, is based on telephone interviews with more than 1,000 employers. Table 1.1 shows a portion of these statistics.

Bureau of Labor Statistics

The Bureau of Labor Statistics is part of the U.S. Department of Labor and maintains many databases for the department. Periodically, the bureau publishes detailed information on the wages, earnings, and benefits of workers. The latest information from the bureau is on its Web site: *www.bls.gov.*

| TABLE 1.1 | Percentage of Employers Offering Selected Group Insurance Benefits, by Size of Employer[4] |

Group Insurance Benefit	Size (by Number of Employees)					
	10–19	20–99	100–499	500–999	1,000–4,999	5,000 or more
Life	56%	78%	94%	98%	98%	99%
Medical expense	79	92	98	98	99	99
Accidental death and dismemberment	37	58	86	91	92	97
Dental	44	68	90	97	98	99
Vision	37	53	65	69	72	82
Short-term disability income	29	41	61	65	68	74
Long-term disability income	26	45	73	86	89	96

The latest survey, conducted in 2003, obtained data from 2,924 private industry establishments, representing nearly 103 million workers. Nearly 79 million of these were full-time workers, and slightly over 24 million were part-time. Table 1.2 shows the percentages of employees participating in life and disability income plans. Before viewing these statistics, note that they are for employees who *participate* in these plans. The number of employees who work for employers that provide such benefits plans to at least some employees is much higher. For example, the LIMRA International statistics cited previously indicate that almost all employers with 100 or more employees offer medical expense and life insurance benefits to employees. There are several reasons for this difference. Many employees may not meet the eligibility requirements for plan benefits. For example, eligibility for long-term disability income benefits may require a minimum length of service, full-time status, and income above a certain amount. In addition, when employees are required to pay all or a portion of the cost of a benefit, they may decline the benefit because they cannot afford it or because they see little value in it. For example, young employees with no dependents may decline life insurance coverage.

Table 1.3 shows the percentage of employees participating in medical expense plans. What some observers view as disturbing about these statistics is that the number of employees participating in medical expense plans is only 45 percent. This percentage has dropped from 63 percent only 10 years ago. A large number of persons who do not have coverage from their own employer have coverage as a dependent under a spouse's or parent's plan. However, many persons are not eligible for benefits, usually because they work part-time. In addition, many low-paid workers fail to elect coverage because they cannot afford the required employee contributions. For both of these reasons, the numbers of Americans who are uninsured for medical expenses continues to grow.

Tables 1.4 and 1.5 show the percentages of workers who have *access* to other selected nonretirement benefits. With the exception of long-term care insurance, these benefits are typically provided to eligible employees without any employee cost-sharing.

| TABLE 1.2 | Percentage of Workers Participating in Life and Disability Income Insurance by Selected Characteristics, Private Industry[5] | | |

Characteristics	Life	Disability Benefits	
		Short-Term Disability	Long-Term Disability
All Employees	47	37	28
Worker Characteristics			
White-collar occupations	54	40	40
Blue-collar occupations	50	44	20
Service occupations	25	20	10
Full time	59	45	36
Part time	9	12	4
Union	61	68	27
Nonunion	46	34	29
Average wage less than $15 per hour	37	27	16
Average wage $15 per hour or higher	64	52	49
Establishment Characteristics			
Goods-producing	58	54	29
Service-producing	44	32	28
1–99 workers	33	26	18
100 workers or more	64	50	40
Geographic Areas			
Metropolitan areas	48	38	30
Nonmetropolitan areas	45	31	17
New England	42	33	29
Middle Atlantic	46	76	27
East North Central	53	37	30
West North Central	46	36	29
South Atlantic	49	29	31
East South Central	59	38	26
West South Central	48	28	28
Mountain	40	19	23
Pacific	41	27	28

In the case of long-term care insurance, employees usually pay all or most of the premium cost for the benefit.

Table 1.6 shows the percentage of workers who participate in retirement plans. Note that the percentage for all plans is less than the sum of the percentages for defined-benefit plans and defined-contribution plans. The discrepancy occurs because some employers have both types of plans.

TABLE 1.3	Percentage of Workers Participating in Medical Expense Plans, by Selected Characteristics, Private Industry[6]		
Characteristics	**Medical Care**	**Dental Care**	**Vision Care**
All Employees	45	32	19
Worker Characteristics			
White-collar occupations	50	37	21
Blue-collar occupations	51	33	20
Service occupations	22	15	9
Full time	56	40	23
Part time	9	6	5
Union	60	51	37
Nonunion	44	30	17
Average wage less than $15 per hour	35	22	12
Average wage $15 per hour or higher	61	47	28
Establishment Characteristics			
Goods-producing	57	42	25
Service-producing	42	29	17
1–99 workers	36	21	11
100 workers or more	55	44	27
Geographic Areas			
Metropolitan areas	45	33	19
Nonmetropolitan areas	44	27	17
New England	43	31	14
Middle Atlantic	47	32	24
East North Central	47	34	17
West North Central	43	31	17
South Atlantic	44	30	14
East South Central	53	37	28
West South Central	47	30	17
Mountain	34	28	17
Pacific	45	33	24

■ FACTORS INFLUENCING THE GROWTH OF EMPLOYEE BENEFITS

No single factor can be identified as the reason for the substantial growth in employee benefits over time. Rather, this growth has resulted from a combination of elements, many of which are applicable to employee benefits in general. Frequently mentioned factors include (1) industrialization, (2) the influence of organized labor, (3) wage controls, (4) cost advantages, (5) inflation, and (6) state and federal legislation.

| TABLE 1.4 | Percentage of Workers with Access to Selected Benefits, by Selected Characteristics, Private Industry[7] |

Characteristics	Paid Holidays	Paid Vacations	Paid Jury Duty Leave	Paid Military Leave
All Employees	79	79	70	50
Worker Characteristics				
White-collar occupations	86	84	79	59
Blue-collar occupations	85	84	69	46
Service occupations	54	61	46	34
Full time	91	91	77	56
Part time	43	40	45	33
Union	91	90	85	56
Nonunion	78	78	68	50
Average wage less than $15 per hour	72	73	60	42
Average wage $15 per hour or higher	91	90	84	64
Establishment Characteristics				
Goods-producing	90	87	76	56
Service-producing	76	77	68	48
1–99 workers	74	73	57	38
100 workers or more	86	87	84	64
Geographic Areas				
Metropolitan areas	79	79	71	51
Nonmetropolitan areas	80	79	61	44
New England	77	79	69	54
Middle Atlantic	83	85	72	54
East North Central	83	81	73	53
West North Central	74	71	70	50
South Atlantic	79	80	71	50
East South Central	81	79	72	45
West South Central	77	79	68	53
Mountain	75	73	71	51
Pacific	80	79	62	41

Industrialization

During the 19th century, the United States made the transition from an agrarian economy to one characterized by increasing industrialization and urbanization. The economic consequences of death, sickness, accidents, and old age became more significant as individuals began to depend more on monetary wages than on self-reliance and

	Child Care	Adoption Assistance	Long-Term Care Insurance	Subsidized Commuting
Characteristics				
All Employees	18	9	11	5
Worker Characteristics				
White-collar occupations	26	13	16	7
Blue-collar occupations	10	6	7	4
Service occupations	10	2	4	2
Full time	21	10	13	6
Part time	11	5	4	2
Union	25	13	16	8
Nonunion	18	19	11	5
Average wage less than $15 per hour	11	5	6	3
Average wage $15 per hour or higher	31	16	19	9
Establishment Characteristics				
Goods-producing	16	9	11	5
Service-producing	19	9	11	5
1–99 workers	7	3	3	2
100 workers or more	32	16	20	9
Geographic Areas				
Metropolitan areas	21	10	12	6
Nonmetropolitan areas	5	2	4	1
New England	22	11	11	8
Middle Atlantic	24	12	12	8
East North Central	21	10	10	2
West North Central	17	7	7	3
South Atlantic	15	9	14	2
East South Central	16	4	7	5
West South Central	14	8	10	6
Mountain	19	7	7	6
Pacific	17	8	14	10

TABLE 1.5 Percentage of Workers with Access to Selected Benefits, by Selected Characteristics, Private Industry[8]

family ties to meet their basic needs. As a result, some employers began to provide retirement, death, and medical benefits to their employees. Although benevolence may have influenced the decision to provide such benefits, the principal reason was probably the employers' realization that it was in their own best interest to do so. Not only did

TABLE 1.6	Percentage of Workers Participating in Retirement Plans, by Selected Characteristics, Private Industry[9]		
Characteristics	**All Plans**	**Defined Benefit**	**Defined Contribution**
All Employees	49	20	40
Worker Characteristics			
White-collar occupations	59	22	51
Blue-collar occupations	20	24	38
Service occupations	21	7	16
Full time	58	24	48
Part time	18	8	14
Union	83	72	39
Nonunion	45	15	40
Average wage less than $15 per hour	35	11	29
Average wage $15 per hour or higher	70	33	57
Establishment Characteristics			
Goods-producing	63	31	49
Service-producing	45	16	37
1–99 workers	35	8	31
100 workers or more	65	33	51
Geographic Areas			
Metropolitan areas	50	21	41
Nonmetropolitan areas	42	14	36
New England	44	15	37
Middle Atlantic	56	30	43
East North Central	56	23	46
West North Central	48	21	37
South Atlantic	46	16	40
East South Central	51	14	46
West South Central	42	18	35
Mountain	38	10	34
Pacific	46	20	37

such benefits improve morale and productivity, they also reduced employee turnover and the expenses associated with it.

Although some of the earlier benefits were paid directly by employers, the development of group insurance enabled these benefits to be funded by systematic payments to an insurance company. As group insurance became more common, employers were faced with adopting new or better plans to remain competitive in attracting and keeping employees. This competition in employee benefits continues to exist.

Industrialization has also led to more government benefits, such as Social Security, Medicare, unemployment insurance, and workers' compensation insurance.

Organized Labor

Since a Supreme Court ruling in 1949, there has been no question about the right of labor unions to legally negotiate for employee benefits. Although union pressures prior to that time frequently resulted in the establishment or broadening of employee benefit plans, this ruling strengthened the influence of labor unions.

Labor unions have also affected benefits for nonunion employees because some employers provide generous benefit plans in an effort to discourage their employees from unionizing. In addition, employers with both union and nonunion employees often provide the same benefits for the nonunion employees as those stipulated in the union contracts.

Wage Controls

Employee benefit plans grew substantially during World War II and the Korean War. Although wages were frozen, no restrictions were imposed on employee benefits, thus making them an important factor in attracting and retaining employees in labor markets with little unemployment. When these conflicts ended, the new and enhanced benefits remained.

Cost Advantages

Because of the economies associated with group underwriting and administration, benefits can usually be obtained at a lower cost through group insurance rather than through separate policies purchased by individual employees. Similar savings can be realized by directly providing employees with certain services, such as financial planning, day-care centers, and subsidized meals. The Internal Revenue Code also provides favorable tax treatment to employer contributions for certain types of group benefits. The employer may deduct most group insurance contributions as usual business expenses, and employees often have no taxable income as a result of employer contributions on their behalf. In addition, employees may receive tax-free benefits from certain types of group insurance plans and payments or services from many other types of group benefit programs, even if provided by employer contributions. However, there are often **nondiscrimination rules** that deny favorable tax treatment to some employees if the benefit plan does not provide equitable benefits to a large cross section of employees.

The extent of the favorable tax treatment applicable to group benefits is discussed in detail in later chapters. Nevertheless, it should be noted here that the types of group benefits with the most favorable tax treatment also tend to be the most prevalent.

Inflation

Inflation also affects group benefits. When benefit levels are related to employees' wages, the level and cost of these benefits increase as wages increase; when benefit levels are stated as fixed amounts, inflation results in employee pressure for increases. For most employers, the cost of group benefits has increased at a rate faster than wages, primarily because of the skyrocketing increase in the cost of providing medical expense benefits.

Legislation

Most states traditionally limited the types of groups that were eligible for group insurance coverage as well as the types, and in some cases the amounts, of coverage that could be written. In recent years, the majority of these states have liberalized their laws and allowed more group insurance products to be available to an increasing variety of groups.

Furthermore, the federal government and many states have passed legislation mandating that certain benefits be included in group insurance contracts or that existing benefits be broadened. Examples include legislation requiring benefits for maternity, alcoholism, and drug abuse. These added benefits have also increased the cost of providing group insurance coverage.

Other benefits, such as family leave, must now be provided by many employers.

■ THE FUTURE

The consensus among employee benefit specialists is that in the absence of adverse economic conditions, group benefits will continue to evolve and grow. Although there is anything but unanimous agreement about what the specifics of these changes will be, there is reasonable agreement about general trends in the near future:

■ Firms with fewer than 50 employees, and especially those with fewer than 10, will continue to be a market for new benefit plans—particularly with sustained economic improvement. Over the last few years, many insurance companies have developed products for this market so that small firms can now obtain products that were previously available only to large employers.

■ Because of increasing benefit costs, employers are more likely to add new benefits by using voluntary plans under which employees who want coverage pay the full cost of the coverage through payroll deduction.

■ The cost of providing medical expense benefits will continue rising faster than will the general rate of inflation. These escalating costs will present a constant challenge to employers and governments seeking to contain them.

■ Employers will continue to make employees pay a greater portion of their medical expenses through the use of consumer-directed medical expense plans and/or increased deductibles, copayments, percentage participation, or premium contributions.

■ Almost all employees will have medical expense coverage provided under managed care plans such as HMOs, PPOs, and various hybrid arrangements.

■ Employers will continue to drop or reduce retiree benefits, particularly medical expense coverage.

■ Defined-benefit retirement plans will continue to be replaced by defined-contribution plans.

■ Benefits for domestic partners will become more common.

■ There will be continued government interest in providing more secure medical expense benefits as well as in making coverage available to a greater number of workers. Change will continue to occur at the federal level, but the change will consist of small steps rather than far-reaching reform. Congress will continue to let the states act as laboratories for health care reform.

■ More employees will have benefits provided under cafeteria plans and will be able to substantially design their own benefit programs.

■ Changing demographics will lead to growth in certain benefits, such as day-care centers for children and retirement planning and long-term care insurance for the aging population.

■ The efforts to contain medical costs and the generally increasing awareness of the importance of good health bode well for the proliferation and lasting success of wellness and employee-assistance programs.

■ The use of technology will increase as employers apply software and technological advances to benefit administration. On-line information will increasingly be made available to employees.

■ OPPORTUNITIES IN EMPLOYEE BENEFITS

A question often asked of the authors of this book is "What opportunities are there for me?" Employee benefits is a broad discipline that offers opportunities for persons with a wide diversity of backgrounds. Some of these are the following:

■ Marketing majors. An important activity of any employee benefit provider is the marketing of its products and services to employers. These sales activities may be performed by commissioned agents of insurance companies, representatives of employee benefit consulting firms, and salaried employees of Blue Cross and Blue Shield plans or HMOs. Marketing departments of employee benefit providers also design and implement the sales activities of their firm.

■ Human resources/management majors. Human resources departments frequently have the task of communicating benefits to employees, and in many firms they may also administer the employee benefit program.

■ Finance majors. The employee benefit departments of many large employers are under the direction of the finance department. The finance department is often involved in the self-funding of benefits. Finance majors are also needed to determine investment strategies for the billions of dollars invested by retirement plans.

■ Insurance majors. Many employee benefits are sold by insurance companies.

■ Accounting majors. Accountants with public and private employers are often involved with employee benefit activities. Accountants in private practice frequently are in a position to advise clients about employee benefit decisions.

■ Communication majors. As employee benefits become increasingly complex and expensive, employers are demanding better communication of benefits to employees. This communication may involve in-house personnel or materials prepared by employee benefit providers or consulting firms.

■ Mathematics majors. The proper pricing of employee benefit products is an important function of the actuarial departments of employee benefit providers.

■ Social science majors. Many job opportunities for social science majors involve interaction with people and the giving of advice about programs to meet their needs. Better advice can be given with an understanding of social insurance programs, wellness programs, employee-assistance programs, dependent-care assistance programs, and the like.

■ Majors in medical fields. Today it is common for medical practitioners to be employed by benefit providers engaged in managed care activities. In fact, this is one of the growth areas for registered nurses.

The above list is merely meant as an example of the many opportunities available in the field of employee benefits. The providers of employee benefit products and services are diverse and, like any industry, need employees from a wide range of backgrounds.

■ WEB SITES AND OTHER ADDITIONAL RESOURCES

Employee benefits is an extensive and complex field of study. Although this book is far more than a broad overview of the field, it is impossible to cover every topic in detail. In addition, changes are always occurring. The Appendix following Chapter 29 contains a list of Web sites and other resources to assist readers who want more detail or to keep abreast of these changes. Relevant Web sites are also mentioned in this text where appropriate.

■ KEY TERMS

employee benefits   nondiscrimination rules   welfare benefits
group benefits   social insurance

■ STUDY QUESTIONS

1. Explain the different ways in which the term *employee benefits* may be defined.

2. The Chamber of Commerce of the United States estimates that the cost of employee benefit programs averages about 42.3 percent of payroll. What factors may account

for a particular firm's having a percentage-of-payroll figure that deviates from the average?

3. Why is the percentage of employees participating in benefit plans often lower than the percentage of employees who are eligible to participate?

4. How has organized labor influenced the growth of employee benefit plans?

5. How does inflation affect the cost of employee benefit plans?

6. Briefly explain how favorable tax laws have contributed to the growth of many types of employee benefits.

■ NOTES

1. The Social Security Administration uses a narrow definition in its studies of employee benefit plans. Its definition includes only benefits not underwritten or paid directly by federal, state, or local governments.

2. These categories are similar to those used by the Chamber of Commerce of the United States in its broad definition of employee benefits. U.S. Department of Labor, Bureau of Labor Statistics, *Employee Benefits in Private Industry, 2003,* Table 2.

3. U.S. Chamber of Commerce, *The 2003 Employee Benefits Study.*

4. LIMRA International, Inc., *The Changing Group Insurance and Health Care Marketplace: Overview 2003,* p. 23.

5. U.S. Department of Labor, Bureau of Labor Statistics, *Employee Benefits in Private Industry, 2003,* Table 2.

6. U.S. Department of Labor, Bureau of Labor Statistics, *Employee Benefits in Private Industry, 2003,* Table 3.

7. U.S. Department of Labor, Bureau of Labor Statistics, *Employee Benefits in Private Industry, 2003,* Table 4.

8. U.S. Department of Labor, Bureau of Labor Statistics, *Employee Benefits in Private Industry, 2003,* Table 5.

9. U.S. Department of Labor, Bureau of Labor Statistics, *Employee Benefits in Private Industry, 2003,* Table 5.

2

Employee Benefit Management and Planning

The significant growth in employee benefits requires increasingly complex decisions. Whether these decisions are made by employers providing benefits, unions negotiating for benefits, or employees selecting benefit options, the need for proper benefit planning is crucial. Employee benefit planning is a dynamic process that must continually be reviewed and modified if an overall benefit plan is to meet the changing needs of a changing environment.

If either a single type of group insurance plan or an overall employee benefit plan is to be properly designed and managed, many questions must be answered. For example, should the plan reflect the wants of employees or the needs of employees as perceived by the employer? Should it have a probationary period for eligibility? Under what circumstances should the plan be self-insured? These questions are only subparts of six much broader issues:

1. What are the employer's objectives?
2. What types of benefits should the plan provide?

3. What provisions for controlling costs should the plan have?
4. How should the plan be communicated to employees?
5. To what extent should administrative functions be outsourced?
6. How should the plan be funded?

Unfortunately for those who like precise answers, plan design and management is an art rather than a science. However, decisions must be made. In some cases, the advantages and disadvantages of the various answers to these questions must be weighed; in other cases, compromises must be made when the answers to two or more questions conflict.

Too often the proper design of a group benefit plan is viewed as a one-time decision rather than as an evolving process. However, benefit plans that were appropriate for yesterday's workforce may not meet the needs of tomorrow's workforce. As times and organizations change, employers' answers to the questions raised in this chapter may also have to change. For this reason, these issues must frequently be restudied to determine whether a group benefit plan is continuing to meet its desired purpose.

Because the question of funding is addressed in detail in Chapter 16, only the remaining questions will be discussed in this chapter.

One difficulty in writing a textbook of this nature is determining where to discuss the many issues and decisions that must be faced if proper planning is to take place. While some issues and decisions can easily be handled at the beginning of a textbook, many others are best discussed along with specific types of benefit plans. Still others are most meaningfully treated only after the basic coverages, provisions, and funding methods have been described. However, a treatment of the benefit-planning process seems appropriate in an introductory chapter to make readers aware that benefit planning is much more than a description of the many types of coverages and provisions that are the subject of most of this book. While this chapter is devoted entirely to planning and is the first and only place where certain issues are discussed, other planning issues are handled where appropriate throughout the book. Readers may wish to return to this chapter after they have completed the remainder of the book.

■ WHAT ARE THE EMPLOYER'S OBJECTIVES?

No benefit plan is properly designed unless it meets the employer's objectives. Although these objectives may be unclear or even nonexistent, particularly in small firms, most large corporations have (and all firms should have) specific written objectives that have been approved by the board of directors (or by the owners of the firm). These objectives vary for each individual organization, depending on such factors as size, location, industry, the results of collective bargaining, and the employer's philosophy. Without such objectives, it is difficult for the agent, broker, benefit consultant, or third-party administrator to make recommendations or for the firm's in-house benefit staff (often part of the human resources department) to make decisions.

Types of Objectives

Objectives for benefit plans can be general and part of a firm's overall compensation objective (that is, cash and fringe benefits in the aggregate) in order to achieve a compensation package that is competitive within the firm's geographic area or industry. Such an "average" objective usually means that the firm wants both its wages and salaries and its fringe benefits to be similar to what the competition is offering its employees. There is usually little room for creativity in the design of a group benefit plan, unless the plans of the competition are quite diverse.

Some firms have separate objectives for cash compensation and employee benefits. For example, a growing firm may want its cash compensation to be competitive, but it may want its overall employee benefit plan to be above average in order to attract new employees. A difficulty for the plan designer with this type of objective is determining whether the firm wants all aspects of the employee benefit plan to be better than average or whether it would be willing to accept, for example, an average program of group insurance benefits but a better-than-average pension plan and more vacation time for its employees. It should be noted that most objectives, even when they are much more detailed, tend to apply to employee benefits in the aggregate rather than to specific types of benefits.

It has become increasingly common for firms, particularly large ones, to maintain a lengthy and often detailed list of objectives for their employee benefit programs. The following are the objectives of one such firm:

■   To establish and maintain an employee benefit program that is based primarily on the employees' needs for leisure time and protection against the risks of old age, loss of health, and loss of life

■   To establish and maintain an employee benefit program that complements the efforts of employees in their own behalf

■   To evaluate the employee benefit plan annually for its effect on employee morale and productivity, giving consideration to turnover, unfilled positions, attendance, employee complaints, and employee opinions

■   To compare the employee benefit plan annually with that of other leading companies in the same field and to maintain a benefit plan with an overall level of benefits (based on cost per employee) that falls within the second quintile of these companies

■   To maintain a level of benefits for nonunion employees that represents the same level of expenditures per employee as for union employees

■   To determine annually the cost of new, changed, and existing programs as a percentage of salaries and wages, and to maintain this percentage as much as possible

■   To self-fund benefits to the extent that long-run cost savings can be expected for the firm and catastrophic losses can be avoided

■   To coordinate all benefits with social insurance programs to which the company makes payments

■   To provide benefits on a noncontributory basis, except benefits for dependent coverage, for which employees should pay a portion of the cost

■ To maintain continual communications with all employees concerning benefit programs

Most lists of objectives contain few, if any, specific details regarding what provisions or what types of benefits should be contained in an employee benefit plan. Rather, they establish guidelines—instead of specific performance goals—within which management must operate. For example, the objectives listed above indicate that this firm wants a plan that is understood and appreciated by employees and that is designed with employee opinions in mind. No mention, however, is made of how this is to be done. As is seen later in this chapter, there may be alternative ways for this firm to achieve its objectives. Similarly, the objectives establish guidelines for the cost of providing benefits. Although the firm wants to have a better-than-average plan, it does not want to be a leader. There is a very specific statement about what the relationship between the cost of benefits for union and nonunion employees should be. However, nothing is mentioned to indicate that the benefits for the two groups must also be identical. If the two groups have different needs, different types and levels of benefits may be desirable.

Three additional points about employer objectives should be made. First, as times change, benefit objectives may need revision.

Second, the frequent lack of specific guidelines in benefit objectives gives the in-house benefit staff great creative latitude to come up with innovative solutions to benefit problems and to respond to the changing benefit environment. Such creativity can often lead to success and financial reward. However, a greater degree of freedom to be creative is also often accompanied by being the scapegoat when benefit decisions do not lead to the desired results.

Third, a firm's primary (and possibly only) objective may be to establish an overall employee benefit plan that channels as large a portion of the benefits as possible to the owner or owners. Although this is a poor objective for an overall plan, it is a reality that must be recognized, most commonly in small firms or in firms that have few owners. Large, publicly held corporations sometimes wish to provide better benefits for their executives than for other employees. However, these extra benefits are likely to be provided under separate executive compensation plans, rather than under the benefit plan that applies to all employees.

Who Should Receive Benefits?

As part of establishing its objectives, an employer must determine its responsibilities to various categories of persons who might be eligible for coverage under the firm's overall benefit program. The list is much longer than one might initially think. It may include the following:

■ Active full-time employees

■ Dependents of active full-time employees

■ Retired employees

■ Dependents of retired employees

■ Part-time employees

■ Dependents of part-time employees

- Disabled employees
- Dependents of disabled employees
- Survivors of deceased employees
- Employees who have terminated employment
- Dependents of employees who have terminated employment
- Employees who are temporarily separated from employment (for example, employees on family leave)
- Dependents of employees who are temporarily separated from employment

Obviously, most benefits are given to employees and some benefits are given to their dependents, such as medical expense coverage. Whether other groups on the list receive any benefits depends on several factors. These include the attitude of the employer and the degree to which protection is available under other programs, such as Social Security. In addition, federal and state laws play a role. For example, some benefits must be continued because of family leave legislation. In addition, medical expense coverage must be continued in many cases as a result of COBRA. The extent to which benefits might be provided to each of these categories of persons is touched upon throughout this book.

■ WHAT TYPES OF BENEFITS SHOULD A PLAN PROVIDE?

A major decision for any employer is what types and levels of benefits to include in an overall employee benefit plan. For those few firms that do not have an employee benefit program, this decision involves choosing which benefits to offer initially. However, in most cases, the decision is ongoing and involves either the offering of new or improved benefits or the redesigning of all or a major portion of the benefit plan. An objective of most employee benefit plans is to meet the "needs" of employees. But what are these needs? If they vary for different groups of employees, should different benefit plans be established? Or should a single plan be designed in which employees are allowed to choose among alternative benefits?

Determining Needs

Every employer wants its employees to appreciate the benefits that are provided. However, employers are becoming increasingly aware that employee benefit programs are failing to achieve this desired level of appreciation. To some extent, this is due to the fact that as employee benefit plans have grown more comprehensive, employees have begun to take the benefits for granted. In addition, the growing consensus seems to be that the traditional methods of determining what types and levels of benefits to offer have lost much of their effectiveness. These traditional methods include basing benefits on the following factors:

- The employer's perception of the employees' needs. This perception is largely based on the opinions of a firm's top management employees, whose compensation is much higher than that of the average employee. Therefore, it is not surprising that many recent studies have shown that management's perception of employees' needs often differs from what the employees themselves feel they need.

- What competitors are doing. Too often, the emphasis is placed on having an employee benefit package that is virtually identical to that of the competition, even though the makeup of the workforce may be different and the employees may have different needs.

- Collectively bargained benefits. Many employers pattern their benefit plans for salaried employees after their negotiated plans for union employees. Again, the needs of salaried employees may be substantially different and may call for a totally different plan.

- Tax laws and regulations. Benefit plans are often designed to include those benefits that are best suited to the high tax brackets of top executives. The average employee who is in a modest tax bracket may actually have a preference for certain benefits even though they result in currently taxable income.

In the last few years, two trends have taken place. First, employers have increasingly taken a marketing-research approach to employee benefit planning. The employees' preferences for benefits are determined similarly to the way that consumers' demands for products are determined. For the most part, this approach has been used only for nonunion employees because benefits for union employees are decided by collective bargaining. However, some employers and some unions use this procedure as a guide in their negotiations over benefits for union employees. Second, employers have increasingly turned to life-cycle and work/life approaches to benefit planning.

Use of Marketing Research. A marketing-research approach to benefit planning can be used for different purposes. Most often it is selected as a way to determine (1) how funds should be allocated to new types of benefits or (2) how funds should be used to improve current benefits. This can be for a one-time change in a firm's benefit plan or for changes that are implemented over time. In addition, a marketing-research approach can also help an employer determine what alternative provisions employees would prefer regarding a specific type of benefit. For example, a firm that allocates additional funds to a long-term disability plan could determine whether employees would prefer a shorter waiting period or an increase in the size of the monthly benefit.

Marketing-research techniques must be used with caution. They can have a negative effect on employee morale unless the employer is committed to using the results of marketing research in benefit decision making. Therefore, this approach should not be undertaken unless the employer intends to base expenditures for benefits on satisfying what employees perceive as their needs. In addition, employees must be made aware that changes in the employer's overall benefit program are subject to financial constraints and possibly to trade-offs among benefits.

Although a variety of marketing-research techniques can be used in benefit planning, the techniques that employers most commonly choose fall into three major categories: personal interviews, simplified questionnaires, and sophisticated research methods.

Personal Interviews.   Personal interviews with employees (either alone or in small groups) are probably the most effective marketing-research technique for a small firm or for a benefit program that is limited to a small number of employees. On this scale, it is also usually the least expensive technique. An advantage of personal interviewing is that it can be used to collect the same type of information as do both simplified questionnaires and sophisticated research techniques. Because it is important in personal interviewing for the employees to feel they can speak candidly, it may be desirable to have the interviews conducted by someone outside the firm and to hold group interviews without the supervisor's presence.

Simplified Questionnaires.   A simplified questionnaire often has two major parts: one determines benefit preferences; the other determines demographic data (such as age, gender, marital status, years of service, and salary range). The questionnaire is called "simplified" because employees are basically asked only to indicate and/or rank their preferences. However, the actual analysis of the data that are gathered may be a complex task. It is important to use a clear, brief questionnaire that is not annoying to employees, so it is best that the questionnaire initially be given to a few employees to determine their reactions.

Figure 2.1 shows a sample of a part of a simplified questionnaire on benefit preferences. The example is typical of most questionnaires because it applies to a broad range of benefits and not just to group insurance.

The questionnaire is essentially a structured one and is not open-ended. Employees are requested only to rank their preferences, and they are not given the opportunity to state whether each benefit is important or whether it should be improved. They are also required to make their preferences known regarding possible trade-offs between benefits and pay. Even though the questionnaire is structured, employees are still given the opportunity to make general comments. Such a feature should be incorporated into any questionnaire as a way of letting employees know that their opinions will be heard. It may also result in useful and sometimes surprising information for the employer.

Sophisticated Research Methods.   One difficulty with simplified questionnaires, and to some extent personal interviews, is that they fail to measure the intensity of employees' preferences. Consequently, some firms have used more sophisticated marketing-research techniques in an attempt to measure the degree of importance that employees place on various benefit alternatives. These more sophisticated research techniques are typically used only when the employer has formulated specific alternatives. Therefore, they are often used as a follow-up to personal interviews and simplified questionnaires, and they frequently involve additional interviews and/or questionnaires.

Figure 2.2 illustrates one example of how preferences might be measured with a questionnaire.

After the information is gathered, the firm must decide which benefits to adopt, based on employees' preferences and other cost and administrative considerations. For example, assume that the firm using the questionnaire is willing to spend up to $400 annually per employee to improve its benefit package. Also assume that the figures in Table 2.1 represent the average importance of each proposed benefit to employees, as well as the expected annual cost per employee of providing each benefit.

FIGURE 2.1	Employee Benefit Questionnaire

1. In the right-hand column below, rank the benefits from 1 to 7 in their importance to you and your family. Use 1 for the most important, 2 for the next most important, etc.

Benefit	Importance
Pension Plan	_____
Life Insurance	_____
Sick Pay	_____
Long-Term Disability Income	_____
Medical Expense Insurance	_____
Holidays	_____
Vacations	_____

2. To the list of benefits below, add the two benefits you would most like to see added by this company. In the right-hand column, rank the benefits listed according to their need for improvement or adoption. Use 1 for the benefit you feel should have the highest priority for improvement or adoption, 2 for the next highest, etc.

Benefit	Need for Improvement or Adoption
Pension Plan	_____
Life Insurance	_____
Sick Pay	_____
Long-Term Disability Income	_____
Medical Expense Insurance	_____
Holidays	_____
Vacations	_____
_____	_____
_____	_____

3. How would you prefer that additional funds for benefits be used? (check one)

_____Improve or add benefit programs.

_____Reduce currently required employee contributions.

4. Which of the following statements reflects your opinion? (check one)

_____More emphasis should be placed on improving wages and salaries and less on improving benefits.

_____More emphasis should be placed on improving benefits and less on improving wages and salaries.

_____The same emphasis as in the past should be placed on improving both benefits and wages and salaries.

5. Please use the back of this form to make any additional comments you feel will be of use to the company in its desire to improve the employee benefit programs.

FIGURE 2.2	Employee Benefit Questionnaire

The company is considering the following benefit changes for adoption in the next fiscal year. Although the company is committed to making improvements in its benefit package, financial considerations dictate that only some of these proposed changes can be adopted at that time. The first item on the list has been given a "value" of 100. Please rank the other items in their relative importance to you. For example, if item 2 is 3 times as important, it should be given a value of 300. If it is only half as important, it should be given a value of 50.

Proposed Change	Value
1. Increase annual dental insurance maximum from $1,000 to $2,000.	100
2. Eliminate employee contributions to long-term disability coverage.	
3. Increase life insurance coverage from 1½ to 2 times base earnings.	
4. Add Columbus Day to list of holidays.	
5. Increase the annual number of sick days from 10 to 12.	

It is clear that the employees feel the second proposed change (which has an annual cost of $200 per employee) is most important by a substantial margin, so it will most likely be adopted. However, it is difficult to determine what other benefit or benefits to offer. The last proposed change will definitely not be made because only $200 per employee remains for additional benefit changes. The firm is therefore faced with two alternatives—either add Columbus Day as a holiday or increase both the life insurance coverage and the annual dental insurance maximum. Because the average importance of each alternative to employees is 240, and only one can be made within the cost constraint, the deciding factor hinges on other considerations. The firm may look at the administrative aspects of each change or the effect of inflation on long-range costs. The firm may also analyze the data in terms of the demographic characteristics of employees. For example, long-time employees may have a slight preference for the insurance benefits, and younger employees would like the extra holiday. If the firm wishes to favor the older employees, it will change the insurance benefits; if morale is low among younger employees, it might decide to add the holiday instead.

TABLE 2.1	Value and Cost of Benefit Changes

Change	Average Value	Annual Cost per Employee
1	100	$100
2	310	200
3	140	100
4	240	200
5	190	250

These other considerations may also be the deciding factor for employers even when employee preferences are clear. However, if employees are led to believe that their preferences are the primary consideration, other considerations should be weighed only when differences in employee preferences are modest.

Life-Cycle Approach to Benefit Planning. The design of employee benefit plans traditionally focused solely on providing active employees with protection against the financial consequences of illness, disability, retirement, and death. Over time, other types of benefits began to be offered, but plan design tended to focus on the employee being part of a traditional family. Over the last two decades, the demographic makeup of the workforce has changed dramatically. As a result, many employers often take a **life-cycle approach** to benefit planning. Traditional benefits are still part of the core of most overall employee benefit plans. However, employers are increasingly designing benefit plans with the realization that benefit needs may differ not only for males and females but also when employees are single, when they have and raise children, when they care for elderly parents, and when they retire. Different benefit needs also arise in today's society because of more family units containing children from prior marriages and more unmarried individuals (of either the same or opposite gender) living together.

Intuition would lead one to believe that a life-cycle benefit plan increases costs because it tends to provide benefits that would be used by all categories of employees. To some extent, this may be true. However, many employers who have taken this approach feel that additional costs are minimal and/or result in offsetting cost savings. For example, flexible work schedules that allow employees to better take care of dependents may cost little or nothing. Other benefits may result in significant cost savings due to less absenteeism and lower employee turnover. In addition, an employer may pass the majority of the cost of some benefits on to the employees who use them. For example, an employer may establish a day-care center but charge a fee for its use to offset some of its operating costs. An employer may also make a voluntary long-term-care insurance plan available on a payroll-deduction basis. Finally, employees may not automatically have all benefits; they might have to elect the benefits they want with a predetermined amount of employer funds under a cafeteria plan.

Many of the benefits employees want at various stages in their lives are probably fairly obvious. However, many employers use questionnaires and personal interviews to determine these varying needs. One employer, in designing its life-cycle benefit plan, used the life-cycle stages shown in Table 2.2 and found the benefits indicated to be of particular value to persons in that category.

Work/Life Approach to Benefit Planning. Employers are increasingly taking a **work/life approach** to benefit planning. They have realized that employees are looking for employers that recognize that their employees have lives away from the workplace. Many of the benefits that appeal to this group of employees are those that have already been mentioned, such as flexible work schedules, child-care plans, elder-care benefits, family leave, and adoption assistance. All of these benefits have seen some growth in prevalence over the last decade.

Employers are also increasingly making on-site personal services available. Some of the more common services are ATMs and other banking activities, access to postal

TABLE 2.2	Life-Cycle Benefits
Life-Cycle Stage	**Desired Benefit**
Young, Unmarried Workers	Extra vacation Fitness programs
Newlyweds	Marriage leave
Employees in Childbearing Years	Prenatal courses Parental leave Adoption assistance
Workers during Child-Rearing Years	Day-care centers Flexible work schedules
Employees Dealing with Divorce	Legal assistance
Workers in Elder-Care Years	Long-term care insurance Support groups
Retirees	Medicare supplements Retiree job banks Preretirement counseling
Employees Facing Death	Grief counseling Funeral leave

services, travel agencies, and dry cleaning pickup. Less common are medical and dental clinics, pharmacies, convenience stores, automobile pickup and delivery for oil changes and state inspections, and take-home meals. In some cases, it is merely a matter of providing space for these types of service providers to rent; in other cases, a rental subsidy might be necessary. In a few cases, the employer can provide these services. For example, the company cafeteria might prepare take-home meals.

Different Plans

From an administrative standpoint, it is easiest for a firm to have a single employee benefit plan that applies to all employees. Nevertheless, some firms have different plans for different groups of employees, especially when the benefits for union employees are determined by collective bargaining. If the benefits for the union employees are provided through a negotiated trusteeship, a separate plan must be designed for the nonunion employees. The employer must then decide whether to play "follow the leader" and provide identical benefits to the nonunion employees or to design a plan that reflects their different needs. When benefits are provided through a negotiated trusteeship, the employer is more likely to develop a "different" plan for nonunion employees than when the employer is required to provide benefits to union employees through group insurance contracts that are purchased by the employer. Under these circumstances, employers often find it simpler administratively to purchase a single contract that covers all employees. Different plans also typically exist for retired employees and other categories of people who are not active full-time employees or their dependents.

Even when unions are not involved, an employer may still decide to have different plans for different groups of employees. Usually, one plan is limited to hourly employees, another to salaried employees. In addition, a plan that offers supplemental benefits to top management may also be provided (but it is often publicized only to those employees who are eligible for these benefits). Some firms that have employees in different parts of the country have also found it desirable to provide somewhat different benefits at some or all locations in order to remain locally competitive. Different plans also typically exist for retired employees and other categories of persons who are not active full-time employees or their dependents.

Having different plans for different groups of employees has its disadvantages. Administrative costs are usually increased, communications with employees become more difficult, and resentment can occur if one group of employees feels its benefit plan is inferior to that of another group. To minimize this latter possibility, some firms have designed their plans so that an overall comparison is difficult. Each plan has its own positive and negative features when examined next to the plans for other groups of employees.

Different plans can also result by giving choices to employees. For example, one group of employees may elect an HMO or PPO option, and another group may elect coverage under a traditional medical expense plan. A trend in recent years has been the growth of cafeteria plans. Because of their popularity and complexity, Chapter 19 is devoted exclusively to them.

■ WHAT PROVISIONS FOR CONTROLLING COSTS SHOULD BE INCLUDED IN THE PLAN?

Employers have always been concerned about the costs of providing employee benefits. Traditionally, this concern has led to plan provisions that transfer these costs to employees rather than reducing the costs. These provisions include probationary periods, benefit limitations, and contributory financing. Many recent attempts to control costs have been directed primarily toward the rapidly increasing costs of medical care, and for the most part these cost-containment provisions have been designed to reduce administrative and claim costs without transferring them to employees. Because methods for controlling the costs of medical expenses are discussed throughout several later chapters, they are not discussed here. Rather, the focus is on provisions and activities that are used with all types of benefit plans.

Probationary Periods

Probationary periods reduce costs to employers because any claims that employees incur during this time must be borne by the employees themselves. In addition, probationary periods reduce the adverse selection that would most likely exist without their use. Administrative costs are also minimized for employees who terminate employment shortly after being hired. However, probationary periods do impose hardship on newer employees who incur claims but find themselves without benefits. (Employees can minimize these hardships by proper use of COBRA and temporary medical expense policies.) Primarily for competitive reasons in attracting employees, the use and length of probationary periods, particularly in medical expense plans, have been decreasing except in high turnover situations.

Benefit Limitations

Benefit limitations in the form of deductibles, coinsurance, maximum benefits, and exclusions for certain types of expenses are common in medical expense insurance. However, some of these techniques can also be used in other types of insurance, as in the following examples:

- The limiting of benefits to a maximum percentage of income in disability income plans. In addition to reducing the amount of the benefits paid by the employer, a maximum percentage also minimizes the possibility of feigned and unnecessarily prolonged disabilities.
- The setting of maximum benefits under dental plans for such expenses as orthodontics. There is little doubt that the availability of benefits encourages treatment of orthodontic conditions, particularly when the treatment is primarily sought for cosmetic reasons. There is also the feeling that dentists encourage the treatment of relatively minor conditions if a patient has coverage for orthodontics.

Contributory Financing

Many benefit plans require that each employee pay a portion of the premium costs for his or her own coverage. This may lower the employer's costs and/or may enable the employer to use these saved dollars to provide additional or improved benefits. There are several arguments both for and against contributory financing, but in many instances it is a moot point because collective bargaining or competition determines the decision.

When contributory financing is used for benefits other than pension plans, employees are generally able to voluntarily elect or decline coverage. To the extent that some employees decline coverage, the cost to the employer is lowered further. However, this savings may be offset by the adverse selection that can result because of those who do elect coverage. Furthermore, having the option to decline coverage could mean that employees or their dependents will be without coverage should a loss occur. Finally, there tend to be greater administrative costs associated with a contributory plan than with a noncontributory plan.

Advocates of contributory plans feel that sharing in the cost increases the employees' awareness and appreciation of both the plan and the contribution the employer is making. This opinion can be countered by the argument that payroll deductions for benefits are a source of employee dissatisfaction because they may view the employer as "cheap" for not paying the entire cost of the plan.

Although there are no empirical studies to support the contention, it has been argued that employees are less likely to misuse medical and dental benefits under a contributory plan because they realize that such misuse will probably lead to an increase in their future contributions.

Contributory financing can be used to encourage desired employee behavior. Employees who elect a managed care plan in lieu of a traditional medical expense plan often have a smaller contribution toward the cost of their coverage or possibly no contribution at all. In many cases, the cost savings to the employer determines the lower contribution. For example, if the cost of coverage to an employer for an unmarried employee is $150 under an HMO and $200 under an indemnity plan, the employee who elects the indemnity plan is required to pay $50 more per month than an employee who elects the HMO. This alone will encourage many employees to elect the managed care plan. However, employers who want to encourage managed care because it tends to have lower annual cost increases might actually make the differential larger, perhaps $75.

Cost Containment

Recent attempts to control benefit costs have concentrated on either reducing the size of claims or minimizing the administrative costs associated with benefit plans. Rather than transfer the costs to employees, these techniques try to lower costs, or at least to lower the rate at which costs are increasing. Although employers are concerned primarily with their own costs, some of the advantages of this cost containment affect the employees in the form of increased benefits or a lower rate of increase for the employees' own out-of-pocket expenses.

Other than provisions or practices associated solely with medical expense plans, which are discussed in detail in other chapters, the following is a list of some of the more common cost-containment techniques that employers are currently using:

- Alternative funding methods that lower administrative costs and improve cash flow
- Competitive bidding among insurance companies and third-party administrators that lowers administrative costs
- Wellness programs and employee-assistance plans that reduce future claims

■ HOW SHOULD THE PLAN BE COMMUNICATED TO EMPLOYEES?

Traditionally, employers have placed a low priority on the communication of their benefit plans to employees. They have taken the attitude that employees appreciated any benefits given to them. The little information that was made available tended to be only the literature that the insurance companies providing the coverage had prepared.

Over the last few years, this situation has changed dramatically. Federal law requires that employers disclose a substantial amount of information to employees about their benefit plans. In addition, employers have come to realize that many employees take their benefits for granted, that they fail to realize the value of these benefits to themselves and their families, and that they are unaware of the employer's dollar outlay.

Not only does effective communication solve this problem, it may also minimize the dissatisfaction that arises from misunderstandings about the benefit program, and it may reduce turnover to the extent that employees realize the true value of their benefits. Employers have also learned that effective communication is necessary to obtain employee support if cost-containment efforts are to be successful.

Finally, benefit communication is increasingly important as employees are given more choice with regard to their own benefits. This is occurring as more employees have alternative medical expense plans, cafeteria plans, and retirement plans that allow investment choices.

Most benefit consultants feel that an effective communication program should have four primary objectives:

1. To create an awareness and appreciation of the way current benefits improve employees' financial security
2. To provide a high level of understanding about available benefits
3. To encourage the wise use of benefits
4. To comply with legal requirements

Because many employees have coverage for dependents under their benefit plan, there is also an increasing awareness of the need to inform spouses of a firm's benefit programs. For example, spouses might be invited to benefit orientations.

Effective Communication

Employees will obtain information about benefits in some manner. Without an effective communications program, an employee is likely to rely on the grapevine, which often provides incomplete and inaccurate information. Good communication rarely just happens. Rather, it requires that employers determine objectives for their communication plans, just as they did for benefit plan design. Although any list of objectives is likely to include the clear and concise dissemination of information about current benefits, other objectives may change over time. For example, an employer may want to encourage employees to switch to a managed care plan.

Depending on the circumstances, communication may be ongoing or on a one-time basis. In either case, benefit consultants feel that it is important for employers to design communication materials so that employees are told that they and their needs are important to the firm, that the employer cares what employees think about benefits, and that the employer wants employees to understand their benefits. A successful long-run communication program also has a method for obtaining feedback so that the employer can determine the effectiveness of its communication. Steps can be taken to rectify inadequate information, and past experience can be of value in designing future communications.

Several factors can complicate the communication process. For example, an employer may have different benefit plans for different groups of employees and therefore may have to design alternative communication strategies. Although it may be possible to have somewhat similar strategies, the sophistication levels of the different employee groups may call for an entirely different approach. A similar problem may occur if an employer has multiple locations. In addition, employers must take the needs of employees who do not speak English into consideration. Finally, communication strategies may vary for new employees and existing employees.

Whatever form a communication plan may take, communication specialists recommend that several basic factors be present:

- The communication should be written in a style that is clear and understandable to the employees. Legalese and benefit jargon should be avoided.

- The communication should make it clear what a benefit means to an employee. For example, if an employer is trying to encourage enrollment in a managed care plan, the lack of any deductibles and minimal (or no) copayments should be emphasized.

- The communication should explain why changes are being made. The effectiveness of the communication is likely to be lessened if an employer is not open and honest. Too many employers fail to realize that employees are smart enough to read between the lines of communication that is less than forthright.

- The communication should make use of graphics and examples. Too often, communication that lacks these features is boring and therefore less effective.

Methods of Communication

The communication of benefit plans to employees is now regarded as a highly sophisticated task. No single method of communication is likely to accomplish all the desired objectives, so several methods must be combined. Benefit plans can be communicated to employees in audiovisual presentations, in face-to-face meetings, through printed materials, and more recently with interactive communication through telephones and computers. To meet these objectives, many employers hire communications experts who generally report to the person responsible for employee benefits. Other employers use the services of benefit-consulting firms, many of which have developed specialized units for advising their clients in this particular area. In addition, to directly communicate benefits to employees, these consulting firms may conduct surveys and train employees to direct focus groups and interact with employees about benefits.

Audiovisual Presentations. Audiovisual presentations are a very effective way to communicate benefit plans to new employees or to explain significant changes in existing benefit plans to current employees. It is much easier to require employees to view audiovisual presentations than to read printed materials. In addition, if properly done, audiovisual presentations can convey the employer's concern for the well-being of its employees, and they can explain proper benefit use more effectively than printed materials. In the past, many audiovisual presentations have been dull and sometimes uninformative. Recently, however, many employers have adopted more sophisticated communications methods, and they view these presentations, if not their entire communication program, as a way of "advertising" their employee benefit plans. In fact, some employers have actually hired advertising firms to design not only their audiovisual programs but other aspects of their communication program as well.

Meetings with Employees. Face-to-face meetings with employees can also be an effective way to explain employee benefit plans and to answer employee questions. For small employers, this technique is generally used to present benefit plans to new employees or to explain the changes in existing plans. Large employers often combine meetings with audiovisual presentations. It is obvious that whoever conducts these meetings (be it the employer, agent, broker, consultant, or group representative) must be truly knowledgeable about the plan. In addition, it is just as important that he or she be able to effectively communicate this knowledge to employees.

The number of employees who attend a meeting may determine its effectiveness. A large meeting may be satisfactory if its purpose is primarily to present information. However, a series of small meetings may be more manageable and appropriate if employee opinions or questions are being solicited. These smaller-sized meetings can be used in lieu of a large meeting or as follow-up meetings to a large group presentation. When employees must make decisions regarding their benefit plans, meetings with individual employees may also be necessary.

Group meetings can be used for other purposes besides explaining new or changed benefit plans. They can be held periodically to reexplain benefits, to answer employee questions, or to listen to employee concerns and suggestions. In addition, every employer should have a procedure by which employees can have ready access to a "knowledgeable" person when they have any problems to discuss or questions to ask. Although this can often be accomplished by telephone, face-to-face meetings should be used when necessary.

The employer's attitude toward a group meeting can influence its effectiveness. Employers should not regard these meetings as necessary formalities, but rather as a way to communicate their concern about the security of their employees and the benefits with which employees are provided. The success of face-to-face meetings may also depend to some degree on their time and location. To achieve maximum employee interest and attention, the facilities should be comfortable and not overcrowded. In addition, meetings should be held during normal working hours, not at the end of the working day, when many employees may be concerned about whether the meeting will end on time.

Printed Materials. Virtually every employer provides employees with some printed materials about its employee benefit plans. Increasingly, this material is available online. At a minimum, this material consists of group insurance certificates and the information that is required under the disclosure provisions of ERISA. The next most commonly provided source of information is the **benefit handbook**. If there is a typical benefit handbook, it is best described as a reference book that summarizes the benefit plans that are available to all employees. In addition to describing group insurance benefits, it includes information about an organization's retirement plan, vacation policy, and possibly other benefits (such as educational assistance). Each plan is described in terms of eligibility, benefits, and what employee contributions are required.

Traditionally, these benefit handbooks merely described each benefit plan separately; they did not discuss the relationship between the various benefit plans or the availability of certain social insurance benefits. Newer benefit handbooks are more likely to focus on the potential causes of lost income to an employee or his or her family. For example, rather than discuss short-term and long-term disability income plans separately, they include a single section on disability income that describes how a short-term disability plan initially pays benefits and at what point it is replaced by the long-term disability plan and Social Security.

Because of the general nature of benefit handbooks, many employers also give each employee a personalized **benefit statement**, usually on an annual basis. Some employers feel that employees will better appreciate the value of their benefits if they are aware of the magnitude of the cost to the employer. Figure 2.3 is an example of one form that is used for reporting this information. However, the most common form of personalized benefit statement specifies the plans for which the employee is eligible and what benefits are available to that particular employee (or his or her family) under each of these plans. Figure 2.4 shows a portion of one such statement.

Other types of printed information (such as company newsletters, personal letters to employees at home, or notices in pay envelopes) may also be of value. This may be the simplest and least expensive way of announcing benefit changes that need little explanation (such as an increase in the annual dental plan maximum). They are also an effective way to advertise or remind employees about the wellness programs that are available or what cost-containment provisions are included in their medical expense coverage. Experience has shown that without occasional reminders, the use of these programs and provisions by employees tends to decrease.

Vendors of employee benefit products and services may also make printed materials available for distribution to employees.

Interactive Voice-Response Systems. Employers are increasingly turning to newer technologies to communicate and manage benefit plans. One of these technologies is the telephone and the use of interactive voice-response systems. At one extreme, a telephone system can be as simple as merely giving information to all employees about such matters as times for employee meetings, enrollment deadlines, and plan changes. However, this use of the telephone requires all employees to have either a telephone or some alternative method to receive the information. From this point, telephone systems can get increasingly complex. At the next level, the system can allow employees, through a menu of options, to request general information and materials such as enrollment forms. Carried even further, the system can enable employees to obtain specific information about their own benefits, such as the amount of life insurance they have or the balance in their 401(k) account. Of course, if personal information is available, employees need to have a personal identification number to access the information. At the most complex extreme, telephones can be used to allow employees to make benefit elections and changes—for example, to change investment options for a 401(k) plan or to change from one medical expense plan to another during open enrollment periods.

There are both advantages and disadvantages to the use of telephone systems for benefit communication. Among the advantages:

■ They can be designed to allow employee access on a 24-hour basis.

■ They enable employees to get quick and accurate responses.

FIGURE 2.3	Sample Benefit Statement

Benefit Statement Review For

_____

Many of us forget that there is more to our paycheck than the amount we take home. The following are the "extras" that were provided in 20___ and their value as determined by the cost to your employer.

	Annual Value	Value per Hour
(1) Social Security and Medicare (employer's contribution)	$ _____	$_____
(2) Workers' Compensation Insurance Premium	_____	_____
(3) State Unemployment Insurance Premium	_____	_____
(4) Paid Holidays	_____	_____
(5) Vacation Days	_____	_____
(6) Pension	_____	_____
(7) Salary Continuation	_____	_____
(8) Long-Term Disability Income Insurance	_____	_____
(9) Life Insurance	_____	_____
(10) Medical Expense Insurance (employer's contribution)	_____	_____
(11) Others		
_____	_____	_____
_____	_____	_____

The $_____ value of those sometimes-forgotten benefits is equal to _____% of the $_____ you received as salary or wages in 20___. These benefits are provided to protect you and your family from certain financial risks and to help provide for your future retirement.

- They make it possible for employees to maintain a degree of anonymity without having to disclose information to in-house personnel.
- They allow human resources personnel to spend more time on issues other than routine phone inquiries.

FIGURE 2.4 Sample Benefit Statement

Personal Statement of Benefits

This Personal Statement of Benefits lists the benefits that protect both you and your family now and provide security for your future. We know you will find this statement informative, and we hope it is useful in your personal planning.

Health Care Benefits
You have elected coverage for
❑ yourself   ❑ your family   ❑ You have not elected coverage

The highlights of your Comprehensive Medical Plan are summarized in the following table. See your employee handbook for further details.

In-Hospital Benefits	Out-of-Hospital Benefits	Special Benefits
$100 deductible per person each calendar year (3-deductible maximum per family)		100% of outpatient emergency treatment of accidental injury (no deductible)
100% of covered expenses, including maternity care, after the deductible is met	80% of first $3,000 of covered expenses, then 100% of remaining covered expenses 50% of psychiatric treatment ($30-per-visit maximum benefit)	100% of diagnostic X-ray and laboratory tests (deductible applies)

Overall Plan Maximum: Unlimited

Disability Income Benefits
Salary Continuation Plan
Your full salary continues for _____ weeks, then 3/4 of your salary continues for _____ weeks.

Long-Term Disability Income Plan
If disabled over 26 weeks, you will receive _____ a month. This is 60 percent of your base pay and includes benefits under the corporation's plan and any Social Security benefits, other than family benefits, for which you are eligible.

If you have eligible dependents, you can receive additional family benefits under Social Security of up to _____ a month.

If total long-term disability income from the above sources exceeds 80 percent of your base pay, disability benefits under the corporation's plan are reduced to bring the total to the 70 percent level.

However, there are also drawbacks and limitations, some of which can be overcome with proper planning and design:

- There is a lack of human interaction. This by itself will discourage some employees from using the telephone system if they can obtain the same information and perform the same transactions by calling someone personally. If a new telephone system is the only way that employees can request certain information or initiate certain transactions, it should be well publicized and possibly established in small increments. A well-designed system is simple to use and does not leave employees in an endless maze of pushing buttons. It also gives employees an option to speak to a real person when they feel it is necessary.

- Telephone systems can become increasingly expensive as they are expanded to allow employees a wider range of options. For some firms, the cost may outweigh the benefits.

- Because employees can make benefit changes and elections by merely pushing a button, mistakes might be made. Therefore, it is necessary for the telephone response system to confirm all transactions over the phone and allow employees to enter needed corrections. In addition, a written confirmation should be sent to employees, possibly requiring the return of a signed copy of the confirmation.

- Telephone systems are not conducive to inputting data, such as the name of a new dependent for purposes of obtaining medical expense coverage.

Computers.   Although telephone systems can be used effectively for obtaining information and simple benefit plan enrollments, computers enable employers to use technology to a much greater extent.

The majority of computer benefits systems are intranet-based over a local area network of company computers. These have the advantage of speed and minimize security concerns, whether they are perceived or real. Firms can also use Internet-based systems over a public network secured by password access. A major advantage of the Internet is that employees can be allowed access from home or while they are traveling. In addition, the Internet is often better for providing employees with links to other useful Web sites because, for security reasons, a firm may not wish to have other links with its intranet site. A few firms have benefit systems on both their intranets and the Internet. Computerized benefit systems can be on either employees' personal computers at their workstations or computer terminals located at centralized stations. Employees may also be able to access these systems from their home computer or from other locations. By pressing the appropriate key, an employee can get a general description of the company's various plans. By inputting appropriate data (including an identification number), an employee may also be able to obtain information about his or her own particular situation. For example, an employee could determine a potential disability income or retirement benefit. An employee may also be able to obtain the answers to "what if" questions. For example, "If I contribute $100 per month to a 401(k) plan that is expected to earn 5 percent annually, how much will I have at age 65?" Or, "If I elect these options under a cafeteria plan, will any additional employer dollars remain for other benefits, or will I have to make an additional contribution through a payroll deduction?"

Employers are increasingly using the computer to allow employees to make benefit selections. To have written verification, a form is either printed on the spot for an employee to sign and return or generated in the personnel office, reviewed, and sent to the employee for signing. Computers also facilitate data input, such as the name of a new beneficiary for life insurance coverage or the name of a new spouse being added to an employee's medical expense coverage.

Computers can be used to educate employees as well as provide benefit information. For example, employees can be given information comparing the pros and cons of a managed care plan with those of a traditional indemnity plan. Employees can also be given information to help them in their overall personal financial planning, often through links to other Internet sites.

Finally, employers are beginning to use computers to disseminate legally required information, such as summary plan descriptions.

Many of the same advantages and disadvantages of using telephone systems also apply to the use of computers. A major drawback to a computerized benefit system has been cost in relation to return on investment. However, this drawback is becoming less of an obstacle as more employees have computer access. Moreover, the success of such a system requires a high level of technical competence at the human resources and management information systems levels. There must be an understanding that computer communications often need to be approached differently from printed communications. Finally, employees need to feel comfortable using computerized benefit systems. This is continuing to occur as employees become more computer literate and intranet and Internet sites evolve.

■ SHOULD BENEFIT ADMINISTRATION BE OUTSOURCED?

Historically, most organizations have fully administered their benefit programs with their own employees. However, it has not been unusual for an organization to turn to **outsourcing,** whereby some administrative functions are performed by other parties. For example, third-party administrators have been used to administer self-funded medical expense plans, and actuaries have been used to perform some of the compliance functions for qualified retirement plans.

More recently, there has been a significant increase in the outsourcing of employee benefit administration, with estimates indicating that between 40 percent and 50 percent of all employers currently use outsourcing to some degree. Surveys also indicate that another 15 percent to 20 percent of employers are actively exploring the use of outsourcing. In this last portion of this chapter, the reasons for outsourcing are identified. In addition, the types of functions commonly outsourced and the types of vendors used for outsourcing are described. Finally, the factors that must be considered when entering into a contract for outsourcing are discussed.

Reasons for Outsourcing

There are many reasons why an employer might decide to outsource benefit administration. The most common reason is that the organization lacks the technical and regulatory expertise to perform many of the necessary functions. For example, few employers have a staff with the expertise to perform actuarial calculations or utilization reviews. Functions of this nature are best left to firms that have a staff of specialists in these areas. Closely correlated with this reason is the desire of firms to seek more value for the dollars spent on benefits. Although outsourcing costs money, it is often cheaper than performing the same functions in house. Some of this savings is because of the high cost of the hardware and software that is increasingly needed. An outside vendor can spread this cost over many customers.

Better service to employees is another often-cited reason for outsourcing. Vendors frequently have 800 numbers and a staff that specializes in specific benefit functions. Persons who answer telephones are typically trained to have the ability to handle 90 percent or more of the inquiries they receive. But more important, they have the ability to transfer the more complex calls to the appropriate person to handle the issue.

Outsourcing also provides a buffer between the employer and disgruntled employees. For example, if an employee is unhappy with disability, medical, or workers' compensation benefits, the outsourcing firm may be blamed rather than the employer.

Another cited reason for outsourcing is so that the organization can focus its attention on the firm's core activities. Outsourcing enables a firm to lower the size of the staff that administers its benefits or at least to have the staff remain stable or grow more slowly in an era when benefit administration is becoming increasingly complex.

Functions Outsourced

Significant variations exist with respect to the benefit functions that are outsourced. Systems, staff, or both can be outsourced. **Systems outsourcing** refers to using an outsourcing organization's computer and other systems but retaining an in-house staff to perform administrative functions. **Staff outsourcing** refers to the outsourcing of people but the continued use of the organization's systems.

Outsourcing can also be classified as either partial or full. With *partial outsourcing,* an employer uses an outsourcing organization's personnel and/or staff for some benefit functions but continues other functions in house. The term *full outsourcing* refers to those situations where most benefit functions are outsourced. Even with full outsourcing, some functions, such as financial management of benefit plans and benefit plan design, remain the responsibility of senior personnel at the firm. Employees, however, typically no longer deal with an employer's benefit or human resources department. Rather, they deal with an outside firm by telephone, mail, or e-mail.

Most employers use partial outsourcing. Among the most common functions to be outsourced are

- COBRA administration,
- administration of medical and dental claims,

- utilization review,
- vision care programs,
- government reporting,
- record keeping and administration of defined-contribution retirement plans,
- record keeping and administration of flexible spending accounts,
- preretirement planning, and
- benefit communication.

Vendors Used for Outsourcing

Many types of organizations operate as vendors for outsourcing. In addition, employers who outsource may use several vendors because each vendor often specializes in a limited number of activities. In fact, some vendors may specialize in only one type of benefit, such as vision care.

The major providers of outsourcing services include benefit consulting firms, insurance companies, stock brokerage firms, mutual funds, and third-party administrators. Stock brokerage firms and mutual funds tend to be involved almost solely in functions relating to retirement plans. Although the other vendors often engage in a wide variety of activities, they may also specialize in a limited number of outsourcing services. For example, benefit consulting firms frequently focus their activities on regulatory compliance, eligibility determination, and enrollment.

Recently, a small number of large organizations have been marketing themselves as having the ability to provide complete outsourcing for an employer. The number of firms that do all their outsourcing with only one vendor is still very small but is likely to grow.

The Decision to Outsource

The decision to outsource is not a simple task, and any such decision needs to incorporate sufficient lead time and preparation for the change. An organization must determine what functions should be outsourced and what functions can best be performed in house. Consideration also needs to be given to the firm's personnel. Outsourcing often involves working with computers and other systems. It is important that people with expertise in these areas be involved. In addition, the help of the internal benefit staff is vital. However, their assistance may be affected by the fact—either real or perceived—that outsourcing may result in the loss of their jobs.

Once a vendor has been selected to provide an outsourcing service, the process of changing vendors can be complex and expensive. Therefore, a high degree of care should go into the vendor-selection process. There should also be contingency plans for changing vendors if that need arises.

A formal outsourcing process begins with a request for proposal (RFP), in which vendors are asked to bid to provide services. The RFP should clearly spell out the goals of outsourcing and identify the major responsibilities of the potential parties to an outsourcing contract.

The outsourcing contract itself needs to clearly establish responsibilities of both the vendor and the employer, yet be flexible enough to address situations that may arise in the future. Proper planning must be done with respect to data to make sure data important to the employer are not destroyed by the vendor—for example, while converting the data to the vendor's systems. It is also important for the employer to be able to retrieve data if the contract with the vendor terminates.

A good outsourcing contract (at least from the employer's standpoint) contains performance guarantees. These guarantees may relate to such factors as timeliness, accuracy, productivity improvements, and employee complaints.

Because the primary purpose of outsourcing is to save money in the long run, it is also very important to address vendor compensation. The contract should not be so open-ended that unforeseen costs are automatically passed on to the employer. Even fixed-price contracts may prove to be expensive if a firm downsizes but the vendor gets the same compensation for servicing a smaller number of employers.

Some other issues that must be addressed include confidentiality and security of data, vendor responsibility for systems upgrades and employer responsibility to pay for them, insurance and/or bonding requirements, and procedures for resolving disputes among the parties.

■ KEY TERMS

benefit handbook	outsourcing	systems outsourcing
benefit statement	staff outsourcing	work/life approach
life-cycle approach		

■ STUDY QUESTIONS

1. Why is it important for an organization to have specific written objectives for its benefit plans?

2. Explain how the benefit objectives of an organization may vary in both length and specific details for realizing the objectives.

3. What are the various categories of persons for whom an employer might have responsibility to provide benefits?

4. Describe the traditional approaches to determine the benefit needs of employees and explain the drawbacks of each approach.

5. What is the potential negative impact of using a marketing research approach to determine the needs of employees?

6. a. What are the advantages of using personal interviews to determine employee needs?

   b. Why should these interviews be conducted without the presence of the employee's supervisor?

7. What advantages does a structured questionnaire have over an open-ended questionnaire for determining employee needs?

8. Some firms have different plans for different groups of employees.

   a. Under what circumstances are different benefits often used?

   b. What are the disadvantages of having different plans?

9. What is the purpose of life-cycle benefits?

10. a. Why are employers increasingly taking a work/life approach to benefit planning?

    b. What types of benefits might be provided under this approach?

11. Identify the potential advantages of requiring that employees pay a portion of the premiums for their own coverage.

12. What should be the objectives of an effective program for communicating benefit plans to employees?

13. What factors should be present in an effective communication plan?

14. Explain why some personalized benefit statements may be more effective techniques than benefit handbooks for communicating with employees.

15. Some firms now use interactive voice-response systems to communicate benefit plans to employees.

    a. How can such systems be used?

    b. What are their advantages and disadvantages?

16. What are some of the ways in which computers can be used to communicate employee benefit plans?

17. Why might an employer decide to outsource benefit administration?

18. What issues must be addressed in the process of outsourcing benefit administration?

Social Insurance

3

Social Security and Medicare

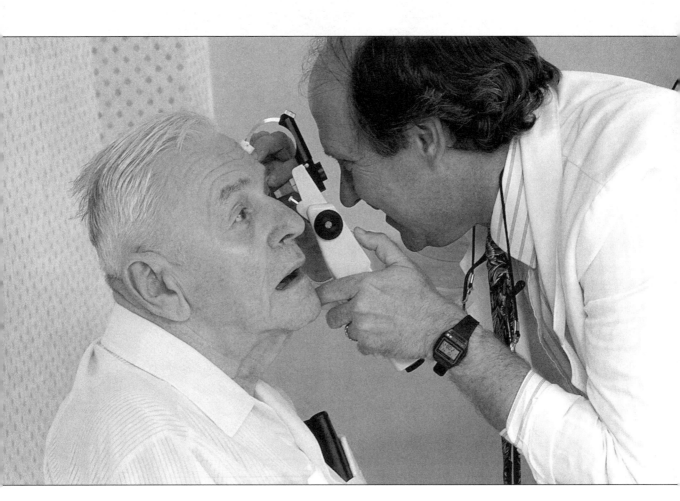

OBJECTIVES

■ Identify the reasons why social insurance exists and describe the basic features of social insurance programs.

■ Describe the financing of Social Security and Medicare benefits, including (1) the purpose and significance of the Social Security and Medicare trust funds and (2) the financial soundness of the programs.

■ Explain the requirements necessary for benefit eligibility under Social Security and Medicare.

■ Identify the types of benefits available under Social Security and Medicare.

■ Explain how Medicare participants may elect coverage under a managed care plan.

■ Explain the extent to which federal tax laws apply to Social Security and Medicare contributions and benefits.

CHAPTER OUTLINE

Reasons for Social Insurance

Characteristics of Social Insurance
Compulsory Employment-Related Coverage
Partial or Total Employer Financing
Benefits Prescribed by Law
Benefits as a Matter of Right
Emphasis on Social Adequacy

Social Security and Medicare
Extent of Coverage
Tax Rates and Wage Bases

Social Security: Eligibility
Fully Insured
Currently Insured
Disability Insured

Social Security: Types of Benefits
Retirement Benefits
Survivors Benefits
Disability Benefits
Eligibility for Dual Benefits
Termination of Benefits

Social Security: Benefit Amounts
Calculating Benefits
Other Factors Affecting Benefits

Social Security: Obtaining Benefit Information

Medicare: Eligibility

Medicare Part A: Hospital Insurance
Hospital Benefits
Skilled-Nursing Facility Benefits
Home Health Care Benefits
Hospice Benefits
Exclusions

Medicare Part B: Medical Insurance
Benefits
Exclusions
Amount of Benefits

Medicare Part C: Medicare Advantage (Medicare+Choice)

Medicare Part D: Prescription Drug Coverage
Drug Discount Cards
Prescription Drug Coverage
Employer Incentives

Adequacy of Financing

Employer and Employee Tax Treatment
Deductibility of Premiums
Tax Treatment of Benefits

Social insurance consists of various programs in which the elements of the insurance technique are present. These programs are designed to help solve the major social problems that affect a large portion of society. Social insurance programs include

- Social Security,
- Medicare,
- unemployment insurance,
- temporary disability insurance, and
- workers' compensation insurance.

Social Security and Medicare are described in this chapter; the remaining three programs are covered in the following chapter. Two other programs, which are not covered, are established by the Railroad Retirement Act and the Railroad Unemployment Insurance Act. These acts provide benefits to railroad workers that are similar to the benefits provided to other persons by Social Security and state unemployment insurance programs.

Social insurance programs are significant for several reasons. First, in the United States, nearly one-quarter of the dollars employers spend on benefits for their employees is used to make legally required payments to social insurance programs. For employers with meager benefit plans, this proportion will be much higher and may even account for the majority of the total benefit package.

Second, the most significant insurance expense for most individuals is their contributions to Social Security and Medicare. For many persons, this contribution will exceed the combined cost of all other types of insurance purchased directly by the individual.

Third, these programs form the foundation on which employee benefit programs and individual insurance plans are built. Employers' medical expense, disability income, and retirement plans are often designed in light of the benefits already available to employees under social insurance programs. Some benefit plans apply only to those employees not adequately covered under comparable social insurance programs; other benefit plans may cover all employees but may provide reduced benefits in those areas where similar social insurance benefits are available. In addition, it is impossible to do a proper job of personal insurance planning without taking potential Social Security and Medicare benefits into consideration.

Many books are devoted entirely to Social Security and Medicare. Because of space limitations, their treatment in this book is rather brief and is devoted primarily to a description of eligibility requirements, financing, and benefits. However, a few words should also be said about the reasons why Social Security, Medicare, and other social insurance programs exist and the general characteristics of such programs.

■ REASONS FOR SOCIAL INSURANCE

The existence and scope of social insurance programs are the result of several factors, probably the most significant of which is the need to solve the major social problems that affect a large portion of society. The industrialization of American society and the decreasing self-sufficiency of families resulted in a greater dependence on monetary income to provide economic security. The widespread lack of such income

during the Great Depression led to the passage of the Social Security Act as an attempt to provide economic security by attacking the sources of economic insecurity, including old age and unemployment.

A second reason for the existence of social insurance programs is the difficulty of privately insuring against certain types of losses. For example, the inability to predict future unemployment rates and the potential for catastrophic losses make the peril of unemployment virtually uninsurable in the private sector. In addition, broad medical expense coverage for the aged can be marketed commercially only at a price beyond the financial means of many retirees.

Finally, many Americans have come to expect the government to provide at least a degree of economic security against the consequences of premature death, old age, disability, and unemployment. As a result, social insurance programs enjoy widespread public acceptance.

■ CHARACTERISTICS OF SOCIAL INSURANCE

Even though there are variations in social insurance programs, and exceptions to the rule always exist, social insurance programs tend to have the following distinguishing characteristics:

- Compulsory employment-related coverage
- Partial or total employer financing
- Benefits prescribed by law
- Benefits as a matter of right
- Emphasis on social adequacy

Compulsory Employment-Related Coverage

Most social insurance programs are compulsory and require that the persons covered be attached—either presently or by past service—to the labor force. If a social insurance program is to meet a social need through the redistribution of income, it must have widespread participation.

Partial or Total Employer Financing

While significant variations exist in social insurance programs, most require that the cost of the program be borne fully or at least partially by the employers of the covered persons. This is the basis for including these programs under the broad definition of employee benefits. The remaining cost of most social insurance programs is paid primarily by the persons covered under the programs. With the exception of Medicare and certain unemployment benefits, the general revenues of the federal government and state governments finance only a small portion of social insurance benefits.

Benefits Prescribed by Law

Although benefit amounts and the eligibility requirements for social insurance benefits are prescribed by law, benefits are not necessarily uniform for everyone. They may vary by such factors as wage level, length of covered employment, or family status. These factors are incorporated into the benefit formulas specified by law, and covered persons are unable to either increase or decrease their prescribed level of benefits.

Benefits as a Matter of Right

Social insurance benefits are paid as a matter of right under the presumption that a need for the benefits exists. This feature distinguishes social insurance programs from public assistance or welfare programs under which applicants, in order to qualify for benefits, must meet a needs test by demonstrating that their income or assets are below some specified level.

Emphasis on Social Adequacy

Benefits under social insurance programs are based more on social adequacy than on individual equity. Under the principle of **social adequacy**, benefits are designed to provide a minimum floor of income to all beneficiaries under the program regardless of their economic status. Above this floor of benefits, persons are expected to provide additional resources from their own savings, employment, or private insurance programs. This emphasis on social adequacy also results in disproportionately large benefits in relation to contributions for some groups of beneficiaries. Under some programs, high-income persons, single persons or small families, and the young are subsidizing low-income persons, large families, and the retired.

If social insurance programs were based solely on **individual equity**, benefits would be actuarially related to contributions just as they are under private insurance programs. While this degree of individual equity does not exist, there is some relationship between benefits and income levels (and thus contributions). Within certain maximum and minimum amounts, benefits are a function of a person's covered earnings under social insurance programs. However, the major emphasis is on social adequacy.

■ SOCIAL SECURITY AND MEDICARE

In a broad sense, the term *Social Security* can be used to refer to any of several programs resulting from the Social Security Act of 1935 and its frequent amendments over the years. The act established four programs aimed at providing economic security for American society:

1. Old-age insurance
2. Unemployment insurance
3. Federal grants for assistance to certain needy groups: the aged, the blind, and children

4. Federal grants for maternal and child welfare, public health work, and vocational rehabilitation

The main focus in this chapter is on the old-age insurance program and the benefits that have been added to that program over the years. These additional benefits include survivors insurance (1939), disability insurance (1956), hospital insurance (1965), and supplementary medical insurance (1965). Taken together, these programs constitute the old-age, survivors, disability, and health insurance (OASDHI) program of the federal government. This program is often separated into two broad parts. The first part is the old-age, survivors, and disability insurance (OASDI) program. Over the years, OASDI has become commonly referred to as **Social Security**, and this is the terminology that will be used in this book. The remainder of the OASDHI program is called **Medicare**, with hospital insurance being called *Part A* and most other medical insurance being called *Part B*. Significant changes were made to Medicare by the passage of the Medicare Prescription Drug, Improvement, and Modernization Act of 2003.

The following discussion of Social Security and Medicare begins with a description of the extent of coverage under the programs and the way the programs are financed. It then focuses on the eligibility requirements and benefits under the various parts of the programs. Because of the many differences between Social Security and Medicare, the discussion largely treats each program separately. This is followed by a discussion of the adequacy of the funding of these programs. Finally, there is a description of the tax implications of Social Security and Medicare benefits and contributions.

More detailed information than is contained in this chapter about Social Security and Medicare can be found on their Web sites: *www.socialsecurity.gov* and *www.medicare.gov*. Throughout this chapter are many dollar amounts that are indicated as being for 2004. These amounts are subject to annual indexing, and the amounts for a given year are posted on these respective Web sites in October or November of the prior year.

Extent of Coverage

More than 90 percent of the workers in the United States are in covered employment under the Social Security program and more than 95 percent under the Medicare program. This means that these workers have wages (if they are employees) or self-employment income (if they are self-employed) on which Social Security and Medicare taxes must be paid. The following are the major categories of workers who are not covered under the programs or who are covered only if they have met specific conditions:

- Civilian employees of the federal government who were employed by the government prior to 1984 and who are covered under the Civil Service Retirement System or certain other federal retirement programs. These workers are covered by government plans that provide benefits similar to those available under Social Security. All federal employees are covered under Medicare.

- Railroad workers. Under the Railroad Retirement Act, employees of railroads have their own benefit system that is similar to Social Security. However, they are covered under Medicare.

- Some state and local government employees if their employers did not elect to bring them under the Social Security and Medicare programs. However, coverage under Medicare is compulsory for state and local employees hired after March 1986, and coverage under Social Security is compulsory for employees hired after July 1, 1991, if they do not participate in a public retirement system.

- American citizens working abroad for foreign affiliates of U.S. employers, unless the U.S. employer owns at least a 10 percent interest in the foreign affiliate and has made arrangements with the secretary of the treasury for the payment of Social Security and Medicare taxes. However, Americans working abroad are covered under Social Security and Medicare if they are working directly for U.S. employers rather than for their foreign subsidiaries.

- Ministers who elect out of coverage because of conscience or religious principles.

- Workers in certain jobs, such as student nurses, newspaper carriers under age 18, and students working for the school at which they are regularly enrolled or doing domestic work for a local college club, fraternity, or sorority.

- Certain family employment. This includes the employment of a child under age 18 by a parent. This exclusion, however, does not apply if the employment is for a corporation owned by a family member.

- Certain workers who must satisfy special earnings requirements. For example, self-employed persons are not covered unless they have net annual earnings of $400 or more. In addition, certain agricultural workers must have annual cash wages of $150 or more, and domestic workers must earn $1,400 or more in cash wages in a calendar year.

Tax Rates and Wage Bases

Part B of Medicare is financed by a combination of monthly premiums paid by persons eligible for benefits and contributions from the federal government. Part A of Medicare and all the benefits of the Social Security program are financed through a system of payroll and self-employment taxes paid by all persons covered under the programs. In addition, employers of covered persons are also taxed. These taxes are often referred to as FICA taxes because they are imposed under the Federal Insurance Contributions Act.

In 2004, an employee and his or her employer each pay a tax of 7.65 percent on the first $87,900 of the employee's wages. Of this tax rate, 6.2 percent is for Social Security; 1.45 percent is for the hospital insurance portion of Medicare. The Medicare tax rate of 1.45 percent is also levied on all wages in excess of $87,900. The tax rates were scheduled to remain the same after 2002. However, the wage bases are adjusted annually for changes in the national level of wages. Therefore, if wage levels increase by 4 percent in a particular year, the wage base for the following year will also increase by 4 percent. The tax rate for the self-employed is 15.3 percent on the first $87,900 of self-employment income and 2.9 percent on the balance of any self-employment income. This is equal to the combined employee and employer rates.

Over the years, both the tax rates and wage bases have risen dramatically to finance increased benefit levels under Social Security and Medicare as well as new benefits that have been added to the program. Table 3.1 shows the magnitude of these increases for selected years.

The adequacy of the current funding structure to pay for Social Security and Medicare benefits continues to be a source of public concern and political debate. The issue is addressed in more detail after the programs are described.

■ SOCIAL SECURITY: ELIGIBILITY

To be eligible for benefits under Social Security, an individual must have credit for a minimum amount of work under the program. This credit is based on quarters of coverage. For 2004, a worker receives credit for one quarter of coverage for each $900 in annual earnings on which Social Security taxes are paid. However, credit for no more than four quarters of coverage may be earned in any one calendar year. Consequently, a worker paying Social Security taxes on as little as $3,600 (that is, $900 × 4) at any time during the year will receive credit for the maximum four quarters. As in the case of the wage base, the amount of earnings necessary for a quarter of coverage is adjusted annually for changes in the national level of wages.

Quarters of coverage are the basis for establishing an insured status under Social Security. The three types of insured status are fully insured, currently insured, and disability insured.

Fully Insured

A person is **fully insured** under Social Security if either of two tests is met. The first test requires credit for 40 quarters of coverage. Once a person acquires such credit, he or she is fully insured for life even if covered employment under Social Security ceases.

Under the second test, a person who has credit for a minimum of six quarters of coverage is fully insured if he or she has credit for at least as many quarters of coverage as there are years elapsing *after* 1950 (or *after* the year in which age 21 is reached, if later) and *before* the year in which he or she dies, becomes disabled, or reaches age 62, whichever occurs first. Therefore, a worker who reached age 21 in 1992 and who died in 2004 would need credit for only 11 quarters of coverage for his or her family to be eligible for survivors benefits under Social Security.

Currently Insured

If a worker is fully insured under Social Security, there is no additional significance to being currently insured. However, if a worker is not fully insured, certain survivors benefits are still available if a currently insured status exists. To be **currently insured**, a worker must have credit for at least 6 quarters of coverage out of the 13-quarter period ending with the quarter in which death occurs.

TABLE 3.1	Changes in Tax Rates and Wage Bases under Social Security and Medicare		
Year	Wage Base	Tax Rate	Maximum Employee Tax
1950	$ 3,000	1.50%	$ 45.00
1960	4,800	3.00	144.00
1970	7,800	4.80	374.40
1980	25,900	6.13	1,587.67
1990	51,300	7.65	3,924.45
1991	first 53,400	7.65	
	next 71,600	1.45	5,123.30
1992	first 55,500	7.65	
	next 74,700	1.45	5,328.90
1993	first 57,600	7.65	
	next 77,400	1.45	5,528.70
1994	first 60,600	7.65	
	additional wages	1.45	‡
1995	first 61,200	7.65	
	additional wages	1.45	‡
1996	first 62,700	7.65	
	additional wages	1.45	‡
1997	first 65,400	7.65	
	additional wages	1.45	‡
1998	first 68,400	7.65	
	additional wages	1.45	‡
1999	first 72,600	7.65	
	additional wages	1.45	‡
2000	first 76,200	7.65	
	additional wages	1.45	‡
2001	first 80,400	7.65	
	additional wages	1.45	‡
2002	first 84,900	7.65	
	additional wages	1.45	‡
2003	first 87,000	7.65	
	additional wages	1.45	‡
2004	first 87,900	7.65	
	additional wages	1.45	‡
2005 and after	*	†	‡

*Subject to automatic adjustment.
†Same as 2004.
‡No determinable maximum due to unlimited wage base for Medicare tax.

Disability Insured

To receive disability benefits under Social Security, it is necessary to be **disability insured**. At a minimum, a disability-insured status requires that a worker (1) be fully insured and (2) have a minimum amount of work under Social Security within a recent time period. In connection with the latter requirement, workers aged 31 or older must have credit for at least 20 of the last 40 quarters ending with the quarter in which disability occurs; workers between the ages of 24 and 30, inclusively, must have credit for at least half the quarters of coverage from the time they turned 21 and the quarter in which disability begins; and workers under age 24 must have credit for 6 out of the last 12 quarters, ending with the quarter in which disability begins.

A special rule for the blind states that they are exempt from the recent-work rules and are considered disability insured as long as they are fully insured.

■ SOCIAL SECURITY: TYPES OF BENEFITS

As its name implies, the Social Security program provides three principal types of benefits:

1. Retirement (old-age) benefits
2. Survivors benefits
3. Disability benefits

Retirement Benefits

A worker who is fully insured under Social Security is eligible to receive monthly retirement benefits as early as age 62. However, the election to receive benefits prior to the full retirement age of 65 results in a permanently reduced benefit.

Full retirement age (sometimes referred to as *normal retirement age*), or the age at which nonreduced retirement benefits are paid, is 65 for workers born in 1937 or before. As shown in Table 3.2, a gradually increasing full retirement age applies to workers born in 1938 and later.

In addition to the retired worker, the following dependents of persons receiving retirement benefits are also eligible for monthly benefits:

■ A spouse aged 62 or older. However, benefits are permanently reduced if this benefit is elected prior to the spouse's reaching full retirement age. This benefit is also available to a divorced spouse under certain circumstances if the marriage lasted at least ten years.

■ A spouse of any age if the spouse is caring for at least one child of the retired worker who is (1) under age 16 or (2) disabled and entitled to a child's benefit as described below. This benefit is commonly referred to as a *mother's* or *father's benefit*.

■ Dependent, unmarried children under age 18. This child's benefit will continue until age 19 as long as a child is a full-time student in elementary or secondary school. In addition, disabled children of any age are eligible for benefits as long as they were disabled before reaching age 22.

TABLE 3.2	Retirement Age for Nonreduced Benefits
Year of Birth	**Full Retirement Age**
1937 and before	65 years
1938	65 years, 2 months
1939	65 years, 4 months
1940	65 years, 6 months
1941	65 years, 8 months
1942	65 years, 10 months
1943–54	66 years
1955	66 years, 2 months
1956	66 years, 4 months
1957	66 years, 6 months
1958	66 years, 8 months
1959	66 years, 10 months
1960 and later	67 years

It is important to note that retirement benefits, as well as all other benefits under Social Security and Medicare, are not automatically paid on eligibility but must be applied for.

Survivors Benefits

All categories of survivors benefits are payable if a worker is fully insured at the time of death. However, three types of benefits are also payable if a worker is only currently insured. The first is a lump-sum death benefit of $255, payable in the following order of priority:

- To a surviving spouse who was living with the deceased worker at the time of death
- To a surviving spouse (other than a divorced spouse) who was not living with the deceased worker at the time of death if the surviving spouse is eligible for or entitled to benefits based on the deceased wage earner's record for the month of death
- To children who are eligible for or entitled to benefits based on the deceased wage earner's record for the month of death

If none of these categories of survivors exists, the benefit is not paid.

There are two categories of persons eligible for income benefits as survivors if a deceased worker was either fully or currently insured at the time of death:

1. Dependent, unmarried children under the same conditions as previously described for retirement benefits
2. A spouse (including a divorced spouse) caring for a child or children under the same conditions as previously described for retirement benefits

The following categories of persons are also eligible for benefits, but only if the deceased worker was fully insured:

■ A widow or widower aged 60 or older. However, benefits are reduced if taken prior to full retirement age. This benefit is also payable to a divorced spouse if the marriage lasted at least ten years. In addition, the widow's or widower's benefit is payable to a disabled spouse at age 50 as long as the disability commenced no more than seven years after (1) the worker's death or (2) the end of the year in which entitlement to a mother's or father's benefit ceased.

■ A parent aged 62 or over who was a dependent of the deceased worker at the time of death.

Disability Benefits

A disabled worker under full retirement age is eligible to receive benefits under Social Security as long as he or she is disability insured and meets the definition of disability under the law. The definition of disability is very rigid and requires a mental or physical impairment that prevents the worker from engaging in any substantial gainful employment. The disability must also have lasted (or be expected to last) at least 12 months or be expected to result in death. A more liberal definition of disability applies to blind workers who are aged 55 or older. They are considered disabled if they are unable to perform work that requires skills or abilities comparable to those required by the work they regularly performed before reaching age 55 or becoming blind, if later.

Disability benefits are subject to a waiting period and are payable beginning with the sixth full calendar month of disability. In addition to the benefit paid to a disabled worker, benefits are also paid to a spouse and children under the same conditions that were described for retirement benefits.

As previously mentioned, certain family members not otherwise eligible for Social Security benefits may be eligible if they are disabled. Disabled children are subject to the same definition of disability as workers. However, disabled widows or widowers must be unable to engage in any gainful (rather than substantial gainful) employment.

Eligibility for Dual Benefits

In many cases, a person is eligible for more than one type of Social Security benefit. Probably the most common situation occurs when a person is eligible for both a spouse's benefit and a worker's retirement or disability benefit based on his or her own Social Security record. In this case and in any other case when a person is eligible for dual benefits, only an amount equal to the higher benefit is paid.

Termination of Benefits

Monthly benefits to any Social Security recipient cease on death of the recipient. When a retired or disabled worker dies, the family members' benefits that are based on the worker's retirement or disability benefits also cease, but the family members are then eligible for survivors benefits.

Disability benefits for a worker technically terminate at full retirement age but are then replaced by comparable retirement benefits. In addition, any benefits payable because of disability cease if medical or other evidence shows that the definition of disability is no longer satisfied. However, the disability benefits will continue during a readjustment period that consists of the month of recovery and two additional months. As an encouragement for them to return to work, disabled beneficiaries for whom there is no evidence that their disability has otherwise terminated are allowed a nine-month trial work period during which benefits are not affected regardless of how much they earn. At the end of that period, a beneficiary's earnings are evaluated to determine if the earnings are substantial ($810 per month in 2004). If earnings then exceed this amount for three months, benefits are suspended but can be reinstated during the next 36 months without starting a new application process should the earnings fall below this level.

As long as children are not disabled, benefits will usually terminate at age 18 but may continue until age 19 if the child is a full-time student in elementary or secondary school.

The benefit of a surviving spouse terminates upon remarriage unless remarriage takes place at age 60 or later.

■ SOCIAL SECURITY: BENEFIT AMOUNTS

Calculating Benefits

With the exception of the $255 lump-sum death benefit, the amount of all Social Security benefits is based on a worker's **primary insurance amount (PIA)**. The PIA is the amount a worker receives if he or she retires at full retirement age or becomes disabled, and it is the amount on which benefits for family members are based. The actual PIA calculation is complex and is done by the Social Security Administration when a beneficiary is eligible for benefits. It involves indexing past wages on which taxes were paid to current wage levels, eliminating some years with the lowest or no earnings, and averaging the indexed wages for the remaining years. The result is then put into a formula that is weighted in favor of lower-income workers.

The average PIA for a worker who retires at normal retirement age in 2004 is about $875. A worker who has continually earned the maximum income subject to Social Security taxes can expect to have a PIA for retirement purposes of about $1,825 if he or she retires at the full retirement age in 2004. The maximum PIA in 2004 for purposes of disability and survivors benefits ranges from approximately $1,825 to $2,025. The higher PIA results for workers who are disabled or die at younger ages. Table 3.3 shows the Social Security Administration's estimated average monthly benefit being received in 2004 for various categories of beneficiaries.

If a worker is retired or disabled, additional benefits are paid to family members as shown in Table 3.4. If the worker dies, survivors benefits are as shown in Table 3.5. However, the full benefits described in the tables may not be payable because of a limitation imposed on the total benefits that may be paid to a family. This family maximum is again determined by a formula and is usually reached if three or more family members (including a retired or disabled worker) are eligible for benefits.

TABLE 3.3	Estimated Average Monthly Social Security Benefits, 2004
Category of Beneficiary	**Amount**
All Retired Workers	$ 922
Aged Couple, Both Receiving Benefits	1,523
Widowed Mother and Two Children	1,904
Aged Widow(er) Alone	888
Disabled Worker, Spouse, and One or More Children	1,442
All Disabled Workers	862

If the total amount of benefits payable to family members exceeds the family maximum, the worker's benefit (in the case of retirement and disability) is not affected, but the benefits of other family members are reduced proportionately. For example, assume a worker dies leaving a spouse under age 65 and three children who are each eligible for 75 percent of the worker's PIA of $1,200. If the family maximum is ignored, the benefits total $3,600 ($900 for each family member). However, the family maximum using the prescribed formula for 2004 is $2,211.98. Therefore, each family member has his or her benefit reduced to $552 (rounded to the next lower dollar). When the first child loses benefits at age 18, each of the other family members has his or her benefit increased to $737 (if any automatic increases in benefit amounts, including the family maximum, are ignored). When a second family member loses eligibility, the remaining two family members each receive the full benefit of $900 because the benefits received by the family now total less than the $2,211.98 calculated by the formula.

Other Factors Affecting Benefits

Special Minimum PIA. There is a minimum PIA for workers who have been covered under Social Security for at least ten years but at very low wages. This PIA is used only if it is higher than a worker's PIA based on actual wages, which is usually not the case. The benefit is first determined by multiplying $11.50 times the number of years of coverage less 10, subject to a maximum of 20. This figure is then adjusted for the cumulative change in the consumer price index (CPI) since 1979. In 2004, a worker

TABLE 3.4	Benefits for Family Members of a Disabled or Retired Worker
Family Member	**Percentage of Worker's PIA**
Spouse at Full Retirement Age	50%
Spouse Caring for Disabled Child or Child under 16	50%
Child under 18 or Disabled	50% each

TABLE 3.5	Benefits for Family Members of a Deceased Worker	
Family Member	**Percentage of Worker's PIA**
Spouse at Full Retirement Age	100%
Spouse Caring for Disabled Child or Child under 16	75%
Child under 18 or Disabled	75% each
Dependent Parent	82.5% for one, 75% each for two

with 30 or more years of coverage under Social Security will have a minimum PIA at age 65 of approximately $640.

Benefits Taken Early.   If a worker elects to receive retirement benefits prior to full retirement age, benefits are permanently reduced by 5/9 of 1 percent for every month that the early retirement precedes full retirement age. For example, for a worker who retires three years before full retirement age, the monthly benefit is only 80 percent of that worker's PIA. A dependent spouse who elects retirement benefits prior to full retirement age has benefits reduced by 25/36 of 1 percent per month, and a widow or widower has benefits reduced by 19/40 of 1 percent per month. In the latter case, benefits at age 60 are 71 1/2 percent of the worker's PIA if the full retirement age is 65. If the widow or widower elects benefits prior to age 60 because of disability, there is no further reduction.

Delayed Retirement.   Workers who delay applying for benefits until after full retirement age are eligible for an increased benefit. Benefits are increased for each month of late retirement until age 70. For persons born in the years from 1917 until 1924, the increase is 1/4 of 1 percent per month, which is equal to 3 percent for delaying application for benefits for one full year. To encourage later retirement, the monthly percentage gradually increases. Table 3.6 shows the percentage for each month of deferral as well as the maximum percentage increase that is available if retirement is postponed until age 70.

It should be pointed out that these increases apply to a worker's PIA as determined at the time a worker applies for retirement benefits. If a person continues to work during the period of delayed retirement and covered wages are sufficiently high, it is possible for a worker's PIA to be higher than it would have been at full retirement age. Therefore, the increased monthly retirement benefit from working past full retirement age may be greater than the percentages in the table.

Earnings Test.   Through the 1999 tax year, benefits were reduced for Social Security beneficiaries under the age of 70 if they had wages that exceeded a specified level. For tax years beginning after 1999, Congress repealed this earnings test in and after the month in which a beneficiary attains the full Social Security retirement age. As shown in Table 3.2, this age is scheduled to increase. However, the **earnings test** still applies to beneficiaries under full retirement age. They are allowed earnings of up to $11,280 in 2002, and this figure is subject to annual indexing for later years. If a beneficiary earns more than this amount, his or her Social Security benefit is reduced by $1 for each $2 of excess earnings. There is one exception to the test. The reduction is $1 for every $3 of earnings in excess of $31,080 (in 2004) in the calendar year a worker attains

	TABLE 3.6	Increase for Delayed Retirement

Year of Birth	Monthly Percentage Increase	Maximum Percentage Increase
1917–24	1/4	15.00
1925–26	7/24	17.50
1927–28	1/3	20.00
1929–30	9/24	22.50
1931–32	5/12	25.00
1933–34	11/24	27.50
1935–36	1/2	30.00
1937	13/24	32.50
1938	13/24	31.42
1939	7/12	32.67
1940	7/12	31.50
1941	15/24	32.50
1942	15/24	31.25
1943–54	2/3	32.00
1955	2/3	30.67
1956	2/3	29.33
1957	2/3	28.00
1958	2/3	26.67
1959	2/3	25.33
1960 and later	2/3	24.00

the full retirement age, for earnings in months prior to such age attainment. Once the beneficiary reaches full retirement age, any amount can be earned without a Social Security reduction.

The reduction in a retired worker's benefits resulting from excess earnings is charged against the entire benefits that are paid to a family and based on the worker's Social Security record. If large enough, this reduction may totally eliminate all benefits otherwise payable to the worker and family members. In contrast, excess earnings of family members are charged against their individual benefits only. For example, a widowed mother who holds a job outside the home may lose her mother's benefit, but any benefits received by her children are unaffected.

Cost-of-Living Adjustments.   Social Security benefits are increased automatically each January as long as there has been an increase in the Consumer Price Index (CPI) for the one-year period ending in the third quarter of the prior year. The increase is the same as the increase in the CPI since the last cost-of-living adjustment, rounded to the nearest 0.1 percent.

There is one exception to this adjustment. In any year that the combined reserves of the Social Security trust funds drop below 20 percent of expected benefits, the cost-of-living adjustment is limited to the lesser of the increase in the CPI or the increase in national wages used to adjust the wage base for Social Security taxes. When benefit

increases are based on wage levels, future cost-of-living increases can be larger than changes in the CPI to make up for the lower benefit increases in those years when the CPI was not used. However, this extra cost-of-living increase is made only in years when the reserve is equal to at least 32 percent of expected benefits.

Offset for Other Benefits. Disabled workers under full retirement age who are also receiving workers' compensation benefits or disability benefits from certain other federal, state, or local disability programs have their Social Security benefits reduced to the extent that the total benefits received (including family benefits) exceed 80 percent of their average current earnings at the time of disability. In addition, the monthly benefit of a spouse or surviving spouse is reduced by two-thirds of any federal, state, or local government pension that is based on earnings not covered under Social Security on the last day of employment.

■ SOCIAL SECURITY: OBTAINING BENEFIT INFORMATION

The Social Security Administration annually sends a **Social Security Statement** to all persons aged 25 or older who have covered employment under Social Security and are not currently entitled to monthly benefits. The statement enables an employee to verify his or her contributions to the Social Security and Medicare programs. It also contains an estimate of benefits that are available upon retirement, disability, or death.

The statement will help employees understand their total benefit package as well as enable any errors in earnings records to be corrected while information is readily available. As a general rule, requests for corrections must be made within 3 years, 3 months, and 15 days following the year in which wages were paid or self-employment income was earned. However, clerical or fraudulent errors can be corrected after that time.

■ MEDICARE: ELIGIBILITY

Part A, the hospital portion of Medicare, is available to any person aged 65 or older as long as the person is entitled to monthly retirement benefits under Social Security or the railroad retirement program. Civilian employees of the federal government aged 65 or older are also eligible. It is not necessary for these workers to actually be receiving retirement benefits, but they must be fully insured for purposes of retirement benefits. The following persons are also eligible for Part A of Medicare at no monthly cost:

- Persons aged 65 or older who are dependents of fully insured workers aged 62 or older.
- Survivors aged 65 or older who are eligible for Social Security survivors benefits.
- Disabled persons at any age who have been eligible to receive Social Security benefits for two years because of their disability. This includes workers under age 65, disabled widows and widowers aged 50 or over, and children 18 or older who were disabled prior to age 22.
- Workers who are either fully or currently insured and their spouses and dependent children with end-stage renal (kidney) disease who require renal dialysis or kidney

transplants. Coverage begins either the first day of the third month after dialysis begins or earlier for admission to a hospital for kidney-transplant surgery.

Most persons aged 65 or over who do not meet the previously discussed eligibility requirements may voluntarily enroll in Medicare. However, they must pay a monthly Part A premium and also enroll in Part B. The monthly Part A premium in 2004 is $343 for individuals with fewer than 30 quarters of Medicare-covered employment and $189 for individuals with 30 to 39 quarters. The premium is adjusted annually, and the $343 amount reflects the full cost of the benefits provided.

Any person eligible for Part A of Medicare is also eligible for Part B. However, a monthly premium must be paid for Part B. This premium, $66.60 in 2004, is adjusted annually to equal 25 percent of the cost of the benefits provided. The remaining cost of the program is financed from the general revenues of the federal government. As a result of the Medicare Prescription Drug, Improvement, and Modernization Act of 2003, the Part B premium will continue to equal 25 percent of Part B benefit costs, but only for beneficiaries with modified adjusted gross income under $80,000 for a single person and $160,000 for a couple. Beginning in 2006, higher income persons will pay a larger premium that increases with income. These increases will be phased in over five years, until persons with incomes above $200,000 ($400,000 for a couple) will have a Part B premium equal to 80 percent of the benefits provided. Starting in 2007, these income figures will also be indexed.

Persons receiving Social Security or railroad retirement benefits are automatically enrolled in Medicare if they are eligible. If they do not want Part B, they must reject it in writing. Other persons eligible for Medicare must apply for benefits. As a general rule, anyone who rejects Part B or who does not enroll when initially eligible may later apply for benefits during a general enrollment period that occurs between January 1 and March 31 of each year. However, the monthly premium is increased by 10 percent for each 12-month period during which the person was eligible but failed to enroll.

Medicare secondary rules, which are covered in detail in Chapter 14, make employer-provided medical expense coverage primary to Medicare for certain classes of individuals who are over 65, who are disabled, or who are suffering end-stage renal disease. These persons (and any other Medicare-eligible persons still covered as active employees under their employer's plans) may not wish to elect Medicare because it largely constitutes duplicate coverage. When their employer-provided coverage ends, these persons have a seven-month special enrollment period to elect Part B coverage, and the late enrollment penalty is waived.

Medicare is also secondary to benefits received by persons (1) entitled to veterans' or black lung benefits, (2) covered by workers' compensation laws, or (3) whose medical expenses are paid under no-fault insurance or liability insurance.

■ MEDICARE PART A: HOSPITAL INSURANCE

Medicare Part A is referred to as the *hospital insurance portion of Medicare*. It, however, also provides benefits for care in skilled-nursing facilities, home health care, and hospice care. For benefits to be paid, the facility or agency providing benefits must

participate in the Medicare program. Virtually all hospitals are participants, as are most other facilities or agencies that meet the requirements of Medicare.

Part A of Medicare, along with Part B, provides a high level of benefits. However, as described in the next few pages, deductibles and copayments may be higher than in prior group or individual coverage. In addition, certain benefits that were previously provided may be excluded or limited. For this reason, persons without supplemental retiree coverage from prior employment may wish to consider the purchase of a Medicare supplement (medigap) policy in the individual marketplace.

Hospital Benefits

Part A pays for inpatient hospital services for up to 90 days in each benefit period (also referred to as a *spell of illness*). A benefit period begins the first time a Medicare recipient is hospitalized and ends only after the recipient has been out of a hospital or skilled-nursing facility for 60 consecutive days. A subsequent hospitalization then begins a new benefit period.

In each benefit period, covered hospital expenses are paid in full for 60 days, subject to an initial deductible of $876 in 2004. This deductible is adjusted annually to reflect increasing hospital costs. Benefits for an additional 30 days of hospitalization are also provided in each benefit period, but the patient must pay a daily copayment ($219 in 2004) equal to 25 percent of the initial deductible amount. Each recipient also has a lifetime reserve of 60 additional days that may be used if the regular 90 days of benefits have been exhausted. However, once a reserve day is used, it cannot be restored for use in future benefit periods. When using reserve days, patients must pay a daily copayment ($438 in 2004) equal to 50 percent of the initial deductible amount.

There is no limit on the number of benefit periods a person may have during his or her lifetime. However, there is a lifetime limit of 190 days of benefits for treatment in psychiatric hospitals.

Covered inpatient expenses include the following:

- Room and board in semiprivate accommodations. Private rooms are covered only if required for medical reasons.
- Nursing services (except private-duty nurses).
- Use of regular hospital equipment, such as oxygen tents or wheelchairs.
- Drugs and biologicals ordinarily furnished by the hospital.
- Diagnostic or therapeutic items or services.
- Operating room costs.
- Blood transfusions after the first three pints of blood. Patients must pay for the first three pints unless they get donors to replace the blood.

There is no coverage under Part A for the services of physicians or surgeons.

Skilled-Nursing Facility Benefits

In many cases, a patient may no longer require continuous hospital care but may not be well enough to go home. Consequently, Part A provides benefits for care in a skilled-nursing facility if a physician certifies that skilled-nursing care or rehabilitative services are needed for a condition that was treated in a hospital within the past 30 days. In addition, the prior hospitalization must have lasted at least three days. Benefits are paid in full for 20 days in each benefit period and for an additional 80 days with a daily copayment ($109.50 in 2004) that is equal to 12.5 percent of the initial hospital deductible. Covered expenses are the same as those described for hospital benefits.

A **skilled-nursing facility** may be a separate facility for providing such care or a separate section of a hospital or nursing home. The facility must have at least one full-time registered nurse, and nursing services must be provided at all times. Every patient must be under the supervision of a physician, and a physician must always be available for emergency care.

One very important point should be made about skilled-nursing facility benefits. Custodial care is not provided under any part of the Medicare program unless skilled-nursing or rehabilitative services are also needed.

Home Health Care Benefits

If a patient can be treated at home for a medical condition, Medicare pays the full cost for **home health care** in the form of an unlimited number of home visits by a home health agency. Such agencies specialize in providing nursing services and other therapeutic services. To receive these benefits, a person must be confined at home and be treated under a home health plan set up by a physician. No prior hospitalization is required. The care needed must include skilled-nursing services, physical therapy, or speech therapy. In addition to these services, Medicare also pays for the cost of part-time home health aides, medical social services, occupational therapy, and medical supplies and equipment provided by the home health agency. There is no charge for these services other than a required 20 percent copayment for the cost of such durable medical equipment as iron lungs, oxygen tanks, and hospital beds. Medicare does not cover home services furnished primarily to assist people in activities of daily living, such as housecleaning, preparing meals, shopping, dressing, or bathing.

If a person has only Part A of Medicare, all home health care services are covered under Part A. If a person has both Parts A and B, the first 100 visits that commence within 14 days of a hospital stay of at least 3 days are covered under Part A. All other home health visits are covered under Part B.

Hospice Benefits

Hospice care benefits are available under Part A of Medicare for beneficiaries who are certified as being terminally ill persons with a life expectancy of six months or less. While a hospice is thought of as a facility for treating the terminally ill, Medicare benefits are available primarily for services provided by a Medicare-approved hospice to patients in their own homes. However, inpatient care can be provided if needed by the patient. In addition to including the types of benefits described for home health care, hospice benefits also include drugs, bereavement counseling, and inpatient respite care when family members need a break from caring for the ill person.

To qualify for hospice benefits, a Medicare recipient must elect such coverage in lieu of other Medicare benefits, except for the services of the attending physician or services and benefits that do not pertain to the terminal condition. There are modest copayments for some services.

The benefit period consists of two 90-day periods followed by an unlimited number of 60-day periods. These periods can be used consecutively or at intervals. A beneficiary may cancel the hospice coverage at any time (for example, to pursue chemotherapy treatments) and return to regular Medicare coverage. Any remaining days of the current hospice benefit period are lost forever, but the beneficiary can elect hospice benefits again. However, the beneficiary must be recertified as terminally ill at the beginning of each new benefit period.

Exclusions

There are some circumstances under which Part A of Medicare does not pay benefits. In addition, there are times when Medicare acts as the secondary payer of benefits. Exclusions under Part A include the following:

- Services outside the United States and its territories or possessions. However, there are a few exceptions to this rule for qualified Mexican and Canadian hospitals. Benefits are paid if an emergency occurs in the United States and the closest hospital is in one of these countries. In addition, persons living closer to a hospital in one of these countries than to a hospital in the United States may use the foreign hospital even if an emergency does not exist. Finally, there is coverage for Canadian hospitals if a person needs hospitalization while traveling the most direct route between Alaska and another state in the United States. However, this latter provision does not apply to persons vacationing in Canada.

- Elective luxury services, such as private rooms or televisions.

- Hospitalization for services not necessary for the treatment of an illness or injury, such as custodial care or elective cosmetic surgery.

- Services performed in a federal facility, such as a veterans' hospital.

- Services covered under workers' compensation.

Medicare is the secondary payer of benefits under these circumstances:

- When primary coverage under an employer-provided medical expense plan is elected by (1) an employee or spouse aged 65 or older or (2) a disabled beneficiary.

- When medical care can be paid under any liability policy, including policies providing automobile no-fault benefits.

■ In the first 30 months for end-stage renal disease when an employer-provided plan provides coverage. By law, employer plans cannot specifically exclude this coverage during this 30-month period.

Medicare pays only if complete coverage is not available from these sources and then only to the extent that benefits are less than would otherwise be payable under Medicare. These Medicare secondary rules are covered in more detail in Chapter 14.

■ MEDICARE PART B: MEDICAL INSURANCE

Benefits

Medicare Part B provides benefits for most medical expenses not covered under Part A. These include the following:

■ Physicians' and surgeons' fees. These fees may result from house calls, office visits, or services provided in a hospital or other institution. Under certain circumstances, benefits are also provided for the services of chiropractors, podiatrists, and optometrists.

■ Diagnostic tests in a hospital or in a physician's office.

■ X-rays.

■ Physical therapy in a physician's office, or as an outpatient of a hospital, skilled-nursing facility, or other approved clinic, rehabilitative agency, or public-health agency.

■ Blood transfusions.

■ Drugs and biologicals that cannot be self-administered.

■ Radiation therapy.

■ Medical supplies, such as surgical dressings, splints, and casts.

■ Rental of medical equipment, such as oxygen tents, hospital beds, and wheelchairs.

■ Prosthetic devices, such as artificial heart valves or lenses after a cataract operation.

■ Ambulance service if a patient's condition does not permit the use of other methods of transportation.

■ Mammograms and Pap smears.

■ Diabetes glucose monitoring and education.

■ Diabetic screening for persons at risk of diabetes (beginning in 2005 as a result of the Medicare Drug, Improvement, and Modernization Act of 2003).

■ Screening blood test for early detection of heart disease (also beginning in 2005).

■ Colorectal cancer screening.

■ Bone mass measurement.

■ Prostate cancer screening.

■ Pneumococcal vaccine and its administration.

- Dilated eye examinations for beneficiaries at high risk for glaucoma.
- Home health care services as described for Part A when a person does not have Part A coverage or Part A benefits are not applicable.

Exclusions

Although the preceding list may appear to be comprehensive, there are numerous medical products and services not covered by Part B, some of which represent significant expenses for the elderly. They include the following:

- Most drugs and biologicals that can be self-administered, except drugs for osteoporosis, oral cancer treatment, and immunosuppressive therapy under specified circumstances. However, benefits will soon be available under Part D, which is discussed later.
- Routine physical, eye, and hearing examinations, except those previously mentioned. However, as part of the Medicare Drug, Improvement, and Modernization Act of 2003, all Medicare beneficiaries will be eligible for a one-time physical examination within six months of enrolling in Part B. This benefit begins in 2005.
- Routine foot care.
- Immunizations, except pneumococcal vaccinations or immunization required because of an injury or immediate risk of infection.
- Cosmetic surgery, unless it is needed because of an accidental injury or to improve the function of a malformed part of the body.
- Dental care, unless it involves jaw or facial bone surgery or the setting of fractures.
- Custodial care.
- Eyeglasses, hearing aids, or orthopedic shoes.

In addition, benefits are not provided to persons eligible for workers' compensation or to those treated in government hospitals. Benefits are provided only for services received in the United States, except for physicians' services and ambulance services rendered for a hospitalization that is covered in Mexico or Canada under Part A. Part B is also a secondary payer of benefits under the same circumstances described for Part A.

Amount of Benefits

The benefits available under Part B are subject to a number of different payment rules. A few charges are paid in full without any cost sharing. These include (1) home health services, (2) pneumococcal vaccine and its administration, (3) certain surgical procedures that are performed on an outpatient basis in lieu of hospitalization, (4) diagnostic preadmission tests performed on an outpatient basis within seven days prior to hospitalization, (5) mammograms, and (6) Pap smears.

For other charges, there is a $100 calendar-year deductible. (As a result of the Medicine Prescription Drug, Improvement, and Modernization Act, the deductible will increase to $110 in 2005 and be indexed for medical inflation beginning in 2006.) When the deductible is satisfied, Part B pays 80 percent of approved charges for most covered medical expenses other than professional charges for mental health care and outpatient services of hospitals and mental health centers. Medicare pays only 50 percent of approved charges for the mental health services of physicians and other mental health professionals. There is a separate payment system under which Medicare determines a set payment for each type of service for outpatient services of hospitals and mental health centers. However, this amount varies across the country to reflect such factors as the level of hospital wages. For some services, Medicare patients are required to pay an amount equal to 20 percent of the set payment amount, with Part B paying 80 percent. For other services, there is a fixed copayment that may be more or less than 20 percent of the set payment amount. In no case can the amount paid by a Medicare patient for a single service exceed a dollar figure equal to the Part A hospital deductible ($876 in 2004).

The approved charge for doctor's services covered by Medicare is based on a fee schedule issued by the Centers for Medicare & Medicaid Services (formerly the Health Care Financing Administration), which administers Medicare. A patient is reimbursed for only 80 percent of the approved charges above the deductible—regardless of the doctor's actual charge. Most doctors and other suppliers of medical services accept an assignment of Medicare benefits and therefore are prohibited from charging a patient in excess of the fee schedule. They can, however, bill the patient for any portion of the approved charges that were not paid by Medicare because of the annual deductible and/or coinsurance. They can also bill for any services that are not covered by Medicare.

Doctors who do not accept assignment of Medicare benefits cannot charge a Medicare patient more than 115 percent of the approved fee for nonparticipating doctors. Because the approved fee for nonparticipating doctors is set at 95 percent of the fee paid for participating doctors, a doctor who does not accept an assignment of Medicare benefits can charge a fee that is only 9.25 percent greater than if an assignment had been accepted (115 percent x 95 percent = 109.25 percent). As a result, some doctors either do not see Medicare participants, or they limit the number of such patients that they treat.

The previous limitation on charges does not apply to providers of medical services other than doctors. Although a provider who does not accept assignment can charge any fee, Medicare pays only what it would have paid if the provider accepted assignment. For example, assume the approved charge for medical equipment is $100 and the actual charge is $190. Medicare reimburses $80 (.80 x $100), and the balance is borne by the Medicare recipient.

■ MEDICARE PART C: MEDICARE ADVANTAGE (MEDICARE+CHOICE)

In 1985, Congress amended the Medicare program to allow a beneficiary to elect coverage under a health maintenance organization (HMO) as an alternative to the original Medicare program. At first, the number of persons electing this option was relatively small. Many of the elderly had not had HMO coverage during their working years and viewed such coverage with some skepticism. In addition, many HMOs continued to focus on expanding their traditional market of younger, healthier lives rather than entering a new and demographically different market. In addition, there were complex federal rules that had to be satisfied to enter the Medicare market.

The situation slowly changed as more HMOs got into the Medicare market and the public became more familiar with HMO coverage. In addition, as medical costs continued to rise, the election of an HMO option made more sense from a cost standpoint. As a result, HMO coverage for Medicare beneficiaries grew rapidly in the middle to late 1990s, and approximately one out of six beneficiaries had such coverage.

Under the 1985 rules, an HMO was basically given 95 percent of what Medicare would expect to pay to provide benefits if a beneficiary electing HMO coverage had stayed in the original Medicare program. In turn, the HMO was expected to provide at least the same benefits as those that are available under Medicare. While an HMO could provide additional benefits and charge an extra premium, many HMOs provided additional benefits, such as prescription drugs, without charging an additional premium. Such zero-premium plans were very popular among Medicare beneficiaries. While they had to continue paying the Part B Medicare premium, these beneficiaries were able to receive coverage that was broader than the original Medicare and thus had no reason to purchase a Medicare supplement policy. Beginning in 2003, such plans can be set up so that the Part B premium can be reduced rather than having benefits increased above what is available under Parts A and B.

In 1999, Part C of Medicare (called **Medicare+Choice**) went into effect. It expands the choices available to most Medicare beneficiaries by allowing them to elect medical expense benefits through one of several alternatives to Parts A and B as long as the providers of these alternatives enter into contracts with the Centers for Medicare & Medicaid Services. However, beneficiaries must still pay any Part B premium.

The Medicare+Choice plans include:

- HMOs. (Most of the HMOs previously in the Medicare market became part of the Medicare+Choice program.)
- Preferred-provider organizations (PPOs).
- Provider-sponsor organizations (PSOs). These are similar to HMOs but established by doctors and hospitals that have formed their own health plans.
- Private fee-for-service plans.
- Private contracts with physicians.

These plans must provide all benefits available under Parts A and B of Medicare. They may include additional benefits as part of the basic plan or for an additional fee.

Through 2004, beneficiaries are able to enroll in a Medicare+Choice plan or switch options (including reenrollment in Parts A and B) at any time during the year. In 2005, changes are allowed only once during the first six months of the year. Beginning in 2006, an annual change will be allowed only during the first three months of the year.

Unfortunately, the initial reaction to Medicare+Choice was less than overwhelming. As of late 2003, few new providers of alternative coverage had entered the marketplace, and the enrollment in alternatives to the original Medicare program had decreased after several years of growth. One reason for this is that the Medicare+Choice rules were extremely complex, and it is questionable if many of the potential providers could have entered the market in a viable way. As a result, there was a decrease in the number of HMOs offering coverage. While some HMOs continued to enter the Medicare market or expand their service areas for Medicare beneficiaries, a larger number of HMOs either ceased providing Medicare coverage or reduced their service areas. While many of those who lost Medicare coverage had other HMOs available, a change to another HMO often required the use of different physicians and hospitals. Other HMO participants had no choice but to return to the original Medicare program. Finally, some HMOs no longer offered zero-premium plans or increased premiums and/or reduced benefits. These changes stem from two factors. First, HMO costs have increased significantly in recent years, partially because of major increases in the cost of prescription drugs, which are a major source of medical expenses for the elderly. Second, the rate of growth of Medicare payments to HMOs has been reduced so that many HMOs are receiving increases that fail to match their increases in expenses.

The situation, however, may change as a result of provisions in the Medicare Prescription Drug, Improvement, and Modernization Act. The act changes the name of Medicare+Choice to **Medicare Advantage**, and all materials for such plans must use this terminology by January 1, 2006. The act makes numerous administrative changes to the program aimed at increasing participation. The method for calculating reimbursement to participating plans has been changed, and many plans are receiving larger reimbursements. This has already resulted in some plans increasing benefits and/or lowering premiums.

Beginning in 2005, PPOs can begin offering Medicare Advantage plans on a regional basis that is broader than the typical service areas for non–Medicare Advantage participants. These regions will be determined by the secretary of Health and Human Services. This will give PPOs a broader base from which to solicit members and should also increase competition. These regional plans must use a single deductible and out-of-pocket limit for Part A and Part B benefits.

In 2006, Medicare Advantage plans will be required to submit proposals to participate in the program. Such proposals are subject to negotiation, and the secretary of Health and Human Services will determine whether a plan can participate in the program based on statutory criteria. This is similar to the procedure used to select the medical expense plans available to employees of the federal government under the Federal Employees Health Benefits Program.

■ MEDICARE PART D: PRESCRIPTION DRUG COVERAGE

Along with numerous other changes to Medicare and the establishment of health saving accounts (discussed in Chapter 13), the Medicare Prescription Drug, Improvement, and Modernization Act adds a prescription drug program to Medicare—Medicare Part D. Until Part D becomes effective in 2006, the act also provides for Medicare-approved drug discount cards. The act also gives employers a financial incentive to provide or continue to provide drug coverage to retirees as an alternative to enrollment in Part D.

Drug Discount Cards

By spring 2004, all Medicare beneficiaries will be able to purchase a drug discount card. The Bush administration estimates that a beneficiary's drug costs will be reduced by 10 to 25 percent, but some critics question if the savings will be this high. These cards can be sponsored by insurance companies, retail pharmacies, Medicare Advantage plans, and pharmacy benefit managers. Sponsors will be required to pass on any discounts they negotiate on the purchase of drugs to cardholders and to publish a price list of the drugs they cover.

Certain low-income seniors will also be eligible for annual subsidies of up to $600 to help them pay the cost of prescription drugs.

Prescription Drug Coverage

In 2006, Medicare Part D will replace Medicare-approved drug discount cards. Part D is a subject of considerable controversy. More liberal members of Congress argue that it does not go far enough in meeting the needs of seniors. More conservative members of Congress contend that its cost will saddle the government with another major entitlement. The program is also viewed by some as a boon to the pharmaceutical industry. In addition, the rules for this program are very complex. Depending on the results of the 2004 elections, Part D may change before it even becomes effective. Even if no changes are made, many regulations still need to be issued to fully implement the program. Therefore, the following discussion is general, and readers should be aware of developments that take place. One source of this information is to look at the Medicare Web site: *www.medicare.gov.*

Eligibility and Cost. Part D is a voluntary prescription drug plan that is available to all Medicare beneficiaries entitled to Part A and enrolled in Part B. This includes persons who participate in any of the various Medicare Advantage plans. The act provides that most eligible persons will have access to at least two privately operated prescription drug plans available in the region in which they live. The plans must meet certain standards and be approved by the secretary of Health and Human Services. There are provisions in the act for the secretary to arrange prescription drug coverage on an alternative basis if fewer than two drug plans are approved. Beneficiaries who participate in Medicare Advantage plans would obtain their prescription drug coverage through that plan as long as it was an approved provider.

It is estimated that the premium will average about $35 per month per person. This represents about 26 percent of the actual cost of coverage, with the balance being paid to the drug plan by the federal government. The premium is partially or totally waived for persons with very low incomes.

Covered Drugs. It is expected that each Medicare prescription drug plan will develop a **formulary**, which is a list of approved drugs that the plan will cover. These formularies do not have to cover every prescription drug. However, they must cover at least two prescription drugs in each therapeutic category and class. Formularies can be changed at any time during the year, but participants may only change drug plans once per year. As a result, some participants may find that there is no longer coverage for a drug that they have been taking.

Benefits.   The act provides for a standard prescription drug program but also allows for alternative plans to be approved if certain requirements are met and the plans are at least actuarially equivalent to the standard plans. The standard prescription drug program will have an annual deductible of $250 in 2006. This amount and other dollar figures mentioned below will increase in later years if the expenditures for prescription drugs by Medicare beneficiaries increase.

After the deductible has been satisfied, the plan will pay 75 percent of the next $2,000 of prescription drug costs covered by the plan. Benefits then cease until a beneficiary's total drug costs (including the deductible) reach $5,100. At this point the beneficiary will have had out-of-pocket costs of $3,600 in addition to the $420 annual premium. The plan will then pay 95 percent of covered drug costs in excess of $5,100.

The following example shows that beneficiaries with $810 or less in annual prescription drug expenditures will receive no net benefit from Part D. Approximately half of Medicare beneficiaries fall into this category and will need to decide whether they should purchase coverage. The negative side of not signing up when initially eligible is that there will be a financial penalty for enrollment at a later date when they might have significantly higher drug costs. This penalty is in the form of a premium that will be higher by at least 1 percent for every month of later enrollment. The percentage increase may actually be higher if the secretary of Health and Human Services determines that a larger penalty is actuarially justified.

EXAMPLE

Roger incurs $810 in covered drug costs during the year.

Payment by drug plan: $.075 \times (\$810 - \$250)$	$420
Less premium ($35/month)	−420
	0
Percentage of drug cost paid by Roger	100%

The next example shows that Medicare beneficiaries with $5,100 or less will also pay a significant percentage of their drug costs.

EXAMPLE

Wendy and her husband Keith have annual prescription drug costs of $2,318 and $5,100 respectively. Wendy's costs are equal to the average prescription drug costs for Medicare recipients in 2003.

Wendy and Keith will each receive $1,500 under their Part D drug plans. This amount is equal to 75 percent of this first $2,000 in drug costs in excess of the deductible. In Wendy's case, she will have out-of-pocket costs equal to $1,238, or 53 percent of her expenditures. This $1,238 figure is calculated as follows:

(continued)

EXAMPLE *(continued)*

Premium	$420
Deductible	250
25% of first $2,000 above deductible	500
100% of expenses in excess of $2,250	68
	$1,238

In Keith's case, his expenses in excess of $2,250 are $2,850, and his total out-of-pocket costs and premium are $4,020, or about 79 percent of his drug expenditures.

The percentage of drug costs will drop as costs exceed $5,100 because Part D plans pay 95 percent of this excess amount.

EXAMPLE

Todd takes several expensive drugs for an assortment of ailments. This year, he expects drug costs to be $20,000. As in the previous example for Keith, Todd will have out-of-pocket costs of $4,020 for the first $5,100 of his drug expenditures. Of the remaining $14,900 in expenditures, he will be responsible for only 5 percent, or $745. Thus his total out-of-pocket costs are $4,765, or about 24 percent of his expenditures.

Qualifications for Drug Plans

The act establishes several criteria for Part D prescription drug plans that are designed to protect beneficiaries. Some of these include the following:

- Plans must provide beneficiaries with information on access to covered drugs, how the plan formulary works, copayment and deductible requirements, and any medication therapy management program.
- Plans must provide a mechanism for responses to beneficiary questions, including toll-free telephone access.
- Plans must provide meaningful procedures for hearing and resolving grievances.
- Plans must allow any willing pharmacy to participate as long as it complies with the terms and conditions of the plan.
- Each pharmacy dispensing drugs must inform the beneficiary of any differential between the price of a drug and the price of the lowest-priced generic that is therapeutically equivalent.
- Plans must include in their provider network a sufficient number of pharmacies that dispense drugs other than by mail order to ensure convenient access.

- Plans must make information on formulary changes available through the Internet and must provide adequate notice of changes to beneficiaries.
- Plans must provide methods for quality-assurance measures and systems to reduce medication errors and adverse drug interaction.
- Plans must provide for medication management programs for beneficiaries with multiple chronic diseases.

Employer Incentives

One concern of Congress was that employers or unions who provided prescription drug coverage to retirees would drop this coverage and, possibly, other retiree medical expense coverage after the act was passed. To minimize this from occurring, the act provides a subsidy to employers or unions that continue drug coverage as long as it is at least actuarially equivalent to the coverage under a standard prescription drug program.

The annual subsidy, which becomes effective in 2004, is equal to 28 percent of the cost of providing a retiree with up to $5,000 in prescription drug benefits, subject to a $250 deductible. After 2006, these dollar amounts will be indexed.

■ ADEQUACY OF FINANCING

Social Security and Medicare are based on a system of funding that the Social Security Administration refers to as **partial advance funding**. Under this system, taxes are more than sufficient to pay current benefits and also provide some accumulation of assets for the payment of future benefits. Partial advance funding falls somewhere between pay-as-you-go financing, which was once the way Social Security and Medicare were financed, and full advance funding as used by private insurance and retirement plans. Under pay-as-you-go financing, taxes are set at a level to produce just enough income to pay current benefits; under full advance funding, taxes are set at a level to prefund all promised future benefits for those persons making current contributions.

All payroll taxes and other sources of funds for Social Security and Medicare are deposited into four trust funds: an old-age and survivors fund, a disability fund, and two Medicare funds. Benefits and administrative expenses are paid out of the appropriate trust fund from contributions to that fund and any interest earnings on accumulated assets. The trust funds have limited reserves to serve as emergency funds in periods when benefits exceed contributions, such as in times of high unemployment. However, current reserves are relatively small and could pay benefits for only a limited time if contributions to a fund ceased. In addition, the reserves consist primarily of IOUs from the Treasury because the contributions have been "borrowed" to finance the government's deficit.

In the early 1980s, considerable concern arose over the potential inability of payroll taxes to pay promised benefits in the future. Through a series of changes, the most significant being the 1983 amendments to the Social Security Act, these problems appeared to have been solved for the Social Security program—at least in the short run. The changes approached the problem from two directions. On one hand, payroll tax rates were increased; on the other hand, some benefits were eliminated and future increases in other benefits were scaled back. However, the solutions of 1983 have not worked. Without further adjustments, the trust funds will have inadequate resources to pay claims in the foreseeable future. The old-age and survivors fund will continue to grow for the time being and will be quite large by the time the current baby boomers begin to retire. Benefits will then exceed income, and the fund will shrink as the percentage of retirees grows rapidly. Current projections indicate that the assets of the Social Security trust funds will run out in 2041.

Because of an increasing number of persons aged 65 or older and medical costs that continue to grow at an alarming rate, there is also concern about the Medicare portion of the program. Estimates are that its trust funds will be depleted by about 2019. The seriousness of this problem was made clear by the fact that one of the earliest actions of the second Clinton administration was the passage of legislation to help maintain the solvency of the Medicare trust funds for a few additional years, primarily through encouraging additional enrollment in managed care plans and trimming projected payments to HMOs, hospitals, and doctors.

It is obvious that changes must be made—either now or later—in the Social Security and Medicare programs. Probably the most important step in finding a solution is to convince the public that changes in this very popular entitlement program must be made. Changes, of course, have significant political implications. While most members of Congress realize the need for reform, neither political party has been willing to compromise and thus take the necessary initiative and risk losing public support.

In the broadest sense, the solution lies in doing one or both of the following: increasing revenue into the trust funds or decreasing benefit costs. Changes that would increase revenue include the following:

- Increasing the Social Security and/or Medicare tax rate
- Increasing the wage base on which Social Security taxes are paid
- Using more general tax revenue to fund the programs
- Increasing the Medicare Part B premium for everyone or possibly only for higher-income retirees.
- Subjecting a greater portion of income benefits to taxation and depositing the increased tax revenue into the trust funds
- Investing all or a portion of trust fund assets in higher-yielding investments than Treasury securities

Suggested changes that have been made for decreasing benefit costs:

- Raising the full retirement age beyond the planned increase to age 67.
- Raising the early retirement age beyond 62.
- Lowering the benefit formula so that future retirees will get somewhat reduced benefits.
- Lowering cost-of-living increases.
- Imposing a means test for benefits.

- Shifting more of the inflation risk to workers through the use of separate accounts for all or part of each worker's contributions. This would give the worker some control over his or her account.

- Increasing the Medicare eligibility age beyond 65.

- Increasing Medicare deductibles and copayments.

- Lowering or slowing the growth of payments to Medicare providers.

- Encouraging or requiring Medicare beneficiaries to enroll in managed care plans.

In May 2001, President Bush announced the establishment of a bipartisan commission to study and report specific recommendations to preserve Social Security for seniors while building wealth for younger Americans. The commission was asked to make its recommendations using the following six guiding principles for modernizing the program:

- Modernization must not change Social Security benefits for retirees or near-retirees.

- The entire Social Security surplus must be dedicated to Social Security only.

- Social Security payroll taxes must not be increased.

- Government must not invest Social Security funds in the stock market.

- Modernization must preserve Social Security's disability and survivors components.

- Modernization must include individually controlled, voluntary personal accounts, which will augment the Social Security safety net.

In late 2001, the commission issued a report. Rather than specifying one specific plan for reforming Social Security, it put forth three alternative proposals that contained the president's guiding principles. Two of the three proposals would also significantly increase benefits for low-income workers over what the current program pays. While each of the various proposals received some degree of support, there were also critics who argued for different changes. The net effect is that no reform has yet taken place.

Any single change to the Social Security program will clearly offend one important group of voters or another. As a result, the ultimate solution (which may or may not follow the commission's recommendations) will probably involve a combination of several of the previously mentioned suggestions for change so that everyone will bear a little of the pain.

EMPLOYER AND EMPLOYEE TAX TREATMENT

Deductibility of Premiums

Employer contributions to the Social Security and Medicare programs are tax deductible for federal income tax purposes. Any employee contributions are paid with after-tax dollars. Self-employed persons can deduct one-half of their Social Security tax as a business expense. In addition, Part B premiums are treated the same as other premiums for individual medical expense insurance and may be deductible as described in Chapter 14.

Tax Treatment of Benefits

Benefits received in the form of monthly income under Social Security are partially subject to income taxation for some Social Security recipients. To determine the amount of Social Security benefits subject to taxation, it is necessary to calculate *modified adjusted gross income,* which is the sum of the following:

- The taxpayer's adjusted gross income (disregarding any foreign income and savings bond exclusions)
- The taxpayer's tax-exempt interest received or accrued during the year
- One-half of the Social Security benefits for the year

If the modified adjusted gross income is $25,000 or less for a single taxpayer ($32,000 or less for a married taxpayer filing jointly), Social Security benefits are not taxable. If the modified adjusted gross income is between the base amount and $34,000 ($44,000 for a married taxpayer filing jointly), up to 50 percent of the Social Security benefit can be included in taxable income. If the modified adjusted gross income exceeds $34,000 ($44,000 for a married taxpayer filing jointly), up to 85 percent of the Social Security benefit can be included in taxable income. The exact amount of the taxable Social Security benefit is determined by complex formulas that are beyond the scope of this discussion.

Medicare benefits and any lump-sum Social Security benefits are received tax free.

■ KEY TERMS

currently insured	hospice care	partial advance funding
disability insured	individual equity	primary insurance amount (PIA)
earnings test	Medicare	skilled-nursing facility
formulary	Medicare Advantage	social adequacy
full retirement age	Medicare+Choice	social insurance
fully insured	Medicare Part A	Social Security
home health care	Medicare Part B	Social Security Statement

■ STUDY QUESTIONS

1. Why are social insurance programs necessary?
2. Describe the characteristics of social insurance programs.
3. How are the Social Security and Medicare programs financed?
4. As of this year, Nancy Westman, aged 37, had 28 quarters of coverage under Social Security. Twenty-four of these quarters were earned prior to the birth of her first child 11 years ago. Four quarters have been earned since she reentered the labor force one year ago.

   a. Is Nancy fully insured? Explain.

  b. Is Nancy currently insured? Explain.

  c. Is Nancy disability insured? Explain.

5. Describe the retirement benefits available under Social Security.

6. What categories of persons are eligible for Social Security survivors benefits?

7. a. What is the definition of disability under Social Security?

  b. What categories of persons may be eligible for disability benefits?

8. a. Explain the relationship between a worker's PIA and the benefits available for dependents and survivors.

  b. What happens if the total benefits for a family exceed the maximum family benefit?

9. Explain how a worker's retirement benefits under Social Security will be affected if that person elects early or delayed retirement.

10. Describe the earnings test applicable to the Social Security program.

11. Describe the automatic cost-of-living adjustment provision under Social Security as it relates to benefit amounts.

12. With respect to the hospital insurance portion of Medicare:

  a. Describe the types of benefits that are available.

  b. Explain the extent to which deductibles and copayments are requirements.

  c. Identify the major exclusions.

13. With respect to the supplementary medical insurance portion of Medicare:

  a. Describe the types of benefits that are available.

  b. Explain the extent to which copayments are requirements.

  c. Identify the major exclusions.

14. Describe the options available under Medicare+Choice and Medicare Advantage.

15. Describe the new Medicare prescription coverage.

16. a. What is the purpose of the Social Security and Medicare trust funds?

  b. Identify possible actions that can better ensure the adequacy of these trust funds.

17. Explain the extent to which Social Security benefits are taxed to recipients.

4

Other Social
Insurance Programs

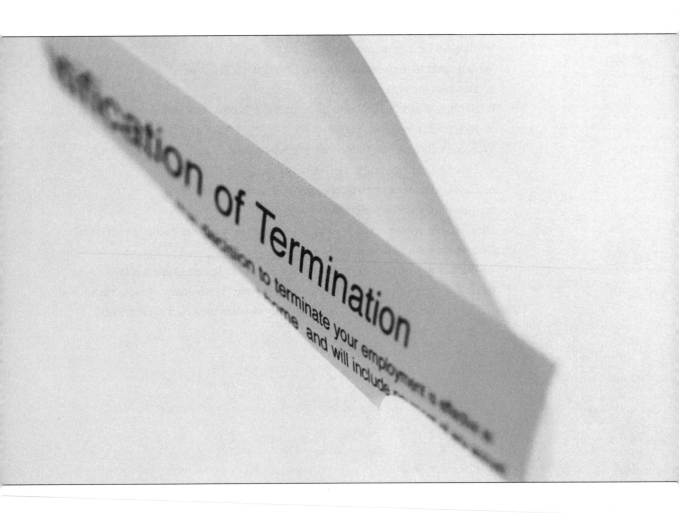

■ Describe unemployment insurance programs with respect to objectives, eligibility requirements, benefits, and financing.

■ Describe the nature of temporary disability insurance.

■ Describe the typical workers' compensation program with respect to type of law, eligibility requirements, benefits, and financing.

■ Explain the extent to which other social insurance benefits are subject to income taxation.

CHAPTER OUTLINE

Unemployment Insurance
Financing of Benefits
Eligibility for Benefits
Benefits
Problems and Issues

Temporary Disability Laws
Eligibility
Benefits

Worker's Compensation Laws
Type of Law
Financing of Benefits
Covered Occupations
Eligibility
Benefits
Problems and Issues

Federal Tax Treatment

This chapter focuses on the three major social insurance programs other than Social Security and Medicare: unemployment insurance, temporary disability laws, and workers' compensation insurance. Unemployment insurance is a joint federal and state program, and workers' compensation insurance and temporary disability laws are solely under state control. Because the programs of each state are unique, the discussion in this chapter is general in nature. Readers should familiarize themselves with the programs in their own state and not assume that these programs always conform to the generalizations that follow. Detailed information on a specific state's program can be obtained from the state agency administering the program.

■ UNEMPLOYMENT INSURANCE

Prior to the passage of the Social Security Act in 1935, relatively few employees had any type of protection for income lost during periods of unemployment. The act stipulated that a payroll tax was to be levied on covered employers for the purpose of financing **unemployment insurance** programs that were to be established by the states under guidelines issued by the federal government. Essentially, the federal law levied a federal tax on certain employers in all states. If a state established an acceptable program of unemployment insurance, the taxes used to finance its program could be offset against up to 90 percent of the federal tax. If a state failed to establish a program, the federal tax would still be levied, but no monies collected from the employers in that state would be returned for purposes of providing benefits to the unemployed there.

Needless to say, all states quickly established unemployment insurance programs. These programs (along with a federal program for railroad workers) now cover more than 95 percent of all working persons, but major gaps in coverage exist for domestic workers, agricultural workers, and the self-employed.

There are several objectives of the current unemployment insurance program. The primary objective is to provide periodic cash income to workers during periods of involuntary unemployment. Benefits are generally paid as a matter of right, with no demonstration of need required. While federal legislation has extended benefits during times of high unemployment, the unemployment insurance program is basically designed for workers whose periods of unemployment are short-term; the long-term and hard-core unemployed must rely on other measures, such as public assistance and job-retraining programs, when unemployment insurance benefits are exhausted.

A second major objective of unemployment insurance is to help the unemployed find jobs. Workers must register at local unemployment offices, and unemployment benefits are received through these offices. Another important objective is to encourage employers to stabilize employment. As described later, this is accomplished through the use of experience rating in determining an employer's tax rate. Finally, unemployment insurance contributes to a stable labor supply by providing benefits so that skilled and experienced workers are not forced to seek other jobs during short-term layoffs, thereby remaining available to return to work when called back.

Financing of Benefits

Unemployment insurance programs are financed primarily by unemployment taxes levied by both the federal and state governments. The federal tax is equal to 6.2 percent of the first $7,000 of wages for each worker, but this tax is reduced by up to 5.4 percentage points for taxes paid to state programs. The practical effect of this offset is that the federal tax is actually equal to 0.8 percent of covered payroll. A few states levy an unemployment payroll tax equal to only the maximum offset (5.4 percent on the first $7,000 of wages), but most states have a higher tax rate and/or levy their tax on a higher amount of earnings.

No state levies the same tax on all employers. Instead, they use a method of experience rating whereby all employers, except those that have been in business for a short time or those with a small number of employees, pay a tax rate that reflects their actual experience within limits. Thus, an employer who has laid off a large percentage of employees has a higher tax rate than an employer whose employment record has been stable.

An employer who has good experience often pays a state tax of less than 1 percent of payroll and possibly even as little as 0.1 percent. On the other hand, some employers pay a state tax as high as 9 or 10 percent. Regardless of the amount of actual state tax paid, the employer still pays the 0.8 percent federal tax.

The major argument for experience rating is that it provides a financial incentive for employers to stabilize employment. However, those who are opposed to its use contend that many employers have little control over economic trends that affect employment. In addition, they argue that tax rates tend to escalate in bad economic times and thus may actually serve as an obstacle to economic recovery.

The entire unemployment insurance tax is collected by the individual states and deposited in the Federal Unemployment Insurance Trust Fund, which is administered by the Secretary of the Treasury. Each state has a separate account that is credited with its taxes and its share of investment earnings on assets in the fund. Unemployment benefits in the state are paid from this account. The federal share of the taxes received by the fund is deposited into separate accounts and is used for administering the federal portion of the program and for giving grants to the states to administer their individual programs. In addition, the federal funds are available for loans to states whose accounts have been depleted during times of high unemployment.

Eligibility for Benefits

To receive unemployment benefits, a worker must meet the following eligibility requirements:

- Have a prior attachment to the labor force
- Be able to work and be available for work
- Be actively seeking work
- Have satisfied any prescribed waiting period
- Be free of disqualification

Prior Attachment to the Labor Force.   The right to benefits depends on the worker's attachment to the labor force within a prior *base period*. In most states, this base period is the 52 weeks or 4 quarters prior to the time of unemployment. During this base period, the worker must have earned a minimum amount of wages, worked a minimum period of time, or both.

Able to Work and Available for Work.   The right to benefits is also contingent on an unemployed worker being both physically and mentally capable of working. The worker must also be available for work. Benefits may be denied if suitable work is refused or if substantial restrictions are placed on the type of work that will be accepted.

Actively Seeking Work.   In addition to registering with a local unemployment office, most states require that a worker make a reasonable effort to seek work.

Waiting Period.   Most unemployment programs have a one-week waiting period before benefits commence. Benefits are not paid retroactively for that time of unemployment.

Free of Disqualification.   All states have provisions in their laws under which a worker may be disqualified from receiving benefits. This disqualification may take the form of (1) a total cancellation of benefit rights, (2) the postponement of benefits, or (3) a reduction in benefits. Following are some common reasons for disqualification:

- Voluntarily leaving a job without good cause.
- Discharge for misconduct.
- Refusal to accept suitable work.
- Involvement in a labor dispute.

■ Receipt of disqualifying income. This includes dismissal wages, workers' compensation benefits, benefits from an employer's pension plan, or primary insurance benefits under Social Security.

Benefits

The majority of states pay "regular" unemployment insurance benefits for a maximum of 26 weeks; the remaining states pay benefits for slightly longer periods. In most states, the amount of the weekly benefit is equal to a specified fraction of a worker's average wages during the highest calendar quarter of the base period. The typical fraction is 1/26, which yields a benefit equal to 50 percent of average weekly earnings for that quarter. Other states determine benefits as a percentage of average weekly wages or annual wages during the base period. Some states also modify their benefit formulas to provide relatively higher benefits (as a percentage of past earnings) to lower-paid workers. Benefits in all states are subject to minimum and maximum amounts. Minimum weekly benefits typically fall within the range of $20 to $100, maximum benefits in the range of $210 to $450, and the average benefit in the range of $200 to $275. In addition, a few states currently provide additional benefits if there are dependents who receive regular support from the worker.

States also provide reduced benefits for partial unemployment. Such a condition occurs if a worker is employed less than full-time and has a weekly income less than his or her weekly benefit amount for total unemployment.

There is a permanent federal-state program of "extended" unemployment benefits for workers whose regular benefits are exhausted during periods of high unemployment. The availability of these benefits is automatically triggered by a state's unemployment rate exceeding a specified level. The federal government and the states involved finance the benefits equally. Workers can be paid for up to 13 weeks, as long as the total of regular and extended benefits does not exceed 39 weeks. This program is operable when the *insured unemployment rate* in a state exceeds a specified level. The insured unemployment rate is the percentage of workers covered by unemployment insurance who are receiving regular benefits. Benefits can also be triggered if a state's *total unemployment rate* exceeds specified criteria. In this case, an additional 20 weeks of benefits can be paid.

In 1988, Congress created a program for the payment of unemployment assistance to individuals whose unemployment is the direct result of a major disaster as declared by the president and who are not otherwise eligible for regular unemployment insurance benefits. To be eligible for benefits under this program, an individual must have worked or be scheduled to work in an area that has been declared a federal disaster area, as were parts of New York after the terrorist attacks on September 11, 2001. In addition, benefits are paid only if the individual cannot work because of the disaster and the work they cannot perform is their primary source of income and livelihood. The benefits are administered by the state where the disaster occurred and the benefit amounts are the same as regular unemployment insurance benefits. The benefits are paid for up to 26 weeks but cease once the disaster assistance period (which is usually also 26 weeks) is over. The funds for these "disaster" benefits are provided by the federal government through the Federal Emergency Management Agency.

In periods of severe economic conditions on a national basis, the federal government often enacts legislation to provide additional benefits that are financed with federal revenue. The most recent such program, which runs through 2003 for new claims, provides up to 13 weeks of benefits to persons whose regular benefits have been exhausted.

Problems and Issues

The current system of unemployment insurance has increasingly become subject to criticism, especially regarding the level of benefits. At current levels, the majority of employees receive benefits that are less than half of their former wages. Because of maximum limits on the amounts of benefits, higher-income employees receive proportionately smaller benefits than lower-paid employees if they are unemployed.

In addition to the level of benefits, the percentage of persons receiving benefits at any point in time has dropped over the last two decades. Typically, fewer than 40 percent of the unemployed receive benefits. Some persons have benefits denied because of more stringent rules, particularly those dealing with initial benefit disqualification. Other persons exhaust the available benefits. Of course, there are those who argue that without disqualifications and limits on benefits, there is little incentive for many of the unemployed to seek work.

Few employers provide any type of supplemental unemployment benefits. The plans that do exist are in highly unionized industries and result from collective bargaining. These plans are briefly discussed in Chapter 18.

There seems to be a feeling among economists that unemployment insurance programs today are less effective in dealing with unemployment issues than they were in the past. In theory, unemployment compensation insurance should be a counterbalance against recessions. In practice, this is often not the case, perhaps because of the low percentage of persons receiving benefits. In addition, the degree of experience rating has declined over time, reducing the incentive for employers to retain employees in bad times rather than laying them off. It also shifts an increasing burden for financing the program to employers in industries with stable employment.

■ TEMPORARY DISABILITY LAWS

At their inception, state unemployment insurance programs were usually designed to cover only unemployed persons who were both willing and able to work. Benefits were denied to anyone who was unable to work for any reason, including disability. Some states amended their unemployment insurance laws to provide coverage to the unemployed who subsequently became disabled. However, five states—California, Hawaii, New Jersey, New York, and Rhode Island—and Puerto Rico each went one step further by enacting a **temporary disability law** under which employees can collect disability income benefits whether their disability begins while they are employed or unemployed. While variations exist among the states, these laws (often referred to as *nonoccupational disability laws*, because benefits are not provided for disabilities covered under workers' compensation laws) are generally patterned after the state unemployment insurance law and provide similar benefits.

In the six jurisdictions that have temporary disability laws, most employers are required to provide coverage for their employees. In most jurisdictions (except Rhode Island, which has a monopolistic state fund), coverage may be obtained from either a competitive state fund or private insurance companies. Private coverage must provide at least the benefits that are prescribed under the law, but the coverage may be more comprehensive. As with workers' compensation insurance, self-insurance is generally permitted. Depending on the jurisdiction, the cost of an employer's program is borne entirely by employee contributions, entirely by employer contributions, or by contributions from both parties.

Eligibility

Before an employee is eligible for benefits under a temporary disability law, the employee must satisfy (1) an earnings or employment requirement, (2) the definition of disability, and (3) a waiting period.

Earnings or Employment Requirement. Every jurisdiction requires that an employee must have worked for a specified time and/or have received a minimum amount of wages within some specific period prior to disability in order to qualify for benefits.

Definition of Disability. Most laws define disability as the inability of the worker to perform his or her regular or customary work because of a nonoccupational injury or illness, including maternity. As with workers' compensation laws, certain types of disabilities are not covered. In most jurisdictions, these include disabilities caused by self-inflicted injuries or by illegal acts.

Waiting Period. The usual waiting period for benefits is seven days. However, in some jurisdictions, the waiting period is waived if the employee is hospitalized.

Benefits

Benefits are a percentage, usually ranging from 50 percent to 66⅔ percent, of the employee's average weekly wage for some period prior to disability, subject to maximum and minimum amounts. Benefits are generally paid for at least 26 weeks if the employee remains disabled that long.

■ WORKERS' COMPENSATION LAWS

Prior to the passage of workers' compensation laws, it was difficult for employees to receive compensation for their work-related injuries or diseases. Group benefits were meager, and the Social Security program had not yet been enacted. The only recourse for employees was to sue their employer for damages. In addition to the time and expense of such actions (as well as the possibility of being fired), the probability of a worker winning such a suit was small because of the three common-law defenses available to employers. Under the *contributory negligence doctrine,* a worker could not collect if his or her negligence had contributed in any way to the injury. Under the *fellow-servant doctrine,* the worker could not collect if the injury had resulted from the negligence of a fellow worker. And finally, under the *assumption-of-risk doctrine,* a worker could not recover if he or she had knowingly assumed the risks inherent in the trade.

To help solve the problem of uncompensated injuries, each state enacted a **workers' compensation law** to require employers to provide benefits to employees for losses resulting from work-related accidents or diseases. These laws are based on the principle of *liability without fault.* Essentially, an employer is absolutely liable for providing the benefits prescribed by the workers' compensation laws, regardless of whether the employer would be considered legally liable in the absence of these laws. However, benefits (with the possible exception of medical expense benefits) are subject to statutory maximums.

In addition to all states, the federal government has enacted several similar laws. The Federal Employees Compensation Act provides benefits for the employees of the federal government and the District of Columbia. Railroad employees and workers aboard ships are covered under the Federal Employer's Liability Act, and stevedores, longshoremen, and workers who repair ships are covered under the United States Longshore and Harbor Workers' Act.

Type of Law

Most workers' compensation laws are compulsory for all employers covered under the law. A few states have elective laws, but the majority of employers do elect coverage. If they do not, their employees are not entitled to workers' compensation benefits and must sue for damages resulting from occupational accidents or diseases. However, the employer loses the right to the three common-law defenses previously described.

Financing of Benefits

Most states allow employers to comply with the workers' compensation law by purchasing coverage from insurance companies. Several of these states also have competitive state funds from which coverage may be obtained, but these funds usually provide benefits for fewer employers than do those provided by insurance companies. Five states have monopolistic state funds that are the only source for obtaining coverage under the law.

Almost all states, including some with monopolistic state funds, allow employers to self-insure their workers' compensation exposure. These employers must generally post a bond or other security and receive the approval of the agency administering the law. While the number of firms using self-insurance for workers' compensation is small, these firms account for approximately one-half the employees covered under such laws.

In virtually all cases, the full cost of providing workers' compensation benefits is borne by the employer. Obviously, if an employer self-insures benefits, the ultimate cost includes the benefits paid plus any administrative expenses.

Employers who purchase coverage pay a premium that is calculated as a rate per $100 of payroll, based on the occupations of their workers. For example, rates for office workers may be as low as $0.10, and rates for workers in a few hazardous occupations may exceed $50. Most states also require that employers with total workers' compensation premiums above a specified amount be subject to experience rating—that is, the employer's premium is a function of benefits paid for past injuries to the employer's workers. To the extent that safety costs are offset or eliminated by savings in workers' compensation premiums, experience-rating laws encourage employers to take an active role in correcting conditions that may cause injuries.

Covered Occupations

Although it is estimated that about 90 percent of the workers in the United States are covered by workers' compensation laws, the percentage varies among the states from less than 70 percent to more than 95 percent. Many laws exclude certain agricultural, domestic, and casual employees. Some laws also exclude employers with a small number of employees. Furthermore, coverage for employees of state and local governments is not universal.

Eligibility

Before an employee can be eligible for benefits under a workers' compensation law, he or she must work in an occupation covered by that law and be disabled or killed by a covered injury or illness. The typical workers' compensation law provides coverage for *accidental occupational injuries (including death) arising out of and in the course of employment*. In all states, this includes injuries arising out of accidents, which are generally defined as sudden and unexpected events that are definite in time and place. Most workers' compensation laws exclude self-inflicted injuries and accidents resulting from an employee's intoxication or willful disregard of safety rules.

Every state has some coverage for illnesses resulting from occupational diseases. While the trend is toward full coverage for occupational diseases, some states cover only those diseases that are specifically listed in the law.

Benefits

Workers' compensation laws typically provide four types of benefits:

1. Medical care
2. Disability income
3. Death benefits
4. Rehabilitative services

Medical Care. Benefits for medical expenses are usually provided without any limitations on time or amount. In addition, they are not subject to a waiting period.

Disability Income. For an employee to collect disability income benefits under workers' compensation laws, his or her injuries must result in one of the following four categories of disability:

1. Temporary total. The employee cannot perform any of the duties of his or her regular job. However, full recovery is expected. Most workers' compensation claims involve this type of disability.
2. Permanent total. The employee will never be able to perform any of the duties of his or her regular job or any other job. Several states also list in their laws certain disabilities (such as loss of both eyes or both arms) that result in an employee automatically being considered permanently and totally disabled even though future employment might be possible.
3. Temporary partial. The employee can perform only some of the duties of his or her regular job but is neither totally nor permanently disabled. For example, an employee with a sprained back might work part-time.
4. Permanent partial. The employee has a permanent injury, such as the loss of an eye, but may be able to perform his or her regular job or may be retrained for another job.

Most workers' compensation laws have a waiting period for disability income benefits that varies from two to seven days. However, benefits are frequently paid retroactively to the date of the injury if an employee is disabled for a specified period of time or is confined to a hospital.

Disability income benefits under workers' compensation laws are a function of an employee's average weekly wage over some time period, commonly the 13 weeks immediately preceding the disability. For total disabilities, benefits are a percentage (usually 66⅔ percent) of the employee's average weekly wage, subject to maximum and minimum amounts that vary substantially by state. Benefits for temporary total disabilities continue until an employee returns to work; benefits for permanent total disabilities usually continue for life but have a limited duration (such as ten years) in a few states.

Benefits for partial disabilities are calculated as a percentage of the difference between the employee's wages before and after the disability. In most states, the duration of these benefits is subject to a statutory maximum. Several states also provide lump-sum payments to employees whose permanent partial disabilities involve the loss (or loss of use) of an eye, an arm, or other body member. These benefits, which are determined by a schedule in the law, may be in lieu of or in addition to periodic disability income benefits.

Death Benefits

Most workers' compensation laws provide two types of death benefits: burial allowances and cash income payments to survivors.

Burial allowances are a flat amount in each state and vary from $300 to $5,000, with benefits of $1,000 and $1,500 common.

Cash income payments to survivors, like disability income benefits, are a function of the worker's average wage prior to the injury resulting in death. Benefits are usually paid only to a surviving spouse and to children under 18. In some states, benefits are paid until the spouse dies or remarries and all of the children have reached 18. In other states, benefits are paid for a maximum time, such as ten years, or until a maximum dollar amount has been paid, such as $50,000.

Rehabilitation Benefits. All states have provisions in their workers' compensation laws for rehabilitative services for disabled workers. Benefits are included for medical rehabilitation as well as for vocational rehabilitation, including training, counseling, and job placement.

A difficulty faced in providing vocational rehabilitation is that employers are reluctant to hire workers with a permanent physical impairment because a subsequent work-related injury may result in their total disability, which would increase the employer's premium for workers' compensation. For example, a worker who lost an arm in a previous work-related accident would probably be totally and permanently disabled if the other arm was lost in a later accident. Consequently, most states have established second-injury funds. If a worker is disabled by a second injury, the employer is responsible only for providing benefits equal to those that would have been provided to a worker who had not suffered the first injury. Any remaining benefits are provided by the second-injury fund.

Problems and Issues

As with unemployment insurance, there are problems and issues associated with workers' compensation insurance. These involve the extent of coverage, the size of benefit payments, and increasing costs. One often-discussed issue is whether a system of 24-hour coverage would be an improvement.

Extent of Coverage. Labor unions have been particularly critical of workers' compensation insurance because of its incomplete coverage of workers. State laws do not cover all workers because of elective laws, numerical exemptions, and exclusions or less-than-full coverage for certain groups, such as agricultural, domestic, and casual workers. It is estimated that nationally between 10 and 15 percent of workers are without coverage and that this figure is as high as 30 percent in some states.

Adequacy of Benefits. Benefits have been criticized as inadequate because they seldom exceed two-thirds of a worker's earnings prior to injury, and most states do not adjust income benefits for inflation. However, some lower-paid workers may have little incentive to return to work because benefits may actually exceed their prior take-home pay. This results from relatively high minimum benefits and the fact that workers' compensation benefits are not subject to Social Security and Medicare taxes or personal income tax. In terms of the replacement of lost income, the situation is worst for higher-paid employees because of the maximum dollar limits on benefits.

Increasing Costs. A major concern of employers is the soaring cost of workers' compensation coverage. Estimates are that these costs have tripled over the past decade. This increase is the result of a combination of several factors, including the following:

■ Soaring increases in the cost of medical care.

■ Increased benefits. Most states have increased benefits faster than average wages have increased. One interesting result of higher benefit levels is that they tend to result in an increased number of claims filed and an increase in the duration of claims.

■ Expansion of coverage to additional workplace injuries and diseases, such as mental stress.

■ Increased litigation. Estimates are that approximately one-quarter of workers' compensation costs are associated with attorneys' fees and other legal costs.

These increasing costs have resulted in large underwriting losses for many insurance companies, leading in turn to higher premiums and more stringent underwriting. As underwriting has tightened, more employers have been forced into the substandard insurance market, where costs are even higher. These higher costs are ultimately passed on to consumers and increase inflationary pressures. Some firms, particularly small ones, are also finding their financial survival threatened by these high costs.

At the state level, there always seems to be talk of workers' compensation reform. However, labor sees reform as increased benefits, and employers see it as lower costs. As a result, fundamental changes often do not occur.

24-Hour Coverage. When workers' compensation laws were first passed, most employees did not have employer-provided benefits for medical expenses or disability income. Today, both types of benefits are common. As a result, there are suggestions that the old systems are obsolete, and the concept of **24-hour coverage** should be adopted. Under this concept, employees have a single benefit plan that responds to injuries whether they occur on or off the job. This concept can be applied to medical expense coverage only or to medical expense coverage and some or all types of disability income coverage. Arguments in favor of 24-hour coverage include the following:

■ The financial needs of employees are the same whether an injury or illness is work-related or not.

■ It is often impossible to determine whether an injury or illness is work-related.

■ Twenty-four-hour coverage would be better at controlling medical costs because cost-containment techniques used in group insurance could also be used for work-related claims.

■ The current system is fragmented and may have both gaps and overlapping benefits. A single comprehensive system may be able to provide better benefits at a lower cost.

Naturally, there are also arguments against 24-hour coverage:

■ The principle of liability without fault would be violated if employees were required to assume deductibles, copayments, or a percentage of work-related claims.

■ Smaller firms that have few employee benefits could not afford 24-hour coverage and might be forced out of business.

■ The strong emphasis on loss control that is associated with workers' compensation insurance might be jeopardized if the program were merged with traditional group insurance programs.

The concept of 24-hour coverage continues to receive a considerable amount of attention. It is an integral part of some proposals for reforms to the nation's health care system. In addition, some states now allow 24-hour coverage to be written for medical expenses, with the employer purchasing a workers' compensation policy to provide benefits other than medical expenses.

■ FEDERAL TAX TREATMENT

Unemployment insurance benefits are included in a recipient's gross income. However, workers' compensation benefits are received free of income taxation.

Benefits received under temporary disability laws must be included in gross income. However, disabled persons with gross incomes below a specified level may be eligible for a federal tax credit. In those jurisdictions where unemployed persons can also receive benefits, any benefits paid to unemployed persons are considered unemployment insurance benefits and are taxed accordingly.

■ KEY TERMS

temporary disability law	unemployment insurance
24-hour coverage	workers' compensation law

■ STUDY QUESTIONS

1. What are the objectives of unemployment insurance?

2. Explain how unemployment insurance benefits are financed.

3. What requirements must be satisfied before a worker is eligible for unemployment insurance benefits?

4. For the extended benefits program of unemployment compensation, explain

   a. the circumstances under which benefits are made available.

   b. the method by which benefits are financed.

5. Why are unemployment benefits viewed by some as being inadequate?

6. How did the passage of workers' compensation laws alter the traditional system of common law with respect to employee injuries?

7. What are the usual eligibility requirements for receiving workers' compensation benefits?

8. Briefly describe the types and amounts of benefits available under workers' compensation laws.

9. Why are workers' compensation benefits viewed by some as being inadequate?

10. What has caused the increase in the cost of providing workers' compensation benefits?

11. What are the pros and cons of 24-hour coverage?

PART THREE

Group Benefits

The Group Insurance Environment

OBJECTIVES

- Identify the ways to structure an employee benefit plan.
- Identify the characteristics that distinguish group insurance from individual insurance.
- Identify the factors that are of concern to group underwriters and explain the significance of each factor.
- Describe voluntary benefit plans, and explain why they have grown in popularity.
- Describe the major aspects of state regulation applying to group insurance.
- Identify the types of groups eligible for coverage under the laws of most states and explain the significant characteristics and regulations pertaining to each.
- Explain the provisions of the Age Discrimination in Employment Act.
- Explain how employee benefit plans are affected by the provisions of the Pregnancy Discrimination Act.
- Explain how the passage of the Americans with Disabilities Act affects employee benefit plans.
- Explain the impact of the Financial Services Modernization Act on employee benefits.

CHAPTER OUTLINE

Structure of Benefit Plans
Group Insurance Arrangements
Self-Funding
Policies of Individual Insurance

Group Insurance Characteristics
The Group Contract
Experience Rating
Group Underwriting

Alternative Funding Methods

Voluntary Benefits
Reasons for Increase in Popularity
Market Characteristics
Portability

State Regulation
Eligible Groups
Contractual Provisions
Benefit Limitations
Tax Treatment
Regulatory Jurisdiction

Federal Regulation
Age Discrimination in Employment Act
Pregnancy Discrimination Act
Employee Retirement Income Security Act
Americans with Disabilities Act
Financial Services Modernization Act

To best understand the field of group insurance, it is first necessary to comprehend certain basic concepts. These include the structure of benefits plans, basic characteristics of group insurance, an introduction to alternative funding methods for group insurance, and the nature of voluntary benefit plans.

The character of group benefits has also been greatly influenced by social insurance programs (covered in Chapters 3 and 4) and the numerous other laws and regulations that both the state and federal governments have imposed. The major impact of state regulation has been felt through the insurance laws governing insurance companies and the products they sell. Traditionally, these laws have affected only those benefit plans funded with insurance contracts. However, as a growing number of employers are turning toward self-funding of benefits, there has been an increasing interest on the part of state regulatory officials to extend these laws to plans using alternative funding methods. The federal laws affecting group benefits, on the other hand, have generally been directed toward any plans that employers establish for their employees, regardless of the funding method used.

■ STRUCTURE OF BENEFIT PLANS

Many types of benefits are available to employees through the workplace. In some cases, the employer pays the entire cost or part of the cost of a benefit. In other cases, the employer merely sets up a benefit plan under which an employee can elect to participate by paying the full cost of his or her coverage. The actual structure of any single benefit plan may take many forms, including group insurance arrangements, self-funding, and policies of individual insurance.

Group Insurance Arrangements

Group insurance is a technique under which many individuals and possibly their dependents are insured under a single policy issued to another entity. In most situations, the entity is an employer, and the individuals are employees. The employer may pay all, some, or none of the cost of the coverage provided. The insurer administers many aspects of the benefit plan, and bears the uncertainty that benefit payments will exceed those expected. Group insurance is the predominant method that employers use to provide their employees with life insurance, disability income expense insurance, medical expense insurance, and dental insurance.

The term *group insurance* is used in a very broad sense in this book. It encompasses the products of traditional insurance companies as well as products of organizations such as Blue Cross and Blue Shield plans, health maintenance organizations (HMOs), preferred-provider organizations (PPOs), and other types of organizations from which employers obtain benefits for their employees. These organizations and their differences are discussed in later chapters.

Self-Funding

In its purest sense, **self-funding** is a method by which an employer pays benefit costs from current revenue, administers all aspects of a benefit plan, and bears the uncertainty that benefit payments will exceed those expected. Self-funding is the typical form for benefits such as vacations, educational assistance, and wellness programs. It has always been a common method for some large employers to finance other benefits such as medical expense coverage. In recent years, smaller and smaller employers are increasingly using some degree of self-funding for some benefits that were once fully insured.

Policies of Individual Insurance

Many employee benefits are funded with policies of individual insurance. In most situations, these policies are part of a *voluntary benefit,* which is usually defined as a benefit plan made available by an employer, but in which employees voluntarily elect to participate and pay the entire cost for the coverage they receive. Voluntary benefit plans often use individual insurance policies for each participant but may also use group insurance contracts. Many supplemental life insurance plans and most long-term care insurance plans are structured as voluntary plans of individual insurance.

Employers may also use individual policies to provide benefits to top executives. In most cases, these executive benefits are limited to the top executives only, and the employer pays the premium for the insurance policies.

■ GROUP INSURANCE CHARACTERISTICS

Group insurance is characterized by a group contract, experience rating of larger groups, and group underwriting. Perhaps the best way to define group insurance is to compare its characteristics with those of individual insurance, which is underwritten on an individual basis.

The Group Contract

In contrast to most individual insurance contracts, the group insurance contract provides coverage to a number of persons under a single contract issued to someone other than the persons insured. The contract, referred to as a **master contract**, provides benefits to a group of individuals who have a specific relationship to the policyowner. Group contracts usually cover individuals who are full-time employees, and the policyowner is either their employer or a trust established to provide benefits for the employees. Although the employees are not actual parties to the master contract, they can legally enforce their rights. Consequently, employees are often referred to as *third-party beneficiaries* of the insurance contract.

Each employee covered under the contract receives a **certificate of insurance** as evidence of his or her coverage. A certificate is merely a description of the coverage provided and is not part of the master contract. In general, a certificate of insurance is not even considered to be a contract and usually contains a disclaimer to that effect. However, some courts have held the contrary to be true when the provisions of the certificate or even the explanatory booklet of a group insurance plan vary materially from the master contract.

In individual insurance, the insured's coverage normally begins with the inception of the insurance contract and ceases with its termination. However, in group insurance, individual members of the group may become eligible for coverage long after the inception of the group contract, or they may lose their eligibility status long before the contract terminates.

Experience Rating

A second distinguishing characteristic of group insurance is the use of experience rating. If a group is sufficiently large, the actual claims experience of that particular group is a factor in determining the premium the policyowner is charged. The experience of an insurance company is also reflected in the dividends and future premiums associated with individual insurance. However, such experience is determined on a class basis and applies to all insureds in that class. This is also true for group insurance contracts when the group's membership is small. The use of experience rating is discussed in detail in Chapter 17.

Group Underwriting

Underwriting is the process of evaluating an insurance applicant, making decisions about the applicant's acceptability for insurance coverage, and determining the appropriate basis on which to determine the price for the coverage. The applicant for individual insurance must generally provide **evidence of insurability.** This means that the applicant must meet the standards that the insurance company has determined are necessary before it will issue a policy. For group insurance, on the other hand, individual members of the group are usually not required to show any evidence of insurability when initially eligible for coverage. This is not to say that there is no underwriting, but rather that underwriting is focused on the characteristics of the group instead of on the insurability of individual members of the group.

The purpose of group insurance underwriting is twofold: (1) to minimize the problem of **adverse selection** (meaning that those who are likely to have claims are also those who are most likely to seek insurance) and (2) to minimize the administrative costs associated with group insurance. Because of group underwriting, coverage can be provided through group insurance at a lower cost than through individual insurance.

Underwriting considerations peculiar to specific types of group insurance are discussed throughout the book where appropriate. However, there are certain general underwriting considerations applicable to all or most types of group insurance that affect the contractual provisions in group insurance contracts as well as insurance company practices pertaining to group insurance. These general underwriting considerations include

- the reason for the group's existence,
- the stability of the group,
- the persistency of the group,
- the method of determining benefits,
- the provisions for determining eligibility,
- the source and method of premium payments,
- the administrative aspects of the group insurance plan,
- the prior experience of the plan,
- the size of the group,
- the composition of the group,
- the industry represented by the group, and
- the geographic location of the group.

Reason for Existence.   Probably the most fundamental group underwriting principle is that a group must have been formed for some purpose other than to obtain insurance for its members. Such a rule protects the group insurance company against the adverse selection that would likely exist if poor risks were to form a group just to obtain insurance. Groups based on an employer-employee relationship present little difficulty with respect to this rule.

Stability.   Ideally, an underwriter would like to see a reasonable but steady flow of persons through a group. A higher-than-average turnover rate among employees results in increased administrative costs for the insurance company as well as for the employer. If turnover exists among recently hired employees, the resulting costs can be minimized by requiring employees to wait a certain period of time before becoming eligible for coverage. However, such a **probationary period** leaves newly hired employees without protection if their previous group insurance coverage has terminated.

A lower-than-average turnover rate often results in an increasing average age for the members of a group. To the extent that a plan's premium is a function of the **mortality** (death rates) and the **morbidity** (sickness and disability rates) of the group, such an increase in average age results in an increasing premium rate for that group insurance plan. This high rate may cause the better risks to drop out of a plan, if they are required to contribute to its cost, and may ultimately force the employer to terminate the plan because of its increasing cost.

Persistency.   An underwriter is concerned with **persistency,** which is the length of time a group insurance contract will remain on the insurance company's books. Initial acquisition expenses of an insurer frequently cause an insurance company to lose money during the first year the group insurance contract is in force. These acquisition expenses include costs associated with marketing and the enrollment of members in a group insurance plan. Only through the renewal of the contract for a period of time, often three or four years, can these acquisition expenses be recovered. For this reason, firms with a history of frequently changing insurance companies or those with financial difficulty are often avoided.

Determination of Benefits. In most types of group insurance, the underwriter requires that benefit levels for individual members of the group be determined in a manner that precludes individual selection by either the employees or the employer. If employees could choose their own benefit levels, there would be a tendency for the poorer risks to select greater amounts of coverage than the better risks would select. Adverse selection could also exist if the employer could choose a separate benefit level for each individual member of the group. As a result, this underwriting rule has led to benefit levels that are either identical for all employees or determined by a benefit formula that bases benefit levels on some specific criterion, such as salary or position.

Benefits based on salary or position may still lead to adverse selection because disproportionately larger benefits are provided to the owner or top executives, who may have been involved in determining the benefit formula. Consequently, most insurance companies have rules for determining the maximum benefit that may be provided for any individual employee without evidence of insurability. Additional amounts of coverage either are not provided or are subject to individual evidence of insurability.

The general level of benefits for all employees is also of interest to the underwriter. For example, benefit levels that are too high may encourage overutilization and malingering, and benefit levels that are unusually low may lead to low participation if a plan is voluntary.

Determination of Eligibility. The underwriter is also concerned with the **eligibility provision** in a group insurance plan. This provision determines who will be eligible for coverage under the plan and when coverage will begin. As previously mentioned, many group insurance plans contain probationary periods that must be satisfied before an employee is eligible for coverage. In addition to minimizing administrative costs, a probationary period also discourages persons with known medical conditions from seeking employment primarily because of a firm's group insurance benefits. This latter problem can also be addressed in other ways—for example, by including a requirement that an employee be actively at work before coverage commences or by limiting coverage for preexisting conditions to the extent allowed by federal and state laws.

Most group insurance plans limit eligibility to regular full-time employees because the coverage of part-time, seasonal, and temporary employees may not be desirable from an underwriting standpoint. In addition to having a high turnover rate, these employees are more likely to seek employment primarily to obtain group insurance benefits.

Premium Payments. Group insurance plans may be contributory or noncontributory. Members of a **contributory plan** pay a portion, or possibly all, of the cost of their own coverage. When employees pay the entire portion, these plans are often referred to as *fully contributory, employee-pay-all,* or *voluntary plans.* Under a **noncontributory plan,** the policyowner pays the entire cost. Because all eligible employees are usually covered, this type of plan is desirable from an underwriting standpoint because it minimizes adverse selection. In fact, most insurance companies and the laws of many states require 100 percent participation of eligible employees under noncontributory plans. In addition, the absence of employee solicitation, payroll deductions, and underwriting of late entrants into the plan results in administrative savings to both the policyowner and the insurance company.

Most state laws prohibit an employer from requiring that an employee participate in a contributory plan. The insurance company is therefore faced with the possibility of adverse selection because those who elect coverage tend to be the poorer risks. From a practical standpoint, 100 percent participation in a contributory plan would be unrealistic because for many reasons some employees neither desire nor need the coverage provided under the plan. However, insurance companies require that a minimum percentage of the eligible members of a group elect to participate before the contract is issued. The common requirement is 75 percent, although a lower percentage is often acceptable for large groups and a higher percentage may be required for small groups. A 75 percent minimum requirement is also often a statutory requirement for group life insurance and sometimes for group health insurance.

A key issue in contributory plans is how to treat employees who did not elect to participate when first eligible but who later desire coverage, or who dropped coverage and want it reinstated. Unfortunately, this desire for coverage may arise when these employees or their dependents have medical conditions that lead to claims once coverage is provided. To control this adverse selection, insurance companies commonly require individual evidence of insurability by these employees or their dependents before coverage is made available. However, there are two exceptions. First, some plans periodically have short open enrollment periods. An **open enrollment period** is an interval during which coverage can be obtained and the evidence-of-insurability requirement is lessened or waived. Second, the *Health Insurance Portability and Accountability Act* (discussed in detail in later chapters) effectively eliminates the use of evidence of insurability for medical expense plans, but not for other types of group insurance.

Insurance companies frequently require that the employer pay a portion of the premium under a group insurance plan. This is also a statutory requirement for group life insurance in most states and occasionally for group health insurance. Many group insurance plans set an average contribution rate for all employees, which in turn leads to the subsidizing of some employees by other employees, particularly in those types of insurance where the frequency of claims increases with age. Without a requirement for employer contributions, younger employees might actually find coverage at a lower cost in the individual market, thereby leaving the group with only the older risks. Even when group insurance already has a cost advantage over individual insurance, its attractiveness to employees is enhanced by employer contributions. With constantly increasing health care costs, employer contributions help cushion rate increases to employees and thus minimize participation problems as contributions are raised. In addition, underwriters feel that the absence of employer contributions may lead to a lack of employer interest in the plan and consequently poor cooperation with the insurance company and inadequate plan administration.

Administration. To minimize the expenses associated with group insurance, the underwriter often requires that the employer carry out certain administrative functions, either with its own employees or through outsourcing. These commonly include communicating the plan to employees, handling enrollment procedures, collecting employee contributions on a payroll-deduction basis, and keeping certain types of records. In addition, employers are often involved in the claims process. Underwriters are concerned not only with the employer's ability to carry out these functions but also with the employer's willingness to cooperate with the insurance company.

Prior Experience. For most insurance companies, a large portion of newly written group insurance consists of business that was previously written by other insurance companies. Therefore, it is important for the underwriter to ascertain the reason for the transfer. If the transferred business is a result of dissatisfaction with the prior insurance company's service, the underwriter must determine whether his or her insurance company can provide the type and level of service desired. Because an employer is most likely to shop for new coverage when faced with a rate increase, the underwriter must evaluate whether the rate increase was due to excessive claims experience. Often, particularly with larger groups, poor claims experience in the past is an indication that there might be poor experience in the future. Occasionally, however, the prior experience may be due to circumstances that will not continue in the future, such as a catastrophe or large medical bills for an employee who died, totally recovered, or terminated employment.

Excessive past claims experience may not result in coverage denial for a new applicant, but it will probably result in a higher rate. As an alternative, changes in the benefit or eligibility provisions of the plan might eliminate a previous source of adverse claims experience.

The underwriter must determine the new insurance company's responsibility for existing claims. Some states prohibit a new insurance company from using a preexisting-conditions clause to deny the continuing claims of persons who were covered under a prior group insurance plan if these claims would otherwise be covered under the new contract. The rationale for this **no-loss no-gain legislation** is that claims should be paid neither more liberally nor less liberally than if no transfer had taken place. Even in states that have no such regulation, an employer may still wish to provide employees with continuing protection. In either case, the underwriter must evaluate these continuing claims as well as any liability of the previous insurance company for their payment.

Finally, the underwriter must be reasonably certain that the employer will not present a persistency problem by changing insurance companies again in the near future.

Size. The size of a group is a significant factor in the underwriting process. With large groups, there is usually prior group insurance experience that can be used as a factor in determining the premium, and considerable flexibility also exists with respect to both rating and plan design. In addition, adjustments for adverse claims experience can be made at future renewal dates under the experience-rating process.

For small groups, coverage is sometimes being written for the first time. Administrative expenses tend to be high in relation to the premium. There is also an increased possibility that the owner or major stockholder might be interested in coverage primarily because he or she or a family member has a medical problem that will result in large immediate claims. As a result, contractual provisions and the benefits available are quite standardized in order to control administrative costs. Furthermore, because past experience for small groups is not necessarily a realistic indicator of future experience, most insurance companies use pooled rates under which a uniform rate is applied to all groups that have a specific coverage. Because poor claims experience for a particular group is not charged to that group at renewal, more restrictive underwriting practices relating to adverse selection are used. These include less liberal contractual provisions and, in some cases, individual underwriting for group members.

Composition.   The age, gender, and income of employees in a group affect the experience of the group. As employees age, the mortality rate increases. Excluding maternity claims, both the frequency and the duration of medical and disability claims also increase with age.

At all ages, the death rate is lower for females than for males. However, the opposite is true for medical expenses and disability claims. Even if maternity claims are disregarded, women as a group tend to be hospitalized and disabled more frequently and to obtain medical and surgical treatment more often than men, except at extremely advanced ages.

Employees at high income levels tend to incur higher-than-average medical and dental expenses. This is partly because practitioners sometimes base charges on a patient's ability to pay. (Because a high percentage of individuals now have health insurance, this practice is less common than in the past.) In addition, higher-income persons are more likely to seek specialized care or care in more affluent areas, where the charges of practitioners are generally higher. On the other hand, low-income employees can also pose problems. Turnover rates tend to be higher, and there is often difficulty in getting and retaining proper levels of participation in contributory plans.

Adjustments can often be made for all these factors when determining the proper rate to charge the policyowner. Some states, however, require the use of unisex rates, in which case the mix of employees by gender becomes an underwriting consideration. A major problem can arise in contributory insurance plans. To the extent that higher costs for a group with a less-than-average mix of employees are passed on to these employees, a lower participation rate may result.

Industry.   The nature of the industry represented by a group is also a significant factor in the underwriting process. In addition to different occupational hazards among industries, employees in some industries have higher-than-average health insurance claims that cannot be directly attributed to their jobs. Therefore, insurance companies commonly make adjustments in their life and health insurance rates based on the occupations of the employees covered as well as on the industries in which they work.

In addition to occupational hazards, the underwriter must weigh other factors as well. Certain industries are characterized by a lack of stability and persistency and thus may be considered undesirable risks. The underwriter must also be concerned with the effect that changes in the economy have on a particular industry.

Geographic Location.   The size and frequency of medical expense and disability income claims vary considerably among geographic regions and must be considered in determining a group insurance rate. For example, medical expenses tend to be higher in the Northeast than in the South and higher in large urban areas than in rural areas. Certain geographic regions also tend to have a higher frequency of disability claims.

A group with geographically scattered employees poses more administrative problems and probably results in greater administrative expense than a group at a single location. In addition, the underwriter must determine whether the insurance company has the proper facilities to service policyowners with multiple worksites.

ALTERNATIVE FUNDING METHODS

As the cost of providing insurance benefits to employees has risen, employers have increasingly turned from fully insured plans to alternative funding methods to minimize this cost. In some cases, these alternative methods consist of variations in group insurance contracts, such as premium-payment delays and reserve-reduction arrangements. At the opposite end of the spectrum are totally self-funded (self-insured) plans, in which no insurance is purchased and benefits are paid from either current revenue or a trust to which periodic payments have been made. Between these two extremes are such programs as minimum-premium plans, stop-loss arrangements, and big-deductible plans that combine various aspects of traditionally insured plans with those of self-funding. Even when self-funding is used, employers often contract with an insurance company or other organization for administrative services.

These alternative funding methods are discussed in detail in Chapter 16. At this point, however, it should be noted that the use of alternative funding methods does not eliminate the need for making decisions regarding such factors as eligibility, benefit levels, and claims handling. In most cases, provisions for these factors are similar, if not identical, to the provisions found in the types of group insurance contracts that are discussed throughout this book.

VOLUNTARY BENEFITS

A major area of growth for insurance companies in recent years has been through the marketing of voluntary benefits for employees, many of which are discussed later in this book. These products—which can be either group insurance or individual insurance—vary considerably among insurance companies. Even the names used to describe these products are not uniform, with terminology like *payroll deduction plans* and *worksite marketing* often being used. For purposes of this book, **voluntary benefits** are defined as products provided by the employer that the employee purchases and for which he or she pays 100 percent of the premium.

It is difficult to measure the precise extent of voluntary benefits because statistics are often included with other group or individual products sold by a company. However, a recent LIMRA International Survey[1] found that 60 percent of employers with 10 to 19 employees make voluntary benefit products available. This figure increases to over 90 percent for employers with 1,000 or more employees. The survey also indicated that more than half of the employers that provide voluntary benefit plans make at least three products available.

Reasons for Increase in Popularity

Voluntary benefits have increased in popularity in recent years, primarily because of employers' attempts to contain the rising costs of employee benefits. For example, an employer may determine that it cannot afford to institute a new group insurance program and pay any portion of the cost of coverage. Even though employees would naturally like to have the employer share in the cost, the ease of payroll deduction and more liberal underwriting still make a payroll deduction plan attractive to them. In addition, **portability** of the coverage is often appealing. Portability allows an employee to continue coverage under an employer-sponsored plan after termination of employment by paying premiums directly to the insurance company.

Voluntary benefits have also grown in popularity as a method of supplementing the benefits provided under a group plan financed by the employer. For example, an employer may pay for a group long-term disability income plan that provides benefits equal to 50 percent of salary. Voluntary benefits then allow employees to purchase additional protection. Or the employer may pay for short-term disability income protection only and make long-term protection available under a voluntary benefit plan.

Changes in demographics make it increasingly difficult for employers to offer an overall benefit plan that meets the needs of all employees. One alternative is to offer a cafeteria plan, under which an employee can allocate the benefit dollars spent by his or her employer among a variety of benefits. Cafeteria plans are covered in detail in Chapter 19. Another option is to provide a basic core of benefits that all employees want. Additional benefits, such as long-term care insurance, can be offered on a voluntary basis.

Another reason for the increase in the popularity of voluntary benefits is the increased availability of products. More insurance companies have entered the market to obtain additional revenue at a time when revenue from other sources has been decreasing. As is often the case, this has sometimes resulted in more competitive premiums and more liberal underwriting.

Market Characteristics

The voluntary benefit market is very diverse. The remainder of this section briefly describes some of the variations.

Insurance Company Involvement. It is estimated that between 150 and 200 insurance companies offer voluntary benefits, with the number of companies offering individual products being about double the number of companies offering group products and with some companies offering both individual and group products. For a few companies, 50 to 100 percent of their premium income is from voluntary products. However, for the majority of companies, the figure is under 10 percent.

As a general rule, individual insurers target employers with fewer employees than do group insurers. However, many insurance companies provide coverage for the employees of almost any size employer. Most companies target employees in the middle-income range.

Types of Products Available. The major goal of most insurance companies in the voluntary market is to sell life insurance to employees and their dependents. Individual insurers are heavily concentrated in this market. Life insurance is also the most popular product of group insurers, but they are more likely to offer health insurance products as well.

Life insurance products run the gamut from basic term insurance to variable universal life insurance and include accidental death and dismemberment insurance. The most prevalent health insurance products are short-term and long-term disability income. Major medical coverage is seldom offered, but some insurers sell specified-disease policies and hospital-indemnity coverage. Dental insurance, prescription drug coverage, and vision coverage are also found, usually in the group insurance market. An increasingly common product is long-term care insurance. A few companies also write property and liability insurance. All these types of benefits are discussed later in this book.

Depending on the size of the employer, group products can be tailored to the employer's needs. In the individual marketplace, some providers of voluntary products sell the standard products that are listed in their rate books. Other insurers market specialized products. This is common for universal life insurance and among companies that specialize in voluntary benefits.

Underwriting. Surveys of both employers and employees indicate that the success of a voluntary benefit plan is affected by insurance company underwriting. Although some voluntary benefits are fully underwritten on an individual basis, most plans are responsive to market demands and use either simplified underwriting or guaranteed issue, with group coverage being more likely than individual coverage to have the latter. **Guaranteed issue** means that coverage is issued without an employee having to provide evidence of insurability. **Simplified issue** means that that coverage is issued with satisfactory responses to questions on an abbreviated application form. Some insurers have a category of underwriting—called **modified guaranteed issue**—that falls somewhere between guaranteed issue and simplified issue. In this case, the insurer accepts most applicants but asks a few medically related questions that may result in the declination of a small number of applicants.

As a general rule, employers want guaranteed-issue coverage unless simplified underwriting results in significant cost savings to employees. Several factors affect the underwriting policy of an insurance company, including size, participation level, and issue limits. For example, an insurance company might use simplified underwriting for its universal life product if there is a minimum 8 percent participation rate among employers with 500 employees and the issue limit is $100,000. For a group of 50 employees, the percentage might be 15 and the issue limit $85,000. For guaranteed issue, the figures might be 35 percent and $80,000 for employers with 500 employees and 55 percent and $50,000 for employers with 50 employees.

Cost. It is estimated that voluntary benefits are about 10 percent less expensive than coverage purchased in the individual marketplace outside the employment relationship. However, significant variations exist. Even when there is no cost differential, the ease of payroll deduction is appealing to employees.

Because both employers and employees have considerable interest in voluntary products being offered on a tax-favored basis, benefits may be provided under a cafeteria plan. However, the use of a cafeteria plan may pose problems, and some benefit consultants feel that voluntary benefits should be kept separate from a firm's cafeteria plan. The issue arises over regulation by ERISA. Most voluntary plans, being employee-pay-all plans, are exempt from ERISA rules, which is a definite plus from the employer's perspective. Any benefits purchased under a cafeteria plan are technically purchased with employer funds, even if made with voluntary salary reductions. It is argued that this would subject a voluntary benefit plan to ERISA rules. In 1996, however, the Pension and Welfare Benefits Administration issued an advisory opinion that ERISA did not apply to premium-conversion plans (also called *premium-only plans*) used in cafeteria plans to allow before-tax salary reductions for medical expense premiums. The government has not yet addressed the issue of other voluntary benefits provided under cafeteria plans.

Methods of Premium Payment.   The vast majority of voluntary benefits use payroll deduction as the method for premium payments, with the employer remitting the premiums to the insurance company. Some insurers bill employees directly if an employer is unwilling to participate in a payroll deduction arrangement. However, payroll deduction is very popular with employees, and direct billing probably has an adverse effect on plan participation, although it may also reduce the rate at which coverage lapses when employment terminates.

Premiums are usually determined by the benefits purchased and the frequency of payroll deductions. However, life insurance is sometimes sold on the basis of the amount of coverage that can be purchased with a given premium, such as $1, $2, or $5 per week (or other period). Because the amount of coverage is a function of the employee's attained age, larger amounts of coverage are available to younger employees than to older employees.

Portability

Individual insurance products are automatically portable when an employee terminates employment. However, there are several possibilities with group coverage. In a few cases, coverage ceases; in some cases, the employee must convert to an individual policy. In most cases, the employee can continue the group coverage on a direct-bill basis.

Premiums often remain the same after termination of employment, but they may have to be paid less frequently. For example, instead of paying a monthly periodic deduction, an individual may be billed quarterly. Under some plans, an extra administrative charge is made for the cost of direct billing.

■ STATE REGULATION

Even though the United States Supreme Court has declared insurance to be commerce and thus subject to federal regulation when conducted on an interstate basis, Congress gave the states substantial regulatory authority by the passage of the **McCarran-Ferguson Act** (Public Law 15) in 1945. The act exempts insurance from certain federal regulations to the extent that individual states actually regulate insurance. In addition, it stipulates that most other federal laws are not applicable to insurance unless they are specifically directed at the business of insurance.

As a result of the McCarran-Ferguson Act, a substantial body of laws and regulations has been enacted in every state. Although no two states have identical laws and regulations, there have been attempts to encourage uniformity among the states. The most significant influence in this regard has been the **National Association of Insurance Commissioners (NAIC),** which is composed of state regulatory officials. Because the NAIC promotes uniformity in legislation and administrative rules affecting insurance, it has developed numerous model laws. Although states are not bound to adopt these model laws, numerous states have enacted many of them.

Some of the more significant state laws and regulations affecting group insurance pertain to the types of groups eligible for coverage, benefit limitations, contractual provisions, and tax treatment. Moreover, because many employers have employees in several states, the extent of each state's regulatory jurisdiction is a matter of some concern.

Eligible Groups

Most states do not allow group insurance contracts to be written unless a minimum number of persons is insured under the contract. This requirement, which may vary by type of coverage and type of group, is most common in group life insurance, where the minimum number required for plans established by individual employers is often ten persons but may be as few as two. A few states have either a lower minimum or no such requirement. A higher minimum (often 100 persons) may be imposed on plans established by trusts, labor unions, or creditors. Only about half the states enforce any minimum number requirement on group health insurance contracts; it is usually either five or ten persons.

Most states also have insurance laws concerning the types of groups for which insurance companies may write group insurance. Most of these laws specify that a group insurance contract cannot be delivered to a policyowner in the state unless the group meets certain statutory eligibility requirements for its type of group. In some states, these eligibility requirements even vary by type of coverage. Although the categories of eligible groups may vary, at least four types of groups involving employees are acceptable in virtually all states: individual employer groups, negotiated trusteeships, trade associations, and labor union groups. Other types of groups, including multiple-employer welfare arrangements, are also acceptable in some states. Some states have no insurance laws regarding the types or sizes of groups for which insurance companies may write group insurance. Rather, eligibility is determined by the underwriting standards of insurance companies.

Individual Employer Groups. The most common type of eligible group is the **individual employer group**, in which the employer may be a corporation, a partnership, or a sole proprietorship. Many state laws are very specific about what constitutes an employee for group insurance purposes. In addition to those usually considered to be employees of a firm, coverage can generally be written for retired employees and employees of subsidiary and affiliated firms. Furthermore, individual proprietors or partners are usually eligible for coverage as long as they are actively engaged in and devote a substantial part of their time to the conduct of the organization. Similarly, directors of a corporation may be eligible for coverage if they are also employees of the corporation.

Negotiated Trusteeships (Taft-Hartley Trusts). A **negotiated trusteeship** is formed as a result of collective bargaining over benefits between a union and the employers of the union members. Generally, the union employees are in the same industry or related ones. For the most part, frequent movement of union members among employers characterizes these industries (such as trucking or construction). The Taft-Hartley Act prohibits employers from paying funds directly to a labor union for the purpose of providing group insurance coverage to members. Payments must be made to a trust fund established for the purpose of providing benefits to employees. The trustees of the fund, who must consist of equal numbers of representatives from both the employers and the union, can elect either to self-fund benefits or to purchase insurance contracts with themselves as the policyowners. Because eligible employees include only members of the collective-bargaining unit (which may include some nonunion members), benefits for other employees must be provided in some other manner.

Negotiated trusteeships differ from other types of groups in how benefits are financed and how eligibility for benefits is determined. Employers often make contributions based on the number of hours worked by the employees covered under the collective-bargaining agreement, regardless of whether these employees are eligible for benefits. Eligibility for benefits during a given period is usually based only on some minimum number of hours worked during a previous period. For example, a union member might receive coverage during a calendar quarter (even when unemployed) if he or she worked at least 300 hours in the previous calendar quarter. This situation, where the employees for whom contributions are made may differ from those who are eligible for benefits, presents a unique problem for the underwriter. Rates must be adequate to build up the contingency reserves necessary to pay benefits in periods of heavy layoffs, during which a large portion of contributions ceases but eligibility for benefits continues.

Although negotiated trusteeships normally provide benefits for the employees of several employers, they can also be established for the employees of a single employer. However, situations involving collective bargaining with a single employer usually result in the employer being required to provide benefits for the employees under a group insurance contract purchased by the employer. Although benefits and eligibility are specified in the bargaining agreement, the employer is the policyowner and the group is an individual employer group rather than a negotiated trusteeship. This approach also enables the employer to provide benefits for nonunion employees under the same contract.

Trade Associations. For eligibility purposes, a **trade association** is an association of employers that has been formed for reasons other than obtaining insurance, such as lobbying, providing education, or setting industry standards for its members. In most cases, these employers are in the same industry or type of business—for example, travel planning, interior decorating, or manufacturing of a specific type of product. Many such associations frequently include a large number of employers without the minimum number of employees necessary to qualify for an individual employer group insurance contract. In some states, the master contract is issued directly to the trade association; most states, however, require that a trust be established. Individual employers may provide coverage for their employees through payment of premiums to the association or trust.

Both adverse selection and administrative costs tend to be greater in trade association groups than in many other types of groups. Therefore, most underwriters and state laws require that a minimum percentage of the employers belonging to the association, such as 50 percent, participate in the plan and that a minimum number of persons, possibly as high as 1,000 or 1,500, be covered. In addition, individual underwriting or strict provisions regarding preexisting conditions may be used to the extent allowed by law, and employer contributions are usually required. To ensure adequate enrollment, the underwriter must determine whether the association has the resources as well as the desire to promote the plan enthusiastically and to administer it properly.

Labor Union Groups. Labor unions may establish group insurance plans to provide benefits for their members, with the master contract issued to the union. In addition to the prohibition by the Taft-Hartley Act of employer payments to labor unions for insurance premiums, state laws generally prohibit plans in which union members pay the entire cost from their own pockets. Consequently, the premiums come solely from union funds or partially from union funds and partially from members' contributions. Labor union groups account for a relatively small amount of group insurance, most of which is life insurance.

Multiple-Employer Welfare Arrangements. The final type of eligible group designed to provide benefits for employees is the **multiple-employer welfare arrangement (MEWA).** MEWAs are a common but often controversial method of marketing group benefits, particularly medical expense coverage, to employers who have a small number of employees. MEWAs are legal entities (1) sponsored by an insurance company, an independent administrator, or some other person or organization and (2) organized to provide group benefits to the employees of more than one employer. Each MEWA must have an administrator that is either an insurance company or a professional administrator. MEWAs may be organized as trusts, in which case there must be a trustee that may be an individual but is usually a corporate trustee, such as a commercial bank.

MEWAs are generally established to provide group benefits to employers within a specific industry, such as construction, agriculture, or banking. However, employers are not required to belong to an association. MEWAs may provide either a single type of insurance (such as medical expense insurance) or a wide range of coverages (for example, life, medical expense, and disability income insurance). In some cases, alternative forms of the same coverage (such as traditional major medical insurance or a preferred-provider organization) are available.

An employer desiring to obtain insurance coverage for its employees from a MEWA must subscribe and become a member of the MEWA. The employer is issued a **joinder agreement,** which spells out the relationship between the MEWA and the employer and specifies the coverages to which the employer has subscribed. It is not necessary for an employer to subscribe to all coverages offered by a MEWA.

A MEWA may either provide benefits on a self-funded basis or fund benefits with a contract purchased from an insurance company. In the latter case, the MEWA, rather than the subscribing employers, is the master insurance contract holder. In either case, the employees of subscribing employers receive benefit descriptions (certificates of insurance in insured MEWAs) in a manner similar to the usual group insurance arrangement.

In addition to alternative methods of funding benefits, MEWAs can also be categorized according to how they are administered—that is, whether by an insurance company or by a third-party administrator. It is generally agreed that there are three types of MEWAs. Unfortunately, the terminology used to describe the three types is not uniform and is often misleading. In this text, the following terminology and definitions are used:

■ *Fully insured multiple-employer trust (MET)*—Benefits are insured, and the MET is administered by an insurance company. (Note: METs are MEWAs, but most insurers use the term **multiple-employer trust** to describe fully insured MEWAs and to distinguish them from the more controversial self-funded MEWAs.)

■ *Insured third-party-administered MEWA*—Benefits are insured, and the MEWA is administered by a third party.

■ *Self-funded MEWA*—Benefits are self-funded, and the MEWA is administered by a third party.

Fully Insured METs. Fully insured METs are established and administered by insurance companies, with a commercial bank usually acting as trustee. Coverage under such METs is normally marketed by the sales force of the insurer involved and may be made available to other licensed producers. It should be noted that a trust purchases coverage from the insurance company, and what is being marketed to employers is the availability of insurance through participation in the trust, not an insurance contract from the insurance company.

Fully insured METs were developed to provide group insurance to small employer groups. A single insurance company may have one MET or several, with each designed for a different industry (such as construction or manufacturing). Through METs, insurance companies have provided group insurance at a cost lower than the cost of a direct sale to the employer or to individual employees. Regulatory restrictions regarding minimum group size are overcome because the employees of many small employers are insured under a single group contract issued to the trust. Costs are also minimized because each type of coverage offered by the trust tends to be standardized for all employers using the trust.

In addition, underwriting standards have been developed to minimize the problems of adverse selection and the higher administrative costs associated with providing coverage to small groups of employees. Although these standards vary among companies, the following are some common examples:

■ More stringent participation requirements, such as 100 percent, for employers with fewer than five employees.

■ A requirement that life insurance coverage be purchased. This tends to be a profitable and stable form of coverage for insurance companies. In some cases, the more life insurance coverage that is purchased, the more comprehensive the medical expense benefits that are made available.

■ Limitations on the period of time for which rates are guaranteed, often no more than six months.

■ Probationary periods, often two or three months, for new employees.

■ Restrictive provisions for preexisting conditions.

■ Limitations on the amounts of life insurance coverage available on a simplified or guaranteed-issue basis (for example, $20,000 for four or fewer employees; $40,000 for five or more). Additional coverage may be available, but individual evidence of insurability is required.

■ Limitations on the amount of long-term disability insurance coverage that is issued, such as 50 percent or 60 percent of income, subject to a $1,500 monthly maximum.

■ Ineligible groups. Most METs have a lengthy list of ineligible groups, including those characterized by poor claims experience or high turnover rates. This list may vary from state to state because of differing laws and regulations.

Because it has generally been accepted under insurance regulatory law that an insurance contract is subject to regulation by the state in which the contract was delivered, many insurers have established METs where they consider the regulatory climate to be favorable. This has allowed an insurance company, in effect, to offer a nationally standardized contract to small employers (through subscribing to the trust) rather than different contracts to comply with the regulatory requirements in each subscriber's state. However, some states require that METs make their coverage conform to applicable state law when an employer from that state becomes a subscriber.

During the 1980s, the importance of METs (and insured, third-party-administered MEWAs) decreased somewhat. Some insurers, primarily because of difficulties in providing medical expense coverage to small employers, left the group insurance business. HMOs increasingly and successfully sought business from smaller employers. In addition, many employers—particularly those with 25 to 100 employees—are more likely to use self-funding. However, in many parts of the country, METs remain a major source of group insurance coverage for small employers.

Insured Third-Party-Administered MEWAs. Insured third-party-administered MEWAs are similar to fully insured METs in that benefits are provided through an insurance contract issued to a trust. However, some person or organization other than an insurance company administers these MEWAs.

The impetus for the establishment of an insured third-party-administered MEWA may come from either the insurance company or the administrator. An insurance company desiring to enter the MEWA field may feel it lacks the expertise or resources to administer MEWAs properly at a competitive cost. Consequently, a number of insurance companies have sought out third-party administrators to perform many of the necessary administrative functions. The third-party administrators under such arrangements are normally organizations specializing in either the administration of various types of insurance programs or solely in the management of MEWAs. In addition to general administrative duties, the third-party administrator (subject to the insurance company's rules) may be involved in any or all of the following functions associated with MEWAs: underwriting, claims administration, benefit design, or marketing.

Third-party administrators desiring to enter the MEWA field or hoping to increase their share of MEWA business might seek out insurance companies to provide the insurance coverages for the MEWAs they wish to establish. Some of these administrators specialize in the administration of insurance programs; others are insurance agents or brokers who desire a product over which they can have marketing control.

Unfortunately, the experience of insured third-party-administered MEWAs was not always satisfactory. There were several instances of mismanagement that caused some of these MEWAs to cease operations. In some cases, eagerness to enter the field resulted in inadequate rates or lax underwriting; in other situations, administrators were more interested in management fees and sales commissions than in making a profit for the insurance company. Although such occurrences have tarnished the image of insured third-party-administered MEWAs in the past, a few still operate successfully and are managed by capable administrators. Two factors have minimized these difficulties in recent years. First, insurance companies, aware of past experiences, are cautious as they enter the field, giving particular regard to the selection of their administrators. Second, some states have passed legislation aimed at regulating administrators of MEWAs and other insurance arrangements.

Self-Funded MEWAs. Self-funded MEWAs are normally established and marketed by the persons or organizations that administer them. The MEWA does not purchase an insurance contract, except possibly to protect against catastrophic claims; instead, benefits are self-funded with premiums paid by subscribing employers. Although many self-funded MEWAs have operated successfully and have been well administered, others have gone bankrupt and left participants with unpaid claims. (Under an insured MEWA, the insurer would be responsible for paying claims even if the MEWA failed.) Again, administrators often did not charge enough to establish proper reserves for future benefits, or they were more concerned with generating management fees and sales commissions than in properly managing the MEWA. In some cases, outright fraud was involved.

Prior to 1982, state insurance departments had tried to obtain the power to shut down mismanaged MEWAs, but the administrators of these plans argued that ERISA (discussed later in this chapter) exempted them from state regulation. In 1982, however, Congress enacted legislation that provides for state regulation of self-funded MEWAs.

Initially, the overall effect of this legislation was to greatly reduce the number of self-funded MEWAs. However, two major factors caused an increase in the number of MEWAs. First, many insurers abandoned the small-group market or became increasingly strict in their underwriting. As a result, self-funded MEWAs became the only alternative for some employers. Second, MEWAs frequently wrote coverage at a cost significantly below the cost of alternative coverage, often because of inadequate actuarial calculations regarding the size of future claims and the need for establishing adequate reserves.

Unfortunately, the resurgence of self-funded MEWAs was accompanied by many bankruptcies and unpaid claims. For example, the General Accounting Office estimated that between 1988 and 1991, almost 200 self-funded MEWAs failed and left nearly 400,000 employees with $132 million of unpaid claims. Although the situation has improved over the last decade, there seems to be little doubt that many states have still been unsuccessful in adequately regulating MEWAs. Even when appropriate laws exist to regulate MEWAs or make them illegal, many MEWAs simply ignore them. The insurance department finds out about a MEWA only when a complaint is received, and by then the MEWA may be in serious financial difficulty or out of business.

Contractual Provisions

Every state regulates contractual provisions through its insurance laws. In many instances, certain contractual provisions must be included in group insurance policies. These mandatory provisions may be altered only if they result in more favorable treatment of the policyowner. Such provisions tend to be most uniform from state to state in the area of group life insurance, primarily because of the widespread adoption of the NAIC model bill pertaining to group life insurance standard provisions. As a result of state regulation, coupled with industry practices, the provisions of most group life and health insurance policies are relatively uniform from company to company. Although an insurance company's policy forms can usually be used in all states, riders may be necessary to bring certain provisions into compliance with the regulations of some states.

Traditionally, the regulation of contractual provisions has focused on provisions pertaining to such factors as the grace period, conversion, and incontestability rather than on those applicable to the types or levels of benefits. These latter provisions have been a matter between the policyowner and the insurance company, but in recent years this situation has changed in many states. In some states, certain benefits, such as well-baby care, treatment for alcoholism or drug abuse, and mental health parity, must be included in any group insurance contract; in other states, they must be offered to group policyowners but are optional. Still other state laws and regulations specify minimum levels for certain benefits if those benefits are included.

With few exceptions the regulation of contractual provisions affects only those employee benefit plans funded with insurance contracts because provisions of ERISA seem to exempt employee benefit plans from most types of state regulation. However, there are exceptions to this exemption, including insurance regulation and, therefore, the provisions in insurance contracts. As a result of ERISA exemption, states have few laws and regulations applying to the provisions of uninsured benefit plans. However, ERISA does not exempt uninsured plans from state regulation in such areas as age and gender discrimination, and laws pertaining to these areas commonly apply to all benefit plans. A few states are also trying to mandate other types of benefits for uninsured plans, and ultimately the issue will probably have to be settled by Congress or the Supreme Court.

Benefit Limitations

The level of benefits that can be provided under group insurance contracts issued to certain types of eligible groups may be subject to statutory limitations. With the exception of group life insurance, these limitations rarely apply in situations involving an employer-employee relationship. In the past, most states limited the amount of group life insurance that an employer could provide for an employee. Today, only Texas still has such a restriction, but its limit is so high that the limit has little practical effect. However, several states limit the amount of coverage that can be provided under contracts issued to groups other than individual employer groups. In addition, some states limit the amount of life insurance coverage that may be provided for dependents.

Tax Treatment

Every state levies a premium tax on foreign (out-of-state) insurance companies licensed to do business in its state, and most states tax the premiums of insurance companies domiciled in their states. These taxes, which are applicable to premiums written within a state, average about 2 percent.

The imposition of the premium tax has placed insurance companies at a competitive disadvantage with alternative methods of providing benefits. Premiums paid to health maintenance organizations are not subject to the tax, nor are premiums paid to Blue Cross and Blue Shield plans in some states. In addition, the elimination of this tax is one cost saving under self-funded plans. Because the trend toward self-funding of benefits by large corporations has resulted in the loss of substantial premium tax revenue to the states, there have been suggestions that all premiums paid to any type of organization or fund for the purpose of providing insurance benefits to employees be subject to the premium tax.

Where state income taxation exists, the tax implications of group insurance premiums and benefits to both employers and employees are generally similar to those of the federal government. Employers may deduct any premiums paid as business expenses, and employees have certain exemptions from taxation with respect to both premiums paid on their behalf and benefits attributable to employer-paid premiums.

Regulatory Jurisdiction

A group insurance contract often insures individuals living in more than one state—a situation that raises the question of which state or states have regulatory jurisdiction over the contract. This issue is a crucial one because such factors as minimum enrollment percentages, maximum amounts of life insurance, and required contract provisions vary among the states.

Few problems arise if the insured group qualifies as an eligible group in all the states where insured individuals reside. Under the **doctrine of comity**, by which states recognize within their own territory the laws of other states, it is generally accepted that the state in which the group insurance contract is delivered to the policyowner has governing jurisdiction. Therefore, the contract must conform only to the laws and regulations of this one state, even though certificates of insurance may be delivered in other states. However, a few states have statutes that prohibit insurance issued in other states from covering residents of their state unless the contract conforms with their laws and regulations. Although these statutes are effective with respect to insurance companies licensed within the state (that is, admitted companies), their effectiveness with respect to nonadmitted companies is questionable, because states lack regulatory jurisdiction over these companies.

This does not mean that the policyowner may arbitrarily seek out a situs (place of delivery) that is most desirable from a regulatory standpoint. Unless the state of delivery has a significant relationship to the insurance transaction, other states may seek to exercise their regulatory authority. Therefore, it has become common practice that an acceptable situs must be at least one of the following:

- The state where the policyowner is incorporated (or the trust is created if the policyowner is a trust)
- The state where the policyowner's principal office is located
- The state where the greatest number of insured individuals are employed
- Any state where an employer or labor union that is a party to a trust is located

Most insurers are reluctant to issue a group contract in any state unless a corporate officer or trustee who can execute acceptance of the contract is located in that state. The principal functions related to the administration of the group contract must also be performed there.

The issue of regulatory jurisdiction is more complex for those types of groups that are not considered to be eligible groups in all states. Multiple-employer welfare arrangements are a typical example. If a state has no regulation to the contrary and if the insured group would be eligible for group insurance in other states, the situation is the same as previously described. In addition, most other states accept the doctrine of comity and do not interfere with the regulatory jurisdiction of the state where the contract is delivered. However, some states either prohibit coverage from being issued or require that it conform with the state's laws and regulations other than those pertaining to eligible groups.

■ FEDERAL REGULATION

Many aspects of federal regulation have affected the establishment and character of group insurance, and many are covered in some detail in this book. The following five acts are discussed in some detail in this chapter because they affect several types of group insurance and other group benefits:

- Age Discrimination in Employment Act
- Pregnancy Discrimination Act
- Employee Retirement Income Security Act
- Americans with Disabilities Act

■ Financial Services Modernization Act

Several other aspects of federal regulation are covered in other chapters of the book:

■ Internal Revenue Code

■ Health Insurance Portability and Accountability Act

■ Newborns' and Mothers' Health Protection Act

■ Women's Health and Cancer Rights Act

■ Mental Health Parity Act

■ Health Maintenance Organization Act

■ Consolidated Omnibus Budget Reconciliation Act (COBRA)

■ Family and Medical Leave Act

■ Uniformed Services Employment and Reemployment Act

The income tax implications of the Internal Revenue Code, which may vary for different types of group insurance coverage, are described in those chapters pertaining to each type of coverage.

The next six acts affect medical expense coverage and are described at various places in the later chapters on group medical expense coverage.

The Family and Medical Leave Act is covered along with the discussion of family leave in Chapter 18. And, finally, the Uniformed Services Employment and Reemployment Act is discussed in Chapters 14 and 18 as it relates to COBRA and family leave.

Age Discrimination in Employment Act

The **Age Discrimination in Employment Act** applies to employers with 20 or more employees and affects employees aged 40 and older. The act, passed in 1967 and amended several times since then, prohibits discrimination against these workers in terms, conditions, or privileges of employment—including wages and benefits. With some exceptions, such as individuals in executive or high policymaking positions, compulsory retirement is not allowed. Employee benefits, which traditionally ceased or were severely limited at age 65, must be continued for older workers. However, some reductions in benefits are allowed. Although the *federal* act does not prohibit such discrimination in benefits for employees under age 40 or for all employees of firms that employ fewer than 20 persons, some *states* may prohibit such discrimination under their own laws or regulations. Detailed information about the act can be found on the Web site of the Equal Employment Opportunity Commission (EEOC), which enforces the act: *www.eeoc.gov.*

The act permits a reduction in the level of some benefits for older workers so that the cost of providing benefits for older workers is no greater than the cost of providing them for younger workers. However, the most expensive benefit—medical expense coverage—cannot be reduced. The following discussion is limited to reductions after age 65—by far the most common age for reducing benefits, even though reductions can start at an earlier age if they are justified on a cost basis. It should be emphasized that these restrictions apply to benefits for active employees only; there are no requirements under the act that any benefits be continued for retired workers.

When participation in an employee benefit plan is voluntary, an employer can generally require larger employee contributions instead of reducing benefits for older employees, as long as the proportion of the premiums paid by older employees does not increase with age. Thus, if an employer pays 50 percent of the cost of benefits for younger employees, it must pay at least 50 percent of the cost for older employees. If employees pay the entire cost of a benefit, older employees may be required to pay the full cost of their coverage to the extent that this is a condition of participation in the plan. However, this provision is not applicable to medical expense benefits—employees over age 65 cannot be required to pay more for their coverage than is paid by employees under age 65.

In cases where benefits are reduced, two approaches are permitted: a benefit-by-benefit approach or a benefit-package approach. Under the more common *benefit-by-benefit approach,* each employee benefit may be reduced to a lesser amount as long as each reduction can be justified on a cost basis. Under a *benefit-package approach,* the overall benefit package may be altered. Some benefits may be eliminated or reduced to a lesser amount than can be justified on a cost basis, as long as other existing benefits are not reduced or the benefit package is increased by adding new benefits for older workers. The only cost restriction is that the cost of the revised benefit package may be no less than if a benefit-by-benefit reduction had been used. The act also places two other restrictions on the benefit-package approach by prohibiting any reduction in medical expense benefits or retirement benefits.

In reducing a benefit, an employer must use data that approximately reflect the actual cost of the benefit to the employer over a reasonable period of years. Unfortunately, such data either have not been kept by employers or are not statistically valid. Consequently, reductions have been based on estimates provided by insurance companies and consulting actuaries. This approach appears to be satisfactory to the EEOC. The act allows reductions to take place on a yearly basis or to be based on age brackets of up to five years. Any cost comparisons must be made with the preceding age bracket. For example, if five-year age brackets are used, the cost of providing benefits to employees aged 65 through 69 must be compared with the cost of providing the same benefits to employees aged 60 through 64.

Although reductions in group insurance benefits for older employees are permissible, they are not required. Some employers make no reductions for older employees, but most employers reduce life insurance benefits at age 65 and long-term disability benefits at age 60 or 65.

Group Term Life Insurance Benefits.   Basing their conclusions on mortality statistics, most insurance companies feel that group term life insurance benefits can be reduced to certain percentages (see Table 5.1) of the amount of coverage provided immediately prior to age 65. However, some insurers recommend different percentage reductions.

Therefore, if employees normally receive $40,000 of group term life insurance, then employees from age 65 through 69 can receive only 45 percent of that amount ($26,000), employees age 70 through 74 can receive 30 percent ($18,000), and so forth. Similarly, if employees normally receive coverage equal to 200 percent of salary, this coverage

Age	Percentage
65–69	65
70–74	45
75–79	30
over 79	20

TABLE 5.1 Group Term Life Insurance Benefit Reductions

may be reduced by 35 percent to 130 percent of salary at age 65, with additional reductions at later ages.

Reductions may also be made on an annual basis. If an annual reduction is used, it appears that a reduction of up to 11 percent of the previous year's coverage can be actuarially justified, starting at age 65 and continuing through age 69. Starting at age 70, the percentage should be 9 percent.

In a plan with employee contributions, the employer may either reduce benefits as described above and charge the employee the same premium as those employees in the previous age bracket, or continue full coverage and require that the employee pay an actuarially increased contribution.

Group Disability Income Benefits. The act allows reductions in insured short-term disability income plans. However, no reductions are allowed in uninsured sick-leave plans. Although disability statistics for those aged 65 and older are limited, some insurance companies feel a benefit reduction of approximately 20 percent is appropriate for employees aged 65 through 69, with additional decreases of 20 percent of the previous benefit for each consecutive five-year period. However, the laws of the few states that require short-term disability income benefits to be provided allow neither a reduction in benefits nor an increase in any contribution rate for older employees.

Under the act, two methods are allowed for reducing long-term disability income benefits for employees who become disabled at older ages. Either the level of benefits may be reduced without altering benefit eligibility or duration or the benefit duration may be reduced without altering the level of benefits. Again, these reductions must be justified on a cost basis. Unfortunately, no rough guidelines can be given because any possible reductions vary considerably, depending on the eligibility requirements and the duration of benefits under a long-term disability plan. For example, one insurance company suggests that if a plan previously provided full benefits until age 70, then the duration of the benefits could be reduced to 12 months for disabilities occurring between the ages of 70 and 74 and 6 months for disabilities occurring after age 74.

Group Medical Expense Benefits. The Age Discrimination in Employment Act requires that employers offer *all* employees over age 65 (and any employees' spouses who are also over age 65) the same medical coverage they provide for younger employees (and their spouses). Consequently, benefits cannot be reduced for older employees because of increasing cost to the employer. In addition, older employees cannot be required to contribute more than younger employees contribute.

For employers with 20 or more employees, the employer's plan is the primary payer of benefits, with Medicare assuming the secondary-payer role. Although employees may reject the employer's plan and elect Medicare as the primary payer of benefits, federal regulations prevent an employer from offering a health plan or option designed to induce such a rejection. This effectively prohibits an employer from paying the Part B premium or offering any type of supplemental plan to employees who elect Medicare as primary. (However, supplemental and carve-out plans can be used for retirees.) Therefore, most employees elect to remain with the employer's plan unless it requires large employee contributions. When Medicare is secondary, the employer may pay the Part B premium for those employees who elect Medicare, but the employer has no legal responsibility to do so.

Pregnancy Discrimination Act

At one time, pregnancy was usually treated differently from other medical conditions under both individual and group insurance policies. However, the 1978 **Pregnancy Discrimination Act** (an amendment to the Civil Rights Act) requires that women affected by pregnancy, childbirth, or related medical conditions be treated the same for employment-related purposes (including receipt of benefits under an employee benefit plan) as other persons who are not so affected but who are similar in their ability to work. The act applies only to the benefit plans (both insured and self-funded) of employers who have 15 or more employees. Although employers with fewer employees are not subject to the provisions of the act, they may be subject to comparable or more stringent state laws. Similarly, because the act applies only to employee benefit plans, pregnancy may be treated differently from other medical conditions under insurance policies that are not part of an employee benefit plan.

Although the act itself is brief, enforcement falls under the jurisdiction of the Equal Employment Opportunity Commission (Web site: *www.eeoc.gov*), which has a lengthy set of guidelines containing its interpretation of the act. The highlights of these guidelines are as follows:

■   If an employer provides any type of disability income or sick-leave plan for employees, the employer must provide coverage for pregnancy and its related medical conditions on the same basis as other disabilities. For example, maternity cannot be treated as a named exclusion in a disability income plan. Similarly, an employer cannot limit disability income benefits for pregnancies to a shorter period than that applicable to other disabilities.

■   If an employer provides medical expense benefits for employees, the employer must provide coverage for the pregnancy-related conditions of female employees (regardless of marital status) on the same basis as for all other medical conditions. For example, an employer cannot limit hospitalization coverage to $5,000 for pregnancy-related conditions and pay up to 80 percent of expenses for other medical conditions, nor can the employer have a preexisting-conditions clause applying to pregnancy unless the clause also applies to other preexisting conditions in the same manner.

- If an employer provides medical expense benefits for dependents, the employer must provide equal coverage for the medical expenses (including those arising from pregnancy-related conditions) of spouses of both male and female employees. The guidelines do allow a lower level of benefits for the pregnancy-related conditions of spouses of male employees than for female employees but only if all benefits for spouses are lower than those for employees. The guidelines also allow an employer to exclude pregnancy-related benefits for female dependents other than spouses as long as such an exclusion applies equally to the nonspouse dependents of both male and female employees.

- Extended medical expense benefits after termination of employment must apply equally to pregnancy-related medical conditions and other medical conditions. Thus, if pregnancy commencing during employment is covered until delivery, even if the employee is not disabled, a similar nondisability extension of benefits must apply to all other medical conditions. However, no extension is required under the guidelines as long as all medical conditions are treated in the same manner.

- Medical expense benefits relating to abortions may be excluded from coverage except when the life of the woman is endangered. However, complications from an abortion must be covered. In addition, abortions must be treated like any other medical condition with respect to sick-leave and other fringe-benefit plans.

Employee Retirement Income Security Act

The **Employee Retirement Income Security Act (ERISA***)* was enacted in 1974 to protect the interests of participants in employee benefit plans as well as the interests of participants' beneficiaries. All sections of the act (sometimes referred to as the *Pension Reform Act*) generally apply to pension plans, but certain sections also apply to employee welfare benefit plans, including most traditional group insurance plans and other non-retirement benefits. The most significant sections dealing with employee welfare benefit plans are those pertaining to (1) fiduciary responsibility and (2) reporting and disclosure. Because of its broader impact on retirement plans, the complete discussion of ERISA is contained in Part Five. The provisions of most relevance to nonretirement plans are found in Chapter 26.

Americans with Disabilities Act

The **Americans with Disabilities Act (ADA)**, which deals with employment, public services, public accommodations, and telecommunications, is the most far-reaching legislation ever enacted in this country to make it possible for disabled persons to join the mainstream of everyday life.

At the time the act went into effect in 1992, it was estimated that almost 45 million Americans were disabled, and nearly $300 billion of government resources was devoted annually to this group. Fifteen million of the disabled were of working age, but only about 30 percent of these were in the workforce, compared with 80 percent of the nondisabled. Most of the working-age disabled who were not in the workforce were dependent on insurance payments or government benefits for support.

As with any social legislation, the act provides benefits, including a better quality of life, for many disabled persons and annual savings in the form of decreased government payments to the disabled. However, there are also costs, many of which are borne by employers and some of which take the form of increased expenditures for physical modifications to the workplace and for employee benefits.

Title I of the ADA, which pertains to employment, makes it unlawful for employers with 15 or more employees to discriminate on the basis of disability against a qualified individual with respect to any term, condition, or privilege of employment. This includes

- payments for private insurance and retirement plans;
- legally required payments for government programs, such as Social Security and Medicare;
- payments for time not worked, such as vacations;
- extra cash payments to employees, such as educational assistance; and
- the cost of services to employees, such as wellness programs and retirement counseling.

Congress gave the responsibility for enforcing Title I to the Equal Employment Opportunity Commission (Web *site: www.eeoc.gov*), which has numerous regulations and a lengthy Technical Assistance Manual to help qualified individuals understand their rights under the act and to facilitate and encourage employer compliance with the act's provisions.

The act, enacted in 1990, has resulted in significant improvements in public accommodations and the availability of telecommunications for the disabled. The percentage of disabled in the workforce has also increased, but the disabled still face greater barriers to employment than do the nondisabled. (However, it should be noted that many employers hired the disabled before the ADA.) Although intuition might suggest that the disabled would be more likely than other employees to have conditions requiring ongoing medical care, many employers who have made an effort to hire the disabled have not found this to be the case. In fact, some employers feel that the disabled make excellent workers and actually save them money. With jobs more difficult to obtain for the disabled, there is the feeling that the disabled are less likely to switch employers (thus minimizing costs to train new employees) and may actually work harder to keep the jobs they have. Whether this situation will continue as more severely disabled persons enter the workforce and have more opportunities to change jobs is an unanswered question.

Effect on Employment Practices.   The ADA defines a disabled person as one who has a physical or mental impairment that substantially limits one or more major life activities, such as caring for oneself, performing manual tasks, walking, seeing, hearing, speaking, breathing, and learning. The EEOC specifically mentions the following as being disabilities: epilepsy, cancer, diabetes, arthritis, hearing and vision loss, AIDS, and emotional illness. A person is impaired even if the condition is corrected, as in the case of a person who is hearing-impaired and wears a hearing aid. The ADA excludes from the definition of disability persons who are currently engaging in the illegal use of drugs. However, anyone who has successfully completed a supervised rehabilitation program or is currently in such a program is subject to the act's protection as long as he or she is not currently engaging in drug use.

The act does not set quotas or require that the disabled be hired. It does, however, provide that a person cannot be discriminated against if he or she is able to perform the essential functions of a job with or without *reasonable accommodation,* which includes making existing facilities that employees use readily accessible and usable by individuals with disabilities. Reasonable accommodation may be as simple as rearranging furniture or changing the height of a workspace to accommodate a wheelchair. (There are estimates that a significant percentage of the disabled can be accommodated with expenditures of $100 or less for each disabled person.) Reasonable accommodations do not include changes that would cause undue hardship to an employer. The act defines *undue hardship* as a significant difficulty or expense by the employer in light of such factors as the cost of the accommodation, the employer's financial resources, and the impact on other employees. With one exception, reasonable accommodation is for specific individuals for an individual job; it need not be made just because a disabled person may someday apply for work. The exception is that an employer must make facilities for *applying* for a job accessible to the handicapped and provide employment information that is usable by persons who are hearing- or vision-impaired.

As a general rule, the ADA prohibits medical examinations or inquiries into a person's disability status prior to an offer of employment. Many questions that were previously asked of prospective employees are no longer allowed. For example, an employer cannot ask about prior illnesses or injuries, sick days used at a previous employer, prescription drugs taken, or the like.

The portion of the ADA pertaining to employment practices is lengthy and complex, and a more detailed discussion is beyond the scope of this book. However, it should be noted that this part of the act continues to be a source of many lawsuits and complaints to the EEOC. The vast majority of these lawsuits and complaints pertain to issues of hiring, termination of employment, and the failure to make reasonable accommodations. Employee benefits, on the other hand, have been a less significant issue.

Effect on Employee Benefits. The ADA specifically allows the development and administration of benefit plans in accordance with accepted principles of risk assessment. EEOC guidelines state that the purpose of the act is not to disrupt the current regulatory climate for self-insured employers or the current nature of insurance underwriting. Furthermore, its purpose is not to alter current industry practices in sales, underwriting, pricing, administrative and other services, claims, and related activities. The act allows these activities based on classification of risks as regulated by the states, unless these activities are being used as a subterfuge to evade the purpose of the act.

The EEOC guidelines stipulate that employees with disabilities be accorded equal access to whatever health insurance coverage the employer provides to other employees. Coverage for dependents is also subject to equal-access rules, but the scope of coverage for dependents can be different from the scope of coverage that applies to employees. In addition, the guidelines state that decisions about the employment of a person cannot be based on concerns about the effect of the person's disability on the employer's health insurance plan.

The guidelines recognize that certain coverage limitations are acceptable. For example, a lower level of benefits is permissible for mental and nervous conditions than is provided for physical conditions. Even though such a limitation may have a greater effect on certain persons with disabilities, the limitation is not considered discriminatory because it applies to the treatment of many dissimilar conditions and affects individuals both with and without disabilities. Similarly, a lower level of benefits for eye care is singled out as acceptable. However, there have been a number of lawsuits on the issue of whether different benefits for mental and physical disabilities violate the ADA. The EEOC feels that such disparities are a violation, but the courts that have heard these lawsuits have not agreed with this position.

The guidelines allow blanket preexisting-conditions clauses that exclude from coverage the treatment of conditions that predate an individual's eligibility for benefits under a plan. The exclusion of experimental drugs or treatment and elective surgery is also permissible. The guidelines allow coverage limits for procedures that are not exclusively, or nearly exclusively, utilized for the treatment of a specific disability. This category includes, for example, limits on the number of blood transfusions or X-rays, even though such limits may adversely affect persons with certain disabilities.

However, "disability-based" provisions are not allowed. These include the exclusion or limitation of benefits for (1) a specific disability, such as deafness, AIDS, or schizophrenia; (2) a discrete group of disabilities, such as cancer, muscular dystrophy, or kidney disease; and (3) disability in general.

If the EEOC determines that a health plan violates the ADA, the burden of proving otherwise is on the employer. To do this, an employer must show that

- the plan is bona fide in that it exists and pays benefits, and its terms have been adequately communicated to employees;
- the plan's terms are not inconsistent with applicable state law as determined by the appropriate state authorities;
- the challenged portion of the plan is not a subterfuge to evade the purpose of the ADA.

The guidelines contain the following "noninclusive list of potential business/insurance justifications" that an employer can use to prove that a plan provision that has been challenged by the EEOC is not a violation of the ADA. Note that the italicized words are taken directly from the guidelines. Although examples used in the guidelines answer some questions about the exact meaning of the words, their precise meaning is open to interpretation until clarified by regulation or the courts.

- The employer may prove that *it has not engaged in the disability-based disparate treatment alleged.* For example, if it is alleged that a benefit cap for a particular catastrophic disability is discriminatory, the employer may prove that its health insurance plan actually treats all similarly catastrophic conditions in the same way.

■ The employer may prove that *the disparate treatment is justified by legitimate actuarial data, or by actual or reasonably anticipated experience, and that conditions with comparable actuarial data and/or experience are treated in the same fashion.* In other words, the employer may prove that the disability-based disparate treatment is attributable to the application of legitimate risk classification and underwriting procedures to the increased risks (and thus increased cost) of the disability, and not to the disability per se.

■ The employer may prove that *the disparate treatment is necessary to ensure that the challenged health insurance plan satisfies the commonly accepted or legally required standards for the fiscal soundness of such an insurance plan.* For example, the employer may prove that it limited coverage for the treatment of a discrete group of disabilities because the high cost of continued unlimited coverage would have caused the health insurance plan to become financially insolvent, and no non-disability-based health insurance plan alternative could have avoided insolvency.

■ The employer may prove that *the challenged insurance practice or activity is necessary to prevent the occurrence of an unacceptable change either in the coverage of the health insurance plan or in the premiums charged for the health insurance plan.* An unacceptable change is a drastic increase in premium payments (or in copayments or deductibles), or a drastic alteration to the scope of coverage or level of benefits provided that would (1) make the health insurance plan effectively unavailable to a significant number of other employees, (2) make the health insurance plan so unattractive as to result in significant adverse selection, or (3) make the health insurance plan so unattractive that the employer could not compete in recruiting and maintaining qualified workers due to the superiority of health insurance plans offered by other employers in the community.

■ *If coverage for a disability-specific treatment is denied, the employer may prove by reliable scientific evidence that the disability-specific treatment does not cure the condition; slow the degeneration, deterioration, or harm attributable to the condition; alleviate the symptoms of the condition; or maintain the current health status of disabled individuals who receive the treatment.*

Financial Services Modernization Act

The **Financial Services Modernization Act (FSMA)** of 1999, also called the *Gramm-Leach-Bliley Act* after its chief sponsors, restructures the financial system in the United States. The act allows affiliations and mergers between securities firms, banks, and insurance companies and allows banks and securities firms to offer insurance products. More significant for group benefits are the act's provisions for the privacy protection of personal financial information.

In general, FSMA's privacy provisions require financial institutions, including insurance companies, to give customers (defined as persons with continuing relationships with a financial institution) with whom they do business a privacy notice if the company collects nonpublic personal financial information about them and shares it with other entities. In turn, these customers have the right to limit some, but not all, information sharing.

Nonpublic personal financial information includes data from the following:

- A customer application
- Third party sources, such as a credit bureau
- Customer transactions with the company, such as a bank balance or the amount or type of insurance purchased

Even the fact that an individual is a customer of a particular financial institution is nonpublic personal financial information. However, FSMA does not restrict the release of such information, if it is lawfully public, such as the public recording of mortgage loans.

FSMA provisions on privacy of nonpublic personal financial information can be summarized with respect to privacy notice requirements, a broad sharing of information, the required opt-out provision, and implementation.

Privacy Notice Requirements.   The privacy notice must provide clear and factual statements that describe an institution's policies and practices for collection and disclosure of information about customers and potential customers, both current and previous. A person should receive a notice automatically when a customer relationship with the institution begins and every year for as long as that relationship continues. The required notice generally presents these statements under the following headings, which also serve to outline the protections a company must implement:

- Confidentiality and security practices
- Types of information collected
- Categories of parties to whom information is disclosed
- Accuracy of information possessed, including a customer's right to access the information and to amend, correct, or delete information that is erroneous
- Notification of privacy policy changes

Depending on the type of information disclosed and the party or parties receiving the information, the notice may also contain an obligatory statement, known as an *opt-out provision,* which allows customers to say "no" to certain disclosures. When the provision is applicable, the privacy notice must explain how and offer a reasonable way a customer can opt out. A company that seeks to disclose information subject to an opt-out provision must also develop a system to track and honor individual opt-out requests. To avoid violating the law or creating unnecessary expense for itself, a financial institution must understand the provisions of the law regarding information that may be shared generally and information that requires an opt-out provision.

Broad Sharing of Information.   FSMA prohibits the disclosure of personal financial information only in very limited circumstances. For example, financial institutions are prohibited from disclosing their customers' account numbers to nonaffiliated companies when it comes to telemarketing, direct mail marketing, or marketing through e-mail— even if a customer has not opted out of sharing the information for marketing purposes.

The act also prohibits obtaining customer information from financial institutions under false pretenses. Otherwise, financial institutions may disclose personal financial information for any legitimate business purpose, including marketing. As previously stated, however, customers may have an opt-out opportunity in certain circumstances.

Generally, an opt-out provision does not apply when personal financial information is shared with an institution's affiliates. An affiliate is an entity that controls another company, is controlled by the company, or is under common control with the company. Moreover, disclosure to a nonaffiliated company—even another financial institution—for joint marketing purposes is also not subject to an opt-out provision. The nonaffiliated company, however, must not use or disclose the information for any purposes other than those specified in the joint marketing agreement.

The FSMA also does not provide an opt-out right to a customer when a financial institution shares financial information with nonaffiliated companies in the following circumstances:

■ To provide essential services such as data processing or servicing accounts

■ To provide other services such as marketing the institution's products or services

■ To satisfy a legally required disclosure

Required Opt-Out Provision. Disclosure of nonpublic personal financial information to nonaffiliated entities for purposes other than those previously mentioned is subject to the opt-out provision. Examples include sharing a customer list with retailers, publishers, or insurance companies for their own business purposes. Through the opt-out notice, FSMA also enforces a provision of the Fair Credit Reporting Act by requiring that credit information collected on a person from outside sources, such as a credit report or credit application information—if shared with an affiliate company—is subject to the opt-out notice. Opt-out does not apply to credit information from a company's own transactions or history with the customer.

If a customer does not exercise the opt-out right and the financial institution legitimately discloses that information to other companies, such as another insurance company, that company may legitimately use the information for its own purposes.

Implementation. Federal regulatory agencies—including the Securities and Exchange Commission, the Commodity Futures Trading Commission, and the Federal Trade Commission—have jurisdiction over most financial institutions for compliance with FSMA provisions. However, state insurance departments with the authority of state statutes and regulations are responsible for implementation and enforcement of this federal law's privacy requirements. The federal requirements, however, are a minimum; a state may legislate stricter provisions.

State implementation of the FSMA became effective as early as July 1, 2001. At the time this book was being updated in early 2004, however, specific questions on the scope and applicability of the privacy of information requirements remain unanswered to some extent in many states. As a result, adherence to the provisions of the NAIC Standards for Safeguarding Customer Information Model Regulation is often recommended as a precaution until a state's regulation in this area becomes final and issues outstanding are addressed.

Under the model regulation as adopted by many states, the requirements for privacy of nonpublic personal financial information apply to all persons or organizations that are part of the financial services industry. This includes insurance companies and insurance agents and brokers, all of whom are referred to as *licensees*. However, if a state follows the model regulation's provisions, licensees may be spared the burden of some of the strict compliance requirements.

Generally, state regulations allow a licensee to provide the required privacy notice to a group benefit policyowner rather than to every employee or certificate holder. However, the licensee may not disclose information about any individual certificate holder to anyone except as allowed for the reasons previously discussed.

A licensee may avoid the privacy notice and opt-out requirements if all the following conditions apply:

- The licensee is an agent of another licensee (as in the case of an agent or broker representing an insurance company)
- The insurance company complies with the law and provides the required notices
- The licensee does not disclose any nonpublic personal information to any other person or organization except the insurance company or its affiliates in the manner permitted by the regulation

However, there is still some uncertainty about whether an agent or broker working on behalf of a client can avoid the act's privacy notice or opt-out requirements, even if these conditions are satisfied.

Most states, in accordance with provisions of the Health Insurance Portability and Accountability Act and their own requirements, also restrict the disclosure of personal health information without an authorization unless it is for treatment, payment, health care operations, or other situations as set forth in federal privacy standards. Indeed, many states include personal health information in the rules that implement the FSMA financial information privacy requirements. The privacy of personal health information is discussed in Chapter 14.

■ KEY TERMS

adverse selection

Age Discrimination in Employment Act

Americans with Disabilities Act (ADA)

certificate of insurance

contributory plan

doctrine of comity

eligibility provision

Employee Retirement Income Security Act (ERISA)

evidence of insurability

Financial Services Modernization Act (FSMA)

group insurance

guaranteed issue

individual employer group

joinder agreement

master contract

McCarran-Ferguson Act

modified guaranteed issue

morbidity

mortality

multiple-employer trust	no-loss no-gain legislation	probationary period
multiple-employer welfare arrangement (MEWA)	noncontributory plan	self-funding
	open enrollment period	simplified issue
National Association of Insurance Commissioners (NAIC)	persistency	trade association
	portability	underwriting
negotiated trusteeship	Pregnancy Discrimination Act	voluntary benefits

■ STUDY QUESTIONS

1. What general characteristics distinguish group insurance from individual insurance?

2. a. What factors do underwriters take into consideration when evaluating group benefit proposals?

   b. What is the significance of each factor?

3. Why have employers turned to alternative funding methods for group benefits?

4. Describe voluntary benefits with respect to each of the following:

   a. Types of products available

   b. Underwriting

   c. Premium payment method

   d. Portability

5. a. How do negotiated trusteeships (Taft-Hartley trusts) differ from other types of groups with respect to financing of benefits and determination of eligibility?

   b. How do labor union groups differ from negotiated trusteeships?

6. Providing group insurance coverage to small groups of employees through trade association plans or MEWAs presents unique problems with respect to adverse selection and high administrative costs. Explain how insurance company underwriting standards have been modified to confront these problems.

7. Describe the alternative ways in which MEWAs may be funded and administered.

8. Explain the extent to which states regulate the provisions found in group insurance contracts.

9. How do state premium taxes put insurance companies at a competitive disadvantage with alternative methods of providing benefits?

10. The Felton Corporation is incorporated in the state of Pennsylvania where it was established. However, its principal office is now located in Wilmington, Delaware, where all administrative functions are performed. While it has some employees in these two states, the majority of its work force of 500 is employed in New Jersey. The corporation has been told by its benefit consultant that most insurance companies will deliver the group insurance contracts for its employees in any of these three states.

    a. Is the agent correct? Explain.

    b. From a practical standpoint, why might the corporation prefer a situs other than the state where its administrative functions are performed?

11. Describe the general approaches that are acceptable for reducing benefits under the Age Discrimination in Employment Act.

12. Explain the extent to which reductions in group term life insurance and group disability income insurance appear justified (using a benefit-by-benefit approach) under the Age Discrimination in Employment Act.

13. The medical expense plan of the Mallory corporation provides benefits for pregnancy-related conditions to married female employees but excludes such coverage for unmarried female employees and unmarried female dependents of employees. Abortions are excluded unless the life of the mother is in danger. In addition, the corporation limits benefits under its short-term disability insurance plan to a maximum of six weeks for pregnancy-related conditions. Assuming the Mallory corporation is subject to the pregnancy provisions of the Pregnancy Discrimination Act, do these plans conform to the requirements of the act? Explain.

14. a. What employers must comply with Title I of the Americans with Disabilities Act?

    b. What type of discrimination is prohibited by the ADA?

15. Under what circumstances must an employer make reasonable accommodations for a disabled person under the Americans with Disabilities Act?

16. To what extent does the Americans with Disabilities Act allow medical expense plans to contain (a) coverage limitations and (b) preexisting-conditions provisions?

17. Describe the Financial Services Modernization Act with respect to each of the following:

    a. The sources of nonpublic personal financial information

    b. Privacy notification requirements

    c. Implementation

■ NOTE

1. LIMRA International, Inc., *Worksite Marketing of Voluntary Benefits: The Employer's Perspective, 2003.*

CHAPTER 6

Group Life Insurance: Term Coverage

- Explain how the benefit schedules under group term life insurance plans might be determined.
- Describe the eligibility requirements usually found in group term life insurance plans.
- Describe other provisions contained in group term insurance contracts.
- Describe the following coverages often written in conjunction with group term insurance for employees:
    1. Supplemental life insurance
    2. Accidental death and dismemberment insurance
    3. Dependent life insurance
- Explain the tax treatment of group term insurance to both employers and employees.

Life insurance is the transfer of part of the financial loss due to the death of an insured person. Upon the insured's death, the insurance company agrees to pay a stated amount or income to the insured's beneficiary. Traditionally, most group life insurance plans were designed to provide coverage during an employee's working years, with coverage usually ceasing upon termination of employment for any reason. Today, the majority of employees are provided with coverage that continues, often at a reduced amount, when termination is a result of retirement. Group term insurance is described

133

in this chapter. The methods and contracts used to extend coverage after retirement are discussed in the following chapter.

SIGNIFICANCE OF GROUP LIFE INSURANCE

Before proceeding further, here are a few statistics that show the significance of group life insurance:

■ Coverage amounting to $6.9 trillion is in force under 164 million certificates of insurance. This amount represents a doubling of the amount of insurance in force since 1989.[1]

■ Group insurance amounts to 42 percent of total life insurance coverage in force, up from 30 percent in 1990.[2]

■ The amount of coverage under the average-size group life insurance certificate is approximately $42,000, compared to about $49,000 under the average-size individual life insurance policy in force.[3]

■ Beneficiaries each year receive a total of more than $17 billion in benefits under group life insurance.[4]

■ Almost 95 percent of the coverage in force is term insurance.[5]

NATURE OF GROUP TERM INSURANCE

The oldest and most common form of group life insurance is **term insurance**, which provides death benefits for a limited period of time. The protection expires at the end of the period without value (that is, it has no cash value) if the insured survives that length of time. Group term insurance consists primarily of **yearly renewable term insurance**, which means that coverage is renewed annually with each successive policy period being for one year. The group insurance marketplace with its widespread use of the yearly renewable term contrasts with the individual marketplace, in which term insurance accounts for slightly more than 40 percent of coverage in force. This lower prevalence of term insurance in the individual marketplace is primarily due to its increasing annual premiums, which become prohibitive for many insureds at older ages. In group life insurance plans, the overall premium, in addition to other factors, is a function of the age distribution of the group's members. Although the premium for any individual employee increases with age, the flow of younger workers into the plan and the retirement of older workers tend to result in a relatively stable age distribution and thus an average group insurance rate that remains constant or rises only slightly.

The following discussion of group term insurance focuses largely on common contract provisions, other coverages that are often added to the basic contract, and relevant federal tax laws.

■ CONTRACT PROVISIONS

The provisions contained in group term insurance contracts are more uniform than those found in other types of group insurance. Much of this uniformity is a result of the adoption by most states of the NAIC Group Life Insurance Standard Provisions Model Bill. This bill, coupled with the insurance industry's attempts at uniformity, has resulted in provisions that are virtually identical among insurance companies. Although the following contract provisions represent the norm and are consistent with the practices of most insurance companies, some states may require slightly different provisions, and some companies may vary their contract provisions. In addition, negotiations between a policyowner and an insurance company may result in the modification of contract provisions.

Benefit Schedules

A **benefit schedule** classifies the employees who are eligible for coverage, and it specifies the amount of life insurance that is provided to the members of each class, thus minimizing adverse selection because the amount of coverage for individual employees is predetermined. A benefit schedule can be as simple as providing a single amount of life insurance for all employees or as complex as providing different amounts of insurance for different classes of employees. For most individual employer groups, the benefit schedules are those in which the amount of life insurance is based on either a multiple of earnings or a specified dollar amount. Benefit schedules may also combine these two approaches.

Benefit schedules usually provide for a change in the amount of an employee's coverage when the employee moves into a different classification or has a change of earnings if a multiple-of-earnings schedule is used, even if this does not occur on the policy anniversary date. Some schedules, however, specify that adjustments in amounts of coverage are only made annually or on monthly premium due dates.

Multiple-of-Earnings Schedules.   The majority of group term life insurance plans use an earnings schedule under which the amount of life insurance is determined as a multiple (or percentage) of each employee's earnings. For example, the amount of life insurance for each employee may be twice (200 percent of) the employee's annual earnings. Most plans use a multiple between one and two, but higher and lower multiples are occasionally used. The amount of insurance is often rounded to the next higher $1,000 and for underwriting and cost purposes may be subject to a maximum benefit, such as $200,000. For purposes of the benefit schedule, an employee's earnings usually consist of base salary only and do not include additional compensation like overtime pay or bonuses.

A few multiple-of-earnings schedules use multiples that vary by earnings, position, or length of service. The larger multiples are used for persons with higher salaries, in higher positions, or with longer service.

Specified-Dollar-Amount Schedules.   There are numerous types of benefit schedules that base benefits on specified dollar amounts: flat-benefit schedules and schedules that vary by such factors as earnings or position.

TABLE 6.1	Dollar-Amount-by-Earnings Schedule	
Annual Earnings	**Amount of Life Insurance**	
Less than $20,000	$ 20,000	
$20,000 to $29,999	40,000	
$30,000 to $39,999	75,000	
$40,000 to $49,999	100,000	
$50,000 and over	150,000	

Flat-Benefit Schedules. By far the most common type of specified-dollar-amount schedule is the flat-benefit schedule, under which the same amount of life insurance is provided for all employees regardless of salary or position. This type of benefit schedule is commonly used in group insurance plans covering hourly paid employees, particularly when benefits are negotiated with a union. In most cases, the amount of life insurance under a flat-benefit schedule is relatively small, such as $10,000 or $20,000; however, it may be as much as $50,000 or higher. When an employer wants to provide only a minimum amount of life insurance for all employees, a flat-benefit schedule is often used.

Dollar-Amount-by-Earnings Schedules. Some benefit schedules provide a specified amount of coverage that varies by earnings, with higher-paid employees typically receiving a proportionally larger benefit than lower-paid employees. Table 6.1 is an example of one such schedule.

Position Schedules. Under position schedules, as Table 6.2 shows, the amount of life insurance is based on an employee's position within the firm.

Because individuals in high positions are often involved in designing the benefit schedule, underwriters are concerned that the benefits for these individuals be reasonable in relation to the overall plan benefits. Position schedules may also pose problems in meeting nondiscrimination rules if excessively large amounts of coverage are provided to persons in high positions.

Even though position schedules are often used when annual earnings can be easily determined, they are particularly useful when it is difficult to determine an employee's annual income. This is the situation when income is materially affected by such factors as commissions earned, number of hours worked, or bonuses that are based on either the employee's performance or the firm's profits.

TABLE 6.2	Position Schedule
Position	**Amount of Life Insurance**
President	$300,000
Vice presidents	150,000
Managers	90,000
Salespersons	60,000
Other employees	30,000

Combination Benefit Schedules.   It is not unusual for employers to have benefit schedules that incorporate elements from several of the various types previously discussed. Although there are numerous possible combinations, a common benefit schedule of this type provides salaried employees with an amount of insurance that is determined by a multiple of their annual earnings and provides hourly employees with a flat amount of life insurance.

Reduction in Benefits.   Group life insurance plans often provide for a reduction in benefits for active employees who reach a certain age, commonly 65 to 70. Such a reduction, which is due to the high cost of providing benefits for older employees, is specified in the plan's benefit schedule. Any reduction in the amount of life insurance for active employees is subject to the provisions of the Age Discrimination in Employment Act, which are discussed in Chapter 5.

Benefit reductions fall into three categories: (1) a reduction to a flat amount of insurance; (2) a percentage reduction, such as to 65 percent of the amount of insurance that was previously provided; or (3) a gradual reduction over a period of years (for example, a 10 percent reduction in coverage each year until a minimum benefit amount is reached).

Eligibility

Group insurance contracts are very precise in their definition of what constitutes an eligible person for coverage purposes. In general, an employee must be in a covered classification, work full-time, and be actively at work. In addition, any requirements concerning probationary periods, insurability, or premium contributions must be satisfied.

Covered Classifications.   All group insurance contracts specify that an employee must fall into one of the categories of employees contained in the benefit schedule. Called **covered classifications**, these categories may be broad enough to include all employees of the organization, or they may be so limited as to exclude many employees from coverage. In some cases, these excluded employees may have coverage through a negotiated trusteeship or under other group insurance contracts provided by the employer; in other cases, they may have no coverage because the employer wishes to limit benefits to certain groups of employees. No employee may be in more than one covered classification, and the responsibility for determining the appropriate covered classification for each employee falls on the policyowner.

Full-Time Employment.   Most group insurance contracts limit eligibility to full-time employees. A **full-time employee** is generally defined as one who works no fewer than the number of hours in the normal workweek established by the employer, which must be at least 30 hours.

Subject to insurance company underwriting practices, an employer can provide coverage for part-time employees. When this is done, part-time is generally defined as less than full-time but more than some minimum number of hours per week. Part-time employees may be subject to more stringent eligibility requirements. For example, full-time hourly paid employees may be provided with $20,000 of life insurance immediately upon employment, but part-time employees may be provided with only $10,000 of life insurance and may be subject to a probationary period.

Actively-at-Work Provision. Most group insurance contracts contain an **actively-at-work provision**, whereby an employee is not covered if absent from work because of sickness, injury, or other reasons on the otherwise effective date of coverage under the contract. Coverage commences when the employee returns to work. This provision is often waived for employers with a large number of employees when coverage is transferred to a different insurance company and the employees involved were insured under the previous insurance company's contract.

Probationary Periods. Group insurance contracts may contain a probationary period, which is a specified length of time that must be satisfied before an employee is eligible for coverage. Such probationary periods are usually either one or three months and rarely exceed six months. An employee is eligible for coverage on either the first day after the probationary period or on the first day of the month following the end of the probationary period.

Insurability. Although most group insurance contracts are issued without individual evidence of insurability, in some instances underwriting practices require evidence of insurability. This commonly occurs when an employee fails to elect coverage under a contributory plan and later wants coverage or when an employee is eligible for a large amount of coverage. In these cases, an employee is not eligible for coverage until he or she submits the proper evidence of insurability and the insurance company determines that the evidence is satisfactory.

Premium Contribution. If a group insurance plan is contributory, an employee is not eligible for coverage until the employee gives the policyowner the proper authorization for payroll deductions. If this is done before the employee otherwise becomes eligible, coverage commences on the eligibility date. During the next 31 days, coverage begins when the policyowner receives the employee's authorization. If the authorization is not received within 31 days, the employee must furnish evidence of insurability at his or her own expense to obtain coverage. Evidence of insurability is also required if an employee drops coverage under a contributory plan and wishes to regain coverage at a future date.

Beneficiary Designation

With few exceptions, an insured person has the right to name the **beneficiary**, who is the person who will receive the death benefits under the group life insurance coverage. These exceptions include credit life insurance, where the creditor is the beneficiary, and dependent life insurance, where the employee is the beneficiary. In addition, the laws and regulations of some states prohibit naming the employer as beneficiary. Unless a beneficiary designation has been made irrevocable, an employee has the right to change the designated beneficiary at any time. All insurance contracts require that the insurance company be notified of any beneficiary change in writing, but the effective date of the change may vary, depending on contract provisions. Some contracts specify that a change is effective on the date it is received by the insurance company; others make it effective on the date the change is requested by the employee.

Under individual life insurance policies, death benefits are paid to an insured person's estate if no beneficiary is named or if all beneficiaries died before the insured.

Some group term insurance contracts contain an identical provision; others stipulate that the death benefits be paid through a **successive beneficiary provision**. Under the successive beneficiary provision, the proceeds are paid (at the option of the insurance company) to any one or more of the following survivors of the insured person: spouse, children, parents, brothers and sisters, or executor of the employee's estate. In most cases, insurance companies pay the proceeds to the person or persons in the first category that includes eligible survivors.

Claims

The provision concerning death claims under group life insurance policies is very simple. It states that the amount of insurance under the contract is payable when the insurance company receives written proof of death. No time period is specified in which a claim must be filed. However, most companies require that the policyowner and the beneficiary complete a brief form before a claim is processed.

Settlement Options

Settlement options are the various methods by which an employee or beneficiary may elect to have life insurance proceeds paid. Group term insurance contracts provide that death benefits are payable in a lump sum unless an optional mode of settlement is selected. Each employee insured under the contract has the right to select and change any available mode of settlement during his or her lifetime. If no optional mode of settlement is in force at the employee's death, the beneficiary generally has the right to elect any of the available options. The most common provision in group term insurance contracts is that the available modes of settlement are those customarily offered by the insurance company at the time the selection is made. The available options are not generally specified in the contract, but information about them is usually given to the group policyowner. In addition, many insurance companies have brochures that describe either all or the most common options available to employees. Any guarantees associated with these options are the guarantees in effect when the option is selected.

In addition to a lump-sum option, most insurance companies offer all the following options and possibly other options as well:

- An interest option. The proceeds are left on deposit with the insurance company, and the interest on the proceeds is paid to the beneficiary. The beneficiary can usually withdraw the proceeds at any time. The amount of any periodic installment is a function of the interest rate paid by the insurance company.

- An installment option for a fixed period. The proceeds are paid in equal installments for a specified period of time. The amount of any periodic installment is a function of the time period and the amount of the death proceeds.

- An installment option for a fixed amount. The proceeds are paid in equal installments of a specified amount until the proceeds plus any interest earnings are exhausted.

■ A life income option. The proceeds are payable in installments during the lifetime of the beneficiary. A choice of guarantee periods is usually available, during which a secondary beneficiary or the beneficiary's estate continues to receive benefits even if the beneficiary dies. The amount of any periodic installment is a function of the age and gender of the beneficiary, the period for which payments are guaranteed, and the amount of the death proceeds.

Premiums

Group insurance contracts stipulate that it is the policyowner's responsibility to pay all premiums to the insurance company, even if the group insurance plan is contributory. Any required contributions from employees are incorporated into the employer's group insurance plan, but they are not part of the insurance contract and therefore do not constitute an obligation to the insurance company by the employees. Rather, these contributions represent an obligation to the employer by the employees and are commonly paid by payroll deduction. Subject to certain limitations, any employee contributions are determined by the employer or as a result of labor negotiations. Most states require that the employer pay at least a portion of the premium for group term insurance (but not for other group insurance coverage), and a few states limit the amounts that may be paid by any employee. The most common restriction limits the contribution of any employee to the greater of 60 cents per month per $1,000 of coverage or 75 percent of the premium rate for that employee. This limitation is adhered to by companies licensed to do business in the state of New York and is often incorporated into their contracts. However, for some hazardous industries, a higher contribution than 60 cents per month is permitted.

Premiums are payable in advance to the insurance company or any authorized agent for the time period specified in the contract. In most cases, premiums are payable monthly but may be paid less frequently. The rates used to determine the premium for any policyowner are guaranteed for a certain length of time, usually one year. The periodic premium is determined by applying these rates to the amount of life insurance in force. Consequently, the premium actually payable changes each month as the total amount of life insurance in force under the group insurance plan varies. A detailed explanation of premium computations is contained in Chapter 17.

Group insurance contracts state that any dividends or experience refunds are payable to the policyowner in cash or may be used at the policyowner's option to reduce any premium due. To the extent that these exceed the policyowner's share of the premium, they must be used for the employees' benefit. This is usually accomplished by reducing employee contributions or increasing benefits.

Assignment

For many years, the owner of an individual life insurance policy has been able to transfer any or all of his or her rights under the insurance contract to another party, including a living trust. Such an **assignment** has been commonly used to avoid federal estate tax by removing the proceeds of an insurance contract from the insured's estate at death. Historically, assignments have not been permitted under group life insurance contracts, often because of state laws and regulations prohibiting them. In recent years, most states have eliminated such prohibitions, and many insurance companies have modified their contracts to permit assignments, or they waive the prohibition upon request. Essentially, an assignment is valid as long as it is permitted by and conforms with state law and the group insurance contract. Generally, insurance companies require that any assignment be in writing and filed with the company.

Grace Period

Group life insurance contracts allow for a **grace period** (almost always 31 days) during which a policyowner may pay any overdue premium without interest. If the premium is not paid, the contract lapses at the end of the grace period unless the policyowner has notified the insurance company that an earlier termination should take place. Even if the policy is allowed to lapse or is terminated during the grace period, the policyowner is legally liable for the payment of any premium due during the portion of the grace period when the contract was still in force.

Entire Contract

The **entire contract clause** states that the insurance policy, the policyowner's application that is attached to the policy, and any individual (unattached) applications of any insured persons constitute the entire insurance contract. All statements made in these applications are considered representations rather than warranties, and the insurance company can use no other statements made by the policyowner or by any insureds as the basis for contesting coverage. When compared with the application for individual life insurance, the policyowner's application that is attached to a group insurance contract may be relatively short. Often, most of the information the insurance company needs is contained in a preliminary application that is not part of the insurance contract. On the delivery of many group insurance contracts, the policyowner signs a final "acceptance application," which in effect states that the coverage as applied for has been delivered. Consequently, a greater burden is placed on the insurance company to verify the statements the policyowner made in the preliminary application.

The entire contract clause also stipulates that no agent has any authority to waive or amend any provisions of the insurance contract and that a waiver of or amendment to the contract is valid only if certain specified corporate officers of the insurance company have signed it.

Incontestability

Like individual life insurance contracts, group insurance contracts contain an **incontestability provision**. Except for the nonpayment of premiums, the validity of the contract cannot be contested after it has been in force for a specified period, generally either one or two years. During this time, the insurance company can contest the contract on the basis of policyowner statements in the application attached to the contract that are considered to be material misrepresentations. Statements by any insured person can be used as the basis for denying claims during the first two years that coverage is in force on the insured but only if such statements relate to the individual's insurability. In addition, the statements must have been made in a written application signed by the individual, and a copy of the application must have been furnished to either the individual or his or her beneficiary. It should be pointed out that the incontestability clause does not concern most covered persons, because evidence of insurability is not usually required and thus no statements about individual insurability are made.

Misstatement of Age

Group insurance contracts contain a **misstatement of age provision**. If the age of any person covered under a policy is misstated, the benefit payable is the amount that is specified under the benefit schedule. However, the premium is adjusted to reflect the true age of the individual. This is in contrast to individual life insurance contracts, where benefits are adjusted to the amount that the premium paid would have purchased at the true age of the individual. Under a group insurance contract, the responsibility for paying any additional premium or the right to receive a refund belongs to the policyowner and not to the individual employee whose age is misstated, even if the plan is contributory. If the misstated age would have affected the employee's contribution, this is a matter to be resolved between the employer and the employee.

Termination

All group insurance contracts stipulate the conditions under which the insurance company or the policyowner may terminate the contract and under which the coverage for a particular insured person terminates.

A group term insurance contract can be terminated for nonpayment of premium at the end of the grace period. Insurance companies may also terminate coverage for an individual employer group on any premium due date if certain conditions exist and notice of termination has been given to the policyowner at least 31 days in advance. These conditions include the failure to maintain a stated minimum number of participants in the plan and, in contributory plans, the failure to maintain a stated minimum percentage participation. The policyowner may also terminate the contract at any time by giving the insurance company 31 days' advance written notice. Moreover, the policyowner has the right to request the amendment of the contract at any time by notifying the insurance company.

The coverage for any insured person terminates automatically (subject to any provisions for a continuation or conversion of coverage) when

- the employee terminates employment;
- the employee ceases to be eligible (for example, if the employee no longer satisfies the full-time work requirement or no longer falls into a covered classification);
- the policyowner or insurance company terminates the master contract; or

■ any required contribution by the employee has not been made (generally because the employee has notified the policyowner to cease the required payroll deduction).

Temporary Interruption of Employment.   Most group term insurance contracts permit the employer to continue coverage on employees during temporary interruptions of active full-time employment arising from leaves of absence, layoffs, or inability to work because of illness or injury. The employer must continue paying the premium, and the coverage may be continued only for a relatively short period of time, such as 3 months, unless the time period is extended by mutual agreement between the employer and the insurance company. Also, in electing to continue coverage, the policyowner must act in a way that precludes individual selection.

Continuation of Coverage for Disabled Employees.   Most group term insurance contracts make some provision for the continuation of coverage on employees whose active employment terminates due to disability. By far the most common provision in use today is the **waiver-of-premium provision**. Under this provision, life insurance coverage is continued without the payment of premium as long as the employee is totally disabled, even if the master contract is terminated. However, certain requirements must be met:

■ The disability must commence while the employee is insured under the master contract.

■ The disability must begin prior to a specified age, commonly age 60.

■ The employee must be totally disabled. Total disability is normally defined as the employee's complete inability to engage in any gainful occupation for which he or she is or becomes qualified by reason of education, training, or experience.

■ The disability must have lasted continuously for a specified time, often six or nine months.

■ The employee must file a claim within a prescribed period (normally 12 months) and must submit annual evidence of continuing disability.

If an employee no longer meets the definition of disability and returns to work, the employee may again be insured under the group insurance contract on a premium-paying basis as long as the employee meets the contract's eligibility requirements. If for any reason the employee is not eligible for insurance under the group insurance contract, he or she can exercise the conversion privilege.

A small but growing trend is for plans to continue disabled employees as eligible employees under a group insurance contract, with the employer paying the periodic cost of their coverage just as if they were active employees. At the termination of the contract, the insurance company has no responsibility to continue coverage unless a disabled employee is eligible, elects to convert coverage, and pays any required premiums. However, depending on the provisions of the group insurance plan, the employer may have a legal responsibility to continue coverage on disabled employees in some manner.

Conversion.   All group term insurance contracts covering employees contain a **conversion provision** that gives any employee whose coverage ceases the right to convert to an individual insurance policy. The terms of the conversion privilege vary, depending on the reason for the termination of coverage under the group contract. The most generous conversion rights are available to those employees who either have terminated employment or no longer fall into one of the eligible classifications still covered by the master contract. These employees have the right to purchase an individual life insurance policy from the insurance company without evidence of insurability, but it is often one without accidental death and dismemberment or other supplementary benefits. However, this right is subject to the following conditions:

- The employee must apply for conversion within 31 days after the termination of employment or membership in an eligible classification. During this 31-day period, the employee's death benefit is equal to the amount of life insurance that is available under the conversion privilege, even if the employee does not apply for conversion. Disability and supplementary benefits are not extended during this period unless they are also subject to conversion. The premium for the individual policy must accompany the conversion application, and coverage is effective at the end of the conversion period.

- The individual policy the employee selects may generally be any form, except term insurance, that the insurance company customarily issues at the age and amount applied for. Some insurance companies also make term insurance coverage available, and a few states require that employees be allowed to purchase term insurance coverage for a limited time (such as one year), after which an employee must convert to a cash value form of coverage.

- The face amount of the individual policy may not exceed the amount of life insurance that terminated under the group insurance contract.

- The premium for the individual policy is determined using the insurance company's current rate applicable to the type and amount of the individual policy for the employee's attained age on the date of conversion and for the class of risk to which the employee belongs. Although no extra premium may be charged for reasons of health, an extra premium may be charged for any other hazards considered in an insurance company's rate structure, such as occupation or avocation.

It is estimated that only 1 or 2 percent of eligible employees actually take advantage of the conversion privilege. Several factors account for this. Many employees obtain coverage with new employers; others are discouraged by the high cost of the permanent insurance to which they must convert. Still others, if they are insurable at standard rates, may find coverage at a lower cost with other insurers and be able to purchase supplementary coverage (such as disability benefits) that is not available under conversion policies. In addition, insurance companies have not actively encouraged group conversions because those who convert tend to be the poorer risks. Finally, because some employers are faced with conversion charges as a result of experience rating (see Chapter 17), they are also unlikely to encourage conversion.

There is a more restrictive conversion privilege if an employee's coverage is terminated because the master contract is terminated for all employees or is amended to eliminate eligible classifications. Under these circumstances, the employee is given a conversion right only if he or she was insured under the contract for a period of time (generally five years) immediately preceding the date on which coverage was terminated. In addition, the amount of insurance that can be converted is limited to the lesser of

(1) $2,000 or (2) the amount of the employee's life insurance under the contract at the date of termination, reduced by any amount of life insurance for which the employee becomes eligible under any group life insurance policy that the same or another insurance company issues or reinstates within 31 days after such termination.

Portability of Term Coverage.   Some insurers issue contracts with a portability provision that allows employees whose coverage terminates to continue coverage at group rates. The rates are age-based and continue to increase as an insured person ages. Employees are billed directly by the insurer.

Significant variations exist among the insurers that offer portable coverage. Some of these variations include the following:

■ Some insurers automatically include a portability provision in their contracts; other insurers make it available as an optional provision that the employer can select.

■ Most insurers allow portability if employment is terminated, and some insurers make it available to retiring employees. Most insurers do not make it available upon termination of a master contract.

■ Some insurers allow portability only if the group contract covers a minimum number of persons, such as 200; other insurers have no minimum size for the group.

■ Some insurers allow the period of coverage to run indefinitely; other insurers terminate the converted coverage after some duration of time or after some age, such as 65 or 70. When coverage continues past age 65, it usually reduces in face amount.

■ Most insurers have some minimum and maximum amount of coverage that can be continued on a portability basis. For employees, the minimum amount is most commonly either $5,000 or $10,000. Maximum amounts vary significantly among insurers, but $300,000 and $500,000 are not unusual. However, amounts in excess of some limit, such as $100,000, are often subject to evidence of insurability.

■ Some insurers charge an additional transaction fee for coverage portability. This might be a one-time charge, such as $25 or $50, or a charge per billing, such as $2 or $3.

Accelerated Benefits

Often what becomes popular in the individual marketplace starts to show up in the group insurance marketplace. Such is the case with accelerated benefits, which are now offered by most group insurers. In fact, many group insurers make accelerated death benefits a part of their standard group term coverage unless an employer does not want the benefit provided.

Under an **accelerated-benefits provision** (sometimes called a *critical-illness rider*), an insured is entitled to receive a portion of his or her death benefit while still living if one or more specified events occur. These events might include

■ a terminal illness that is expected to result in death within 6 or 12 months;

■ a specified catastrophic illness, such as cancer, renal failure, AIDS, a stroke, or Alzheimer's disease; or

■ the incurring of nursing home and possibly other long-term-care expenses.

The categories of triggering events and the specific definitions of each vary among insurers. However, most group insurers allow accelerated benefits for terminal illnesses only. Some insurers use a life expectancy of 6 months or less; most use a life expectancy of 12 months or less. In either case, a doctor must certify the life expectancy.

The amount of the accelerated benefit is expressed as a percentage of the basic life insurance coverage and may range from 25 percent to 100 percent. In addition, many insurers limit the maximum benefit to a specified dollar amount. This amount varies widely among insurers and can be as low as $25,000 or as high as $500,000 or more. Any amount not accelerated is paid to the beneficiary upon the insured's death.

A few insurers charge the policyowner an additional premium for the inclusion of accelerated death benefit coverage and make no additional charge when a benefit is accelerated. The majority of insurers, however, follow one of two alternative approaches. Some insurers charge no additional premium but often levy a transaction charge each time a benefit is accelerated. Other insurers also charge no additional premium but shift the cost of the benefit to the insured by either (1) discounting the accelerated benefit to reflect lost interest or (2) treating the advance payment as a lien against the coverage and charge interest on the amount advanced. A few insurers allow the insured to select whether the discounting or lien approach will be used.

There are no limitations on how the accelerated benefit can be used. It might be used to pay medical expenses and nursing home care not covered by other insurance, or it could even be used to prepay funeral expenses.

■ ADDED COVERAGES

Group term insurance contracts often provide additional insurance benefits. Historically, these benefits have been obtained through the use of a **rider**, which is an endorsement to an insurance policy for the purpose of adding, deleting, or classifying coverage. Many companies, however, now incorporate some or all of the benefits into their basic term insurance contracts. These benefits are also forms of group term insurance and consist of (1) supplemental life insurance, (2) accidental death and dismemberment insurance, (3) survivor income benefit insurance, and (4) dependent life insurance. These added benefits can be provided for all employees insured under the basic group term contract or may be limited to certain classes of employees. With the exception of dependent life insurance, these coverages may also be written as separate contracts.

Supplemental Life Insurance

The majority of group life insurance plans enable all or certain classes of employees to purchase additional amounts of life insurance, commonly referred to as **supplemental life insurance**. Generally, the employer provides a basic amount of life insurance to all eligible employees on a noncontributory basis. This is commonly a flat amount of coverage or a multiple of annual earnings. The supplemental coverage is contributory and may be either incorporated into the basic group life insurance contract or contained

TABLE 6.3 Supplemental Life Insurance	
Type of Coverage	**Amount of Life Insurance**
Basic Insurance	$25,000
Supplemental Insurance	50,000

in a separate contract. The latter method tends to be more common when the supplemental coverage is available to only a select group of employees. Although the employee may pay the entire cost of the supplemental coverage, either state laws that require employer contributions or insurance company underwriting practices often result in the employer's paying a portion of the cost. It is not unusual for there to be two sets of rates—one for smokers and another for nonsmokers.

The amount of supplemental coverage available is specified in a benefit schedule. Under some plans, an employee must purchase the full amount of coverage; under other plans, an employee may purchase a portion of the coverage. Tables 6.3 and 6.4 are two examples of benefit schedules for a basic-plus-supplemental life insurance plan.

Because giving employees the right to choose their benefit amounts leads to adverse selection, more stringent underwriting requirements usually accompany supplemental coverage. These may include requiring individual evidence of insurability for the full amount of coverage. However, many insurers will issue a specific amount of supplemental coverage on a guaranteed-issue basis, with the guaranteed amount based on the size of the group and the amount of basic coverage. Larger amounts of supplemental coverage are subject to individual underwriting. Higher rates may be charged for the supplemental insurance than for the basic coverage.

Accidental Death and Dismemberment Insurance

Many group life insurance contracts contain an **accidental death and dismemberment (AD&D)** provision that gives additional benefits if an employee dies accidentally or suffers certain types of injuries. Traditionally, this group coverage was available only as a rider to a group life insurance contract. Now, however, it is common to find these benefits in separate group insurance contracts in which coverage is usually contributory

TABLE 6.4 Supplemental Life Insurance	
Type of Coverage	**Amount of Life Insurance**
Basic Insurance	1 times salary
Supplemental Insurance	½, 1, 1½, or 2 times salary, subject to a maximum (including basic insurance) of $250,000

TABLE 6.5	AD&D Schedule of Benefits
Type of Injury	**Benefit Amount**
Loss of (including loss of use of):	
Both hands or both feet	The principal sum
The sight of both eyes	The principal sum
One hand and sight of one eye	The principal sum
One foot and sight of one eye	The principal sum
One foot and one hand	The principal sum
One hand	One-half the principal sum
One foot	One-half the principal sum
The sight of one eye	One-half the principal sum

on the part of employees. Such contracts are referred to as *voluntary accidental death and dismemberment insurance.* There are also separate contracts that employers can purchase to replace the employer-paid coverage available from their group term life insurance carrier. These contracts are used because of more favorable provisions and/ or lower premiums. Such an arrangement is referred to as a **carve-out**, which is a term that is used when one or more classes of employees or a specific benefit is excluded from a benefit plan and an alternative arrangement is used to provide coverage. Carve-outs are generally used to contain employee costs or to provide broader or more tax-favored benefits to key employees and executives. The use of this form of carve-out is found in all types of group insurance plans.

Traditional Coverage. Under the usual traditional form of accidental death and dismemberment insurance, an employee eligible for group life insurance coverage (and electing the life insurance coverage if it is contributory) automatically has the accidental death and dismemberment coverage if the employer adds it (or purchases an AD&D carve-out) or if the insurer includes it as a standard part of its group term life insurance contract. A few plans impose a probationary period, such as six months, before coverage begins. Under the typical accidental death and dismemberment rider, the insurance company pays an additional amount of insurance that is equal to the amount of coverage under the basic group life insurance contract (referred to as the *principal sum*) if an employee dies as a result of accidental bodily injuries while he or she is covered under the policy. It is specified that death must occur within a certain time, often 90 days, following the date that injuries are sustained, but some courts have ruled this time period is invalid and have required insurance companies to pay claims when longer periods have been involved. In addition to an accidental death benefit, the benefit schedule shown in Table 6.5 is provided for certain specific types of injuries.

In some cases, the accidental death and dismemberment rider is written to provide the same benefits for any accident covered under the contract. However, it is not unusual to have a higher level of benefits for accidents that occur while the employee is traveling on business for the employer. These larger travel benefits may apply to death benefits only. They may also be limited to accidents that occur while the employee is occupying

TABLE 6.6	AD&D Schedule of Benefits	
Type of Loss	**Benefit Amount**
Death While Traveling on Business When Occupying, Boarding, Alighting from, or Struck by Any Motor Vehicle, Airplane, or Other Conveyance, Including Company-Owned or Personally Owned Vehicles	3 times the principal sum
Death at All Other Times	2 times the principal sum
Dismemberment	Up to the principal sum (as shown in the previous schedule)

(or entering, alighting from, or struck by) a public conveyance and possibly a company-owned or personally owned vehicle. Table 6.6 is an example of a benefit schedule reflecting some of these variations.

Death benefits are paid in accordance with the beneficiary provision of the group life insurance contract, and dismemberment benefits are paid to the employee. Coverage is usually written to cover both occupational and nonoccupational accidents. However, when employees are in hazardous occupations, coverage may apply only to nonoccupational accidents, in which case employees still have workers' compensation coverage for any occupational accidents.

Some insurers also pay an additional benefit if an insured suffers a covered loss as the result of an automobile accident as long as the insured is wearing a properly fastened seat belt and is not under the influence of alcohol. Other insurers may include additional educational benefits for dependent children. For competitive reasons, some insurers make available a number of additional benefits for purchase by the employer if an employee is injured or killed in a covered accident. Some of these additional benefits include the following:

- A benefit to help cover the costs of the employer to make worksite adaptations that are necessitated by the Americans with Disabilities Act to accommodate a disabled employee
- A benefit to return an injured employee or the body of a deceased employee home if death or disability occurs elsewhere
- Rehabilitation benefits for an injured employee
- Monthly income benefits for an employee who is permanently disabled
- Monthly income benefits for an employee who becomes a paraplegic or quadriplegic
- Monthly income benefits for an employee who is in a coma
- Education benefits for a spouse who needs to enter or reenter the workforce

Coverage is usually not subject to a conversion privilege, although an increasing number of insurers are allowing conversion, but possibly only up to specified limits that are lower than the former group coverage. When life insurance coverage is continued after retirement, accidental death and dismemberment benefits are normally no longer available. As with the life insurance coverage, however, this coverage may be continued during temporary periods of unemployment. In contrast to the group term insurance policy to which it is attached, group accidental death and dismemberment insurance does contain some exclusions. These exclusions include losses resulting from the following situation and events:

- Suicide at any time (It is interesting to note that, except for a few multiple-employer trusts, group term insurance does not contain a suicide provision.)
- Disease or bodily or mental infirmity, or medical or surgical treatment thereof
- Ptomaine or any infection other than one occurring simultaneously with and through an accidental cut or wound
- War
- Travel or flight in any type of aircraft either as a pilot, as a student pilot, or as an officer or member of the crew (However, there is a trend toward eliminating this exclusion, particularly when coverage is written on large groups.)

Voluntary AD&D Coverage. The provisions of voluntary group accidental death and dismemberment insurance are practically identical to those in a group life insurance contract with an accidental death and dismemberment insurance rider. However, there are a few differences. Voluntary plans usually require that the employee pay the entire cost of coverage, and they virtually always provide both occupational and nonoccupational coverage. Subject to limitations, the employee may select the amount of coverage desired, and the maximum amount of coverage available tends to be larger than when coverage is provided through a rider. For example, one plan allows coverage to be purchased at the following levels: $50,000, $75,000, $100,000, $200,000, $300,000, or $500,000, as long as the amount selected does not exceed ten times annual salary. The amount of coverage often decreases after age 65 or 70, just as the amount of traditional coverage decreases when it is a function of a life insurance benefit that is lowered at older ages.

Another difference is the frequent use in voluntary plans of a common accident provision, whereby the amount payable by the insurance company is limited to a stipulated maximum for all employees killed or injured in any single accident. If this exceeds the sum of the benefits otherwise payable for each employee, benefits are prorated.

A final difference is that some voluntary plans allow an employee to purchase accidental death and dismemberment coverage on dependents. For example, under one plan the coverage on a spouse is equal to 40 percent of the coverage on the employee, and coverage on each child is 10 percent of the employee's coverage. When dependent coverage is purchased, some insurers make a variety of optional benefits available. Some of these include

- education benefits for dependent children enrolled in a university, college, or trade school following an employee's death;

- additional dismemberment benefits for children who periodically need to be refitted with prosthetic devices as they grow;

- day care expense coverage for children if the day care is necessitated by the death of a parent;

- benefits to pay the cost of a family's COBRA coverage after the death of an employee; and

- an additional benefit to the children if both parents are killed in the same accident.

Dependent Life Insurance

Some group life insurance contracts provide insurance coverage on the lives of employees' dependents. **Dependent life insurance** has been viewed as a method of giving the employee resources to meet the funeral and burial expenses associated with a dependent's death. Consequently, the employee is automatically the beneficiary. The employee also elects and pays for this coverage if it is contributory. Coverage for dependents is almost always limited to employees who are themselves covered under the group contract. Thus, if an employee's coverage is contributory, the employee must elect coverage for himself or herself in order to be eligible to elect dependent coverage.

For purposes of dependent life insurance coverage, dependents are usually defined as an employee's spouse who is not legally separated from the employee and an employee's unmarried dependent children (including stepchildren and adopted children) who are over 14 days of age and younger than some specified age, commonly 19 or 21. This is sometimes extended to a later age, such as 23 or 25, if the dependent is a full-time student. To prevent adverse selection, an employee usually cannot select coverage on individual dependents. A few policies do allow an employee to elect coverage for the spouse only or for children only. If dependent coverage is selected, all dependents fitting the definition are insured. When dependent coverage is in effect for an employee, any new eligible dependents are automatically insured.

The amount of coverage for each dependent is usually quite modest. Some states limit the maximum amount of life insurance that can be written, and a few states actually prohibit writing any coverage on dependents. Employer contributions used to purchase more than $2,000 of coverage on each dependent result in income to the employee for purposes of federal taxation. However, amounts in excess of $2,000 may be purchased with employee contributions without adverse tax consequences. In some cases, the same amount of coverage is provided for all dependents; in other cases, a larger amount is provided for the spouse than for the children. It is also not unusual for the amount of coverage on children to be less until the children attain some specified age, such as six months. Tables 6.7 and 6.8 are examples of benefit schedules under dependent coverage.

A single premium applies to the dependent coverage for each employee and is unrelated to the number of dependents. In some cases, the premium may vary, depending on the age of the employee (but not the dependents), but more commonly it is the same

TABLE 6.7	Dependent Life Insurance Benefits Schedule
Class	**Amount of Insurance**
Each Dependent	$2,000

amount for all employees regardless of age. Dependent coverage usually contains a conversion privilege that applies only to the coverage on the spouse. However, some states require that the conversion privilege apply to the coverage on all dependents. Some insurers also have portability provisions so that the group coverage can continue on a direct-bill basis.

Assignment is almost never permitted, and no waiver of premium is available if a dependent becomes disabled. However, if the basic life insurance contract contains a waiver-of-premium provision applicable to the employee, the employee's disability sometimes results in a waiver of premium for the dependent coverage. A provision similar to the actively-at-work provision pertaining to employees is often included for dependents. It specifies that dependents are not covered when otherwise eligible if they are confined in a hospital (except for newborn children, who are covered after 14 days). Coverage commences when the dependent is discharged from the hospital.

■ TAX TREATMENT

A discussion of group term life insurance is incomplete without an explanation of the tax laws affecting its use. Although discussions of these laws are often limited to federal income and estate taxation, federal gift taxation and taxation by the states should also be considered.

Federal Tax Treatment

The growth of group term insurance has been greatly influenced by the favorable tax treatment afforded it under federal tax laws. This section is devoted to the effects of these tax laws on basic group term insurance and on coverages that may be added

TABLE 6.8	Dependent Life Insurance Benefits Schedule
Class	**Amount of Insurance**
Spouse	50% of the employee's insured amount, subject to a maximum of $5,000
Dependent Children:	
at Least 14 Days Old but	
Less Than 6 Months	$ 500
6 Months or Older	$1,000

to a basic group term insurance contract. A complete explanation of the federal tax laws pertaining to group term insurance and their interpretation by the Internal Revenue Service (IRS) is lengthy and beyond the scope of this book. Consequently, this discussion and subsequent discussions of federal tax laws only highlight these laws. Appendix A contains a summary of the relevant tax laws, as well as references to the Internal Revenue Code for those who wish to investigate the subject further.

Deductibility of Premiums. In general, employer contributions for an employee's group term insurance coverage (as well as for most other types of employee benefits) are fully deductible under Code Section 162 to the employer as an ordinary and necessary business expense as long as the employee's overall compensation is reasonable. The following persons, however, are considered self-employed persons for income tax purposes and no deduction is allowed: sole proprietors, partners, members of limited liability companies (LLCs), and more-than-2-percent shareholders of an S corporation. The reasonableness of compensation (which includes wages, salary, and other fringe benefits) is usually only a potential issue for the owners of small businesses or the stockholder-employees of closely held corporations. For income tax purposes, a firm may not deduct any compensation that the IRS determines to be unreasonable. In addition, the Internal Revenue Code does not allow a firm to take an income tax deduction for contributions that are made in behalf of stockholders unless they are providing substantive services to the corporation. Finally, no deduction is allowed under Code Section 264 if the employer is named as beneficiary of an employee's life insurance coverage.

Contributions by any individual employee are considered payments for personal life insurance and are not deductible for income tax purposes by that employee. Thus, the amount of any payroll deductions authorized by an employee for group term insurance purposes is included in the employee's taxable income.

Employees' Income Tax Liability. In the absence of tax laws to the contrary, the amount of any compensation for which an employer receives an income tax deduction (including the payment of group insurance premiums) represents taxable income to the employee. However, **Section 79** of the Internal Revenue Code gives favorable tax treatment to employer contributions for life insurance that qualifies as group term insurance.

Section 79 Requirements. To qualify as group term insurance under Section 79, life insurance must meet the following conditions:

- It must provide a death benefit excludible from federal income tax.

- It must be given to a group of employees, defined to include all employees of an employer. If all employees are not covered, membership must be determined on the basis of age, marital status, or factors relating to employment.

- It must be provided under a policy carried directly or indirectly by the employer. This includes any policy for which the employer pays any part of the cost. If the employer pays no part of the cost, it also includes any policy arranged by the employer if at least one employee is charged less than his or her cost (using Uniform Premium Table I, which is discussed later) and at least one other employee is charged more than his or her cost.

- A policy is defined to include a master contract or a group of individual policies. The term *carried indirectly* refers to those situations when the employer is not the policyowner but rather provides coverage to employees through master contracts issued to organizations, such as negotiated trusteeships or multiple-employer welfare arrangements.

- The plan must be arranged to preclude individual selection of coverage amounts. However, it is acceptable to have alternative benefit schedules based on the amount an employee elects to contribute. Supplemental plans that give an employee a choice, such as either 1, 1½, or 2 times salary, are considered to fall within this category. An employee can be allowed to reject coverage in excess of $50,000 if he or she does not want any imputed income.

All life insurance that qualifies under Section 79 as group term insurance is considered to be a single plan of insurance, regardless of the number of insurance contracts used.

EXAMPLE
The Grant Corporation provides coverage for its union employees under a negotiated trusteeship, coverage for its other employees under an individual employer group insurance contract, and additional coverage for its top executives under a group of individual life insurance policies. Under Section 79, these all constitute a single plan.

This plan must be provided for at least ten full-time employees at some time during the calendar year. For purposes of meeting the ten-life requirement, employees who have not satisfied any required waiting periods may be counted as participants. Employees who have elected not to participate are also counted as participants—but only if they would not have been required to contribute to the cost of other benefits besides group term insurance if they had participated. As described later, a plan with fewer than ten full-time employees may still qualify for favorable tax treatment under Section 79 if it meets more restrictive requirements.

Exceptions to Section 79. Even when all the previous requirements are met, there are some situations in which Section 79 does not apply. In some cases, different sections of the Internal Revenue Code provide alternative tax treatment. For example, when group term insurance is issued to the trustees of a qualified pension plan and is used to provide a death benefit under the plan, the full amount of any life insurance paid for by employer contributions results in taxable income to the employee.

There are three situations in which employer contributions for group term insurance do not result in taxable income to an employee, regardless of the amount of insurance:

1. If an employee has terminated employment because of disability
2. If a qualified charity (as determined by the Internal Revenue Code) has been named as beneficiary for the entire year

3. If the employer has been named as beneficiary for the entire year

Coverage on retired employees is subject to Section 79, and these persons are treated in the same manner as active employees. Thus, they have taxable income in any year in which the amount of coverage received exceeds $50,000. However, a grandfather clause to this rule stipulates that it does not apply to group term life insurance plans (or to comparable successor plans or plans of successor employers) in existence on January 1, 1984, for covered employees who (1) retired before 1984 or (2) were at least 55 years of age before 1984 and were employed by the employer any time during 1983. There is one exception to this grandfather clause: It does not apply to persons (either key or nonkey employees) retiring after 1986 if a plan is discriminatory. The factors that make a plan discriminatory are discussed later.

General Tax Rules.   Under Section 79, the cost of the first $50,000 of coverage is not taxed to the employee. Because all group term insurance provided by an employer that qualifies under Section 79 is considered to be one plan, this exclusion applies only once to each employee.

EXAMPLE
John has $5,000 of coverage that is provided to all nonunion employees under a group insurance policy of the Grant Corporations. He also has $200,000 of coverage provided to executives under a separate insurance policy. For purpose of Section 79, John has a single $50,000 exclusion.

The cost of coverage in excess of $50,000, minus any employee contributions for the entire amount of coverage, represents taxable income to the employee. For purposes of Section 79, the cost of this excess coverage is determined by a government table called the **Uniform Premium Table I** (see Table 6.9).

TABLE 6.9 Uniform Premium Table 1	
Age	**Cost per Month per $1,000 of Coverage**
24 and under	$ .05
25–29	.06
30–34	.08
35–39	.09
40–44	.10
45–49	.15
50–54	.23
55–59	.43
60–64	.66
65–69	1.27
70 and over	2.06

To calculate the cost of an employee's coverage for one month of protection under a group term insurance plan, the Uniform Premium Table I cost shown for the employee's age bracket (based on the employee's attained age at the end of the tax year) is multiplied by the number of thousands in excess of 50 of group term insurance on the employee. The monthly costs are then totaled to obtain an annual cost.

EXAMPLE

Theresa, aged 57, is provided with $150,000 of group term insurance by her employer. The Table I monthly cost for someone her age is $43 per $1,000 of coverage. The monthly cost of her coverage (assuming no employee contributions) is calculated as follows:

Coverage provided	$150,000
Minus Section 79 exclusion	– 50,000
Amount subject to taxation	$100,000

Monthly cost = $.43/$1,000 x $100,000 = $43

Annual cost (assuming no change in the amount of coverage during the year) = $516

Finally, any employee contributions for the entire amount of coverage are deducted from the annual cost to determine the taxable income that an employee must report. If Theresa contributes $.25 per month ($3 per year) per $1,000 of coverage, her total annual contribution for $150,000 of coverage is $450. This reduces the amount reportable as taxable income from $516 to $66. If her employee contribution is $.30 rather than $.25 per month, the annual contribution is $540. Because $540 exceeds the Table I cost, there is no imputed income.

One final point is worthy of attention. The use of Uniform Premium Table I results in favorable tax treatment for the cost of group term insurance when the monthly costs in the table are lower than the actual cost of coverage in the marketplace. However, group term insurance coverage can often be purchased at a lower cost than Table I rates. There are some who argue that in these instances the actual cost of coverage can be used in place of the Table I cost for determining an employee's taxable income. From the standpoint of logic and consistency with the tax laws, this view makes sense. However, the regulations for Section 79 are very specific: Only Table I costs are to be used.

Nondiscrimination Rules.   Any plan that qualifies as group term insurance under Section 79 is subject to nondiscrimination rules, and the $50,000 exclusion is not available to key employees if a plan is discriminatory. Such a plan favors key employees in either eligibility or benefits. In addition, the value of the full amount of coverage for key employees, minus their own contributions, is considered taxable income, based on the greater of actual or Table I costs. (The actual cost of discriminatory coverage is determined by a complex process that is not covered in this book. See Internal Revenue Code Reg. 1.79-4T.)

A **key employee** of a firm is defined as any person (either active or retired) who at any time during the plan year containing the discrimination date is any of the following:

- An officer of the firm who earns more than $130,000 (in 2004) in annual compensation from the firm. This amount is subject to periodic indexing. For purposes of this rule, the number of employees treated as officers is the greater of 3 employees or 10 percent of the firm's employees, subject to a maximum of 50. In applying the rule, the following employees can be excluded: persons who are part-time, persons who are under 21, and persons with less than six months of service with the firm.

- A 5 percent owner of the firm. For a corporation, a 5 percent owner is a person who owns (1) more than 5 percent of the firm's outstanding stock or (2) stock that has more than 5 percent of the combined voting power of all the firm's stock. For a noncorporate entity, it is any person who owns more than 5 percent of the firm's capital or profits.

- A 1 percent owner of the firm who earns more than $150,000 in annual compensation from the firm. The definition of a 1 percent owner is the same as that of a 5 percent owner with 1 percent substituted for 5 percent.

Eligibility requirements are not discriminatory if (1) at least 70 percent of all employees are eligible, (2) at least 85 percent of all employees who are participants are not key employees, (3) participants constitute a classification that the IRS determines is nondiscriminatory, or (4) the group term insurance plan is part of a cafeteria plan and Section 125 requirements are satisfied. For purposes of the 70 percent test, employees with less than three years' service, part-time employees, and seasonal employees may be excluded. Employees covered by collective-bargaining agreements may also be excluded if plan benefits were the subject of good-faith bargaining.

Benefits are not discriminatory if neither the type nor amount of benefits discriminates in favor of key employees. It is permissible to base benefits on a uniform percentage of salary.

Groups with Fewer than Ten Full-Time Employees. A group insurance plan that covers fewer than ten employees must satisfy an additional set of requirements before it is eligible for favorable tax treatment under Section 79. These rules predate the general nondiscrimination rules previously described, and it was assumed that the under-ten rules would be abolished when the new rules were adopted. However, that was not done, so smaller groups are subject to two separate and somewhat overlapping sets of rules. Again, note that Section 79 applies to an employer's overall plan of group insurance, not to separate group insurance contracts. For example, an employer providing group insurance coverage for its 50 hourly employees under one group insurance contract and for its six executives under a separate contract is considered to have a single plan covering 56 employees and thus is exempt from the under-ten rules. Although the stated purpose of the under-ten rules is to preclude individual selection, their effect is to prevent the group insurance plan from discriminating in favor of the owners or stockholder-employees of small businesses.

With some exceptions, plans covering fewer than ten employees must provide coverage for all full-time employees. For purposes of this requirement, employees who are not customarily employed for more than 20 hours in any one week or five months in any calendar year are considered part-time employees. It is permissible to exclude full-time employees from coverage under the following circumstances:

- The employee has reached age 65.
- The employee has not satisfied the probationary period under the plan, which may not exceed six months.
- The employee has elected not to participate in the plan, but only if the employee would not have been required to contribute to the cost of other benefits besides group term life insurance if he or she had participated.
- The employee has not satisfied the evidence of insurability required under the plan. An employee's eligibility for insurance (or the amount of insurance on the employee's life) may be subject to evidence of insurability. However, this evidence of insurability must be determined solely on the basis of a medical questionnaire completed by the employee and not by a medical examination.

The amount of coverage must be a flat amount, a uniform percentage of compensation, or an amount based on different employee classifications. These employee classifications, which are referred to as *coverage brackets* in Section 79, may be determined in the manner described earlier in this chapter in the section on benefit schedules. The amount of coverage for each employee in any classification may be no greater than 2½ times the amount of coverage provided to each employee in the next lower classification. In addition, each employee in the lowest classification must be provided with an amount of coverage that is equal to at least 10 percent of the amount for each employee in the highest classification. There must also be a reasonable expectation that there will be at least one employee in each classification.

EXAMPLE

The Lindsay Corporation has nine employees—a president, two salaried supervisors, and six hourly employees. It has the following benefit schedule for its group term life insurance plan:

President	$100,000
Supervisor	40,000
Hourly employees	5,000

This schedule is unacceptable for favorable tax treatment under Section 79 for two reasons. First, the amount of coverage provided for the hourly employees is only 5 percent of the amount of coverage provided for the president. Second, the amount of coverage on the supervisor is more than 2 1/2 times the amount of coverage provided for the hourly employees.

The following schedule, however, would be acceptable:

President	$100,000
Supervisor	40,000
Hourly employees	20,000

If a group insurance plan that covers fewer than ten employees does not qualify for favorable tax treatment under Section 79, any premiums paid by the employer for such coverage represents taxable income to the employees. The employer, however, still receives an income tax deduction for any premiums paid on behalf of the employees as long as overall compensation is reasonable.

Tax Treatment of Proceeds.   In most instances, Code Section 101 provides that the death proceeds under a group term insurance contract do not result in any taxable income to the beneficiary if they are paid in a lump sum. If the proceeds are payable in installments over more than one taxable year, only the interest earnings attributable to the proceeds are included in the beneficiary's income for tax purposes.

Under certain circumstances, the proceeds are not exempt from income taxation if the coverage was transferred (either in whole or in part) for a valuable consideration. Such a situation arises when the stockholder-employees of a corporation name each other as beneficiaries under their group term insurance coverage as a method of funding a buy-sell agreement. The mutual agreement to name each other as beneficiaries is the valuable consideration. Under these circumstances, any proceeds paid to a beneficiary constitute ordinary income to the extent that the proceeds exceed the beneficiary's tax basis, as determined by the Internal Revenue Code.

In many cases, benefits paid by an employer to employees or their beneficiaries from the firm's assets receive the same tax treatment as benefits provided under an insurance contract. This is not true for death benefits. If they are provided other than through an insurance contract, the amount of the proceeds represents taxable income to the beneficiary. (Until late 1996, up to $5,000 of benefits could be provided from the firm's assets on a tax-free basis.) For this reason, employers are less likely to use alternative funding arrangements for death benefits than for disability and medical expense benefits.

Under Code Section 2042 proceeds of a group term insurance contract, even if paid to a named beneficiary, are included in an employee's gross estate for federal estate tax purposes, as long as the employee possessed incidents of ownership in the coverage at the time of death. However, no estate tax is levied on any amounts, including life insurance proceeds, left to a surviving spouse. In addition, taxable estates of $1.5 million or less (in 2004 and 2005) are generally free of estate taxation regardless of the beneficiary. This figure increases to $2 million in 2006 and continues to $3.5 million in 2009. In 2010, the estate tax is scheduled for repeal.

When an estate is otherwise subject to estate taxation, an employee may remove the proceeds of group term insurance from his or her taxable estate by absolutely assigning all incidents of ownership to another person, usually the beneficiary of the coverage. Incidents of ownership include the right to change the beneficiary, to terminate coverage, to assign coverage, or to exercise the conversion privilege. For this favorable treatment, however, the Internal Revenue Code requires that such an assignment be permissible under both the group term insurance master contract and the laws of the state having jurisdiction. The absolute assignment is usually in the form of a gift, which has its own tax implications. The amount of insurance is considered a gift made each year by the employee to the person to whom the absolute assignment was granted.

Consequently, if the value of the gift is of sufficient size, federal gift taxes are payable. Because the Code and the IRS regulations are silent on the specific gift tax consequences of assigned group term insurance, there is disagreement about whether the gift is valued at Table I costs or at the actual premium for the coverage.

The assignment of group term life insurance also results in the inclusion of some values in the employee's estate. If the employee dies within three years of making the assignment, the full amount of the proceeds is included in the employee's estate. If death occurs more than three years after the assignment is made, only the premiums paid within the three years prior to death are included in the employee's taxable estate. In the past, a problem arose if the employer changed group insurance carriers, thus requiring that the employee make a new assignment and again be subject to the three-year time limit. However, the IRS now considers this type of situation to be a continuation of the original assignment, as long as the amount and provisions of the new coverage are essentially the same as those of the old coverage.

If certain requirements are satisfied, accelerated death benefits paid to persons who are either terminally or chronically ill receive favorable tax treatment. Benefits received because of a terminal illness are treated as income-tax-free death benefits, as long as a physician has certified that the insured has an illness or physical condition that can reasonably be expected to result in death within 24 months or less after the date of certification. If a group contract provides accelerated death benefits to other categories of individuals, benefits can also be received with favorable tax treatment if a person is chronically ill and the coverage qualifies as a long-term care insurance contract. The definition of *chronically ill* and the conditions to qualify as a long-term care insurance contract are discussed in detail when group long-term care insurance is covered in Chapter 15.

Treatment of Added Coverages.   It is also important to discuss the tax treatment of supplemental life insurance, accidental death and dismemberment insurance, and dependent life insurance.

Supplemental Life Insurance.   Supplemental life insurance can be written either as a separate contract or as part of the contract providing basic group term life insurance coverage. If it is a separate contract and if the supplemental group life insurance meets the conditions of qualifying as group term insurance under Section 79, the amount of coverage provided is added to all other group term insurance for purposes of calculating the Uniform Premium Table I cost. Any premiums the employee pays for the supplemental coverage are included in the deduction used to determine the final taxable income. In all other ways, supplemental life insurance is treated the same as group term insurance.

Many separate supplemental contracts are fully contributory, and do not qualify as group term insurance under Section 79. This occurs only if all employees are charged rates that are either (1) equal to or lower than Table I costs or (2) equal to or greater than Table I costs. In either of these cases, the value of the coverage is not included in an employee's income.

When supplemental life insurance coverage is written in conjunction with a basic group life insurance plan, employers have the option of treating the supplemental coverage as a separate policy of insurance, as long as the premiums are properly allocated among the two portions of the coverage. There is no advantage in treating the supplemental coverage as a separate policy if it would still qualify by itself as group term insurance under Section 79. However, this election minimizes taxable income to employees if the cost of the supplemental coverage is paid totally by the employees and all employees are charged rates at or below Table I costs.

Accidental Death and Dismemberment Insurance. Premiums paid for AD&D insurance are considered to be health insurance premiums rather than group term insurance premiums. However, these are also deductible to the employer as an ordinary and necessary business expense, just like group term insurance. Benefits paid to an employee under the dismemberment portion of the coverage are treated as benefits received under a health insurance contract and are income tax free. Death benefits received under the coverage are treated like death benefits received under group term life insurance.

Dependent Life Insurance. Employer contributions for dependent life insurance coverage are fully deductible by the employer as an ordinary and necessary business expense if the employee's overall compensation is reasonable. Employer contributions do not result in taxable income to an employee as long as the value of the benefit is *de minimis*. This means that the value is so small that it is administratively impractical for the employer to account for the cost on a per-person basis. Dependent coverage of $2,000 or less on any person falls into this category. The IRS considers amounts of coverage in excess of $2,000 on any dependent to be more than *de minimis*. If more than $2,000 of coverage is provided for any dependent from employer contributions, the cost of the entire amount of coverage for that dependent (as determined by Uniform Premium Table I costs) is considered taxable income to the employee.

Death benefits are free of income taxation and are not included in the dependent's taxable estate for estate tax purposes.

State Tax Treatment

In most instances, state tax laws affecting group term insurance are similar to the federal laws. However, two major differences do exist. In most states, the payment of group term insurance premiums by the employer does not result in any taxable income to the employee, even if the amount of coverage exceeds $50,000. In addition, death proceeds receive favorable tax treatment under the estate and inheritance tax laws of most states. Generally, the proceeds are at least partially, if not totally, exempt from such taxation.

■ KEY TERMS

accelerated-benefits provision	dependent life insurance	settlement options
accidental death and dismemberment (AD&D)	entire contract clause	successive beneficiary provision
	full-time employee	
	grace period	supplemental life insurance
actively-at-work provision	incontestability provision	term insurance
assignment	key employee	Uniform Premium Table I
beneficiary	life insurance	waiver-of-premium provision
benefit schedule	misstatement of age provision	
carve-out		yearly renewable term insurance
conversion provision	rider	
covered classifications	Section 79	

■ STUDY QUESTIONS

1. Describe the following types of benefit schedules:
   a. Earnings schedules
   b. Position schedules
   c. Flat-benefit schedules

2. What are the criteria that generally must be satisfied before an employee is eligible for group term insurance coverage?

3. a. Under what circumstances is the assignment of group life insurance coverage valid?
   b. What requirements do insurance companies impose on assignments of group life insurance coverage?

4. The owner of the Midtown Garage decided to amend his group insurance contract to provide coverage for part-time employees. His agent said such a change presented no problem and wrote the owner a letter stating that the change had been made. Two weeks later, the agent called and informed the owner that the insurance company had refused to amend the contract. Can the insurance company overrule its agent? Explain.

5. Describe the methods for continuing group term life insurance coverage for disabled employees.

6. Because of severe business difficulties, the Newtown Manufacturing Company permanently laid off 20 percent of its employees last March. All had been employed by the company for less than three years. In June, salaries and fringe benefits were reduced for the remaining employees. This included amending the company's group term insurance contract to eliminate all eligible classifications except those pertaining to four executives. Explain the extent, if any, to which the following

groups of employees would have had the right to convert any coverage that was terminated under the plan:

   a. Employees who were laid off in March.

   b. Employees whose coverage was terminated in June.

7. What is the purpose of an accelerated death benefit?

8. How have insurance companies handled the problem of adverse selection associated with supplemental life insurance?

9. How may the amount of an accidental death benefit vary depending on when and how an employee dies?

10. How does dependent life insurance differ from group term life insurance for employees with respect to

   a. Conversion privilege?

   b. Ability to assign benefits?

   c. Availability of a waiver-of-premium provision?

11. What requirements must be met in order for life insurance to qualify as group term insurance under Code Section 79?

12. a. Last year, Sarah Robbins, aged 32, was provided with $75,000 of group term insurance by her employer for the entire year. Sarah is not a key employee, and the employer paid the entire premium. Using Table I, calculate the amount of federal taxable income Sarah had because of this coverage.

   b. What if Sarah had contributed $3 per month for her coverage?

13. a. To what extent are group life insurance proceeds included in an employee's gross estate for federal estate tax purposes?

   b. What are the potential tax implications for an employee if an absolute assignment is used to remove life insurance proceeds from his or her estate?

■ NOTES

1. American Council of Life Insurance, *Life Insurance Fact Book 2003*. This publication is updated annually.

2. Ibid.

3. Ibid.

4. Ibid.

5. LIMRA International, Inc., *U.S. Group Life Insurance: Industry Highlights,* 2003.

7

Group Life Insurance: Postretirement Coverage

Group term insurance plans were traditionally designed to provide employees with preretirement life insurance coverage. At retirement, an employee was faced with the decision of whether to let coverage terminate or to convert to an individual policy at an extremely high premium rate. In recent years, however, an increasing number of group life insurance plans have been designed to provide postretirement as well as preretirement life insurance coverage. In some cases, this has been accomplished by continuing group term insurance coverage, often at a reduced amount, after retirement. In other cases, it has been done through life insurance that provides permanent benefits funded during employees' working years.

The popularity of various approaches for providing postretirement life insurance coverage has changed over time, primarily because of changes in tax laws. Older and once-popular products, such as group paid-up insurance and group ordinary insurance, are no longer written. Newer products like group universal life insurance and group variable universal life insurance have come on the scene and grown in popularity. This chapter discusses four approaches that are currently used:

1. Continuation of group term insurance
2. Group universal life insurance
3. Group variable universal life insurance
4. Group term carve-outs

■ CONTINUATION OF GROUP TERM LIFE INSURANCE

Most postretirement life insurance coverage consists of the continuation of group term insurance. This requires that the employer make two important decisions: the amount of coverage to be continued and the method of paying for the continued coverage. Although the full amount of coverage prior to retirement may be continued, the high cost of group term insurance coverage for older employees frequently results in a reduction in the amount of coverage. In some cases, employees are given a flat amount of coverage (such as $2,000 or $5,000); in other cases, employees are given a percentage (such as 50 percent) of the amount of coverage they had on the date of retirement.

Current Revenue Funding

Current revenue funding is most commonly used to provide postretirement life insurance. Each periodic premium to the insurance company is paid from the employer's current revenue and is based on the lives of all employees covered, both active and retired. Because retired employees have no salary or wages from which payroll deductions can be made, most postretirement life insurance coverage is noncontributory.

The tax implications for both the employer and the employee of providing postretirement group term insurance on a current-revenue basis are the same as those discussed in the previous chapter.

Retired-Lives Reserve To Continue Coverage

In the late 1970s and early 1980s, increasing interest was shown in prefunding the cost of postretirement group term insurance coverage through retired-lives-reserve arrangements. Much of this interest stemmed from the IRS changing Section 79 regulations and making previously popular products less attractive. The concept was not new; retired-lives reserves, although not extensively used prior to that time, had been in existence for many years, primarily for very large employers. However, the trend in the 1970s was to establish them for smaller employers because the tax laws allowed the plans to be designed so that they often provided significant benefits to the firm's owners or key employees. Because the Tax Reform Act of 1984 imposed more stringent requirements on retired-lives reserves and because of the availability of newer products for postretirement coverage, there is little interest in establishing new plans. Nevertheless, plans still exist, primarily in heavily unionized industries and usually for employers with 2,000 to 5,000 employees. In addition, other plans still exist for employees and retirees previously covered under them, but other arrangements are used for newer employees.

A **retired-lives reserve** is best defined as a fund established during employees' working years to pay all or a part of the cost of their group term insurance after retirement. The fund may be established and maintained through a trust or with an insurance company. If properly designed, a retired-lives reserve (1) enables an employer to make currently tax-deductible contributions to the fund during employees' working years and (2) does not result in any taxable income to employees before retirement. However, an employer may take current deductions only for prefunding coverage that is received tax free by retired employees under Section 79. This amount is generally $50,000 but may be higher for certain employees, subject to a grandfather clause. In addition, contributions on behalf of key employees cannot be deducted if the plan is discriminatory under Section 79.

At retirement, the assets of the fund can be used to pay the cost of maintaining the postretirement coverage. If assets are withdrawn from a trust, there is the possibility of the fund being inadequate in the long run because of higher premiums and/or shorter life expectancies than anticipated. However, insurance company products typically assume this uncertainty and guarantee that the fund will be adequate to maintain the promised benefits as long as the prescribed contributions have been deposited with the insurer.

As long as an employee has no rights in a retired-lives reserve except to receive postretirement group term insurance coverage until his or her death, the employee incurs no income taxation as a result of either employer contributions to the reserve or investment earnings on the reserve. In addition, up to $50,000 can be received income tax free by beneficiaries.

In those instances when death benefits are paid directly from trust assets, the tax consequences to the employee are the same as if death benefits are provided through group term insurance contracts, except that death proceeds represent taxable income to the beneficiary.

■ GROUP UNIVERSAL LIFE INSURANCE

Group universal life insurance is a flexible-premium policy that, unlike traditional cash value life insurance, divides the pure insurance protection and the cash value accumulation into separate and distinct components. The employee is required to pay a specified initial premium, from which a charge is subtracted for one month's insurance protection. This mortality charge in effect is used to purchase the required amount of pure or term insurance (often referred to as the *amount at risk*) at a cost based on the insured's current age. Under some policies, an additional deduction is made for expenses. The balance of the initial premium becomes the initial cash value of the policy, which, when credited with interest, becomes the cash value at the end of the period. The process continues in succeeding periods. New premiums are added to the cash value, charges are made for expenses and mortality, and interest is credited to the remaining cash value. Employees receive periodic disclosure statements showing all charges made for the period as well as any interest earnings.

Group universal life insurance offers an employee considerable flexibility to meet several life-cycle financial needs with a single type of insurance coverage. The death benefit can be increased because of marriage, the birth of a child, or an increase in income. The death benefit can be reduced later when the need for life insurance decreases. Cash withdrawals can be made for the down payment on a home or to pay college tuition. Premium payments can be reduced during those periods when a young family has pressing financial needs. As financial circumstances improve, premiums can be increased so that an adequate retirement fund can be accumulated. The usual settlement options found in traditional cash value life insurance are available, so an employee can periodically elect to liquidate the cash accumulation as a source of retirement income.

Group universal life insurance products are being marketed primarily as supplemental life insurance plans—either to replace existing supplemental group term life insurance plans or as additional supplemental plans. Some insurers are selling them as a way of providing the basic life insurance plan of the employee as well. Marketing efforts tout group universal life insurance as having the following advantages to the employer:

- No direct cost other than that associated with payroll deductions and possibly enrollment, because the entire premium cost is borne by the employee. In this sense, group universal life insurance plans are much like voluntary benefit plans that offer individual universal life insurance policies.

- No ERISA filing and reporting requirement if the master contract is issued to a trust and there are no employer contributions for the cost of coverage. The current products are marketed through multiple-employer trusts, with the trust being the policy-owner.

- The ability of employees to continue coverage into retirement, alleviating pressure for the employer to provide postretirement life insurance benefits.

The following advantages are being claimed for employees:

- The availability of a popular life insurance product at group rates

- The opportunity to continue insurance coverage after retirement, possibly without any postretirement contributions

- Flexibility in designing coverage to best meet the needs of the individual employee

The current plans being marketed are still evolving, and differences do exist among the plans being offered by competing insurance companies. Due to the flexibility given policyholders, the administrative aspects of a group universal plan are formidable, and most insurers originally designed their plans only for employers with a large number of employees, usually at least 1,000. However, some insurers now make the product available for as few as 50 lives or less.

There has been steady growth in the sales of group universal life insurance over the last decade, but it still constitutes a relatively small part of the group life insurance business. In 2002, universal life accounted for about 2.7 percent of group life insurance certificates in force and about 5.6 percent of the face amount of group life insurance.[1]

Types of Group Universal Products

Two approaches have been used in designing group universal life insurance products. Under the first approach, there is a single group insurance plan. An employee who wants only term insurance can pay a premium equal to the mortality and expense charges so that there is no accumulation of cash values. Naturally, an employee who wants to accumulate cash values must pay a larger premium.

Under the second approach, there are actually two group insurance plans—a term insurance plan and a universal life insurance plan. An employee who wants only term insurance contributes to the term insurance plan, and an employee who wants only universal life insurance contributes to the universal life insurance plan. With this approach, an employee purchasing universal life insurance must make premium payments that are sufficient to generate a cash value accumulation. Initially, the employee may be required to make minimum premium payments, such as two or three times the cost of the pure insurance. If an employee who has only the term insurance coverage later wants to switch to universal life insurance coverage, the group term insurance certificate is canceled, and the employee is issued a new certificate under the universal life insurance plan. An employee can also withdraw his or her cash accumulation under the universal life insurance plan and switch to the term insurance plan or can even have coverage under both plans. Typically, an employee is eligible to purchase a maximum aggregate amount of coverage under the two plans. For example, if this amount is three times annual salary, the employee can purchase term insurance equal to two times salary and universal life insurance that has a pure insurance amount equal to one times salary.

Underwriting

Insurers that write group universal life insurance have underwriting standards concerning group size, the amounts of coverage available, and insurability.

Currently, most group universal life insurance products are being limited primarily to employers who have at least 100 or 200 employees. However, a few insurers write coverage for even smaller groups. Some insurance companies also have an employee percentage-participation requirement, such as 20 or 25 percent, that must be satisfied before a group can be installed. Other insurance companies feel their marketing approach is designed so that adequate participation results and therefore have no participation requirements.

Employees can generally elect amounts of pure insurance equal to varying multiples of their salaries, which typically start at one-half or one and range as high as three or five. There may be a minimum amount of coverage that must be purchased, such as $10,000. The maximum multiple an insurance company offers is influenced by such factors as the size of the group, the amount of insurance provided under the employer's basic employer-pay-all group term insurance plan, and the percentage of employees that participate in the plan. In general, the rules regarding the amounts of coverage are the same as those that have been traditionally applied to supplemental group term life insurance plans. The initial premium, which is a function of an employee's age and death benefit, is frequently designed to accumulate a cash value at age 65 equal to approximately 20 percent of the total death benefit.

Other approaches for determining the death benefit may be used, depending on insurance company practices and employer desires. Under some plans, employees may elect specific amounts of insurance, such as $25,000, $50,000, or $100,000. Again, an employee's age and the death benefit selected determine the premium. Some plans allow an employee to select the premium he or she wants to pay. The amount of the premium and the employee's age then automatically determine the amount of the death benefit.

The extent to which evidence of insurability is required of individual employees is also similar to that found under most supplemental group term life insurance plans. When an employee is initially eligible, coverage is usually issued on a guaranteed basis up to specified limits, which again are influenced by the size of the group, the amount of coverage provided under the employer's basic group term insurance plan, and the degree of participation in the plan. If an employee chooses a larger death benefit, simplified underwriting is used up to a second amount, after which regular underwriting is used. Guaranteed issue is often unavailable for small groups, in which case underwriting on the basis of a simplified questionnaire is used up to a specific amount of death benefit, after which regular underwriting is used.

With some exceptions, future increases in the amount of pure insurance are subject to evidence of insurability. These exceptions include additional amounts resulting from salary increases as long as the total amount of coverage remains within the guaranteed issue limit. A few insurance companies also allow additional purchases without evidence of insurability when certain events occur, such as marriage or the birth of a child.

FIGURE 7.1   Universal Life Insurance—Death Benefit Option A

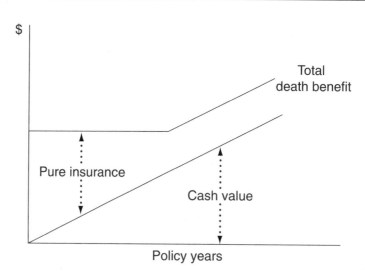

Death Benefit

The policyowner under an individual group universal life insurance policy typically has a choice of two death benefit options. Option A provides a level death benefit in the early policy years. As the cash value increases, the amount of pure insurance decreases so that the total amount paid to a beneficiary upon the insured's death remains constant. Without any provision to the contrary, the cash value would eventually approach the amount of the total death benefit. To prevent this from occurring, and also to keep the policy from failing to qualify as a life insurance policy under existing tax regulations, the amount of pure insurance does not decrease further once the cash value reaches a predetermined level. Thereafter, the total death benefit increases unless the cash value decreases. Figure 7.1 graphically demonstrates option A. Note that this and the following figure are for illustrative purposes only. The actual death benefit for a particular individual varies by such factors as the amount of interest credited, premiums paid, loans, and withdrawals.

Under option B, the amount of pure insurance is constant, and the death benefit increases each period by the change in the policy cash value. This is shown graphically in Figure 7.2.

With group universal life insurance products, an employee usually has only one death benefit option available, and whether it is option A or option B depends on which one the employer has selected. In general, there seems to be a feeling that the availability of

---

FIGURE 7.2   Universal Life Insurance—Death Benefit Option B

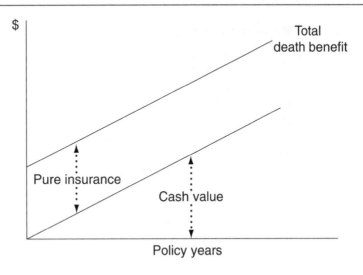

both options makes a plan more difficult to explain to employees and more costly to administer. Most employers have selected option B, which is usually easier to market to employees because the increasing total death benefit is a visible sign of any increase in their cash value or "investment." As a result, several insurers now make only option B available with their group products.

Universal life insurance products give the insured the right to increase or decrease the death benefit from the level originally selected as circumstances change. For example, the policyowner might have initially selected a pure death benefit of $100,000 under option B. Because of the birth of a child, this amount might be increased to $150,000. Increases, but not decreases, typically require that the insured provide evidence of insurability.

Mortality Charges

Most products have a guaranteed mortality charge for three years, after which the mortality charge is based on the experience of each particular group. As with experience rating in general, the credibility given to a group's actual experience is greater for larger groups. Most insurance companies guarantee that any future increases in the mortality charge will not exceed a stated maximum.

The products designed for small groups typically use pooled rates that apply to all groups insured through a particular trust. Therefore, the mortality charge for any employer varies, not with the employer's overall experience but rather with the overall experience of the trust.

Expense Charges

Probably the greatest variations among group life insurance products occur in the expense charges that are levied. Typically, a percentage of each premium, such as 2 percent, is deducted for expenses. In addition, there is a flat monthly charge, normally ranging from $1 to $3, to maintain the accumulation account. Some insurance companies levy this charge against all certificate holders, even those who are contributing only enough to have the pure insurance coverage. Other insurance companies levy the charge only against those accounts that have a positive cash value accumulation. A few insurance companies also load their mortality charges for expenses.

Finally, many companies levy a transaction charge, such as $25, that often applies to withdrawals in early policy years. A transaction charge may also apply to policy loans and additional lump-sum contributions. In evaluating the expense charges of different insurers, one should remember that an insurer with a lower-than-average charge may be subtly compensating for this charge by having a higher mortality charge or crediting a lower interest rate to cash value accumulations than would otherwise be paid.

Interest Rates

Insurance companies guarantee that the initial interest rate credited to cash value accumulations will remain in effect for a minimum period of time, often one year. After that time, the rate is typically adjusted quarterly or semiannually but cannot fall below some contractual minimum, typically in the range of 3 to 3½ percent for newer policies. The interest rate credited is usually determined on a discretionary basis but is influenced by the insurance company's investment income and competitive factors. However, some insurers stipulate that it be linked to some money market instrument, such as three-month Treasury bills. In general, the same interest is credited to all groups that an insurance company has underwritten.

Premium Adjustments

Employees are allowed considerable flexibility in the amount and timing of premium payments. Premiums can be raised or lowered and even suspended. In the latter case, the contract terminates if an employee's cash value accumulation is inadequate to pay current mortality and expense charges. Of course, premium payments could be reinstated to prevent this from happening. Additional lump-sum contributions may also be made to the accumulation account.

Two restrictions are placed on premium adjustments. First, the premium payment cannot be such that the size of the cash value accumulation becomes so large in relationship to the pure protection that an employee's coverage fails to qualify as a policy of insurance under IRS regulations. Second, because changes in premium payments through payroll deductions are costly to administer, many employers limit the frequency with which adjustments are allowed.

Loans and Withdrawals

Employees are allowed to make loans and withdrawals from their accumulated cash values, but for administrative reasons the frequency of loans and withdrawals may be limited. There are also minimum loan and withdrawal amounts, such as $250 or $500. In addition, an employee is usually required to leave a minimum balance in the cash value account sufficient to pay mortality and expense charges for some time period, possibly as long as one year. If an option A death benefit is in effect, the amount of the pure insurance is increased by the amount of the loan or withdrawal so that the total death benefit remains the same. With an option B death benefit, the amount of the total death benefit is decreased.

The interest rate charged on policy loans is usually pegged to some index, such as Moody's composite bond yield. In addition, the interest rate credited to an amount of the cash value equal to the policy loan is reduced. This reduced interest rate may be the guaranteed policy minimum or may also be based on some index, such as 2 percent less than Moody's composite bond yield.

An employee can withdraw his or her entire cash value accumulation and terminate coverage. Total withdrawals are subject to a surrender charge during early policy years. The charge decreases with policy duration and is usually in addition to any transaction charge that might also be levied.

Dependent Coverage

Most products allow an employee to purchase a rider that provides term insurance coverage on his or her spouse and children. For example, one insurance company allows an employee to elect spousal coverage of $10,000 to $50,000 in $10,000 increments and coverage on children in the amount of either $5,000 or $10,000. Other insurers make varying amounts available.

Some insurance companies allow separate universal life insurance coverage to be elected, but often only for the spouse. In such cases, the coverage is provided under a separate group insurance certificate rather than a rider.

Accidental Death and Waiver of Premium

A group universal life insurance plan may provide accidental death benefits and a disability waiver of premium. These benefits are not optional for each employee; they are part of the coverage only if the employer has elected to include them in the plan. When a waiver of premium is included, all that is waived in case of disability is the portion of the premium necessary to pay the cost of the pure insurance protection for the employee and any dependents.

Employee Options at Retirement and Termination

Several situations may arise in which an employee is no longer actively working, or a group universal plan might be terminated by the employer.

Several options are available to the retiring employee. First, the employee can continue the group insurance coverage like an active employee. However, if premium payments are continued, the insurance company bills the employee, probably on a quarterly basis. Because of the direct billing, the employee may also be subject to a higher monthly expense charge. Second, the employee can terminate the coverage and completely withdraw his or her accumulated cash value. Third, the employee can elect one of the policy settlement options for the liquidation of the cash value in the form of annuity income. Finally, some insurers allow the retiring employee to decrease the amount of pure insurance so that the cash value is adequate to keep the policy in force without any more premium payments. In effect, the employee then has a paid-up policy.

The same options are generally available to an employee who terminates employment prior to retirement. In contrast to most other types of group insurance arrangements, the continuation of coverage does not involve a conversion and the accompanying conversion charge; instead, the employee usually remains in the same group. If former employees who continue coverage have higher mortality rates, this is reflected in the mortality charge for the entire group. However, at least one insurer places terminated employees into a separate group consisting of terminated employees from all plans. These persons are subject to a mortality charge based solely on the experience of this group. Thus, actively working employees do not share in any higher mortality due to adverse selection from terminated employees.

If the employer terminates the group insurance arrangement, some insurance companies keep the group in force on a direct-bill basis, even if the coverage has been replaced with another insurer. Other insurance companies continue the group coverage only if the employer has not replaced the plan. If replacement occurs, the insurance company terminates the pure insurance amount and either gives the cash value to participants or transfers it to the trustee of the new plan.

Enrollment and Administration

Variations exist in the method by which employees are enrolled in group universal life insurance plans. Some early plans used agents who were compensated in the form of commissions or fees, but several insurance companies have dropped this practice. The employer typically handles the actual enrollment with materials the insurance company provides. However, salaried or commissioned representatives of the insurer usually conduct group meetings with the employees to explain the plan.

The employer's main administrative function is to process the payroll deductions associated with a plan. As previously mentioned, employee flexibility may be somewhat limited to minimize the costs of numerous changes in payroll deductions.

The insurance company or a third-party administrator performs other administrative functions, including providing employees with annual statements about their transactions and cash value accumulation under the plan. Toll-free telephone lines are often maintained to give information and advice to employees.

Tax Treatment

Group universal life insurance products are not designed to be policies of insurance under Section 79. In addition, each employee pays the full cost of his or her coverage. Therefore, the tax treatment is the same to employees as if they had purchased a universal life insurance policy in the individual insurance marketplace.

■ GROUP VARIABLE UNIVERSAL LIFE INSURANCE

In the mid-1990s, most major insurers that wrote group universal life insurance introduced a variable product, usually called **group variable universal life insurance**. It has the same basic characteristics that were previously described for group universal life, with one major difference—employees have a series of investment accounts to which they may allocate their net premiums. Once an employee elects the initial allocation, all future net premiums are allocated in the same proportion unless the employee makes a written request for a change. With the one exception described below, there are no minimum guarantees, and the full investment risk rests solely with the employee.

Group variable universal life insurance plans may offer up to 20 or more differing types of investment funds. These typically include at least one and possibly more of the following: growth funds, bond funds, money market funds, index funds, international stock funds, mortgage securities funds, and small company stock funds. Employers can choose the investment options that are made available to employees. For ease of administration and communication, this number is often in the range of four to six.

Many group variable universal life insurance products also have an account that has a minimum interest-rate guarantee. An employee who is selecting a 100 percent allocation to this account in effect has the equivalent of coverage under a group universal life insurance contract rather than a variable contract. This feature leads some observers to predict that if the variable product should gain more widespread acceptance, there may be little need for insurers to maintain both a group universal life product and a group variable universal life product. However, group variable universal life insurance currently accounts for only a minute percentage of new group life insurance certificates issued.

■ GROUP TERM CARVE-OUTS

Prior to 1984, employees had no taxable income if they were provided with post-retirement coverage under a group term life insurance plan. At that time, coverage in excess of $50,000 became subject to the imputed income rules of Section 79, based on Table I costs, which are relatively high at older ages. As a result, many employers turned to group term carve-outs. Although carve-outs can be used for any employee with more than $50,000 of group term coverage, they typically apply only to shareholders and key executives.

Bonus Plans

In the simplest sense, a group term carve-out works like this: The employer decides which employees are covered under the carve-out plan and limits coverage for these employees under its group term plan to the $50,000 that is received tax free. The employer then gives any premium savings to each "carved-out" employee in the form of a bonus, which is fully deductible to the employer as long as the employee's overall compensation is reasonable. The bonus amounts are either paid directly to an insurance company for individual coverage on the lives of the participants in the carve-out plan or in some cases provided to the employees as compensation to pay life insurance premiums. In most cases, the coverage purchased under the carve-out plan is some form of permanent life insurance protection that provides paid-up coverage at retirement. Traditional whole life insurance, universal life insurance, variable universal life insurance, and variable life insurance are all viable alternatives. At retirement, the employee can either keep the coverage in force (possibly at a reduced paid-up amount) or surrender the policy for its cash value.

The popularity of carve-out plans lies in the fact that a comparable or greater amount of life insurance coverage can often be provided to participants at a lower cost than if the participants were to receive all their coverage under the group term life insurance plan. Because the carve-out plan does not qualify as a plan of insurance under Section 79, each participant has taxable income in the amount of the bonus. However, this income is offset by the absence of any imputed income from Table I.

In reality, carve-out plans are more complex. In many cases, the cost of permanent coverage for an employee may actually be greater than the cost of group term coverage during the working years. However, this high cost is often more than compensated for by the cash value at retirement and the absence of imputed income after retirement. Under some carve-out plans, participants must pay this increased premium cost with after-tax dollars. Under other plans, the employer increases the bonus amount. In effect, the employer is now paying more than if the carve-out plan did not exist, but this arrangement is often acceptable to the employer as a way of providing shareholders and key executives with a benefit that is not available to other employees. In many plans, the bonus is also increased to compensate the employee for any additional income taxes that must be paid because of the carve-out plan. Such an arrangement is commonly referred to as a *zero-tax approach*.

A carve-out plan can pose a potential problem if there are rated or uninsurable employees, but the problem is ameliorated if the plan has enough participants that the insurance company will use simplified underwriting or grant concessions on impaired risks. Any employee who is still uninsurable can be continued in the group term plan.

Other Types of Carve-Out Plans

A bonus arrangement is the most common type of carve-out plan, but other alternatives are available. A carve-out plan is sometimes designed as a **death-benefit-only plan**, under which the employer agrees only to pay a death benefit to the employee's beneficiary out of corporate assets. The employer often funds the plan with corporate-owned life insurance on the employee's life. With this approach, the employee has no taxable income, but death benefits result in taxable income to the beneficiary. In addition, the employer is unable to deduct the premiums as a business expense but does receive the death proceeds tax-free.

Some firms also use split-dollar life insurance in carve-out plans. The most common approach is to use a collateral assignment arrangement under which the employer pays most of the premium, and the employee collaterally assigns a portion of the cash value and death benefit to the employer equal to the employer's premium payments. At retirement (or any other predetermined time), the employee withdraws the cash value necessary to repay the employer, who then removes the collateral assignment. At that time, the employee has full control of the policy, and the remaining cash value can be used to keep coverage in force. Many split-dollar arrangements are also used to provide nonqualified retirement benefits to key employees as a supplement to the benefits under the employer's qualified retirement plan.

Determining the Best Plan

In many instances, carve-out plans are the most cost-effective approach for providing benefits to key employees. The best plan depends on the employer's overall benefit objectives. A proper analysis of alternatives involves a complex consideration of many factors, including the employer's tax bracket, the effect on the employer's financial statements, the employee's tax bracket, premium costs, and the time value of money.

■ KEY TERMS

current revenue funding

death-benefit-only plan

group universal life insurance

group variable universal life insurance

retired-lives reserve

■ STUDY QUESTIONS

1. Why is postretirement life insurance coverage usually noncontributory?

2. Describe the nature of a retired-lives reserve.

3. What are the tax implications of retired-lives reserves?

4. What are the advantages of group universal life insurance for (a) the employer and (b) employees?

5. What underwriting requirements are often found in group universal life insurance products with respect to

   a. group size?

   b. amounts of coverage available?

   c. insurability?

6. Briefly describe the typical group universal life insurance product with respect to

   a. guarantees of mortality charges.

   b. types of expense charges.

   c. interest rates applied.

   d. premium flexibility.

   e. loans and withdrawals.

   f. dependent coverage.

   g. waiver of premiums for accidental death.

7. What options are available under group universal life insurance plans to employees who retire or terminate employment?

8. Why is group universal life insurance not treated as group term life insurance for tax purposes?

9. How do group variable universal life insurance products differ from group universal life insurance products?

10. Briefly describe the types of group carve-out plans.

11. What factors should be considered in designing a group term carve-out plan?

■ NOTE

1. LIMRA International, Inc., *U.S. Group Life Insurance Highlights,* 2003.

8 Group Disability Income Benefits

The purpose of **disability income benefits** is to partially (and sometimes totally) replace the income of employees who are unable to work because of sickness or accident. Although an employee may miss a few days of work from time to time, there is often a tendency to underestimate both the frequency and severity of disabilities that last for longer periods. At all working ages, the probability of being disabled for at least 90 consecutive days is much greater than the chance of dying. One of every three employees will have a disability that lasts at least 90 days during his or her working years, and one of every ten employees can expect to be permanently disabled prior to age 65.

All too often, the importance of adequate disability income coverage is overlooked. In terms of its financial impact on the family, long-term disability is more severe than death. In both cases, income from employment ceases. In the case of long-term disability, however, family expenses—instead of decreasing because of one fewer family member—may actually increase because of the cost of providing care for the disabled person.

Employers are less likely to provide employees with disability income benefits than with either life insurance or medical expense benefits. Thus, many employees may need to buy individual policies on their own. It is difficult to estimate the exact extent of disability coverage because often benefits are not insured and workers are sometimes covered under overlapping plans. However, a reasonable estimate would be that at least 75 percent of all employees have some form of short-term employer-provided protection, and only about 40 percent have protection for long-term disabilities. This does not mean that almost all employees have some sort of disability income coverage, because many employees have both short-term and long-term protection and thus are included in both estimates. These estimates are also somewhat misleading because most employees have long-term disability income coverage under Social Security as well as coverage for certain types of disabilities under other government programs.

Group disability income protection consists of two distinct products:

1. **Short-term disability (STD) income plans**, which provide benefits for a limited period of time, usually six months or less. Benefits may be provided under uninsured sick-leave plans or under insured plans, often referred to as *accident and sickness insurance* or *weekly indemnity benefits*.

2. **Long-term disability (LTD) income insurance**, which provides extended benefits (possibly for life) after an employee has been disabled for a period of time, frequently six months.

An important task in designing and underwriting insured group disability income plans is to coordinate them with each other (if both a short-term and a long-term plan are provided for employees). An equally important task is to coordinate them with other benefits to which employees might be entitled under social insurance programs, uninsured sick-leave plans, and employer-sponsored retirement plans. A lack of coordination can lead to such a generous level of benefits for employees that absences from work because of disability might be either falsified or unnecessarily prolonged. Alternatively, a lack of coordination can lead to an employee having a gap in coverage from the time a short-term plan ends until a long-term plan or Social Security benefits begin.

■ SICK-LEAVE PLANS

Employers use two approaches to provide short-term disability benefits to employees: sick-leave plans and short-term disability income insurance plans. A **sick-leave plan** (often called a *salary continuation plan*) is uninsured and generally fully replaces lost income for a limited period of time, starting on the first day of disability or a short time period later. In contrast, a *short-term disability income insurance plan* (which is covered in the next section of this chapter) usually provides benefits that replace only a portion of an employee's lost income and often requires a period of time before benefits start, particularly for sickness. It is impossible to obtain precise statistics, but surveys indicate that about half of the employees with short-term coverage obtain benefits under sick-leave plans, about one-quarter under insured plans, and about one-quarter under plans that combine the two approaches.

Traditionally, many sick-leave plans were informal, with the availability, amount, and duration of benefits for an employee being discretionary on the part of the employer. Although some plans used by small firms or for a limited number of executives still operate this way, informal plans are generally inappropriate. There is a possibility that the IRS will consider benefit payments to be either a gift or a dividend and therefore not tax deductible by the employer. In addition, an informal plan increases the likelihood of suits brought by persons who are disabled but who do not receive benefits. As a result, the vast majority of sick-leave plans are now formalized and have specific written rules concerning eligibility and benefits.

TABLE 8.1	Sick Leave Benefit Schedule
Length of Service	**Amount of Sick Leave***
Less than 3 Months	None
3 or More Months	1 day at full pay for each month of service (retroactive to date of employment)

* Maximum unused sick leave: 130 days.

In recent years, a few employers have combined their sick-leave plans with other types of payments for time not worked, such as vacations, holidays, and personal leave, into a single **paid time off (PTO) program**. One rationale for such programs is that many employees view sick days as a right and will take the maximum number of days available, whether sick or not. With a PTO, an employee is given a specified bank of days off with full pay and can take this paid time off for any reason. The bank of days is usually slightly less than the total number of days under the prior programs, but within the range of the number of days that most employees took off. PTO programs have generally had the effect of lowering the number of days that employees call in sick, because these days can be used for other purposes. This lowers an employer's benefit costs and minimizes other problems associated with unscheduled absences.

Eligibility

Almost all sick-leave plans are limited to regular full-time employees, but benefits may also be provided for regular part-time employees. Most plans also require that an employee satisfy a short probationary period (commonly one to three months) before being eligible for benefits. Sick-leave plans may also be limited to certain classes of employees, such as top management or nonunion employees. The latter is common when the union employees are covered under a collectively bargained, but insured, plan.

Benefits

Most sick-leave plans are designed to provide benefits equal to 100 percent of an employee's regular pay. Some plans, however, provide a reduced level of benefits after an initial period of full pay.

Several approaches are used in determining the duration of benefits. The most traditional approach credits eligible employees with a certain amount of sick leave each year, such as ten days. The majority of plans using this approach allow employees to accumulate unused sick leave up to some maximum amount, which rarely exceeds six months (sometimes specified as 180 days or 26 weeks). A variation of this approach is to credit employees with an amount of sick leave, such as one day, for each month of service. Table 8.1 is an example of a benefit schedule that uses this variation.

Another approach, illustrated in Table 8.2, bases the duration of benefits on an employee's length of service.

An alternative to this approach provides benefits for a uniform length of time to all employees, except possibly those with short periods of service. However, benefits are reduced to a level less than full pay after some period of time that is related to an employee's length of service. Table 8.3 is an illustration of this increasingly common approach.

In some instances, an employee is not eligible for sick-leave benefits if he or she is eligible for benefits under social insurance plans, such as workers' compensation. However, most sick-leave plans are coordinated with social insurance programs. For example, if an employee is entitled to 100 percent of pay and receives 60 percent of pay as a workers' compensation benefit, the sick-leave plan pays the remaining 40 percent.

A problem for the employer is how to verify an employee's disability. In general, the employee's word is accepted for disabilities that last a week or less. Most sick-leave plans have a provision that benefits for longer periods are paid only if the employee is under the care of a physician, who certifies that the employee is unable to work.

■ INSURED DISABILITY INCOME PLANS

As mentioned, insured disability income plans consist of two distinct products: short-term coverage and long-term coverage. In many respects, the contractual provisions of both short-term and long-term disability income contracts are the same or very similar. In other respects—notably, the eligibility requirements, the definition of disability, and the amount and duration of benefits—there are significant differences.

Eligibility

The eligibility requirements in group disability income insurance contracts are similar to those found in group term insurance contracts. In addition to being in a covered classification, an employee usually must work full-time and be actively at work before coverage commences. Any requirements concerning probationary periods, insurability, and premium contributions must also be satisfied.

TABLE 8.2	Sick Leave Benefit Schedule
Length of Service	**Maximum Days of Sick Leave per Year**
Less than 3 Months	0
3 Months to 1 Year	5
2 Years	10
3 Years	15
5 Years	20
7 Years	25
10 Years	30

TABLE 8.3	Sick Leave Benefit Schedule		
	Weeks of Sick Leave per Disability		
Length of Service	**100% of Pay**	**50% of Pay**	**Total Weeks**
Less than 6 Months	0	0	0
6 Months to 1 Year	2	0	2
1 Year	4	22	26
2 Years	8	18	26
3 Years	12	14	26
4 Years	16	10	26
5 Years	20	6	26
6 Years or More	26	0	26

Short-term and long-term disability income insurance plans frequently differ in both the classes of employees who are eligible for coverage and the length of the probationary period. Employers are more likely to provide short-term benefits to a wider range of employees, and it is not unusual for short-term plans to cover all full-time employees. However, these plans may be a result of collective bargaining and apply only to union employees. In this situation, other employees frequently have short-term disability benefits under uninsured sick-leave plans.

Long-term disability plans often limit benefits to salaried employees, but they may include employees with commission-based income such as stockbrokers and other sales-related occupations. Claims experience has traditionally been less favorable for hourly paid employees for a number of reasons. Claims of hourly paid employees tend to be more frequent, particularly in recessionary times when the possibility of temporary layoffs or terminations increases. Such claims also tend to be of longer duration, possibly because of the likelihood that these employees hold repetitive and nonchallenging jobs. Some long-term plans also exclude employees below a certain salary level because this category of employees, like hourly paid employees, is considered to have a reasonable level of benefits under Social Security.

Long-term disability income plans usually have longer probationary periods than short-term disability income plans. Although the majority of short-term disability plans (as well as group term insurance plans and medical expense plans) either have no probationary period or have a probationary period of three months or less, it is common for long-term disability plans to have probationary periods ranging from three months to one year. Short-term plans require only that an employee be actively at work on the date he or she is otherwise eligible for coverage, but long-term plans sometimes require that the employee be on the job for an extended period (such as 30 days) without illness or injury before coverage becomes effective.

Definition of Disability

Benefits are paid under disability income insurance contracts only if the employee meets the definition of disability as specified in the contract. Virtually all short-term disability income insurance contracts define disability as *the total and continuous inability of the employee to perform each and every duty of his or her regular occupation.* A small minority of contracts use a more restrictive definition, requiring that an employee be unable to engage in any occupation for compensation. Partial disabilities are usually not covered, but a few newer plans do provide such benefits. **Partial disability** is usually defined to mean that an employee is neither permanently nor totally disabled but can perform only some of the duties of his or her job. For example, an employee with a sprained back might work part time.

The majority of short-term contracts limit coverage to nonoccupational disabilities, because employees have workers' compensation benefits for occupational disabilities. This limitation tends to be most common when benefits under the short-term contract are comparable to or lesser in amount than those under the workers' compensation law. In those cases, where workers' compensation benefits are relatively low and the employer desires to provide additional benefits, coverage may be written for both occupational and nonoccupational disabilities.

A few long-term disability income contracts use the same liberal definition of disability that is commonly used in short-term contracts. However, the term *material duties* often replaces the term *each and every duty.* Some other contracts define disability as *the total and continuous inability of the employee to engage in any and every gainful occupation for which he or she is qualified or shall reasonably become qualified by reason of training, education, or experience.* However, most long-term disability contracts use a dual definition that combines these two. Under a dual definition, benefits are paid for some period of time (usually 24 or 36 months) as long as an employee is unable to perform his or her regular occupation. After that time, benefits are paid only if the employee is unable to engage in any occupation for which he or she is qualified by reason of training, education, or experience. The purpose of this combined definition is to require and encourage a disabled employee who becomes able after a period of time to adjust his or her lifestyle and earn a livelihood in another occupation.

Another popular definition of disability found in long-term contracts contains an occupation test and an earnings test. Under the occupation test, a person is totally disabled if he or she meets the definition of disability as described in the previous paragraph. However, if the occupation test is not satisfied, a person is still considered disabled as long as an earnings test is satisfied. This means that the person's income has dropped by a stated percentage, such as 20 percent, because of injury or sickness. This definition makes a group insurance contract similar to an individual disability income policy that provides residual benefits.

The definition of disability in long-term contracts may differ from that found in short-term contracts in several other respects. Long-term contracts are somewhat more likely to provide benefits for partial disabilities. However, the amount and duration of such benefits may be limited when compared with those for total disabilities, and the receipt of benefits is usually contingent on a previous period of total disability. In addition, most long-term contracts provide coverage for both occupational and nonoc-cupational disabilities. Finally, short-term contracts usually have the same definition of disability for all classes of employees. Some long-term contracts use different definitions for different classes of employees—one for most employees and a more liberal definition for executives or salaried employees.

Exclusions

An **exclusion** is a provision in an insurance contract that indicates situations that the insurer does not intend to cover. Under certain circumstances, disability income benefits are not paid even if an employee satisfies the definition of disability. Common exclusions under both short-term and long-term disability income contracts specify that no benefits are paid in the following cases:

- For any period during which the employee is not under the care of a physician.
- For any disability caused by an intentionally self-inflicted injury.
- Unless the period of disability commenced while the employee was covered under the contract. For example, an employee who previously elected not to participate under a contributory plan cannot obtain coverage for an existing disability by decid-ing to pay the required premium.
- If the employee is engaged in any occupation for remuneration. This exclusion applies in those situations when an employee is totally disabled with respect to his or her regular job but is engaged in other employment that can be performed despite the employee's condition.
- If (or to the extent) benefits are payable under workers' compensation or similar laws.

Additional exclusions are often found in long-term contracts. These commonly deny benefits for disabilities resulting from the following:

- War, whether declared or undeclared.
- Participation in an assault or felony. Some insurers have recently expanded this exclusion to include the commission of any crime.
- Mental disease, alcoholism, or drug addiction. However, many contracts provide employees with benefits but limit their duration (such as for 24 months per disabil-ity); other contracts provide benefits for an employee who is confined in a hospital or institution that specializes in the care and treatment of such disorders.
- Preexisting conditions.

Until the Pregnancy Discrimination Act, it was common for disabilities resulting from pregnancy to be excluded. Such an exclusion is now illegal under federal law if an employer has 15 or more employees. Employers with fewer than 15 employees may still exclude pregnancy disabilities unless they are subject to state laws to the contrary.

The exclusion for preexisting conditions is designed to counter the adverse selection and potentially large claims that could occur if an employer established a group disability income plan or if an employee elected to participate in the plan because of some known condition that is likely to result in disability. Although variations exist, a common **preexisting-conditions provision** excludes coverage for any disability that commences during the first 12 months an employee is covered under the contract if the employee received treatment or medical advice for the disabling condition both (1) prior to the date the employee became eligible for coverage and (2) within 90 consecutive days prior to the commencement of the disability.

When coverage is transferred from one insurance company to another, it is not unusual, particularly in the case of large employers, for the new insurance company to waive the limitation for preexisting conditions for those employees who were insured under the previous contract. This situation is often referred to as *prior coverage credit* or a *no-loss no-gain provision*. In some instances, the provision is modified so that benefits are limited to those that would have been provided under the previous contract, possibly for a specified period of time, such as one year. Note that a transfer of coverage has no effect on the responsibility of the prior insurance company to continue paying benefits for claims that have already occurred, except in rare instances in which some arrangement is made for the new contract to provide benefits.

Benefits

A discussion of the benefits under disability income contracts is more complex than a discussion of the benefits under group life insurance contracts. A similarity exists in that there are benefit schedules that classify employees and specify the amount of disability income to be provided. However, the relationship between an employee's earnings and the employee's potential benefits is more important in disability income insurance than in group life insurance. In addition, disability benefits are subject to several provisions not found in group life insurance contracts. These pertain to the length of time that benefits are paid and the coordination of benefits with other available types of disability income.

Benefit Schedules. As in group life insurance, there is a variety of benefit schedules found in group disability income contracts. Benefits may be available to all employees or limited to specific groups of employees. In addition, benefits may be expressed as flat-dollar amounts, varying dollar amounts by classification, or a percentage of earnings.

A major difficulty in disability insurance is determining the appropriate level of benefits to provide. Absenteeism is encouraged and the incentive to return to work is diminished if a disabled employee is given a level of income that is comparable to his or her regular earnings. In general, disability income plans are designed to provide a level of benefits that replaces between 50 and 70 percent of an employee's gross income. Although this may appear to represent a substantial reduction of regular earnings, it should be remembered that a disabled employee does not have the usual expenses associated with working, such as transportation costs. In addition, disability income benefits are not subject to Social Security and Medicare taxation after a period of time and, depending on the source and amount, may be free of income taxation. Despite the logic in providing a reduced level of income, some short-term disability income plans provide employees with 100 percent of their predisability earnings. In most cases, this level of benefits is either a result of collective bargaining or an effort by employers to provide nonunion employees with a level of benefits that is comparable to that of union employees.

Many short-term disability income plans and the majority of long-term plans base benefits on a single percentage of regular earnings (excluding bonuses, overtime, commissions, and other incentive-based income). This percentage varies widely for short-term plans, and benefits as low as 50 percent or as high as 100 percent are not unusual. However, many insurers are reluctant to underwrite plans that provide benefits higher than 70 percent of earnings. In some instances, short-term plans, like sick-leave plans, may use different percentages, such as 100 percent of earnings for four weeks and 70 percent of earnings for the remaining benefit period. The length of time for which the higher level of benefits is provided may also be a function of the length of an employee's service.

Long-term plans typically provide benefits that range from 50 to 70 percent of earnings, with 60 and 66⅔ being the most prevalent percentages. Some plans also use a sliding scale, such as 66⅔ percent of the first $4,000 of monthly earnings and 40 percent of earnings in excess of $4,000.

It is common for plans that determine benefits as a percentage of earnings to also place a maximum dollar amount on the benefit that is provided, regardless of earnings. For example, a short-term plan covering hourly employees may have a benefit equal to 70 percent of earnings that might be subject to a maximum of $500 per week. Similarly, a long-term plan may provide benefits equal to 66⅔ percent of earnings, but might be subject to a monthly maximum that may vary from $3,000 or $4,000 for some small groups to as much as $6,000 to $10,000 for large groups. A few plans for large groups of executives may, however, have limits of up to $25,000. The purpose of such a maximum is to prevent the absolute benefit from being so high that an employee, by adjusting his or her lifestyle, could live comfortably on the disability income benefit and thus have no financial incentive to return to work.

Other types of benefit schedules are found in short-term disability income plans, particularly when these plans are designed for hourly paid employees. If the weekly earnings of most employees fall within a narrow range, the benefit might be expressed as a flat-dollar amount. For example, if all employees earn between $400 and $500 per week, a benefit of $270 per week might be used. If earnings vary widely, a benefit schedule like the one in Table 8.4 might be used.

TABLE 8.4 Short-Term Disability Income Benefits	
Weekly Earnings	**Weekly Benefit**
$341 to $380	$250
$381 to $420	280
$421 to $460	310
$461 to $500	340
Over $500	370

TABLE 8.5	Short-Term Disability Income Benefits
Monthly Earnings	**Monthly Benefit**
$1,500 to $2,500	$1,200
$2,501 to $3,500	1,800
$3,501 to $4,500	2,400
$4,500 to $5,500	3,000
Over $5,500	4,000

A similar approach is occasionally used in long-term disability income plans, as shown in the Table 8.5 benefit schedule for salaried employees earning in excess of $18,000 per year.

Period of Benefits. To determine the period for which disability income benefits are paid, it is necessary to determine when benefits begin and how long they are paid. In both respects, there are differences between short-term and long-term plans.

Short-Term Plans. Short-term disability income contracts commonly contain a **waiting period** (often referred to in such contracts as an *elimination period*). The waiting period is the length of time for which an employee covered under the contract must be disabled before benefits begin. In the typical short-term contract, there is no waiting period for disabilities resulting from accidents, but a waiting period of one to seven consecutive days is used for disabilities resulting from sicknesses. However, some plans have a single waiting period that applies to disabilities from either accidents or sicknesses; a few plans have no waiting periods for either. Waiting periods longer than 7 days are occasionally used, particularly when there is a sick-leave plan to provide benefits during the initial portion of a disability. Besides lowering the cost of a disability income plan, the waiting period discourages unwarranted absences from work due to sickness. In a few cases, benefits are paid retroactively to the date of disability if the disability lasts for a predetermined period of time. However, it is generally felt that retroactive benefits cause employees to prolong their return to work in order to receive benefits for the full period of their disability.

Once an employee begins receiving benefit payments under a short-term disability contract, the benefits continue until the end of the benefit period specified in the contract if the employee remains disabled for that long. Although short-term contracts may provide benefits up to two years (with long-term contracts providing benefits for periods over two years), benefits rarely continue for more than a year. In fact, the majority of short-term contracts stipulate that benefits are paid for either 13 or 26 weeks, with the latter period being most prevalent. Short-term plans are often described in terms of their waiting period and their duration of benefits. For example, a "1-8-26" plan pays benefits for a maximum of 26 weeks beginning with the first day of disability in the case of an accident and with the eighth day of disability in the case of sickness.

TABLE 8.6	Duration of Long-Term Disability Income Benefits
Age at Commencement of Disability	**Benefits Duration**
59 and Younger	To age 65
60–64	5 years
65–69	To age 70
70–74	1 year
75 and Older	6 months

In a few cases, the maximum period of benefits applies to a specified duration of time (such as any consecutive 12 months) regardless of the number of separate disabilities. However, in most plans, both the maximum benefit period and the waiting period apply to each separate disability. Moreover, successive periods of disability caused by the same accident or the same or related sickness are generally considered to be a single disability unless they are separated by a period (normally two weeks) of continuous resumption of active employment. This provision prevents an employee from briefly returning to work in order to obtain a second maximum period of benefits for the same disability.

Although reducing short-term disability income benefits for older employees may be justifiable on a cost basis, few plans have done so.

Long-Term Plans.   Although waiting periods in long-term disability income plans may be as short as 30 days or as long as a year or more, most plans use periods of three to six months, with six months most common. The length of the waiting period often corresponds to the length of time benefits are paid under a firm's short-term disability income plan or sick-leave plan. Unlike short-term plans, the waiting periods for sicknesses and accidents are the same.

Long-term disability income benefits may be paid for as short a period as two years or as long as the lifetime of the disabled employee. In a few cases, the length of the benefit period may differ, depending on whether the disability was a result of an accident or a sickness. Benefits are commonly reduced for older employees, and several different approaches are acceptable under the Age Discrimination in Employment Act. In a few cases, benefits are paid until age 70 for any disability that occurred before that age. For disabilities occurring at age 70 or later, benefits are paid for a reduced duration. A more common approach is to use a graded benefit period and give benefits to age 65 for employees who are disabled before a specified age. Employees disabled after the specified age get benefits for a limited duration, as shown in Table 8.6.

A similar approach uses a sliding level of benefit durations after a certain age. For example, a plan may provide that employees disabled prior to age 60 will receive benefits until age 65. The schedule shown in Table 8.7 might then be used for employees who are disabled at age 60 or older.

As do short-term disability income plans, long-term plans typically provide for successive disabilities. The majority of contracts stipulate that successive periods of

TABLE 8.7	Duration of Long-Term Disability Income Benefits	
Age at Commencement of Disability		**Benefit Duration (in Years)**
60		5
61		4
62		3½
63		3
64		2½
65		2
66		2
67		1
68		1
69		1

disability that are separated by less than some period (usually varying from three to six months) of continuous, active full-time employment are considered a single disability, unless the subsequent disability (1) arises from an unrelated cause and (2) begins after the employee has returned to work.

Coordination with Other Benefits. To minimize the possibility that an employee will receive total benefits higher than his or her predisability earnings, disability income plans commonly stipulate that benefits be coordinated with other sources of disability income. The effect of this coordination (often referred to as *integration*) is to reduce (either totally or partially) the benefits payable under the disability income contract to the extent that certain other benefits are available. In general, the insurance laws or regulations of most states allow such reductions to be made as a result of benefits from social insurance programs and group insurance or retirement plans provided by the employer. Reductions as a result of benefits from individual disability income contracts are not usually allowed unless the policies were purchased by the employer. Employers and employees often resent the fact that disability income benefits that they have "paid for" may be reduced. However, such reductions are considered in determining the rates charged for disability income insurance. In effect, the employer is purchasing a contract that is only a supplement to these other available sources of disability income rather than being penalized because these resources are available.

For various reasons, including the limited duration of benefits and the desire for simplified operating procedures, coordination with other benefits is less common for short-term plans than for long-term plans. If a short-term plan covers only nonoccupational disabilities, there is no need for coordination with workers' compensation benefits; also, unless benefits are provided for disabilities lasting longer than five months, there is no need to coordinate benefits with Social Security. In general, benefits under short-term plans are coordinated with the following:

■ Workers' compensation benefits, if the plan covers occupational disabilities

■ Temporary disability laws, if they are applicable

■   Social Security benefits, if the maximum benefit period is longer than five months

Some insurance companies sell long-term disability income coverage without any provision for coordination with other disability income benefits; however, the availability and potential magnitude of other benefits is an underwriting factor in determining the maximum amount of coverage that is written. Usually, long-term disability income benefits are coordinated with benefits provided under the following:

■   Social Security

■   Workers' compensation laws

■   Temporary disability laws

■   Other insurance plans for which the employer makes a contribution or payroll deduction

■   Pension plans for which the employer has made a contribution or payroll deduction to the extent that the employee elects to receive retirement benefits because of disability

■   Sick-leave plans

■   Earnings from employment, either with the employer or from other sources

A few insurers also coordinate group long-term coverage with individual disability income policies.

The coordination with Social Security may be based solely on the benefit a disabled worker receives for himself or herself (referred to as the *employee's primary insurance amount*). It may also be based on the employee's total family benefit if the employee has eligible dependents.

Two basic approaches to Social Security coordination of disability income benefits are used: a full-coordination approach and a dual-percentage approach. Under the *full-coordination approach,* long-term disability income benefits are reduced to the extent that any benefits subject to coordination are received.

EXAMPLE:
Theresa earns $2,500 per month and is entitled to a disability income benefit of 60 percent, or $1,500 per month. In addition, she is entitled to a disability benefit of $900 under Social Security, as well as additional family benefits of $450 (a total of $1,350). If her long-term disability income benefit plan provides for coordination with total family benefits, she will receive $1,500 ($1,350 from Social Security and the remaining $150 from the long-term plan). However, if full coordination is provided only with respect to the primary insurance amount (in other words, the $450 of family benefits is not considered), she will receive $1,950 ($1,350 from Social Security and $600 from the long-term disability plan).

Under the *dual-percentage approach,* two percentages are used. The first is applicable to benefits that are provided under the long-term plan when there are no other

EXAMPLE
Assume Theresa's disability income plan provides benefits equal to 60 percent of earnings in the absence of other benefits subject to coordination. If there are benefits subject to coordination, benefits under the insured plan are reduced to the extent that the sum of the benefits under the long-term disability plan and the benefits subject to coordination exceeds 70 percent. Using these percentages and the previous example, 70 percent of earnings is $1,750. Because the long-term disability benefit and all the Social Security benefits total $2,850, the long-term disability benefit is reduced by $1,100 if the plan provides for coordination with total family benefits. Therefore, she will receive a total benefit of $1,750 ($1,350 from Social Security and $400 from the long-term plan).

benefits subject to coordination. A second and higher percentage is applicable to total benefits payable from the long-term plan and other sources subject to coordination.

Coordination with other benefits has the potential to totally eliminate a long-term disability benefit. To prevent this from happening, many plans provide (and some states require) that a minimum benefit, such as $50 or $100 per month, be paid. Most plans also contain a provision freezing the amount of any reduction because of Social Security at the initial level that was established when the claim began. Without such a provision, the intended effect of increases in Social Security benefits would be erased by equivalent reductions in other disability income benefits provided to the employee. This is seen by some regulators as contrary to public policy and thus a reason for requiring that insured plans contain a freeze on the amount of the reduction.

EXAMPLE
Herb is entitled to receive $1,000 per month in disability income benefits under a long-term plan that contains a provision for full coordination with Social Security. If he initially receives $400 from the long-term plan and $600 from Social Security, the $400 continues to be paid under a provision that freezes this amount even if Social Security benefits are increased. If a 5 percent increase is later granted in Social Security benefits, he will receive a total benefit of $1,030.

As a general rule, both the insured and the insurer are better off if the insured is able to collect Social Security benefits for a disability. The insured has an increased overall benefit, and the insurer has a substantially lower claim to pay. Consequently, insurers are often willing to provide assistance to claimants by helping them with the filing of Social Security claims and the appealing of decisions denying claims.

Supplemental Benefits. It is becoming increasingly common to find group long-term disability income plans that provide employees with a base of employer-paid benefits and that allow each covered employee to purchase additional coverage at his or her own expense. For example, a plan may provide basic benefits of 50 percent of earnings and an option for an employee to increase this amount to 60, 66⅔, or 70 percent of earnings. Such a supplemental or **buy-up plan** is becoming more popular because employers feel the need to control the costs of benefits by shifting a greater burden of the cost to employees.

Some plans are also designed to "carve out" benefits for certain employees, frequently key executives. For example, an employer might design one plan to cover most of its employees, but top executives might be covered with another group plan that provides enhanced benefits in the form of a larger percentage of earnings and a more liberal definition of disability. Another variation of a carve-out plan would provide the executives with a lower benefit percentage than other employees receive, but it could provide supplemental benefits in the form of individual disability income policies. In addition to more favorable policy provisions, a carve-out plan might offer better rate guarantees and an overall higher benefit than a group plan could offer. Furthermore, the portability of the individual policy might be attractive to executives, although it might not necessarily appeal to the employer. In addition, individual policies might be available on a guaranteed-issue basis if the group of executives is large enough.

Catastrophic Benefits Rider.   A few disability insurers that also sell long-term care insurance have recently started to make available additional benefits in the form of a **catastrophic benefits rider** if the insured suffers a severe disability that includes cognitive impairment or the inability to perform two or more of six activities of daily living. These are the same criteria that trigger benefits in long-term care policies, which are discussed in Chapter 15.

The employer can typically purchase benefits that range from an additional 10 to 40 percent of earnings, as long as total disability benefits do not exceed a specified limit that may be as high as 100 percent of earnings. The length of time the catastrophic benefits are paid is also selected by the employer and can vary from one year to the duration of the regular disability benefits provided by the policy. In addition, an employer may have the option of adding a flat monthly benefit that is payable if an employee's spouse suffers a cognitive impairment or is unable to perform two or more activities of daily living.

Other Contract Provisions

Many provisions in group disability income contracts are similar to those in group life insurance contracts and are not discussed further in this chapter. These provisions pertain to incontestability, a grace period, the entire contract, and the payment of premiums. The provisions that are discussed either are unique to group disability income benefit contracts or differ in certain respects from similar provisions found in group life insurance contracts.

Claims.   The provisions concerning claims under both short-term and long-term disability income contracts are essentially the same. The insurance company must be notified within a relatively short time period—20 or 30 days (or as soon as is reasonably possible)—after the disability for which benefits are being claimed begins. A claim form must then be filed with the insurance company, usually within 90 days after the commencement of the disability or after the end of the week, month, or other time period for which benefits are payable. The claim form normally consists of three statements; one by the employee concerning the disability, another by the attending physician, and a third by the employer indicating the date and reason that active employment ceased. Provisions also require periodic reports from the attending physician or permit the insurance company to request such reports at reasonable intervals. The insurance company also has the right to have the employee examined by a physician of its own choice (and at its own expense) at reasonable time periods during the duration of the claim.

Payment of Benefits. The insurance company is not obligated to make benefit payments until a proof of loss has been filed. Although benefits are usually payable to the employee, a facility-of-payment provision is included to allow payments to a guardian if the employee is physically, mentally, or otherwise incapable of giving a valid release for any payment received. Benefits may be assigned to another party if such an assignment is permissible under state law and the insurance contract.

Rehabilitation. As an incentive to encourage disabled employees to return to active employment as soon as possible, but perhaps at a lower-paying job, most insurance companies include a **rehabilitation provision** in their long-term disability income contracts. This provision permits the employee to enter a trial work period (sometimes referred to as a *return-to-work program*) of one or two years in rehabilitative employment. During this time, disability benefits continue but are reduced by some percentage (varying from 50 to 80 percent) of the earnings from rehabilitative employment. For example, with a 50 percent reduction, an employee who is otherwise entitled to a disability benefit of $1,500 per month will have this benefit reduced by only $600 if he or she can earn $1,200 in the new job. If the trial work period indicates that the employee is unable to perform the rehabilitative employment, the original long-term benefits continue and the employee is not required to satisfy a new waiting period.

Often, there are no other provisions in long-term disability income contracts that require the insurance company to aid in the rehabilitation of disabled employees. Insurance companies, however, sometimes provide benefits for rehabilitation when it is felt that the cost of these benefits is offset by shortening an employee's disability period. These benefits may be in the form of physical therapy, job training, adaptive aids to enable a disabled person to perform job functions, or even the financing of a business venture.

In the past, the decision to seek rehabilitation was left to the disabled person. A number of insurers now require that the person undertake rehabilitation or have benefits reduced or stopped.

The rehabilitation of disabled workers is continuing to grow in importance among insurance companies. In fact, the rehabilitative services provided are often used as a selling feature for a company's product. More and more companies are taking a proactive role in managing disability claims by employing more skilled professionals and by intervening earlier in the claims process. In addition to providing rehabilitation benefits, insurance companies are monitoring claims data more closely so that they can better advise employers of areas where action can be taken to reduce the number of future claims.

Integrated Disability Management. Because early intervention is a key to getting disabled employees back to work sooner, more and more employers are turning to

integrated disability management. These employers use the same organization to manage the rehabilitation of disabled employees under all their disability programs—short-term, long-term, and workers' compensation. The organization may be the insurance company that provides insurance coverage to the employer or a firm that specializes in disability management. This approach is commonly referred to as integrated disability management and applies to both insured and self-funded benefits.

Integrated disability management has several advantages to both the employer and the employees. There is a single centralized claims-reporting system that is easier to understand and less expensive than duplicate programs for each type of coverage. There are consistent treatment protocols for all disabilities, no matter where or when they occurred, and it is easier to measure and track outcomes of return-to-work programs. In addition, there is a lower incidence of fraudulent claims from employees trying to collect under disability plans and workers' compensation at the same time.

Termination.   For the most part, the provisions in disability income contracts concerning either the termination of the master contract or an employee's coverage are the same as those found in group life insurance. However, there is one notable exception: A conversion privilege is rarely included, based on the theory that the termination of employment also terminates an employee's income and thus the need for disability income protection. If a conversion privilege is available, an extra charge is made for the coverage.

One other situation should be mentioned. When an employee meets the definition of total disability under a disability income contract, the employee is considered to have terminated employment by reason of ceasing to be an active, full-time employee. Without some provision to the contrary, an employee who resumes work is then required to resatisfy any eligibility requirements, including a new probationary period. However, most group disability income contracts allow the employer to consider disabled employees as not having terminated employment for insurance purposes. The employer may continue coverage as long as it is done on a nondiscriminatory basis and as long as the required premiums are paid. In short-term contracts, coverage is generally continued by the payment of premiums on the same basis as for active employees, although it is common for long-term contracts to contain a waiver-of-premium provision. This waiver normally begins at the time benefit payments start, not at the beginning of the waiting period.

The only practical effect of continuing coverage on a disabled employee is to guarantee that the employee will again be eligible for disability income benefits after he or she has returned to active employment. The continuation of coverage (or termination of coverage) has no effect on the future disability income benefits to an employee who is currently disabled and therefore entitled to receive benefits.

Additional Benefits.   Several types of additional benefits are occasionally found under long-term disability income contracts. The most common are a cost-of-living adjustment, a pension supplement, and a survivor's benefit.

Some disability income plans have a **cost-of-living adjustment (COLA)** so that inflation does not erode the purchasing power of disability income benefits being received. Under the typical COLA formula, benefits increase annually along with changes in the consumer price index.

Many firms make provisions in their pension plan for treating disabled employees as if they were still working and accruing pension benefits. Such a **pension supplement** requires that contributions on behalf of disabled employees be made to the pension plan, usually from the employer's current revenues. However, some disability income contracts stipulate that the contributions to fund a disabled employee's accruing pension benefits be paid from the disability income contract.

Some retirement plans also provide disability income benefits by allowing disabled employees to begin receiving retirement benefits when they are totally and permanently disabled. It is common, however, to limit these early retirement benefits to employees who have satisfied some minimum period of service or who have reached some minimum age. In recent years, the feeling among employee benefit consultants seems to be that it is preferable to have separate retirement and disability income plans.

Some long-term contracts provide a benefit to survivors in the form of continued payments after the death of a disabled employee. In effect, the disability income payments continue, possibly at a reduced amount, for periods ranging up to 24 months, with three to six months being most common. Payments are generally made only to eligible survivors, who commonly are the spouse and unmarried children under age 21.

Other less common types of additional benefits may also be found. Examples include child-care payments for disabled employees who can work on a part-time basis, spousal disability benefits payable to the employee, benefits to pay premiums for medical expense coverage, and benefits for worksite modification.

FEDERAL TAX TREATMENT

As with group life insurance, employer contributions for an employee's disability income insurance are fully deductible to the employer as an ordinary and necessary business expense under Code Section 162 if the employee's overall compensation is reasonable. Sick-leave payments are similarly tax deductible. Contributions by an individual employee are considered payments for personal disability income insurance and are not tax deductible.

Income Tax Liability of Employees

In contrast to group life insurance, for which employer contributions may result in some taxable income to an employee, Code Section 106 provides that employer contributions for disability income insurance result in no taxable income to an employee. However, the payment of benefits under an insured plan or sick-leave plan may or may not result in the receipt of taxable income. To make this determination, it is necessary to look at whether the plan is fully contributory, noncontributory, or partially contributory.

Fully Contributory Plan. Under a fully contributory plan, the entire cost is paid by employee contributions and benefits are received free of income taxation.

Noncontributory Plan. Under a noncontributory plan, the employer pays the entire cost and benefits are included in an employee's gross income. However, the Internal Revenue Code provides a tax credit to persons who are permanently and totally disabled.

A tax credit is better than a tax deduction in that it is subtracted from an individual's federal income tax liability rather than deducted from gross income to determine taxable income. For purposes of this tax credit, the IRS uses the Social Security definition of disability; that is, an employee must be unable to engage in any kind of gainful work because of a medically determinable physical condition that has lasted or is expected to last at least 12 months or to result in death.

The maximum credit is $750 for a single person, $1,125 for a married person filing jointly, and $562.50 for a married person filing separately. The credit cannot exceed the taxable disability benefit actually received. The maximum credit is reduced if a single individual has an adjusted gross income (including the disability benefit) over $7,500, if a married person filing jointly has an adjusted gross income over $10,000, or if a married person filing separately has an adjusted gross income over $5,000. The reduction is equal to 7½ percent of any income over the limit. In addition, the credit is reduced by 15 percent of any tax-free income received as a pension, an annuity, or a disability benefit from certain government programs, including benefits from Social Security. Because disability income plans are usually coordinated with Social Security, the tax credit available to most individuals who receive disability benefits from employer plans is substantially reduced or may be eliminated altogether.

Partially Contributory Plan. Under a partially contributory plan, benefits attributable to employee contributions are received free of income taxation. Benefits attributable to employer contributions are includible in gross income, but employees are eligible for the tax credit described previously.

The portion of the benefits attributable to employer contributions (and thus subject to income taxation) is based on the ratio of the employer's contributions to the total employer-employee contributions for an employee who has been under the plan for some period of time. For example, if the employer paid 75 percent of the cost of the plan, 75 percent of the benefits would be considered attributable to employer contributions and 25 percent to employee contributions. The time period used to calculate this percentage varies, depending on the type of disability income plan and the length of time that the plan has been in existence. Under group insurance policies, the time period used is the three policy years ending prior to the beginning of the calendar year in which the employee is disabled. If coverage has been in effect for a shorter time, IRS regulations specify the appropriate time period that should be used. Similar provisions pertain to contributory sick-leave plans. There is one major exception, however, that stipulates when the time period should be based on calendar years rather than policy years. If benefits are provided under individual disability income insurance policies, the proportion is determined on the basis of the premiums paid for the current policy year.

Tax Withholding and Social Security Taxes

Benefits paid directly to an employee by an employer under a sick-leave plan are treated like any other wages for purposes of tax withholding. Disability income benefits paid by a third party (for instance, an insurance company or a trust) are subject to the withholding tax rules and regulations only if the employee requests that taxes be withheld.

In both cases, benefits that are attributable to employer contributions are subject to Social Security and Medicare taxes. However, taxes are payable only during the last calendar month in which the employee worked and during the six months that follow.

■ STATE TAX TREATMENT

For income tax purposes, some states consider an individual's taxable income to be the figure shown on the individual's federal income tax return, and those states treat disability income and sick-leave benefits as the federal government does. Although considerable variations exist in other states, disability income and sick-leave benefits are generally treated more favorably than under the federal tax laws and are often totally exempt from state income taxation.

■ KEY TERMS

buy-up plan

catastrophic benefits rider

cost-of-living adjustment (COLA)

disability income benefits

exclusion

integrated disability management

long-term disability (LTD) income insurance

paid time off (PTO) program

partial disability

pension supplement

preexisting-conditions provision

rehabilitation provision

short-term disability (STD) income plans

sick-leave plan

waiting period

■ STUDY QUESTIONS

1. Why is it important to coordinate insured group disability income plans with other sources of disability income benefits?

2. Describe the approaches used to determine the duration of benefits under sick-leave plans.

3. Why are long-term disability income plans less likely to cover all employees than are short-term disability income plans?

4. What is the rationale for providing disability benefits that are less than an employee's earnings prior to disability?

5. Compare insured short-term and long-term disability income contracts with respect to

   a. definition of disability.

   b. coverage for partial disabilities.

   c. coverage for nonoccupational disabilities.

6. Compare insured short-term and long-term disability income contracts with respect to

   a. exclusions.

   b. waiting (elimination) period.

   c. duration of benefits.

   d. extent to which benefits are usually reduced for older employees.

   e. extent to which benefits are usually coordinated with other disability income benefits.

7. Lindsay Grant, who earns $1,600 per month, is covered under a group long-term disability income plan that provides benefits equal to 60 percent of predisability earnings. If disabled, she will also receive Social Security disability benefits of $780: $520 as her primary insurance amount and an additional $260 as a family benefit. If the group plan contains an integration provision that reduces benefits to the extent that the long-term disability income benefit and the primary insurance amount exceed 75 percent of earnings, how much will Lindsay receive from each source if she is disabled?

8. Describe the rehabilitation provision often found in long-term disability income contracts.

9. Explain how long-term disability income contracts are sometimes modified to provide

   a. a pension supplement.

   b. survivor benefits.

10. Under the federal income tax laws, to what extent are employer contributions for disability income insurance

    a. deductible to the employer?

    b. taxable as income to an employee?

Introduction to Medical Expense Benefits

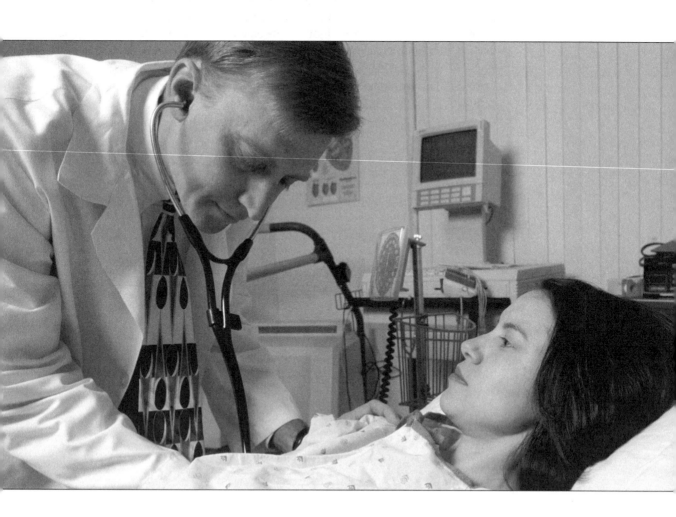

- Describe the development of medical expense coverage.
- Explain the reasons for the increasing cost of health care.
- Identify the measures used by employers to contain health care costs.
- Describe the possible approaches that have been proposed for a national health insurance program.
- Explain how the Health Insurance Portability and Accountability Act affects the availability of medical expense coverage.

CHAPTER OUTLINE

Comments on Terminology

Development of Medical Expense Coverage
Birth of the Blues
Early HMOs
Early Efforts of Insurance Companies
The 1960s—Era of Government Involvement
The 1970s—First Reactions to Spiraling Costs
The 1980s and 1990s—Continued Change
Into the New Millennium

Cost Containment
Benefit Plan Design
Alternative Providers
Alternative Funding Methods

Claims Review
Health Education and Preventive Care
Encouragement of External Cost-Control Systems
Managed Care
Consumer-Directed Health Care

State Reforms
NAIC Model
Other State Reforms

National Health Insurance
Some Basic Questions
Possible Approaches
Increased Availability of Medical Expense Coverage

The purpose of **medical expense insurance** is to provide protection against financial losses that result from medical bills because of accident and/or illness. Medical expense insurance is the most significant type of group insurance in terms of both the number of persons covered and the dollar outlay. With the exception of employers with a very small number of employees, virtually all employers offer some type of medical expense plan. In almost all cases, coverage identical to that offered for employees is also available for eligible dependents. In the absence of employee contributions, the cost of providing medical coverage for employees is several times greater for most employers than the combined cost of providing life insurance and disability income insurance.

Group medical expense contracts are not as standardized as group life insurance and group disability income insurance. Coverage may be provided through Blue Cross and Blue Shield plans, health maintenance organizations (HMOs), and preferred-provider organizations (PPOs), as well as insurance companies. In addition, a large and increasing percentage of the benefits is provided under plans that are partially or totally self-funded (self-insured). An overall medical expense plan may be limited to specific types of medical expenses, or it may be broad enough to cover almost all medical expenses. Even when broad coverage is available, benefits may be provided under either a single contract or a combination of contracts. Furthermore, in contrast to other types of group insurance, benefits may be in the form of services rather than cash payments. Finally, the skyrocketing cost of providing medical expense benefits over a long period of time has led to changes in coverage and plan design aimed at controlling these costs. Many of these changes have resulted in more similarities among the providers of medical expense coverage than existed in the past.

Over the past 15 years, two major issues—affordability and accessibility of medical care—have led to profound changes in the health care industry. Not only has there been a continued shift to managed care plans but the entire character of the health care industry has changed. Where once there was a distinction between the providers of care (such as doctors and hospitals) and the organizations that financed the care (such as insurers, the Blues, and HMOs), this distinction is becoming blurred. Physicians and hospitals are establishing HMOs and PPOs. Physicians may be employees of managed care plans. There are those who feel that in the not-too-distant future most Americans will receive their medical expense coverage from one of a small number of large organizations that both provide medical care and finance the cost of that care.

The issues surrounding medical care have also become a concern of government. Many states have enacted programs to make coverage available to the uninsured, including those who work for employers with a small number of employees. At the federal level, lively debate over health care has occurred and is likely to continue.

This chapter, the first of six chapters devoted to group medical expense coverage, discusses the following topics:

■ A brief history of the development of medical expense coverage and the environment in which this development continues to take place

■ An overview of the trend toward cost containment and managed care

■ State initiatives to make medical expense coverage more available

■ A discussion of national health insurance—the extent to which it already exists and proposals to expand its scope

Chapter 10 is devoted to traditional medical expense plans, and managed care approaches are discussed in Chapters 11 and 12. Consumer-directed medical expense plans are covered in Chapter 13. Common provisions of medical expense plans and the tax treatment of medical expense premiums and benefits are covered in Chapter 14.

■ COMMENTS ON TERMINOLOGY

Medical expense is often referred to as *health insurance*. However, in this book, **health insurance** is used in a broad sense to mean protection against the financial consequences of poor health. These consequences include incurring medical and dental bills. But poor health can also result in lost income and additional expenses. In this context, health insurance includes medical expense insurance, dental insurance, disability insurance, and long-term care insurance.

This introductory chapter on medical insurance briefly lays the groundwork for later chapters and introduces many terms. To precisely define all these terms at this point would defeat the purpose of a brief introduction. Some readers will be familiar with most of these terms. However, for readers who are not familiar, rest assured that these terms are soon defined and discussed in detail. In addition, this book contains an extensive glossary of terms just before the index.

■ DEVELOPMENT OF MEDICAL EXPENSE COVERAGE

To understand the wide array of medical expense plans available today, it is appropriate to review their historic development. There is further discussion of each type of plan in later chapters.

Until the 1930s, medical expenses were borne primarily by ill or injured persons or their families. It was not unusual, however, for hospitals and physicians to provide care on a charity basis if the patient lacked the resources to pay. What have been described as the earliest "health insurance" plans were in reality disability income coverage. At that time, however, medical costs were relatively low, and the continuation of income was often the difference between a person's ability to pay medical bills and the need to rely on charity.

Birth of the Blues

The Great Depression saw the development of the first organizations that would later be called Blue Cross plans. These organizations, which were initially controlled by hospitals, were designed to provide first-dollar coverage for hospital expenses, but with a limited duration of benefits. In the late 1930s, physicians followed the hospitals' approach and established Blue Shield plans. Through the 1940s, the Blues (the term used to describe these two types of plans) were the predominant providers of medical expense coverage.

Early HMOs

Although it is often thought that HMOs were a product of the 1970s, some HMOs were among the earliest providers of medical expense coverage. What is usually considered to be the first HMO, the Ross-Loos Clinic, was founded in Los Angeles in 1929. Other HMOs, such as the Kaiser Plans, had their beginnings in the 1930s. However, HMOs played only a small role in the marketplace for medical expense coverage until the past two decades.

Early Efforts of Insurance Companies

Insurance companies, seeing the success of Blue Cross, entered the market for hospital insurance in the 1930s and later added coverage for surgical expenses and physicians' expenses. However, insurance companies were only modestly successful in competing with the Blues until a new product was introduced in 1949—major medical insurance. As a result, by the mid-1950s insurance companies surpassed the Blues in premium volume and number of persons covered.

The 1960s—Era of Government Involvement

The number of persons covered by medical expense insurance plans grew rapidly during the 1950s and 1960s. Much of this growth was in employer-sponsored plans as a result of a 1949 Supreme Court ruling that employee benefits were subject to collective bargaining.

Although the types of products available underwent little change during this period, there were two major developments in the mid-1960s. For the first time, the federal government became a major player in providing medical expense coverage by creating national health insurance programs for the elderly and the poor. Medicare provides benefits for persons aged 65 and older. The financing of the benefits under this program comes from three sources: government revenue, premiums of Medicare beneficiaries, and the Social Security and Medicare taxes paid by most working persons and their employers.

The second program—**Medicaid**—provides health benefits for certain classes of low-income individuals and families. There is little doubt that both Medicare and Medicaid provide benefits to major segments of the population with large numbers of persons who would otherwise be unable to receive adequate medical care. However, the effect of so many additional persons with coverage beginning at the same time created shortages of medical facilities and professionals. This increased demand for medical care is one reason for the high rate of inflation for health care costs that soon developed.

The 1970s—First Reactions to Spiraling Costs

In 1950, expenditures for health care equaled 4.4 percent of the gross national product (GNP); they increased to 5.4 percent in 1960 and 7.3 percent in 1970. These spiraling costs received the attention of employers and the federal government. Large employers started turning to the self-funding of medical expense benefits. In addition to improved cash flow, savings were achieved by the avoidance of state-mandated benefits and state premium taxes. The passage of ERISA in 1974 thwarted initial state attempts to bring self-funded plans under their insurance regulations. This federal legislation freed self-funded plans from state regulation and hastened the growth of this financing technique.

The 1970s also saw the first large-scale debate over national health insurance. As in the mid-1990s, the majority of the members of Congress supported one of the many plans that were introduced, but opinions were diverse and little common ground was found. However, one significant piece of legislation was passed—the Health Mainte-nance Organization Act of 1973. This legislation sought to encourage the growth of HMOs by providing funding for their development costs and mandating that certain employers make these plans available to employees. There is little doubt that the growth of HMOs is a result of this legislation.

The 1980s and 1990s—Continued Change

Attempts to rein in the cost of medical care in the 1970s seemed to have little effect. By 1980, expenditures for health care reached 9.2 percent of GNP. This figure was 12.2 percent by 1990 and nearly 14 percent by the end of the decade. In addition, about 14 percent of the population, including many employed persons and their families, remained uninsured.

Reactions to these statistics came from many sources. Many state governments adopted programs to make coverage more available and affordable to the uninsured. At the federal level, there were suggestions that the entire health care system needed an overhaul. Although the national health insurance proposal of the Clinton administra-tion was not adopted, there was still continued support by members of Congress for changes in the nation's approach to providing and financing health care. Significant federal legislation was enacted in 1996, but little new and significant legislation was enacted until 2003.

The many efforts by employers to contain costs included the following:

- Growth in the self-funding of benefits. Much of this growth came from small- and medium-sized employers.

- Cost-shifting to employees. It became increasingly common for employers to raise deductibles and require employees to pay a larger portion of their medical expense coverage.

- Requiring or encouraging managed care plans. Some employers dropped traditional medical expense plans and offered managed care alternatives only. A more prevalent approach was to offer employees a financial incentive to join managed care plans.

- Increased use of managed care plans that are alternatives to HMOs, such as PPOs and point-of-service plans. These approaches often overcome the reluctance of some employees to participate in managed care plans.

Many of these reactions are reflected in the changing prevalence of varying types of medical expense coverage; unfortunately, however, precise data are difficult to obtain. For example, many Blue Cross and Blue Shield plans and HMOs report only the total number of persons covered and make no distinction between individual coverage and group coverage. Many persons receive portions of their coverage from different types of provid-ers, such as hospital coverage from a Blue Cross plan and other medical expense coverages from an insurance company under a supplemental major medical contract. In addition, self-funded plans may operate as HMOs, purchase stop-loss coverage, and/or utilize PPOs.

Even though precise data cannot be obtained, there is no doubt that a significant change took place in the 1990s. In 1980, approximately 90 percent of all insured workers were covered under "traditional" medical expense plans, and 5 percent were covered under HMOs. Under a traditional plan, if a worker or family member was sick, he or she had complete freedom in choosing a doctor or a hospital. Medical bills were paid by the plan, and no attempts were made to control costs or the utilization of services. It is estimated that between 10 percent and 15 percent of the employees under these traditional plans were in plans that were totally self-funded by the employer; the remainder of the employees were split fairly evenly between plans written by insurance companies and the Blues.

By the end of the 1990s, the figures had changed dramatically, with the majority of employees covered under plans that control costs and the access to medical care. More than 90 percent of employees were enrolled in managed care plans—either HMOs, PPOs, or point-of-service plans often owned by insurance companies or the Blues. Of the remaining employees, few were in traditional plans. Many were still with insurance companies and the Blues, but under traditional plans that had been redesigned to incorporate varying degrees of managed care.

One important change is hidden in these statistics—the increasing trend toward self-funding of medical expenses by employers. It is estimated that more than 50 percent of all workers are covered under plans that are totally or substantially self-funded. Self-funding is more prevalent as the number of employees increases, with between 80 percent and 90 percent of persons who work for employers with more than 20,000 employees being covered under self-funded plans. However, employers with as few as 25 to 50 employees also use self-funding. It should be noted that the way benefits are provided under a self-funded plan can vary—the employer may design the plan to provide benefits on a traditional basis or as an HMO or PPO.

Despite the difficulty in obtaining precise statistics, the data collected by the Kaiser Family Foundation[1] is similar to that found in surveys conducted by other organizations. The Kaiser survey shows that enrollment in medical expense plans that can be characterized as traditional plans dropped from more than 70 percent to 5 percent since 1990. During the same time period, the number of enrollees in plans that use PPOs increased significantly to 54 percent. Point-of-service plans and HMOs grew more slowly and now account for about 24 percent and 17 percent, respectively, of the number of enrollees.

Into the New Millennium

Just as in past decades, the health care system will continue to evolve in the first decade of the new millennium. What the changes will be is only speculation, but a few observations can be made about the current environment:

■ Renewal rates in 2002 and 2003 for employer-provided medical expense plans increased at the highest percentage since the early 1990s; these high percentage increases are predicted to continue in the foreseeable future.

■ Surveys indicate that a large majority of Americans are satisfied with their own health care plans. The relatively low degree of dissatisfaction, however, is higher for plans with the greatest degree of managed care.

■ Despite satisfaction with their own coverage, surveys also indicate that Americans are becoming less satisfied with and less confident about the health care system.

■ There is still a backlash against managed care, particularly HMOs. Two observations can be made about this trend. First, many persons appear to have based their opinions on media reports and stories from friends, not on their own experiences. In this regard, opinions about managed care and Congress tend to be somewhat similar, with a high percentage of negative attitudes. However, most persons give high ratings to their own managed care plans and their own congresspersons. Second, this backlash has gotten the attention of Congress and the states. Some legislation has resulted at the state level. Managed care plans, however, are also becoming increasingly flexible and consumer friendly, possibly to prevent further legislation aimed at managed care reform. Managed care reform is discussed in Chapter 11.

■ Until 2003, there had been little federal health care legislation during the previous few years. In Clinton's second term, this was at least partially due to a congressional majority of a different political party from the president. Although there seemed to be bipartisan agreement that there were some problems with the current system, there was bipartisan disagreement about what should be done. Initially, it looked like the situation might change during the early months of the Bush administration, but the congressional agenda was initially altered as a result of the terrorist attacks of September 2001 and a faltering domestic economy. However, this changed in 2003 with the passage of the Medicare Prescription Drug, Improvement, and Modernization Act. Not only did this legislation make the most significant changes to Medicare since its enactment in 1965, it also encouraged the growth of consumer-directed medical expense plans with the creation of health savings accounts.

■ COST CONTAINMENT

Between 1970 and the early 1990s, the average annual increases in the cost of medical care were approximately twice the average annual increases in the consumer price index. No single factor accounts for these increases. Rather, it was a combination of the following reasons:

■ Technological advances. Many exciting technological advances took place. Numerous lives are now being saved by such techniques as CAT scans, MRIs, fetal monitoring, and organ transplants. As miraculous as many of these techniques are, they are also very expensive. Technological advances can also prolong the life of the terminally ill and increase associated medical expenses.

■ Increasing malpractice suits. The providers of care were much more likely to be sued than in the past, and malpractice awards outpaced the general rate of inflation. This development resulted in higher malpractice insurance premiums, a cost that is ultimately passed on to consumers. The increase in malpractice suits also led to an increase in defensive medicine, with routine tests likely to be performed more often.

■ Design of medical expense plans. Many medical expense plans provided first-dollar coverage or had low out-of-pocket costs for many health care services. There was often little incentive for patients to avoid the most expensive forms of treatment.

■ Increases in third-party payments. Private health insurers or the government paid a growing portion of the country's health care expenditures. The expansion of coverage and benefits shielded providers and patients from the true cost of health care.

■ Underutilization of medical facilities. The United States had an overabundance of hospital beds, and a surplus of physicians was also beginning to develop. Empty hospital beds are expensive to maintain, and an oversupply of physicians tends to drive up the average costs of medical procedures so that physicians' average income does not decrease.

■ AIDS. The increase in the number of AIDS cases resulted in increasing costs to employers. Costs in excess of $100,000 for an employee with AIDS are not unusual.

■ An aging population. The incidence of illness increases with age. Current demographics indicate that this trend will be a source of cost increases for several years to come.

During the period from 1994 to 1996, several factors caused the cost of medical expense coverage to remain uncharacteristically stable, particularly for managed care plans. Many providers of medical services and medical expense plans were reluctant to raise costs while the health care proposal of the Clinton administration was being debated. In addition, managed care plans were holding down premiums while actively increasing enrollments.

However, the late 1990s started to see significant increases in health care costs, particularly because of skyrocketing costs for prescription drugs. There is a feeling among benefit consultants that managed care plans have saturated the market to the point that savings resulting from additional employees moving to managed care plans will be modest. There is also an interesting trend occurring among medical providers. The large number of mergers of hospitals and other providers of medical services in many parts of the country may in fact shift the balance of bargaining power to these providers from managed care plans and other buyers of medical services. In addition, costs will increase somewhat because of federal and state legislation that continues to mandate benefits.

Increasing health care costs have become the concern of almost everyone—government, labor, employers, and consumers. In this introduction to cost containment, many of the measures employers use are enumerated. Some of the following measures are discussed in more detail throughout the next four chapters (with others discussed later in the book):

■ Benefit plan design

■ Alternative providers

■ Alternative funding methods

■ Claims review

■ Health education and preventive care

■ Encouragement of external cost-control systems

■ Managed care

■ Consumer-directed plans

Benefit Plan Design

Numerous design features of a medical expense plan can control costs. These have traditionally been in the form of contractual provisions that shift costs to employees. Examples are

■ deductibles,

■ coinsurance,

■ copayments,

■ exclusions and limitations, and

■ maximum benefits.

In recent years, design features have been aimed at reducing costs rather than shifting them. In fact, benefit plans are often structured to provide a higher level of benefits if less costly alternatives are used. Examples of these cost-containment features are

■ preadmission testing,

■ second surgical opinions,

■ coordination of benefits,

■ the use of alternatives to hospitals (such as skilled-nursing facilities, home health care, hospice care, birthing centers, and ambulatory care centers), and

■ the use of medical savings accounts and other consumer-directed medical expense plans.

Alternative Providers

The use of HMOs and PPOs has been popular for some years as a cost-containment method. These methods have now been joined by point-of-service plans, usually designed as variations of HMOs. HMOs are described in more detail in Chapter 11 and PPOs in Chapter 12.

Alternative Funding Methods

Employers are increasingly turning to funding methods that are alternatives to the traditional insurance company plan or Blue Cross and Blue Shield plan. Chapter 16 is devoted to a discussion of these techniques.

Claims Review

There is no doubt that claims review can generate substantial cost savings. In general, the employer does not do this review. Rather, the provider of medical expense benefits, a third-party administrator, or some independent outside organization performs this function. At a minimum, claims should be reviewed for patient eligibility, eligibility of the services provided, duplicate policies, and charges that are in excess of usual, customary, and reasonable amounts. Many medical expense plans routinely audit hospital bills, particularly those that exceed some stipulated amount, such as $5,000 or $10,000. They check for errors in such items as length of stay, services performed, and billed charges. Many insurance companies have found that each dollar spent on this type of review results in two or three dollars of savings.

Good claims review should also look at ongoing claims. For example, is hospice care or home health care a less expensive alternative to hospitalization? Many providers of medical expense benefits pay for such alternative forms of treatment even if they are not specifically covered under the medical expense plan as long as their cost is lower than the cost of continued hospitalization.

Health Education and Preventive Care

Persons who lead healthy lifestyles tend to have fewer medical bills, particularly at younger ages. Healthier employees save an employer money by taking fewer sick days and having fewer disability claims. For these reasons, employers are increasingly establishing wellness programs and employee-assistance plans, both of which are discussed in Chapter 18. With increasing health awareness among the general population, the existence of these programs has a positive side effect—the improvement of employee morale.

Encouragement of External Cost-Control Systems

Although a certain degree of cost containment is within the control of employers, the proper control of costs is an ongoing process that requires participation by consumers (both employers and individuals), government, and the providers of health care services. Many agencies and committees of the Department of Health and Human Services carry out these activities at the federal level. This government department has the primary responsibility for identifying health care needs, monitoring resources, establishing priorities, recommending courses of action, and overseeing laws that pertain to health care.

At the state and local level, many employers are active in coalitions whose purpose is to control costs and improve the quality of health care. These groups—which may also involve unions, providers of health care, insurance companies, and regulators—are often catalysts for legislation, such as laws authorizing PPOs and establishing hospital budget-review programs. Some coalitions act as purchasing groups to negotiate lower-cost coverage for members. For example, one Midwestern coalition consists of several large corporations and offers a uniform health plan to the 50,000 employees of its members. The plan is self-funded by the coalition and utilizes the services of about

1,000 primary care physicians and 4,000 specialists. Another coalition, an example of a different approach, represents over 10,000 companies with fewer than 150 employees each. The coalition negotiates with providers of medical expense coverage and offers its members a choice of about a dozen different group plans. The annual increase in cost to coalition members has been significantly less than the annual increase in cost for other companies in the area that do not belong to the coalition.

Managed Care

For many years, the buzzword with respect to cost containment has been **managed care**. In a general sense, the term can be defined to include any medical expense plan that attempts to contain costs by controlling the behavior of participants. However, in practice many persons use the term to mean different things. At one extreme are traditional plans that require second opinions and/or hospital precertification. At the other extreme are HMOs and PPOs that limit a participant's choice of medical providers, negotiate provider fees, and manage utilization of medical services.

Managed care plans have evolved over the last few years. Today, it is generally felt that a true managed care plan should have five basic characteristics:

1. *Controlled access to providers.* It is difficult to control costs if participants have unrestricted access to physicians and hospitals. Managed care plans attempt to encourage or force participants to use specified providers. Because a major portion of medical expenses results from referrals to specialists, managed care plans tend to use primary care physicians as gatekeepers to determine the necessity and appropriateness of specialty care. By limiting the number of providers, managed care plans are better able to control costs by negotiating provider fees.

2. *Comprehensive utilization management.* Successful managed care plans perform utilization review at all levels. This involves reviewing a case to determine the type of treatment necessary, monitoring ongoing care, and reviewing the appropriateness and success of treatment after it has been given.

3. *Preventive care.* Managed care plans encourage preventive care and the attainment of healthier lifestyles.

4. *Risk sharing.* Managed care plans are most successful if providers share in the financial consequences of medical decisions. Newer managed care plans have contractual guarantees to encourage cost-effective care. For example, a physician who minimizes diagnostic tests may receive a bonus. Ideally, such an arrangement will eliminate unnecessary tests, not discourage tests that should be performed.

5. *High-quality care.* A managed care plan is not well received nor often selected by participants if there is a perception of inferior or inconvenient medical care. In the past, too little attention was paid to this aspect of cost containment. Newer managed care plans not only select providers more carefully but also monitor the quality of care on a continuing basis.

There seems to be a reasonable consensus among employers and benefit specialists that there is a negative correlation between benefit costs and the degree of managed care—that is, the greater the degree of managed care, the lower the cost. For example, studies generally rank benefit plans in the following order (from highest to lowest) with respect to annual benefit costs:

- Traditional insurance company and Blue Cross and Blue Shield plans without utilization management
- Traditional insurance company and Blue Cross and Blue Shield plans with utilization management
- PPOs
- Point-of-service plans
- Independent practice association HMOs
- Closed-panel HMOs

It is interesting to note that the degree of managed care increases as one goes down the list. There also seems to be a high correlation between annual benefit costs and the rate of cost increases. For example, the cost of traditional benefit plans has been increasing recently at an annual rate in excess of the annual increase in cost for closed-panel HMOs.

Consumer-Directed Health Care

The beginning of the new decade has seen considerable interest in the concept of consumer-directed health care. With this approach, employees are put in charge of managing the health care dollars provided by their employers. It exposes employees to the true cost of care and involves them in keeping health care expenditures under control.

Chapter 13 is devoted to a discussion of consumer-directed medical expense plans.

■ STATE REFORMS

Often overlooked in the debate over national health policy is the role of the states in health care reform. In recent years, all states have passed some type of legislation to make medical expense coverage more available and less costly to certain segments of the population. Some of this legislation has been incorporated into both proposed and enacted legislation at the federal level. There has been and continues to be considerable support in Congress for having the states, rather than the federal government, take the initiative in health care reform.

State reforms fall into two categories. One category is laws and regulations aimed at uninsured individuals other than employees. These are not discussed in this book. The other category is those laws and regulations that constitute what is commonly referred to as *small-group reform.* It is in these groups of fewer than 25 or 50 employees that the majority of employees without employer-sponsored coverage is found. Most states have passed National Association of Insurance Commissioners (NAIC) model legislation, and a few states have gone even farther with other types of legislation. Unfortunately, the results seem to be somewhat mixed. Some states report modest results, but the national percentage of employees with medical coverage under small-employer plans has remained static. In addition, several insurers no longer choose to write business for small groups because of the limitations imposed by the legislation. Although coverage is still more readily available, the legislation does not make it more affordable. Some small employers cannot afford to pay a significant share of the cost for their employees, and the employee share under contributory plans is often in excess of what employees can or are willing to pay.

NAIC Model

The most common approach to state reform has been the adoption of one of the versions of the NAIC Small Employer Health Insurance Availability Model Act. The stated purpose and intent of the model act are the following:

- To promote the availability of health insurance to small employers regardless of their health status or claims experience
- To prevent abusive rating practices
- To require disclosure of rating practices to purchasers
- To establish rules regarding renewability of coverage
- To establish limitations on the use of preexisting-conditions exclusions
- To provide for development of basic and standard health benefit plans to be offered to all small employers
- To provide for establishment of a reinsurance program
- To improve the overall fairness and efficiency of the small-group health insurance market

Although some provisions of the model act may result in lower costs for certain employers, the main emphasis of the model act is on the availability of coverage, not on the employer's or employees' ability to afford the coverage.

While the following discussion focuses on the provisions of the NAIC model act, it is important to remember that states often adopt model acts with variations. Some of the more significant variations are described.

Plans Subject to the Act.   The model act defines a *small employer* as one who had 25 or fewer employees working on at least 50 percent of the days during the previous calendar quarter. Several states extend their legislation to employers with as many as 50 employees and/or exclude groups of one or two employees.

The model act applies to most medical expense products provided by insurance companies, HMOs, and prepaid service plans such as Blue Cross and Blue Shield. Certain types of coverage are specifically excluded from the act's provisions: dental insurance, vision insurance, Medicare supplements, long-term care insurance, and disability income insurance. In addition, voluntary plans of individual medical expense insurance under which the employer pays no portion of the cost may or may not be subject to a specific state's legislation.

The small-group legislation does not force the providers of medical expense coverage to operate in the small-employer market. However, if a provider of coverage does sell medical expense coverage to small employers, the provisions of the legislation must be followed.

Benefit Provisions. The model act establishes a committee that represents providers of medical expense coverage, employers, employees, health care practitioners, and agents to recommend the form and level of coverage to be made available to small employers. The committee must recommend a basic plan and a more comprehensive standard plan and make decisions regarding benefit levels, cost-sharing levels, exclusions, and limitations. In designing the basic plan, the committee can ignore any state mandates for benefits unless the small-group legislation specifically requires them.

Preexisting-conditions provisions are allowed but with limitations. A medical condition can be treated as preexisting if it was treated (or if a prudent person would have sought treatment) within a specified prior period, which cannot exceed six months. Coverage for preexisting conditions cannot be excluded for more than 12 months following the effective date of coverage. Preexisting conditions must be covered as any other medical conditions if a person had benefits for the medical condition under a prior medical expense plan for at least 90 continuous days prior to the effective date of the new coverage.

One unfortunate and probably unintended side effect of the small-group legislation is that the policies that must be made available in many states are very precisely prescribed, making it impossible for insurance companies to use the same policies in multiple states. The expense of designing and refiling policies for many states, coupled with rate controls and the inability to underwrite for medical conditions, has resulted in several insurers leaving the small-group market.

Underwriting. With few exceptions, coverage must be written for all small employers. An insurance company or other provider of medical expense coverage is permitted to have requirements for minimum participation and minimum employer contributions as long as these requirements are the same for all similarly sized groups. These requirements cannot be increased after an employer has been accepted for coverage.

Coverage must be made available to all employees and their dependents. However, persons who did not enroll when initially eligible can be denied coverage for up to 18 months or have coverage excluded for preexisting conditions for up to 18 months.

Rates and Renewability. The model act prescribes a procedure for determining an "index rate" to be charged by each provider of medical expense coverage. Under certain circumstances, such as the use of more than one type of marketing system, the provider can use different rates for different classes of business to reflect substantial differences in expected claims experience or administrative costs. However, the index rate for any class of business cannot be more than 20 percent higher than the index rate for any other class of business.

Although the act allows rate differences among groups due to variations in age, gender, industry, geographic area, family composition, and group size, far fewer refinements are allowed than would be the case without this legislation. Some states have adopted more restrictive legislation and require community rating.

At annual renewals, rates can be increased because of changes in the index rate, changes in the mix of employees, and possibly group experience. In the latter case, the size of the adjustment is limited to a modest amount. The provider of medical expense coverage must renew all policies subject to certain exceptions, such as nonpayment of premium or the failure to meet any minimum participation requirement. The provider may also elect not to renew all policies for small employers in a state. However, proper notification (usually 180 days) must be given to the insurance commissioner and all employers.

Relation to Federal Legislation.   The Health Insurance Portability and Accountability Act (HIPAA) contains provisions that are similar to many provisions of the NAIC model act. State law continues to apply to insured medical expense plans unless it interferes with the federal legislation. Provisions of the state law supersede the federal legislation if they are more generous toward insured individuals. For example, the maximum allowable length of preexisting-conditions periods may be shorter in some states than under the federal legislation.

Other State Reforms

Other reforms passed by the states:

- Tort reform. Several states have passed legislation to control medical malpractice suits. This legislation ranges from limiting recovery for noneconomic loss to mandatory arbitration.

- Claim administration reform. A few states now require the use of standardized claim forms, including a uniform system of coding diagnoses and procedures.

- The establishment of health insurance purchasing cooperatives (HIPCs). Several states have laws that establish HIPCs, entities that act as brokers between the purchasers and providers of medical expense coverage. They negotiate alternative plans of coverage on the basis of price and quality. Those eligible to use the HIPC, which may vary from all purchasers to small employers only, may elect one of the available plans directly from the HIPC. With some HIPCs, an employer deals directly with the cooperative without using agents or brokers. In one state, however, an employer can purchase coverage through an agent or broker or deal directly with the cooperative and receive a discount equal to the commission that would be paid to an agent or broker. An unexpected result of this arrangement is that almost 70 percent of the employers have elected to use an agent or broker. Clearly, these employers feel that the services agents and brokers provide are worth the extra cost.

A few states have considered the adoption of even more radical reforms to the health care market, such as the adoption of single-payer plans, which are discussed in the next section of this chapter.

■ NATIONAL HEALTH INSURANCE

Few issues in recent years have gotten as much attention as the debate over national health insurance. With health care expenditures taking nearly one of every six dollars spent in this country and about 15 percent of the population without adequate coverage for medical expenses, the magnitude of the problem cannot be overemphasized. There are no easy solutions to the problems of increasing costs and the lack of coverage for everyone. Health care is an emotional issue, and any reform will be complex and affect almost all Americans to varying degrees.

The following discussion of national health insurance does not give any precise answers or solutions. Rather, it addresses many aspects of the issue, describes some approaches suggested for solving current problems, and attempts to predict what is most feasible in the short term. The major goal of this discussion is to provide readers with a better framework for following—and perhaps participating in—the debate that will undoubtedly continue for many years to come.

Some Basic Questions

The issue of national health insurance is best addressed by having an understanding of its many dimensions. This discussion is organized around several questions, not all of which have precise or easy answers.

Don't We Already Have National Health Insurance? The answer is yes for many Americans. Unlike most other industrialized countries, however, the United States does not have a system of national health insurance that covers everyone. Although national health insurance does exist in the form of Medicare, Medicaid, certain veterans' benefits, and coverage of military personnel and their families, each of these programs addresses the issue of health insurance for a specific group and each takes a different approach.

Some people would say that most other Americans are also covered under a national health insurance program. Although the role of the federal government is probably not extensive enough for most persons to agree with this observation, the federal government does in fact have an influence on the design of employer-provided medical expense plans of almost all but the smallest employers. This influence comes from numerous pieces of federal legislation, such as ERISA, COBRA, the Family and Medical Leave Act, the Age Discrimination in Employment Act, the Americans with Disabilities Act, and HIPAA.

Many Americans feel that the federal government should have no role in health care reform. But approximately 50 percent of all medical care expenditures are for persons who are either employees of the federal government or covered under the national health insurance programs previously mentioned. Therefore, the government and the taxpayers who fund its activities have a direct stake in controlling the cost of medical care. Nevertheless it is easy for many observers to become a bit cynical when they compare their own medical expense plan with the generous plan available to members of Congress.

What Is the Objective of National Health Insurance? It is difficult to determine exactly what a national health insurance program should accomplish. Alternative proposals either have different objectives or place varying degrees of emphasis on a combination of objectives. There are two primary concerns with the current health care system—rapidly increasing costs and the lack of coverage for a large segment of the population. Some programs are essentially a proposed solution to only one of these concerns; other proposals address both concerns in varying degrees. It would be much easier to find a solution if there were consensus on the scope of the actual problem.

Unfortunately, the two problems are not independent, and solving one problem may actually exacerbate the other. For example, making broad coverage available to everyone might so increase the demand for medical treatment that costs would go up because of a shortage of medical care providers. This situation occurred after the passage of Medicare and Medicaid. In addition, efforts to control costs could lead to rationing of medical care so that some types of care would be available only to the more affluent segment of the population who could afford supplemental insurance protection.

Do Americans Want Reform? This is a difficult question to answer. During health care debates over the last few years, numerous polls were taken. There seemed to be overwhelming agreement among the American people that the health care system is broken and needs fixing. Some proponents of national health insurance inferred from this opinion that there was support for radical reform.

As the debate continued and more polls about the underlying mood of the public were conducted, a different picture began to emerge. Most Americans were happy with their own medical expense coverage. They were also aware of rapidly rising costs, but those in managed care plans had been less significantly affected by them. In fact, as many employees elected managed care options, they actually saw their out-of-pocket medical expenses decrease. Although the public was not in favor of changes that would affect their relationships with providers of medical care, a surprisingly large percentage of the public was aware that reform carried a financial cost, and within limits many Americans were willing to foot the bill.

These further surveys also indicated that the major concern of Americans was the lack of security surrounding their own medical expense coverage, particularly if they became unemployed or changed jobs. There was fear that the loss of employment would put them in the category of uninsured. Even if coverage could be continued under COBRA, its high cost would make it unaffordable. Considerable concern was also expressed over the lack of coverage when changing jobs because of preexisting-conditions provisions in the new employer's coverage. Although Congress is often considered out of touch with the electorate, these, in fact, were significant issues addressed by recent major health insurance legislation.

One final observation: These surveys showed that the majority of Americans do not want another program as bureaucratic as they view Medicare to be.

Is the Goal Universal Coverage or Universal Access? Some national health insurance programs call for **universal coverage,** which means that all Americans would be covered. Unfortunately the cost of universal coverage would be very expensive, and it is questionable whether such a program could be accomplished voluntarily. As long as some people are in a position of voluntarily electing coverage, there are those who would be unwilling to pay the price, even if it were subsidized. Therefore, universal coverage probably requires a program similar to Medicare and the accompanying tax revenue to support the program. With the majority of the public wanting a nongovernment program of health insurance, many other national health insurance proposals focus on universal access and realize that a goal of slightly less than universal coverage is all that is realistically attainable. But even this goal will require subsidies for some segments of the population.

Who Should Pay the Cost? A majority of the uninsured have inadequate resources to pay the cost of voluntary coverage, even if it were suddenly available. As a result, there will be some need to subsidize the cost of coverage if the number of uninsured is going to be reduced substantially. Who pays? The alternatives are many, but they can largely be summed up in one word—*taxes.* There have been numerous suggestions about the form of these taxes, but in all cases they will fall on some or all taxpayers. These alternatives include general tax revenue, additional Social Security taxes, and taxes on cigarettes because smoking is the source of many medical problems.

The fact that many of the uninsured do receive medical treatment is sometimes overlooked. Even though uninsured persons may be unable to pay, treatment by hospitals and physicians is usually not denied for serious illnesses or injuries. However, when the hospital or physician writes off a large portion of these bills as uncollectible, the cost is in effect being passed on to those who do pay their bills (usually through insurance) in the form of higher charges than would otherwise be made. In theory, the cost to many individuals or employers will decrease if a larger portion of the population has the resources to pay their own expenses. This is used as the rationale for taxing employers or individuals to pay the cost of providing protection for the uninsured.

What Benefits Should Be Available? One of the major debates in designing a national health insurance program involves the scope of the benefits that will be included. At one extreme in the debate are those who feel the government should guarantee only a minimum level of health care. Private medical expense insurance or personal resources would be necessary to obtain broader benefits. At the other extreme are those who feel that a comprehensive level of health care should be available to all Americans. This group views complete health care protection as a basic right that belongs to everyone regardless of income.

The current system of health insurance falls somewhere between these two extremes, and this is probably where any ultimate solution will be found. Most Americans do not have coverage for long-term care; many have limitations on such benefits as mental health and substance abuse treatments. Some plans limit coverage for prescription drugs. Such limitations exist not because employers see no value in these benefits but because realistic cost constraints dictate the benefits that are provided. Employers cannot afford a medical expense plan that does everything for everyone, and it is questionable whether Americans are willing to pay the cost of a national health insurance program that has such a lofty goal.

Another issue is whether a uniform package of benefits should be available nation-wide. Under some proposals, benefits would be determined on a state-by-state basis;

under others, a national benefit standard would be established for the plans of employers. These proposals typically call for the abolishment of state benefit mandates.

Does Cost Containment Harm Quality? Although there are undoubtedly inefficiencies in the health care system, many of these inefficiencies have been addressed in recent years. For example, hospitals, faced with limits on Medicare and Medicaid reimbursements, have had to operate in a more cost-effective manner. However, future efforts to control costs probably need to be more severe and may come with a high price. Americans arguably have the best and most innovative health care system in the world. Can this quality be continued if prices are controlled? Or will it continue only for those who have additional resources to pay? Control of costs, if taken beyond a certain point, will lead to the situation that exists in most countries with national health insurance programs—rationing of medical care. Questions like the following will then need to be answered: Should organ transplants be limited to persons under age 50? Should very expensive health care continue to be provided to premature babies who have a less than 25 percent chance of survival? To what extent should medical treatment be provided to persons with AIDS and other terminal illnesses? Will controls on the cost of prescription drugs eliminate the resources needed to develop the next generation of medicines?

Are Employer Mandates the Proper Approach? National health care proposals differ with respect to the employer's role in making coverage available to its employees. Some proposals argue for an **employer mandate,** which would require virtually all employers to make coverage available to employees (including part-time employees) and their dependents and to pay a portion of the cost. Under all such proposals, there are additional programs for the unemployed and subsidies to some employers for whom the cost exceeds a certain limit. However, small employers would be hit hard by most of these proposals and have lobbied against employer mandates. There is considerable support for the argument that the cost of employer mandates would result in some small employers going out of business.

One major argument for employer mandates that has been used, however, is that the alternative is a government-run program with its accompanying bureaucracy.

What Is the Role of Medicare and Medicaid? Many differences exist over the role of Medicare and Medicaid in health care reform. Although some argue for a single system to cover all Americans, opponents argue that the Medicare and Medicaid programs serve specific groups and are working reasonably well. Why alter the part of the system that is already closest to the concept of universal coverage?

National health insurance proposals are much more likely to fold Medicaid recipients into a new program than they are to include Medicare recipients. This fact reflects the reality that tinkering with Medicare can have grave consequences because of the high turnout of older voters.

What Are the Political Realities? The possibility of any national health insurance program depends on whether Congress can design a program that receives broad-based support. Although a Republican administration is unlikely to offer solutions that are as far-reaching as the proposal of the Clinton administration and that will offend as many segments of society, public clamor for change will undoubtedly lead to continued reform of the current health care system, modest though it may be. Clearly any change will be designed to appeal to a different class of constituents. Although the initial Clinton administration's proposal appealed to such groups as organized labor, the Republicans are much more likely to be influenced by the concerns of small businesses. However, no program will be successful and politically palatable unless it receives support from many diverse groups, including employers, insurers, hospitals, physicians, drug companies, and the general public.

Possible Approaches

One difficulty for the author of any textbook is the extent to which current proposals should be covered in detail. In a debate like the continuing one occurring over health insurance, new proposals are continually replacing old ones, and those that are around for any length of time undergo revision. For this reason, the discussion is general and describes the following generic approaches that are being discussed:

- Managed competition plans
- Single-payer plans
- Reform on a state-by-state basis
- Modest reform of the current system

It is important to remember that the use of any one of these approaches does not dictate a specific national health insurance plan. Within each approach, there is wide latitude to address many of the issues that have been discussed in the previous pages.

Managed Competition Plans. The term **managed competition** received considerable attention because it was the approach taken by the Clinton administration in designing its initial national health insurance proposal. However, the term and the concept have been discussed since the 1970s. The basic philosophy behind the idea of managed competition is that competition for medical expense insurance should be based on price rather than on the risk characteristics of those needing coverage. A managed competition plan would create a new type of organization—often referred to as a **health insurance purchasing cooperative (HIPC)**. An HIPC would act as a purchasing agent and negotiate with insurance companies, HMOs, and other providers of medical expense coverage to offer a menu of different insurance plans to employers and individuals who subscribe to the HIPC. In addition to price, subscribers would be given information on each plan's quality of care. Note that some states have now adopted HIPCs, as was discussed earlier in this chapter. In addition, this is similar to the approach used by the Federal Employees Health Benefits Program.

Under most managed care proposals, HIPCs would be established under state regulation, would operate in a specified geographic region, and would not compete with each other. Some proposals require that all employers be subscribers to the HIPC in their area, which would be the only source for providing coverage to employees. To varying degrees, however, most managed competition proposals allow larger employers to establish their own HIPCs for self-funding benefits.

All employers (and also unemployed and self-employed persons) would be eligible for coverage from the HIPC, and there would be no preexisting-conditions provisions for employees. Some proposals use community rating, which would establish a set price per covered person for the plan selected. Other proposals would adjust rates by such factors as age or gender.

Although individual proposals for national health insurance may vary, there is nothing in the basic idea of managed competition that dictates any specific benefit package, level of employer contribution to the cost of the coverage for employees, or government price controls.

There are many critics of managed competition. Because it involves a fundamental change in the delivery of health care, managed competition has been opposed by many physicians who fear that their ability to treat patients will come under government control. Insurance agents have been particularly vocal because their role would be virtually eliminated. However, there would still be a modest role for benefit consultants to advise employers on the selection of alternative plans under the HIPC. HIPCs are also unappealing to persons who are not already in managed care plans and wish to retain control over their choice of medical practitioners. Employers that operate in many regions would also be required to deal with several HIPCs.

Managed competition has also been criticized for creating another level of health care bureaucracy by the formation of HIPCs and the additional regulation that would be needed. It has been suggested that this might also negate the effect of any cost-saving features of the approach.

Single-Payer Plans. Several proposals for national health insurance can be categorized as single-payer plans, which is the approach taken in Canada and many European countries. Under a **single-payer plan**, a single program run by the government automatically covers everyone, and the same benefit package is provided to everyone. Some proposals have a totally federal program; other proposals call for each state to administer the program for its residents, but under specific federal guidelines.

Single-payer plans eliminate the employer's role in providing medical expense benefits to employees. The agent's role is also eliminated unless the plan benefits are at a level where there is a market for supplemental insurance. However, most proposals call for very comprehensive coverage with few if any copayments.

Most proposals for a single-payer plan call for the financing of the program through taxes rather than premiums. Although the taxes could take a variety of forms, a Social Security type of payroll tax on both employers and employees is most commonly mentioned.

In some respects, a single-payer plan can be viewed as a Medicare-type program that covers everyone. The single-payer approach, however, goes further and calls for more government control of medical care. A national health care budget would be established, and reimbursement schedules to providers would be determined at the state or federal level within the constraints of this budget. In addition, the budget would result in the government's exercising controls over the types of treatment available for specific conditions and the extent to which monies would be spent on new technology and medical facilities. In effect, a single-payer plan rejects market forces as the allocator of medical resources and implies that there would be some rationing of medical care under government guidelines.

Although the broad nature of a single-payer plan would result in additional costs because of increased demand for health care, these costs would be offset by efficiencies associated with the approach. For example, the claim process would be dramatically streamlined, and marketing costs would be virtually eliminated. Furthermore, the widespread availability of medical care would probably lead to more preventive care, which would minimize the need for more expensive treatments in the future.

Much of the support for a single-payer approach to the health care problem arises from the perception that Americans have of the Canadian health care system. There is no doubt that Canadians overwhelmingly believe they have a good system, but just as in the United States the system is becoming a subject of national debate. Costs are lower than in the United States, but they are increasing at a rapid rate. Moreover, there is rationing of care, which can lead to lengthy waits to schedule surgeries. As a result, some Canadians come to the United States for treatment that privately insured Americans can receive on demand. These facts, coupled with the American public's concern over bigger government and its bureaucracy, make the adoption of a single-payer approach unlikely.

State Reform.   There is increasing support in Congress for the idea that national health insurance should take the form of a series of state programs rather than a single federal program. This support comes from many new members of Congress who are more amenable to having the states rather than the federal government solve some of the nation's problems. Support also comes from some state governors. Some other members of Congress, who might otherwise prefer a federal solution, feel that reform at the state level is preferable to partisan debate at the national level with little chance of any real reform.

To give the states flexibility in health care reform, it will be necessary for the states to be free of such constraints as ERISA. Without an ERISA preemption, states will be unable to apply reform to employees who are in self-funded plans. Employers who self-fund benefits, particularly those who have been successful with cost containment, will be reluctant to support such a change in federal law because it may ultimately result in increased costs, particularly if a state adopts some type of community rating. Self-funded employers that operate in many states would also be burdened by having to comply with each state's mandates.

Reform of the Current System.   The 1994 elections, which resulted in a more conservative Congress, effectively ended any hopes of the Clinton administration for a major comprehensive restructuring of the nation's health care system. However, despite very divergent views in Washington, 1996 saw the most far-reaching federal legislation to affect medical expense insurance in many years. It was clear to all sides that the public strongly supported certain changes, and these changes were enacted with bipartisan support. In addition, each side seemed willing to give the other side a little bit of what it wanted. Although the overall result is not a basic restructuring of the health care system, it clearly represents significant reform and change.

The primary piece of legislation in 1996 was the **Health Insurance Portability and Accountability Act (HIPAA)**. Although a detailed discussion of many of the act's provisions appears in the appropriate sections of later chapters, these provisions can be summarized as follows:

- Increased availability of medical expense coverage, discussed in the next section of this chapter
- A trial program of tax-favored MSAs, discussed in Chapter 13
- Increased portability of medical expense coverage, discussed in Chapter 14
- Expansion of eligibility for COBRA benefits, discussed in Chapter 14
- Broader tax deductibility of medical expense premiums for the self-employed, discussed in Chapter 14
- Favorable income tax treatment for long-term care insurance, discussed in Chapter 15
- Requirements for wellness programs, discussed in Chapter 18
- Administrative rules pertaining to privacy, security, and transaction standards for personal health information, discussed in Chapter 14

HIPAA was not the only 1996 legislation to affect group medical expense coverage. The Mental Health Parity Act requires that many employers provide increased benefits for mental illnesses. In addition, the Newborns' and Mothers' Health Protection Act may increase the length of inpatient benefits for childbirth in many cases. The effect of each act on medical expense plans is discussed in Chapter 10. It is interesting to note that much of this federal legislation and many recent state health reforms (such as the establishment of HIPCs and small-group legislation) incorporate aspects of the original Clinton proposal for national health insurance.

For the foreseeable future, it appears that changes to the health care system will continue on a piecemeal approach to address specific issues and problems. For example, at the time this book is being revised, there are bills in Congress that would make medical expense benefits available to more children, establish a patients' bill of rights, and establish association health plans. An **association health plan (AHP***)* would allow small businesses to band together through trade and professional associations to purchase medical expense benefits. AHPs would be free of state regulations so that one standardized policy could be offered across the country. Proponents of AHPs, including the Bush administration, argue that these plans would make medical expense coverage available to small businesses at a lower cost and encourage more small businesses to provide coverage for their employees. However, there are opponents who question if AHPs would destroy state plans that already address the needs of small employers. There is also concern that these plans would operate largely unregulated by the federal government and be subject to fraud and abuse.

Increased Availability of Medical Expense Coverage

HIPAA contains several provisions designed to help both employees and employers obtain coverage more easily. Portions of the act that deal with preexisting conditions are covered in Chapter 14 when the issue of eligibility is discussed. The discussion in this chapter focuses on the plans covered by the act and portions of the act that address nondiscrimination rules, special enrollment periods, renewability, and small groups.

Covered Plans. The act applies to group health plans that cover two or more employees, whether insured or self-funded. However, the act does not apply to a long list of excepted benefits. The following are excepted benefits in all circumstances:

- Coverage for accidents, including accidental death and dismemberment
- Disability income insurance
- Liability insurance
- Coverage issued as a supplement to liability insurance
- Workers' compensation or similar insurance
- Automobile medical payments insurance
- Credit-only insurance, such as mortgage insurance
- Coverage for on-site medical clinics

In addition, certain other benefits are excepted benefits under specified circumstances:

- Limited vision or dental benefits, long-term care insurance, nursing home insurance, home health care insurance, and insurance for community-based care if these benefits are offered separately rather than as an integral part of a medical expense plan.
- Coverage for a specific disease or illness or for hospital or other fixed indemnity insurance if the benefits (1) are provided under a separate policy, certificate, or contract of insurance and (2) are not coordinated with other coverage under a medical expense plan.
- Medicare supplement insurance or other similar supplemental coverage if the policy is offered as a separate insurance policy rather than as a continuation of coverage under a plan that also covers active employees.
- Flexible spending accounts (FSAs) under cafeteria plans, as long as (1) the employee has other coverage available under a group health plan of the employer and (2) the maximum payment under the FSA for the year does not exceed the greater of two times the employee's salary reduction or the amount of the employee's salary reduction plus $500. Virtually all FSAs, which are discussed in Chapter 19, meet these requirements.

With one exception, all employers—including the federal government—must comply with the act's provisions. State and local government plans can elect to be excluded from most of HIPAA's provisions.

Nondiscrimination Rules. The act prohibits the use of any of the following health-related factors as a reason to exclude an employee or dependent from coverage under a group health plan or to charge the individual or dependent a higher premium:

- Health status
- Medical condition, including both physical and mental condition

- Claims experience
- Receipt of health care
- Medical history
- Genetic information
- Evidence of insurability, including conditions caused by domestic violence and participation in such activities as motorcycling, snowmobiling, all-terrain vehicle riding, horseback riding, skiing, and other similar activities
- Disability

It is important to note that these factors relate to coverage for specific individuals under a plan. The overall plan itself (except for plans in the small-group market, as explained later) can still be subject to traditional underwriting standards. In addition, a group health plan is not required to offer any specific benefits. It can also limit benefit levels or exclude coverage for certain types of injuries as long as any limitations or exclusions apply uniformly to all similarly situated individuals and are not directed at individual participants based on any health factor. However, the act does not prohibit different benefit structures for different groups of employment classifications. Examples of acceptable classifications are full-time versus part-time, different geographic locations, membership in a collective bargaining unit, date of hire, length of service, current employee versus former employee status, and different occupations.

The act does not restrict the amount an insurance company or other provider of health care coverage can charge an employer for coverage. The act does allow an employer or provider of medical expense coverage to establish premium discounts or to modify copayments or deductibles for persons who participate in bona fide programs of health promotion or disease prevention.

Special Enrollment Periods. For various reasons, employees and their dependents may elect not to enroll in an employer's plan when they are initially eligible for coverage. For example, a new employee may have coverage under a spouse's plan. The act requires that employers allow these employees and dependents to enroll in the employer's plan under any one of several specified circumstances as long as the employee had previously stated in writing that the original declination was because there was other coverage. However, the requirement of a written declination does not apply unless the employer requires it and notifies the employee that it is a requirement for future coverage. The following are the circumstances for special enrollment:

- The other coverage was lost because of loss of eligibility under the other plan. This loss of eligibility can result from such circumstances as divorce, the spouse's termination of employment, or the spouse's death.
- The other coverage was lost because employer contributions for the coverage terminated.
- The other coverage was COBRA coverage that is exhausted. (COBRA is discussed in detail in Chapter 14.)

The employee has 30 days following the loss of coverage to request enrollment in the employer's plan.

In addition, new dependents (including children placed for adoption) are also eligible for coverage under special enrollment rules. The employee must enroll the dependent within 30 days of his or her gaining dependent status. Coverage for a new spouse must become effective no later than the first month beginning after the employee's request; coverage for children must go into effect as of the date of birth, adoption, or placement for adoption.

Guaranteed Renewability. All group health insurers must renew existing health insurance coverage unless one of the following circumstances exists:

- The plan sponsor failed to pay premiums or the issuer of health insurance coverage failed to receive timely premiums.

- The plan sponsor performed an act of fraud or made an intentional misrepresentation of material fact under the terms of the coverage.

- The plan sponsor failed to comply with a material plan provision relating to employer contribution or group participation rules, as long as these rules are permitted under applicable state or federal law. For example, an employer might fail to maintain a minimum required percentage of participation under a plan.

- There is no covered employee who lives or works in the service area of a network plan, such as an HMO.

- The employer is no longer a member of the association that sponsors a plan.

- The issuer of coverage ceases to offer coverage in a particular market. The issuer must notify each plan sponsor, participant, and beneficiary at least 90 days prior to the discontinuation of coverage, and the issuer must offer each plan sponsor the option to purchase other health insurance coverage currently being offered by the issuer to a group health plan in the market. If the issuer exits the market entirely, the period of notice is 180 days, and the issuer cannot reenter the market and sell health insurance coverage for at least five years.

Similar rules require multiemployer plans and multiple-employer welfare arrangements to renew coverage for employers. It also establishes guaranteed-issue and renewal rules for the individual marketplace.

Guaranteed Issue for Small-Group Plans. With some exceptions, the act requires that insurers, HMOs, and other providers of health care coverage that operate in the small-group market accept all small employers—defined as employers with 2 to 50 employees—that apply for coverage. In addition, all employees of small employers and their dependents must be accepted for coverage as long as they enroll during the period in which they are first eligible. This rule is in line with the small-group legislation of many states. However, some states have similar rules for groups as small as one employee, and some stipulate an upper limit of 25, above which the small-group legislation does not apply.

Exceptions to this guaranteed-issue requirement are allowed if a provider of coverage in the small-group market has inadequate network or financial capacity or if applicants are not in a plan's service area.

Minimum participation or employer contribution requirements are acceptable as long as they are permitted under applicable state law.

Interrelationship of State and Federal Legislation. For the most part, the new federal legislation does not preempt state laws pertaining to group health insurance (which might be more stringent than HIPAA) except in those situations where any state standard or requirement would prevent the application of the federal law. To prevent any preemption, many states have had to make some modifications to their laws and regulations. (As explained in Chapter 14, the situation is different for the rules pertaining to preexisting conditions.)

The act permits a state to enforce the act's provisions with respect to insurance companies and other medical expense providers. However, the federal government can take over enforcement if a state does not perform its duties. In that case, enforcement is by the secretary of health and human services. The secretary of labor has enforcement power for the act's provisions as they apply to group health plans themselves, including the act's portability provisions. When there is federal enforcement, the penalty for noncompliance can be up to $100 per day for each individual with respect to whom a plan or issuer is in noncompliance.

■ KEY TERMS

association health plan (AHP)	health insurance purchasing cooperative (HIPC)	medical expense insurance
employer mandate		single-payer plan
health insurance	managed care	universal coverage
Health Insurance Portability and Accountability Act (HIPAA)	managed competition Medicaid	

■ STUDY QUESTIONS

1. a. How did the federal government become a major player in providing medical expense coverage during the 1960s?

   b. What effect did this have on health care costs?

2. How was medical expense coverage affected by legislation in the 1970s?

3. Describe the efforts that employers have used in recent years to control the cost of medical expense coverage.

4. What are some of the reasons for the significant increases in the cost of health care?

5. What are the major components of health care cost containment?

6. What characteristics should be contained in a managed care plan?

7. Describe the provisions of the NAIC Small Employer Health Insurance Availability Model Act.

8. In addition to making coverage more available and affordable for small employers, what other types of health care reform are being adopted by the states?

9. What are the two primary objectives of national health insurance?

10. Why is the goal of universal coverage probably unobtainable?

11. What is the rationale for taxing employers and individuals to pay the cost of providing medical expense coverage for the uninsured?

12. What are the arguments for and against managed competition as an approach for designing a national health insurance program?

13. a. How does a single-payer plan affect the role of the employer and the agent in providing medical expense coverage?

    b. What effects would a single-payer plan likely have on costs for medical care and medical expense insurance?

14. a. What are the arguments for giving an ERISA preemption to the states?

    b. Why are certain groups opposed to such preemptions?

15. What types of provisions are contained in the Health Insurance Portability and Accountability Act (HIPAA)?

16. What health-related factors does HIPAA prohibit as a reason to exclude an employee from coverage under a group health plan or to charge an individual or dependent a higher premium?

17. Describe the circumstances under which HIPAA requires a group health plan to have special enrollment periods.

18. Under what circumstance does HIPAA allow an insurer to not renew a group health plan?

19. What is the relationship between HIPAA and state laws?

■ NOTE

1. The Henry J. Kaiser Foundation and Health Research and Education Trust, *Employer Health Benefits, 2003.*

CHAPTER

10

Traditional Medical
Expense Plans

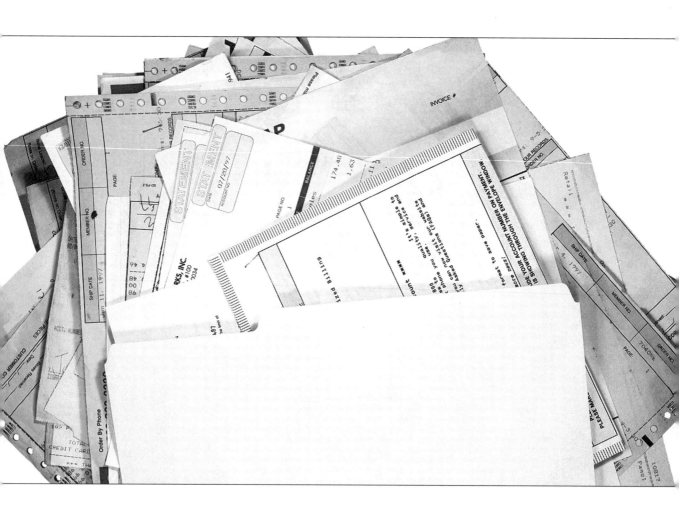

■ Identify the providers of traditional medical expense coverage in today's market-place.

■ Describe each of the following types of basic medical expense coverages:
1. Hospital expense benefits
2. Surgical expense benefits
3. Physicians' visits expense benefits

■ Describe the approaches used to provide major medical coverage.

■ Describe the characteristics of major medical insurance.

■ Describe the types of managed care provisions used in traditional medical expense insurance plans.

CHAPTER OUTLINE

Providers of Traditional Coverage
Blue Cross and Blue Shield Plans
Insurance Companies
Comparison of the Blues and Insurance Companies
The Blues and Insurance Companies in Today's Environment

Basic Medical Expense Coverages
Hospital Expense Benefits
Surgical Expense Benefits
Physicians' Visits Expense Benefits

Major Medical Coverage
Types of Major Medical Coverage
Supplemental versus Comprehensive
Characteristics of Major Medical Coverage

Managed Care Provisions in Traditional Plans
Preadmission Testing
Hospital Precertification
Second Surgical Opinions
Alternative Facilities for Treatment
Preapproval of Visits to Specialists
Benefits for Preventive Care

Coverage for Complementary and Alternative Medicine

Prior to the mid-1970s, most employees were covered by what is commonly referred to as a **traditional (or indemnity) medical expense plan**. Medical expenses were incurred, and patients had considerable freedom in choosing the providers of medical care. Claims were paid on the basis of charges billed by providers with virtually no attempts to control costs. As a result, a traditional plan is also referred to as a **fee-for-service plan**.

As was pointed out in Chapter 9, some employees are still covered under plans that are largely traditional in nature. However, these plans have evolved. Although they are still far from what might be called managed care plans, these plans contain provisions designed to control costs, influence the behavior of persons needing medical care, and provide preventive care.

This chapter begins with a brief discussion of the providers of traditional medical expense coverage. It continues by first analyzing plans that provide basic coverage and then discussing major medical coverage. The chapter next reviews some managed care techniques that might be found in traditional plans. Other techniques are described where appropriate throughout the chapter. This is followed by a brief discussion of coverage for complementary and alternative medicine.

Before proceeding further, three comments need to be made about the importance of this chapter. First, interest in traditional plans will undoubtedly vary by the state in which a reader resides. The previous chapter pointed out that only a small percentage of employees and their families are still covered under traditional plans. However, this percentage varies significantly by state. For example, HMO enrollments are small (10 percent or less) in about 20 percent of the states—mostly states with small and heavily rural populations. In these states, most employees and their families are covered by traditional plans or PPOs, which can be viewed as traditional major medical plans that have adopted a wide range of managed care characteristics. In another 20 percent of the states—typically populous and urban states—35 percent to 50 percent of employees and their families are covered by HMOs. Almost all of the remaining employees and families in these states are covered by other forms of managed care—most frequently PPOs, which again are patterned after traditional major medical plans.

Second, traditional major medical plans are still offered by a significant number of employers. Although participation by employees is small, one major survey indicated that 14 percent of employees still have the option of selecting such plans.[1] However, many employees are unlikely to do so because of higher premiums, deductibles, and copayments than those found in managed care plans.

Third, the discussion of medical expense plans in this and the following chapters largely follows the historical development of medical expense plans. Much of the terminology and coverage of legislation introduced here also applies to the managed care approaches to medical care that are discussed in Chapters 11 and 12.

■ PROVIDERS OF TRADITIONAL COVERAGE

Providers of traditional coverage include Blue Cross and Blue Shield plans, insurance companies, and employers using self-funded arrangements, which are discussed in more detail in Chapter 16. Although the plans described in this chapter are characteristic of those offered by the Blues and insurance companies, self-funded plans must be properly designed to be effective. Such plans have "borrowed" liberally from insured plans and contain similar—if not identical—provisions.

Blue Cross and Blue Shield Plans

Prior to the Great Depression, "health" insurance contracts provided by insurance companies were primarily designed to give income benefits to persons who were disabled by accidents and, to a limited degree, illnesses. It was generally accepted that individuals should pay their own medical expenses from their savings. During the Depression, however, the savings of many individuals disappeared, unemployment was severe, and most insurance companies ceased writing disability income contracts. Faced with financial difficulties arising from the inability of many patients to pay their bills, many hospitals established plans for the prepayment of hospital expenses. By paying a monthly fee to the hospital, a member was entitled to a limited number of days of hospitalization per year. Note that **member** is the term most often used to describe persons covered by Blue Cross and Blue Shield plans and other plans that use network providers, although the terms *subscriber* and *enrollee* are also used.

The early plans were limited to a single hospital, but by the mid-1930s many plans had become communitywide or statewide operations, offering members the choice of using any participating hospital. Much of this expansion resulted from actions by the American Hospital Association to promote and control this type of plan. In the late 1930s, the American Hospital Association adopted the Blue Cross name and emblem and permitted them to be used only by plans that met standards established by the association. As a general rule, only one plan within a geographic area was allowed to use the Blue Cross name. Eventually, the Blue Cross activities of the American Hospital Association were transferred to a separate national organization, the Blue Cross Association.

The success of the early Blue Cross plans resulted in the development of Blue Shield plans, established by local medical associations to prepay physicians' charges. The evolution of Blue Shield plans paralleled that of Blue Cross plans, with the American Medical Association acting similarly to the American Hospital Association. Eventually, the role of the American Medical Association was transferred to the National Association of Blue Shield Plans, which then became the national coordinating body.

To a large extent, the persons covered by Blue Shield plans were the same ones whose hospital charges were covered by Blue Cross plans, and in many geographic regions this overlapping led to a close working relationship between the two. For many years in some areas of the country, one plan administered the other. However, this administration was typically on a fee-for-administration basis, with the two plans being separate legal entities. In recent years, there has been a consolidation of most Blue Cross and Blue Shield plans. Usually, this consolidation has taken the form of a complete merger; in a few cases the consolidation has only been partial. These partial consolidations have resulted in Blue Cross and Blue Shield plans that operate under a single staff but with separate governing boards.

There has been consolidation at the national level as well. In 1978, the staffs of the two national organizations were merged, and a new organization—the Blue Cross and Blue Shield Associations—was formed to act on matters of mutual interest to both Blue Cross plans and Blue Shield plans. It was governed by members of the boards from both the Blue Cross Association and the National Association of Blue Shield Plans. In

1982, a complete merger took place, with the resulting organization called the Blue Cross and Blue Shield Association.

As of early 2004, there were 41 plans in existence. Most jointly wrote Blue Cross and Blue Shield coverage, but there were a few separate Blue Cross plans and Blue Shield plans. Although a single Blue Cross and Blue Shield plan serves most states, in a few states there is more than one plan, each operating within a specific geographic region. In some instances, plans may cover more than one state. Only in a few cases is there any overlapping of the geographic areas served by individual plans.

Each local Blue Cross, Blue Shield, or Blue Cross and Blue Shield plan is a legally separate entity operated by a governing board, which establishes specific practices for the plan in accordance with the broad standards of the national Blue Cross and Blue Shield Association. Consequently, individual plans may differ substantially from one another. Providers of coverages used to dominate the boards of these plans, but now "nonproviders," including representatives of consumer organizations, foundations, labor unions, businesses, and the general public, dominate the boards of most plans.

Traditionally, Blue Cross and Blue Shield plans have been nonprofit corporations and acted as insurers of last resort in most states. This meant that they wrote coverage on almost anyone at competitive rates. For this, the Blues tended to receive favorable tax treatment. However, as insurance companies and HMOs expanded their market share, they tended to take the better business and leave the Blues with books of business that had an increasing number of unhealthy lives. As a result, the Blues have become more restrictive in their underwriting practices. In addition, a large number of the Blues have changed to for-profit status to raise the capital necessary to compete more effectively with other types of providers of medical expense coverage. Many of the Blues also own subsidiaries that are run to make a profit.

Insurance Companies

For many years, Blue Cross and Blue Shield plans were the predominant providers of medical expense coverage; insurance companies were much slower to enter the market and took a different approach. Rather than emphasizing basic first-dollar coverage for hospital or physicians' charges, most insurers chose to write major medical coverage with deductibles and coinsurance. By the mid-1950s, insurance companies surpassed the Blues in premium volume for medical expense coverage.

As with other types of insurance, both stock and mutual insurance companies write medical expense coverage. Insurers that specialize in the medical expense market write some coverage, but much of the premium volume for group coverage is written by large life insurance companies. It is interesting to note that medical expense coverage is also a line of insurance sometimes written by property-casualty insurance companies.

Comparison of the Blues and Insurance Companies

Perhaps the best way to describe the nature of Blue Cross and Blue Shield plans and insurance company plans is to compare their characteristics. Traditionally, the similarities between the Blues and insurance companies were overshadowed by their differences. Over time, however, intense competition has often caused one type of provider to adopt the more popular but differing practices of the other. As a result, insurance companies and the Blues are becoming increasingly similar, in spite of their many distinctly different characteristics.

The following comparison of the Blues and insurance companies focuses on their operation with respect to traditional medical expense insurance coverage. It is followed by a brief treatment of how both types of organizations have expanded into managed care.

Regulation and Tax Treatment.   In a few states, Blue Cross and Blue Shield plans are regulated under the same laws that apply to insurance companies. In most states, though, the Blues are not-for-profit organizations and are regulated under special legislation. Typically, the same body that regulates insurance companies carries out this regulation. However, in some respects the Blues receive preferential treatment over insurance companies, probably the most significant example being their exemption from premium taxation and income taxation by many states. Because premium taxes (usually about 2 percent of premiums) are passed on to consumers, this gives the Blues a cost advantage but in many other respects, the Blues are subject to more stringent regulation than insurance companies. For example, their rates are subject to regulatory approval in most states. With recent trends toward consumerism, this approval has become more burdensome and expensive.

In addition, the Blues are also accorded favorable tax treatment under federal income tax laws. Prior to the Tax Reform Act of 1986, the Blues (except the few plans that were incorporated as insurance companies) were exempt from federal income taxation. The tax act eliminated this complete exemption. Because of various deductions that can be taken, however, the average effective tax rate for the Blues is significantly lower than the average tax rate for insurance companies.

Form of Benefits.   Traditionally, the Blues offered benefits in the form of services, and insurance companies offered benefits on an indemnity (or reimbursement) basis. Under the **service-benefit concept**, benefits are expressed in terms of the services that are provided by the hospitals or physicians participating in the plan rather than in terms of dollar maximums. For example, a Blue Cross plan might provide up to 90 days of hospitalization per year in semiprivate accommodations. Under the **indemnity concept**, an insured would be reimbursed for covered medical expenses incurred up to a maximum dollar amount. For example, an insurance company might provide reimbursement for hospital charges subject to both dollar and duration limits, such as $600 per day for 90 days. In both cases, any charges in excess of the benefits must be borne by the covered person.

Blue Cross and Blue Shield plans involve two separate types of contractual relationships: A plan promises to provide specified services to a member for whom a premium has been paid, and it has contracts with providers of services whereby the providers are reimbursed for the cost of services rendered to members. In general, members are not billed for the cost of covered services or required to file claim forms. Rather, this cost is negotiated between the plan and the providers. This type of arrangement generally requires that members receive their services from providers participating in the plan; however, most hospitals and physicians are participants. If nonparticipating providers can be used (such as for emergencies), benefits are usually paid on an indemnity basis, as is done by insurance companies.

In contrast, an insurance company that writes traditional medical expense coverage agrees to reimburse a covered person for medical expenses only up to the limits specified in the insurance contract. There is no contractual relationship between the providers of medical services and the insurance company. Thus, covered persons must file the appropriate claim forms. Although covered persons have a legal obligation to pay their medical bills, the insurance company's obligation (unless benefits are assigned) is to reimburse only the covered person, not to actually pay the providers. However, most hospitals and many other providers require that a patient assign any potential insurance benefits to them before they will render services. In effect, such an assignment requires that the insurance company pay benefits directly to the provider on behalf of the covered person.

In the past, insurance companies incorporated maximum daily room and board limits into their contracts that did not cover medical expenses in full. However, to compete with the Blues, many insurance companies now frequently write contracts that provide full reimbursement for certain medical expenses. Even though a covered person may see little difference in the benefits received from either type of provider, the traditional distinction still exists: The Blues are providing services, whereas insurance companies are providing reimbursement for the cost of services.

Types of Benefits. Over the years, the Blues have specialized in providing basic medical benefits, with Blue Cross providing coverage for hospital expenses and Blue Shield providing coverage for surgical expenses and physicians' visits. Major medical benefits were rarely available. However, competition from insurance companies and increased cooperation between Blue Cross and Blue Shield have resulted in the Blues now offering virtually the same coverages as insurance companies. As the Blues have expanded the scope of benefits offered, they have frequently included deductible and coinsurance provisions similar to those used by insurance companies. When there is a deductible, a covered person is required to pay expenses up to some limit (such as $100 per year or per illness) out of his or her own pocket before benefits are paid. When coinsurance is used, the medical expense plan pays a percentage (such as 80 percent) of some or all expenses, the remaining portion being paid by the covered person. Deductibles and coinsurance are more precisely defined and discussed in greater detail later in this chapter.

The advantage many insurance companies have had over the Blues has been their ability to offer a wide variety of group benefits, including life insurance coverage and disability income coverage. Until a few years ago, most states had laws and regulations that prevented the Blues from offering any coverage other than medical expense benefits. However, because of changes in these laws and regulations, the Blues can now offer a wider range of group benefits to their members. Although competition between the Blues and insurance companies over writing these other benefits is increasing, the Blues currently write relatively little coverage other than medical expense benefits.

Reimbursement of Providers. The method by which the Blues reimburse providers often gives them a competitive advantage over insurance companies. Most Blue Cross plans pay participating hospitals on a per diem basis for each day a member is hospitalized. Periodic negotiations with Blue Cross determine the amount of this payment (which includes room-and-board charges as well as other covered charges) for each hospital. For example, if the per diem amount is $900, the hospital receives $900 for each day a member is hospitalized, regardless of what the actual charges are. Although this per diem amount is adequate on average, the hospital will "lose money" on some patients but "make money" on others.

In addition to the administrative simplicity of this method of reimbursement, the per diem amount is often less than the average daily hospital charges. Frequently, it is determined by excluding such hospital costs as bad debts, charity care, and nursing school costs. These costs are used in determining charges for patients who are not Blue Cross members or members of managed care plans that have entered into similar arrangements. Therefore, Blue Cross members in effect receive a discount on the charges made to some other patients, including those whose benefits are provided by insurance companies under many traditional medical expense plans. However, insurance companies often also reimburse hospitals on a per diem basis under their managed care plans.

Under some Blue Shield plans, physicians may also be reimbursed at less than their actual charges, as is discussed later in this chapter.

National Coverage. Although Blue Cross and Blue Shield plans operate in precise geographic regions, many insurance companies have historically operated on a national basis. In the era of traditional medical expense plans, the Blues had a more difficult time competing with insurance companies for the group insurance business of employers whose employees were located in areas served by several different Blue Cross and Blue Shield plans. Today, the situation has changed. It is more difficult for insurance companies to operate on a national basis because of differences in the state regulation of medical expense insurance. In addition, in this era of managed care, a national presence requires the ability to set up provider networks everywhere. As a result, many insurance companies have withdrawn from the medical expense market or do not sell products in all states. The Blues, on the other hand, have developed procedures on a cooperative basis among themselves for providing coverage to "national accounts." For example, an employer can arrange a medical expense plan that allows any employee to have coverage through the HMO or PPO of the Blue Cross and Blue Shield organization that operates in the area where the employee resides.

Flexibility. Benefit consultants seem to feel that insurance companies have a greater degree of flexibility than Blue Cross and Blue Shield plans in modifying their group contracts to meet employers' needs and desires. Blue Cross and Blue Shield contracts have traditionally been quite standardized, with few, if any, variations allowed. One major reason for this rigidity is that changes in the benefits promised to members also have an effect on the contracts between the Blues and the providers. However, with employers increasingly wanting new approaches to medical expense benefits, often for cost-containment reasons, many Blue Cross and Blue Shield plans have taken a more flexible approach. Many variations exist among plans, and some have been very innovative in meeting the demands of the marketplace, even going as far as to administer benefit plans that are self-funded by employers.

Rating. In their early years, the Blues used only a community-rating approach in determining what premium rates to charge. With **community rating**, each plan uses the same rate structure for all members, regardless of their past or potential loss experience and regardless of whether coverage is written on an individual or a group basis. Usually, the only variations in the rate structure result from variations in coverage: whether it is for an individual, a couple without children, or a family. The philosophy behind the community-rating approach is that coverage should be available to the widest range of persons possible at an affordable cost. Charging lower premium rates to segments of the community with better-than-average loss experience is thought to result in higher and possibly unaffordable premium rates for other segments of the community.

Community rating placed Blue Cross and Blue Shield plans at a competitive disadvantage when insurance companies began to aggressively market group medical expense insurance and use experience rating, which allowed them to charge certain employer groups much lower premiums than those charged by the Blues. As a result, by the mid-1950s, insurance companies surpassed the Blues in the number of persons covered. Faced with the growing dilemma that rate increases necessary to compensate for the loss of better-than-average business tended to drive even more business to the insurance companies, the Blues initiated the use of experience rating for groups. Today, there is little difference in this regard between these two major providers with respect to group business. However, the Blues still use community rating in pricing products for smaller employers and for the individual marketplace.

Marketing. The Blues tend to have lower acquisition expenses than insurance companies, and salaried employees market most coverage. However, more than half of the plans also market coverage through agents and/or brokers in addition to their own sales forces. In general, the commissions paid to agents or brokers are below the commissions paid by insurance companies.

The Blues and Insurance Companies in Today's Environment

Today, the Blues and insurance companies have moved far beyond writing only traditional medical expense plans and are major players in the managed care marketplace. Together they write the majority of PPO coverage and a significant portion of HMO coverage.

Most of the Blues now have their own HMOs, PPOs, and point-of-service plans. In fact, national statistics show that more than one-half of Blue Cross and Blue Shield members are covered under PPOs, and this is the fastest-growing market segment. About one-third of their members are covered under traditional plans, and a little less than one-third are covered under HMOs. As the Blues have expanded into broader markets, many of them have changed their names and do not use Blue Cross or Blue Shield in the new names.

Similarly, insurance companies have expanded their offerings. Most insurers that write traditional medical expense coverage also offer PPO products. Some insurers have actually left the market for traditional products and offer only PPOs. A relatively small number of insurers have entered the HMO market—sometimes through mergers with existing HMOs—but these insurers account for about 20 percent of HMO coverage written. Insurance companies also offer a wide array of products and services for use with self-funded plans.

■ BASIC MEDICAL EXPENSE COVERAGES

Historically, medical expense coverage consisted of separate benefits for hospital expenses, surgical expenses, and physicians' visits. Coverage was limited, and many types of medical expenses were not covered, although covered expenses were paid in full without deductibles and coinsurance. (Today, however, deductibles and coinsurance are sometimes used.) Over time, employers began to offer more extensive benefits to employees. Although this broader coverage is usually provided through a single major medical contract, some employees are still covered under medical expense plans that consist of selected basic coverages typically provided by Blue Cross and/or Blue Shield. In most cases, these basic coverages are supplemented by a major medical contract so that the effect is essentially the same as if a single major medical contract were used. The exclusions and limitations found in basic medical expense coverages are fundamentally the same as those discussed later for major medical contracts.

Basic coverages consist of three traditional coverages:

1. Hospital expense benefits
2. Surgical expense benefits
3. Physicians' visits expense benefits

Hospital Expense Benefits

Hospital expense coverage provides benefits for charges incurred in a hospital by a covered person (that is, the employee or his or her dependents) who is an inpatient or, in some circumstances, an outpatient. Every medical expense contract discussed in this book defines what is meant by a hospital. The actual wording may vary among insurance companies and in some states, but the following definition is typical:

> The term hospital means (1) an institution that is accredited as a hospital under the hospital accreditation program of the Joint Commission on Accreditation of Healthcare Organizations or (2) any other institution that is legally operated under the supervision of a staff of physicians and with 24-hour-a-day nursing service. In no event should the term hospital include a convalescent nursing home or include any institution or part thereof that (1) is used principally as a convalescent facility, rest facility, nursing facility, or facility for the aged; or (2) furnishes primarily domiciliary or custodial care, including training in the routines of daily living; or (3) is operated primarily as a school.

Inpatient Benefits.   Hospital inpatient benefits fall into two categories: coverage for room-and-board charges and coverage for "other charges."

Room and Board. Coverage for room-and-board charges includes the cost of the hospital room, meals, and services normally provided to all inpatients, including routine nursing care. Benefits are normally provided for a specific number of days for each separate hospital confinement; this number may vary from 31 to 365 days. Some contracts provide coverage for an unlimited number of days.

The amount of the daily room-and-board benefit may be expressed in one of two ways: either a flat-dollar maximum or more commonly the full cost of semiprivate accommodations. Under the first approach, benefits are provided for actual room-and-board charges up to a maximum daily amount, such as $750. Many hospital expense contracts include additional room-and-board benefits for confinement in an intensive care unit.

Other Charges. Coverage for "other charges" (often called *miscellaneous charges, ancillary charges*, or *hospital extras*) provides benefits for certain services and supplies ordered by a physician during a covered person's hospital confinement, such as drugs, operating room charges, laboratory services, and x-rays. With a few exceptions, only the hospital portion of these charges is covered; any associated charges for such professional services as physicians' fees are not covered. The exceptions often include charges for ambulance services and anesthesia if it is not covered as part of surgical expense benefits.

The amount of the benefit for other charges is usually expressed in one of the following three ways:

1. Full coverage up to a dollar maximum. This approach is most commonly found in contracts when the daily room-and-board benefit is also subject to a dollar limit. In most cases, this maximum is some multiple (often 20) of the daily room-and-board benefit. For example, a contract with a daily room-and-board benefit of $750 might have a $15,000 maximum for other charges.

2. Full coverage up to a dollar maximum (again, often expressed as a multiple of the room-and-board benefit) and partial coverage for a limited amount of additional expenses.

3. Full payment subject only to the duration for which room-and-board benefits are payable.

When coverage for ambulance services is provided, it is common to limit the benefit to a dollar maximum, such as $50 per hospital confinement. A few plans have a mileage limit in lieu of a dollar limit.

Outpatient Benefits. Although hospital expense contracts did not originally cover outpatient expenses, today it is common to find coverage for such expenses arising from surgery. The purpose of this benefit is to provide comparable coverage and thus lower hospital utilization when surgical procedures can be performed on an outpatient basis. It should be noted that this benefit covers only hospital charges or charges of outpatient surgical centers (such as the use of operating room facilities), not the surgeon's fee.

Hospital expense contracts commonly provide coverage for emergency room treatment of accidental injuries within some specified time period (varying from 24 to 72 hours) after an accident. Any emergency room charges incurred immediately prior to hospitalization are usually considered inpatient expenses.

Surgical Expense Benefits

Surgical expense coverage provides benefits for physicians' charges associated with surgical procedures. Although one tends to think of a surgical procedure as involving cutting, insurance contracts typically define the term broadly to include such procedures as suturing, electrocauterization, removal of a stone or foreign body by endoscopic means, and the treatment of fractures or dislocations.

Even though surgical expense coverage is frequently sold in connection with hospital expense coverage, surgical expense coverage normally provides benefits for surgery performed not only in the hospital (either as an inpatient or an outpatient) but also as an outpatient in a freestanding (that is, separate from a hospital) ambulatory surgical center and in a physician's office. To discourage unnecessary hospitalization, some surgical expense benefit contracts actually provide larger benefits if a procedure is performed as outpatient surgery.

Outpatient surgery also results in charges for medical supplies, nurses, and the use of facilities. As mentioned, these charges are often covered if surgery is performed on an outpatient basis in a hospital or outpatient surgical facility.

Surgical expense coverage traditionally provided benefits only for the primary surgeon's fee. However, newer contracts often provide separate benefits for assistant surgeons and anesthesiologists as well. Because both hospital expense coverage and surgical expense coverage often pay for anesthesia, it is important that an overall medical expense plan be properly designed to make sure this benefit is neither omitted nor overlapping. The major difficulty in this regard occurs when different providers of coverage are used for the hospital and surgical benefits.

In providing basic surgical expense benefits, some insurance companies and some Blue Shield plans use a **surgical fee schedule** in which charges are paid up to the maximum amounts specified in the schedule of surgical procedures in the master contract. However, the majority of surgical expense plans follow the approach used in major medical contracts and provide benefits to the extent that surgical charges are reasonable and customary. Unfortunately, the precise meaning of these terms in insurance contracts is vague, and each company determines for itself what it considers reasonable and customary. In general, a **reasonable-and-customary charge** (sometimes referred to as a *usual, customary, and reasonable charge,* or *prevailing charge*) is considered to be a charge that falls within the range of fees normally charged for a given procedure by physicians of similar training and experience within a geographic region.

The usual practice of insurance companies is to pay charges in full as long as they do not exceed some percentile (usually ranging from the 85th to the 95th) of the range of charges for a specific surgical procedure within a certain geographic region. For example, if an insurance company uses the 90th percentile and if for a certain procedure 90 percent of the charges are $300 or less, this is the maximum amount that is paid. The covered person is required to absorb any additional charges if he or she uses a more expensive physician. Through the use of computers, insurance companies now have statistics that categorize expenses by geographic regions that are as small as the zip codes of medical-care providers. Thus, $300 may be the maximum reasonable-and-customary amount in one part of a metropolitan area, and $350 may be considered reasonable and customary in another part of the same metropolitan area.

Blue Shield plans often use a somewhat modified approach in determining the maximum amount that is paid. Each year, physicians file their charges for the coming year with the Blue Shield plan, and during that year the plan pays charges in full up to some percentile of these filed charges. Under most plans, the physicians agree not to charge Blue Shield patients amounts in excess of their filed fees.

Physicians' Visits Expense Benefits

Physicians' visits expense coverage (often referred to as *medical expense coverage* or *regular medical expense coverage*) provides benefits for fees of attending physicians other than surgeons (because the charges of the latter are paid under surgical expense benefits coverage). Benefits are usually provided only for physicians' visits while a covered person is hospitalized. However, coverage may also include office and home visits.

In-Hospital Coverage. In-hospital coverage is designed to provide benefits for physicians' charges when a covered person is hospitalized as an inpatient. Three general approaches determine the amount and duration of benefits. Under one approach, physicians' fees are paid on a reasonable-and-customary basis, up to a specific number of visits per hospitalization. Under the second approach, benefits are limited to a daily maximum that is expressed as a dollar amount (such as $70). The third approach expresses the total benefit as a lump-sum amount equal to the daily benefit times the number of days hospitalized. For example, if the daily benefit is $60 and the covered person is hospitalized for ten days, physicians' charges would be paid in full up to $600, regardless of the charges incurred on any specific day or the number of visits made by the physician.

Three additional types of benefits are sometimes included when in-hospital coverage is provided:

1. Coverage for physicians' visits when a covered person is in an intensive care unit. If benefits are paid on a reasonable-and-customary basis, these charges are covered in the same manner. Under plans with a daily maximum, the maximum may be increased to reflect the more expensive charges normally associated with intensive care.

2. Coverage for consultation services. Although most plans cover only the charges of attending physicians, some plans provide benefits for the consultation services of other physicians. This benefit may be subject to a dollar maximum, or it may be paid on a reasonable-and-customary basis.

3. Coverage for physicians' visits in other types of medical care facilities, such as extended care centers. This benefit is most commonly provided when room-and-board charges for alternative facilities are also covered.

In-Hospital and Out-of-Hospital Coverage. In addition to the benefits previously described, coverage for physicians' visits may also include physicians' charges incurred in a physician's office or in a covered person's home. This broader coverage is usually not written as a separate and distinct benefit but rather as a single overall coverage for all types of physicians' visits. Benefits may be paid on a reasonable-and-customary basis or be subject to a dollar maximum per visit. In the latter case, it is not unusual to have two different dollar maximums: one for hospital visits and home visits and a lesser one for office visits. Benefits are subject to some overall maximum limit, which may be expressed as either a dollar amount (such as $1,000) or a specified number of visits (such as 60). This limit may be applied on an annual basis or for any single illness or injury. Most plans contain a waiting period, commonly ranging from one to five visits, before benefits for home and office visits are paid. However, this waiting period is often waived in the case of an accident.

Some plans also provide coverage for well-baby care, which includes benefits for inoculations and physicians' examinations (both in and out of the hospital) of healthy infants for a limited period of time, such as three months after birth. In addition, coverage sometimes includes benefits for hospital nursery charges. Some states require that medical expense contracts cover these benefits for newborns only until the infant is discharged from the hospital.

■ MAJOR MEDICAL COVERAGE

Most employees have some type of **major medical coverage** that protects against catastrophic medical expenses, with few exclusions or limitations. However, employees must often pay part of the cost of these medical expenses because of deductibles and coinsurance provisions.

Types of Major Medical Coverage

There are two general types of plans for providing major medical coverage—supplemental (or superimposed) plans and comprehensive plans. **Supplemental major medical coverage** coordinates major medical coverage with various basic medical expense coverages. Figure 10.1 shows one example of such a plan.

Subject to its own limitations and exclusions, a supplemental major medical plan covers the following expenses:

■ Expenses not within the scope of the basic coverages. For example, benefits for office visits to a physician may be included if the basic coverages provide benefits for in-hospital visits only.

■ Expenses no longer covered under the basic coverages because those benefits have been exhausted. For example, if the basic coverages provide room-and-board benefits

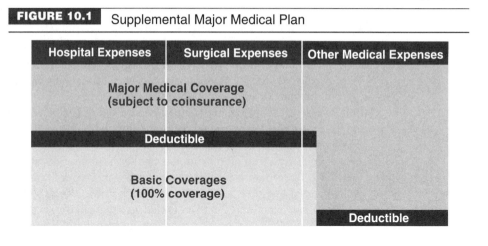

FIGURE 10.1 Supplemental Major Medical Plan

in full, but only for a maximum of 60 days, the major medical plan covers the cost of room and board beginning on the 61st day.

■ Expenses specifically excluded under the basic coverages. For example, if the basic coverages exclude hospital charges for the treatment of alcoholism, the major medical coverage may provide benefits. However, expenses that are excluded under the basic coverages are often excluded under the major medical plan.

With **comprehensive major medical coverage**, a single major medical contract covers all medical expenses, as illustrated in Figure 10.2. In this example, once the deductible is satisfied, most medical expenses are covered subject to a coinsurance provision. Although Figure 10.2 shows a comprehensive major medical plan in its purest form, most comprehensive medical expense contracts contain modifications of deductibles and/or coinsurance provisions for certain expenses, often resulting in payment of 100 percent of reasonable and customary charges. These variations are discussed later in this chapter.

Supplemental versus Comprehensive

At first glance, it might appear that the simplicity of a comprehensive major medical plan makes it preferable to a supplemental plan. However, supplemental plans continue to cover a large percentage of employees insured under traditional medical expense plans, even though most newly written plans are of the comprehensive type. The reasons for choosing separate coverages include the employer's desire to (1) use more than one provider of coverage, (2) offer first-dollar coverage, or (3) use different contribution rates for the basic and supplemental coverages. There are also disadvantages to using supplemental plans, including more difficult administration and communication.

More than One Provider of Coverage. Sometimes, the provider of a supplemental major medical plan is different from the provider of the underlying basic coverages. For example, Blue Cross or Blue Shield may provide the basic coverages, and an insurance

FIGURE 10.2	Comprehensive Major Medical Plan

Hospital Expenses	Surgical Expenses	Other Medical Expenses
	Major Medical Coverage (subject to coinsurance)	
	Deductible	

company may provide the supplemental coverage. In the past, only a few of the Blues offered major medical coverage because (1) some of them felt such coverage was not within the scope of their traditional benefit structure, (2) some states legally prohibited it, and (3) some Blues experienced administrative difficulties with effectively and efficiently coordinating these broader benefits. Although Blue Cross and Blue Shield plans now offer major medical coverage (sometimes referred to as *extended benefits*), insurance companies are still the largest providers of major medical benefits.

The most common type of supplemental plan is the one shown in Figure 10.1, but occasionally a major medical plan is designed to supplement only a basic Blue Cross plan.

First-Dollar Coverage. Under the traditional comprehensive major medical plan, a deductible and coinsurance apply to all covered expenses. However, because of competition or labor negotiations, employers frequently offer their employees **first-dollar coverage** for certain medical expenses. With first-dollar coverage, there is no deductible and usually no coinsurance provision, and the basic medical expense plan consists only of those benefits provided on a first-dollar basis. Because first-dollar coverage has been characteristic of the Blues, they are frequently used as the providers of basic coverages. Therefore, to compete with them, most insurance companies now offer comprehensive major medical plans that are modified to provide similar first-dollar coverage.

It should be emphasized that, all other things being equal, first-dollar coverage increases the cost of a medical expense plan. Employers have become increasingly concerned with the cost of providing medical expense coverage and are less likely than in the past to provide first-dollar coverage.

Different Contribution Rates. A few employers still maintain separate basic medical and major medical expense plans, because different employer contributions are made for each plan. The most common arrangement under these circumstances has the employer paying the entire cost of the basic coverages for the employee (and possibly his or her dependents) and the employee paying a portion, if not all, of the costs of the major medical coverage. However, most employers have a single plan even when the contribution rates for the basic and major medical coverages differ.

Administration and Communication. Most employers want to have benefit plans that minimize administrative problems and that can be easily communicated to employees. In both respects, comprehensive plans have the advantage. With supplemental plans, the employer must often deal with two providers of coverage, so two plans must be properly coordinated so that no undesired gaps in coverage exist. In addition, processing claims becomes more burdensome for both the employer and the employees. The complexity of medical expense plans in general makes them difficult to communicate to employees, and the task becomes even more challenging when two plans are used.

Even when a single provider supplies both the basic medical expense plan and a supplemental major medical plan, the same problems may exist. The employer may need to negotiate the plans with separate divisions of the provider's organization, and separate claims forms and departments may have to be used.

Characteristics of Major Medical Coverage

The distinguishing features of major medical expense plans—either supplemental or comprehensive—include a broad range of covered expenses, exclusions, limitations, deductibles, coinsurance, and high overall maximum benefits.

Covered Expenses. Major medical plans give broad coverage for necessary expenses incurred for medical services and supplies that a physician has ordered or prescribed. The services and supplies, which are specified in the contract, generally include the following:

■ Hospital room and board. Traditionally, coverage has not been provided either for confinements in extended care facilities or for home health care. However, major medical plans now often include such coverage. Some plans also provide benefits for room and board in alternative facilities, such as birthing centers. These types of facilities and the benefits for them are covered later in this chapter.

■ Other hospital charges.

■ Charges of outpatient surgical centers.

■ Anesthetics and their administration.

■ Services of doctors of medicine or osteopathy.

■ Professional services of a registered nurse. The services of a nurse midwife, nurse practitioner, and nurse anesthetist may also be covered.

■ Services of certain other types of providers. Most states mandate that the services of certain types of providers other than physicians and nurses must be covered as long as the service is a covered benefit and the provider is operating within the scope of his or her license. The list of providers varies from state to state and may include one or more of the following: acupuncturists, audiologists, chiropractors, dentists, marriage and family therapists, dietitians, optometrists, physical therapists, physicians' assistants, podiatrists, psychologists, social workers, and speech pathologists.

- Prescription drugs. This benefit, as discussed in Chapter 12, is often carved out and provided through a separate prescription drug program.
- Physical and speech therapy.
- Diagnostic x-ray and laboratory services.
- Radiation therapy.
- Blood and blood plasma.
- Artificial limbs and organs.
- Pacemakers.
- Casts, splints, trusses, braces, and crutches.
- Rental of wheelchairs, hospital beds, and iron lungs.
- Ambulance services.

Dental care expenses may also be included as a major medical benefit. However, dental benefits (discussed in Chapter 15) are usually provided under a separate dental expense plan.

Even though coverage is broad, major medical contracts contain certain exclusions and limitations.

Exclusions. The list of exclusions varies, but exclusions found in most major medical contracts include charges arising from the following:

- Occupational injuries or diseases to the extent that benefits are provided by workers' compensation laws or similar legislation.
- Services furnished by or on behalf of government agencies unless there is a requirement for either the patient or the patient's medical expense plan to pay for the services. Under federal law, medical expense plans must generally pay benefits to the government for care in Veterans Health Administration or military hospitals on the same basis as they pay for care received elsewhere. However, if a plan does not pay charges in full because of deductibles, coinsurance, or plan limitations, the patient is not responsible for the balance. The exceptions to the law—meaning that the plan is not responsible for payment—include treatment in Veterans Health Administration hospitals for service-connected disabilities and treatment of active-duty members of the armed services in military hospitals.
- Care provided by family members or when no charge would be made for the care received in the absence of the insurance contract.
- Cosmetic surgery, except as required by the Women's Health and Cancer Rights Act, unless such surgery is to correct a condition resulting from either an accidental injury or a birth defect (if the parent has dependent coverage when the child is born).
- Most physical examinations, unless such examinations are necessary for the treatment of an injury or illness. Although most major medical plans contain this exclusion, some plans (as discussed later in this chapter) do provide coverage for some

forms of preventive medicine, which might involve specific types of physical examinations.

- Experimental or investigational drugs and treatment.
- Convalescent, custodial, or rest care.
- Dental care except for (1) treatment required because of injury to natural teeth and (2) hospital and surgical charges associated with hospital confinement for dental surgery. This exclusion is not included if dental coverage is provided under the major medical contract.
- Eye refraction, or the purchase or fitting of eyeglasses or hearing aids. Like the dental care exclusion, this exclusion is not included if the major medical coverage provides benefits for vision and hearing care. These benefits, however, are most likely to be provided under a separate plan. Separate vision care plans are discussed in Chapter 12.
- Expenses either paid or eligible for payment under Medicare or other federal, state, or local medical expense programs.
- Benefits provided by any other benefit program to which the employer makes a contribution. This includes any benefits provided under basic medical expense plans if a supplementary major medical plan is used.

To minimize the problem of adverse selection, most major medical plans also contain an exclusion for preexisting conditions. However, this exclusion applies only for a limited time, after which the condition is no longer considered preexisting and is covered in full, subject to any other contract limitations or exclusions.

A preexisting condition for medical expense insurance is typically defined as any illness or injury for which a covered person received medical care during the three-month period prior to the person's effective date of coverage. Usually, the condition is no longer considered preexisting after the earlier of (1) a period of three consecutive months during which no medical care is received for the condition or (2) 12 months of coverage under the contract by the individual.

The use of preexisting-conditions provisions in group medical expense plans was affected by the passage of the Health Insurance Portability and Accountability Act (HIPAA), but the traditional time periods that apply to such conditions are within the act's guidelines. HIPAA allows preexisting-conditions provisions as long as they apply uniformly to individuals within the same group of similarly situated employees and are not based on any health factors of employees or their dependents. However, the act does limit the use of preexisting-conditions provisions with respect to newborn or adopted children. In addition, preexisting-conditions provisions cannot apply to pregnancy. The topic of preexisting conditions as they relate to HIPAA is discussed in more detail in Chapter 14.

Some insurance companies limit rather than exclude coverage for preexisting conditions. During the time a condition is considered preexisting, benefits may be paid subject to limitations, such as a 50 percent coinsurance provision or a calendar-year maximum of $1,000. It is also not unusual, particularly with large employers, for the preexisting-conditions clause to be waived for persons eligible for coverage on the date a master contract becomes effective. However, future employees will be subject to the provision.

Finally, there are certain types of medical expenses that may or may not be excluded. Although these exclusions are not found in most major medical contracts, they are found in many. Examples include charges arising from the following:

■ Treatment for weight reduction and morbid obesity.

■ Treatment of injuries resulting from attempted suicide or self-inflicted injury. However, HIPAA regulations do not allow such an exclusion to apply to injuries that result from a medical condition, such as depression.

■ Sexual transformation or sexual dysfunction.

■ Procedures to restore or enhance fertility, reversal of sterilizations, artificial insemination, or in vitro fertilization.

■ Treatment of injuries incurred while committing a felony.

Maternity. Until the passage of the Pregnancy Discrimination Act, it was not unusual to exclude maternity-related expenses from medical expense contracts. However, the act requires that benefit plans of employers with 15 or more employees treat pregnancy, childbirth, and related conditions the same as any other illness. (See the discussion in Chapter 5.)

In the absence of state laws to the contrary, pregnancy may be and is sometimes excluded under group insurance contracts written for employers with fewer than 15 employees. If these employers wish to provide such coverage, it can usually be added as an optional benefit. In some cases, pregnancy is treated like any other illness covered under the contract. In other cases, benefits are determined in accordance with a schedule that most commonly provides an all-inclusive benefit for hospital, surgical, and certain other expenses associated with delivery. Regular physician visits and diagnostic tests may or may not be covered. Table 10.1 is an example of a maternity schedule.

An expense associated with maternity is the nursery charge for a newborn infant, which in most cases is equal to at least 50 percent of a hospital's normal room-and-board charge. This expense is not part of a maternity benefit, and a few medical expense contracts do not cover the expense if the infant is healthy (because the contract covers only expenses associated with accidents and illnesses). However, most contracts do cover nursery charges, and a number of states require that they be covered.

TABLE 10.1 Maternity Schedule

Type of Pregnancy	Benefit
Normal Delivery	$2,000
Cesarean	4,000
Miscarriage	1,000

Since 1998, group medical expense plans have been subject to the provisions of the **Newborns' and Mothers' Health Protection Act**. This federal act is very broad and, with one exception, applies to all employers regardless of size and to self-funded plans as well as those written by health insurers and managed care plans. The exception is for plans subject to similar state legislation, which exist in more than half the states. The impetus for such legislation at both the state and federal levels arose over consumer backlash from the practice of an increasing number of HMOs and insurance companies limiting maternity benefits to 24 hours after a normal vaginal birth and 48 hours after a cesarean section. The act affects maternity benefits if they are provided. It does not mandate that such benefits be included in benefit plans. Of course, many employers are subject to other state and federal laws that do mandate maternity benefits.

The act prohibits a group medical expense plan or insurer from restricting hospital benefits to less than 48 hours for both the mother and the newborn following a normal vaginal delivery and 96 hours following a cesarean section. In addition, a plan cannot require that a provider obtain authorization from the plan or insurer for a stay within these minimums. Although a new mother, in consultation with her physician, might agree to a shorter stay, a plan or insurer cannot offer a monetary or nonmonetary incentive to the mother for this purpose. For example, follow-up visits from a home health nurse cannot be provided to mothers and children who are discharged early unless these visits are also provided to mothers and children who stayed in the hospital for the full period specified in the act. In addition, the plan or insurer cannot limit provider reimbursement because care was provided within the minimum limits or make incentives available to providers to render care inconsistent with the minimum requirements.

If a plan has deductibles or other benefit restrictions, these cannot be greater during the 48-hour or 96-hour period than those imposed on any preceding portion of the hospital stay prior to the birth.

Effect of Women's Health and Cancer Rights Act. The **Women's Health and Cancer Rights Act** amended ERISA and applies to group medical expense plans as well as individual medical expense insurance. Under the provisions of the federal act, any benefit plan or policy that provides medical and surgical benefits for mastectomy must also provide benefits for the following:

- Reconstruction of the breast on which the mastectomy has been performed
- Surgery and reconstruction of the other breast to produce a symmetrical appearance
- Prostheses and physical complications of all stages of mastectomy, including lymphedemas

Prior to the act's taking effect, such coverage was often not available because of exclusions, particularly exclusions that applied to cosmetic surgery. This coverage can be subject to deductibles and coinsurance provisions, as long as they are consistent with those provided for other procedures under the plan or policy. Plan participants must be notified of the existence of these benefits on an annual basis.

Limitations. Major medical plans also contain **limitations** or internal limits for certain types of medical expenses. Although the expenses are covered, the amounts that are paid under the contract are limited. Benefits are very rarely paid for charges that exceed what is reasonable and customary. In addition, limitations are often placed on the following expenses:

■ Hospital room and board. Benefits are generally limited to the charge for semiprivate accommodations unless other accommodations are medically necessary. In some cases, a flat-dollar maximum is placed on the daily semiprivate accommodation rate.

■ Treatment in alternative facilities, if provided. These facilities (described later in this chapter) include extended care facilities, home health care benefits, and hospice benefits. Benefits for extended care facilities are often subject to a dollar limit per day for room-and-board charges as well as a time limit on the number of days that coverage is provided. Similarly, home health care benefits are often subject to a maximum daily benefit and limited to a certain number of visits within a specific time period. Hospice benefits are usually limited to a specified maximum amount.

■ Dental care, vision and hearing care, and physical examinations. When these are covered under major medical contracts, benefits are frequently subject to schedules and annual limitations.

■ Ambulance service, such as $250 per trip.

■ Rental or purchase of durable equipment, such as $5,000.

Some plans also have limits on outpatient prescription drugs, such as $2,500 per year per person.

Treatment of Mental Illness, Alcoholism, and Drug Addiction. It is common for major medical plans to provide limited benefits for treatment of mental and nervous disorders, alcoholism, and drug addiction. Unless state laws require that such conditions be treated like any other medical condition, inpatient coverage is often limited to a specific number of days each year (commonly 30 or 60). Outpatient benefits, which are even more limited, are usually subject to 50 percent coinsurance and to a specific dollar limit per visit. One unfortunate effect of more stringent limitations on outpatient care is that it encourages many persons to seek inpatient treatment, which is significantly more expensive but no more effective in the eyes of many medical experts. As a result, some plans have started to carve out coverage from the major medical plan. Benefits are then coordinated by a managed care plan that specializes in mental health and/or substance abuse problems. These plans are discussed in Chapter 12.

It was once common for major medical plans to impose an annual maximum (such as $1,000) and/or an overall maximum lifetime limit (such as $25,000) on benefits for mental and nervous disorders, alcoholism, and drug addiction. Under federal legislation, such limitations are no longer allowed for mental health benefits in many employee benefit plans.

At the time of the 1996 debate over HIPAA, there was considerable disagreement over the issue of requiring mental illness to be treated as any other illness for purposes of medical expense coverage. With estimates that complete parity would raise the cost of providing medical expense benefits by 4 percent to 10 percent (depending on whose estimate one believed), Congress left the issue unresolved. The debate continued after the passage of the previously mentioned act and resulted in the passage of another act the following month—the **Mental Health Parity Act**. Because of cost considerations, however, its provisions are limited and the use of the term *parity* is probably a misnomer.

The provisions of the act apply only to employers that have more than 50 employees. The act prohibits a group health plan, insurance company, or HMO from setting annual or lifetime dollar limits on mental health benefits that are less than the limits applying to other medical and surgical benefits. If there are no such dollar limitations for substantially all other (meaning two-thirds or more) medical and surgical benefits under a plan, there can be none for mental health benefits. If substantially all benefits are subject to an annual or lifetime limit, the parity requirements can be satisfied by either having separate dollar limits that are equal for mental health benefits and other medical and surgical benefits or applying a uniform dollar limit to all benefits in the aggregate. If a plan has different limits for different categories of benefits, the act calls for the use of a weighted average of all the limits to be used for the mental health limitations.

The act does not prohibit limitations on benefits for alcoholism or drug addiction. The act is also noteworthy for other things it does not do. It does not require that employers make any benefits available for mental illness, and it does not prohibit any other restrictions on mental health benefits. Employers can still impose limitations, such as an annual maximum on number of visits or days of coverage, and different cost-sharing provisions for mental health benefits from those that apply to other medical and surgical benefits.

Any employer who can prove that the act's provisions increase its group health plan costs by more than 1 percent is exempt from the act. However, this exemption is available only if the employer has complied with the act for six months and uses a prescribed formula for measuring the cost increase.

The act is subject to a sunset provision of December 31, 2004. As of that date, any benefits required by the act can be eliminated unless Congress extends the date, removes the sunset provision prior to that time, or passes alternative legislation.

Deductibles. A **deductible** is the initial amount of covered medical expenses an individual must pay before he or she receives benefits under a major medical plan.

EXAMPLE
Kirk is covered under a major medical plan that has an annual deductible of $200. He is responsible for the first $200 of medical expenses incurred each year. Covered expenses in excess of $200 are then paid by the major medical plan, subject to any limitations or coinsurance.

In addition to the different types of deductibles, there are variations in (1) the amounts of the deductible, (2) the frequency with which it must be satisfied, and (3) the expenses to which it applies.

Types of Deductibles. Probably the simplest form of deductible is the **initial (or straight) deductible** commonly used in comprehensive major medical plans (see

Figure 10.2). Essentially, a covered person must satisfy this deductible before the plan pays any insurance benefits.

Most supplemental medical expense plans use a **corridor deductible** (see Figure 10.1), under which no benefits are paid by the major medical plan until an individual has incurred a specific amount of covered expenses above those paid under his or her basic coverages.

In those situations when no benefits are paid under the basic coverages, the corridor deductible operates as if it were an initial deductible.

Deductible Amounts. Deductible amounts for any covered person under group benefit plans tend to be relatively small. Most deductibles are fixed-dollar amounts that apply separately to each person and usually fall within the range of $100 to $500. A few major medical expense plans contain deductibles that are based on a percentage of an employee's salary (such as 1 percent or 2 percent), possibly subject to a maximum annual limit (such as $250).

> **EXAMPLE**
> Marilyn incurs $4,000 of covered medical expenses, $2,500 of which is paid by her basic coverages. If her supplemental major medical plan has a $200 corridor deductible, the plan pays $1,300 of the expenses, subject to any limitations or coinsurance. This is determined as follows:
>
> | | |
> |---|---:|
> | Covered expenses | $4,000 |
> | Minus expenses covered under basic protection | − 2,500 |
> | | $1,500 |
> | Minus deductible | − 200 |
> | | $1,300 |

In most major medical expense plans, the deductible must be satisfied only once during any given time period (usually a calendar year), regardless of the number of causes from which medical expenses arise. This type of deductible is often referred to as an **all-causes deductible**. A few plans have a **per-cause deductible** (also referred to as a *per-disability deductible*), under which the deductible amount must be satisfied for each separate accident or illness before major medical benefits are paid.

Deductibles apply to each covered individual, including the dependents of an employee. To minimize the family's burden of satisfying several deductibles, most major medical expense plans also contain a **family deductible**. Once the family deductible is satisfied, future covered medical expenses of all family members are paid just as if each member of the family had satisfied his or her individual deductible.

Two basic types of family deductibles are found in major medical expense plans. The most common type waives any deductible requirements for other family members once a certain number of family members (generally two or three) have satisfied their individual deductibles. Two important points should be noted. First, major medical benefits are paid for each individual family member once his or her individual deductible is satisfied, even though the family deductible has not been met. Second, the waiver of any deductible requirements that results from the satisfaction of the family deductible does not apply to medical expenses incurred prior to the date the deductible is satisfied.

> **EXAMPLE**
> Assume a family deductible is satisfied when each of three family members incurs $200 in covered medical expenses. If a fourth family member has had $60 in medical expenses up to that point, future medical expenses for that person will be paid under the major medical coverage. The $60, however, is not covered. In effect, the satisfaction of the family deductible freezes the deductible for each family member at the lesser of the individual deductible or the amount of medical expenses incurred up to that time.

Another approach taken in some major medical plans is to have a fixed-dollar amount for the family deductible (such as $500). In addition, each family member has to meet an individual deductible (such as $200). Major medical benefits are paid for any given family member once his or her deductible is satisfied, and future deductible requirements for all family members are waived once the family maximum has been reached. Although the same expenses can satisfy both the family deductible and an individual deductible, any amount that is applied toward the family deductible cannot exceed the individual deductible.

> **EXAMPLE**
> If a family has deductibles of $200 for an individual and $500 for the family and if one family member incurs $1,000 in covered medical expenses, the $800 exceeding the individual deductible is paid under the major medical plan, subject to any limitations and coinsurance. The $200 used to satisfy the individual deductible, but no more, can also be applied to the family deductible. The family deductible will not be completely satisfied until other family members incur another $300 in covered expenses (but no more than $200 from any one family member).

Most major medical expense contracts contain a **common accident provision**, whereby if two or more members of the same family are injured in the same accident, the covered medical expenses for all family members are at most subject to a single deductible, usually equal to the individual deductible amount. This deductible establishes the maximum amount of medical expenses an employee must bear for his or her family before major medical benefits are paid. Sometimes the employee may actually bear a smaller portion of the medical expenses if the amount satisfies the family or individual deductibles.

Deductible Frequency. An all-causes deductible usually applies to medical expenses incurred within a 12-month period, typically a calendar year (January 1 to

EXAMPLE
If each of three family members incurs $300 of medical expenses in an accident under a plan that contains a $200 deductible, at least $700 of these expenses is covered under the major medical coverage. If due to previous medical expenses only $40 is needed to satisfy the family deductible, then $860 of these expenses is covered under the major medical plan.

December 31). Under such a **calendar-year deductible**, expenses incurred from January 1 apply toward the deductible. Once it has been satisfied, the balance of any covered expenses incurred during the year is then paid by the major medical plan, subject to limitations and coinsurance.

Many plans with a calendar-year deductible also have a **carryover provision** that allows any expenses (1) applied to the deductible and (2) incurred during the last three months of the year also to be applied to the deductible for the following year. No carryover is allowed if the deductible for the year is satisfied prior to the last three months of the year.

EXAMPLE
Assume Ed satisfies only $150 of a $200 deductible prior to October 1. If less than $50 of covered expenses are incurred in the last three months of the year, the deductible is not totally satisfied for the year, but this amount can be applied to the deductible for the following year. If $50 or more of covered expenses are incurred in this three-month period, not only is the deductible satisfied for the year but this amount ($50) can also be applied to the deductible for the following year.

With a per-cause deductible, a different approach is normally taken. Medical expenses used to satisfy the deductible for each illness or accident must be incurred within a specified **accumulation period**. Although the accumulation period can be a calendar year or some other 12-month period, most accumulation periods consist of any consecutive two-month, three-month, or six-month period. Once the deductible for an accumulation period has been met, benefits are paid for a **benefit period**. In medical expense insurance, this period usually begins when the deductible is satisfied, but sometimes begins on the date the first expense toward the deductible is incurred. (In the latter case, expenses used to satisfy the deductible are not paid by the major medical plan.) The benefit period typically lasts until the earlier of (1) two years or (2) the end of some time period (usually 60 or 90 days) in which covered medical expenses from that cause are less than a small but specified dollar amount (such as $25 or $50). Once the benefit period ends, an individual must again satisfy the deductible before a new benefit period begins.

Expenses to Which the Deductible Applies. Most major medical plans have a single deductible that applies to all medical expenses. However, some plans have two (or more) deductibles that apply separately to different categories of medical expenses. Many variations exist, but the most common plan of this type has a small deductible (such as $50) that applies to those expenses over which individuals have the least control (for example, hospital charges, surgical charges, and charges resulting from accidents). A larger deductible (such as $100) applies to all other medical expenses.

In some major medical plans, the deductible does not apply to certain expenses, in effect giving the covered person first-dollar coverage for these charges. Insurance companies sometimes write comprehensive major medical expense plans without any deductible for hospital and/or surgical expenses as their way of competing with the first-dollar coverage offered by the Blues. In addition, these expenses may be paid in full but possibly up to certain maximums. Above these maximums, coinsurance applies.

Coinsurance. Major medical expense plans contain a coinsurance provision, whereby the plan pays only a specified percentage (in most cases, 80 percent) of the covered expenses that exceed the deductible. The term **coinsurance** as used in this book refers to the percentage of covered expenses paid by a medical expense plan. Thus, a plan with 80 percent coinsurance, sometimes referred to as an 80/20 plan, pays 80 percent of covered expenses, and a person who receives benefits under the plan must pay the remaining 20 percent. It has been argued that having such provisions is a financial incentive for employees to control their use of medical care because they must bear a portion of the cost of any expenses incurred.

In some plans, a percentage participation, such as 20 percent, is specified. As commonly used, **percentage participation** refers to the percentage of covered medical expenses that is not paid by a medical expense plan and that must be paid by a person receiving benefits. Note that percentage participation is sometimes referred to as a **copayment**, but that terminology usually implies a fixed-dollar amount that an insured must pay for a covered service. To make the matter even more confusing, some insurers refer to the percentage participation, rather than their portion of the benefit payment, as coinsurance.

EXAMPLE

Karl's comprehensive major medical expense plan has a $200 calendar-year deductible and an 80 percent coinsurance provision that applies to all expenses. If Karl incurs $1,200 of covered medical expenses during the year, he will receive an $800 reimbursement from the insurance company, calculated as follows:

Covered expenses	$1,200
Minus deductible	– 200
	$1,000
Times coinsurance percentage	× .80
	$ 800

Karl will have to pay the remaining $400 from his own pocket (that is, the deductible plus 20 percent of those expenses exceeding the deductible).

Just as deductibles vary, so do coinsurance provisions. Sometimes different coinsurance percentages apply to different categories of medical expenses. For example, outpatient psychiatric charges may be subject to 50 percent coinsurance, and other covered medical expenses may be subject to 80 percent coinsurance. In addition, certain medical expenses may be subject to 100 percent coinsurance (and usually no deductible), which in effect means that the expenses are paid in full, subject to any limitations. Such full coverage is most likely to exist (1) for those expenses over which an individual has little control, (2) when there is a desire to provide first-dollar coverage for certain expenses, or (3) when there is a desire to encourage the use of the most cost-effective treatment (such as outpatient surgery, preadmission testing, or birthing centers).

In the case of catastrophic medical expenses, the coinsurance provision could result in an individual having to assume a large dollar amount of his or her own medical expenses. Consequently, many major medical expense plans have a **stop-loss (or coinsurance) limit** on the amount of out-of-pocket expenses that a covered person must bear during a specified time period. It is sometimes specified that the coinsurance provision applies only to a limited amount of expenses and that expenses over this limit are paid in full.

> **EXAMPLE**
> Eve's medical plan has a $200 deductible, an 80 percent coinsurance provision that applies to the next $3,000 of covered expenses, and full coverage for any remaining covered expenses. Therefore, the most she will pay out of pocket in any year is the $200 deductible and 20 percent of $3,000 (for a total of $800).

Occasionally, this type of plan is modified to allow a gradual increase in the coinsurance percentage, such as 80 percent of the first $2,000 of covered expenses above the deductible, 90 percent of the next $2,000, and 100 percent of the remainder.

Another way of limiting out-of-pocket expenses is to state the maximum dollar amount that any individual (or a family) must bear during a specific period. Once this limit is reached, by paying either deductibles or a percentage of medical expenses, additional expenses are paid in full.

> **EXAMPLE**
> Trevor's medical expense plan has a $200 deductible and an 80 percent coinsurance provision. A $1,000 stop-loss limit is met if total medical expenses reach $4,200. Of this amount, Trevor is responsible for the $200 deductible and 20 percent of the remaining $4,000 (for a total of $1,000). Any medical expenses in excess of $4,200 are paid in full.

Maximum Benefits.   The maximum benefits that will be paid for any covered person under a major medical contract may be determined in one of two ways. Although the use of a lifetime maximum is most common, a few contracts contain a per-cause maximum. In both instances, the benefit maximum applies separately to each employee and each dependent covered under the contract.

Lifetime Maximum. When a **lifetime maximum** is used, the specified overall maximum applies to all medical expenses paid (after the application of deductibles and coinsurance) during the entire period an individual is covered under the contract. Benefit maximums of less than $1 million are no longer common, and most benefit maximums fall within the range of $1 million to $2 million. Higher maximum benefits (such as $5 million) or even an unlimited maximum benefit are sometimes available, but their availability is much less common with traditional major medical contracts than it is with PPO products. The lifetime maximum is reduced by the amount of any benefits paid.

EXAMPLE

Sarah's major medical plan has a $200 calendar-year deductible, an 80 percent coinsurance provision, and a $100,000 lifetime maximum. If she incurs $4,000 of medical expenses in her first year of coverage (assuming it corresponds with the calendar year), she will receive benefits of $3,040 (that is, 80 percent of $3,800). This reduces her remaining lifetime benefit to $96,960.

Until recently, it was common to include one or more provisions in major medical contracts that restored (either partially or totally) the lifetime maximum to its original level. In some cases, this restoration required showing evidence of insurability or having no claims for a period of time. This type of provision has largely been dropped because it appears to be in conflict with state and federal regulations that prohibit the basing of benefits on health status.

A few plans still have an automatic annual restoration of a small amount of benefits, varying from $1,000 to $5,000 per year. Such a restoration was of significant value a few years ago when lifetime maximums were much lower. However, there is little practical value in such a restoration with today's maximum lifetime benefits of $1 million or more. As a result, a majority of plans have dropped this type of provision.

In addition to the overall lifetime maximum, an **internal maximum** is sometimes found in major medical contracts. For example, a plan may have a $1 million overall lifetime maximum, but a $10,000 lifetime maximum for benefits relating to alcoholism and drug addiction. In other words, only $10,000 of the $1 million will be paid for expenses relating to these conditions. Such a limitation was once also common for mental and nervous disorders, but the provisions of the Mental Health Parity Act prohibit this type of maximum for many employee benefit plans. A few plans do contain calendar-year or per-disability internal maximums.

Per-Cause Maximum. A few plans contain a maximum limit, or **per-cause maximum,** for each cause of medical expenses, but in general this type of maximum limit is used only when the deductible is also applied on a per-cause basis. Although coverage terminates for any cause for which the maximum benefit has been paid, it remains in force for medical expenses arising from other causes.

■ MANAGED CARE PROVISIONS IN TRADITIONAL PLANS

Historically, traditional medical expense plans contained few provisions aimed at managing the care of covered persons, but this situation continues to evolve. Provisions such as preadmission testing, hospital precertification, and second surgical opinions have been around for many years. It is also common for benefits to be provided for treatment in facilities other than hospitals. These types of facilities and the benefits for them are discussed below.

Other managed care provisions and practices that may be found in traditional plans include the following:

■ Preapproval of visits to specialists.

■ Increased benefits for preventive care.

■ Carve-outs of benefits that can be provided cost effectively under arrangements that employ various degrees of managed care. Examples include prescription drugs, mental illness, substance abuse, and maternity management. These types of carve-outs are discussed in Chapter 12.

Some traditional major medical plans actually make wide use of managed care techniques; the primary factor that prevents them from being called managed care plans is that there are few restrictions on access to providers.

Preadmission Testing

The first day or two of hospital confinement, particularly for surgical procedures, were historically devoted to necessary diagnostic tests and x-rays. **Preadmission testing** requires the performance of these procedures on an outpatient basis prior to hospitalization and covers the costs as if the person were an inpatient. For benefits to be paid, these procedures must generally be (1) performed after a hospital confinement for surgery has been scheduled, (2) ordered by the same physician who ordered the hospital confinement, (3) performed in the hospital where the confinement will take place, and (4) accepted by the hospital in lieu of the same tests that would normally be performed during confinement. Benefits are paid even if the preadmission testing leads to a cancellation of the scheduled confinement.

Hospital Precertification

As a method of controlling costs, most medical expense plans have adopted utilization review programs. One aspect of these programs, which were discussed in the previous chapter, is **hospital precertification**. Such a program requires that a covered person or his or her physician obtain prior authorization for any nonemergency hospitalization. Authorization usually must also be obtained within 24 to 48 hours of admissions for emergencies.

The initial reviewer, typically a registered nurse, determines whether hospitalization or some type of alternative care is most appropriate and what the length of stay for the medical condition should be. If the preapproved length of stay is insufficient, the patient's physician must obtain prior approval for any extension.

Most plans reduce benefits if the hospital precertification procedure is not followed. Probably the most common reduction is to pay only 50 percent of the benefit that would otherwise be paid. If a patient enters the hospital after a hospital precertification has been denied, many plans do not pay for any hospital expenses, whereas other plans provide a reduced level of benefits.

Second Surgical Opinions

In an attempt to control medical costs by eliminating unnecessary surgery, many medical expense plans, both traditional and managed care, provide benefits for a **second surgical opinion**. Although such opinions undoubtedly cause some patients to decide against surgery, it is still unclear whether the cost savings of second surgical opinions are illusory. For example, surgery may still be required at a later date or long-term costs for alternative treatment may be incurred.

A voluntary approach for obtaining second surgical opinions is often used. If a physician or surgeon recommends surgery, a covered person can seek a second opinion; the cost is borne by the medical expense plan. Sometimes the benefit is limited to a specific maximum, but usually the costs of the second opinion, including x-rays and diagnostic tests, are paid in full. Some plans also pay for a third opinion if the first two opinions disagree. When there are divergent opinions, the final choice is up to the patient, and the plan's regular benefits are usually paid for any resulting surgery. As an incentive to encourage second opinions, some plans actually provide larger benefits for a covered person who has obtained a second opinion, even if it does not agree with the first opinion.

In the last few years, it has become increasingly common for medical expense plans to require mandatory second opinions, which may apply to any elective and nonemergency surgery but frequently apply only to a specified list of procedures. In most cases, a surgeon selected by the insurance company or other provider of benefits must give the second opinion. If conflicting opinions arise, a third opinion may be obtained. The costs of the second and third opinions are paid in full. In contrast to voluntary provisions, mandatory provisions generally specify that benefits are paid at a reduced level if surgery is performed either without a second opinion or contrary to the final opinion.

The trend toward mandatory second opinions has had an interesting result. Because many employers felt money was being saved under their voluntary programs, wouldn't it be logical to save more money by making the program mandatory? Unfortunately, the opposite situation has often been the case: people who voluntarily seek a second opinion are frequently looking for an alternative to surgery, and those who obtain a second opinion only because it is required are more likely to accept surgery as the best alternative. Employers have also found that a second opinion by a surgeon is still likely to call for surgery. As a result, there seems to be a growing feeling that the cost of mandatory second opinions may exceed any decrease in surgical benefits paid. Consequently, some employers have returned to voluntary programs or stopped providing coverage for second opinions altogether.

Alternative Facilities for Treatment

Many traditional medical expense plans provide coverage for treatment in facilities that are alternatives to hospitals. Initially, this coverage was provided primarily to the extent that it reduced hospital benefits that were otherwise covered. Although this is still the primary effect of this coverage, it is often an integral part of medical expense plans, and benefits are provided even if they might not have been covered under a plan limited solely to treatment received in hospitals. The following types of coverage are discussed:

- Extended care facility benefits
- Home health care benefits
- Hospice benefits
- Birthing centers

Extended Care Facility Benefits. Many hospital patients recover to a point where they no longer require the full level of medical care provided by a hospital, but they cannot be discharged because they still require a period of convalescence under supervised medical care. An **extended care facility** (often called a *convalescent nursing home* or *skilled-nursing facility*) often exists to provide this type of care. To the extent that patients can be moved to such a facility (which are often adjacent to hospitals), daily room-and-board charges can be reduced—often substantially.

Extended care facility coverage provides benefits to the person who is an inpatient in an extended care facility, which is typically defined as an institution that furnishes room and board and 24-hour-a-day skilled-nursing care under the supervision of a physician or a registered professional nurse. It does not include facilities that are designed as a place for rest or domiciliary care for the aged. In addition, facilities for the treatment of drug abuse and alcoholism are often excluded from the definition.

To receive benefits, the following conditions must usually be satisfied:

- A physician must recommend the confinement.
- Twenty-four-hour-a-day nursing care must be needed.
- The confinement must commence within (1) 14 days after termination of a specified period of hospital confinement (generally three days) for which room-and-board benefits were payable or (2) 14 days of a previous confinement in an extended care facility for which benefits were payable. A few (but increasing number of) contracts include benefits for situations where extended care facilities are used in lieu of hospitalization.
- The confinement must be for the same or a related condition for which the covered person was hospitalized.

Benefits are provided in much the same manner as under hospital expense coverage. If hospital expense benefits are paid on a semiprivate accommodation basis, extended care facility benefits are generally paid on the same basis. If hospital expense benefits are subject to a daily dollar maximum, extended care facility benefits are usually likewise subject to a daily dollar maximum, most typically 50 percent of the daily hospital benefit.

The maximum period for which extended care facility benefits are paid may be independent of the period for which a person is hospitalized, in which case a maximum of 60 days' coverage is fairly common. Alternatively, the benefit period may be related to the number of unused hospital days. The most common approach in this instance is to allow two days in an extended care facility for each unused hospital day. For example, if a hospital expense plan provides benefits for a maximum period of 90 days and if a covered person is hospitalized for 50 days, the 40 unused hospital days can be exchanged for 80 days of benefits in an extended care facility. Other charges incurred in an extended care facility may be treated in one of several ways. They may be covered in full, subject to a separate dollar limit, or treated as part of the maximum benefit payable for other charges under hospital expense coverage.

Home Health Care Benefits.   **Home health care coverage** is similar to extended care facility benefits but designed for when the necessary part-time nursing care ordered by a physician following hospitalization can be provided in the patient's home. Coverage is for (1) nursing care (usually limited to a maximum of two hours per day) under the supervision of a registered nurse; (2) physical, occupational, and speech therapy; and (3) medical supplies and equipment, such as wheelchairs and hospital beds.

In most cases, the benefits payable are equal to a percentage, frequently 80 percent, of reasonable-and-customary charges. Benefit payments are limited to either a maximum number of visits (such as 60 per calendar year) or to a period of time (such as 90 days after benefits commence). In the latter case, the time period may be a function of the unused hospital days, such as 3 days of home visits for each unused hospital day.

Hospice Benefits.   Hospices for the treatment of terminally ill persons are a recent development in the area of medical care. **Hospice care** does not attempt to cure medical conditions but rather is devoted to easing the physical and psychological pain associated with death. In addition to providing services for the dying patient, a hospice may also offer counseling to family members. Although a hospice is usually thought of as a separate facility, this type of care can also be provided on an outpatient basis in the dying person's home. Where hospice care is available, the cost of treating terminally ill patients is usually much less than the cost of traditional hospitalization. Hospice benefits may be subject to a specified maximum benefit, such as $5,000.

Birthing Centers.   Another recent development in medical care is birthing centers, separate from hospitals. The cost of using birthing centers is considerably less than using hospitals. Nurse-midwives perform deliveries, and mothers and babies are released shortly after birth. Benefits may be paid as if the mother had used a hospital and obstetrician, but charges are frequently paid in full as an incentive to use these lower-cost facilities.

Preapproval of Visits to Specialists

Many persons elect to bypass primary-care physicians, such as family physicians and pediatricians, and use specialists and the emergency room as their primary access to medical care; this results in additional costs but does not improve medical outcomes, in the opinion of much of the medical community. To counter this practice, some traditional medical expense plans require that a visit to a specialist be preceded by a visit to a primary-care physician. It is not necessary for the primary-care physician to actually certify that a trip to a specialist is necessary, only that he or she has been told that the patient plans to make such a visit. The rationale for this procedure is that the primary-care physician may convince the patient that he or she is able to treat the condition and that a specialist is unnecessary, at least at that time. If a specialist is needed, the primary-care physician is also in a better position to recommend the right type of specialist and to coordinate health care for persons seeing multiple specialists.

Failure to use the primary-care physician as a quasi-gatekeeper will result in a reduction in benefits. Usually, benefits will still be paid but at a lower level.

Benefits for Preventive Care

Most traditional medical expense plans provide at least a few benefits for preventive care. Probably the most frequently found benefits, because of state mandates for group insurance contracts, are well-baby care, childhood immunizations, and mammograms. Plans may also go as far as providing routine physicals for children at specified ages and, perhaps, for all covered persons, typically subject to an annual maximum benefit, such as $150 or $200. However, coverage for routine adult physicals is much more likely to be covered under managed care plans.

■ COVERAGE FOR COMPLEMENTARY AND ALTERNATIVE MEDICINE

During the 1990s, the use of **complementary and alternative medicine (CAM)** increased dramatically, with estimates that more than half of the population has used one or more of these types of services as alternatives to conventional treatments covered under medical expense plans. In addition, the majority of physicians have recommended CAM techniques, particularly for treatment of neck and back problems, anxiety, depression, and headaches. Examples of CAM services include the following:

- Acupuncture
- Biofeedback
- Chiropractic treatment
- Herbal medicine
- Naturopathy
- Homeopathy
- Hypnosis
- Massage therapy
- Meditation
- Relaxation
- Therapeutic touch
- Vitamin therapy
- Yoga

The attractiveness of these programs has increased over the past few years for a number of reasons. For example, patients appreciate the rapport they develop with their CAM practitioners, and this is indicated by a higher degree of satisfaction with these practitioners than with their physicians. Patients also like the fact that CAM practitioners are more likely than traditional medical practitioners to actively involve patients in the development of treatment plans. As a result, patients are more likely to follow plans of CAM than they are to follow conventional medical treatment plans. Finally, complications from treatment are less likely than from conventional medical treatment, possibly because of the less invasive nature of CAM.

Insurers and plan administrators have typically been leery of adding benefits for CAM because they fear increases in claims costs. This will obviously occur if CAM is used in addition to traditional medical treatment. However, it is often used as a replacement for traditional medical treatment. If successful, costs might decrease. There is also concern over the qualifications and training of many of the persons who provide CAM.

Many insurance contracts and managed care plans provide limited benefits for chiropractic treatment, and a smaller number cover acupuncture, sometimes as a result of state mandates. However, benefits are often subject to limitations. Some providers of medical benefits will add other types of CAM to their insurance contracts or managed care plans if the employer is willing to pay an increased premium. Employers may be willing to pay this cost as a response to employee interest or to differentiate their medical expense plan from those of other employers. Results of surveys vary, but it appears that more than half of employers have benefit plans that cover chiropractic services, about 20 percent have plans that cover acupuncture, and about 10 percent have plans that cover some other forms of CAM.

To control costs, coverage of CAM is subject to a variety of controls. These include one or more of the following:

- Annual or lifetime dollar limits
- Limits on the number of annual visits
- A requirement that treatment be for specified medical conditions
- A requirement for a referral from a primary care physician

■ KEY TERMS

accumulation period	complementary and alternative medicine (CAM)	family deductible
all-causes deductible		fee-for-service plan
benefit period		first-dollar coverage
calendar-year deductible	comprehensive major medical coverage	home health care coverage
carryover provision		hospice care
coinsurance	copayment	hospital expense coverage
common accident provision	corridor deductible	hospital precertification
community rating	deductible	indemnity concept
	extended care facility	

initial (or straight) deductible

internal maximum

lifetime maximum

limitations

major medical coverage

member

Mental Health Parity Act

Newborns' and Mothers' Health Protection Act

per-cause deductible

per-cause maximum

percentage participation

physicians' visits expense coverage

preadmission testing

reasonable-and-customary charge

second surgical opinion

service-benefit concept

stop-loss (or coinsurance) limit

supplemental major medical coverage

surgical expense coverage

surgical fee schedule

traditional (or indemnity) medical expense plan

Women's Health and Cancer Rights Act

■ STUDY QUESTIONS

1. Compare Blue Cross and Blue Shield organizations and private insurance companies with respect to each of the following features:
   a. Regulation and taxation
   b. Form of benefits provided
   c. Types of benefits provided
   d. Reimbursement of providers
   e. Rating
   f. Marketing

2. Describe the nature of each of the following basic medical expense coverages:
   a. Hospital expense
   b. Surgical expense
   c. Physicians' expense

3. a. What is the difference between a supplemental major medical contract and a comprehensive major medical contract?
   b. Why are supplemental major medical contracts still used?

4. What types of exclusions are commonly found in major medical contracts?

5. a. How does the Newborns' and Mothers' Health Protection Act affect coverage for maternity under medical expense plans?
   b. How does the Women's Health and Cancer Rights Act affect exclusions under medical expense plans?

6. What types of limitations are usually placed on the benefits provided under major medical contracts?

7. Why are benefits for mental illness, alcoholism, and drug addition often carved out of major medical plans?

8. How is medical expense coverage for mental illness affected by the Mental Health Parity Act?

9. What types of deductibles are found in major medical contracts?

10. Why do different coinsurance percentages sometimes apply to different categories of medical expenses?

11. Describe the methods used to place a limit on the amount of out-of-pocket medical expenses that must be borne by an individual under the coinsurance provision of a major medical contract.

12. a. What is the purpose of hospital precertification?

    b. What are the possible penalties if the precertification process is not followed?

13. Explain how surgical benefits may be affected by (a) voluntary provisions and (b) mandatory provisions for second surgical opinions.

14. What conditions must usually be satisfied before an individual is eligible to receive benefits for care in an extended care facility?

15. What types of benefits are typically provided under home health care coverages?

16. How does hospice care often lower the cost of health care?

17. Explain how medical expense plans might use each of the following to control medical expenses:

    a. Birthing centers

    b. Preapproval of specialists

18. What types of benefits for preventive care might be found in a traditional medical expense plan?

19. Why have benefits for complementary and alternative medicine become more attractive in recent years?

■ NOTE

1. The Henry J. Kaiser Foundation and Health Research and Education Trust, *Employer Health Benefits, 2003.*

Managed Care:
Introduction and HMOs

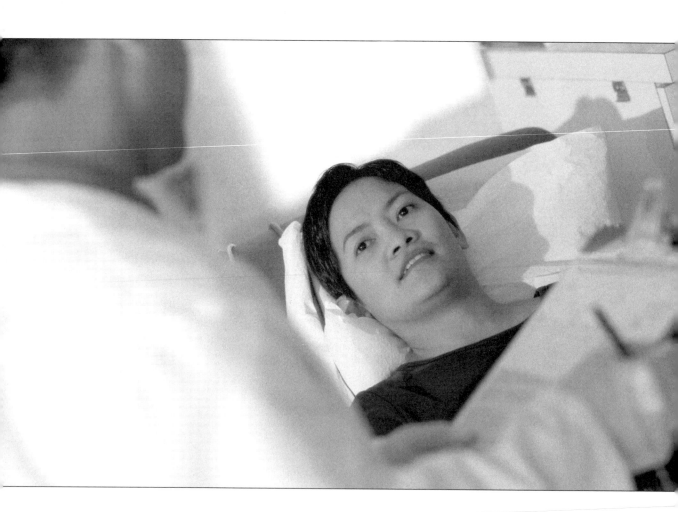

- Explain how managed care plans differ from traditional medical expense plans.
- Describe the reasons for using managed care plans.
- Explain the role of provider networks in managed care plans.
- Explain the role of utilization management in managed care plans.
- Describe the characteristics of health maintenance organizations and explain the effect of the Health Maintenance Organization Act of 1973.
- Compare HMOs with traditional major medical expense plans.

The concept of managed care was introduced in Chapter 9. This and the following chapter are devoted primarily to an analysis of the various types of managed care plans. The chapter begins with an introduction to managed care plans and why a person might select managed care in general or a particular managed care plan. There is also a discussion of major aspects of managed care plans—provider networks and utilization review. The chapter concludes with an analysis of health maintenance organizations (HMOs). Preferred-provider organizations (PPOs), point-of-service (POS) plans, and other forms of managed care are covered in Chapter 12.

Before proceeding further, it is important to note that managed care continues to evolve and is very different today from what it was just a few years ago.

■ INTRODUCTION TO MANAGED CARE PLANS

It was pointed out in Chapter 9 that a true managed care plan should have five main characteristics:

1. Controlled access to providers
2. Comprehensive utilization management
3. Preventive care
4. Risk sharing
5. High-quality care

The major characteristic of managed care plans that differentiates them from traditional medical expense plans is probably the limitations on the choice of medical care providers that may be used. The question arises as to whether these choice limitations lead to a different quality of care. Despite these apparent or perceived differences, more than three-quarters of the population is now in some type of managed care plan, and the majority seem reasonably satisfied with the arrangement. In the past few years, much of the growth in managed care has come from employers with fewer than 50 employees. Unlike larger employers, who usually give employees a choice between one or more managed care plans and a traditional indemnity plan, small employers are more likely to offer a single managed care plan rather than any options.

Despite the relatively high level of satisfaction, there has been some recent consumer backlash against managed care that has led to plan changes and legislation, particularly at the state level.

Limited Choice of Medical Providers

Managed care plans attempt to eliminate the unrestricted use of medical care providers by either requiring or encouraging members to use preapproved network providers. The earliest managed care plans, which were HMOs, usually provided no coverage for treatment outside the managed care network, discouraging enrollment because many Americans valued the choice that had traditionally been available when medical treatment was needed.

The concept of managed care received considerable attention in the late 1960s and early 1970s, culminating in the passage of the Health Maintenance Organization Act of 1973. The act resulted in modest growth of HMO plans, but the real growth that came later for managed care was encouraged by several developments that gave members more choice in selecting providers of medical care. One of these changes was more flexibility under HMO plans. For example, many of the early HMOs assigned a primary physician to a new member. Gradually, new forms of HMOs developed and existing

HMOs were modified to allow members to select a primary care physician from a list of primary care providers.

At the same time, the traditional insurance industry was entering managed care, primarily through the marketing of PPO products, which allowed more flexibility than most HMOs with respect to selection of specialists. In addition, benefits were usually available for treatment received outside a managed care network, although at a reduced payment level.

The popularity of PPO products with both employers and employees forced the HMOs to adopt even more flexibility. They did this through the establishment of POS plans, which covered nonnetwork treatment. The typical POS plan is more flexible than a typical HMO but more restrictive than a typical PPO product. However, the variations in all three types of plans today are so significant that it is sometimes difficult to determine exactly what is typical.

Survey statistics on the availability of managed care plans to employees vary. One recent survey, however, estimated that 77 percent of employees had PPO plans available to them.[1] The percentages for traditional HMO and POS plans were 47 and 30, respectively.

Quality of Care

A difficult question to answer is whether persons covered by managed care plans receive the same quality of care as persons covered under traditional medical expense plans. If the sole objective of a managed care plan is to offer coverage at the lowest possible cost, the quality of care may decline. However, some type of quality assurance program is one aspect of any managed care plan. If properly administered, this type of program can weed out providers who give substandard and unnecessary care. In this regard, managed care plans may be more progressive than the medical field as a whole.

The results of numerous surveys and studies on the quality of medical care plans have been mixed. Some studies show that persons in managed care plans are less likely than persons in traditional medical expense plans to receive treatment for a serious medical condition from specialists, and they are also likely to have fewer diagnostic tests. There are those who argue that family physicians can treat a wide variety of illnesses and avoid unnecessary diagnostic tests and referrals to specialists. On the other hand, an opposing argument contends that the decline in the use of specialists and frequency of diagnostic tests is also a clear indication that there is a decline in the level of medical care. Other studies show that persons in managed care plans are much more likely than the rest of the population to receive preventive care and early diagnosis and treatment of potentially serious conditions, such as high blood pressure and diabetes. In addition, managed care plans are viewed as having been successful in coordinating care when it is necessary for a person to see several different types of specialists. There is no doubt that there are some small provider networks with a limited choice of specialists, but most networks are relatively large or allow persons to select treatment outside the network. There are also many managed care plans that do refer members to highly regarded physicians and hospitals or have these providers as part of their networks.

In evaluating the quality of medical care, it is also interesting to look at surveys of participants in the various types of medical expense plans. Most persons in traditional medical expense plans are convinced they receive better care because of their unlimited ability to choose providers of medical care as needed. Although surveys of members in managed care plans usually show a high degree of satisfaction with the medical care received, there are some concerns that have resulted in recent plan changes and legislative actions and interest.

Two recent developments relate to the quality of care provided by managed care organizations—an increased interest in accreditation and a consumer backlash against some aspects of managed care. This backlash has led to the introduction or passage of laws in many states aimed at solving consumer and provider concerns about access to care, quality of care, and choice.

Accreditation

As managed care matures and becomes more widespread, there is an increasing focus by government, employers, and consumers on quality. This has led many employers, particularly large employers, to require that managed care organizations for their employees meet some type of **accreditation** standards. Accreditation does more than just provide consumers with information about health plans. The process, which may cost a managed care organization several thousand dollars, compares it with what are considered benchmark standards of quality care. The organization knows where it stands in relation to its competitors and also what must be done to become accredited or to achieve a higher level of accreditation.

The leading organization for accrediting appears to be the **National Committee for Quality Assurance (NCQA)**, an independent, not-for-profit organization that has been accrediting managed care plans since 1991. (The NCQA's Web site is *www.ncqa.org*.) It also accredits or certifies physician organizations and organizations that provide behavioral health care, utilization management, disease management, and credentials verification. Unlike some accrediting organizations, NCQA makes detailed information available to the general public. The NCQA rates managed care organizations by evaluating each of the following five areas of performance:

1. *Access and service.* Do plan members have access to the care and service they need? For example, are physicians in the health plan free to discuss all treatment options available? Do patients report problems getting needed care? How well does the health plan follow up on grievances?

2. *Qualified providers.* Does the plan assess each physician's qualifications, and what do plan members say about their providers? For example, does the plan regularly check the licenses and training of physicians? How do plan members rate their personal physician or nurse?

3. *Staying healthy.* Does the plan help people maintain good health and avoid illness? Does it give its physicians guidelines about how to provide appropriate preventive health services? Are members receiving tests and screenings as appropriate?

4. *Living with illness.* How well does the plan care for people with chronic conditions? Does the plan have programs in place to assist patients in managing chronic conditions such as asthma? Do diabetics, who are at risk for blindness, receive eye exams as needed?

5. *Getting better.* How well does the plan care for people when they become sick? How does the plan evaluate new medical procedures, drugs, and devices to ensure that patients have access to safe and effective care?

The possible ratings for each area of performance are best, very good, good, fair, or poor. From this information, the NCQA also gives managed care plans one of the following overall accreditation outcomes:

■ Excellent

■ Commendable

■ Accredited

■ Provisional

■ Denied

The NCQA has also developed a set of performance measures that are designed to enable purchasers and consumers to have necessary information to reliably compare the performance of managed care plans. These measures are commonly referred to as the **Health Plan Employer Data and Information Set,** or **HEDIS**. The current version (which tends to change almost annually) has more than 50 measures that fall into the following categories:

■ Effectiveness of care

■ Access/availability of care

■ Satisfaction with the experience of care

■ Health plan stability

■ Use of services

■ Health plan descriptive information

Examples of a few of the measures that HEDIS reports, which can then be compared with suggested norms, are the following:

■ Percentage of adolescents receiving immunizations

■ Percentage of patients receiving beta blocker treatment following a heart attack

■ Percentage of patients receiving appropriate treatment for asthma

■ Percentage of women receiving counseling at the onset of menopause

There are also other bodies that accredit various types of health care organizations, including managed care plans, and make their data available to consumers. The Joint Commission on Accreditation of Healthcare Organizations (JCAHO) has accredited hospitals for many years. It also accredits health care networks (including PPOs), home care organizations, assisted-living facilities, long-term care facilities, behavioral health care organizations, ambulatory care organizations, and pathological and clinical laboratory services (Web site: *www.jcaho.org*).

Another major accrediting organization is URAC (formerly the Utilization Review Accreditation Commission). URAC focuses on accrediting specific aspects of managed care, such as health utilization management. Managed care organizations, such as HMOs and PPOs, can have their own utilization management activities accredited if prescribed standards are met. In addition, URAC accredits the activities of organizations that specialize solely in utilization management and that sell their services to managed care plans that do not have their own utilization management staffs. URAC also accredits organizations with respect to other aspects of managed care, including the following: case management standards, call center standards, network standards, plan standards, and network credentialing standards (Web site: *www.urac.org*).

Reactions to Consumer and Provider Concerns

As previously mentioned, the majority of employers and employees are reasonably satisfied with managed care plans but have increasing concerns. However, the satisfaction of physicians and other providers is much more negative, primarily because of decreased control over medical decisions for their patients and a loss of income. As a result, there has been what the media describe as a "backlash against managed care." In some ways, this terminology is inaccurate. First, some of the public's concerns, such as the lack of complete mental health parity and the issue of coverage sometimes being denied as unnecessary, apply to the entire health care system. Second, although some of the concerns are aimed at all types of managed care plans, many are aimed solely at practices of HMOs.

This backlash has had several results:

■ States continue to enact legislation that addresses many of the concerns.

■ Managed care organizations voluntarily modify their practices in light of legislative activity and competitive forces.

■ The federal government continues to grapple with consumer legislation.

State Reform. State legislatures in recent years have passed several types of laws aimed at managed care reform. Many of these laws, which have been passed by anywhere from 12 to almost all states, include the following:

■ Antigag-clause rules

■ Grievance, review, and appeal procedures

■ Any-willing-provider laws

■ Mandatory POS options

■ Continuity of care

■ Provider protection

■ Emergency room coverage

■ Mental health parity

- Diabetes health benefits
- Minimum stays for certain procedures
- Plastic surgery mandates
- Direct access to providers

A smaller number of states have also passed other types of reform legislation.

Some of these changes tend to bring managed care plans closer to traditional indemnity plans in terms of both coverage and cost.

Antigag-Clause Rules.   Almost all states have adopted **antigag-clause legislation** that prohibits managed care organizations from including provisions in their contracts that prevent physicians from discussing with patients treatment options that may not be covered under their health plans or from referring very ill patients for specialized care by providers outside the plan.

Grievance, Review, and Appeal Procedures.   A concern of many consumers over the years has been that managed care plans did not have adequate procedures to receive complaints or appeals about denials of coverage or to make decisions in a timely fashion. As a result, all states have passed some type of legislation that requires that managed care plans follow specified grievance, review, and appeal procedures. At a minimum, this legislation requires that members be informed of the procedures, usually in writing. There is often a specific time period in which a plan must respond to a grievance, particularly when emergency care is needed. Some states have gone further and require an independent external review process if a member is dissatisfied after going through the plan's grievance and appeal process. The decision of the independent review organization is usually binding on the parties, but it is nonbinding in a few states.

Any-Willing-Provider Laws.   There has been some concern, often by physicians, that managed care organizations unnecessarily limit the access of patients to physicians. As a result, several states have passed an **any-willing-provider law**. These laws require that HMOs and other networks of medical care providers accept any provider who is willing to agree to the plan's basic terms and fees. This legislation has been opposed by managed care plans on the basis that it will prevent them from negotiating for the best possible terms with highly qualified and efficient providers.

Mandatory POS Options.   As is discussed later, closed-panel HMOs have traditionally required that members seek treatment from network providers. Several states have recently adopted legislation that requires managed care organizations to permit members to seek treatment from nonnetwork providers. The managed care organization must pay a portion, but not all, of the expenses incurred with these providers. In effect, such legislation turns a traditional HMO into a POS plan. POS plans are discussed later in this chapter. In some states, this legislation applies only to HMOs with a minimum number of members, such as 10,000. In other states, a POS option must be made available to employer groups above a certain size, such as 25 employees.

Continuity of Care.   One drawback to receiving care through a managed care plan is that continuity of care may be lost if the provider ceases to be a part of the provider network, for whatever reason. Several states have recently addressed this issue through this legislation. For example, one state requires that the managed care plan continue to pay for care for up to 60 days, as long as such a continuation is appropriate. Many of the state laws deal primarily with pregnant patients and may, for example, require coverage to be continued until birth or shortly thereafter for any woman who is in the third trimester of a pregnancy at the time of her obstetrician's departure from the network.

Provider Protection. Most states now require that managed care plans disclose their criteria for selecting medical care providers, give these providers advance notice of contract termination, and provide them with procedures for contesting the termination. One purpose of this legislation is to address the concern that providers who give quality care might lose their provider contract if this care was more expensive or extensive than the managed care plan deemed necessary.

Emergency Room Coverage. Managed care organizations have been criticized for often refusing to pay for emergency room care, claiming that emergency room treatment was unnecessary. For example, some plans do not pay if a member who goes to an emergency room with chest pains is found to have indigestion rather than a heart attack. The majority of states now require that a plan pay emergency room charges whenever a prudent layperson considers a situation to be an emergency. In addition, care cannot be delayed to get plan authorization for treatment.

Mental Health Parity. Some states have passed mental health parity laws that go beyond the federal law in that they require either complete parity for benefits arising from physical illnesses and mental illnesses or complete parity for physical illnesses and certain severe mental illnesses, such as schizophrenia, depression, or bipolar disorder. These types of laws apply to benefits provided under both traditional insurance contracts and managed care contracts.

Diabetes Health Benefits. Many states require that insurance contracts or managed care plans pay for certain education, equipment, and supplies required by diabetics. With proper care, diabetics can often avoid many serious complications of the disease, such as blindness, amputations, strokes, heart disease, and kidney disease. It is interesting to note one difference between the passage of the laws for mental health parity and diabetes health benefits. The push for mental health parity was partially a result of some managed care plans providing more restrictive benefits than many traditional major medical contracts. On the other hand, the diabetes legislation was probably encouraged by the publicity and success of practices adopted by some managed care plans that were not used in traditional major medical contracts.

Minimum Stays for Certain Procedures. As a result of concerns that some HMOs were compromising proper health care by forcing new mothers and their babies to leave the hospital too soon, most states adopted laws requiring coverage of mandated minimum stays for mothers and newborns following deliveries. As a rule, these time periods coincide with those required by the federal legislation. Most states also mandate that coverage be provided for minimum stays following surgery for breast cancer. For example, several states mandate coverage for stays of 48 hours for mastectomies and 24 hours for lymph node dissection.

Plastic Surgery Mandates. As a result of publicity over several cases in which HMOs denied coverage for reconstructive surgery—for example, to deformed children—several states enacted legislation to require all health insurance contracts or health plans to provide coverage for certain types of reconstructive surgery. This legislation may apply to the repair of birth defects only, or it may apply to a broader list of situations in which reconstruction might be needed as a result of mastectomies, trauma, infections, tumors, or disease.

Direct Access to Providers. Most states have passed laws to allow women covered under managed care plans to have direct access to obstetricians/gynecologists without obtaining approval or a referral from their health plan. A few states require direct access to other types of providers, such as dermatologists.

Other Legislation. Other types of legislation have been introduced in several states, but the number of states adopting the legislation has been small to date. Examples include the following:

- Allowing managed care organizations to be sued for medical malpractice if their denial of medically necessary treatment results in harm or injury to a patient. Under many typical state laws, a managed care plan cannot be sued for medical malpractice because it is not considered to be practicing medicine.

- Requiring that patients and/or state regulators be informed of financial incentives offered to providers.

- Granting patients access to all prescription drugs approved by the government for sale.

- Making health care plans disclose their policies for covering experimental treatments.

- Improving state monitoring of managed care plans by requiring that these plans report the status of patient grievances to the states.

Voluntary Reform by Managed Care Organizations. Many managed care reforms have been initiated voluntarily by managed care organizations. Some reforms are probably a result of the natural evolving of a new form of financing and providing health care. Other changes have occurred because of competition among managed care organizations for market share. However, most of the reforms probably are reactions to legislation that is proposed or passed by the states. After a few states pass a certain type of managed care legislation, there is often a tendency for managed care organizations nationwide to revise their plans to address the concerns that resulted in the legislation. There then may be little need for other states to adopt similar legislation, and, in fact, managed care bills introduced in state legislatures are often not enacted if the legislature learns that the managed care industry has already resolved the problem.

The threat of legislation at either the state or federal level is also a major impetus for voluntary changes by managed care plans. Just as with other types of businesses, such voluntary reform may dampen the likelihood that more restrictive government regulation will result.

Federal Reform. Congress has addressed some health care concerns with the passage of such legislation as the following acts, which have been discussed earlier in this book: the Mental Health Parity Act, the Newborns' and Mothers' Health Protection Act, and the Women's Health and Cancer Rights Act.

At the time this book was being revised in early 2004, there were bills in Congress that would add significant federal legislation to the health care environment. Sometimes referred to as a *patients' bill of rights*, this type of legislation seems to have bipartisan support. However, there are differences of opinion as to what should be done, and these often vary by political party. The following discussion addresses a few of these issues.

There is disagreement whether the legislation should apply to all health insurance plans or to self-funded plans only. For the most part, ERISA exempts self-funded benefit plans from state regulation and, therefore, the types of state reforms previously described apply only to "insured" plans in the sense that they apply to insurance contracts and managed care plans over which the states have legislative control. There are arguments that federal legislation should apply only to self-funded plans because the states are already regulating the plans that are not self-funded. There are other arguments that federal legislation should apply to all health insurance plans because of a lack of legislation in some states and less stringent regulation in many states.

Much of the proposed federal regulation is in fact broader than that found in most states, and even the Congressional Budget Office agrees that a federal bill would increase the cost of health care plans. Unfortunately, increased health plan costs lead to an increase in the number of employers and employees who are unable to afford coverage. This has resulted in a debate over what should be the proper balance between availability and cost.

There is also disagreement over the issue of health plan and employer liability. Some proposed legislation would allow employees to sue medical expense plans and their employers if a delay or denial of benefits injures them. There are concerns that this type of legislation would benefit trial lawyers more than consumers. In addition, there are concerns that the potential liability might result in many employers terminating health care plans and giving employees pay increases with which they would have to arrange their own health insurance coverage. Such a result would undoubtedly increase the number of uninsureds because some employees would find other uses for the money. Some bills do not impose liability on employers; rather, they provide a process of external review over medical decisions of managed care plans.

Readers should follow legislative developments and their potential effect on health care plans.

■ REASONS FOR USE OF MANAGED CARE

There are many reasons why employees elect coverage under a managed care plan. First, it may be the only plan the employer provides, although most employers allow a choice of benefit plans. In those situations, the following factors have been identified as reasons why a managed care plan in general, or a particular managed care plan might be selected:

■ The reputation of the managed care plan. To some extent, this is a function of the managed care plan's experience. In areas where managed care plans have been established for many years, a larger percentage of employees participate. Employees are also concerned with perceived quality of care and are less likely to choose a plan known for frequent coverage denials and difficulty in obtaining referrals to specialists.

- The extent to which employees have established relationships with physicians. Employees are reluctant to elect a managed care option if it requires that they give up a physician with whom they are satisfied. In some cases, of course, this physician may also participate in the managed care plan. In general, new employees are more likely to elect a managed care option if they are new residents of the area or are just entering the labor force.

- Costs. Managed care plans are obviously more attractive to employers when they offer a less expensive alternative to coverage under insurance company plans. As a rule, managed care plans are less expensive, and any employee share of the premium is lower. Even when the premium cost is comparable, there is often broader coverage and no deductibles or percentage participation. If employees view a managed care alternative as being less expensive in the long run, their participation is greater.

In the early days of the growth of managed care, employers were concerned primarily with cost savings when they adopted managed care plans. In a more mature managed care marketplace, employers are concerned with the same factors when they change plans as are employees: reputation, availability of providers, and cost. Throughout most of the late 1990s, the economy was booming, labor markets were tight, and employers faced relatively modest premium increases from year to year. As a result, employers were much more likely than in the past to modify managed care plans or to adopt new plans that were less restrictive, and therefore somewhat more expensive, in their management of care. With greater premium increases and a downturn in the economy as the new millennium began, this trend started to reverse itself.

■ PROVIDER NETWORKS

Networks of providers of health care services and the contracts that establish them are essential to managed care plans. These plans manage care primarily through the **provider network** that members in the plan are encouraged to use. Members may be required to receive covered medical care services from network providers only, or they must use these providers to obtain full plan benefits. To be successful, a managed care plan must create and maintain provider networks that do the following:

- Contain qualified providers of health care services
- Meet member needs for medical care services
- Compensate network providers in a manner that encourages efficient use of resources

Qualified Providers of Health Care Services

Managed care plans specify the qualifications, known as **credentials**, that providers must have and maintain to be a network participant. Physicians, for example, must document their training, licensure, certification in a specialty, and malpractice insurance coverage. In addition, they must be free of limitations, suspensions, or impairments that would affect their practice of medicine and hospital admitting privileges. Hospitals and other institutions must be licensed, accredited, and approved for participation in the Medicare program. Generally, a credentialing verification organization hired by the managed care plan obtains the information to determine if a provider has the qualifications that the plan requires. The credentialing process is repeated periodically to make sure that network providers continue to meet the required qualifications.

Member Needs for Medical Care Services

A managed care plan's provider network must encompass the broad scope of health services that members may need and must be conveniently accessible to those members.

Network providers include physicians, hospitals and other institutions, diagnostic radiology and laboratory services, and therapy services. Among the other institutions in a network are facilities that provide outpatient care, including surgery, rehabilitation, and skilled-nursing care. Although a few managed care plans may hire their health care professionals and own their facilities, most managed care plans establish their networks through contracts with providers. These providers may be either solo practitioners or participants in various types of groups under a variety of organizational structures. A provider often participates in several networks and also treats patients who are not members of managed care plans. Plans may also contract with specialty care organizations for specific services. These services may include psychiatric care, substance abuse treatment, rehabilitation, radiology, laboratory and pathology services, transplant surgeries, and prescription drug services.

Networks must be designed to allow members to have reasonably convenient access to the broad range of services that the managed care plan offers. Therefore, managed care plans must develop and maintain sufficient numbers and types of providers to meet member health care needs in a geographic area. In addition, most network physicians must remain open to accepting as patients those members who are new to the plan as well as those who may wish to change providers. As a result, most plans maintain active recruitment and management programs to make sure that their networks keep pace with the needs of their ever-changing member populations in the areas and regions where these members reside. However, competition for members frequently requires that managed care plans expand their networks to offer members a choice of physicians, specialists, and hospitals beyond that required by scope of service and convenience alone.

Provider Compensation

A major objective of managed care plans is cost containment through the efficient use of health care resources. The method of provider compensation is one major component of this objective.

Providers are willing to grant preferred rates to managed care plans because as participants in the plan's network they anticipate an increased number of patients who will utilize their services. Or conversely, they will not lose patients to providers who are network providers. The specific payment method for network providers varies by the type of provider and the negotiating strength of the plan. However, the managed care plan's objective remains the same under any payment arrangement: to control the price of services and the overall increase in the cost of services utilized.

The price to be paid for services is determined by agreement in advance of the provision of services and cannot be changed for a specified period without notification. It also usually requires the agreement of each party. An important part of the contract with a provider outlines the provider's obligation to accept the agreed-on amount as payment in full, except for copayments and other clearly identified amounts that the provider must collect from plan members.

The payment method also intends, if possible, to have providers participate to some degree in the increased cost of services utilized, either through incentive payments for meeting utilization targets or penalties for failure to do so. Among the payment methods managed care plans use are capitation, modification of the traditional fee-for-service payment system, and per-day and per-case rates.

Capitation. Although far from dominant, the payment method historically associated with managed care plans is **capitation**. HMOs frequently employ this method for the payment of primary care physicians if each HMO member is required to select or is assigned a primary care physician who is responsible for the member's care. Primary care physicians provide members with basic health care services and coordinate additional care needs through referrals to other network physicians for certain medical specialist services. Under capitation, these physicians receive a fixed payment per month for each member without regard to the services a member may receive in any particular month. These rates reflect likely utilization of services by the plan's members based on age and gender and the cost of care in the area. Capitation provides physicians no financial incentives to overtreat patients.

In conjunction with capitation, a managed care plan commonly establishes an **incentive payment program** that rewards physicians who meet budgeted cost and utilization levels for hospital and ancillary services. This program may include other criteria such as meeting member satisfaction and quality standards. Such an incentive program is called a **withhold arrangement** if it imposes financial penalties or decreases compensation for failure to meet these same criteria.

Capitation may be used in some cases for the payment of specialty physicians and for services such as substance abuse care and chronic condition management. Although infrequent, payment arrangements for inpatient hospital services may also use capitation.

Modified Fee-for-Service Payments. Despite the cost containment advantages of capitation, a **modified fee-for-service payment system** is the dominant method for compensating physicians in managed care plans. Many specialty physicians in managed care plans and most physicians in PPO networks are paid in this manner. It is also occasionally used with hospitals.

With this method of compensation, providers are paid on a fee-for-service basis, subject to negotiated maximums per procedure. In most cases, this involves a discount from what the physician would charge a patient who did not participate in the managed care plan.

Modified fee-for-service payment arrangements employed by managed care plans often include some element of physician financial involvement in cost containment through rewards or penalties based on success in achieving the plan's utilization and cost targets. These rewards and penalties are similar to the incentive and withhold arrangements discussed previously under capitation payment.

Per-Day and Per-Case Payments.　The dominant arrangement used by managed care plans for payment of inpatient hospital services is a negotiated **per-day rate**. With this approach, a hospital is paid a specified amount for each day a plan member is hospitalized, regardless of the actual cost of services on any particular day. The rate usually differs by type or level of care such as intensive care, obstetrics, or rehabilitation. The rate may decrease in relation to the days the member stays in the hospital or the aggregate days of stay for all plan members.

A managed care plan may be able to control costs more effectively by using a **per-case rate** to pay for hospital stays. With this approach, a specified fee is paid for all inpatient costs, regardless of a member's length of stay. This fee is based on such factors as a member's principal diagnosis, secondary diagnosis, surgical procedures, age, gender, and presence of complications. This system of classification of services is often referred to as **diagnosis-related groups**.

A per-case rate is also often used to reimburse hospitals and other providers for nonphysician services that are received by members on an outpatient basis.

■ UTILIZATION MANAGEMENT

Utilization management is the process by which a managed care plan ensures that members use health services effectively and efficiently. Such programs are essential to a managed care plan's control of medical care resource use and plan costs overall. The provider compensation methods previously discussed should be designed to reinforce utilization management objectives or at least be compatible with them.

Utilization management programs may be categorized as demand management, referral management, and management of institutional services. Case management and disease management are also important classes of utilization programs that cut across these categories.

Demand Management

Demand management is a category of utilization management that guides members with respect to their personal health conditions. This category, which aims to reduce member need and use of medical services, includes wellness programs, health risk assessments, and provision of medical information.

Wellness Programs.　A wellness program promotes the well-being of plan members. One goal of a wellness program is to discover and treat medical conditions before they become severe. This goal may be accomplished through such plan benefits as routine physicals and immunizations as well as screening for breast and prostate cancer, high cholesterol, high blood pressure, and diabetes.

A second goal of a wellness program is to reduce health risks by conforming personal behavior to a healthy lifestyle with healthy habits. Exercise and nutrition programs for weight management and fitness as well as smoking cessation programs are common plan benefits to achieve this goal.

Wellness programs are discussed in more detail in Chapter 18.

Health Risk Assessments.   A **health risk assessment** is an evaluation of a member's health status using self-reported information. In addition to gathering data on health history and current medical conditions, the evaluation also elicits information on a member's behavior and habits. Members may have the option of using the Internet or an intranet to supply the assessment information. Taken together, this information identifies the member's potential health care risks and gives the plan the opportunity to advocate member lifestyle and health habit changes that reinforce prevention and wellness programs. The extent to which counseling is required is usually left to the primary care physician who receives the health risk assessment from the managed care plan.

Medical Information Programs.   Managed care plans have a variety of **medical information programs** that manage utilization by providing professional medical information that members can use for self-care of common conditions or to decide when to seek professional care. This service also provides members with in-depth information on specific diseases and treatment alternatives via newsletters, pamphlets, and authoritative texts. Plans may offer computer programs and Internet Web sites with interactive features to tailor the information to the member's needs. This technology can assist members in conjunction with their physicians to make informed decisions regarding their course of treatment.

Telephone advice lines also provide members with guidance from qualified professionals, usually nurses, regarding their medical care. Advice lines and the other sources of medical information also reinforce prevention and wellness programs while educating members on self-care.

Referral Management

Referral management is a major function of many managed care plans, usually HMOs and POS plans that require members to select a primary care physician. With this approach, a primary care physician acts as a **gatekeeper**, or **care manager**, in that the physician serves as a member's initial contact for medical care and referral for any additional medical services the member may need. The primary care physician must authorize the use of specialty physicians such as dermatologists, cardiologists, and urologists. The authorization, known as a **referral**, means that the primary care physician believes the member's health condition requires treatment by a specialist who is also a participant in the plan's network. Without a referral, the specialist receives no payment or a reduced payment from the plan. In this way the cost of specialists' services and the services they may order are controlled and unnecessary utilization is avoided.

The managed care plan does not intervene in the referral decision, but it must capture the authorization information to process the specialist's claim for full payment as a network service. The plan also uses the same information to report to the primary care physician on referral rates and the costs they generate. This may affect the physician's compensation under incentive or penalty payment arrangements.

Management of Institutional Services

Management of institutional services includes three types of review: prospective, concurrent, and retrospective. If a coverage decision is disputed by the plan, the member, or the provider, the plan usually has an external review process. In this process, outside specialists who do not work directly for the managed care plan determine whether denied benefits should be paid after a review of the facts of the case. Disputes typically involve disagreements over medically necessary care or experimental treatments. Many states require external review programs.

Prospective Management. **Prospective management** of hospital and other institutional services is a standard part of a plan's utilization management program. Both inpatient admissions and outpatient procedures may require an authorization. When the plan's medical management department receives an authorization request, a utilization manager, usually a nurse, compares the proposed course of treatment or procedure with medical criteria for care based on the member's diagnosis. If the request for an inpatient admission is approved, the plan usually assigns an expected length of stay that approves benefits for that period and sets the anticipated discharge date.

Although the main purpose of the authorization is to avoid unneeded institutional care, the process serves additional purposes. If the course of treatment promises to be complicated and expensive, the plan may earmark the episode for case management. A member initially assigned to inpatient care may be diverted to an outpatient care setting or to a specialty care organization where services may cost less and/or be more effective.

The participating network provider, either the institution or physician, is responsible for obtaining the authorization, not the member. Under the terms of the contract with the plan, if the institutional care proceeds without an authorization, the network providers may incur a payment reduction or be denied payment. If the member seeks treatment outside the provider network, which would still be covered under a PPO or a POS plan, the plan may still require an authorization. In this case, the member may be responsible for obtaining the authorization and is subject to a benefit penalty for failure to obtain it. In emergency situations, a penalty is not imposed as long as the plan is notified within a reasonable time.

Concurrent Management. **Concurrent management**, also known as *continued stay review*, is the management of inpatient utilization during a hospital stay. The plan's utilization manager conducts it by telephone or in person. Initially the utilization manager confirms the member's status to be sure that discharge is planned within the assigned length of stay for which benefits are approved. If the member is recovering more quickly, the utilization manager may pursue an earlier discharge. However, if the hospital stay is expected to exceed the approved period, the utilization manager must reach a decision using medical criteria to authorize or deny coverage for additional days. Rather than deny coverage, the utilization manager usually tries to expedite the discharge. For example, the member's physician and the hospital's own utilization review and discharge-planning departments may agree that home care services and outpatient treatments will allow an earlier discharge. Nevertheless, resolution of disagreements may require a plan's medical director or consulting physician to contact the member's physician regarding the appropriateness of the care with referral to the plan's external review process if necessary.

Retrospective Management.   The **retrospective management** of utilization is an evaluation of the patterns of medical care services that members received over a prior period to determine their appropriateness and to take corrective action as needed. The evaluation of utilization patterns, which may be done on a provider-specific or plan-wide basis, may show that certain tests and procedures are performed more or less frequently than the norm. The length of stay and charges incurred for certain surgeries at some hospitals may be higher than expected. Retrospective evaluation of utilization patterns allows a plan to concentrate its utilization management efforts more effectively on problem areas. For example, retrospective evaluation might lead to a more stringent concurrent management program for a hospital with excessive lengths of stay. Data shared with providers might also cause some of them to modify their practices when they compare their treatment patterns with those of their peers.

Case Management and Disease Management

Case management and disease management are both programs of a health plan's utilization management department that actively coordinate the care of members who incur or are expected to incur unusually high medical care costs from complex courses of treatment resulting from injury or illness. The coordination often applies to a spectrum of the professional and institutional services previously mentioned with the goal of providing cost-effective care.

Case management frequently involves a single episode of inpatient care that may occur, for example, as a result of an automobile accident or a high-risk pregnancy. By contrast, **disease management** focuses on selected medical conditions that are chronic, severe, and expensive to treat. It attempts to control the course of the disease and avoid the need for expensive medical care services. Disease management is covered in more detail later in Chapter 12.

Education of members to effectively manage their conditions is an integral part of these programs.

■ HEALTH MAINTENANCE ORGANIZATIONS

A **health maintenance organization (HMO)** is generally regarded as an organized system of health care that provides a comprehensive array of medical services on a prepaid basis to voluntarily enrolled persons living within a specified region. HMOs act like insurance companies and the Blues in that they finance health care. However, unlike insurance companies and the Blues, they also deliver medical services.

Even though the term is relatively new, the concept of the HMO is not. For many years, prepaid group practice plans (as they were called) operated successfully in many parts of the country. However, growth was relatively slow until the passage of the Health Maintenance Organization Act of 1973. This act resulted from a belief on the part of the federal government that HMOs were a viable alternative method of financing and delivering health care and thus should be encouraged. In fact, the act also resulted in many employers being required to offer their employees the option of coverage by an HMO instead of by a more traditional medical expense plan. There are approximately 650 HMOs in existence, with the 25 largest plans enrolling nearly 40 percent of all HMO participants. In addition, a large majority of HMO members are in plans that belong to one of about 50 chains of HMOs.

Characteristics of HMOs

HMOs have several characteristics that distinguish them from traditional medical expense contracts that are offered by insurance companies and the Blues.

Comprehensive Care. HMOs offer their members a comprehensive package of health care services, generally including benefits for outpatient services as well as for hospitalization. Members usually get many of these services at no cost except the periodically required premium. However, in some cases, a copayment may be imposed for certain services, such as $5 or $10 per physician's visit or per drug prescription. HMOs emphasize preventive care and include such services as routine physicals and immunizations. The cost of such preventive care was historically not covered under the contracts of insurance companies or the Blues, even when major medical coverage was provided. Today, however, as a result of legislation and consumer demand, these plans also provide some preventive care and immunizations but to a lesser degree than HMOs.

Delivery of Medical Services. HMOs provide for the delivery of medical services, which in some cases are performed by salaried physicians and other personnel employed by the HMO. Although this approach is in contrast to the usual fee-for-service delivery system of medical care, some HMOs do contract with providers on a fee-for-service basis.

Members are required to obtain their care from providers of medical services who are affiliated with the HMO. Because HMOs often operate in a geographic region no larger than one state or a single metropolitan area, this requirement may result in limited coverage for members if treatment is received elsewhere. Most HMOs do have "out-of-area coverage," but usually only in the case of medical emergencies.

HMOs emphasize treatment by primary care physicians to the greatest extent possible. These practitioners provide a gatekeeper function and historically have controlled access to specialists. The traditional HMO covers benefits provided by a specialist only if the primary care physician recommends the specialist. This specialist may be a fellow employee in a group-practice plan or a physician who has a contract with the HMO. The member has little or no say regarding the specialist selected, which has been one of the more controversial aspects of HMOs and one that has discouraged larger enrollment. In response to consumer concerns, many HMOs now make the process of seeing a specialist easier. Referrals can often be made by nurses in physicians' offices or by staff members of the HMO whom members can contact by telephone. Some HMOs, referred to as **direct-access** (or **self-referral**) **HMOs**, allow members to see network specialists without going through a gatekeeper. However, the specialist may have to contact the HMO for authorization before proceeding with tests or treatment. A variation of an HMO, called a *POS plan,* allows even more choice. This type of managed care plan is discussed in Chapter 12.

Cost Control.   A major emphasis of HMOs is the control of medical expenses. By providing and encouraging preventive care, HMOs attempt to detect and treat medical conditions at an early stage, thereby avoiding expensive medical treatment in the future. HMOs have also attempted to provide treatment on an outpatient basis whenever possible. Because insurance companies and the Blues have provided more comprehensive coverage for a hospitalized person in the past, less expensive outpatient treatments were often not performed. This emphasis on outpatient treatment and preventive medicine has resulted in a lower hospitalization rate for HMO members than for the population as a whole. However, some of this decreased hospitalization rate over the years appears to be a result of younger and healthier employees having been more likely to elect HMO coverage. This increased emphasis on outpatient treatment has resulted in HMOs often providing better coverage than other types of plans for mental health, alcoholism, or drug addiction if the treatment is received outside a hospital setting. However, if hospitalization is needed, HMOs often have more limited benefits than other types of plans.

HMOs practice a greater degree of utilization management and control than do other types of health plans. In addition to the usual types of prospective review, such as hospital preadmission certification or second surgical opinions, other techniques are often used, such as controlled access to specialists by gatekeepers and preauthorization for certain outpatient procedures. Note that the burden for obtaining preadmission certification or preauthorization for medical procedures lies with the plan physician, not the plan member. This is in contrast to traditional medical expense plans and nonnetwork PPO coverage, where that responsibility is on the plan member.

HMOs are more likely than other types of health plans to conduct a high degree of concurrent management while patients are hospitalized. In addition, HMOs closely monitor the practice patterns of physicians. If a physician, for example, orders a higher-than-average number of diagnostic tests or admits more patients to hospitals than do other physicians, the HMO reviews the situation with the physician to determine whether proper practice standards are being followed. If they are not, the HMO may help the physician adopt better standards.

Physicians sometimes are not aware of all alternatives to hospitalization or that the medical community has changed its standards regarding the effectiveness and frequency of some diagnostic tests. Working with the physician may result in an effective change in practice patterns or, in the most extreme cases, the termination of the physician from the plan. HMOs that monitor practice patterns closely may also contact physicians who do not seem to be ordering enough diagnostic tests or who provide lower-than-usual amounts of preventive care.

HMOs also tightly control payments to physicians and other providers of medical services. In some cases, these providers are employees of the HMO. In other cases, providers' compensation is controlled by capitation or by other arrangements under which the providers share some of the risk that costs will exceed certain levels.

Sponsorship of HMOs

Traditionally, most HMOs operated as nonprofit organizations and had the majority of members until a few years ago. The majority of new HMOs are profit making, and almost two-thirds of members are covered under this type of organization. Although many members are covered by HMOs that have been sponsored by consumer groups, a sizable and increasing portion is covered by plans sponsored by insurance companies or the Blues. Sponsorship may also come from physicians, hospitals, labor unions, or private investors. Some recently established HMOs have been formed by **physician-hospital organizations (PHOs)**. A PHO is a legal entity that is formed by one or more physicians' groups and hospitals. It negotiates, contracts, and markets the services of the physicians and the hospitals. PHOs may form their own HMOs, or they may contract with existing HMOs or other types of managed care organizations.

The issue of whether insurance companies and the Blues should be involved with HMOs was once a source of disagreement within the industry. Some insurance companies viewed HMOs as competitors with the potential of putting them out of the health insurance business. Other insurance companies viewed them as a viable alternative method of financing and delivering health care that could be offered to employers as one of the products in their portfolio.

Over time, the latter viewpoint prevailed. In addition to actually sponsoring and owning HMOs, some insurance companies are actively involved with them in a variety of ways. These include

- consulting on such matters as plan design and administration.

- administrative services, such as actuarial advice, claims monitoring, accounting, and computer services.

- marketing assistance, such as designing sales literature. In a few cases, the agents of insurance companies have been used to market HMOs in conjunction with the marketing of the insurance company's hospitalization plan when the HMO does not provide hospitalization coverage to its members.

- providing hospitalization coverage. HMOs that do not control their own hospital facilities may provide this benefit by purchasing coverage for their members.

- providing emergency out-of-area coverage. An insurance company operating on a national basis may be better equipped to administer these claims than an HMO.

- providing financial support in a variety of ways, including reinsurance if an HMO experiences greater-than-expected demand for services and agreements, to bail out financially troubled HMOs.

Types of HMOs

There are several types of HMOs. The earliest plans can best be described as **closed-panel plans**, under which members must use physicians employed by the plan or by an organization with which it contracts. With most closed-panel plans having several general practitioners, members can usually select their physician from among those accepting new patients and make medical appointments just as if the physician were in private practice. However, there is frequently little choice among specialists because a plan may have a contract with only one physician or a limited number of physicians in a given specialty.

The number of closed-panel plans is relatively small, but they account for almost 20 percent of all HMO members. The three different types of closed-panel plans—staff-model HMOs, group-model HMOs, and network-model HMOs—are discussed in more detail below.

Many newer HMOs have been formed as individual practice associations (IPAs), which can be described as **open-panel plans**. This type of plan has more flexibility with respect to members choosing physicians and the ability of physicians to participate in the plan. About 45 percent of HMO members are in IPAs.

Most of the remaining members of HMOs receive their coverage in a variety of ways under mixed-model plans. Some members are also in open-ended HMOs, which are discussed in Chapter 12 as POS plans.

Staff-Model HMO.   Under a **staff-model HMO**, the HMO owns its own facilities and hires its own physicians. It may own hospitals, laboratories, or pharmacies, or it may contract for these services. The HMO may also have contracts with specialists to treat members if it is not large enough to justify hiring its own specialists in a given medical field.

Employees of staff-model HMOs are paid a salary and possibly an incentive bonus. A staff-model HMO offers a great degree of control over costs because it controls the salaries of the physicians who might find themselves unemployed if the HMO is unprofitable or if they do not provide care within the cost and utilization parameters of the HMO.

Despite the potential for cost savings in staff-model HMOs, few have actually been established, primarily because of high start-up costs and high fixed costs once they are operating.

Group-Model HMO.   The most common type of closed-panel plan is the **group-model HMO**. Under this arrangement, physicians (and other medical personnel) are employees of another legal entity that has a contractual relationship with the HMO to provide medical services for its members. In most cases, this is an exclusive arrangement and the entity's physicians treat only members of the HMO. These physicians also typically operate out of one or more common facilities.

Under a group-model plan, the HMO may contract with a single provider of medical services or with different providers for different types of services (for example, one contract for physicians' services and another for hospital services). The HMO often pays for services on a capitation basis, which means that the provider of services gets a predetermined fee per month for each member and must provide any and all covered services for this capitation fee. The fee is independent of how the provider compensates its own employees. Under this arrangement, the provider shares the risk in that it loses money if utilization is higher than expected or increases its profit if utilization is lower than expected. Therefore, the provider has a very real incentive to control costs.

Network-Model HMO. A **network-model HMO** differs from a group-model HMO in that it contracts with two or more independent groups of physicians to provide medical services to its members. Physician groups that enter into this type of arrangement often treat non-HMO patients on a fee-for-service basis.

Individual Practice Associations. In an **individual practice association (IPA)**, participating physicians practice individually or in small groups at their own offices. In most cases, these physicians accept both non-HMO patients on a traditional fee-for-service basis and HMO members. IPAs are often referred to as *open-panel plans* because members choose from a list of participating physicians. The number of physicians participating in this type of HMO is frequently larger than the number participating in group practice plans and may include several physicians within a given specialty. In some geographic areas, most physicians may participate; in other geographic areas, only a relatively small percentage of physicians may participate. Because most of the newer HMOs are IPAs, the percentage of HMO members served by these plans continues to grow.

Several methods may be used to compensate physicians participating in an IPA. The most common is a fee schedule based on the services provided to members. To encourage physicians to be cost effective, it is common for plans to have a provision for reducing payments to physicians if the experience of the plan is worse than expected. On the other hand, the physicians may receive a bonus if the experience of the plan is better than expected. Particularly with respect to general practitioners, some IPA plans pay each physician a flat annual amount for each member who has elected to use him or her. For this annual payment, the physician must see these members as often as necessary during the year.

It is unusual for IPAs to own their own hospitals. Instead, they enter into contracts with local hospitals to provide the necessary services for their members.

Mixed-Model HMOs. An increasing number of HMOs are now operating as **mixed-model HMOs**, which means that the organization of the plan is a combination of two or more of the approaches previously described. Such a combination generally occurs as a plan continues to grow. For example, a plan might have been established as a staff-model HMO, and at a later time the HMO decided to expand its capacity or geographic region by adding additional physicians under an IPA arrangement. Some mixed models have also resulted from the merger of two plans that each used a different organizational form.

Extent of HMO Use

It is estimated that more than 70 million employees and dependents are covered under HMOs, with the enrollment varying considerably by geographic region. For example, one state (California) has more than 50 percent of its population enrolled in HMOs, but four other states have enrollments of 2 percent or less. There are also significant variations by metropolitan area, with approximately two-thirds of all members living in 30 metropolitan areas. In several metropolitan areas, the majority of persons are covered by HMOs.

Except in rare instances, employees covered by HMO plans have elected this form of coverage as an alternative to their employer's insurance company plan or Blue Cross and Blue Shield plan. Although state law may require certain employers to offer an HMO option, other employers voluntarily offer it. The administrative details of such an option may be burdensome and expensive for small employers, but they seem to pose few problems for large employers with specialized employee benefit staffs. In many cases, the financial consequences to the employer of such an option are insignificant because the employer makes the same contribution on an employee's behalf regardless of which plan is selected. Until recently, the general attitude of employers toward HMOs seems to have been somewhat ambivalent: Some employers had been in favor of them, others against, and the majority indifferent. However, according to several recent studies, most employers feel that HMOs have been a very effective technique for controlling benefit costs.

Where there is a choice of medical expense plans, most employees do not elect an HMO option unless there is a financial incentive to do so. However, studies have revealed that employees who have elected HMOs are for the most part satisfied with their choice and are unlikely to switch back to an insurance company plan or Blue Cross and Blue Shield plan as long as the HMO option remains available.

Health Maintenance Organization Act of 1973

The **Health Maintenance Organization Act** of 1973 has had a significant influence on both the interest in and the growth of HMOs. The act introduced the concept of the **federally qualified HMO**. For several years after the act's passage, most HMOs were formed to take advantage of this federal qualification, which entitled them to federal grants for feasibility studies and development (including grants to solicit members) and federal loans (or loan guarantees) to assist them in covering initial operating deficits. In addition, many employers were required to make federally qualified HMOs available to their employees until late 1995. Federal qualification also exempted federally qualified HMOs from restrictive laws in many states that had effectively prevented the establishment of HMOs. Such state laws have now essentially disappeared.

The need now for a federal HMO law is debatable. Most states have similar legislation. Although newer HMOs may forgo federal qualification, the majority of older HMOs still retain that status. It is felt that this grants them a "seal of approval" from the federal government. In addition, many employers will deal only with federally qualified HMOs. However, this practice is changing as employers are increasingly requiring some type of accreditation (either solely or as an alternative to federal qualification) as their measure of quality. Finally, federal qualification continues to be one way that HMOs can satisfy certain qualifications necessary to provide coverage for Medicare recipients. Today, about two-thirds of HMO members are covered by federally qualified plans.

An HMO might have more than one line of business, with some lines being federally qualified and other lines not being federally qualified.

Requirements for Federal Qualification. To become federally qualified, an HMO must meet certain requirements (set forth in the act) to the satisfaction of the secretary of health and human services. In return for a periodic prepaid fee, an HMO must provide the following basic benefits to its members at no cost or with nominal copayments:

- Physicians' services, including consultant and referral services, up to 10 percent of which may be provided by physicians who are not affiliated with the HMO
- Inpatient and outpatient hospital services
- Medically necessary emergency health services
- Short-term (up to 20 visits) outpatient mental health services
- Medical treatment and referral services for alcohol or drug abuse or addiction
- Diagnostic laboratory services and diagnostic and therapeutic radiological services
- Home health services
- Preventive health services, such as immunizations, well-baby care, periodic physical examinations, and family-planning services
- Medical social services, including education in methods of personal health maintenance and in the use of health services

The HMO may also provide the following supplemental benefits, either as part of its standard benefit package or as optional benefits for which an additional fee may be charged:

- Services of intermediate-care and long-term care facilities
- Vision care
- Dental care
- Additional mental health services
- Rehabilitative services
- Prescription drugs

In addition to the benefits that either are required or may be included, an HMO must meet the following other requirements with respect to its operations:

- A fiscally sound operation, including provisions against the risk of insolvency
- Annual open enrollment periods
- An ongoing quality assurance program

The HMO Act permits HMOs to establish rates based on an employer's past and projected claims experience if a group has 100 or more employees. Experience rating can also be used for groups of fewer than 100 employees, but the initial rate cannot be more than 10 percent higher than the HMO's community rates. In contrast to the usual practice of experience rating (see Chapter 17), HMOs are *not* allowed to make retrospective rate adjustments if actual claims turn out to be higher or lower than had been expected.

Open Enrollment Periods.   Once an HMO option is made available, an employer must provide for a group enrollment period of at least ten working days each year in which eligible employees may transfer between any available health insurance plans without the application of waiting periods, exclusions, or limitations based on health status. During this open enrollment period and at least 30 days prior to it, an employer must allow any participating HMOs to have fair and reasonable access to eligible employees for purposes of presenting and explaining their programs.

A problem may arise if an HMO ceases operations because of financial difficulties. Unfortunately, this has occurred in some cases, even among HMOs that have met the standards for federal qualification. Unless the cessation of HMO coverage coincides with an open enrollment period, these employees may not be able to join or rejoin their employer's insurance company plan or Blue Cross and Blue Shield plan without showing evidence of insurability. However, under these circumstances, many insurance companies and Blue Cross and Blue Shield plans include provisions in their contracts for coverage without evidence of insurability for these employees. In fact, many HMOs also have a similar provision in case other plans available to employees cease operations for any reason.

Contributions.   Employers who voluntarily offer federally qualified HMOs are required to make nondiscriminatory contributions to the HMOs. Under regulations issued in 1996 by the Health Care Financing Administration, the following five employer contribution practices are considered nondiscriminatory:

1. The employer may contribute the same amount it contributes to non-HMO alternatives.
2. The employer's contributions may vary by class of enrollee on the basis of attributes, such as age, gender, and family status, that are reasonable predictors of utilization, experience, costs, or risks. For each enrollee in a class, the employer would contribute the same amount, regardless of the plan that an employee chooses.
3. If the employer requires employee contributions, the employee contribution rate to the HMO plan cannot be greater than 50 percent of the contribution rate to the most popular non-HMO plan.
4. The employer may pay the same percentage of the cost of all available health plans.
5. The employer and an HMO may negotiate a payment schedule that is mutually acceptable as long as it meets the basic criteria for nondiscrimination against employees who enroll in HMOs.

State Regulation

HMOs are heavily regulated by the states. All states have numerous laws that are enforced by various state officials, often including both the insurance and public health commissioners. In many cases, the state legislation largely duplicates the federal HMO act.

Almost all states have adopted the NAIC Health Maintenance Organization Model Act, which focuses substantially on issues relating to licensing of HMOs and the maintenance of their financial solvency. However, it also addresses numerous other issues, such as the types of activities in which HMOs can engage, the requirement of a quality assurance program, standards for materials given to members, grievance procedures, enrollment periods, and coordination-of-benefits provisions.

HMO Coverage as an Alternative to Major Medical

Most HMOs include broad protection for medical expenses. In fact, federally qualified HMOs often give more comprehensive protection than most major medical plans, because in addition to covering such items as routine examinations and immunizations, they tend to require fewer out-of-pocket expenses by the members. HMOs that meet the requirements for federal qualification are allowed to use copayments for services as long as two criteria are met. First, the copayment for any single service cannot exceed 50 percent of the cost for that service. Second, the total of all copayments cannot exceed more than 20 percent of the cost of supplying all basic health services. In practice, copayments (if used at all) are usually substantially below these permissible limits. In addition, no member is required to copay more than 50 percent of the annual member fee that would have been charged if coverage had been written without any copayments.

Table 11.1 on the following pages compares the major medical plan and two HMOs that are offered to the employees of one organization. All three plans are reasonably representative of their respective plan type.

TABLE 11.1	A Comparison: Insured Plan versus HMOs		
	Insured Comprehensive Major Medical Expense Plan	**Group-Model HMO**	**Individual Practice Association HMO**
Choice of Physician	Member may select any licensed physician or surgeon	Member selects a personal physician from the medical group, who coordinates and directs all health care needs, including referrals to specialists	Members select a personal primary care physician from among the health plan physicians
Where Primary Care and Specialty Care Are Available	Care provided in physician's office or outpatient facility	Care provided at four multispecialty centers	Care provided in participating private physicians' offices
Choice of Hospitals	Member may select any accredited hospital—choice depends on where physician has admitting privileges	Selection from participating hospitals	Selection from participating hospitals

TABLE 11.1	A Comparison: Insured Plan versus HMOs (continued)		
	Insured Comprehensive Major Medical Expense Plan	**Group-Model HMO**	**Individual Practice Association HMO**
Annual Deductible and Coinsurance	There is a $200 deductible; plan pays 100% of expenses for hospitalization, but does have 80% coinsurance for other covered services; coinsurance provision is subject to a $3,000 out-of-pocket limit	There is no deductible and 100% coinsurance (except for small copayments for home visits and outpatient mental health)	There is no deductible and 100% coinsurance (except for small copayments for home visits, outpatient mental health, and a deductible for prescription drugs)
Maximum Benefit	$1 million lifetime maximum	No overall maximum limit	No overall maximum limit
Preventive Care Routine			
physicals	Not covered	Covered in full	Covered in full
Well-baby care	Covered in full	Covered in full	Covered in full
Pap smears	Routine exams not covered	Covered in full	Covered in full
Immunizations	Not covered	Covered in full	Covered in full
Eye exams	Not covered	Covered in full, including written prescriptions for lenses	Paid in full for children up to age 18
Hearing exams	Not covered	Covered in full	Covered in full
Health education	Available through some physicians' offices	Periodic classes held on diet, prenatal care, physical fitness, etc.	Covered in full through participating hospital programs
Physician Care Surgery	Covered at 80% after satisfying deductible	Covered in full	Covered in full
Inpatient visits	Covered at 80% after deductible	Covered in full	Covered in full
Office and home	Covered at 80% after deductible	Covered in full after a $10 copayment per visit	Covered in full after a $15 copayment per visit
X-rays and lab	Covered at 80% after deductible	Covered in full	Covered in full
Hospital Services Room and board	Covered in full for unlimited days in semiprivate room after satisfying deductible	Covered in full for unlimited days in semiprivate room	Covered in full for unlimited days in semiprivate room
Supplies, tests, medication, etc.	Covered in full for covered benefit days	Covered in full	Covered in full
Private-duty nurse	Covered in full while hospitalized (outpatient licensed practical nurse services covered at 50% up to $250 per year)	Covered in full	Covered in full

TABLE 11.1	A Comparison: Insured Plan versus HMOs (continued)		
	Insured Comprehensive Major Medical Expense Plan	**Group-Model HMO**	**Individual Practice Association HMO**
Emergency Room Care	Covered in full for care received in hospital outpatient department within 24 hours of an accident; $100 copayment for other types of care	Covered in full for around-the-clock emergency care by plan physicians and in participating hospitals; emergency care by nonplan physicians or hospitals is also covered when obtaining plan care not reasonable because of distance and urgency	Covered in full for around-the-clock emergency care by participating physicians and in participating hospitals; emergency care by nonparticipating physicians or hospitals also covered when obtaining plan care not reasonable because of distance and urgency
Ambulance service	Covered in full for local transportation after satisfying deductible	Covered in full	Covered in full
Maternity Care			
Hospital	Covered in full after deductible	Covered in full	Covered in full
Physician	Covered at 80% after deductible	Covered in full	Covered in full
Mental Health Care			
Hospital	Covered as regular hospitalization, i.e., 365-day/lifetime limitation	Covered in full for 45 days per year	Covered in full for 30 days during 12-month period
Inpatient physician	Covered as regular inpatient physician care	Covered in full for 45 days per year	Covered in full for 30 days during 12-month period
Outpatient physician	Covered at 50% up to $30 per visit	Covered for 30 visits per year; first 3 visits covered in full, member pays $20 per visit for next 27 visits	Covered for 20 visits per period; first 3 visits covered in full, member pays 25% of regular fee for next 7 visits, member pays 50% of regular fee for next 10 visits
Alcohol and drug addiction	Covered like other mental health services	No special limits; covered as other medical and mental health services	After detoxification treatment, covered as for mental health problems
Dental Care			
Hospital	Covered for hospital costs when confinement necessary for dental care	Covered for hospital costs when confinement necessary for dental care	Covered for hospital costs when confinement necessary for dental care
Dentist or dental surgeon	Covered for treatment of accidental injury to natural teeth	Covered for treatment of accidental injury to natural teeth and certain oral surgical procedures (e.g., impacted wisdom teeth)	Covered for treatment of diseases and injuries to the jaw and removal of impacted wisdom teeth

TABLE 11.1	A Comparison: Insured Plan versus HMOs (continued)		
	Insured Comprehensive Major Medical Expense Plan	**Group-Model HMO**	**Individual Practice Association HMO**
Outpatient Medication Prescription drugs	Covered at 80% after deductible, if related to treatment of non-occupational illness or injury	Covered subject to a $10 co-payment per prescription for generic drugs, $15 for brand-name formulary drugs, and $25 for nonformulary drugs	Covered subject to a $5 copay-ment per prescription for generic drugs and $10 copay-ment for nongeneric drugs. Prior authorization required for certain high-cost drugs
Injections	Covered at 80% after deductible, if related to treatment of non-occupational illness or injury	Covered in full	Covered in full
Prescribed Home Health Services	Covered at 80% after deductible	Covered in full	Covered in full
Allergy Care	Covered at 80% after deductible	Covered in full	Covered in full
Eligibility	Spouse and unmarried depen-dent children to age 19 or age 23 if a full-time student	Spouse and unmarried depen-dent children to age 19 or 23 if a full-time student	Spouse and unmarried depen-dent children through age 19 or 23 if a full-time student
Conversion	Conversion to individual coverage available	Conversion to nongroup coverage available	Conversion to individual enroll-ment available at same benefit level

■ KEY TERMS

accreditation
antigag-clause legislation
any-willing-provider law
capitation
case management
closed-panel plans
concurrent management
credentials

demand management
diagnosis-related groups
direct-access (self-referral) HMOs
disease management
federally qualified HMO
gatekeeper (care manager)
group-model HMO

health maintenance organization (HMO)
Health Maintenance Organization Act
Health Plan Employer Data and Information Set (HEDIS)
health risk assessment
incentive payment program

individual practice
association (IPA)

medical information
programs

mixed-model HMOs

modified fee-for-service
payment

National Committee for
Quality Assurance
(NCQA)

network-model HMO

open-panel plans

per-case rate

per-day rate

physician-hospital
organizations (PHOs)

prospective management

provider network

referral

referral management

retrospective management

staff-model HMO

utilization management

wellness program

withhold arrangement

■ STUDY QUESTIONS

1. How do managed care plans attempt to eliminate the unrestricted use of medical care providers?

2. What are the arguments for and against the proposition that persons covered by managed care plans receive the same quality of care as persons covered by traditional medical expense plans?

3. a. Why may the terminology "backlash against managed care" be somewhat inaccurate?

   b. In a general sense, what have been the results of this backlash?

4. What types of legislation are states adopting to address consumer and provider concerns about managed care?

5. What are the factors that might lead an employee to elect a particular managed care plan?

6. What is the role of provider networks in managed care plans?

7. How does a managed care plan determine whether it has qualified providers of medical care services?

8. How do managed care plans address member needs for medical care services?

9. a. Why are providers willing to grant preferred rates to managed care plans?

   b. What are the important aspects of a provider contract?

10. What is the relationship between a managed care plan's utilization management and its provider compensation methods?

11. How do each of the following demand management programs guide members with respect to their personal health conditions?

    a. Wellness programs

    b. Health risk assessments

    c. Medical information programs

12. What is the role of a gatekeeper in a managed care plan?

13. How do managed care plans usually settle disputes about coverage decisions?

14. What is the role of each of the following?

    a. Prospective management

    b. Concurrent management

    c. Retrospective management

15. Describe the characteristics of HMOs that distinguish them from insurance companies.

16. Explain how HMOs may vary with respect to each of the following:

    a. Choice of medical providers

    b. Reimbursement of physicians

17. What provisions are contained in the HMO Act of 1973 with respect to each of the following?

    a. Open enrollment periods

    b. Level of employer contributions

18. What type of state regulation applies to HMOs?

■ NOTE

1. The Henry J. Kaiser Foundation and Health Research and Education Trust, *Employer Health Benefits, 2003.*

12

Managed Care: PPOs and Other Types of Managed Care

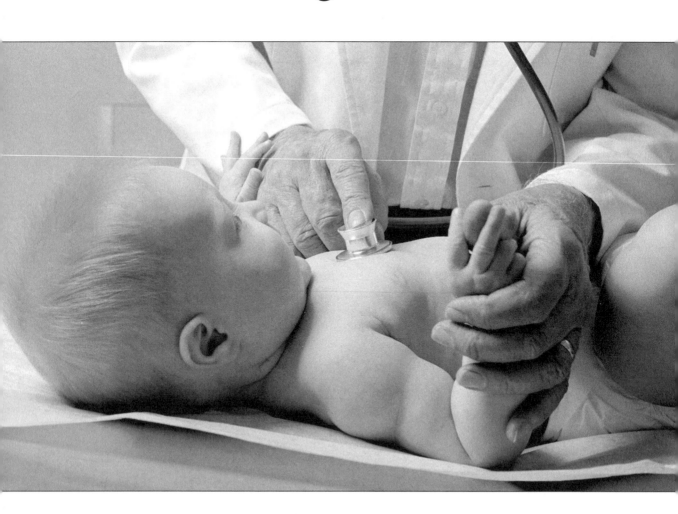

This second chapter devoted exclusively to managed care begins by looking at preferred-provider organizations, which are now the most prevalent type of managed care plan. Point-of-service plans and multiple-option plans are also described. The chapter concludes with a discussion of benefit carve-outs that incorporate managed care.

■ PREFERRED-PROVIDER ORGANIZATIONS

A concept that continues to receive considerable attention from employers and insurance companies is the preferred-provider organization. A few of these organizations have existed on a small scale for many years, but since the early 1980s they have grown steadily in number and in membership. Today, they provide coverage for medical expenses to more Americans than do health maintenance organizations, or HMOs, primarily because of the flexibility of covered persons to choose their own medical providers.

What Is a PPO?

The term **preferred-provider organization (PPO)** tends to be used in two ways. One way is to apply it to health care providers that contract with employers, insurance companies, union trust funds, third-party administrators, or others to provide medical care services at a reduced fee. Using this definition, a PPO may be organized by the providers themselves or by other organizations, such as insurance companies, the Blues, HMOs, or employers. Like HMOs, they may take the form of group practices or separate individual practices. They may provide a broad array of medical services, including physicians' services, hospital care, laboratory costs, and home health care, or they may be limited only to hospitalization or physicians' services. Some of these organizations are very specialized and provide specific services such as dental care, mental health benefits, substance abuse services, maternity care, or prescription drugs. In this book, these providers are referred to not as *PPOs* but as *preferred providers* or *network providers.*

The second use of the term *PPO,* and the one generally assumed when the term is used throughout this book, is to apply it to benefit plans that contract with preferred providers to obtain lower-cost care for plan members. PPOs typically differ from HMOs in several respects. First, the preferred providers are generally paid on a fee-for-service basis as their services are used. However, fees are usually subject to a schedule that is the same for all similar providers within the PPO, and providers may have an incentive to control utilization through bonus arrangements. Second, employees and their dependents are not required to use the practitioners or facilities that contract with the PPO; rather, a choice can be made each time medical care is needed, and benefits are also paid for care provided by nonnetwork providers. However, employees are offered incentives to use network providers; they include lower or reduced deductibles and copayments as well as increased benefits, such as preventive health care. Third, most PPOs do not use a primary care physician as a gatekeeper; employees do not need referrals to see specialists.

Employers were disappointed with some of the early PPOs. Although discounts were received, they seemed to have little effect on benefit costs, either because discounts were from higher-than-average fees or because providers were more likely to perform diagnostic tests or prolong hospital stays to generate additional fees to compensate for the discounts. Needless to say, these PPOs seldom lasted long. Successful PPOs today emphasize quality care and utilization review. In selecting physicians and hospitals, PPOs look not only at the type of care provided but also at the provider's cost effectiveness. In this era of fierce competition among medical care providers, these physicians and hospitals are often willing to accept discounts in hopes of increasing patient volume. It is also important for a PPO to monitor and control utilization on an ongoing basis and to deal with groups of preferred providers that monitor their own costs and utilization. As a general rule, however, PPOs do not monitor their preferred providers as closely as HMOs do.

Variations. Over time, PPOs have continued to evolve. A few PPOs compensate providers on a capitation basis, and a few others perform a gatekeeper function. If a member's primary care physician does not recommend a specialist, benefits may be reduced. With these changes, it is sometimes difficult to determine the exact form of a managed care organization. However, those that operate as traditional HMOs generally provide medical expense coverage at a slightly lower cost than do those that operate as traditional PPOs, but there are wide variations among HMOs as well as among PPOs. Therefore, a careful analysis of quality of care, cost, and financial stability is necessary before a particular HMO or PPO is selected.

Another variation of the PPO is the **exclusive-provider organization**, or EPO. The primary difference is that an EPO does not provide coverage outside the preferred-provider network, except in those infrequent cases when the network does not contain an appropriate specialist. This aspect of an EPO makes it very similar to an HMO. The number of EPOs is small.

Sponsorship

Insurance companies established most of the early PPOs to provide products to compete with HMOs. In the 1990s, the number of PPOs grew significantly to about 1,100, with about 60 percent still owned by insurance companies. Another 10 percent are owned by HMOs to give them another product in their health plan portfolios to offer employers. The remaining 30 percent have a variety of ownership forms, including the Blues, third-party administrators, private investors, and groups of physicians and/or hospitals.

Benefit Structure

The basic benefit structure of a PPO is very similar to that of the traditional comprehensive major medical contract, which is discussed in Chapter 10. The most significant difference is that there is a higher level of benefits for care received from network providers than there is for care received from nonnetwork providers. Many PPOs have extensive networks of preferred providers, particularly in the geographic areas in which they operate, and there is little reason to seek care outside the network. Some of these PPOs also have reciprocity agreements elsewhere with networks of other PPOs and hospitals (called **centers of excellence**) that have excellent outcomes and reputations for certain types of medical procedures, such as cancer treatment, organ transplants, or burn treatment. Under these agreements, benefits are paid as if care had been received from network providers. Other PPOs have more limited networks, and the need and desire for treatment from nonnetwork providers is greater.

The level of benefits under PPOs may vary because of differences in deductibles, coinsurance, maximum lifetime benefits, and precertification rules. There may also be a few additional benefits that are available only if care is received from a network provider. Finally, the procedures for filing claims also differ. The major purpose of these differences is to encourage an employee or dependent to receive care from preferred providers who have agreed to charge the plan a discounted fee.

Deductibles. A PPO may have annual deductibles that apply separately to network and nonnetwork charges. For examples, these might be $100 and $250, respectively.

However, many PPOs have no deductible for network charges. As mentioned in Chapter 10, deductibles may be waived for some medical services, such as emergency or preventive care.

Coinsurance. Most PPOs use coinsurance percentages that are 20 percent (and occasionally 30 percent) lower when care is received from nonnetwork providers. The most frequently found provision applies 90 percent coinsurance to network charges and 70 percent coinsurance to nonnetwork charges. Coinsurance provisions of 100/80, 90/80, and 100/70 are also frequently used. As with deductibles, the percentage participation may be waived for certain medical services. In addition, different stop-loss limits or coinsurance caps, such as $1,000 and $3,000, may apply to network and nonnetwork charges.

Although PPOs typically have higher coinsurance percentages for network charges than do traditional major medical plans, a covered person may be responsible for modest copayments in some circumstances. For example, there might be a copayment of $5, $10, or $15 for each visit to a primary care physician.

In evaluating PPOs, it is important to determine the basis the PPO uses to apply the coinsurance percentage. For example, assume a plan uses 80 percent coinsurance for nonnetwork charges and that a charge of $100 is incurred for a medical procedure from a nonnetwork provider. Most PPOs first determine whether this charge is usual, customary, and reasonable. If it is, the plan pays $80. If the plan determines that the usual, customary, and reasonable charge is $90, it will be 80 percent of that amount, or $72. However, some plans apply the coinsurance percentage to what is often referred to as an **allowable charge**. In most cases, this is the amount that is paid to network providers for the same procedure. In some cases, network discounts are quite large and, for example, the allowable charge in this example might be only $60. For a nonnetwork charge, the plan pays 80 percent of this amount, or $48. Thus the insured has an out-of-pocket expense of $52. Needless to say, few employees and their families will seek nonnetwork care under this type of plan. For this reason, plans that pay nonnetwork charges on this basis are sometimes referred to as *phantom PPOs*.

Maximum Benefits. Although there are variations, most PPOs have a lifetime maximum of $1 million for nonnetwork benefits. The lifetime maximum for network benefits is seldom less that $2 million and may even be unlimited.

Precertification Rules. PPOs often have precertification requirements for many types of hospitalizations, outpatient procedures, and medical supplies. For network benefits, the person responsible for obtaining the needed certification is the network provider, and the covered person is not penalized if the network provider fails to obtain the proper precertification. (This becomes an issue between the PPO and the provider.) However, this responsibility shifts to the employee or family member for nonnetwork services. If precertification is not obtained when required, there usually is a reduction in benefits. For example, what was once 80 percent coinsurance might shrink to 60 percent.

Additional Network Benefits. For the most part, PPOs pay benefits for the same medical procedures, whether they are performed by a network or a nonnetwork provider. However, a few procedures may be covered only if they are received from network providers. For example, routine physical exams may be covered only in the network. In addition, there might be coverage for more outpatient psychiatric visits if a network provider is used.

Claims.   No claim forms are required for network services. The covered person merely pays any required copayment, and the provider of medical services does the paperwork needed to receive the additional amounts payable by the plan. Just as in traditional major medical plans, it is the ultimate responsibility of the covered person to file the claims forms necessary to receive benefits for nonnetwork care. Of course, the provider may do much of the paperwork and accept an assignment of benefits.

> **EXAMPLE**
> Table 12.1 shows excerpts of the benefit structure from an actual PPO.

Regulation

PPOs have been subject to much less stringent regulation than HMOs with respect to their managed care activities. In fact, until recently, they were largely unregulated. As a result, the NAIC created the Preferred Provider Arrangements Model Act, which has now been adopted by more than half the states. The act is relatively brief and establishes only a minimal regulatory framework. The act requires that PPOs incorporate cost-containment mechanisms, such as utilization review, to determine whether a service is medically necessary. Covered persons must be given reasonable access to medical services. The act also allows PPOs to provide incentives for persons to use the preferred-provider network and to place limitations on the number and types of providers with whom they contract.

It should be noted that most PPO contracts also meet the definition of insurance and are subject to the same regulation by state insurance departments as traditional insurance contracts with respect to contract provisions and benefit mandates.

■ POINT-OF-SERVICE PLANS

A newer and fast-growing type of managed care arrangement is the **point-of-service (POS) plan**. A POS plan is a hybrid arrangement that combines aspects of a traditional HMO and a PPO. With a POS plan, participants in the plan elect, at the time medical treatment is needed, whether to receive treatment within the plan's tightly managed network, usually an HMO, or outside the network. Expenses received outside the network are reimbursed in the same manner as described earlier for nonnetwork services under PPO plans.

There are two basic types of POS plans: the open-ended HMO and the gatekeeper PPO. An **open-ended HMO** is by far the most common form and is the HMO industry's response to the demand for more consumer flexibility in the choice of providers, even though it increases costs somewhat. It essentially consists of traditional HMO coverage with an endorsement for nonnetwork coverage. It can take the basic form of any of the

TABLE 12.1	Selected Benefits Under a PPO	
	Network Benefit	**Nonnetwork Benefit**
Deductible	None	$250 per person per year; family deductible equals 2 times the individual deductible; deductible does not apply to emergency care, pediatric immunizations, routine gynecological examinations, Pap smears, or routine mammograms
Coinsurance	100% for most services	70% for most services
Out-of-Pocket Limit	None	$1,000
Lifetime Maximum	Unlimited	$1 million per covered person
Hospital Services	100% with a $250 copayment per hospitalization	70% with a $500 copayment per admission
Emergency Room	100% with $50 copayment per visit	100% with $50 copayment per visit
Surgical Services	100%	70%
Outpatient Diagnostic Services	100%	70%
Cardiac Rehabilitation Therapy (limit 18 sessions per benefit period)	100% with $15 copayment per session	70%
Psychiatric Services		
Inpatient	100% for 30 days per benefit period	70% for 20 days per benefit period
Outpatient	100% for 9 visits with $10 copayment; $20 copayment for visits 10–30; no coverage for more than 30 visits	50% for up to 20 visits per benefit period
Outpatient Diabetic Education	100%	70%
Physician Service	100% with $10 copayment per visit for primary care physicians; $20 copayment for specialists	70%
Prescription Drugs	100% with $10 copayment for generic drugs and $20 for non-generic drugs	50%

HMOs previously described. However, at any time a member can elect to go outside the HMO network of medical care providers.

While it can be argued that any PPO is actually a POS plan, the normal usage of the term *POS* implies a higher degree of managed care than is found in most PPOs. A **gatekeeper PPO** requires that the PPO participant elect a primary care physician in the manner of an HMO participant. This physician acts as a gatekeeper to control utilization and refer members to specialists within the PPO network. However, any time that care is needed, a covered person can elect to go outside the network. This type of PPO is generally formed by a traditional PPO or insurance company that does not own an HMO.

Under some POS plans, a covered person can go outside the plan's network without informing the plan of this fact. In other POS plans, the person must notify the gatekeeper that such treatment will be sought. Even though the gatekeeper has no power to prevent the nonnetwork treatment, the gatekeeper may be able to convince the person that proper treatment is available within the network. Furthermore, the gatekeeper can better manage future medical care by being aware of all medical treatment that a person is receiving.

■ MULTIPLE-OPTION PLANS

Until recently, an employer who wanted to make an HMO or a POS option available to employees had to enter into a separate contractual arrangement with an HMO. Unless the insurance company or Blue Cross and Blue Shield plan of an employer sponsored a PPO, a similar contractual arrangement was also required. Several insurance companies and Blue Cross and Blue Shield plans are now providing all these options under a single medical expense contract, referred to as a **multiple-option plan**. For example, one insurer markets a so-called quadruple-option plan that gives employees the choice of a traditional major medical contract, a PPO, an HMO, or a POS plan. In most cases, the HMOs and PPOs used in such arrangements have been formed or purchased by the insurance company or Blue Cross and Blue Shield plan, but occasionally a contractual relationship has been established with an existing HMO or PPO. HMOs, in addition to offering POS options, also frequently offer PPO products to employers as part of a multiple-option plan.

These plans offer certain advantages to the employer. First, administration is easier because all elements of the plan are purchased from a single provider. Second, costs may be lower because the entire plan, including the HMO, may be subject to experience rating. Because federally qualified HMOs cannot fully use experience rating (particularly on a retrospective basis), nonfederally qualified HMOs are often used in multiple-option plans.

■ COMPARISON OF TYPICAL MEDICAL EXPENSE PLANS

The various types of medical expense plans, and how they differ, have been discussed throughout the last three chapters. Although variations within each type of plan exist, some generalizations can be made. These are summarized in Table 12.2. The degree of managed care increases as one moves from left to right in the table. However, the cost of the plans, on the average, decreases as the degree of managed care increases. In addition, a higher degree of managed care is generally associated with lower annual premium increases by a plan.

■ BENEFIT CARVE-OUTS

The use of benefit carve-outs by medical expense plans has grown in recent years, often as a method of cost containment through the use of managed care techniques. In addition, many medical expense plans have come to realize that they cannot always provide as high a quality of care as can a well-managed specialty provider. Carve-outs for prescription drugs, vision care, dental care, and behavioral health have been common for a

TABLE 12.2	Comparison of Health Insurance Plans			
	Traditional Major Medical Contracts	**PPOs**	**POS Plans**	**HMOs**
Provider Choice	Unlimited	Unlimited in network, but benefits are greater if network provider is used	Unlimited in network, but benefits are greater if network provider is used	Network of providers must be used; care from nonnetwork providers covered only in emergencies
Use of Gate-keeper	None	None	Used for care by network specialists	Used for access to specialists
Out-of-Pocket Costs	Deductibles and percentage participation	Deductibles and percentage participation, which are lower if network providers are used; may have small copayment for network services	Small copayments for network services; deductibles and percentage participation for nonnetwork services	Small copayments for some services
Utilization Review	Traditionally little, but a few techniques are likely to be used now	More than traditional plans, but less than HMOs; network provider may be subject to some controls	Like HMOs for network services; like PPOs for nonnetwork services	Highest degree of review, including financial incentives and disincentives for providers
Preventive Care	Little covered other than that required by law	Usually, more coverage than traditional major medical plan but less coverage than HMOs and POS plans	Covered	Covered
Responsibility for Claims Filings	Covered person	Plan provider for network services; the covered person for non-network services	Plan provider for network services; the covered person for non-network services	Plan providers

number of years. Increasingly, carve-outs are being used to better manage a wide variety of medical conditions, such as pregnancy, asthma, and diabetes. The final section of this chapter is devoted to a discussion of the nature of such carve-outs, the reasons for their use, possible concerns, and a few of the more common types of carve-out arrangements.

Nature

A benefit carve-out can best be defined as coverage under a medical expense plan for a health care service that has been singled out for individual management by a party other than the employer's health plan (or the employer if a plan is self-funded). Some types of carve-outs predate managed care as it is now known. For example, many employees have long been covered under separate prescription drug plans. However, the early emphasis under these plans was on discounts with preferred providers of prescription drugs. Today, prescription drug plans and other types of carve-outs use a wider variety of managed care techniques.

An employer can purchase a medical expense plan to provide benefits to its employees for most types of medical care and then enter into a separate contract with another provider for the carved-out benefit. However, in most cases, it is the insurance company, Blue Cross and Blue Shield plan, HMO, or PPO that enters into the carve-out arrangement with a "subcontractor" that manages the benefits. From the standpoint of employers and employees, the benefit is part of the provider's plan.

Vendors who provide carve-outs often act as managed care plans for a single medical expense benefit and take on the characteristics of HMOs or PPOs. They also have learned over time that their type of specialty care should sometimes be accompanied by a unique benefit structure. This is one reason why mental health and prescription drug benefits are often subject to different deductibles, copayments, or benefit limitations than those used for most types of medical expenses.

Reasons for Use

There are several reasons for using benefit carve-outs. These include the following:

- The carve-out can save money. A good carve-out vendor should be able to provide products and services in a cost-effective manner and pass along savings from these efficiencies.

- The carve-out may result in a shifting of financial risk and a better ability to budget. It is often difficult for a benefit plan to control costs. One way of doing this is to select a carve-out vendor that is paid on a capitated basis. This shifts much of the financial risk of higher-than-average claims to the carve-out vendor.

- The carve-out vendor may be better able to build a network of specialists. For some diseases or medical conditions, even very large HMOs or PPOs have too few claims to justify the establishment of their own in-plan network. The carve-out vendor may also be able to provide better outcomes data because of the vendor's size and expertise.

- The carve-out vendor may increase employer and employee satisfaction by lowering plan costs, providing high-quality care through the use of well-regarded specialists, and providing easier access to medical products and services.

Possible Concerns

A carve-out arrangement must be entered with care. Today, many vendors claim they can properly perform the required tasks, but benefit plans sometimes find themselves dissatisfied. Therefore, proper evaluation of vendors is vital. Questions that need to be answered include the following:

■ How does the carve-out vendor credential providers?

■ Is the carve-out vendor financially able to deliver what it promises?

■ Does the carve-out vendor have the management expertise to deliver what it promises?

■ Why is the carve-out vendor in business? Providers of medical products and services often market carve-out arrangements, and this may result in their having the expertise to run a high-quality operation. On the other hand, it is important to distinguish these arrangements from those whose primary goal is to increase sales of the provider's products and services.

■ Will the carve-out vendor keep a patient's primary-care physician informed about the patient's treatment? This information is essential if the primary-care physician is to properly coordinate patient care.

Types of Carve-Outs

There are numerous types of benefit carve-outs. Those discussed in this chapter include

■ prescription drugs,

■ vision benefits,

■ behavioral health,

■ disease management, and

■ maternity management.

Prescription Drugs. The cost of prescription drugs is more than 15 percent of all medical expense claims, and the percentage continues to grow. This increase results from several factors. One is the availability and prescribing of high-priced new pharmaceutical products. Another factor is increased use arising from several sources, which include (1) the aging population, which uses more prescription drugs; (2) increased advertising to consumers; and (3) the shift from inpatient to outpatient treatment, resulting in more intensive pharmaceutical treatments. Finally, new drugs have been found for many previously untreatable conditions. As a result, prescription drug benefits are often carved out in an attempt to control costs.

Although separate prescription drug plans have existed for many years, the initial focus was on obtaining lower costs through discounts with participating pharmacies and mail-order suppliers of drugs. However, the situation changed significantly in the early 1980s when pharmacy benefit managers (PBMs) appeared in the marketplace. It is estimated that more than 75 percent of prescription drugs are provided through PBMs, and that fewer than 10 large PBMs cover more than 80 percent of the health plan participants who received drugs in this manner. PBMs may be affiliated with pharmaceutical companies or health care providers, such as insurance companies. They may also be independently owned.

Pharmacy Benefit Managers. A **pharmacy benefit manager** administers prescription drug plans on behalf of self-funded employers, HMOs, PPOs, insurance companies, Blue Cross and Blue Shield plans, and third-party administrators. The online capabilities of PBMs enable them to offer considerable flexibility in designing a prescription drug program for a specific employer or benefit plan provider.

In addition to developing networks for the dispensing of prescription drugs, PBMs typically also do the following:

- Drug utilization review. This practice compares information gathered from a patient's medical and prescription drug records to determine such factors as overutilization, underutilization, drug-to-drug interactions, improper drugs for pregnant patients, early refills, and therapeutic duplication.

- Physician profiling and education. For example, physicians whose prescribing patterns lie outside acceptable variations from established benchmarks can be identified and counseled.

- Pharmacy profiling and education. For example, pharmacies that recommend large amounts of brand-name drugs might be contacted about making more use of generic substitutions.

- Patient profiling and education. For example, patients treated for hypertension can be identified and sent educational materials on their condition. This material focuses on the risks associated with the condition, safety issues associated with drug treatment, and the importance of complying with prescribed drug regimens. Patients who fail to refill needed medication can also be identified and contacted.

PBMs are also increasingly developing disease management programs that focus on diagnostic aids identification, treatment guidelines, education, and outcomes measurement for specific diseases. PBMs may also be involved in the overall case management of a patient.

PBMs have been leaders in the integration of formularies into prescription drug plans. A **formulary** is a list of preferred medications for a specific medical condition developed by a committee of pharmacists and physicians. This list is provided to physicians with the hopes that it will positively affect their prescribing behavior. A formulary, for example, informs physicians of approved uses of new drugs on the market, appropriate uses for existing drugs, and appropriate times for generic and therapeutic substitutions. A **therapeutic substitution** is a drug with a similar therapeutic effect as to the prescribed drug. Unlike generic substitution, which can often be made by patients or pharmacists, a physician's permission is needed for a therapeutic substitution.

Many prescription drug plans do not have a price differential for a patient if formulary drugs are not prescribed. However, PBMs will offer plans that either cover formulary drugs only (referred to as *closed formularies*) or provide a financial incentive for patients to use them.

Nature of Plans. The typical **prescription drug plan** covers the cost of drugs (except those dispensed in a hospital or in an extended care facility) that are required by either state or federal law to be dispensed by prescription. Drugs for which prescriptions are not required by law are usually not covered even if a physician orders them on a prescription form. One frequent exception to this general rule is injectable insulin, which is generally covered despite the fact that in many states it is a nonprescription drug. No coverage is provided for charges to administer drugs or the cost of the therapeutic devices or appliances, such as bandages or hypodermic needles. It is also common to exclude benefits for a quantity of drugs in excess of a specified amount. In some plans, this quantity is expressed as the amount normally prescribed by physicians; in other plans, it is expressed as a supply for a certain time period, often 34 days. However, refills are considered new prescriptions.

Contraceptive drugs are usually covered but may be excluded. Some prescription drug plans take a middle approach by covering these drugs only when they are prescribed for treating a medical condition rather than for preventing conception. (It should be noted that some recent court decisions and the position of the Equal Employment Opportunity Commission would seem to indicate that an employer will have a more difficult time defending a challenge by female employees of the failure to provide less-than-complete coverage for prescription contraceptives.) Drugs for treatment of infertility or sexual dysfunction, such as Viagra, may or may not be covered.

Drug plans are increasingly requiring precertification for the use of certain expensive drugs. Some plans also use **step therapy** under which approval for higher-cost medications is contingent on a member's first trying lower-cost, often well-established drugs to see if they are effective.

Most prescription drug plans have a copayment that a covered person pays for any prescriptions filled; in some cases, it is a flat amount that usually varies from $5 to $15 per prescription. Other plans have one copayment amount for generic drugs and a higher one for brand-name drugs. A three-tier structure, such as a $10 copayment for generic drugs, $20 for brand-name formulary drugs, and $30 for brand-name nonformulary drugs, has rapidly become the most widely used option since the start of the decade. Some plans provide financial incentives for prescriptions filled by mail-order pharmacies or on the Internet. A few plans have quarterly, semiannual, or annual spending caps. For example, benefits might be limited to $500 per person per quarter or $3,000 per year per family.

Two basic methods are used to provide prescription drug coverage: a reimbursement approach and a service approach. Under plans using a reimbursement approach, a covered individual personally pays the cost of prescription drugs. The person may be able to use any pharmacy he or she chooses or may be required to use a participating pharmacy. A claim for reimbursement is then filed with the provider of benefits, either by the employee or electronically by the pharmacy. Reimbursement (subject to any copayments) is made to the covered person on the basis of either billed charges or reasonable-and-customary charges.

Although coverage for prescription drugs under major medical plans is often on a reimbursement basis, the majority of prescription drug plans use a service approach. Under this approach, drugs are provided to covered persons by participating pharmacies upon receipt of prescriptions, proper identification (usually a card issued by the plan), and any required copayments. The pharmacy then bills the provider of coverage (usually electronically) for the remaining cost of any prescription filled. This provider may be a PBM, a Blue Cross and Blue Shield association, an HMO, an insurance company, or a third-party administrator acting on behalf of either an insurance company or an employer with a self-insured plan. Because of the specialization that can be used in handling many small claims and the need to establish a system of participating pharmacies, most insurance companies, except for a few large ones, use PBMs for their prescription drug plans.

Under virtually all service plans, the provider of coverage or the third-party administrator negotiates a contract with participating pharmacies to provide drugs at a reduced cost, usually equal to the wholesale cost of the drug plus a flat dispensing fee, such as $3 for each prescription. Prescriptions filled at nonparticipating pharmacies are often covered, but on a reimbursement basis. In addition, reimbursement in these cases is typically less than the cost of the prescription. In some cases, the plan pays up to the amount that would have been paid to a participating pharmacy. In others, benefits may be limited to some percentage (for example, 75 percent) of the cost of a prescription purchased at a nonparticipating pharmacy, minus any copayment.

Vision Benefits.   Carve-out vision benefits may be provided by insurance companies, Blue Cross and Blue Shield plans, plans of state optometric associations patterned after Blue Shield, closed-panel HMO–type plans established by local providers of vision services, vision care PPOs, or third-party administrators.

More than half of the persons covered under employer-provided medical expense plans have some type of **vision plan**, and the majority of this coverage is provided under some type of carve-out arrangement. Despite concerns with rising benefit costs in recent years, vision care is one type of benefit that employers continue to add. Routine eye exams can result in better overall health care because certain other types of health problems—such as high blood pressure, diabetes, and kidney problems—may be discovered during the course of such routine exams. Proper vision correction can also result in fewer accidents and greater productivity by minimizing eyestrain and headaches.

Benefits are occasionally provided on a reasonable-and-customary basis or are subject to a flat benefit per year that may be applied to any covered expenses. Normally, however, a benefit schedule will be used that specifies the type and amounts of certain benefits and the frequency with which they will be provided. Table 12.3 is an example of one such schedule. If a provider of vision services writes a plan, it is common for a discount, such as 20 percent, to be available for costs incurred with the provider that are not covered by the schedule of benefits. Under some plans, most benefits are provided on a service basis rather than being subject to a maximum benefit. However, these plans usually cover only the cost of basic frames, which the covered persons can upgrade at an additional expense.

Exclusions commonly exist for any extra charge for plastic lenses or the cost of safety lenses or prescription sunglasses. Benefits are generally provided for eye examinations by either an optometrist or an ophthalmologist, and larger benefits are sometimes provided if the latter is used. Vision care plans do not pay benefits for necessary eye surgery or treatment of eye diseases because these are covered under the regular coverage of a medical expense plan. However, many vision plans make benefits available for elective procedures to improve vision, such as LASIK surgery. The benefit is usually in the form of a discounted fee from a provider who has a relationship with the plan.

TABLE 12.3 Vision Benefits	
Type of Benefit	**Maximum Amount**
Any 12-Month Period	
Eye examination	$ 45
Lenses, pair	
single vision	45
bifocal	75
trifocal	125
lenticular	200
contact (when medically necessary)	300
contact (when not medically necessary)	125
Any 24-Month Period	
Frames	60

Behavioral Health. Providing behavioral health benefits has always been an area of difficulty for medical expense plans. There is less uniformity in treatment standards for mental health, alcoholism, and drug addiction than for most other medical conditions. This, and the difficulty of monitoring treatment, has often led to unnecessary, expensive, and dangerous treatment by less-than-scrupulous providers of behavioral health care. Historically, benefit plans addressed these problems by having very limited benefit levels. But even these benefit levels still tend to encourage more expensive inpatient care over outpatient treatment, which in most cases appears to be as clinically effective. In addition, there was little follow-up care after treatment. With rapidly increasing costs for behavioral health, employers and providers of benefit plans are increasingly carving out this benefit by contracting with vendors that use managed care techniques. However, even with the use of carve-outs, benefit plans still continue to limit behavioral health benefits to a level significantly below that for other medical conditions.

Characteristics of a successful **behavioral health program,** whether it be a carve-out arrangement or not, should include the following:

■ The use of case management to design and coordinate treatment plans and to monitor the need for follow-up care.

■ A mechanism for referring a patient to the program. In many cases, this is through a primary-care physician gatekeeper. However, behavioral health programs are increasingly being coordinated with employee-assistance programs, which are discussed in Chapter 18.

■ The development of a provider network that specializes in behavioral health. In addition to physicians, the network will include psychologists and therapists. It will also include alternatives to hospital treatment, such as residential centers, halfway houses, and structured outpatient programs. Benefits may or may not be provided if nonnetwork treatment is sought. If it is covered, there is usually a lower benefit level than for network treatment.

■   Patient access to care on a 24-hour basis. Persons who have behavioral health problems often need immediate crisis intervention. Of course, the availability of such care needs to be well communicated to patients.

Disease Management.   Traditionally, medical expense plans have focused on the treatment of sickness rather than prevention and education. Even though this philosophy changed with managed care, there has often been less-than-complete attention paid to controlling chronic conditions that can lead to frequent and often expensive medical intervention. The list of chronic conditions is lengthy; a few of the conditions on this list are asthma, diabetes, heart disease, high blood pressure, arthritis, allergies, back pain, and multiple sclerosis. Many chronic conditions are high maintenance, and most are not curable. However, with proper control, hospitalization for the condition and related complications can be reduced. In addition, the patient's longevity and quality of life can be increased. As managed care has evolved, the concept of disease management has taken on increasing importance, sometimes through the use of carve-outs for certain chronic conditions. The two most commonly carved out chronic conditions are probably diabetes and asthma.

Traditional case management begins with an episode of illness, whereas disease management begins prior to it. Disease management programs attempt to identify persons with chronic conditions as early as possible so that proper treatment can minimize future spells of illness. In this regard, it is important to work with primary care physicians so that they can steer patients toward the disease management program.

Disease management programs have a network of providers who deliver the needed care and prevention. These include physicians as well as nurses who provide patient counseling and education and who may even make home visits. Education about a chronic condition is crucial in that a disease management program is much more effective if a patient understands how to manage his or her lifestyle in light of the condition. It is also important for a disease management program to involve pharmacists, because patients with chronic diseases are often on maintenance drugs, the effectiveness of which can be influenced by prescription drugs that might be prescribed for other illnesses. A disease management program also has procedures for reacting to emergencies and providing ambulatory care following a hospitalization.

Maternity Management.   The identification of high-risk pregnancies and proper medical treatment can result in significant cost savings to a benefit plan. For example, the expenses associated with premature birth can amount to several hundred thousand dollars. As a result, many plans have begun to incorporate **maternity management**, which focuses on low-frequency, high-cost claims in contrast to many cost-containment efforts. Although there is a cost in providing this coverage, this cost will usually be more than offset if only one large claim is avoided. Some providers of medical expense plans provide maternity management with their own staff, but others carve out the benefit.

A maternity-management provision requires a patient or her primary care physician to notify the maternity management program within some prescribed time period after confirmation of pregnancy. Failure to obtain this precertification may result in a reduction of benefits. A case manager, usually a registered nurse, works closely with the expectant mother and her physician throughout the pregnancy to see that a complete assessment of the mother's health is made so that unfavorable risk factors can be monitored. Individualized maternity education is provided through brochures and telephone contact. This education focuses on such aspects of prenatal care as nutrition, alcohol use, and smoking.

■ KEY TERMS

allowable charge

behavioral health program

centers of excellence

exclusive-provider organization

formulary

gatekeeper PPO

maternity management

multiple-option plan

open-ended HMO

pharmacy benefit manager

point-of-service (POS) plan

preferred-provider organization (PPO)

prescription drug plan

step therapy

therapeutic substitution

vision plan

■ STUDY QUESTIONS

1. What must a successful PPO do in addition to seeking discounts from preferred providers?

2. What are the differences between the benefit structure of a traditional major medical contract and a PPO?

3. What are the characteristics of PPOs with respect to each of the following?
   a. Deductibles
   b. Coinsurance
   c. Maximum benefits

4. How may each of the following differ under a PPO, depending on whether network or nonnetwork services are used?
   a. Precertification rules
   b. Benefits received
   c. Claims

5. To what extent are PPOs subject to state regulation?

6. How does a POS plan differ from a traditional PPO?

7. What advantages do multiple-option plans have for employers?

8. a. What are the reasons for using benefit carve-outs?
   b. What are the concerns about benefit carve-outs?

9. What are the functions performed by pharmacy benefits managers?

10. Describe the variations that are often found in prescription drug plans.

11. Why do employers continue to add vision plans?

12. Describe the nature of vision care plans.

13. What are the characteristics of a successful behavioral health program?

14. a. How does disease management differ from traditional case management?

    b. What are the characteristics of a typical disease management program?

15. Describe the nature of a maternity management program.

13 Consumer-Directed Medical Expense Plans

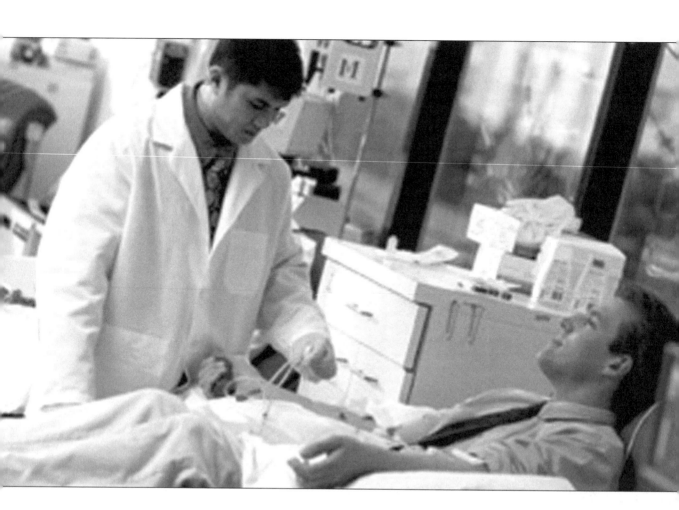

The beginning of the new decade has seen considerable interest in the concept of the **consumer-directed medical expense plan**. Such plans, also referred to by such names as *consumer-driven health care* and *consumer-choice plans,* give the employee increased choices and responsibilities with the selection of his or her own medical expense coverage. Some consumer-directed models also have a greater accountability for health plans and providers.

■ GENERAL APPROACHES

There are two general approaches to consumer-directed medical expense plans—defined-contribution medical expense plans and the use of savings accounts.

Defined-Contribution Medical Expense Plans

Even though some consumer-directed approaches for medical expense plans are in their infancy or still in the proposal stage, they have existed in the form of the **defined-contribution medical expense plan** for some time. For example, many employers make two or more medical expense plans available to their employees, such as an HMO, a PPO, and an indemnity plan. The employer contribution to the cost of coverage for each plan may be a dollar amount that is pegged to a fixed percentage of the cost of the least expensive plan, usually an HMO. Therefore, an employee who elects a more expensive PPO or indemnity plan must make a greater out-of-pocket contribution for his or her coverage than if the HMO had been selected. Certain forms of cafeteria plans, which are discussed in detail in Chapter 19, also incorporate a defined-contribution approach for medical expense plans.

EXAMPLE

The Weir Corporation makes three medical expense plans available to its employees—an HMO, a point-of-service plan, and a PPO. For a single employee, the corporation pays an amount equal to 90 percent of the cost of the least expensive plan, which is the HMO. For the three plans, the employee contribution is as follows:

	Total Monthly Premium	Employee Contribution	Employee Contribution
HMO	$275.70	$248.13	$27.57
POS Plan	330.67	248.13	82.54
PPO	419.09	248.13	170.96

A similar approach is used to determine the cost of dependent coverage, for which the corporation contributes an amount equal to 50 percent of the cost of HMO coverage.

There is no question that defined-contribution plans have driven large numbers of employees to medical expense plans with higher degrees of managed care. However, managed care plans historically have provided a broad scope of coverage, including prescription drugs, yet limited the member's payment for these services to a modest copayment, such as $10. In doing so, these plans greatly diminish the motivation of their members to contain costs when they seek services. From a member's viewpoint, the broad array of services is available for only the cost of the copayment. Even as many managed care plans have become less restrictive, copayment levels have usually changed little. Such marginal copayments applicable to the wide array of more easily available services may explain, at least in part, the decline in overall personal out-of-pocket payments from nearly 25 percent of health care spending in 1980 to less than 15 percent today.[1]

Use of Savings Accounts

Newer types of defined-contribution medical expense plans have features other than just fixed employer contributions. At a minimum, these approaches force employees to make financial decisions involving their health care. Typically, an employer might provide employees with a medical expense plan that has a very high deductible, perhaps as much as $5,000 per year. This type of plan is often referred to as a **high-deductible health plan**. The employer also contributes a lower or equal amount, such as $2,500 per year, to some type of savings account from which the employee can make withdrawals to pay medical expenses that are not covered because of the deductible. The employee can carry forward any unused amount in the account and add it to the next year's employer contribution. Such a plan gives the employee an immediate incentive to purchase medical care wisely because, if the amount in the account is exceeded, the employee will have to pay the full cost of medical expenses out of his or her own pocket until the deductible is satisfied. The plan often incorporates a preferred-provider network of health care professionals. As long as an employee receives medical treatment within the network, any charges that the employee must pay because of the deductible are limited to the amount negotiated with the preferred provider.

Employers might use this approach for all employees, but most employers make it available as an option to a more traditional medical expense plan. In addition, because of the newness of the approach to providing medical expense coverage, employers often limit these plans to a select group of employees on a trial basis.

The rationale for using a high-deductible medical expense plan along with a savings account is that significant cost savings can occur for two primary reasons. First, the expensive cost of administering and paying small claims is largely eliminated, as demonstrated by the fact that a major medical policy with a $2,500 deductible can often be purchased for about one-half the cost of a policy with a $250 deductible. Second, employees now have a direct financial incentive to avoid unnecessary care and to seek out the most cost-effective form of treatment.

A very small number of employers have used this approach for some time with positive results. Costs have been lowered or have risen less rapidly than would otherwise be expected. Reactions of employees have generally been favorable, but until federal legislation in 1996 there was one major drawback—employer contributions to a savings account constituted taxable income to employees.

As with almost any approach to cost containment, this type of medical expense plan has its critics. It is argued that employees will minimize treatment for minor medical expenses and preventive care that would have been covered under a plan without a high deductible. Critics contend that this avoidance of medical care may lead to major expenses that could have been averted or minimized with earlier treatment. However, some types of consumer-directed medical expense plans are permitted to waive the deductible for preventive care. Another criticism is that a high-deductible plan tends to favor healthy individuals and those in high tax brackets. A final criticism is that this type of medical expense plan does not focus on the problem of the uninsured. In rebuttal to this criticism, proponents argue that any technique that lowers costs for employers will ultimately benefit everyone and encourage small employers to provide coverage that would have previously been unaffordable.

Some consumer-directed medical expense plans using the savings-account approach have been designed so that employer decisions about specific benefit plans are eliminated, or at least minimized. Some employers view this as a way of minimizing their legal exposure for health care decisions because a certain level of responsibility is transferred back to employees and health care providers. Under such a plan, an employee can use an employer contribution (along with any additionally needed employee contribution) to shop at some type of "health care supermarket," where many different types of medical expense plans are available. These plans are often required to provide detailed information about their operations so that consumers can make more informed decisions in selecting a medical expense plan. An insurer or some type of Internet provider may offer these plans, and the employer may or may not be involved in the selection of the supermarket that an employee uses. Most consumer-directed medical expense plans that use the savings-account approach, however, only make a single medical expense plan available to employees.

There are still legal, regulatory, and tax issues that need to be addressed for some types of consumer-directed medical expense plans that use savings plans. Whether employers will embrace these newer types of plans on a large scale is still open to conjecture. So far there seems to be more interest in the approach than in implementation, but that is often the way with new concepts. It should be remembered that it took many years for managed care plans to be widely used, even with legislative encouragement.

The remainder of this chapter is devoted to three tax-favored approaches that use savings accounts:

1. Archer medical savings accounts
2. Health reimbursement arrangements
3. Health savings accounts

■ ARCHER MEDICAL SAVINGS ACCOUNTS

The Health Insurance Portability and Accounting Act provided favorable tax treatment for medical savings accounts (MSAs) under a pilot project that began on January 1, 1997, and continued through 2003. In 2001, these MSAs were given the name *Archer MSAs*. During this period, the act allowed for the establishment of up to 750,000 Archer MSAs. However, fewer than 100,000 were actually established despite great initial enthusiasm about their potential success. No more Archer MSAs can be established, but those in existence at the end of 2003 can remain in effect.

During this seven-year pilot project, Archer MSAs were evaluated and debated. With the basic concept receiving strong support from the insurance industry and the more conservative members of Congress, Archer MSAs were retooled and became health savings accounts (HSAs) as part of the Medicare Prescription Drug, Improvement, and Modernization Act of 2003. HSAs and how they differ from Archer MSAs are discussed later in this chapter.

General Nature

An **Archer MSA** is a personal savings account from which unreimbursed medical expenses, including deductibles, percentage participation, and copayments can be paid. Coverage can be limited to an individual or include dependents. The Archer MSA must be in the form of a tax-exempt trust or custodial account established in conjunction with a high-deductible health (that is, medical expense) plan. An Archer MSA is established with a qualified trustee or custodian in much the same way that an IRA is established. Any insurance company or bank (as well as certain other financial institutions) can be a trustee or custodian, as can any other person or entity already approved by the IRS as a trustee or custodian for IRAs. Some insurers that sell high-deductible health plans for use with Archer MSAs also market the Archer MSA accounts; other insurers leave it to the purchasers of a high-deductible health plan to establish their Archer MSAs with other institutions.

Even though employers can sponsor Archer MSAs, these accounts are established for the benefit of individuals and are portable. If an employee changes employers or leaves the workforce, the Archer MSA remains with the individual.

Eligibility

Two types of individuals were eligible to establish and now maintain existing Archer MSAs:

1. An employee (or spouse) of a small employer that maintains an individual or family high-deductible health plan covering that individual. These persons established their Archer MSAs under an employer-sponsored plan.
2. A self-employed person (or spouse) maintaining an individual or family high-deductible health plan covering that individual. These persons needed to seek out a custodian or trustee for their Archer MSAs.

A small employer is defined as an employer who has an average of 50 or fewer employees (including employees of controlled-group members and predecessor employers) on business days during either of the two preceding calendar years. After the initial qualification as a small employer is satisfied, an employer can continue to make contributions to employees' Archer MSAs until the first year following the year in which the employer has more than 200 employees. At that time, participating employees may take over contributions to their accounts, but no employer contributions can be made.

A high-deductible health plan, for purposes of Archer MSA participation, is a plan that has the following deductibles and annual out-of-pocket limitations. These amounts are for 2004 and are subject to inflation adjustments.

- In the case of individual coverage, the deductible must be at least $1,700 and cannot exceed $2,600. The maximum annual out-of-pocket expenses cannot exceed $3,450.

- In the case of family coverage, the deductible must be at least $3,450 and cannot exceed $5,150. The maximum annual out-of-pocket expenses cannot exceed $6,300.

The deductible must apply to all medical expenses covered by the plan.

An insurance company or a managed care organization, such as an HMO, can write a high-deductible plan. Currently, the high-deductible plans are written by insurance companies, sometimes in the form of traditional major medical products but usually as PPO products. No HMOs have yet established high-deductible plans.

A high-deductible plan can be part of a cafeteria plan, but the Archer MSA must be established outside the cafeteria plan.

With some exceptions, a person who is covered under a high-deductible health plan is denied eligibility for an Archer MSA if he or she is covered under another health plan that does not meet the definition of a high-deductible plan but that provides any benefits that are covered under the high-deductible health plan. The exceptions include coverage for accident, disability, dental care, vision care, and long-term care as well as liability insurance, insurance for a specified disease or illness, and insurance paying a fixed amount per period of hospitalization.

Contributions

Either the account holder of an Archer MSA or the account holder's employer, but not both, may make a contribution to an Archer MSA. If the employer makes a contribution, even one below the allowable limit, the account holder may not make a contribution. Contributions must be in the form of cash.

Contributions by an employer are tax deductible to the employer and are not included in an employee's gross income or subject to Social Security and other employment taxes. Employee contributions are deductible in computing adjusted gross income. As with IRAs, individuals' contributions must generally be made by April 15 of the year following the year for which the contributions are made.

The amount of the annual tax-deductible contribution to an employee's account is limited to 65 percent of the policy deductible for the health coverage if the Archer MSA is for an individual. The figure is 75 percent if an Archer MSA covers a family. If each person in a married couple has an Archer MSA and if one or both of the Archer MSAs provide family coverage, the aggregate contribution is equal to 75 percent of the deductible for the family coverage with the lowest deductible. The contribution is split equally between the two persons unless they agree to a different division.

The actual Archer MSA contribution that can be deducted in a tax year is limited to $\frac{1}{12}$ of the annual amount, as described in the previous paragraph, times the number of months that an individual is eligible for Archer MSA participation. For example, assume that the deductible under an individual's health plan is $1,800. The maximum annual contribution to the Archer MSA is then 65 percent of this amount, which is $1,170, and the monthly amount is $97.50. If the individual is covered under a high-deductible plan for only the first eight months of the year, then the annual deductible contribution is eight times $97.50, or $780. Note, however, that there are no requirements that contributions be made on a monthly basis or at any particular time. In this example, the full $1,170 could have been made early in the year. The amount over $780 would then be an excess contribution.

An excess contribution occurs to the extent that contributions to an Archer MSA exceed the deductible limits or are made for an ineligible person. Any excess contribution made by the employer is included in the employee's gross income. In addition, account holders are subject to a 6 percent excise tax on excess contributions for each year these contributions are in an account. This excise tax can be avoided if the excess amount and any net income attributable to the excess amount are removed from the Archer MSA prior to the last day prescribed by law, including extensions, for filing the account holder's income tax return. The net income attributable to the excess contributions is included in the account holder's gross income for the tax year in which the distribution is made.

An employer that makes contributions to Archer MSAs is subject to a nondiscrimination rule that requires that the employer make comparable contributions for all employees who have Archer MSAs. However, full-time employees and part-time employees (those working fewer than 30 hours per week) are treated separately. The comparability rule requires that the employer contribute either the same dollar amount for each employee or the same percentage of each employee's deductible under the health plan. Failure to comply with this rule subjects the employer to an excise tax equal to 35 percent of the aggregate amount contributed to Archer MSAs during the period when the comparability rule was not satisfied.

Employer contributions belong to the employee and are nonforfeitable.

Account Growth

Unused Archer MSA balances carry over from year to year, and there is no prescribed period in which they must be withdrawn. Earnings on amounts in an MSA are not subject to taxation as they accrue.

Distributions

An individual can take distributions from an Archer MSA at any time. The amount of the distribution can be any part or all of the account balance. Subject to some exceptions, distributions of both contributions and earnings are excludible from an account holder's gross income if used to pay medical expenses of the account holder and the account holder's family as long as these expenses are not paid by other sources of insurance. For the most part, the eligible medical expenses are the same ones that would be deductible, ignoring the 7.5 percent of adjusted gross income limitation, if the account holder itemized his or her tax deductions. (See the discussion on deductibility of medical expenses in Chapter 14.) However, tax-free withdrawals are not permitted for the purchase of insurance other than long-term care insurance, COBRA continuation coverage, or health coverage while an individual receives unemployment compensation. In addition, in any year a contribution is made to an Archer MSA, tax-free withdrawals can be made to pay the medical expenses of only those persons who were eligible for coverage under an Archer MSA at the time the expenses were incurred. For example, Archer MSA contributions cannot be withdrawn tax free to pay the unreimbursed medical expenses of an account holder's spouse who is covered under a health plan of his or her employer that is not a high-deductible plan.

Distributions for reasons other than paying eligible medical expenses are included in an account holder's gross income and are subject to a 15 percent penalty tax unless certain circumstances exist. The penalty tax is not levied if the distribution is made after the account holder turns 65 or because of the account holder's death or disability. In addition, the penalty tax does not apply to funds rolled over to a new Archer MSA as long as the rollover is done within 60 days. Transfers of Archer MSA accounts as a result of divorce are also tax free.

Estate Tax Treatment

Upon death, the remaining balance in an Archer MSA is includible in the account holder's gross estate for estate tax purposes. If the beneficiary of the account is a surviving spouse, the Archer MSA belongs to the spouse and he or she can deduct the account balance in determining the account holder's gross estate. The surviving spouse can then use the Archer MSA for his or her medical expenses. If the beneficiary is anyone else, or if no beneficiary is named, the Archer MSA ceases to exist.

■ HEALTH REIMBURSEMENT ARRANGEMENTS

For several years, a few employers have used high-deductible medical expense plans and created a savings account for each employee under which he or she could obtain reimbursement for certain medical expenses that were not covered under a high-deductible plan. However, there was uncertainty about the tax treatment of such reimbursements, particularly if account balances were carried over to subsequent plan years. This uncertainty was settled in 2002 when the IRS issued a ruling that specifically allowed such tax-favored **health reimbursement arrangements (HRAs)** as long as specified criteria were satisfied.

Requirements for Health Insurance Policies

Although HRAs are almost always used with high-deductible insurance policies, there is no requirement for the size of the deductible. In fact, a policy with any size deductible can be used. The deductible can also be waived for preventive services such as physical exams, immunizations, and mammograms.

Eligibility

HRAs can be established by any size employer for its employees, but they cannot be established by or for self-employed persons.

Contributions

Contributions to an HRA must be made solely by the employer. However, employees may be required to pay part of the underlying medical expense coverage.

There is no requirement that contributions be made to a trust or custodial account. In fact, HRAs are typically unfunded, and the employer contributions are merely credits to a savings account. Reimbursements are then paid from the employer's current revenue, at which time the employer receives an income tax deduction.

Contributions in an employee's account can be carried over to subsequent years to the extent they have not been withdrawn to reimburse medical expenses.

Distributions

Employees can take tax-free distributions from an HRA as reimbursement for medical expenses that are not paid by any other medical expense plan. The medical expenses may be for the employee, his or her spouse, or any other persons who are dependents for tax purposes. The reimbursements may be for any medical expenses that would be deductible, ignoring the 7.5 percent of adjusted gross income limitation, if the employee itemized his or her income tax deductions.

Distributions under any other circumstances are not permitted.

HRAs that are unfunded (as is usually the case) are treated as self-funded medical reimbursement plans and are subject to the nondiscrimination rules applicable to such plans (discussed in Chapter 14). Therefore, if HRAs are set up on a discriminatory basis, highly compensated employees may be taxed on all or a portion of any benefits they receive.

Termination of Employment

At termination of employment, an employee's HRA usually terminates. With one exception, the employee cannot receive any taxable or nontaxable benefit from the account after termination. The exception is that the employer can (but is not required to) allow a terminated employee to spend down an HRA balance for unreimbursed medical expenses incurred after termination of employment.

Unlike Archer MSAs and HSAs, HRAs are treated as group health plans and are generally subject to COBRA requirements (see Chapter 14). If any employee elects this option, he or she has access to unused balances in the HRA account during the COBRA continuation period.

■ HEALTH SAVINGS ACCOUNTS

In addition to providing prescription drug coverage for older Americans, the Medicare Prescription Drug, Improvement, and Modernization Act established **health savings accounts (HSAs).** Like Archer MSAs, HSAs are savings accounts for use with high-deductible medical expense plans and from which certain unreimbursed medical expense can be paid. They are designed to be successors to Archer MSAs and have many features in common. However, they also have some notable differences that make them more attractive than Archer MSAs and available to a much larger pool of consumers.

HSAs can be established as early as 2004. While there is considerable interest in these products among health insurers, their development is proceeding cautiously, and growth will probably be slow in the employer market before 2005. First, there are still many concerns that must be addressed by IRS regulations that have yet to be issued as of spring of 2004. The IRS, however, is expected to have these regulations in place during 2004. Second, employer plans often have plan years that are on a calendar-year basis. Therefore, 2005 is the earliest that many employers can establish medical expense plans that incorporate HSAs.

The extent of HSA use in the near future is open to conjecture. Many insurers, third-party administrators, and benefit consultants—particularly those who want to market the product—are extolling their virtues. Many employers, however, seem to be taking more of a wait-and-see attitude. They want to analyze the products that are being developed and be certain that these products will in fact better control health care costs.

Employers also are looking for products that will appeal to employees and realize that it will take time before employees understand HSAs. The situation is not unlike the early days of HMOs and PPOs. There was considerable interest and slow, but steady, growth over a number of years. But eventually the products dominated the medical expense marketplace. Only time will tell if the same is true for HSAs.

Even though many details still need to be resolved, the basic character of HSAs is spelled out in the new Medicare act. The following discussion focuses on how HSAs are similar to MSAs and how they differ.

General Nature

Like an Archer MSA, an HSA is a personal savings account fully owned by the account holder. Participation can be limited to an individual or include dependents, and the account can be used to pay unreimbursed medical expenses. HSAs must be funded, and the funds are held by a qualified trustee or custodian under the same rules that apply to Archer MSAs.

Some of the many insurers that intend to sell high-deductible health plans for use with HSAs also plan to market the HSAs. Other insurers will only market the high-deductible health plans.

Eligibility

The eligibility rules for HSAs are much broader than those for Archer MSAs. HSAs can be established by employees, the self-employed, and anyone else who meets the following rules for qualification:

- The individual must be covered by a high-deductible health plan.
- With certain exceptions, the individual must not be covered by another health insurance plan. These exceptions are the same as those for Archer MSAs and include policies that provide coverage for specified disease or illness, a fixed payment for a period of hospitalization, accidents, disability, dental care, vision care, or long-term care.
- The individual is not eligible to be claimed as a dependent on another person's federal income tax return.
- The individual is not entitled to Medicare benefits because of attaining age 65 or disability.

An employer can establish HSAs for its employees, or an individual (whether employed or not) may establish his or her own HSA.

For purposes of HSA participation, a high-deductible health plan is defined as having the following deductibles and annual out-of-pocket limitations:

■ In the case of individual coverage, the deductible must be at least $1,000, and annual out-of-pocket expenses cannot exceed $5,000.

■ In the case of family coverage, the deductible must be at least $2,000, and annual out-of-pocket expenses cannot exceed $10,000.

As with high-deductible health plans for use with Archer MSAs, the above figures are subject to annual indexing for inflation. However, high-deductible health plans used with HSAs are permitted to waive any deductible requirements for preventive care. If these high-deductible plans use preferred-provider networks, they can have higher out-of-pocket limits for services provided outside the network, and any deductibles for nonnetwork services are not taken into account when determining the out-of-pocket limits specified above.

One point should be emphasized about the deductible for family coverage. It is not a family deductible as was described in Chapter 10. In that situation, there is an individual deductible that applies to each family member as well as a separate deductible for the family. This is sometimes referred to as a *stacked deductible*, and policy benefits are paid for any family member once his or her deductible is satisfied, even if the family deductible has not been met.

In the case of a high-deductible policy used with an HSA, there will usually not be an individual deductible if a policy is written for a family. Rather, there will be a single deductible—referred to as a *common deductible*—that must be satisfied before any benefits are payable, even if all claims are for one family member. It is permissible, however, to use a stacked deductible, but only if the individual deductible is equal to at least the required HSA family deductible of $2,000. For example, a policy with an individual deductible of $2,500 and a family deductible of $5,000 would be acceptable.

Contributions

Contributions to an HSA for a self-employed or unemployed individual are made directly by that person. For an employed person, contributions can be made by the employer, the employee, or a combination of the two. Family members may also make contributions to an HSA on behalf of other family members. Contributions can also be made under a cafeteria plan. No contributions, however, can be made after an individual is eligible for Medicare.

Contributions by an individual are deductible for federal income tax purposes even if the individual does not itemize deductions. Employer contributions are deductible by the employer and do not represent taxable income to an employee. If an employer makes contributions, the same nondiscrimination rule for comparable contributions that was described for Archer MSAs applies.

The maximum annual contribution to an HSA in 2004 is $2,600 for an individual and $5,150 for families. These amounts are subject to annual indexing for inflation and are not a function of the deductible amount for the high-deductible policy. The amounts, however, are aggregate amounts that apply to all HSAs and MSAs that an individual or family might have.

Individuals aged 55 or older are also permitted an additional annual catch-up contribution of up to $500 in 2004. This amount will increase by $100 per year until it reaches $1,000 in 2009. If both a husband and wife are aged 55 or older, the catch-up contribution is available to each of them.

Account balances from Archer MSAs can be rolled over to HSAs on a tax-free basis.

As with Archer MSAs, the contribution is limited to $\frac{1}{12}$ of these amounts for each month of participation in an HSA. However, the full contribution for a year can be made at any time. Excess contributions are treated in the same manner as for Archer MSAs.

Account Growth

Unused amounts in an HSA accumulate on a tax-free basis and carry over to subsequent years without limit. The size of an HSA balance carried over from prior years has no effect on a current year's contribution.

Distributions

Distributions from HSAs are tax free as long as they are used to pay for qualified medical expenses. These medical expenses are the same as those described for Archer MSAs. Tax-free distributions can also be used to pay premiums for long-term care insurance, COBRA continuation coverage, and health insurance while an individual receives unemployment insurance.

Even though contributions cannot be made after an individual reaches age 65, tax-free distributions can still be used for qualified medical expenses, which include Medicare premiums and premiums for medical expense coverage under employer-sponsored plans. However, tax-free distributions cannot be used to pay premiums for Medicare supplement policies.

Distributions are permitted for other reasons, but they are subject to income taxation and possibly to a 10 percent penalty tax. However, the penalty tax does not apply in the case of distributions after an individual's death, disability, or the attainment of age 65.

Estate Tax Treatment

Upon death, the remaining balance in an HSA is treated in the same manner as the balance in an Archer MSA if a spouse is the beneficiary. If the beneficiary is anyone else, the beneficiary must include the fair market value of the account in his or her gross income for tax purposes.

TABLE 13.1	Savings Accounts Comparisons		
	Archer MSA	**HRA**	**HSA**
Persons Eligible	Employees of employer with 50 or fewer employees and self-employed	All employees	Anyone
Use of High-Deductible Health Plan with Account	Required	Not required, but usually used	Required
Waiver of Deductible Requirement for Preventive Care	Not allowed	Permitted	Permitted
Contribution	By employer or employee but not both	By employer	By employer, employee, or both
Taxation of Distribution to Participants	Tax free if for qualified medical expenses; other distributions subject to taxation and possibly penalty tax	Tax free if for qualified medical expense only	Tax free if for qualified fixed medical expenses; other distributions subject to taxation and possibly penalty tax
Portability	Yes, account owned by employee	No, account usually terminates with employment	Yes, account owned by employee
COBRA	Does not apply	Applies	Does not apply
Funding	Account must be funded	Account usually unfunded and paid from employer's current revenue	Account must be funded

A COMPARISON CHART

Table 13.1 compares Archer MSAs, HRAs, and HSAs.

KEY TERMS

Archer MSA
consumer-directed medical expense plan

defined-contribution medical expense plan
health reimbursement arrangements (HRAs)

health savings accounts (HSAs)
high-deductible health plan

STUDY QUESTIONS

1. Why have defined-contribution medical expense plans failed to contain medical care expenses?
2. One technique for containing medical expenses is to use a savings account with a high-deductible medical expense policy.

      a. What is the nature of this savings account?

      b. What is the rationale for this technique?

      c. What are the criticisms of this technique?

3. Describe the general nature of Archer MSAs.

4. a. Explain the income tax treatment of Archer MSA contributions.

      b. Describe the nondiscrimination rule that applies to employer contributions.

5. a. When can distributions be taken from an Archer MSA?

      b. How are distributions taxed?

6. a. Who is eligible for an HRA?

      b. Who can make contributions to an HRA?

7. a. What is the usual source of distributions from an HRA?

      b. How are these distributions taxed?

8. What happens to an employee's HRA at termination of employment?

9. Who is eligible for a health savings account (HSA)?

10. What is the nature of the high-deductible health plan that must be used with an HSA?

11. a. Who can make contributions to an HSA?

      b. What limits are placed on these contributions?

12. a. What types of distributions from an HSA are tax free?

      b. What types of distributions are subject to taxation but free of any penalty tax?

13. How is an HSA treated for estate tax purposes?

■ NOTE

1. Centers for Medicare & Medicaid Services, Office of the Actuary, National Health Statistics Group.

14

Provisions and Tax Treatment of Medical Expense Plans

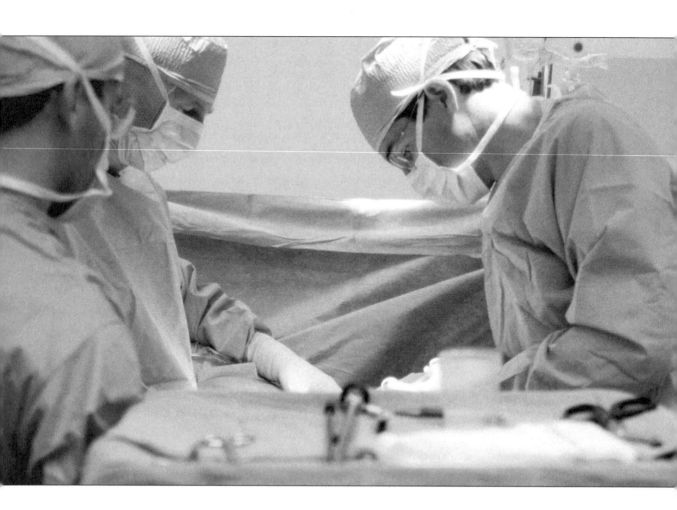

- Describe the eligibility provisions found in medical expense plans.
- Explain the coordination-of-benefits process.
- Explain the relationship between employer-provided medical expense coverage and Medicare.
- Identify the circumstances under which employer-provided coverage may terminate, and explain how coverage can be continued.
- Describe the procedures for processing medical expense claims.
- Explain the HIPAA administrative standards.
- Explain the tax implication of group medical expense premiums and benefits for the employer and employees.

CHAPTER OUTLINE

Eligibility
   Dependent Eligibility
   Federal Rules for Children's Coverage
   Portability
   Benefits for Domestic Partners

Coordination of Benefits
   Determination of Primary Coverage
   Determination of Benefits Payable:
     Some Examples
   Determination of Benefits: Some
     Complexities

Relationship with Medicare
   Medicare Secondary Rules
   Medicare Carve-Outs and Supplements

Termination of Coverage
   Continuation of Coverage under
     COBRA
   Continuation of Coverage in Addition
     to COBRA
   Extension of Benefits
   Conversion
   Group-to-Individual Portability

Claims
   Indemnity Benefits
   Service Benefits
   Subrogation

HIPAA Administrative Standards
   Privacy Standards
   Security Standards
   Identifier Standards
   Transaction and Code Set Standards

Federal Tax Treatment
   Deductible Employee Contributions
   Self-Funded Plans
   Health Coverage Tax Credit

This chapter is devoted primarily to a discussion of many of the major provisions in medical expense plans, whether the plan benefits are self-funded or provided through a traditional insurance contract, HMO, or PPO. Although these provisions may stand alone as part of the employer's plan, most of them are incorporated into the contracts of the providers that fund the plan's benefits. To a large extent, these provisions are similar—if not identical—to those discussed in Chapter 6 for group term life insurance. However, certain provisions are either unique to medical expense plans or different from those found in other types of group benefits. These provisions pertain to eligibility, coordination of benefits, the effect of Medicare, termination (including postretirement benefits), and claims. Several of the provisions have changed in recent years as a result of the passage of the Health Insurance Portability and Accountability Act (HIPAA) in 1996.

The last portion of the chapter describes the tax treatment of medical expense benefits. One unusual characteristic of this tax treatment is the difference in the way that insured benefits and self-funded benefits are treated.

■ ELIGIBILITY

The eligibility requirements for medical expense coverage are essentially the same as those discussed earlier for group term insurance—an employee must usually be in a covered classification, must satisfy any probationary period, and must be full time. Coverage is rarely made available to part-time employees. In addition, medical expense contracts often contain an actively-at-work provision. This provision may be waived, particularly for larger employers for whom adverse selection tends to be less of a problem than for smaller groups, because any adverse selection for a large group is reflected in future premiums through the experience-rating process.

It is important to note the effect of HIPAA on actively-at-work provisions. HIPAA allows the use of an actively-at-work provision that requires that an employee be at work on the first day of his or her employment. Thus, an employee who is absent on the initial day of employment, even because of health reasons, can be denied coverage until he or she begins work. However, if there is a probationary period, such as 90 days of being actively at work, an actively-at-work provision cannot be used to lengthen the probationary period after an employee is actively at work. Furthermore, it cannot be used to postpone eligibility at the end of the probationary period if there has been an absence for reasons of the employee's health.

Eligibility requirements may vary somewhat if an employer changes providers of a plan's benefits. Note that the following discussion refers to the employer's plan with benefits paid by the previous provider as the "old plan" and the employer's plan with benefits paid by the new provider as the "new plan." In actuality, the employer still has the same medical expense plan. It has only been modified with the use of a new provider and, possibly, a different level of benefits. This is a material modification to a group health plan, and ERISA requires that participants be notified of this change by a summary of material modification. The ERISA rules are covered in Chapter 27.

Even though it has been adopted by only a few states, most providers follow the procedures established by the National Association of Insurance Commissioners (NAIC) Group Coverage Discontinuance and Replacement Model Regulation for medical expense coverage (and possibly other group coverages). This regulation stipulates that coverage be provided (but possibly limited) under a new plan to anyone who (1) was covered under the old plan at the date it was discontinued and (2) is in an eligible classification of the new plan. Employees actively at work on the date coverage is transferred are automatically covered under the new plan and are exempt from any probationary periods. If the new plan contains a preexisting-conditions provision, benefits applicable to an individual's preexisting conditions are limited to the lesser of (1) the maximum benefits of the new plan (ignoring the preexisting conditions) or (2) the maximum benefits of the old plan.

When employers adopt a new plan, they often negotiate with the provider of benefits to ensure the availability of coverage for employees who are covered under the old plan but who are not actively at work on the date coverage is discontinued. Such employees may be disabled by illness or injury or having temporary interruptions of employment. Benefits for these employees, however, are frequently limited to the old plan's level until they meet the new plan's actively-at-work requirement.

Two final points should be made concerning the transfer of coverage. First, the new plan will not pay benefits for expenses that were covered by the old plan under an extension-of-benefits provision (discussed later). Second, when applying any deductibles or probationary periods under the new plan, credit is often given for the satisfaction (or partial satisfaction) of the same or similar provisions during the last three months of the old plan. For example, assume that coverage is transferred in the middle of a calendar year and the new plan contains the same $200-a-year calendar deductible as the old plan. If an employee has already satisfied the deductible under the old plan, no new deductible is required for the remainder of the calendar year, provided that (1) the expenses used to satisfy the deductible under the old plan satisfy the deductible under the new plan and (2) the expenses were incurred during the last three months of the old plan. If only $140 of the $200 was incurred during those last three months, an additional $60 deductible is required under the new plan for the remainder of the calendar year.

Dependent Eligibility

Typically, the same medical expense benefits that are provided for an eligible employee are also available for that employee's dependents. Conversely, dependent coverage is rarely available unless the employee also has coverage. As long as any necessary payroll deductions have been authorized, dependent coverage is typically effective on the same date as the employee's coverage. If coverage under a contributory plan is not elected within 31 days after dependents are eligible, future coverage is available only during an open enrollment period or when satisfactory evidence of insurability is provided. However, if an employee was previously without dependents (and therefore had no dependent coverage), any newly acquired dependents (by birth, marriage, or adoption) are eligible for coverage as of the date they gain dependent status.

The term **dependent** most commonly refers to an employee's spouse who is not legally separated from the employee and any unmarried dependent children (including stepchildren and adopted children) under the age of 19. However, coverage is usually provided for children to age 23 if they are full-time students. In addition, coverage may also continue (and is required to be continued in some states) for children who are incapable of earning their own living because of a physical or mental infirmity. Such children are considered dependents as long as this condition exists, but periodic proof of the condition may be required. If an employee has dependent coverage, all newly acquired dependents (by birth, marriage, or adoption) are automatically covered.

Some persons that meet the definition of a dependent may be ineligible for coverage because they are in the armed forces or they are eligible for coverage under the same plan as the employees themselves. This latter restriction, however, may not apply to a spouse unless the spouse is actually covered under the plan. Some plans also exclude coverage for any dependents residing outside the United States or Canada.

At one time, some medical expense plans contained a "nonconfinement" provision for dependents, which was similar to the actively-at-work provision for employees. Under this provision, a dependent was not covered if he or she was confined for medical care or treatment in a hospital or at home at the time of eligibility. Such a provision is no longer allowed as a result of HIPAA regulations.

Federal Rules for Children's Coverage

Until the passage of the Omnibus Budget Reconciliation Act of 1993 (OBRA '93), provisions regarding eligibility were determined by the employer, provider underwriting practices, and/or any applicable state laws. OBRA '93 brought the federal government into the picture with a series of rules designed to better guarantee that benefits are available to children. Some of these rules pertain to eligibility.

Coverage for Adopted Children. If a work-related group medical expense plan provides coverage for dependent children of participants or beneficiaries, it must provide benefits for adopted children or children placed for adoption under the same terms and conditions that apply to natural children. For purposes of this change, a *child* is defined as a person under the age of 18 at the time of adoption or placement for adoption. Placement for adoption occurs at the time in the adoption process when the plan participant or beneficiary assumes and retains the legal duty for the total or partial support of a child to be adopted.

In addition to providing coverage, a plan cannot restrict benefits because of a preexisting condition at the time coverage is effective as long as the adoption or placement for adoption occurs while the parent is eligible for plan participation.

Medical Child Support Orders. One goal of the act was to shift Medicaid costs from the government to the private sector by requiring employer-provided benefit plans to pick up more of the cost of providing medical expense benefits to the children of divorced and separated parents. As a result, employer-sponsored medical expense plans must recognize qualified medical child support orders by providing benefits for a participant's children in accordance with the requirements of such an order.

The act defines a **medical child support order** as a court judgment, decree, or order that (1) provides for child support with respect to the child of a group plan participant or provides benefit coverage to such a child, is ordered under state domestic relations law, and relates to benefits under the plan or (2) enforces a state medical support law enacted under the new Medicaid rules discussed below. The support order then becomes *qualified* if two additional requirements are met. First, the order must create or recognize the right of the child to receive benefits to which the plan participant or other beneficiary is entitled under a group plan. Second, the order must include such information as the name and last known mailing address of the plan participant and the child, a reasonable description of the coverage to be provided, the period for which coverage must be provided, and each plan to which the order applies. However, a qualified order cannot require a plan to offer any benefit that is not already available under the plan unless the benefits are necessary to meet the requirements of a state medical child support law established under the Social Security Act.

Because of a lack of uniformity among medical child support orders and difficulty for employers in determining whether they are qualified, the Department of Labor and the Department of Health and Human Services have jointly developed a National Medical Support Notice (NMSN) that must be used by state courts and agencies. When properly completed, the NMSN meets the requirements of a qualified medical child support order. The NMSN has two parts, both of which are sent to the employer. Within 20 days, the employer must respond to the agency that sent the order if coverage is not available for any reason. If coverage is available, part B of the form must be sent to the plan administrator if it is not the employer. Within 40 days after receiving the NMSN, the dependent child must be added to the employer's coverage. If the plan administrator is not the employer, the administrator must notify the employer of the amount to withhold from the worker's pay.

Information about medical child support can be found on the Web site of U.S. Department of Health and Human Services' Administration for Children & Families: *www.acf.hhs.gov.*

Medicaid Rules.   The act encouraged the states (under threat of losing some Medicaid reimbursement) to adopt a series of laws relating to medical child support. One of these laws prohibits plan administrators from denying enrollment of a child under a parent's insurance plan on any of the following grounds:

■   The child was born out of wedlock

■   The child is not claimed as a dependent on the parent's federal income tax return

■   The child does not reside with the parent or in the insurer's service area

In addition, a second law provides that if a court orders a parent to provide medical support, the parent's plan must enroll the child without regard to any enrollment restrictions. If the parent fails to enroll the child, enrollment can be made by the child's other parent or by the state Medicaid agency. The employer is required to withhold from the parent's compensation any payments that the parent must make toward the cost of coverage.

Portability

Some of the most significant parts of HIPAA are the provisions dealing with portability of medical expense coverage. These provisions do not allow employees to take specific insurance from one job to another; they put limitations on preexisting-conditions exclusions and allow employees to use evidence of prior insurance coverage to reduce or eliminate the length of any preexisting-conditions exclusion when employees move to another medical expense plan. These provisions should minimize job lock for employees by eliminating the fear that medical expense coverage will be lost if an employee changes jobs.

The portability provisions apply to almost all group health insurance plans (either insured or self-funded) as long as they have at least two active participants on the first day of the plan year. Note that the same definition of *group health plan* mentioned in the initial discussion of HIPAA in Chapter 9 applies to the portability provisions.

Limitations on Preexisting Conditions. Restrictions for preexisting conditions are limited to a maximum of 12 months (18 months for late enrollees). In addition, the period for preexisting conditions must be reduced for prior creditable coverage as defined below. It should be noted that there is nothing in the act that prohibits an employer from imposing a probationary period before a new employee is eligible to enroll in a medical expense plan. (Note: Although HIPAA refers to the probationary period as a waiting period, the term *probationary* is consistent with the terminology used in this book and is therefore used in this discussion.) However, any probationary period must be applied uniformly without regard to the health status of potential plan participants or beneficiaries. In addition, the probationary period must run concurrently with any preexisting-conditions period. For example, an employee might be subject to a preexisting-conditions period of seven months because of prior coverage. If the employer's plan had a three-month probationary period for enrollment, the length of the preexisting-conditions period after enrollment could be only four months. An HMO is also permitted to have an affiliation period of up to two months (three months for late enrollees) if the HMO does not impose a preexisting-conditions provision and if the affiliation period is applied without regard to health status-related factors.

Under the act, a *preexisting condition* is defined as a mental or physical condition for which medical advice, diagnosis, care, or treatment was recommended or received within the six-month period ending on the enrollment date. No preexisting-conditions exclusions can apply to pregnancy or to newborn children or, if under age 18, to newly adopted children or children newly placed for adoption as long as they become covered for creditable coverage within 30 days of birth, adoption, or placement. In addition, the use of genetic information as a preexisting condition is prohibited unless there is a diagnosis of a preexisting medical condition related to the information.

The 12-month limitation for preexisting conditions applies if an employee enrolls when he or she is initially eligible for coverage. It also applies in the case of special enrollment periods (discussed in Chapter 9) that are required by the act for employees and dependents who lose other coverage and for new dependents. Anyone who does not enroll in an employer's plan during the first period he or she is eligible or during a special enrollment period is a late enrollee and can be subject to a preexisting-conditions period of 18 months.

Creditable Coverage. The act defines **creditable coverage** as coverage under an individual policy, an employer-provided group plan (either insured or self-funded), an HMO, Medicare, Medicaid, or various public plans, regardless of whether the coverage is provided to a person as an individual, an employee, or a dependent. However, coverage is not creditable if there has been a break in coverage of 63 days or more.

In determining the length of a person's preexisting-conditions period, the period of prior creditable coverage must be subtracted.

> **EXAMPLE**
> Assume that an employer's plan has a preexisting-conditions period of 12 months. If a new employee has 12 months or more of creditable coverage, the preexisting-conditions period is satisfied. If the period of creditable coverage is only seven months, then the preexisting-conditions period runs five more months. Note, however, that if the employee has been without coverage for at least 63 days between jobs, the full preexisting-conditions period applies.

Employers have two ways in which they can apply creditable coverage: on a blanket basis to all categories of medical expense coverage or on a benefit-specific basis. For example, if an employee had prior coverage that excluded prescription drugs, this particular coverage could be subject to the full preexisting-conditions period, and the period for other benefits would be reduced because creditable coverage had applied to them. For administrative ease, an employer usually picks the first method.

The act requires that an employer automatically give persons losing group coverage a certificate that specifies the period of creditable coverage under the plan they are leaving, including any period of COBRA coverage. In addition, the employer must provide the certificate to anyone who requests it within 24 months after coverage ceased. If an individual is eligible for COBRA coverage, the certificate must be provided no later than the time when a COBRA election notice must be provided. In other cases, the employer must provide the certificate within a "reasonable" time. This certificate of creditable coverage must include the following information:

- The date the certificate was issued
- The name of the health plan that provided the coverage
- The name and identification number of any individual(s) whose coverage has ceased
- The name, address, and telephone number of the administrator responsible for the certificate
- A statement that the individual(s) had at least 18 months of creditable coverage
- The date any probationary period began and the date coverage began

■ The date coverage ended

One certificate may include coverage for the employee and all dependents, or the employer may issue separate certificates for each person.

Sample certificates of creditable coverage are readily available, including blank ones that can be downloaded from the Internet. This has led to a high incidence of fraudulent certificates. As a result, many plans contact the prior employer to verify the accuracy of any certificates they are given.

State Options. The act's provisions on portability generally override state laws. However, state laws that provide greater portability are not overridden. For example, a look-back period of less than 6 months might be required, or the maximum preexisting-conditions period could be less than 12 months.

Benefits for Domestic Partners

In the mid-1980s, the plans of a few employers began to make coverage available for unmarried **domestic partners**. For example, one plan covers unmarried couples as long as they live together, show financial interdependence and joint responsibility for each other's common welfare, and consider themselves life partners. This type of requirement is fairly typical, as is the additional requirement that the employee's relationship must have lasted some specified minimum period of time, such as 6 or 12 months. The employee must usually give the employer an affidavit that these requirements have been satisfied.

Most surveys indicate that at least 25 percent of employers now provide medical expense benefits to domestic partners. (A smaller percentage of employers offer other types of group benefits.) Most plans provide benefits to domestic partners engaged in either heterosexual or homosexual relationships. Some plans provide benefits only to persons of the opposite gender of the employee, and a small number of plans limit benefits only to persons of the same gender. The rationale for the latter is that persons of opposite genders can obtain benefits by marrying, whereas this option is not usually available to persons of the same gender. Most plans that provide benefits for domestic partners require that the partners live together, but a few plans provide benefits even if the partners live apart. The rationale used is that a cohabitation requirement is not necessary for a married partner to receive benefits.

In some cases, plans provide domestic-partner benefits to persons who are related. For example, benefits may be available to a parent or sibling who lives with and is supported by an employee.

The number of employees obtaining coverage for domestic partners has been relatively small, with many employers experiencing enrollment of less than 1 percent when only partners of the same gender are covered. Some employers have experienced enrollment of up to 4 percent if partners of either gender are covered. (Enrollments of partners of the opposite gender are more than double the enrollments of partners of the same gender.) This low enrollment is due primarily to two factors. First, the domestic partner is probably also working and has medical expense coverage from his or her employer.

Second, some employees are unwilling to make their living arrangement or sexual orientation known in the workplace.

Despite predictions that domestic partners would have adverse claims experience, the claims experience has been good. This is probably due in part to the fact that domestic partners, on the average, tend to be younger and therefore are healthier than employees in general. Also, same-gender partners have few maternity claims. Most, if not all, insurers that levied surcharges on premiums for domestic partners when the coverage was new have now dropped the surcharges.

■ COORDINATION OF BENEFITS

In recent years, the percentage of individuals having duplicate group medical expense coverage has increased substantially and is estimated to be about 10 percent. Probably the most common situation is the one in which a husband and wife both work and have coverage under their respective employers' noncontributory plans. If the employer of either spouse also provides dependent coverage on a noncontributory basis, the other spouse (and other dependents if both employers provide such coverage) is covered under both plans. If dependent coverage is contributory, it is necessary for a couple with children to elect such coverage under one of their plans. However, because a spouse is considered a dependent, he or she also has duplicate coverage when the election is made. Note that this duplicate coverage can be avoided if dependent coverage can be elected for children only. This option exists under many but not all plans. Duplicate coverage may also arise when

- an employee has two jobs.
- children are covered under both a parent's and a stepparent's plans.
- an employee elects coverage under a contributory plan even though the employee is covered as a dependent under another plan. This could result from ignorance or from an attempt to collect double the amount if a claim should occur. In many cases, this coverage is elected because it is broader, even though it still results in an element of duplicate coverage.

Duplicate coverage can also occur if the individual has coverage under a group plan that is not provided by an employer, as with children whose parents have purchased accident coverage for them through their schools.

In the absence of any provisions to the contrary, group medical expense plans are obligated to provide benefits in cases of duplicate coverage as if no other coverage exists. However, to prevent individuals from receiving benefits that exceed their actual expenses, group medical expense plans contain a **coordination-of-benefits (COB) provision**, under which priorities are established for the payment of benefits by each plan covering an individual.

Most states do not require medical expense products of insurance companies, the Blues, HMOs, or PPOs to have a COB provision. If one is used, however, it must comply with the appropriate state rules. Most COB provisions are based on the Group Coordination of Benefits Model Regulation promulgated by the NAIC. This regulation, which applies to traditional insurance products and other products subject to insurance regulation, is periodically revised, and all or portions of one of the versions have now been adopted by almost all states. As with all NAIC model legislation and regulations, some states have adopted the COB provisions with variations. Most states also have adopted a virtually identical COB provision for use by HMOs.

Although some flexibility is allowed, virtually all COB provisions apply when other coverage exists through the group insurance plans or other group benefit arrangements (such as the Blues, HMOs, or self-funded plans) of another employer. They may also apply to no-fault automobile insurance benefits and to student coverage that is either sponsored or provided by educational institutions. However, these provisions virtually never apply (and cannot in most states) to any other coverages provided under contracts purchased on an individual basis outside the employment relationship.

Determination of Primary Coverage

The usual COB provision stipulates that any other plan without the COB provision is primary and that any plan with it is secondary. If more than one plan has a COB provision, the following priorities are established:

- Coverage as an employee is usually primary to coverage as a dependent. The exception occurs if a retired person is covered (1) by Medicare, (2) under a retiree plan of a former employer, and (3) as a dependent of a spouse who is an active employee. In this case, coverage as a dependent is primary, Medicare is secondary, and the retiree plan pays last.

- Coverage as an active employee (or that person's dependent) is primary to coverage as a retired or laid-off employee (or that person's dependent). This rule is ignored unless both plans contain it.

- Coverage as an active employee (or that person's dependent) is primary to a plan that provides COBRA continuation benefits. This rule is also ignored unless both plans contain the rule.

- If the specific rules of a court decree state that one parent must assume responsibility for his or her child's health care expenses, and the plan of that parent has actual knowledge of the terms of the court decree, then that plan is primary.

- If the parents of dependent children are married or are not separated (regardless of whether they have ever been married) or if a court awards joint custody without specifying that one parent has the responsibility to provide health care coverage, the plan of the parent whose birthday falls earlier in the calendar year is primary and the plan of the parent with the later birthday is secondary.

- If the parents of dependent children are not married, are separated (regardless of whether they have ever been married), or are divorced and if there is no court decree allocating responsibility for the child's health care expenses, the following priorities apply:
    - The plan of the parent with custody is primary.

- The plan of the stepparent who is the spouse of the parent with custody is secondary.

- The plan of the parent without custody is tertiary.

- The plan of the stepparent who is the spouse of the parent without custody pays last.

■ If none of the previous rules establishes a priority, the plan covering the person for the longest period of time is primary. If this rule also fails to determine the primary plan, then allowable expenses are shared equally among the plans.

Determination of Benefits Payable: Some Examples

The actual mechanics of the previously described COB provision are demonstrated with some examples.

EXAMPLE

Myra is covered under two medical expense plans, neither of which contains a COB provision.

Plan A provides PPO coverage that pays allowable expenses in full as long as network preferred providers are used. If nonnetwork providers are used, there is (1) a $500 annual deductible, (2) 80 percent coinsurance subject to a $3,000 out-of-pocket limit, and (3) a $1 million lifetime maximum.

Plan B provides traditional comprehensive major medical expense coverage with (1) a $200 calendar-year deductible, (2) 80 percent coinsurance subject to a $1,000 out-of-pocket limit, and (3) a $2 million lifetime maximum.

Assume that Myra incurs the following expenses for a surgical procedure:

Semiprivate room for 5 days at $800 per day	$4,000
Other hospital charges	3,500
Surgeon's fees	3,000
Total expenses	$10,500

Assume also that (1) plan A is primary and (2) network providers were used. In this case, plan A would pay the full $10,500, and plan B would pay $9,300 after deductions for the $200 deductible and the $1,000 out-of-pocket limit that applies to the coinsurance provision. Consequently, Myra would collect a total of $19,800, or $9,300 in excess of her actual expenses.

If the example is changed so that plan B is primary and nonnetwork providers are used for plan A, plan B will still pay $9,300. However, plan A will only pay $8,000, which is 80 percent of the expenses above the nonnetwork deductible. In this case, Myra would collect $17,300, still significantly more than her actual expenses.

If a COB provision is used, it must first be determined whether the provision applies to a given claim. It applies only if the sum of the benefits under the plans involved (assuming there is no provision) exceeds an individual's allowable expenses. **Allowable expenses** are defined as any necessary, reasonable, and customary items of expense, all or a portion of which are covered under at least one of the plans that provides benefits to the person for whom the claim is made. However, under a primary plan, the amount of any benefit reductions resulting from a covered person's failure to comply with the plan's provisions (such as second opinions or precertification) is not considered an allowable expense. In addition, the difference between the cost of a private hospital room and the cost of a semiprivate hospital room is not considered an allowable expense unless the patient's stay in a private room is medically necessary. When the allowable expenses are determined, any deductibles, percentage participation resulting from coinsurance provisions, and plan maximum are ignored.

When the COB provision applies, a person can receive benefits equal to 100 percent of his or her allowable expenses and no more.

EXAMPLE

Assume the same facts as in the previous example, except that each plan contains a COB provision. The entire $10,500 of expenses incurred by Myra is considered allowable expenses. Because the sum of the benefits otherwise payable under the two plans (either $19,800 or $17,300, depending on which plan is primary) exceeds this amount, the COB provision applies. The primary plan pays its benefits as if no other coverage exists, and the secondary plan (or plans) pays the remaining benefits. If plan A in this example is primary, it will pay $10,500, and plan B will pay nothing because 100 percent of Myra's allowable expenses have been paid. If plan B is primary, it will pay $9,300, and plan A will pay the remaining $1,200 of Myra's allowable expenses.

Determination of Benefits: Some Complexities

In actual practice, the determination of benefits payable may be much more complex than the previous simple example. Although many of these complexities are beyond the scope of this book, a few issues are addressed. These include the following:

- Determination of benefits payable by each plan
- Benefit banks
- Coordination of benefits with self-funded plans

Before proceeding further, however, one important point needs to be made: Coordination of benefits is between two (or more) specific plans, each of which has its own rules. Although generalizations can be made, the ultimate benefits paid depend on the specific rules of each plan.

Determination of Benefits Payable by Each Plan. The earlier example lumped expenses together into three broad categories and assumed that they were fully covered by each plan, except for any deductibles and percentage participation by the insured. An actual benefit calculation looks at every charge billed by the hospital and surgeon and determines to what extent that charge is covered. It is possible that some charges will not be paid in full because they exceed reasonable and customary charges or because of exclusions. In addition, some managed care plans limit benefits for nonnetwork services to what is paid to network providers. It is common for this to be significantly below billed charges.

Benefit Banks. Some medical expense plans have a **benefit bank** (also called a *benefit reserve*) in which COB savings from being a secondary payer accumulate for future claims when the plan is also the secondary payer. Balances in the benefit bank usually revert to zero at the end of a specified period, most commonly a calendar year.

EXAMPLE
Assume that a medical expense plan is secondary and pays $1,000 of a claim for which the plan would have paid $15,000 if it had been primary. The $14,000 savings is credited to an account for the insured and can be withdrawn for reimbursement of future allowable medical expenses to the extent they that are not 100 percent reimbursed. Assume further that there is $4,000 of allowable expenses resulting from a future claim, and for some reason the primary and secondary payers pay only a total of $3,500. This $500 shortfall will be withdrawn from the $14,000 balance in the benefit bank so that the insured has a 100 percent reimbursement.

Coordination of Benefits with Self-Funded Plans. Self-funded plans are not bound by the state COB rules that apply to insurance contracts and HMO plans, but as a rule they use provisions that are identical or very similar. However, they are free to use any type of COB provision.

Some self-funded plans use a provision so that their payment as a secondary payer is limited to the amount that would reach the limits of their own plan. For example, assume that two self-funded plans each cover only 80 percent of an insured's medical expenses after a $250 deductible. The secondary payer would pay nothing because the limits of its own plan had already been reached by the primary plan. If the secondary plan had a lower deductible, such as $200, the secondary plan would pay $50. This type of provision, which in effect preserves deductible and coinsurance in the COB process, is not allowed under the NAIC model regulation previously discussed for insured plans.

A few self-funded plans coordinate benefits with plans under which an individual is eligible for coverage, even if the individual is not covered under that plan. For example, the self-funded plan might provide coverage for an employee's dependents. If a dependent spouse works outside the home and is eligible for his or her own employer-provided coverage, the self-funded plan would pay on a secondary basis, whether or not the spouse signed up for his or her employer's plan.

Finally, self-funded plans have been designed so that they are excess or "always secondary" to any other medical expense plan. The most extreme situation occurs if a person is covered under two self-funded plans, each of which takes an always-secondary approach. Each plan pays as if it were secondary. In the earlier example where the insured has $10,500 of covered expenses, this means that plan A pays $2,200 and plan B pays nothing. This total of $2,200 is less than either plan would pay if it were primary. This issue has been the subject of several court cases, and some (but not all) courts have stated that the always-secondary position cannot prevail. Although these courts have ordered an equitable payment of benefits to the covered person, that person has been forced to take the matter to court.

A similar situation exists if a person is covered under a self-funded plan that is always secondary (but would be primary if the state's rules applied) and an insured plan that is legitimately secondary because of the state's COB rules. However, the results are usually somewhat different. In most states, the insured plan must pay the covered person two amounts. The first amount is what the insured plan is obligated to pay as the secondary plan. The second is the difference between what the self-funded plan pays on a secondary basis and what it would have paid if it had settled the claim as the primary payer of benefits. This second amount is considered an advance to the covered person, and the insured plan receives a right of subrogation. In other words, the insured plan has the right to take legal action to recover the amount of the advance from the self-funded plan. If the amount is recovered, the advance is in effect repaid. If there is no recovery, the covered person has no obligation to repay the insured plan.

■ RELATIONSHIP WITH MEDICARE

Because most employees and their dependents are eligible for Medicare on reaching age 65 (and possibly under other circumstances), a provision that eliminates any possible duplication of coverage is necessary. The simplest solution is to exclude any person eligible for Medicare from eligibility under the group contract. However, in most cases this approach conflicts with the Age Discrimination in Employment Act, which prohibits discrimination in welfare benefit plans for active employees.

Medicare Secondary Rules

As mentioned in Chapter 3, Medicare is often the secondary payer to employer-provided medical expense coverage. Under the **Medicare secondary rules**, employers with 20 or more employees must make coverage available under their medical expense plans to active employees aged 65 or older and to active employees' spouses who are eligible for Medicare. Unless an employee elects otherwise, the employer's plan is primary and Medicare is secondary. Except in plans that require large employee contributions, it is doubtful that employees will elect Medicare to be primary because employers are prohibited from offering active employees or their spouses a Medicare carve-out, a Medicare supplement, or some other incentive not to enroll in the employer's plan.

Medicare is the secondary payer of benefits in two other situations. The first involves persons who are eligible for Medicare benefits to treat end-stage renal disease with dialysis or kidney transplants. Medicare provides these benefits to any insured workers (either active or retired) and their spouses and dependent children, but the employer's plan is primary only during the first 30 months of treatment; after that, Medicare is primary and the employer's plan is secondary. It should be noted that the employer's plan could totally exclude dialysis and/or kidney transplants, in which case Medicare would pay. However, federal regulations prevent the employer from excluding these benefits for the first 30 months if they are covered thereafter. This rule for renal disease applies to medical expense plans of all employers, not just those with 20 or more employees.

Medicare is also the secondary payer of benefits to disabled employees (or the disabled dependents of employees) under age 65 who are eligible for Medicare and who are covered under the medical expense plan of large employers (defined as plans with 100 or more employees). Medicare, however, does not pay anything until a person has been eligible for Social Security disability income benefits for two years. The rule applies only if an employer continues medical expense coverage for disabled persons; such continuation is not required.

When an employer's plan is primary, Medicare payments are made for any expenses that are covered by Medicare but not by the employer's plan. For purposes of these payments, Medicare deductibles, copayments, and percentage participation generally do not apply. However, Medicare benefits are limited to what would have been paid in the absence of the employer's plan.

Medicare Carve-Outs and Supplements

An employer's plan may cover certain persons aged 65 or older who are not covered by the provisions of the Age Discrimination in Employment Act—specifically, retirees and active employees of firms with fewer than 20 employees. Although there is nothing to prevent an employer from terminating coverage for these persons, many employers provide them with either a Medicare carve-out or Medicare supplement.

With a **Medicare carve-out**, plan benefits are reduced to the extent that benefits are payable under Medicare for the same expenses. (Medicare may also pay for some expenses not covered by the group plan.)

> **EXAMPLE**
> If Karen incurs $1,000 of covered expenses and is not eligible for Medicare, $720 in benefits is paid under her medical expense plan that has a $100 deductible and an 80 percent coinsurance provision. However, if she is eligible for Medicare, and if Medicare pays $650 for the same expenses, the employer's plan pays only $70, for a total benefit of $720.

Some medical expense plans use a more liberal carve-out approach and reduce covered expenses (rather than benefits payable) by any amounts received under Medicare.

> **EXAMPLE**
> In the previous example, the $650 paid by Medicare would be subtracted from the $1,000 of covered expenses, which would leave $350. After the deductible and coinsurance are applied to this amount, the employer's plan would pay $200, so Karen would receive a total of $850 in benefits, or $130 more than a person not eligible for Medicare.

As an alternative to using a carve-out approach, some employers use a **Medicare supplement** that provides benefits for certain specific expenses not covered under Medicare. These include (1) the portion of expenses not paid by Medicare because of deductibles, coinsurance, or copayments and (2) certain expenses excluded by Medicare, such as prescription drugs. Such a supplement may or may not provide benefits similar to those available under a carve-out plan.

■ TERMINATION OF COVERAGE

In the absence of any provisions for continuation or conversion, the group medical expense coverage of an employee generally ceases upon the earliest of

- the date on which employment terminates. In some plans, coverage ceases on the last day of the month in which employment terminates.
- the date on which the employee ceases to be eligible.
- the date on which the master contract terminates.
- the date on which the overall maximum benefit of major medical coverage is received.
- the end of the last period for which the employee has made any required contribution.

Coverage of any dependent usually ceases on the earliest of the following:

- The date on which he or she ceases to meet the definition of dependent
- The date on which the coverage of the employee ceases for any reason except the employee's receipt of the overall maximum benefit
- The date on which the dependent receives the overall maximum benefit of major medical coverage
- The end of the last period for which the employee has made any required contribution for dependent coverage

However, coverage often continues past these dates because of federal legislation or employer practices.

Continuation of Coverage under COBRA

The Consolidated Omnibus Budget Reconciliation Act of 1985 (**COBRA**) requires that group health plans allow employees and certain beneficiaries to elect to have their current health insurance coverage extended at group rates for up to 36 months following a "qualifying event" that results in the loss of coverage for a "qualified beneficiary." The term *group health plan* as used in the act is broad enough to include medical expense plans, dental plans, vision care plans, and prescription drug plans, regardless of whether benefits are self-insured or provided through other entities, such as insurance companies, HMOs, or PPOs. Long-term care and disability income coverages are not included in the definition of group health plan and are not subject to COBRA.

COBRA also applies to voluntary group health plans even if the employee pays the entire premium as long as an employee would not be able to receive the coverage at the same cost if the employment relationship ended. If the voluntary plan has a portability provision whereby an employee can continue the coverage on an individual basis at no increase in cost, then COBRA does not apply.

Certain church-related plans and plans of the federal government are exempt from COBRA, but the act applies to all other employers who had the equivalent of 20 or more full-time employees on at least 50 percent of its typical business days during the preceding calendar year. For example, an employer who has 10 full-time and 16 half-time employees throughout the year has the equivalent of 18 full-time employees and is not subject to COBRA.

Failure to comply with the act results in an excise tax of up to $100 per day for each person denied coverage. The tax can be levied on the employer as well as on the entity (such as an insurer or HMO) that provides or administers the benefits. In addition, employers face a significant liability risk if they fail to notify qualified beneficiaries about the availability of COBRA coverage. There have been legal judgments under which employers have been required to pay uninsured claims that would have been covered if a qualified beneficiary had known about COBRA and elected coverage.

Since the passage of COBRA, a **qualified beneficiary** has been defined as any employee, or the spouse or dependent child of the employee, who on the day before a qualifying event was covered under the employee's group health plan. HIPAA expanded the definition to include any child who is born to or placed for adoption with the employee during the period of COBRA coverage. This change gives automatic eligibility for COBRA coverage to the child as well as the right to have his or her own election rights if a second qualifying event occurs.

Under the act, each of the following is a **qualifying event** if it results in the loss of coverage by a qualified beneficiary or an increase in the amount the qualified beneficiary must pay for the coverage:

- The death of the covered employee.

- The termination of the employee for any reason except gross misconduct. This includes quitting, retiring, or being fired for anything other than gross misconduct.

- A reduction of the employee's hours so that the employee or dependent is ineligible for coverage.

- The divorce or legal separation of the employee and his or her spouse.

- For spouses and children, the employee's eligibility for Medicare.

- A child's ceasing to be an eligible dependent under the plan.

The act specifies that a qualified beneficiary is entitled to elect continued coverage without providing evidence of insurability. The beneficiary must be allowed to continue coverage identical to that available to employees and dependents to whom a qualifying event has not occurred. Coverage for persons electing COBRA continuation can be changed when changes are made to the plan covering similarly situated active employees and their dependents. In addition, a qualified beneficiary who moves out of an area served by a region-specific plan must be given the right to change coverage if the employer is able to provide coverage under another of its existing plans.

Each qualified beneficiary must be allowed to continue coverage from the qualifying event until the earliest of the following:

- 18 months for employees and dependents when the employee's employment has terminated or coverage has been terminated because of a reduction in hours. This period is extended to 29 months for a qualified beneficiary if the Social Security Administration determines that the beneficiary was or became totally disabled at any time during the first 60 days of COBRA coverage.

- 36 months for other qualifying events.

- The date the plan terminates for all employees.

- The date the coverage ceases because of a failure to make a timely payment of premium for the qualified beneficiary's coverage. COBRA regulations prohibit a plan from discontinuing coverage because a payment is short by an insignificant amount, which is defined as the lesser of $50 or 10 percent of the amount due. The plan must either accept the amount received as satisfying the plan's payment requirement, or it must notify the beneficiary of the amount of the deficiency and grant a reasonable time for it to be paid.

- The date the qualified beneficiary subsequently becomes entitled to Medicare or becomes covered (as either an employee or dependent) under another group health plan, provided the group health plan does not contain an exclusion or limitation with respect to any preexisting condition. If the new plan does not cover a preexisting condition, the COBRA coverage can be continued until the earlier of (1) the remainder of the 18-month or 36-month period or (2) the time when the preexisting-conditions provision no longer applies. Note that COBRA coverage is not affected by entitlement to benefits under Medicare or coverage under another group plan if this entitlement or coverage existed at the time of the qualifying event.

If a second qualifying event (such as the death or divorce of a terminated employee) occurs during the period of continued coverage, the maximum period of continuation is 36 months. For example, if an employee terminates employment, the employee and family are eligible for 18 months of COBRA coverage. If the employee dies after 15 months, a second qualifying event has occurred for the employee's spouse and dependent children. The normal period of COBRA continuation resulting from the death of an employee is 36 months. However, because the spouse and children have already had COBRA coverage for 15 months, the second qualifying event extends coverage for an additional 21 months.

At the termination of continued coverage, a qualified beneficiary must be offered the right to convert to an individual insurance policy if a conversion privilege is generally available to employees under the employer's plan.

Notification of the right to continue coverage must be made at two times by a plan's administrator. First, when a plan becomes subject to COBRA or when a person becomes covered under a plan subject to COBRA, notification must be given to an employee as well as to his or her spouse, generally within 90 days. This requirement can be satisfied by a single letter to the employee and spouse as long as they reside at the same location. Second, when a qualifying event occurs, the employer must notify the plan administrator, who then must notify all qualified beneficiaries within 14 days. In general, the employer has 30 days to notify the plan administrator. However, an employer may not know of a qualifying event if it involves divorce, legal separation, or a child ceasing to be eligible for coverage. In these circumstances, the employee or family member must notify the employer within 60 days of the event, or the right to elect COBRA coverage is lost. The time period for the employer to notify the plan administrator begins when the employer is informed of the qualifying event, as long as this occurs within the 60-day period.

Recent changes to COBRA rules also require that plan administrators provide notification to qualified beneficiaries in two other circumstances. First, if a plan beneficiary receives a notice of a qualifying event and the qualified beneficiary is ineligible for COBRA coverage, the plan administrators must explain why the qualified beneficiary is not entitled to coverage. Second, if COBRA coverage is terminated before the end of the maximum duration, the plan administrator must explain when and why the coverage is being terminated and inform the qualified beneficiary of any available rights to other coverage.

The continuation of coverage is not automatic; a qualified beneficiary must elect it. The election period starts on the date of the qualifying event and may end not earlier than 60 days after actual notice of the event to the qualified beneficiary by the plan administrator. Once coverage is elected, the beneficiary has 45 days to pay the premium for the period of coverage prior to the election.

Under COBRA, the cost of the continued coverage may be passed on to the qualified beneficiary, but the cost cannot exceed 102 percent of the cost to the plan for the period of coverage for a similarly situated active employee to whom a qualifying event has not occurred. The extra 2 percent is supposed to cover the employer's extra administrative costs. The one exception to this rule occurs for months 19 through 29 if an employee is disabled, in which case the premium can then be as high as 150 percent.

Qualified beneficiaries must have the option of paying the premium in monthly install-ments. In addition, there must be a grace period of at least 30 days for each installment.

COBRA has resulted in significant extra costs for employers. Precise statistics are difficult to obtain, but one insurer indicates that coverage is elected by approximately 20 percent of those persons who are entitled to a COBRA continuation. The length of coverage averages almost one year for persons eligible for an 18-month extension and almost two years for persons eligible for a 36-month extension. Although significant variations exist among employers, claim costs of persons with COBRA coverage gen-erally run about 150 percent of claim costs for active employees and dependents. Moreover, administrative costs are estimated to be about $20 per month for each person with COBRA coverage.

Coverage for Active Duty Military Personnel. In many cases, employees called to active military duty are eligible for COBRA. Employees who work for employers with fewer than 20 employees, however, are not. As a result, the Uniformed Services Employment and Reemployment Rights Act (described in more detail in Chapter 18) requires all employers to make COBRA-type coverage available to any person whose health plan coverage terminates because of an absence due to military service. The duration of available coverage is the shorter of (1) 18 months or (2) the period of service plus any time allowed to apply for reemployment with the employer. The person cannot be required to pay more than 102 percent of the cost of the coverage. If the military service is for 30 or fewer days, however, the cost cannot exceed the normal employee share of any premium.

Special Rules for Persons Eligible for Health Care Tax Credit. The Trade Adjust-ment Assistance Act of 2002 provides a health care tax credit (discussed later) to workers who have lost their jobs or whose hours of work and wages have been reduced as a result of imports. Workers are entitled to a second COBRA election period when they become eligible for the tax credit as long as the eligibility for the tax credit is within six months after the loss of their medical expense coverage. This second election period is available even if COBRA coverage was initially declined. COBRA coverage, however, commences on the first day of the month in which a worker becomes eligible for the tax credit. Coverage can continue until the end of the period that would have applied to the original COBRA election period.

Continuation of Coverage in Addition to COBRA

Even before the passage of COBRA, it was becoming increasingly common for employers (particularly large employers) to continue group insurance coverage for certain employees—and sometimes their dependents—beyond the usual termination dates. Obviously, when coverage is continued now, an employer must at least comply with COBRA. However, an employer can be more liberal than COBRA by paying all or a portion of the cost, providing continued coverage for additional categories of persons, or continuing coverage for a longer period of time. Some states have continu-ation laws for insured medical expense plans that might require coverage to be made available in situations not covered by COBRA. One example is coverage for employees of firms with fewer than 20 employees; another is coverage for periods longer than those required by COBRA.

Retired Employees.   Although not required to do so by the Age Discrimination in Employment Act, many employers continue coverage on retired employees. The majority of these employers continue coverage for the life of an employee, but some employers provide coverage only until the employee is eligible for Medicare. Although coverage can also be continued for retirees' dependents, it is often limited only to spouses. Retired employees under age 65 usually have the same coverage as active employees have. However, coverage for employees aged 65 or older (if included under the same plan) may be provided under a Medicare carve-out or a Medicare supplement. The lifetime maximum for persons eligible for Medicare is often much lower (such as $5,000 or $10,000) than for active employees.

The subject of retiree benefits has become a major concern to employers since the Financial Accounting Standards Board (FASB) phased in new rules between 1993 and 1997 for the accounting of postretirement benefits other than pensions. These rules require that employers do the following:

■ Recognize the present value of future retiree medical expense benefits on the firm's balance sheet with other liabilities.

■ Record the cost for postretirement medical benefits in the period when an employee performs services. This is comparable to the accounting for pension costs.

■ Amortize the present value of the future cost of benefits accrued prior to the new rules.

These rules are in contrast to the long-used previous practice of paying retiree medical benefits or premiums out of current revenue and recognizing these costs as expenses when paid. Although the rules are logical from a financial accounting standpoint, the effect on employers has been significant. Employers who elected to immediately recognize the liability had to show reduced earnings and net worth. Firms that elected to amortize the liability (often because immediate recognition would wipe out net worth) will be affected for years to come.

The FASB rules, along with the increasing cost of medical expense coverage, have resulted in two major changes by employers. First, many employers have reduced or eliminated retiree benefits or are considering such a change. Since 1993, the number of employers providing coverage to early retirees has dropped from about 45 percent to 25 percent, and the number of employers providing coverage after Medicare eligibility has declined from about 40 percent to 20 percent. However, there are legal uncertainties as to whether benefits that have been promised to retirees can be eliminated or reduced. Some employers also feel that there is a moral obligation to continue these benefits. As a result, many employers are not altering plans for current retirees or active employees who are eligible to retire. Instead, the changes apply to future retirees only. These changes, which seem to run the gamut, include the following:

- Eliminating benefits for future retirees.

- Shifting more of the cost burden to future retirees by reducing benefits. Such a reduction may be accomplished by providing lower benefit maximums, covering fewer types of expenses, or increasing copayments.

- Adding or increasing retiree sharing of premium costs after retirement.

- Shifting to a defined-contribution approach to funding retiree benefits. For example, an employer might agree to pay $5 per month toward the cost of coverage after retirement for each year of service by an employee. Thus, an employer would make a monthly contribution of $150 for an employee who retired with 30 years of service, but the employer would make a contribution of only $75 for an employee with 15 years of service. Many plans of this nature have been designed so that the employer's contribution increases with changes in the consumer price index, subject to maximum increases (such as 5 percent per year).

- Encouraging retirees to elect benefits from managed care plans. With this approach, retirees are required to pay a significant portion of the cost if coverage is continued through a traditional indemnity plan.

A second change is that employers have increasingly explored methods to prefund the benefits. However, there are no alternatives for prefunding that are as favorable as the alternatives for funding pension benefits. One alternative is the use of a 501(c)(9) trust (or VEBA). As discussed in Chapter 16, there are limitations on the deductibility of contributions to a 501(c)(9) trust. Furthermore, a 501(c)(9) trust can be used to fund retiree benefits only if it is currently being used to fund benefits for active employees.

Another alternative is to prefund medical benefits within a pension plan. Contributions are tax deductible, and earnings accumulate tax free. The IRS rules for qualified retirement plans permit the payment of benefits for medical expenses from a pension plan if the following requirements are satisfied:

- The medical benefits must be subordinate to the retirement benefits. This rule is met if the cost of the medical benefits provided does not exceed 25 percent of the employer's aggregate contribution to the pension plan. For many employers, this figure is too low to allow the entire future liability to be prefunded.

- A separate account must be established and maintained for the monies allocated to medical benefits. Nonkey employees can have an aggregate account, but separate individual accounts must be maintained for key employees, and medical benefits attributable to a key employee (and his or her family members) can be made only from the key employee's account.

- The employer's contributions for medical benefits must be ascertainable and reasonable.

Although the rules for funding retiree medical benefits in a pension plan are restricted and administratively complex, they offer an employer the opportunity to deduct at least a portion of the cost of prefunded benefits.

Surviving Dependents. Coverage can also be continued for the survivors of deceased active employees and/or deceased retired employees. However, coverage for the survivors of active employees is not commonly continued beyond the period required by COBRA, and coverage for the survivors of retired employees may be limited to surviving spouses. In both instances, the continued coverage is usually identical to what was provided prior to the employee's death. It is also common for the employer to continue the same premium contribution level.

Laid-Off Employees. Medical expense coverage can be continued for laid-off workers, and large employers frequently provide such coverage for a limited period. Few employers provide coverage beyond the period required by COBRA, but some employers continue to make the same premium contribution, at least for a limited period of time.

Disabled Employees. Medical expense coverage can be continued for an employee (and dependents) when he or she has a temporary interruption of employment, including one arising from illness or injury. Many employers also cover employees who have long-term disabilities or who have retired because of a disability. In most cases, this continuation of coverage is contingent on satisfaction of some definition of total (and possibly permanent) disability. When continuing coverage for disabled employees, an employer must determine the extent of employer contributions. For example, the employer may continue the same premium contribution as for active employees, although there is nothing to prevent a different contribution rate—either lower or higher.

Domestic Partners. Domestic partners do not meet the definition of qualified beneficiary for purposes of COBRA. However, some employers provide domestic partners who have coverage under the employer's plan with continuation coverage that is similar or identical to what is available under COBRA.

Extension of Benefits

When coverage is terminated rather than continued, most medical expense plans have an **extension of benefits** for any covered employee or dependent who is totally disabled at the time of termination. However, the disability must have resulted from an illness or injury that occurred while the person was covered under the provider's contract. Generally, the same level of benefits is available as before termination. Although some contracts cover only expenses associated with the same cause of disability, other contracts cover any expenses that would have been paid under the terminated coverage, regardless of cause.

As a general rule, the extension of benefits generally ceases after 12 months, or when the individual is no longer totally or continuously disabled, whichever comes first.

Conversion

Except when termination results from the failure to pay any required premiums, medical expense contracts usually contain (and are often required to contain) a conversion provision. With such a provision, most covered persons whose group coverage terminates are allowed to purchase individual medical expense coverage without evidence of insurability and without any limitation of benefits for preexisting conditions. Covered persons commonly have 31 days from the date of termination of the group coverage to exercise this conversion privilege, and coverage is then effective retroactively to the date of termination.

This conversion privilege is typically given to any employee who has been insured under the group contract (or under any group contract it replaced) for at least three months, and it permits the employee to convert his or her own coverage as well as any dependent coverage. In addition, a spouse or child whose dependent coverage ceases for any other reason may also be eligible for conversion (for example, a spouse who divorces or separates and children who reach age 19).

A person who is eligible for both the conversion privilege and the right to continue the group insurance coverage under COBRA has two choices when eligibility for coverage terminates. He or she can either elect to convert under the provisions of the policy or elect to continue the group coverage. If the latter choice is made, the COBRA rules specify that the person must again be eligible to convert to an individual policy within the usual conversion period (31 days) after the maximum continuation-of-coverage period ceases. Policy provisions may also make the conversion privilege available to persons whose coverage terminates prior to the end of the maximum continuation period.

The provider of the medical expense coverage has the right to refuse the issue of a "conversion" policy to anyone (1) who is covered by Medicare or (2) whose benefits under the converted policy, together with similar benefits from other sources, would result in overinsurance according to the insurance company's standards. These similar benefits may be found in other coverages that the individual has (either group or individual coverage) or for which the individual is eligible under any group arrangement.

The use of the word *conversion* is often a misnomer. In actuality, a person whose coverage terminates is given only the right to purchase a contract on an individual basis at individual rates. Most Blue Cross and Blue Shield plans and some HMO plans offer a conversion policy that is similar or identical to the terminated group coverage. However, most insurance companies offer a conversion policy (or a choice of policies) that contains a lower level of benefits than existed under the group coverage. Traditionally, the conversion policy contained only basic hospital and surgical coverages even if major medical coverage was provided under the group contract. Now many insurance companies provide (and are required to provide in many states) a conversion policy that includes major medical benefits, which do not necessarily have to be as broad as those under the former group coverage. To protect themselves from legal liability, employers should emphasize any lower level of coverage to individuals electing conversion.

Some plans offer a conversion policy that is written by another entity. For example, an HMO might enter into a contractual arrangement with an insurance company. In some cases, the HMO and insurance company are commonly owned or have a parent-subsidiary relationship.

Self-funded plans, which are exempt from state laws mandating a conversion policy, may still provide such a benefit. Rather than providing coverage directly to the terminated employee, an agreement is usually made with an insurance company to make a policy available. This agreement is typically part of a broader contract with the insurer to also provide administrative services and/or stop-loss protection. Because the availability of a conversion policy results in a charge (such as $0.65 per employee per month), most self-funded plans do not provide any continuation of coverage beyond what is required by COBRA.

Group-to-Individual Portability

HIPAA makes it easier for individuals who lose group medical expense coverage to find alternative coverage in the individual marketplace. The purpose of the federal legislation seems to be to encourage states to adopt their own mechanisms to achieve this goal. The federal rules apply in a state only if the state fails to have its own plan in effect.

Most states have adopted their own plans so that the federal rules does not apply. However, the state alternative must do all the following:

- Provide a choice of health insurance coverage to all eligible individuals
- Not impose any preexisting-conditions restrictions
- Include at least one policy form of coverage that is either comparable to comprehensive health coverage offered in the individual marketplace or comparable to or a standard option of coverage available under the group or individual laws of the state

In addition, the state must implement one of the following:

- One of the NAIC model laws on individual market reform
- A qualified high-risk pool
- Certain other mechanisms specified in the act
- If a state fails to adopt an alternative to federal regulation, then insurance companies, HMOs, and other health plan providers in the individual marketplace are required to make coverage available on a guaranteed-issue basis to individuals with 18 or more months of creditable coverage and whose most recent coverage was under a group health plan. However, coverage does not have to be provided to an individual who has other health insurance or who is eligible for COBRA coverage, Medicare, or Medicaid. No preexisting-conditions exclusions can be imposed. Health insurers have three options for providing coverage to eligible individuals:

- They may offer every health insurance policy they offer in the state.
- They may offer their two most popular policies in the state, based on premium volume.
- They may offer a low-level and a high-level coverage as long as they contain benefits that are similar to other coverage offered by the insurer in the state.

Rules similar to those described in Chapter 9 for group medical expense insurance coverage require the renewal of individual coverage.

■ CLAIMS

Medical expense claims are handled differently, depending on whether benefits are provided on an indemnity basis or on a service basis. Subrogation provisions may also apply.

Indemnity Benefits

Medical expense contracts that provide benefits on an indemnity basis typically require that the insurance company (or other provider) be given a written proof of loss (that is, a claim form) concerning the occurrence, character, and extent of the loss for which a claim is made. This form usually contains portions that must be completed and signed by the employee, a representative of the employer, and the provider of medical services.

The period during which an employee must file a claim depends on the provider of coverage and any applicable state requirements. An employee generally has at least 90 days (or as soon as is reasonably possible) after medical expenses are incurred to file. Some insurance companies require that they be notified within a shorter time (such as 20 days) about any illness or injury on which a claim may be based, even though they give a longer time period for the actual filing of the form itself.

Individuals have the right to assign their benefits to the providers of medical services. Such an assignment, which authorizes the insurance company to make the benefit payment directly to the provider, is generally made by completing the appropriate portion of the claim form. In addition, the insurance company has the right (as it does in disability income insurance) to examine any person for whom a claim is filed at its own expense and with the physician of its own choice.

Service Benefits

Medical expense contracts that provide benefits on a service basis (such as HMOs and the Blues) generally do not require that covered persons file claim forms. Rather, the providers of services perform any necessary paperwork and are then reimbursed directly.

For example, when a physician presents a claim, the plan must determine one or more of the following: the physician's status as a network participant, the primary or specialty care nature of the service if rendered by a network participant, and the applicability of an authorization requirement. Depending upon the plan's stringency, the provider's reimbursement may be denied altogether or be far less than the amount charged if the enrollee receives services from a nonnetwork provider or if a specialist is seen without a required referral. In turn, the payment made to the provider determines whether the enrollee must pay a modest copayment, a more substantial amount under an indemnity benefit as described above, or the total amount if a claim is denied.

Network providers with capitation payment arrangements file patient encounter forms which, in effect, are claims that produce no payment for a specific service.

Subrogation

Most self-funded plans contain subrogation provisions. If state law allows, they are also commonly contained in the group medical expense contracts of HMOs, PPOs, the Blues, and insurance companies. A subrogation provision gives the plan (or the organization providing plan benefits) the right to recover from a third party who is responsible through negligence or other wrongdoing for a covered person's injuries that result in claims being paid. If a covered person receives a settlement from the third party (or his or her liability insurance company) for medical expenses that the plan has already paid, the covered person must reimburse the plan. The plan also has the right to seek a recovery for benefits paid if the person who receives benefits does not take legal action.

■ HIPAA ADMINISTRATIVE STANDARDS

Another important result of HIPAA is the various administrative standards that it imposes on medical expense plans. The act authorizes the secretary of the Department of Health and Human Services (HHS) to set administrative standards for the privacy, security, and electronic exchange of personal health information, which is referred to in the act as **protected health information (PHI).** PHI is individually identifiable health information that is transmitted or maintained in electronic or other media, including both written and oral communications.

Entities subject to these standards include health plans, health information data processors (known as *clearinghouses*), and health care providers. For purposes of the standards, *health plans* are very broadly defined to include essentially all individual policies and group plans that provide or pay the cost of medical care, both public and private. However, self-administered plans with fewer than 50 participants are not included in the definition. The definition extends to most insurance companies that provide medical, dental, vision, prescription drug, and long-term care insurance. Employers and plan sponsors are also subject to the rules to the extent they handle PHI.

The administrative standards impose significant penalties for noncompliance. There are civil penalties of $100 per violation, up to $25,000 per person, for each requirement or prohibition violated. There are also criminal penalties for violations relating to PHI protected under the standards. These penalties can be as high as (1) $50,000 and one year in prison for obtaining or disclosing PHI; (2) $100,000 and five years in prison for obtaining PHI under false pretenses; and (3) $250,000 and ten years in prison for obtaining or disclosing PHI information with the intent to sell, transfer, or use it for commercial advantage, personal gain, or malicious harm.

The HIPAA provisions that authorize the creation of these standards are known collectively as *administrative simplification* because of the consistency and efficiency they seek to achieve. These provisions generate extensive regulations that are summarized under the following headings:

■ Privacy standards

■ Security standards

■ Identifier standards

■ Transaction and code set standards

Privacy Standards

Privacy standards, which are now in effect, provide the first comprehensive federal protection for the privacy of personal health information. At the same time, many states have their own privacy rules, and federal standards do not override those rules if they contain stricter provisions. The federal privacy standards extend protection to all PHI relating to physical or mental health condition, the provision of health care, or the payment for the provision of health care.

The standards give covered entities flexibility to design their own policies and procedures to meet the privacy requirements. Covered entities, however, will generally have to adopt written procedures regarding certain privacy issues. These include who has access to protected information, how it will be used by the entity, and when the information may be disclosed. Covered entities must also train their employees in privacy procedures and designate a privacy officer who is responsible for ensuring that the procedures are followed.

Under the privacy standards, individuals have significant rights to control and understand how their health information is used. These rights include the following:

■ Providers and health plans must give patients and members a clear written explanation of how the covered entity may use and disclose health information.

■ Patients must be able to see and obtain copies of their health records and to make amendments. In addition, a history of nonroutine disclosures of personal health information must be made available to patients.

■   A separate authorization must be obtained from an individual for nonroutine and most nonhealth-care-related disclosures of their personal health information. Individuals have the right to request restrictions on the uses and disclosures of their information.

■   Individuals have the right to file a formal complaint with a covered provider or health plan, or with HHS, about violations of the privacy regulations or the policies and procedures of the covered entity.

The standards do allow use and disclosure of PHI without authorization for specified purposes. All other purposes require an individual's authorization. A covered entity must also establish an agreement with any business associate to which it discloses personal health information in the conduct of the covered entity's business.

Use and Disclosure Without Specific Authorization.   A covered entity may use or disclose PHI without written authorization for treatment, payment, or health care operations, or in other situations permitted by the privacy standards.

Treatment, Payment, or Health Care Operations.   *Treatment* includes the provision, coordination, and management of health care and related services by health care providers. *Payment* consists of a health plan's activities to obtain premiums, determine or fulfill responsibilities for coverage and provision of benefits, and provide reimbursement for health care services to an individual. Payment also extends to the activities of a health care provider to obtain payment for services. *Health care operations* covers a broad spectrum of administrative services that support or otherwise relate to the delivery of health care services including such insurance functions as underwriting, rating, and reinsurance.

Other Situations.   The privacy standards allow disclosure of personal health information without an individual's authorization for several other purposes or situations that include the following:

■   Informal situations in which the individual may be asked directly or has the opportunity to agree or object, such as in the case of a pharmacist dispensing a prescription to a person acting on the patient's behalf

■   Incidental uses and disclosures such as when a health plan employee discusses a patient's health claim on the phone and may be overheard by another employee who is not authorized to handle personal health information

■   Public interest and benefit activities such as research, public health and safety, and law enforcement

Authorized Use and Disclosure.   For purposes other than those previously identified, a covered entity must request an individual's written authorization. *Authorization* is defined as a specific written permission from individuals to use and disclose their personal health information. Examples of situations that would require an individual's authorization are disclosures to an insurer for coverage purposes, to an employer of results of a preemployment physical, or to a pharmaceutical firm for its own marketing purposes. Although the specific form is not dictated, an authorization must be in plain language and contain specific items among which are the information to be disclosed, persons disclosing and receiving the information, expiration date, and right to revoke the authorization.

In limited circumstances, a covered entity may condition treatment, payment, enrollment, or benefits on an individual's granting an authorization. For instance, a health plan may condition enrollment on an authorization to obtain personal health information to establish eligibility for enrollment or for underwriting or premium determination.

Business Associate Agreements. The privacy standards not only require that a covered entity ensure compliance by its workforce, but they also contain requirements for agreements between a covered entity and its business associates. A **business associate** is a person or organization, other than a member of the covered entity's workforce, that performs services for a covered entity that involve PHI. These services may be legal, actuarial, accounting, consulting, data aggregation, management, administrative, accreditation, or financial functions. A covered entity's agreement with a business associate must do the following:

- Ensure that the business associate establishes safeguards to protect the confidentiality of, integrity of, and appropriate access to PHI
- Assure that the agents and subcontractors to whom the business associate provides PHI meet the same standards and report to the covered entity any security incident of which they become aware
- Authorize termination of the contract if the business associate commits a material violation of the privacy provisions

The privacy standards do not specifically mention agents and brokers, and the HHS has issued no guidance on their role under the standards at the time this book is being revised. There seems to be a general (but not unanimous) consensus, however, that agents or brokers are business associates. As a result, agents or brokers may be asked to sign a business associate contract with the covered entities with which they deal.

Security Standards

The **security standards** require that covered entities implement measures to maintain reasonable and appropriate administrative, physical, and technical safeguards for electronic PHI. These safeguards aim to protect the integrity, confidentiality, and availability of the PHI that a covered entity creates, receives, stores, or transmits. They must also protect against reasonably anticipated threats or hazards to the security or integrity of the data and unauthorized use or disclosure of the information. Policies and procedures must effectively control physical access to the data and establish technical security measures to protect networks, computers, and other electronic devices. Business associate agreements as required by the privacy standards must also contain these safeguards.

Although the scope of the security standards is limited to PHI in electronic form, the privacy standards, previously discussed, provide a security requirement for all PHI, regardless of form or medium.

Except for small health plans (defined as those with less than $5 million in annual receipts), which are granted an additional year, covered entities must comply with the electronic security standards by April 21, 2005.

Identifier Standards

Historically, providers, employers, and health plans have used nonstandard identification formats when conducting business with each other. Each physician, for example, has a different provider number with each insurer or health plan to which he or she submits claims. The **identifier standards** will ensure the use of uniform identifiers among these health care organizations in order to reduce errors, uncertainty, and duplication. The employer identification standard adopted for electronic transactions is an employer's tax identification number or employer identification number assigned by the Internal Revenue Service. Health care providers will be issued a single unique identification number. With the exception of small health plans that have an additional year, the identifier standards must be used by May 23, 2007, for transactions among health plans and providers.

Transaction and Code Set Standards

Standard data elements and electronic processes are expected to promote cost-effective, efficient, accurate, and prompt health care transactions. The **transaction and code set standards** apply to code systems for diagnosis and treatment as well as data fields and electronic formats for transmitting data. Transactions subject to the national electronic standards include health claims or claims status, patient encounters, benefit eligibility inquiries, enrollments and disenrollments, provider and premium payments, referral certifications and other authorizations, and related communications. Providers that use nonelectronic transactions with private health plans are not required to adopt and use the standards.

Even though these standards became effective in late 2003, health plans, including Medicare, are continuing to accept noncompliant electronic claims submission from health care providers at the time this book is being revised in early 2004.

■ FEDERAL TAX TREATMENT

In many respects, the federal tax treatment of group medical (including group dental) expense premiums and benefits parallels that of other group coverage if they are provided through an insurance company, a Blue Cross and Blue Shield plan, an HMO, or a PPO. Contributions by the employer for an employee's coverage or the coverage of the employee's dependents are tax deductible to the employer under Code Section 162 as long as the employee's overall compensation is reasonable. Code Section 106 provides that employer contributions do not create any income tax liability for an employee. Moreover, benefits are not taxable to an employee under Code Section 105 except when they exceed any medical expenses incurred. The value of any employer-provided coverage for an employee's domestic partner, minus any employee contributions, represents taxable income to the employee unless the partner qualifies under IRS rules as the employee's dependent. There are, however, some tax aspects of the tax treatment of medical expense coverage that are unique to this type of employee benefit. These include deductible employee contributions, special rules for self-funded medical expense plans, and a credit for certain individuals.

Deductible Employee Contributions

One major difference between group medical expense coverage and other forms of group insurance is that a portion of an employee's contribution for coverage may be tax deductible as a medical expense if that individual itemizes his or her income tax deductions. Under the Internal Revenue Code, individuals are allowed to deduct certain medical care expenses (including dental expenses) for which no reimbursement was received. This deduction is limited to expenses (including amounts paid for insurance) that exceed 7.5 percent of the person's adjusted gross income.

As mentioned earlier in this book, a sole proprietor, partner, member of a limited liability company (LLC), or more-than-2-percent shareholder of an S corporation is considered a self-employed person. If an organization pays the cost of medical expense coverage for a self-employed person (including dependent coverage), this amount constitutes taxable income to the self-employed person. However, the self-employed person is entitled to an income tax deduction for this amount, but the deduction cannot exceed the individual's earned income from the organization that provides the medical expense plan. In addition, the deduction is available only if the self-employed person is not eligible to participate in any subsidized medical expense plan of another employer of the self-employed person or the person's spouse. It is important to recognize that this is not an itemized deduction; rather, it is a deduction in arriving at adjusted gross income. The remainder of the cost of the medical expense coverage can be deducted as an itemized expense to the extent that it and other medical expenses exceed the 7.5 percent threshold that was previously described.

There is one circumstance under which a self-employed person, other than a more-than-2-percent owner-employee of an S corporation, can receive a 100 percent deduction for his or her medical expense coverage. This occurs only if the spouse is a bona fide employee of the self-employed person. The medical coverage is then provided to the spouse, who elects dependent coverage for the self-employed person. The self-employed person then pays the entire premium and takes a business deduction for the medical expense coverage provided to an employee. However, the IRS has indicated that such an arrangement will be challenged if the spouse's involvement in the business consists of nominal or insignificant services that have no economic substance or independent significance. Note that if there is a significant investment of the spouse's separate assets in the business, the spouse is employed in the business as a joint owner and treated as a self-employed person rather than an employee for purposes of the medical expense insurance.

Self-Funded Plans

The tax situation may be different if an employer provides medical expense benefits through a self-funded plan (referred to in the Internal Revenue Code as a **self-insured medical reimbursement plan**), under which employers either (1) pay the providers of medical care directly or (2) reimburse employees for their medical expenses. If a self-funded plan meets certain nondiscrimination requirements for highly compensated employees, the employer can deduct benefit payments as they are made, and the employee has no taxable income. If a plan is discriminatory, the employer still receives an income tax deduction. However, Code Section 105 specifies that all or a portion of the benefits received by "highly compensated individuals," but not by other employees, is treated as taxable income. A **highly compensated individual** is defined as (1) one of the five highest-paid officers of the firm, (2) a shareholder who owns more than 10 percent of the firm's stock, or (3) one of the highest-paid 25 percent of all the firm's employees. There are no nondiscrimination rules if a plan is not self-funded and provides benefits through an insurance contract, a Blue Cross and Blue Shield plan, an HMO, or a PPO.

To be considered nondiscriminatory, a self-funded plan must meet certain requirements regarding eligibility and benefits. The plan must provide benefits (1) for 70 percent or more of "all employees" or (2) for 80 percent or more of all eligible employees if 70 percent or more of all employees are eligible. The following can be excluded from the all-employees category without affecting the plan's nondiscriminatory status:

- Employees who have not completed three years of service.
- Employees who have not attained age 25.
- Part-time employees. Anyone who works fewer than 25 hours per week is automatically considered a part-time employee. Persons who work 25 or more but fewer than 35 hours per week may also be counted as part-time as long as other employees doing similar work for the employer have substantially more hours.
- Seasonal employees. Anyone who works fewer than seven months of the year is automatically considered a seasonal employee. Persons who work between seven and nine months of the year may also be considered seasonal as long as other employees have substantially more months of employment.
- Employees who are covered by a collective-bargaining agreement if accident-and-health benefits were a subject of collective bargaining.

Even if a plan fails to meet the percentage requirements regarding eligibility, it can still qualify as nondiscriminatory as long as the IRS is satisfied that the plan benefits a classification of employees in a manner that does not discriminate in favor of highly compensated employees. This determination is made on a case-by-case basis.

To satisfy the nondiscrimination requirements for benefits, the same type and amount of benefits must be provided for all employees covered under the plan, regardless of their compensation. In addition, the dependents of other employees cannot be treated less favorably than the dependents of highly compensated employees. However, because diagnostic procedures are not considered part of a self-funded plan for purposes of the nondiscrimination rule, a higher level of this type of benefit is permissible for highly compensated employees.

If a plan is discriminatory in either benefits or eligibility, highly compensated employees must include the amount of any "excess reimbursement" in their gross income for income tax purposes. If highly compensated employees receive any benefits that are not available to all employees covered under the plan, these benefits are considered an excess reimbursement. For example, if a plan pays 80 percent of covered expenses for employees in general, but 100 percent for highly compensated employees, the extra 20 percent of benefits constitutes taxable income.

If a self-funded plan discriminates in the way it determines eligibility, highly compensated employees have excess reimbursements for any amounts they receive. The amount of this excess reimbursement is determined by a percentage that is calculated by dividing the total amount of benefits highly compensated employees receive (exclusive of any other excess reimbursements) by the total amount of benefits paid to all employees (exclusive of any other excess reimbursements). Using the previous example, assume a highly compensated employee receives $2,000 in benefits during a certain year. If other employees receive only 80 percent of this amount (or $1,600), the highly compensated employee has received an excess reimbursement of $400. If the plan also discriminates in the area of eligibility, the highly compensated employee incurs additional excess reimbursement. For example, if 60 percent of the benefits (ignoring any benefits already considered excess reimbursement) are given to highly compensated employees, 60 percent of the remaining $1,600 ($2,000 − $400), or $960, is added to the $400, for a total excess reimbursement of $1,360.

If a plan provides benefits only for highly compensated employees, all benefits received are considered an excess reimbursement, because the percentage is 100 percent.

Health Coverage Tax Credit

As a result of trade legislation passed in 2002, a tax credit is available to certain taxpayers. These include the following:

- Individuals who receive a trade adjustment allowance or would receive the allowance except that they had not exhausted unemployment benefits. This allowance is for individuals who are certified as having lost their jobs because of trade-related reasons such as competition from foreign imports.

- Individuals who are at least 55 years of age and receiving benefits from the Pension Benefit Guaranty Corporation. These benefits are for persons whose pension plans (and often their employers) have become insolvent.

The credit is equal to 65 percent of the cost of the premium to continue coverage under COBRA and possibly for the purchase of other medical expense coverage. The credit, however, is not available to a taxpayer who has medical expense coverage under Medicare, Medicaid, the Federal Employees Health Benefits Program, or an employer-sponsored plan for which the employer pays at least 50 percent of the cost of the coverage.

Detailed information about the tax credit can be found on the IRS Web site: *www.irs.gov.* Search for IRS Form 8885 and its instructions.

■ KEY TERMS

allowable expenses	highly compensated individual	protected health information (PHI)
benefit bank	identifier standards	qualified beneficiary
business associate	medical child support order	qualifying event
COBRA		security standards
coordination-of-benefits (COB) provision	Medicare carve-out	self-insured medical reimbursement plan
creditable coverage	Medicare secondary rules	transaction and code set standards
dependent	Medicare supplement	protected health information (PHI)
domestic partners	privacy standards	
extension of benefits		

■ STUDY QUESTIONS

1. Explain the effect of the NAIC Model Regulation on Group Coverage Discontinuance and Replacement when group insurance coverage is transferred.

2. What dependents are typically eligible for coverage under a medical expense plan?

3. a. What is a medical child support order?

   b. What makes such an order *qualified*?

   c. What are the obligations of a plan administrator who receives a medical child support order?

4. What is the meaning of the term *portability* as used in HIPAA?

5. How does HIPAA limit the use of preexisting conditions in medical expense plans?

6. What is the relationship between creditable coverage and the length of a person's preexisting-conditions period?

7. What are the rules that apply to the issuance of a certificate of creditable coverage?

8. a. What requirements must often be satisfied for an individual to be considered a domestic partner?

   b. How do plans differ with respect to the groups of persons who might be eligible for domestic-partner benefits?

9. A child in the custody of her mother is covered as a dependent under the major medical coverage of both her father and her stepfather. Explain which coverage is primary if both coverages are subject to a coordination-of-benefits provision that conforms to the NAIC model provisions.

10. Edith incurred $5,000 of medical expenses that, except for deductibles and coinsurance, are fully covered under the medical expense plan provided by her employer. She is also covered as a dependent under her husband's plan. Edith's plan has a $100 deductible and an 80 percent coinsurance provision; her husband's plan has a

$200 deductible and a 90 percent coinsurance provision. How much will Edith collect from each plan if the traditional coordination-of-benefits approach is used?

11. a. Under what circumstances is Medicare the secondary payer of medical expense benefits?

   b. What does Medicare pay if it is secondary?

12. a. What employers are subject to the health insurance continuation provisions of COBRA?

   b. What are the penalties for noncompliance?

13. With respect to the health insurance continuation provisions of COBRA, answer each of the following questions:

   a. Who are eligible qualified beneficiaries?

   b. What is a qualifying event?

   c. For what length of time must coverage be continued?

14. What special rights to continue medical expense coverage are granted to each of the following:

   a. Persons who are covered by the Uniformed Services Employment and Reemployment Act

   b. Persons who have rights under the Trade Adjustment Assistance Act of 2002

15. Briefly describe how medical expense coverage provided to retired employees may differ from that provided to active employees.

16. a. Under what circumstances is an employee or dependent eligible to convert medical expense coverage that has terminated?

   b. What type of coverage can be obtained under the conversion provision?

17. Describe the group-to-individual portability rules of HIPAA.

18. How does the claims process differ with respect to medical expense plans providing benefits on a service basis and medical expense plans providing benefits on an indemnity basis?

19. How do the HIPAA privacy standards give patients the right to control and understand how their personal health information is used?

20. What is required by employers under each of the following HIPAA administrative standards?

   a. Security

   b. Identifier

   c. Transaction and code sets

21. To what extent and under what circumstances are contributions for group medical expense coverage deductible for federal income tax purposes if paid by

   a. the employer?

   b. the employees?

15

Dental, Long-Term Care, and Other Group Insurance Benefits

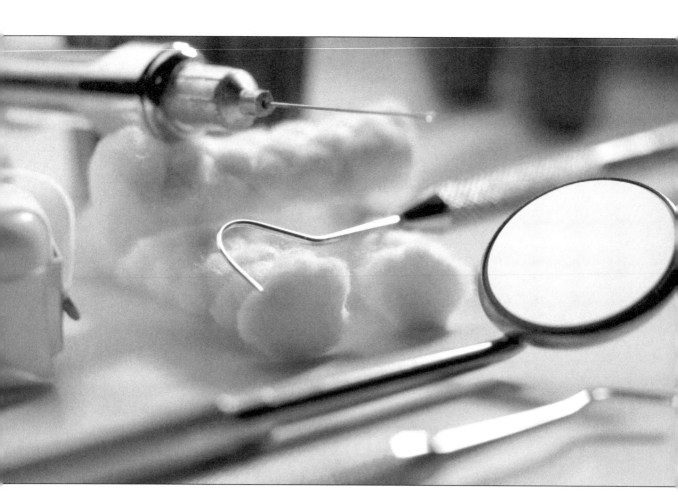

OBJECTIVES

■ Identify the sources of group dental insurance benefits and explain the provisions contained in dental insurance contracts.

■ Explain the reasons why long-term care insurance is needed and describe the provisions found in group long-term care products.

■ Describe the approaches used to provide group legal expense benefits.

■ Briefly describe the status of property and liability insurance as an employee benefit.

CHAPTER OUTLINE

Group Dental Insurance
  Providers of Dental Coverage
  Contractual Provisions
  Examples of Major Plan Types

Group Long-Term Care Insurance
  Need for Long-Term Care
  Sources of Long-Term Care Financing
  NAIC Model Legislation
  Effect of Health Insurance Portability
    and Accountability Act (HIPAA)
  Policy Characteristics

Group Legal Expense Plans
  Types of Plans
  Current Tax Treatment

Group Property and Liability Insurance
  Reasons for Slow Growth
  Types of Plans

Previous chapters have considered the three traditional types of group insurance: life insurance, disability income insurance, and medical expense insurance. This chapter focuses on four of the newer and/or less common types of group insurance coverage: group dental insurance, long-term care insurance, legal expense insurance, and property and liability insurance, all of which have experienced growth in recent years.

■ GROUP DENTAL INSURANCE

Dental insurance is a specialized form of health insurance that is designed to pay for normal dental care as well as care needed as a result of accidents.

The percentage of employees with dental benefits has grown significantly during the last 25 years. As was shown in Chapter 1, the Bureau of Labor Statistics indicates that 68 percent of employers with 20 to 90 employees make such coverage available. This figure increases to more than 90 percent for larger employers. The Bureau, however, also indicates that only 32 percent of workers actually participate in such plans. The reasons for this lower percentage include the reasons mentioned in Chapter 1 for a similar disparity in medical expense coverage. For dental insurance, there is an additional reason: a large percentage of plans are voluntary and require 100 percent employee contributions.

To a great extent, group dental insurance contracts have been patterned after group medical expense contracts, and they contain many similar, if not identical, provisions. Like group medical expense insurance, however, group dental insurance has many variations. Dental plans may be limited to specific types of services, or they may be broad enough to cover virtually all dental services. In addition, coverage can be obtained from various types of providers, and benefits can be in the form of either services or cash payments.

Managed care has significantly affected the evolvement of group dental insurance plans. However, this evolvement has been somewhat different from that of medical expense plans. Group dental plans are more likely to provide benefits on a traditional fee-for-service basis, although these traditional plans are also more likely to take a managed care approach to providing benefits. The most common example of this is the emphasis on providing a higher level of benefits for preventive care. As group dental plans have become more prevalent, the percentage of persons receiving preventive care has continued to increase. As a result, the percentage of persons needing care for more serious dental problems has continued to decrease.

One other difference between group medical expense plans and group dental plans is that providers of managed dental care arrangements have been more likely to offer coverage to very small groups.

The federal tax treatment of dental insurance premiums and benefits is the same as the tax treatment that is described in Chapter 14 for medical expense premiums and benefits.

Providers of Dental Coverage

Group dental benefits are offered by insurance companies, dental service plans, the Blues, and managed care plans. Like medical expense coverage, a significant portion of dental coverage is also self-funded. An employer may self-administer the plan or use the services of a third-party administrator. In either case, the plan may use a preferred-provider network to provide dental services. Many employees also are eligible for discounted services under discount plans.

Insurance Companies.   Insurance companies are major providers of dental coverage, often on an indemnity or PPO basis. Coverage is usually offered independently of other group insurance coverages, but it may be incorporated into a major medical contract. However, if it is part of a major medical contract, the benefits are frequently subject to the same provisions and limitations as benefits that are available under a separate dental plan. Although there has been little recent growth in traditional dental indemnity plans, they still account for about 30 percent of overall dental enrollment.

Dental Service Plans.   Most states have dental service plans, often called **Delta Dental Plans** or *Delta Plans,* that write approximately one-quarter of the dental coverage, along with the Blues. However, the extent of their use varies widely by state, and western states generally have larger and more successful plans than states in other parts of the country. The majority of these plans are nonprofit organizations that are sponsored by state dental associations. In addition, they are often patterned after Blue Shield plans, and dentists provide service benefits on a contractual basis. Also like Blue Shield, state Delta Dental Plans are coordinated by a national board—Delta Dental Plans, Inc.

Blue Cross and Blue Shield Plans. Many Blue Cross and Blue Shield plans also provide dental coverage. In some cases, the Blues have contractual arrangements that are similar to those that dental service plans have with dentists; in other cases, benefits are paid on an indemnity basis just as if an insurance company were involved. Finally, a few of the Blues market dental coverage through Delta Dental Plans in conjunction with their own medical expense plans.

Managed Care Plans. A majority of dental coverage is now provided through managed care plans, often sponsored by insurance companies, the Blues, or Delta Dental Plans. Because dental expenses are more predictable than medical expenses, the emphasis on preventive care by managed care plans provides a real potential to hold down future costs.

Coverage can be obtained from PPOs, which have enjoyed rapid growth in recent years and account for about 40 percent of dental plan enrollment. Coverage can also be obtained from a **dental health maintenance organization (DHMO)**, which operates like a health maintenance organization but provides dental care only. Like HMOs, DHMOs can take the form of closed-panel plans or individual practice associations. Point-of-service plans have also become increasingly common for providing dental coverage.

Self-Funded Plans. For several years, it has been common for large employers to self-fund dental benefits. Their plans typically have the same characteristics as insured plans except that they are administered by a third party, often a dental insurer. The plan, on a contractual basis, usually has access to a dental insurer's provider network and utilization management. More recently, the concept of self-funding has spread to smaller employers. Under the technique, often used in this market, called **direct reimbursement**, the employee visits the dentist, pays the bill, and then submits the bill to the employer for reimbursement. This process often generates significant savings for the employer, largely because of lower administrative costs. The claims process is relatively simple because most reimbursements are small in size, large claims do not exist because of caps on benefit amounts, and plan design tends to be relatively simplistic. The number of claims is also fairly stable from year to year. One problem that often occurs in the self-funding of benefits is the lack of control over utilization. However, this has been a minimal problem in direct reimbursement plans because employees seem to have a natural reluctance to visit the dentist unless it is absolutely necessary and benefits are limited.

EXAMPLE
The Matthews Company has a direct reimbursement dental plan for its 55 employees. The plan pays 100 percent of the first $100 of annual dental bills submitted for each employee or eligible dependent. The plan reimburses the employee for 80 percent of the next $500 of dental bills, resulting in a total annual maximum benefit of $500 per covered person.

Discount Plans. Although they cannot be classified as an insurance plan, dental discount plans play a role in providing dental services to many Americans. A **discount plan**, often referred to as a *referral* or *access plan*, provides members with a discount on the purchase of professional services. Discount plans usually have a modest monthly fee—such as $5 or $7 per person—that may be paid by an employer. In return, the employee receives a discount on specified dental services as long as the services are received from providers affiliated with the discount plan's network. The employee pays the discounted fee. There is no other reimbursement to either the dental provider or employee.

Discounts are often in the range of 20 to 30 percent, but may be higher or lower. The discounts may also vary by type of dental procedure. Dental professionals are willing to grant these discounts in anticipation of an increased volume of business.

Contractual Provisions

Although group dental insurance contracts have been patterned after group medical expense contracts, some of their provisions are different, and others are unique to dental coverage. These provisions pertain to eligibility, benefits, exclusions, benefit limitations, predetermination of benefits, and termination.

Eligibility. In contributory plans, most employers use the same eligibility requirements for dental coverage as they use for medical expense coverage. However, some employers have different probationary periods for the two coverages. Probationary periods are used because members of a group who previously had no dental insurance usually have a large number of untreated dental problems. In addition, because many dental care expenditures are postponable, an employee who anticipates coverage under a dental plan in the future will be inclined to postpone treatment that is not crucial. Depending on the group's characteristics, the number of first-year claims for a new plan or for new employees and their dependents under an existing dental plan can be expected to run between 20 and 50 percent more than long-run annual claims. Therefore, to counter this higher-than-average number of claims, some employers use a longer probationary period for dental benefits than for medical expense benefits. Other employers may have the same probationary period for both types of coverage but impose waiting periods before certain types of dental expenses are covered (such as 12 months for orthodontics and/or other major services).

Longer-than-usual probationary periods or waiting periods initially minimize claims, but unless an organization has a high turnover rate, the result may be false economy. Many persons who do not have coverage merely postpone treatment until they do have coverage. This postponement may actually lead to increased claims, because existing dental conditions only become more severe and then require more expensive treatment. For this reason, some benefit consultants feel that dental plans should at most contain relatively short probationary and waiting periods.

Because dental expenditures are postponable and somewhat predictable, the problem of adverse selection under contributory plans is more severe for dental insurance than for many other types of group insurance. To counter this adverse selection, insurance companies impose more stringent underwriting (including eligibility) requirements on contributory dental plans than they do on other types of group insurance. In addition, most insurance companies insist on a high percentage of participation (such as 80 or 85 percent), and a few do not write contributory coverage. Many insurance companies also insist on having other business besides dental coverage from the employer.

The problem of adverse selection is particularly severe when persons desire coverage after the date on which they were initially eligible to participate. These persons most likely want coverage because they or someone in their family needs dental treatment. Dental insurance contracts contain several provisions that try to minimize this problem, including one or a combination of the following:

■ Reducing benefits (usually by 50 percent) for a period of time (such as one year) following the late enrollment.

■ Reducing the maximum benefit to a low amount (such as $100 or $200) for the year following the late enrollment.

■ Excluding some benefits for a certain period (such as one or two years) following the late enrollment period. This exclusion may apply to all dental expenses except those that result from an accident, or it may apply only to a limited array of benefits (such as orthodontics and prosthetics).

Benefits. Most dental insurance plans pay for almost all types of dental expenses, but a particular plan may provide more limited benefits. One common characteristic of dental insurance is the inclusion of benefits for both routine diagnostic procedures (including oral examinations and x-rays) and preventive dental treatment (including teeth cleaning and fluoride treatment). In fact, a few dental plans actually require periodic oral examinations as a condition for continuing eligibility. There is clear evidence that the cost of providing these benefits is more than offset by the avoidance of the expensive dental procedures that are required when a condition is not discovered early or when a preventive treatment has not been given.

In addition to benefits for diagnostic and preventive treatment, benefits for dental expenses may be provided for these types of dental treatment:

■ Restoration (including fillings, crowns, and other procedures used to restore the functional use of natural teeth)

■ Oral surgery (including the extraction of teeth as well as other surgical treatment of diseases, injuries, and defects of the jaw)

■ Endodontics (treatment for diseases of the dental pulp within teeth, such as root canals)

■ Periodontics (treatment of diseases of the surrounding and supporting tissues of the teeth)

■ Prosthodontics (the replacement of missing teeth and structures by artificial devices, such as bridgework and dentures)

■ Orthodontics (the prevention and correction of dental and oral anomalies through the use of corrective devices, such as braces and retainers)

For benefit plan design purposes, these treatments are usually divided into the following categories of dental services:

- Service level I—preventive and diagnostic services
- Service level II—basic services, including minor restorative procedures (fillings), and endodontic, periodontic, and oral surgery services
- Service level III—major services, including major restorations (crowns, inlays, onlays, veneers), and prosthodontic procedures (dentures, bridges)
- Service level IV—orthodontic services

Most dental plans provide benefits for the first three service levels; some plans provide benefits for service level IV. These service levels are key to designing plans in which members have focused financial incentives to seek routine services for prevention of future expenses and have a greater stake in more costly major services decisions. Thus, for example, a typical dental plan will aim to provide its most complete payment for level I services and somewhat less complete payment for level II services, while providing the least complete benefit for level III and level IV services (if covered).

Benefit Payment Methods. Several types of benefit payment methods are found in dental plans. Plans that pay benefits on an indemnity basis usually make payments on the basis of reasonable-and-customary charges. Most plans have annual deductibles in the neighborhood of $50 to $100. However, the deductible typically does not apply to level I services. Coinsurance is also common. It is typically 80 percent or higher for level I services, with 100 percent being the most common. Level II services are usually subject to coinsurance in the range of 70 percent to 85 percent. Level III and level IV services typically have coinsurance of between 50 percent and 60 percent.

A very few indemnity plans have scheduled maximum benefits. These benefits are provided on a first-dollar basis with no deductibles or specified coinsurance percentage. Benefit maximums, however, are usually lower than reasonable-and-customary charges, thereby forcing employees to bear a portion of the costs of their dental services.

Dental plans that are structured as PPOs usually have deductibles and coinsurance similar to indemnity plans except that higher coinsurance percentages are used when services are received from network providers. In-network benefits are also paid on the basis of negotiated charges with providers.

Deductibles and coinsurance are usually not used for most service levels in DHMO plans as long as network providers are used. However, the member may be responsible for varying copayments for level II and level III services. Level IV services are usually subject to coinsurance, often 50 percent or 60 percent.

Exclusions. Exclusions are found in all dental plans, but their number and type vary. Some of the more common exclusions are charges for the following:

- Services that are purely cosmetic, unless necessitated by an accidental bodily injury sustained while a person is covered under the plan (Orthodontics, although often used for cosmetic reasons, can usually also be justified as necessary to correct abnormal dental conditions.)

- Replacement of lost, missing, or stolen dentures or other prosthetic devices
- Duplicate dentures or other prosthetic devices
- Oral hygiene instruction or other training in preventive dental care
- Services that do not have uniform professional endorsement
- Occupational injuries to the extent that benefits are provided by workers' compensation laws or similar legislation
- Services furnished by or on behalf of government agencies, unless there is a requirement to pay
- Certain services that began prior to the date that coverage for an individual became effective (for example, a crown for which a tooth was prepared prior to coverage)

Limitations. Dental insurance plans also contain numerous limitations that are designed to control claim costs and to eliminate unnecessary dental care. In addition to deductibles and coinsurance, virtually all dental plans have overall benefit maximums. Except for DHMOs, which usually do not have a calendar-year limit, most plans contain a calendar-year maximum (varying from $500 to $2,500) but no lifetime maximum. However, some plans have only a lifetime maximum (such as $5,000), and a few plans contain both a calendar-year maximum and a large lifetime maximum. These maximums may apply to all dental expenses, or they may be limited to all expenses except those that arise from orthodontics (and occasionally periodontics). In the latter case, benefits for orthodontics are subject to a separate, lower lifetime maximum, typically between $500 and $2,000.

Most dental plans limit the frequency with which some benefits are paid. Routine oral examinations and teeth cleaning are usually limited to once every six months and full-mouth x-rays to once every 24 or 36 months. The replacement of dentures may also be limited to one time in some specified period (such as five years).

The typical dental plan also limits benefits to the least expensive type of accepted dental treatment for a given dental condition. For example, if either a gold or amalgam (silver) filling can be used, benefit payments are limited to the cost of an amalgam filling, even if a gold filling is inserted.

Predetermination of Benefits. About half of dental contracts provide for a pretreatment review of certain dental services by the insurance company. Although this procedure is usually not mandatory, it does allow both the dentist and the patient to know just how much will be paid under the plan before the treatment is performed. In addition, it enables the insurance company (or other provider of benefits) to have some control over the performance of unnecessary or more-costly-than-necessary procedures, by giving patients an opportunity to seek less costly care (possibly from another dentist) if they learn that benefits are limited.

In general, the **predetermination-of-benefits provision** (which goes by several names, such as *precertification* or *prior authorization*) applies only in nonemergency situations and when a dentist's charge for a course of treatment exceeds a specified amount (varying from $200 to $300). The dentist in effect files a claim form (and x-rays if applicable) with the insurance company just as if the treatment had already been performed. The insurance company reviews the form and returns it to the dentist. The form specifies the services that are covered and the amount of reimbursement. If and when the services are actually performed, the insurance company makes payment to the dentist after the claim form has been returned with the appropriate signatures and the date of completion.

When the predetermination-of-benefits provision has not been followed, benefits are still paid. However, neither the dentist nor the covered person will know in advance what services are covered by the insurance company or how much the insurance company will pay for these services.

Termination.   Coverage under dental insurance plans typically terminates for the same reasons it terminates under medical expense coverage (described in Chapter 14).

Benefits for a dental service received after termination may still be covered as long as (1) the charge for the service was incurred prior to the termination date and (2) treatment is completed within 60 or 90 days after termination. For example, the charge for a crown or bridgework is incurred once the preparation of the tooth (or teeth) has begun, even though the actual installation of the crown or bridgework (and the billing) does not take place until after the coverage terminates. Similarly, charges for dentures are incurred on the date the impressions for them are taken, and charges for root canal therapy are incurred on the date the root canal is opened.

Rarely is there any type of conversion privilege for dental benefits. However, dental coverage is subject to the continuation rules of COBRA.

Examples of Major Plan Types

Dental benefit plans can be classified as indemnity plans or managed care plans. As with medical expense insurance, different plan types may be available.

According to one source,[1] 31 percent of current dental program members are covered under traditional fee-for-service indemnity plans; 37 percent are enrolled in dental PPOs and 13 percent in DHMOs. An additional 19 percent are estimated to be participants in noninsured discount dental plans. Managed care is by far the fastest-growing type of dental benefit plan, and this growth has been at the expense of indemnity plans. Within managed care, PPOs have overtaken and surpassed DHMOs, which are the more structured and integrated managed dental care option.

Table 15.1 is an example of an indemnity plan. Table 15.2 is an example of a PPO plan. Table 15.3 is an example of a DHMO plan with a point-of-service option. All three plans can be classified as typical of their plan types, but variations do exist.

■ GROUP LONG-TERM CARE INSURANCE

In the 1980s, insurance companies started to market long-term care insurance policies to individuals. **Long-term care insurance** is designed to provide coverage for at least 12 months to persons who need nonacute care for personal care services. Many of the earlier policies had limited benefits and expensive premiums. As the products have evolved, benefits have improved while premiums have remained stable or decreased. As is often the case, success in the individual marketplace led to interest in long-term care insurance

TABLE 15.1	Dental Indemnity Plan Benefits Summary	
Service Level	**Benefits**	
Level I—Preventive	100% of R & C*	
Level II—Basic	80% of R & C*	
Level III—Major Restorative	50% of R & C*	
Level IV—Orthodontia	50% of R & C*	
Deductible†	$75 (individual)	
	$150 (family)	
Orthodontia Lifetime Maximum	$2,000	
Annual Maximum for Other Benefits	$2,000	

*Reasonable and customary—charge determined by the plan based on prevailing fees charged by dentists in the area.
†Not applicable to service level I.

as an employee benefit. The first group long-term plan was written in 1987, and a growing number of employers continue to make coverage available.

The current products available in the group long-term care insurance market fall into two basic categories—group insurance policies and voluntary benefit plans. Insurers that write other types of group life and health insurance tend to issue group contracts. Insurers that specialize in the individual market—often life insurers—tend to write voluntary products. Some insurers that have historically written both group and individual life and health insurance coverage may offer both types of long-term care insurance products. For the most part, the coverage available to employees and other eligible persons is similar regardless of the type of product used.

TABLE 15.2	Dental PPO Plan Benefits Summary	
Service Level	**In-Network Benefits**	**Out-of-Network Benefits**
Level I—Preventive	100% of negotiated charge*	100% of R & C†
Level II—Basic	85% of negotiated charge*	75% of R & C†
Level III—Major Restorative	50% of negotiated charge*	50% of R &C†
Level IV—Orthodontia	50% of negotiated charge*	50% of R & C†
Deductible‡	$50 (individual)	$75 (individual)
	$100 (family)	$100 (family)
Orthodontia Lifetime Maximum	$2,000	$2,000
Annual Maximum for Other Benefits	$2,000	$2,000

*Negotiated charge—fee that the dentist participating in the network accepts as payment in full.
†Reasonable and customary—charge determined by the plan based on prevailing fees charged by dentists in the area.
‡Not applicable to service level I.

TABLE 15.3	DHMO with Point-of-Service (POS) Option Plan Benefits Summary	
Service Level	**DHMO Benefits**	**POS Benefits**
Level I—Preventive	Fully paid	100% of R & C[*]
Level II—Basic	$10 copay	80% of R & C[*]
Level III—Major Restorative	$50 to $250 copay[†]	50% of R & C[*]
Level IV—Orthodontia	50% of negotiated charge[‡]	50% of R & C[*]
Deductible	Not applicable	$75 (individual)[§] $150 (family)[§]
Orthodontia Lifetime Maximum	Not applicable	$2,000
Annual Maximum for Other Benefits	Not applicable	$2,000

[*]Reasonable and customary—charge determined by the plan based on prevailing fees charged by dentists in the area.
[†]Amount varies depending on treatment or service.
[‡]Negotiated charge—fee that the DHMO-participating dentist accepts as payment in full.
[§]Not applicable to service level I.

The growth of group long-term care insurance can be described as slow and cautious for several reasons. First, the individual long-term care insurance market is still in an evolving state, due partially to the lack of adequate actuarial data to design and price coverage. The situation is not unlike the early days of disability income insurance.

Second, the tax status of group long-term care coverage has been uncertain, with most tax experts feeling that employer-provided benefits, unlike medical expense benefits, would result in taxation to employees. To the extent that employers want to spend additional benefit dollars, they want to spend them on benefits for which employees receive favorable tax benefits. As a result, most group long-term care plans have been financed solely by employee contributions. However, the Health Insurance Portability and Accountability Act (HIPAA) now provides favorable tax treatment for long-term care insurance. The effect of this act is discussed later in this chapter.

Third, there has been uncertainty about whether long-term care can be included in a cafeteria plan on a tax-favored basis. This issue was also addressed by HIPAA (which states that long-term care cannot be included).

Finally, participation in group plans has been modest because older employees often do not see the need for coverage, or it is too expensive. A surprise, however, with many of the early plans has been the higher-than-expected participation by employees in the 40-to-50 age bracket. Despite this modest participation, almost 1.5 million persons obtain their long-term care insurance through an employer-sponsored plan.[2] This represents about 25 percent of the long-term care insurance in force.

Before a description of the existing plans is undertaken, it is important to discuss the need for long-term care protection, the sources already available to meet this need, NAIC model legislation, and the effect of HIPAA.

Need for Long-Term Care

An Aging Population.   Long-term care has traditionally been thought of as a problem primarily for the older population. The population aged 65 or over is the fastest-growing age group; today it represents about 11 percent of the population, a figure that is expected to increase to between 20 percent and 25 percent over the next 50 years. The segment of the population aged 85 and over is growing at an even faster rate. While less than 10 percent of the over-65 group is over 85 today, this percentage is expected to double over the next two generations.

An aging society presents changing problems. Those who needed long-term care in the past were most likely to have suffered from strokes or other acute diseases. With longer life spans today and in the future, a larger portion of the elderly are or will be incapacitated by chronic conditions such as Alzheimer's disease, arthritis, osteoporosis, and lung and heart disease—conditions that often require continuing assistance with day-to-day needs. The likelihood that a person will need to enter a nursing home increases dramatically with age. One percent of persons aged 65 through 74 reside in nursing homes, and the percentage increases to 6 percent of those aged 75 through 84. At age 85 and over, the figure rises to approximately 25 percent. Statistics of the Department of Health and Human Services indicate that persons aged 65 or older face a 40 percent chance of entering a nursing home at some time during the remainder of their lives. Nearly half of the persons who enter nursing homes remain longer than one year, and the average nursing home stay is about 2½ years.[3]

Nursing home statistics tell only part of the story. An even greater percentage of the elderly have age-related conditions that require varying degrees of assistance to enable them to perform normal daily activities. In some cases, this assistance is provided in other types of supportive-living arrangements such as assisted living facilities and adult foster homes. In many cases, however, the elderly remain in their own homes or the homes of relatives and receive their care from relatives, home health agencies, and community-based programs. The latter programs include meals on wheels and adult day care centers.

The elderly are not the only group of persons who need long-term care. Many younger persons are unable to care for themselves because of handicaps resulting from birth defects, mental conditions, illnesses, or accidents.

Increasing Costs.   Almost $100 billion is spent each year on nursing home care, and home health care costs exceed $30 billion.[4] These costs, about 11 percent of national health care expenditures, are increasing faster than inflation because of the growing demand for nursing home beds and the shortage of skilled medical personnel. The cost of complete long-term care for an individual can be astronomical, with annual nursing home costs of $30,000 to $60,000 and more not unusual. Costs of $2,500 or more per month can easily be incurred in part-time home health care. By 2030, the annual cost of nursing home care is expected to approximate $200,000 with comparable increases in home care charges.[5]

Inability of Families to Provide Full Care.   Traditionally, family members have provided long-term care, often at considerable personal sacrifice and stress. However, it is becoming more difficult for families to provide long-term care for these reasons:

- Geographic dispersion of family members
- Increased participation in the paid workforce by women and children
- Fewer children in the family
- More childless families
- Higher divorce rates
- Inability of family members to provide care because they, too, are growing old

Inadequacy of Insurance Protection. Private medical expense insurance policies (both group and individual) almost always have an exclusion for convalescent, custodial, or rest care. Some policies do provide coverage for extended-care facilities and for home health care. In both cases, the purpose is to provide care in a manner that is less expensive than care in a hospital. However, coverage is provided only if a person also needs medical care; benefits are not provided if a person is merely "old" and needs someone to care for him or her.

Medicare is also inadequate because it does not cover custodial care unless this care is needed along with the medical or rehabilitative treatment provided in skilled-nursing facilities or under home health care benefits.

Sources of Long-Term Care Financing

There are several sources other than insurance that are available for financing long-term care; however, there are drawbacks associated with each.

One source is to rely on personal financial resources. Few individuals have sufficient retirement income to fully meet their potential long-term care expenses. Unless a person has substantial assets on which to draw, this approach may force an individual and his or her dependents into poverty. It may also mean that the person will not meet the financial objective of leaving assets to heirs.

An often overlooked source of providing or financing long-term care is relatives, or even friends. In some cases, family members may act as caregivers themselves; in other cases, they may give financial support to provide care or pay for long-term care insurance premiums. The support of relatives, however, may not last forever. For example, a spouse may no longer be able to provide care because of his or her own physical condition. And aging children may not have the financial resources to continue the same level of support because of their own long-term care needs.

Another source is to rely on public assistance. The Medicaid program in most states provides benefits, which usually include nursing home care and home health care (and possibly assisted living care), to the "medically needy." A person, however, is not eligible unless he or she is either poor or has a low income and has exhausted most other assets (including those of a spouse). There is also often a social stigma associated with accepting public assistance. In addition, reliance on Medicaid eliminates many decisions an individual would like to be able to make about his or her own care. For example, nursing home care may be available only in an approved facility that is far from a person's home and of a lower quality than the person might prefer to occupy.

One strategy that is sometimes used to qualify for Medicaid is to give a person's assets away at the time nursing home care is needed and ultimately rely on Medicaid. (This will work only if income, including pensions and Social Security, is below specified limits.) However, Medicaid benefits are reduced (or their onset postponed) if assets were disposed of at less than their fair market value within a specific time period (called the *look-back period*) prior to Medicaid eligibility. One approach is to purchase long-term care insurance in an amount sufficient to provide protection for the length of the look-back period. If care is needed, a person can rely on the insurance coverage and transfer assets to heirs. When the insurance coverage runs out and the look-back period is over, the person can apply for Medicaid.

Several states have attempted to encourage better coverage for long-term care by waiving or modifying certain Medicaid requirements if a person carries a state-approved long-term care policy. For example, in Connecticut a person can apply for and receive Medicaid benefits without having to exhaust current assets if the individual has maintained an approved long-term care policy and its benefits have run out. In essence, these programs increase the assets that a person can retain and still collect Medicaid benefits, with the increase in the allowable asset threshold related to the amount of long-term care coverage carried and exhausted.

The concept of the **continuing-care retirement community (CCRC)**, also referred to as a *life care facility*, is growing in popularity as a source of meeting long-term care needs. Residents in a CCRC pay an "entrance fee" that allows them to occupy a dwelling unit but usually does not give them actual ownership rights. The entrance fee may or may not be refundable if the resident leaves the facility voluntarily or dies. As a general rule, the higher the refund is, the higher the entrance fee is. Residents pay a monthly fee that includes meals, some housecleaning services, and varying degrees of health care. If a person needs long-term care, he or she must give up the independent living unit and move to the assisted-living or nursing home portion of the CCRC, but the monthly fee normally remains the same.

The disadvantages of this option are that the cost of a CCRC is beyond the reach of many persons, and a resident must be in reasonably good health and able to live independently at the time he or she enters the facility. Therefore, the decision to use a CCRC must be made in advance of the need for long-term care. Once such care is needed or is imminent, this approach is no longer viable.

A few insurers now include long-term care benefits in some cash value life insurance policies. Essentially, an insured can begin to use these accelerated benefits while he or she is still living. For example, if the insured is in a nursing home, he or she might be able to elect a benefit equal to 25 percent or 50 percent of the policy face amount. However, any benefits received reduce the future death benefit payable to heirs. One potential problem with this approach is that the acceleration of benefits may result in the reduction of the death benefit to a level that is inadequate to accomplish the purpose of life insurance—the protection of family members after a wage earner's death. If benefits are accelerated, there is less left for the surviving family. In addition, the availability of an accelerated benefit may give the insured a false sense of security that long-term care needs are being met when in fact the potential benefit may be inadequate to cover extended nursing home stays.

NAIC Model Legislation

Because of its widespread adoption by the states, it is appropriate to discuss the NAIC model legislation regarding long-term care. The legislation consists of a model act that is designed to be incorporated into a state's insurance law and model regulations that are designed to be adopted for use in implementing the law. This discussion is based on the latest version of the model legislation, which, as mentioned earlier, seems to be amended almost annually. Even though most states have adopted the NAIC legislation, some states may not have adopted the latest version. However, the importance of the model legislation should not be overlooked. With most insurers writing coverage in more than one state, it is likely that the latest provisions have been adopted by one or more states where an insurer's coverage is sold. Because most insurance companies sell essentially the same long-term care product everywhere they do business, the NAIC guidelines are often, in effect, being adhered to in states that have not adopted the legislation.

Before proceeding with a summary of the major provisions of the NAIC model legislation, it is important to make two points. First, the model legislation establishes guidelines. Insurance companies still have significant latitude in many aspects of product design. Second, many older policies are still in existence that were written prior to the adoption of the model legislation or under one of its earlier versions.

The model legislation focuses on two major areas—policy provisions and marketing. Highlights of the criteria for policy provisions include the following:

- Many words or terms cannot be used in a policy unless they are specifically defined in accordance with the legislation. Examples include adult day care, home health care services, personal care, and skilled-nursing care.

- No policy can contain renewal provisions other than guaranteed renewable or non-cancelable.

- Limitations and exclusions are prohibited except in the following cases:

  - Preexisting conditions
  - Mental or nervous disorders (but this does not permit the exclusion of Alzheimer's disease)
  - Alcoholism and drug addiction
  - Illness, treatment, or medical condition arising out of war, participation in a felony, service in the armed forces, suicide, and aviation if a person is a non-fare-paying passenger
  - Treatment in a government facility and services available under Medicare and other social insurance programs

- No policy can provide coverage for skilled-nursing care only or provide significantly more coverage for skilled care in a facility than for lower levels of care.

- The definition of preexisting condition can be no more restrictive than to exclude a condition for which treatment was recommended or received within six months prior to the effective date of coverage. In addition, coverage can be excluded for a confinement for this condition only if it begins within six months of the effective date of coverage.

- Eligibility for benefits cannot be based on a prior hospital confinement or higher level of care.

- Insurance companies must offer the applicant the right to purchase coverage that allows for an increase in the amount of benefits based on reasonable anticipated increases in the cost of services covered by the policy. The applicant must specifically reject this inflation protection if he or she does not want it.

- Insurance companies must offer the applicant the right to purchase a nonforfeiture benefit.

- A policy must contain a provision that makes a policy incontestable after two years on the grounds of misrepresentation alone. The policy can still be contested on the basis that the applicant knowingly and intentionally misrepresented relevant facts pertaining to the insured's health.

The following provisions of the model legislation pertain to marketing:

- An outline of coverage must be delivered to a prospective applicant at the time of initial solicitation. Among the information this outline must contain is (1) a description of the coverage; (2) a statement of the principal exclusions, reductions, and limitations in the policy; (3) a statement of the terms under which the policy can be continued in force or terminated; (4) a description of the terms under which the policy may be returned and the premium refunded; (5) a brief description of the relationship of cost of care and benefits, and (6) a statement whether the policy is intended to be tax qualified.

- A shopper's guide must be delivered to all prospective applicants.

- The policy must allow covered persons to have a free 30-day look at their policy or certificate of insurance. If they are not satisfied, they may terminate the policy or enrollment in the group plan as of the initial date of coverage.

- An insurance company must establish procedures to ensure that any comparisons of policies by its agents or other producers are fair and accurate and to prohibit excessive insurance from being sold or issued.

- Applications for insurance must be clear and unambiguous so that an applicant's health condition can be properly ascertained. The application must also contain a conspicuous statement near the place for the applicant's signature that says the following: "If your answers to this application are incorrect or untrue, the company has the right to deny benefits or rescind your policy."

Effect of Health Insurance Portability and Accountability Act (HIPAA)

The Health Insurance Portability and Accountability Act (HIPAA) made the tax treatment of long-term care insurance more favorable. However, this favorable tax treatment is given only if long-term care insurance policies meet prescribed standards. It should be emphasized that the long-term care changes in the act are primarily changes in the income tax code. States still have the authority to regulate long-term care insurance contracts.

Eligibility for Favorable Tax Treatment. The act provides favorable tax treatment to a **qualified long-term care insurance contract**. Most, if not all, group and voluntary contracts used in the employer marketplace are designed to be this type of contract, which is defined as any insurance contract that meets all the following requirements:

- The only insurance protection provided under the contract is for qualified long-term care services.

- The contract cannot pay for expenses that are reimbursable under Medicare. However, this requirement does not apply to expenses that are reimbursable if (1) Medicare is a secondary payer of benefits or (2) benefits are payable on a per diem basis.

- The contract must be guaranteed renewable.

- The contract does not provide for a cash surrender value or other money that can be borrowed or paid, assigned, or pledged as collateral for a loan.

- All refunds of premiums and policyowner dividends must be applied as future reductions in premiums or to increase future benefits.

- The policy must comply with various consumer protection provisions. For the most part, these are the same provisions contained in the NAIC model legislation and already adopted by most states.

The act defines **qualified long-term care services** as necessary diagnostic, preventive, therapeutic, curing, treating, and rehabilitative services, and maintenance or personal care services that are required by a chronically ill person and are provided by a plan of care prescribed by a licensed health care practitioner.

A **chronically ill individual** is one who has been certified as meeting one of the following requirements, often referred to as *benefit triggers*:

- The person is expected to be unable to perform, without substantial assistance from another person, at least two **activities of daily living (ADLs)** for a period of at least 90 days due to a loss of functional capacity. The act allows six ADLs: eating, bathing, dressing, transferring from bed to chair, using the toilet, and maintaining continence. A qualified long-term care insurance contract must contain at least five of the six.

- Substantial supervision is required to protect the individual from threats to health and safety because of severe cognitive impairment.

Federal Income Tax Provisions. A qualified long-term care insurance contract, typically referred to as *tax qualified*, is treated as accident and health insurance. With some exceptions, expenses for long-term care services, including insurance premiums, are treated like other medical expenses. That is, self-employed persons may deduct the premiums paid, and persons who itemize deductions can include the cost of long-term care services, including insurance premiums, for purposes of deducting medical expenses in excess of 7.5 percent of adjusted gross income. However, there is a cap on the amount

TABLE 15.4	Long-Term Care Deductible Limits
Age	**Annual Deductible Limit per Covered Individual**
40 or Younger	$ 260
41–50	490
51–60	980
61–70	2,600
Older than 70	3,150

of personally paid long-term care insurance premiums that can be claimed as medical expenses. These limits, which are based upon a covered individual's age and subject to cost-of-living adjustments, are shown for 2004 in Table 15.4. Deductions cannot be taken for payments made to a spouse or relative who is not a licensed professional with respect to such services.

Any employer contributions for group contracts are deductible to the employer and do not result in any taxable income to an employee. Coverage cannot be offered through a cafeteria plan on a tax-favored basis. In addition, if an employee has a flexible spending account for unreimbursed medical expenses, any reimbursements for long-term care services must be included in the employee's income.

Benefits received under a qualified long-term care insurance contract are received tax free by an employee with one possible exception. Under contracts written on a per diem basis, proceeds are excludible from income up to $230 per day in 2004. (This figure is indexed annually.) Amounts in excess of $230 are also excludible to the extent that they represent reimbursement for actual long-term care services.

Policy Characteristics

Eligibility for Coverage.   The typical eligibility rules (that is, full time, actively at work, and so on) apply to long-term care products. At a minimum, coverage can be purchased for an active employee and/or spouse. Many products also provide coverage to retirees and to other family members, such as children, parents, parents-in-law, and possibly adult children. There is a maximum age for eligibility, but it is frequently as high as 85 and may be higher.

Cost.   As previously mentioned, the cost of long-term care coverage is almost always borne by the employee. Initial premiums are usually in five-year age brackets and increase significantly with age. For example, the annual premium for persons aged 40 to 44 is usually only one-third to one-half the premium for persons aged 60 to 64. Once coverage is elected, premiums remain level and do not increase when a person enters another age bracket. Coverage is guaranteed renewable, so premiums can be increased by class.

Under most plans, premiums are payable for life. Under other plans, premiums are higher but cease at retirement age. Such a plan is analogous to a life insurance policy that is paid up at age 65. Virtually all plans contain a waiver-of-premium provision that becomes effective when a covered person starts to receive benefits.

Types of Care Covered. There are many types of care for which benefits may be provided under a long-term care policy. By broad categories, these can be categorized as nursing home care, assisted-living care, hospice care, Alzheimer's facilities, home health care, care coordination, and alternative sources of care. A long-term care policy may provide benefits for one, several, or all of these types of care.

Nursing Home Care. **Nursing home care** encompasses skilled care, intermediate care, and custodial care in a licensed facility. **Skilled care** (also called *skilled-nursing care*) consists of daily nursing and rehabilitative care that can be performed only by, or under the supervision of, skilled medical personnel and must be based on a doctor's orders. **Intermediate care** involves occasional nursing and rehabilitative care that must be based on a doctor's orders and can be performed only by, or under the supervision of, skilled medical personnel. **Custodial care** is primarily to handle personal needs, such as walking, bathing, dressing, eating, or taking medicine, and can usually be provided by someone without professional medical skills or training.

Policies that provide nursing home care often also provide a **bed reservation benefit**, which continues payments to a long-term care facility for a limited time (such as 20 days) if a patient temporarily leaves because of hospitalization or any other reason. Without a continuation of payments, the bed may be assigned to someone else and unavailable upon the patient's release from the hospital.

Assisted-Living Facility Care. **Assisted-living care** is provided in facilities that care for the frail elderly who are no longer able to care for themselves but do not need as high a level of care as is provided in a nursing home.

Hospice Care. Hospice care does not attempt to cure medical conditions but rather is devoted to easing the physical and psychological pain associated with death. In addition to providing services for the dying patient, a hospice may offer counseling to family members. A hospice may be a separate facility, but this type of care can also be provided on an outpatient basis in the dying person's home. Most long-term care insurance policies that provide benefits for hospice care make no distinction in the setting.

Alzheimer's Facilities. The states require long-term care insurance policies to cover Alzheimer's disease and related forms of degenerative diseases and dementia under the same terms as they cover other conditions that qualify an individual as chronically ill. Therefore, coverage is provided if an individual receives services in a nursing home, in an assisted-living facility, or at home—as long as the specific type of care is covered in the policy. Most policies, however, have some specific reference to Alzheimer's facilities. In some cases, they are included as part of the definition for assisted-living facilities. In other cases, they are referred to separately but defined as a facility that must meet the policy's definition of either a nursing home or an assisted-living facility.

Home Health Care. Home health care is much broader than just part-time skilled care, therapy, part-time services from home health aides, and help from homemakers. It may also include benefits for one or more of the following:

■ The purchase or rental of needed medical equipment and emergency alert systems.

■ Modifications to the home such as a ramp for a wheelchair or bathroom modifications.

■ **Adult day care**, which is received at centers specifically designed for the elderly who live at home but whose spouses or families cannot be available during the day.

■ **Respite care**, which allows occasional full-time care for a person who is receiving home health care. Such persons are often also receiving care from a family member or friend. This benefit gives them a needed break. Respite care can be provided in a person's home or by moving the person to a nursing facility for a short stay.

■ Caregiver training, which is the training of a family member or friend to provide care so that a person can remain at home.

■ A homemaker companion, who is an employee of a state-licensed home health care agency. The companion may assist with such tasks as cooking, shopping, cleaning, bill paying, or other household chores.

■ Prescription drugs and laboratory services typically provided in hospitals and nursing homes.

Care Coordination.   Many policies provide **care coordination,** which is the services of a care coordinator who works with an insured, his or her family, and licensed health care practitioners to assess a person's condition, evaluate care options, and develop an individualized plan of care that provides the most appropriate services. The care coordinator may also periodically reevaluate ongoing plans of care and act as an advocate for the insured. Some long-term care policies mandate that the insured use the services of the care coordinator to receive benefits.

Alternative Plans of Care.   Many policies provide benefits for an **alternative plan of care**, even though the types of care might not be covered in the policy. For example, a policy covering only nursing home care might provide benefits for care in an assisted-living facility if these benefits are an appropriate and cost-effective alternative to care in a nursing home. As a general rule, the alternative plan must be acceptable to the insurance company, the insured, and the insured's physician.

Benefit Variations.   There are almost as many variations among long-term care policies as there are insurance companies writing the product. Much of this variation is related to the types of care for which benefits are provided. These benefit variations fall into three broad categories: facility-only policies, home health care only policies, and comprehensive policies.

Facility-Only Policies.   Many early long-term care policies were designed to provide benefits only if the insured was in a nursing home. This type of policy was frequently referred to as a *nursing home policy*. Such policies still exist, but they frequently also provide benefits for care in other settings such as assisted-living facilities and hospices. The term **facility-only policy** is often used to describe this broader type of policy, and the term, in its most generic sense, also includes nursing home policies.

Home Health Care Only Policies.   Home health care only policies were originally developed to be used either as an alternative to nursing home policies or to complement such policies if more comprehensive coverage was desired. A **home health care only policy** is designed to provide benefits for care outside an institutional setting. Some home health care policies also provide benefits for care in assisted-living facilities, and this is one area in which they often overlap with facility-only policies.

Although a few insurers still write stand-alone home health care policies in the employer marketplace, many other insurers only write the coverage as part of a broader comprehensive policy.

Comprehensive Policies. Most group long-term care policies written today can be described as comprehensive policies. A **comprehensive long-term care insurance policy,** sometimes referred to as an *integrated policy*, combines benefits for facility care and home health care into a single contract.

Benefit Amounts. When purchasing long-term care coverage, the employee selects the level of benefit he or she desires from the available options. Most group plans have fewer options than are available in the individual marketplace, but most plans offer at least three daily benefits such as $100, $150, or $200.

The same level of benefits is usually provided for all types of institutional care. Many comprehensive policies that provide home health care benefits once limited the daily benefit to one-half the amount payable for institutional stays. However, some policies automatically provide or allow applicants to select home health care limits that are as high as 75 percent to 100 percent of the benefit for institutional care. If a policy provides home health care benefits only, the daily amount of that benefit is what the applicant selected.

Policies pay benefits in one of two basic ways: reimbursement or per diem.

Reimbursement Policies. The majority of group policies pay benefits on a **reimbursement basis**. These contracts reimburse the insured for actual expenses up to the specified policy limit. For example, a policy with a daily benefit amount of $200 will pay only $150 if that was the insured's actual charge for care. Tax-qualified policies that provide benefits on a reimbursement basis must be coordinated with Medicare except when Medicare is the secondary payer of benefits.

Per Diem Policies. Some policies provide benefits on a **per diem basis** once care is actually being received. This means that benefits are paid regardless of the actual cost of care. In this case, a policy with a daily benefit of $200 will pay $200 even if actual long-term care charges for the day are only $150. Per diem contracts are seldom coordinated with any benefits that are payable under Medicare. If home health care benefits are provided, most per diem policies pay benefits regardless of the service provider. In such cases, benefits are paid even if a family member provides care at no charge. Some policies, however, define the type of service provider from whom care must be received.

Note that per diem policies are sometimes referred to as *indemnity policies,* even though the usual insurance meaning of indemnity implies payment of benefits for actual expenses up to policy limits. In this sense, reimbursement policies, not per diem policies, are actually policies of indemnity.

A few insurers offer a variation of the per diem policy that pays benefits as long as the insured satisfies the policy's benefit triggers, even if no long-term care is being received. Such a policy is referred to as a **disability-based policy**.

Period of Benefits. To determine the period of benefits under a long-term care insurance policy, it is necessary to look at the waiting period and the maximum duration of benefits.

Waiting Period. The applicant is required to select a period of time that must pass after long-term care commences but before benefit payments begin. Many long-term care insurers refer to this period as a *waiting period*. However, some insurers call it an *elimination period* or a *deductible period*. Most insurers allow an applicant to select from among three to five optional waiting periods. For example, one insurer allows the choice of 20, 60, 100, or 180 days. Choices may be as low as 0 days or as high as 365 days.

In a comprehensive policy, there is normally a single waiting period that can be met by any combination of days during which the insured is in a long-term care facility or receiving home health care services.

There are several ways that home health care services can be counted toward the waiting period. Some policies count only those days when actual services are received for which charges are made and that will be covered after the waiting period is satisfied. If an insured receives services three days during the week, this counts as three days. If the insured's policy has a 60-day waiting period, benefit payments will not begin until the insured has been receiving services for 20 weeks (or 140 days). Some policies count each week as seven days toward the satisfaction of the waiting period if services were received on any number of days in the week, even one day. In this case, the insured will start receiving benefit payments after 60 days have elapsed from the first service.

Another variation in reimbursement policies is for the insurer to start counting days toward satisfaction of the waiting period as soon as long-term care is certified as being necessary, even if services are received from someone who does not make a charge. Therefore, family members or friends could provide the services until the waiting period is satisfied, and the insurer will then start paying benefits for the services of a paid caregiver.

One final comment about the waiting period concerns its relationship to the requirement that tax-qualified policies cannot pay benefits for the inability to perform ADLs unless this inability is expected to last at least 90 days. Actually, despite what some people think, there is no relationship! If an insured is certified as being unable to perform the requisite number of ADLs for at least 90 days, benefit payments will start after the satisfaction of the waiting period, be it 0, 20, 60, or any other specified number of days. If the insured makes a recovery after the waiting period is satisfied but before the end of the 90-day period, the insured is fully entitled to any benefits received because the period was *expected* to be at least 90 days.

Maximum Duration of Benefits. The applicant is also given a choice as to the maximum period for which benefits are paid, often referred to as the *benefit period*. This period begins from the time benefit payments start after satisfaction of the waiting period. In addition, the benefit period does not necessarily apply to each separate period for which long-term care services are received. Rather, it is a period that applies to the aggregate time benefits are paid under the policy. When the maximum benefits are paid, the policy will terminate. However, if benefits are only partially exhausted during a course of long-term care, they may be restored under certain circumstances, as explained later. Also, as explained later, the length of the benefit period may actually differ from the period chosen if a policy uses a pool-of-money concept.

Most insurers require that the applicant select the benefit period, which is the length of time benefits will be paid after the waiting period is satisfied. Several options are available. For example, one insurer offers durations of three, five, and six years as well as lifetime benefits. In most cases, a single benefit period applies to long-term care, no matter where it is received. A few policies, however, have separate benefit periods for facility care and home health care. There are also a few policies, usually the per diem type, that specify the maximum benefits as a stated dollar amount such as $100,000.

There are actually two ways that the benefit period is applied in the payment of benefits. Under one approach, benefit payments are made for exactly the benefit period chosen. If the applicant selects a benefit period of four years and collects benefits for four years, the benefit payments cease. The other approach, most commonly but not exclusively used with reimbursement policies, uses a **pool of money**. Under this concept, there is an amount of money that can be used to make benefit payments as long as the pool of money lasts. The applicant does not select the amount in the pool of money; it is determined by multiplying the daily benefit by the benefit period selected. For example, if the daily benefit is $200 and the benefit period is 1,460 days (or four years), then the pool of money is $292,000 ($200 × 1,460). Several important points about this pool of money should be mentioned:

■ Daily benefit payments from the pool of money cannot exceed the daily policy benefits.

■ Under comprehensive policies, the pool of money is typically determined by using the daily benefit amount for institutional care.

■ Adjustments are made to the pool of money during periods of benefit payments to reflect any inflation protection that applies to the policy benefits.

A few insurers use the concept of a **shared benefit** when a husband and wife are insured under the same policy or with the same insurer. Under this concept, each spouse can access the other spouse's benefits. For example, if each spouse has a four-year benefit period and one spouse has exhausted his or her benefits, benefit payments can continue by drawing on any unused benefits under the other spouse's policy. In effect, one spouse could have a benefit period of up to eight years as long as the other spouse receives no benefit payments.

Prepackaged Benefit Options. Some plans limit employee choice by having a series (most commonly three) of prepackaged benefit options. These options are often referred to as *low, medium,* and *high* to reflect the level of benefits and the cost. The low option offers the lowest level of benefits and lowest cost, while the high option has the highest level of benefits and the highest cost. Tables 15.5 and 15.6 show two such prepackaged plans.

Restoration. Many policies written with less than a lifetime benefit period provide for restoration of full benefits if the insured previously received less-than-full policy

TABLE 15.5 Prepackaged Benefit Options	Low	Medium	High
Type of Policy	Comprehensive	Comprehensive	Comprehensive
Waiting Period	90 days	60 days	30 days
Daily Benefit Amount (80% for home health care)	$100	$150	$200
Benefit Duration	3 years	6 years	Lifetime
Inflation Protection	No	Yes	Yes
Nonforfeiture Benefits	No	No	Yes

benefits and has not required long-term care for a certain time period, often 180 days. If a policy does not have this provision, maximum benefits for a subsequent claim are reduced by the benefits previously paid.

Inflation Protection.   Most states require that a long-term care policy offer some type of automatic inflation protection. Under some group contracts, the employer is given the choice to select the option or decline the option. However, in most products, the employee makes the selection. The applicant is given the choice to select this option, decline the option, or possibly select an alternative option. The cost of an automatic-increase option is built into the initial premium, and no additional premium is levied at the time of an annual increase. As a result of the NAIC model act and HIPAA, the standard provision found in almost all policies is a 5 percent benefit increase that is compounded annually over the life of the policy. Under such a provision, the amount of a policy's benefits increases by 5 percent each year over the amount of benefits available in the prior year.

A common alternative that many insurers make available is based on simple interest, with each annual automatic increase being 5 percent of the original benefit amount. Other options that are occasionally found are increases (either simple or compound) based on different fixed percentage amounts such as 3 or 4 percent.

TABLE 15.6 Prepackaged Benefit Options	Low	Medium	High
Type of Policy	Facility only	Comprehensive	Comprehensive
Waiting Period	90 days	90 days	90 days
Daily Benefit Amount (all care settings)	$150	$150	$200
Benefit duration	3 years	5 years	Lifetime
Inflation Protection	Yes	Yes	Yes
Nonforfeiture Benefits	No	No	No

If an automatic-increase option is not selected, some insurers allow a policyowner to increase benefits without evidence of insurability on a pay-as-you-go basis at specified intervals such as every one, two, or three years. Each benefit increase is accompanied by a premium increase that is based on attained-age rates for the additional coverage.

The amount of the periodic benefit increase under a pay-as-you-go option may be a fixed dollar amount, such as a daily benefit increase of $20 every third year, or be based on a specified percentage or an index such as the consumer price index (CPI). Some insurers have an aggregate limit on the total amount of benefit increases or an age beyond which they are no longer available. Failure to exercise a periodic increase or a series of increases over a specified period typically terminates the right to purchase additional benefits in the future.

Increases in benefits are often inadequate to offset actual inflation in the annual cost of long-term care, which has been in the double digits over the last decade.

Eligibility for Benefits.   Almost all tax-qualified contracts use the same two criteria for determining benefit eligibility, with the insured being required to meet only one of the two. The first criterion is that the insured is expected to be unable, without substantial assistance from another person, to perform two of the six ADLs that are acceptable under HIPAA for a period of at least 90 days due to loss of functional capacity. The second criterion is that substantial supervision is required to protect the individual from threats to health and safety because of severe cognitive impairment.

Exclusions.   Most long-term care policies contain the exclusions permitted under the NAIC model act. One source of controversy is the exclusion for mental and nervous disorders. These are conditions that insurers frequently do not cover because of the possibility of fraudulent claims and the controversies that often arise over claim settlements. The usual exclusion is stated as follows: "This policy does not provide benefits for the care or treatment of mental illness or emotional disorders without a demonstrable organic cause." Many policies also specifically stipulate that Alzheimer's disease and senile dementia, as diagnosed by a physician, are considered as having demonstrable organic cause, even though state law frequently requires these disorders to be covered.

Underwriting.   There are several levels of underwriting that may apply to employer-sponsored groups for long-term care insurance. These levels include guaranteed issue, modified guaranteed issue, simplified issue, and full underwriting. From the standpoint of applicants, employees are often subject to less stringent underwriting than their family members. Adverse selection tends to be less of a problem with employees because they tend to be healthier as a result of their being actively at work.

Insurers occasionally use guaranteed-issue underwriting for employees but only if the group meets certain criteria that minimize adverse selection. Guaranteed-issue underwriting is seldom used for applicants other than employees.

When modified guaranteed-issue underwriting is used, the insurer accepts most applicants. However, some medical questions are asked on the application, and the answers to these questions may result in the declination of the application. These questions are often aimed at determining whether the applicant has recently received long-term care services or requires assistance with any activities of daily living. Questions may also ask whether the applicant has certain specified medical conditions such as Parkinson's disease, multiple sclerosis, cancer, or AIDS. As long as there are no unsatisfactory answers to these questions, no further medical information is requested and coverage is issued. There may also be some underwriting of the group itself but on a less stringent basis than if guaranteed-issue underwriting is used. Modified guaranteed-issue underwriting may also be limited to employees.

With simplified-issue underwriting, the insurer tends to ask more medically related questions than are used with modified guaranteed-issue underwriting. Only if the answers to these questions are unsatisfactory does the insurer request further medical information—such as an attending physician's statement—or further medical assessments. Simplified-issue underwriting might be used for all applicants, or it might be used for all applicants other than employees when the employees are subject to less stringent underwriting.

In some cases, a group plan will use the same underwriting as in the individual marketplace. This type of underwriting is most likely to be used in the group marketplace for very small groups and for persons other than employees.

Renewability.   Long-term care policies currently being sold are guaranteed renewable, which means that an individual's coverage cannot be canceled except for nonpayment of premiums. While premiums cannot be raised on the basis of a particular applicant's claim, they can (and often are) raised by class.

Nonforfeiture Options.   Most companies give an applicant for long-term care insurance the right to elect a nonforfeiture benefit, and some states require that such a benefit be offered. With a **nonforfeiture benefit,** the policyowner will receive some value for a policy if the policy lapses because the required premium is not paid in the future. Few applicants, however, elect this option.

The most common type of nonforfeiture option is a shortened benefit period. With this option, coverage is continued as a paid-up policy, but the length of the benefit period (or the amount of the benefit if stated as a maximum dollar amount) is reduced. Under the typical provision, the reduced coverage is available only if the lapse is on or after the policy's third anniversary. The amount of the benefit is equal to the greater of the total premiums paid for the policy prior to lapse or 30 times the policy's daily nursing home benefit.

Portability.   If an insured is no longer eligible for employer-sponsored coverage, he or she can elect to continue coverage. If the insured's coverage is in the form of an individual policy paid through payroll deductions, the insured needs only to make arrangements with the insurer to pay the premium on a direct-bill basis.

If the coverage is under a group policy, the NAIC model regulations require that the insurer provide the insured with a basis for continuation or conversion of coverage. Under a continuation of coverage, the insured retains coverage under the group contract but pays premiums directly to the insurer. Under a conversion of coverage, the insured is issued an individual policy that must be identical or substantially equivalent to the group coverage. The premium for the converted policy is based on the rates for the individual policy at the insured's attained age when the original group coverage was obtained.

■ GROUP LEGAL EXPENSE PLANS

Legal expense plans, which cover the legal expenses of employees, have been a common benefit in several European countries for many years. However, until the mid-1970s, the concept was not widely used in the United States. The plans that did exist were almost always established by unions and were financed from general union funds. Usually, attorneys who were employed by the unions provided the legal services, and the only services covered were those limited to job-related difficulties, such as suspensions or workers' compensation disputes.

Over the last 25 years, the number of employees has continued to grow. This growth, however, has been modest, primarily due to the fact that legal expense benefits cannot be offered to employees on a tax-favored basis. Despite this fact, it is estimated that about 25 percent of employers make some type of plan available to at least some of their employees.[6]

Types of Plans

The types of group legal expense plans vary significantly in the ways they provide legal services. When an employer or a negotiated trusteeship for union employees establishes a group legal expense plan, benefits can be self-funded or purchased from another organization. These other organizations include state bar associations, groups of attorneys, or other organizations (either profit or nonprofit) formed for this purpose. However, most group legal expense coverage is purchased from a relatively small number of organizations, several of which have recently affiliated with insurance companies.

Existing plans fall into one of three types of arrangements:

1. Referral and discount plans
2. Access plans
3. Comprehensive plans

Referral and Discount Plans.   The most basic form of legal expense plan is a **referral and discount plan**. Plan members are referred to an attorney who provides services based on a fee schedule or at a discount from his or her usual fees, but the plan member pays the attorney's charges. In some cases, plan members may be eligible to be referred to attorneys who provide free services, such as a clinic for low-income persons or an attorney hot line of a local bar association.

Access Plans.   This form of legal expense plan, sometimes also called a **telephone access plan**, provides plan members with unlimited legal consultation over the telephone for most legal matters. The plan may also provide simple legal services, such as the preparation of wills or powers of attorney or the review of legal documents.

Plan members are referred to an attorney for more complex legal matters. The attorney will often provide a free initial consultation (usually either one-half or one hour), after which the attorney will bill at some discount (often 25 percent) from normal fees. A plan member is responsible for paying this discounted fee.

Access plans can often be provided for $5 to $10 per month per member.

Comprehensive Plans.   Most legal expense plans can be categorized as comprehensive plans, and premiums usually fall in the range of $10 to $25 per month per member, depending on the level of services provided. This type of plan is increasingly being referred to as a **legal HMO**.

In addition to telephone consultation, comprehensive plans cover in-office and trial work of attorneys. The term *comprehensive* may be a slight misnomer because most plans are not designed to cover 100 percent of a member's potential legal services; 80 to 90 percent is probably a better figure.

Comprehensive plans usually contain a list of covered services. Although there are significant variations among plans, most cover at least the following:

- Unlimited legal advice by telephone
- Document review and preparation
- Name changes
- Adoptions
- Purchase or sale of primary residences
- Eviction defense
- Civil actions
- Driver's license suspension
- Juvenile court proceedings
- Consumer protection
- Bankruptcy
- IRS audits
- Debt collection
- Child custody and support
- Divorce, but possibly only for the covered employee and not dependents

If a particular legal service that is required is not on the list of covered services, there may be some limited coverage as long as the service is not otherwise excluded. This limited service, for example, may be in the form of telephone consultation or a limited amount of work by the attorney, such as two to four hours per family per year. Additional services may be available at discounted rates.

Legal expense plans have exclusions, and common exclusions include the following:

- Business activities or transactions
- Preparation of tax returns
- Class-action suits
- Actions involving the legal expense plan
- Actions involving the employer
- Actions involving the union that bargained for the coverage
- Cases that have contingent fees

Comprehensive plans take three approaches to the method by which a plan member may select an attorney. Many plans use a closed-panel approach, under which a panel of attorneys has agreed to provide covered services at a predetermined fee or hourly rate for which they bill the plan. The plan member selects the attorney, and benefits are generally available at little or no additional cost. However, plans may limit some benefits to a scheduled maximum (such as $500) and usage limitation (such as four hours). A few plans also have deductibles and copayments.

Other plans are open-panel. A plan member can choose any licensed attorney; however, benefits are usually subject to scheduled dollar maximums.

Many plans are modified-panel plans. Under such plans, a plan member may choose either a panel attorney as in a closed-panel plan or select his or her own attorney. The election of a panel attorney often results in benefits being paid in full, and the election of a nonpanel attorney results in the use of benefit maximums.

Current Tax Treatment

The cost of a legal expense plan is deductible for the employer. Employees, however, have taxable income to the extent of employer payments. If the plan is prefunded, the employee is taxed on his or her share of the premium paid and benefits are received tax free. If a plan is self-funded by the employer, the employee's taxable income is the value of the benefits paid by the plan.

■ GROUP PROPERTY AND LIABILITY INSURANCE

In the mid-1960s, it was thought that property and liability insurance, especially automobile insurance, would be the next major employee benefit. However, by the late 1970s, most of the insurance companies that had entered this market were no longer willing to write property and liability coverage as an employee benefit. In fact, many began to dismiss this benefit as an idea whose time might never come. The current status of property and liability insurance as an employee benefit is that for several years it has been offered by a few large employers. Only a small percentage of personal property and liability insurance is provided as the result of an employer-arranged plan. Estimates, however, indicate that plans that offer automobile insurance are provided by about 15 percent of employers.[7]

Reasons for Slow Growth

The slow growth of group property and liability plans can be traced to several factors, namely unfavorable tax treatment, a low potential for cost savings, a lack of employer enthusiasm, and regulatory restrictions.

Unfavorable Tax Treatment. The Internal Revenue Code specifically exempts employer contributions for certain employee benefits from inclusion in employees' taxable income. This exemption does not apply to property and liability insurance. Although the employer is allowed an income tax deduction, employees must report as taxable income any contributions made in their behalf for property and liability coverage. Note, however, that the portion of any premium that applies to medical or no-fault benefits is treated as health insurance and is not included in income.

In general, employers, unions, and employees prefer that employer dollars be used to provide nontaxable benefits. Therefore, without employer contributions, it is often difficult to offer employees property and liability insurance at a substantial enough saving to encourage significant participation.

Lower Potential for Cost Savings. The potential for savings under group property and liability insurance plans is typically less than it is under group insurance plans that provide life insurance, disability income, or medical expense benefits. Under these latter plans, there is a substantial reduction in agents' commissions when compared with commissions received on individual coverage. Such savings do not occur in property and liability insurance because commission scales for individual insurance are lower as a percentage of premium. The main reason for this lower scale is that a less intense marketing effort is required by agents because consumers are more likely to seek out property and liability coverage on their own, rather than be solicited by agents. Therefore, a higher portion of commissions are for services that are performed for the client, rather than for the agents' marketing efforts. These services (for example, financial responsibility filings, automobile changes, and certificates of insurance for mortgagees) must still be performed for coverage that is provided on a group basis.

A second source of savings under most types of group insurance coverage results from the reduction or elimination of individual underwriting, which, together with other savings, more than offsets the cost of covering poor risks at group rates. However, this is not the case in property and liability insurance, particularly in automobile insurance. Not only are savings lower, but there are proportionately many more substandard drivers who must pay surcharged premiums in the individual property and liability insurance marketplace than there are persons with poor health in the individual life and health insurance marketplace. The lack of individual underwriting in property and liability insurance usually means that the average rate for the group members is higher than some persons would pay in the individual marketplace. Consequently, to avoid getting only the poor risks, group property and liability insurance plans generally use individual—but possibly liberalized—underwriting. As a result, poorer risks are charged a higher premium or are ineligible for coverage in some cases.

Under the most successful group property and liability plans, savings have averaged only between 5 and 15 percent when compared with the same insurance company's rates for individual coverage. However, property and liability rates vary widely among insurance companies, and this group rate may still be higher than what many employees are paying for their individual coverage. Without a significant cost advantage, there is little incentive for an employee to switch to a group property and liability plan, except perhaps for the simplicity of paying premiums on a payroll-deduction basis. This is particularly true when the employee has an established relationship with his or her current property and liability insurance company or agent. Consequently, it may be difficult to enroll the minimum percentage (usually 30 or more) of employees required by the insurance company.

Lack of Employer Enthusiasm. In addition to the unfavorable tax treatment of employer contributions to the employee, many employers feel that group property and liability plans will place a strain on their relationship with employees. Although the magnitude of the problem varies among employers that offer group property and liability plans, it is an undisputed fact that dissatisfaction with the plan and the employer does occur when employees (1) are ineligible for coverage because of underwriting considerations, (2) find the coverage more expensive than their current individual coverage, or (3) have disputes over claims. In spite of this dissatisfaction, however, some employers view property and liability insurance as a desirable benefit because of high visibility.

Regulatory Restrictions. Once common in almost all states, some type of regulation or statute that hinders the marketing of group property and liability insurance still exists in several states. These **fictitious group insurance statutes**, or similar regulations, prohibit the grouping of individual risks in order to give them favorable treatment in underwriting, coverage, or rates, with the possible exception of rate reductions that are the result of savings in expenses. In effect, what is done for group life insurance, medical expense, and disability coverages cannot be done for property and liability insurance. These laws apply only to true group insurance products; voluntary plans are not affected. In addition, the laws of some states effectively prohibit true group insurance products because there is no specific statute that allows these products to be written.

Many states also have regulations that prohibit any person who is not a licensed insurance agent from advising in the sale of property and liability insurance. This prevents the employer from performing any other functions besides those of a purely administrative nature, such as accepting applications or deducting premiums from payroll.

Federal regulatory restrictions are another reason for lack of union interest, because the Federal Labor Code prohibits a negotiated trusteeship from providing property and liability coverage. However, the benefit can still be bargained for and provided under a plan established by the employer.

Types of Plans

Most employer-provided property and liability insurance plans are not true group insurance but are voluntary plans of individual insurance. The cost of these plans is usually borne entirely by the participating employees and paid by payroll deduction. Besides handling the payroll deductions, the employer has little, if any, responsibility for plan administration. Representatives of the insurance company solicit employees, usually by mail or telephone. Some insurance companies may actually have agents on or near the employer's premises, but most insurance companies give group members toll-free numbers to contact their representatives.

Voluntary property and liability insurance plans are usually not experience rated but are offered at a slight discount because of the administrative savings associated with mass marketing. Premiums for employees vary because they are based on the same factors as individual property and liability insurance (such as age, driving record, or value of the home), which also means that some employees may be ineligible for coverage. Most plans offer automobile insurance, and a few also offer other coverages, such as homeowners' insurance and umbrella liability insurance. Employees usually have the same choices regarding the amount and type of coverage that they would have in the individual marketplace, and the contracts offered are usually identical. However, modifications that attempt to decrease the cost of the payroll deduction coverage are sometimes made. These include larger deductibles and provisions in the automobile insurance policy that eliminate coverage for medical expenses to the extent that they are paid under the employer's medical expense plan.

A few companies offer property and liability insurance on a true group basis and use both a master contract and experience rating for the group. All employees are usually eligible. The coverages offered to the employees are usually the same as those offered under voluntary plans, but the rating structure tends to be less refined, particularly for automobile insurance. Instead of having several dozen classifications that are based on such factors as age, gender, and driving record, there may only be three or four classifications based solely on driving record. In virtually all cases when true group property and liability plans are made available, the insurance company insists on employer contributions of between 25 and 50 percent of the cost of the coverage and on participation by a large percentage of employees, possibly as high as 75 percent.

■ KEY TERMS

activities of daily living
  (ADLs)
adult day care
alternative plan of care
assisted-living care
bed reservation benefit
care coordination
chronically ill individual
comprehensive long-term
  care insurance policy
continuing-care retirement
  community (CCRC)
custodial care
Delta Dental Plans
dental health maintenance
  organization (DHMO)

dental insurance
direct reimbursement
disability-based policy
discount plan
facility-only policy
fictitious group insurance
  statutes
home health care
  only policy
intermediate care
legal HMO
long-term care insurance
nonforfeiture benefit
nursing home care
per diem basis

pool of money
predetermination-of-benefits
  provision
qualified long-term care
  insurance contract
qualified long-term care
  services
referral and discount plan
reimbursement basis
respite care
shared benefit
skilled care
telephone access plan

■ STUDY QUESTIONS

1. What types of limitations are often imposed upon benefits for a person enrolling in a dental insurance plan after his or her initial eligibility period has ended?

2. Why are dental insurance plans more likely than medical expense plans to include benefits for routine examinations and preventive medicine?

3. Describe the exclusions and limitations often contained in dental expense plans to control claims costs and to eliminate unnecessary dental treatment.

4. a. What factors result in the need for long-term care insurance?

   b. What are the reasons for the cautious growth of group long-term care insurance?

5. What sources other than long-term care insurance coverage are available to meet the need for long-term care?

6. Describe the broad categories of care for which benefits might be provided by a long-term care insurance policy.

7. Compare facility-only policies, home health care only policies, and comprehensive long-term care insurance policies.

8. What are the usual criteria to receive benefits under a tax-qualified long-term care insurance policy?

9. a. What types of legal services are covered under most comprehensive legal expense plans?

   b. What are the common exclusions?

   c. What are the approaches by which a plan member may be able to select an attorney?

10. What is the current tax treatment of group legal expense plans?

11. Explain the reasons for the slow growth of group property and liability insurance.

12. Describe the types of plans that may be used to provide group property and liability insurance.

■ NOTES

1. National Association of Dental Plans, *Background on Dental Benefits*, 2003.

2. LIMRA International, Inc., *U.S. Group Long-Term Care Insurance Sales, 2003*.

3. American Council of Life Insurance, *What Long-Term Care Insurance Can Do for You/Tips on Buying Long-Term Care Insurance, 1997*.

4. Congressional Budget Office, *Projected Long-Term Care Expenditures for the Elderly*.

5. American Council of Life Insurance, *Can Aging Baby Boomers Avoid the Nursing Home?*, 2003.

6. Society for Human Resource Management, *2003 Benefits Survey*, p. 26.

7. Ibid., p. 39.

16 Alternative Funding Methods

- Explain the reasons why employers may use alternative funding methods.
- Describe the characteristics and appropriateness of modifications to traditional funding methods for group insurance arrangements.
- Describe the characteristics and appropriateness of the methods for self-funding group benefits.

CHAPTER OUTLINE

Reasons for Alternative Funding
    Cost Savings
    Improved Cash Flow
Methods of Alternative Funding
    Premium-Delay Arrangements
    Reserve-Reduction Arrangements
    Minimum-Premium Plans

Cost-Plus Arrangements
Retrospective-Rating Arrangements
Total Self-Funding and Self-
    Administration
Self-Funding with Stop-Loss Coverage
    and/or ASO Arrangements
Funding Through a 501(c)(9) Trust

In recent years, employers have increasingly considered—and often adopted—benefit funding methods that are alternatives to the traditional fully insured group insurance contract. Under the traditional group insurance contract, the employer pays premiums in advance to the insurance company, which then has the financial responsibility both for paying claims (if and when they occur) and for assuming the administrative expenses associated with the contract. In addition, the insurance company bears the risk that claims will be larger than anticipated.

■ REASONS FOR ALTERNATIVE FUNDING

The increasing interest in alternatives to the traditional fully insured group arrangement has focused on two factors: cost savings and improved cash flow. To a large extent, this interest has grown in response to the rising cost of medical care that has resulted in an increase in the cost of providing medical expense benefits. Even though alternative funding methods are most commonly used for providing medical expense benefits, many of the methods described here are also appropriate for other types of benefits.

Cost Savings

Savings can result to the extent that either claims or the insurance company's retention can be reduced. Retention—the portion of the insurance company's premium over and above the incurred claims and dividends—includes such items as commissions, premium taxes, risk charges, and profit. Traditionally, alternative funding methods have not focused on reducing claims because the same benefits are normally provided (and therefore the same claims are paid) regardless of which funding method is used. However, this focus has changed as state laws and regulations increasingly mandate the types and levels of benefits that must be contained in medical expense contracts. To the extent that these laws and regulations apply only to benefits that are included in insurance contracts, employers can avoid providing these mandated benefits by using alternative funding methods that do not involve insurance contracts. Federal mandates apply to benefit plans, not just insurance contracts, and cannot be avoided by self-funding.

Modifications of fully insured contracts are usually designed either to lower or eliminate premium taxes or to reduce the insurance company's risk and consequently the risk charge. Alternative funding methods that involve a degree of self-funding also may be designed to reduce other aspects of retention and to reduce claims by excluding mandated benefits.

Improved Cash Flow

Under a fully insured contract, an employer has the ability to improve cash flow because premiums are collected before the funds are actually needed to pay claims. The employer is generally credited with interest while these funds are held in reserves. Alternative funding arrangements that are intended to improve cash flow are designed either to postpone the payment of premiums to the insurance company or to keep the funds that would otherwise be held in reserves in the employer's hands until the insurance company needs them. Such an arrangement is particularly advantageous to the employer when the employer can invest these funds at a rate of return that is higher than the interest rate credited by the insurance company to reserves. It must be remembered, however, that earnings on funds invested by the employer are generally subject to income taxation, but interest credited to reserves by the insurance company is tax free.

■ METHODS OF ALTERNATIVE FUNDING

Totally self-funded (or self-insured) employee benefit plans are the opposite of traditional fully insured group insurance plans. Under totally self-funded plans, the employer is responsible for paying claims, administering the plan, and bearing the risk that actual claims will exceed those expected. However, very few employee benefit plans that use alternative methods of funding have actually turned to total self-funding. Rather, the methods used typically fall somewhere between the two extremes.

The methods of alternative funding can be divided into two general categories: those that primarily modify traditional fully insured group insurance contracts and those that have some self-funding (either partial or total). The first category includes the following:

■ Premium-delay arrangements

■ Reserve-reduction arrangements

■ Minimum-premium plans

■   Cost-plus arrangements

■   Retrospective-rating arrangements

These alternative funding methods are regarded as modifications of traditional fully insured plans because the insurance company has the ultimate responsibility for paying all benefits promised under the contract. Although practices differ among insurance companies, generally a group insurance plan must generate between $150,000 and $250,000 in claims or have a minimum number of covered persons, such as 50 or 100, before these funding methods are available to the employer.

The second category of alternative funding methods includes the following:

■   Total self-funding from current revenue and self-administration

■   Self-funding with stop-loss coverage and/or administrative-services-only arrangements

■   Funding through a 501(c)(9) trust

In contrast to the first category of alternative funding methods, small employers can use some of these alternatives.

Premium-Delay Arrangements

A **premium-delay arrangement** allows the employer to defer payment of monthly premiums for some time beyond the usual 30-day grace period. In fact, this arrangement lengthens the grace period, most commonly by 60 or 90 days. The practical effect of a premium-delay arrangement is that it enables the employer to have continuous use of the portion of the annual premium that is approximately equal to the claim reserve. For example, a 90-day premium delay allows the employer to use three months (or 25 percent) of the annual premium for other purposes. This amount roughly corresponds to what is usually in the claim reserve for medical expense coverage. Generally, the larger this reserve is on a percentage basis, the longer the premium payment can be delayed. Because the insurance company still has a statutory obligation to maintain the claim reserve, it must use other assets besides the employer's premiums for this purpose. In most cases, these assets come from the insurance company's surplus.

A premium-delay arrangement has a financial advantage to the extent that an employer can earn a higher return by investing the delayed premiums than by accruing interest on the claim reserve. In actual practice, interest is still credited to the reserve, but an interest charge on the delayed premiums or an increase in the insurance company's retention offsets the credit.

On termination of an insurance contract with a premium-delay arrangement, the employer is responsible for paying any deferred premiums. However, the insurance company is legally responsible for paying all claims incurred prior to termination, even if the employer fails to pay the deferred premiums. Consequently, most insurance companies are concerned about the employer's financial position and credit rating. For many insurance companies, the final decision of whether to enter into a premium-delay arrangement, or any other alternative funding arrangement that leaves funds in the hands of the employer, is made by the insurer's financial experts after a thorough analysis of the employer. In some cases, this may mean that the employer will be required to submit a letter of credit or some other form of security.

Reserve-Reduction Arrangements

A **reserve-reduction arrangement** is similar to a premium-delay arrangement. Under the usual reserve-reduction arrangement, the employer is allowed (at any given time) to retain an amount of the annual premium that is equal to the claim reserve. Generally, such an arrangement is allowed only after the contract's first year, when the pattern of claims and the appropriate amount of the reserve can be more accurately estimated. In succeeding years, if the contract is renewed, the amount retained will be adjusted according to changes in the size of the reserve. As with a premium-delay arrangement, the monies retained by the employer must be paid to the insurance company on termination of the contract. Again, the advantage of this approach lies in the employer's ability to earn more on these funds than it would earn under the traditional insurance arrangement.

A few insurance companies offer another type of reserve-reduction arrangement for long-term disability income coverage. Under a so-called **limited-liability arrangement,** the employer purchases from the insurance company a one-year contract in which the insurer agrees to pay claims only for that year, even though the employer's "plan" provides benefits to employees for longer periods. Consequently, enough reserves are maintained by the insurance company to pay benefits only for the duration of the one-year contract. At renewal, the insurance company agrees to continue paying the existing claims as well as any new claims. In effect, the employer pays the insurance company each year for existing claims as the benefits are paid to employees, rather than when disabilities occur. A problem for employees under this type of arrangement is the lack of security for future benefits. For example, if the employer goes bankrupt and the insurance contract is not renewed, the insurance company has no responsibility to continue benefit payments. For this reason, several states do not allow this type of arrangement.

The limited-liability arrangement contrasts with the usual group contract in which the insurance company is responsible for paying disability income claims to an employee for the length of the benefit period (as long as the employee remains disabled). On average, each disability claim results in the establishment of a reserve equal to approximately five times the employee's annual benefit.

Minimum-Premium Plans

A **minimum-premium plan** is designed primarily to reduce state premium taxes. However, many minimum-premium plans also improve the employer's cash flow.

Under the typical minimum-premium plan (sometimes called *limited self-funding*), the employer assumes the financial responsibility for paying claims up to a specified level, usually from 80 to 95 percent of estimated claims (with 90 percent most common). The specified level may be determined on either a monthly or an annual basis. The funds necessary to pay these claims are deposited into a bank account that belongs to the employer. However, the actual payment of claims is made from this account by the insurance company, which acts as an agent of the employer. When claims exceed the specified level, the balance is paid from the insurance company's own funds. No premium tax is levied by the states on the amounts the employer deposits into such an account, as it would have been if these deposits had been paid directly to the insurance company. In effect, for premium-tax purposes, the insurance company is considered to be only the administrator of these funds and not a provider of insurance. Unfortunately, the IRS considers these funds to belong to the employer, and death benefits represent taxable income to beneficiaries. Consequently, minimum-premium plans are used to insure disability income and medical expense benefits rather than life insurance benefits.

Under a minimum-premium plan, the employer pays a substantially reduced premium, subject to premium taxation, to the insurance company for administering the entire plan and for bearing the cost of claims above the specified level. Because such a plan may be slightly more burdensome for an insurance company to administer than would a traditional group arrangement, the retention charge may also be slightly higher. Under a minimum-premium arrangement, the insurance company is ultimately responsible for seeing that all claims are paid, and it must maintain the same reserves that would have been required if the plan had been funded under a traditional group insurance arrangement. Consequently, the premium includes a charge for the establishment of these reserves, unless some type of reserve-reduction arrangement is also negotiated.

Some insurance regulatory officials view the minimum-premium plan primarily as a loophole used by employers to avoid paying premium taxes. In several states, there have been attempts to seek court rulings or legislation that would require that premium taxes be paid either on the funds deposited in the bank account or on claims paid from these funds. Most of these attempts have been unsuccessful, but court rulings in California require that the employer pay premium taxes on the funds deposited in the bank account. If similar attempts are successful in the future, the main advantage of minimum-premium plans will be lost.

Cost-Plus Arrangements

A **cost-plus arrangement** (often referred to by other names, such as *flexible funding*) may be used to fund other types of employee benefits, but large employers generally use this to provide life insurance benefits. Under such an arrangement, the employer's monthly premium is based on the claims paid by the insurance company during the preceding month, plus a specified retention charge that is uniform throughout the policy period. To the extent that an employer's loss experience is less than that assumed in a traditional premium arrangement, the employer's cash flow is improved. However, an employer with worse-than-expected experience, either during the early part of the policy period or during the entire policy period, could also have a more unfavorable cash flow than if a traditional insurance arrangement were used. To prevent this from occurring, many insurance companies place a maximum limit on the employer's monthly premium. The effect of this limit is that the aggregate monthly premiums paid at any time during the policy period do not exceed the aggregate monthly premiums that would have been paid if the cost-plus arrangement had not been used.

Retrospective-Rating Arrangements

Under a **retrospective-rating arrangement,** the insurance company charges the employer an initial premium that is less than what would be justified by the expected claims for the year. In general, this reduction is between 5 and 10 percent of the premium for a traditional group insurance arrangement. However, if claims plus the insurance company's retention exceed the initial premium, the employer is called upon to pay an additional amount at the end of the policy year. Because an employer will usually have to pay this additional premium, one advantage of a retrospective-rating arrangement is the employer's ability to use these funds during the year.

This potential additional premium is subject to a maximum amount based on some percentage of expected claims. For example, assume that a retrospective-rating arrangement bases the initial premium on the fact that claims will be 93 percent of those actually expected for the year. If claims in fact are below this level, the employer receives an experience refund. If they exceed 93 percent, the retrospective-rating arrangement is "triggered," and the employer has to reimburse the insurance company for any additional claims paid, up to some percentage of those expected, such as 112 percent. The insurance company bears claims in excess of 112 percent, so some of the risk associated with claims fluctuations is passed on to the employer. This reduces both the insurance company's risk charge and any reserve for claims fluctuations. The amount of these reductions depends on the actual percentage specified in the contract, above which the insurance company is responsible for claims. This percentage and the one that triggers the retrospective-rating arrangement are subject to negotiations between the insurance company and the employer. In general, the lower the percentage that triggers the retrospective arrangement, the higher the percentage above which the insurance company is fully responsible for claims. In addition, the better the cash-flow advantage of the employer, the greater the risk of claims fluctuations.

In all other respects, a retrospective-rating arrangement is identical to the traditional group insurance contract.

Total Self-Funding and Self-Administration

The purest form of a self-funded benefit plan is one in which the employer pays benefits from current revenue (rather than from a trust), administers all aspects of the plan, and bears the risk that benefit payments will exceed those expected. In addition to eliminating state premium taxes, avoiding state-mandated benefits, and improving cash flow, the employer has the potential to reduce its operating expenses to the extent that the plan can be administered at a lower cost than the insurance company's retention (other than premium taxes). A decision to use this kind of self-funding plan is generally considered most desirable when all of the following conditions are present:

■ Predictable claims. Budgeting is an integral part of the operation of any organization, and it is necessary to budget for benefit payments that will need to be paid in the future. This can best be done when a specific type of benefit plan has a claim pattern that is either stable or shows a steady trend. Such a pattern is most likely to occur in those types of benefit plans that have a relatively high frequency of low-severity claims. Although a self-funded plan may still be appropriate when the level of future benefit payments is difficult to predict, the plan will generally be designed to include stop-loss coverage (discussed later in this chapter).

■ A noncontributory plan. Several difficulties arise if a self-funded benefit plan is contributory. Some employees may resent paying "their" money to the employer for benefits that are contingent on the firm's future financial ability to pay claims. If claims are denied, employees under a contributory plan are more likely to be bitter toward the employer than they would be if the benefit plan were noncontributory. Finally, ERISA requires that a trust must be established to hold employee contributions until the plan uses the funds. Both the establishment and maintenance of the trust result in increased administrative costs to the employer.

■ A nonunion situation. Self-funding of benefits for union employees may not be feasible if a firm is subject to collective bargaining. Self-funding (at least by the employer) clearly cannot be used if benefits are provided through a negotiated trusteeship. Even when collective bargaining results in benefits being provided through an individual employer plan, unions often insist that benefits be insured to guarantee that union members actually receive them. An employer's decision about whether to use self-funding is most likely motivated by the potential to save money. When unions approve of self-funding, they also frequently insist that some of these savings be passed on to union members through additional or increased benefits.

■ The ability to effectively and efficiently handle claims. One reason that many employers do not use totally self-funded and self-administered benefit plans is the difficulty in handling claims as efficiently and effectively as an insurance company or other benefit-plan administrator would handle them. Unless an employer is extremely large, only one person or a few persons are needed to handle claims. Who in the organization can properly train and supervise these people? Can they be replaced if they should leave? Will anyone have the expertise to properly handle the unusual or complex claims that might occur? Many employers want some insulation from their employees in the handling of claims. If employees are unhappy with claim payments under a self-administered plan, dissatisfaction (and possibly legal actions) is directed toward the employer rather than toward the insurance company. The employer's inability to handle claims, or its lack of interest in wanting to handle them, does not completely rule out the use of self-funding. As discussed later, employers can have claims handled by another party through an administrative-services-only contract.

■ The ability to provide other administrative services. In addition to claims, the employer must determine whether the other administrative services normally included in an insured arrangement can be provided in a cost-effective manner. These services are associated with plan design, actuarial calculations, statistical reports, communication with employees, compliance with government regulations, and the preparation of government reports. Many of these costs are relatively fixed, regardless of the size of the employer, and unless the employer can spread them out over a large number of employees, self-administration is not economically feasible. As with claims administration, an employer can purchase needed services from other sources.

■ The ability to obtain discounts from medical care providers if medical expense benefits are self-funded. To obtain much of the cost savings associated with managed care plans, the employer must be able to secure discounts from the providers of medical care. Large employers whose employees live in a relatively concentrated geographic region may be able to enter into contracts with local providers. Other employers often use the services of third-party administrators who have either entered into contracts with managed care plans to use their networks or possibly established their own networks.

The extent of total self-funding and self-administration differs significantly among the different types of group benefit plans. Plans that provide life insurance or accidental death and dismemberment benefits do not usually lend themselves to self-funding because of infrequent and large claims that are difficult to predict. Only very large employers can expect stable and predictable claims on an annual basis. In addition, federal income tax laws impede the use of self-funding for death benefits because any payments to beneficiaries are considered taxable income to the beneficiaries. Such a limitation does not exist if the plan is insured.

The most widespread use of self-funding and self-administration occurs in short-term disability income plans, particularly those that limit the maximum duration of benefits to six months or less. For employers of almost any size, the number and average length of short-term absences from work are relatively predictable. In addition, the payment of claims is fairly simple because benefits can be (and usually are) made through the employer's usual payroll system.

Long-term disability income benefits are occasionally self-funded by large employers. Like death claims, long-term disability income claims are difficult to predict for small employers because of their infrequent occurrence and potentially large size. In addition, because small employers receive only a few claims of this type, it becomes economically unjustifiable to self-administer such claims.

The larger the employer is, the more likely that its medical expense plan is self-funded. In fact, statistics indicate that about two-thirds of employers with 500 or more employees self-fund their traditional indemnity plans and PPOs. About half of point-of-service plans are also self-funded. However, self-funding is only used with fewer than 15 percent of HMO plans.

The major problem with a self-funded medical expense plan is not the prediction of claims frequency but rather the prediction of the average severity of claims. Although infrequent, claims of $500,000, $1,000,000, or more do occasionally occur. Most small- and medium-sized employers are unwilling to assume the risk that they might have to pay such a large claim. Only employers with several thousand employees are large enough to anticipate that such claims will regularly occur and to have the resources necessary to pay any unexpectedly large claims. This does not mean that smaller employers cannot self-fund medical benefits. To avoid the uncertainty of catastrophic claims, these employers often self-fund basic medical expense benefits and insure major medical expense benefits or self-fund their entire coverage but purchase stop-loss protection. Many employers that self-fund, regardless of size, also purchase at least some administrative services.

It is not unusual to use self-funding and self-administration in other types of benefit plans, such as those providing coverage for dental care, vision care, prescription drugs, or legal expenses. Initially, it may be difficult to predict the extent to which these plans will be utilized. However, once the plans have "matured," the level of claims tends to be fairly stable. Furthermore, these plans are commonly subject to maximums so that the employer has little or no risk of catastrophic claims. Although larger employers may be able to economically administer the plans themselves, smaller employers commonly purchase administrative services.

Self-Funding with Stop-Loss Coverage and/or ASO Arrangements

Two of the problems associated with self-funding and self-administration are the risk of catastrophic claims and the employer's inability to provide administrative services in a cost-effective manner. For each of these problems, however, solutions have evolved—namely stop-loss coverage and administrative-services-only (ASO) contracts—that still allow an employer to use elements of self-funding. Although an ASO contract and stop-loss coverage can be provided separately, they are commonly written together. In fact, most insurance companies require an employer with stop-loss coverage to have a self-funded plan administered under an ASO arrangement, either by the insurance company or by a third-party administrator.

Until recently, stop-loss coverage and ASO contracts were generally provided by insurance companies and were available only to employers with at least several hundred employees. However, these arrangements are increasingly becoming available to small employers, and in many cases the administrative services are purchased from third-party administrators who operate independently from insurance companies.

Stop-Loss Coverage. **Aggregate stop-loss coverage** is one form of protection for employers against an unexpectedly high level of claims. If total claims exceed a specified dollar limit, the insurance company assumes the financial responsibility for those claims that are over the limit, subject to the maximum reimbursement specified in the contract. The limit is usually applied on an annual basis and is expressed as some percentage of expected claims (typically between 115 percent and 135 percent). The employer is responsible for the paying of all claims to employees, including any payments that are received from the insurance company under the stop-loss coverage. In fact, because the insurance company has no responsibility to the employees, no reserve for claims must be established.

Aggregate stop-loss coverage results in (1) an improved cash flow for the employer and (2) a minimization of premium taxes because they must be paid only on the stop-loss coverage. However, these advantages are partially (and perhaps totally) offset by the cost of the coverage. In addition, many insurance companies insist that the employer purchase other insurance coverages or administrative services to obtain aggregate stop-loss coverage.

Stop-loss plans may also be written on a "specific" basis, similar to the way an insured plan with a deductible is written. In fact, this **specific stop-loss coverage** (most commonly used with medical expense plans) is sometimes referred to as a *big-deductible plan* or as *shared funding*. The deductible amount may vary from $1,000 to $250,000 but is most commonly in the range of $10,000 to $20,000. It is usually applied on an annual basis and pertains to each person insured under the contract. Although stop-loss coverage was once written primarily for large employers, more recently it has also been written for employers with as few as 25 employees. These plans have particular appeal for small employers who have had better-than-average claims experience but who are too small to qualify for experience rating and the accompanying premium savings.

The deductible specified in the stop-loss coverage is the amount the employer must assume before the stop-loss carrier is responsible for claims and is different from the deductible that an employee must satisfy under the medical expense plan. For example, employees may be given a medical expense plan that has a $200 annual deductible and an 80 percent coinsurance provision. If stop-loss coverage with a $5,000 stop-loss limit has been purchased, an employee assumes the first $200 in annual medical expenses, and the plan will then pay 80 percent of any additional expenses until it has paid a total of $5,000. At that time, the stop-loss carrier reimburses the plan for any additional amounts that the plan must pay to the employee. The stop-loss carrier has no responsibility to pay the employer's share of claims under any circumstances, and most insurance companies require that employees be made aware of this fact.

Misunderstandings often arise over two variations in specific stop-loss contracts. Most contracts settle claims on a *paid* basis, which means that only those claims paid during the stop-loss period under a benefit plan are taken into consideration in determining the liability of the stop-loss carrier. Some stop-loss contracts, however, settle claims on an *incurred* basis. In these cases, the stop-loss carrier's liability is determined on the basis of the date a loss took place rather than when the benefit plan actually made payment. For example, assume an employee was hospitalized last December, but the claim was not paid until this year. This is an incurred claim for last year but a paid claim for this year.

A second variation affects an employer's cash flow. Assume an employer has a medical expense plan with a $20,000 stop-loss limit and that an employee has a claim of $38,000. If the stop-loss contract is written on a *reimbursement* basis, the employer's plan must pay the $38,000 claim before the plan's administrator can submit an $18,000 claim to the stop-loss carrier. If the stop-loss contract is written on an *advance-funding* basis, the employer's plan does not actually have to pay the employee before seeking reimbursement.

Most insurance companies that provide stop-loss coverage for medical expense plans also agree to provide a conversion contract to employees whose coverage terminates. However, the employer must pay an additional monthly charge to have this benefit for employees.

ASO Contracts.   Under an **ASO contract**, the employer purchases specific administrative services from an insurance company or from an independent third-party administrator. These services usually include the administration of claims, but they may also include a broad array of other services, such as COBRA administration, prescription drug cards, employee communications, and government reporting. In effect, the employer has the option to purchase services for those administrative functions that can be handled more cost effectively by another party. It should also be noted that an employer may purchase different administrative services from more than one source. In addition, third-party administrators often subcontract some of the services they provide employers to other administrators that provide specialized services, such as case management and hospital audits.

Under ASO contracts, the administration of claims is performed in much the same way as it is under a minimum-premium plan; that is, the administrator has the authority to pay claims from a bank account that belongs to the employer or from segregated funds in the administrator's hands. However, the administrator is not responsible for paying claims from its own assets if the employer's account is insufficient.

In addition to listing the services that are provided, an ASO contract also stipulates the administrator's authority and responsibility, the length of the contract, the provisions for terminating and amending the contract, and the manner in which disputes between the employer and the administrator are settled. The charges for the services provided under the contract may be stated in one or some combination of the following ways:

- A percentage of the amount of claims paid
- A flat amount per processed claim
- A flat charge per employee
- A flat charge for the employer

Payments for ASO contracts are regarded as fees for services performed, and they are therefore not subject to state premium taxes. However, one similarity to a traditional insurance arrangement may be present: The administrator may agree to continue paying any unsettled claims after the contract's termination but only with funds provided by the employer.

Funding Through a 501(c)(9) Trust

Section 501(c)(9) of the Internal Revenue Code provides for the establishment of *voluntary employees' beneficiary associations* (commonly called **501(c)(9) trusts** or *VEBAs*), which are funding vehicles for the employee benefits that are offered to members. The trusts have been allowed for many years, but until the passage of the 1969 Tax Reform Act, they were primarily used by negotiated trusteeships and association groups. The liberalized tax treatment of the funds accumulated by these trusts resulted in their increased use by employers as a method of self-funding employee benefit plans. However, the Tax Reform Act of 1984 imposed more restrictive provisions on 501(c)(9) trusts, and their use has diminished somewhat, particularly by smaller employers who previously had overfunded their trusts primarily as a method to shelter income from taxation.

Advantages. The use of a 501(c)(9) trust offers the employer some advantages over a benefit plan that is self-funded from current revenue. Contributions can be made to the trust and can be deducted for federal income tax purposes at that time, just as if the trust were an insurance company. Appreciation in the value of the trust assets or investment income earned on the trust assets is also free of taxation. The trust is best suited for an employer who wishes to establish either a fund for claims that have been incurred but not paid or a fund for possible claims fluctuations. If the employer does not use a 501(c)(9) trust in establishing these funds, contributions cannot be deducted by the employer for federal income tax purposes until they are paid in the form of benefits to employees. In addition, earnings on the funds are subject to taxation.

The Internal Revenue Code requires that certain fiduciary standards be maintained regarding the investment of the trust assets. The employer, however, does have some latitude and does have the potential for earning a return on the trust assets that is higher than what is earned on the reserves held by insurance companies. A 501(c)(9) trust also lends itself to use by a contributory self-funded plan because ERISA requires that, under a self-funded benefit plan, a trust must be established to hold employees' contributions until they are used to pay benefits.

There is also flexibility regarding contributions to the trust. Although the Internal Revenue Service does not permit a tax deduction for "overfunding" a trust, there is no requirement that the trust must maintain enough assets to pay claims that have been incurred but not yet paid. Consequently, an employer can "underfund" the trust in bad times and make up for this underfunding in good times with larger-than-normal contributions. However, any underfunding must be shown as a contingent liability on the employer's balance sheet.

Disadvantages. A 501(c)(9) also has its drawbacks. The cost of establishing and maintaining the trust may be prohibitive, especially for small employers. In addition, the employer must be concerned about the administrative aspects of the plan and the fact that claims might deplete the trust's assets. However, as long as the trust is properly funded, ASO contracts and stop-loss coverage can be purchased.

Requirements for Establishment. To qualify under Section 501(c)(9), a trust must meet certain requirements—some of which may hinder its establishment—including the following:

- Membership in the trust must be objectively restricted to those persons who share a common employment-related bond. Internal Revenue Service regulations interpret this broadly to include active employees and their dependents, surviving dependents, and employees who are retired, laid off, or disabled. Except for plans maintained pursuant to collective-bargaining agreements, benefits must be provided under a classification of employees that the IRS does not find to be discriminatory in favor of highly compensated individuals. It is permissible for life insurance, disability, severance pay, and supplemental unemployment compensation benefits to be based on a uniform percentage of compensation. In addition, the following persons may be excluded in determining whether the discrimination rule has been satisfied: (1) employees who have not completed three years of service, (2) employees under age 21, (3) seasonal or less-than-half-time employees, and (4) employees covered by a collective-bargaining agreement if the class of benefits was subject to good-faith bargaining.

■ With two exceptions, membership in the trust must be voluntary on the part of employees. Members can be required to participate (1) as a result of collective bargaining or (2) when participation is not detrimental to them. In general, participation is not regarded as detrimental if the employee is not required to make any contributions.

■ The trust must provide only eligible benefits. The list of eligible coverages is broad enough that a trust can provide benefits because of death, medical expenses, disability, and unemployment. Retirement benefits, deferred compensation, and group property and liability insurance cannot be provided.

■ The sole purpose of the trust must be to provide benefits to its members or their beneficiaries. Trust assets can be used to pay the administrative expenses of the trust, but they cannot revert to the employer. If the trust is terminated, any assets that remain after all existing liabilities have been satisfied must either be used to provide other benefits or be distributed to members of the trust.

■ The trust must be controlled by (1) its membership, (2) independent trustees (such as a bank), or (3) trustees or other fiduciaries, at least some of whom are designated by or on behalf of the members. Independent trustees selected by the employer control most 501(c)(9) trusts.

Limitation on Contributions.   The contributions to a 501(c)(9) trust (except collectively bargained plans for which Treasury regulations prescribe separate rules) are limited to the sum of (1) the qualified direct cost of the benefits provided for the taxable year and (2) any permissible additions to a reserve (called a *qualified asset account*). The qualified direct cost of benefits is the amount that would have been deductible for the year if the employer had paid benefits from current revenue.

The permissible additions may be made only for disability, medical, supplemental unemployment, severance pay, and life insurance benefits. In general, the amount of the permissible additions includes (1) any sums that are reasonably and actuarially necessary to pay claims that have been incurred but remain unpaid at the close of the tax year and (2) any administration costs with respect to these claims. If medical or life insurance benefits are provided to retirees, deductions are also allowed for funding these benefits on a level basis over the working lives of the covered employees. However, for retirees' medical benefits, current medical costs must be used rather than costs based on projected inflation. In addition, a separate account must be established for postretirement benefits provided to key employees. Contributions to these accounts are treated as annual additions for purposes of applying the limitations that exist for contributions and benefits under qualified retirement plans.

The amount of certain benefits for which deductions are allowed is limited. Life insurance benefits for retired employees cannot exceed amounts that are tax free under Section 79. Annual disability benefits cannot exceed the lesser of (1) 75 percent of a disabled person's average compensation for the highest three years or (2) $165,000. Supplemental unemployment compensation benefits and severance benefits cannot exceed 75 percent of average benefits paid plus administrative costs during any two of the immediately preceding seven years. In determining this limit, annual benefits in excess of $60,000 cannot be taken into account. (The $165,000 and $62,250 amounts are for 2004 and subject to periodic indexing.)

In general, it is required that the amount of any permissible additions be actuarially certified, although deductible contributions can be made to reserves without such certification as long as certain specified limits on the size of the reserve are not exceeded. The specified limits for supplemental unemployment compensation benefits and severance benefits are the same as the amounts previously mentioned. For short-term disability benefits, the limit is equal to 17.5 percent of benefit costs (other than insurance premiums for the current year), plus administrative costs for the previous year. For medical benefits, the limit is 35 percent. The Internal Revenue Code provides that the limits for life insurance benefits and long-term disability income benefits will be those prescribed by regulations. However, no regulations have been issued.

Employer deductions cannot exceed the limits as previously described. However, any excess contributions may be deducted in future years to the extent that contributions for those years are below the permissible limits.

There are several potential adverse tax consequences if a 501(c)(9) trust does not meet prescribed standards. If reserves are above permitted levels, additional contributions to the reserves are not deductible and earnings on the excess reserves are subject to tax as unrelated business income. (This effectively negates any possible advantage of using a 501(c)(9) trust to prefund postretirement medical benefits.) In addition, an excise tax is imposed on employers maintaining a trust that provides disqualified benefits. The tax is equal to 100 percent of the disqualified benefits, which include (1) medical and life insurance benefits provided to key employees outside the separate accounts that must be established, (2) discriminatory medical or life insurance benefits for retirees, and (3) any portion of the trust's assets that revert to the employer.

■ KEY TERMS

aggregate stop-loss coverage	minimum-premium plan	retrospective-rating arrangement
ASO contract	premium-delay arrangement	specific stop-loss coverage
cost-plus arrangement	reserve-reduction arrangement	501(c)(9) trusts
limited-liability arrangement		

■ STUDY QUESTIONS

1. What are the reasons for increased employer interest in using alternative methods to fund employee benefit plans?

2. Why is an insurance company concerned with the financial position and credit rating of an employer to whom it issues a group insurance contract that contains a premium-delay arrangement?

3. a. Why are reserve-reduction arrangements usually not used during the first year of a group insurance contract?

   b. What is the responsibility of the employer under a reserve-reduction arrangement if an insurance contract is terminated?

4. a. Explain how minimum-premium plans minimize premium taxes.

   b. What is the responsibility of the insurance company under a minimum-premium plan for paying claims and maintaining reserves?

5. Explain the mechanics of retrospective rating.

6. Explain the conditions that are generally considered desirable before an employer should use total self-funding.

7. Why are life insurance benefits usually not self-funded?

8. What is the difference between aggregate stop-loss coverage and specific stop-loss coverage?

9. a. What are the tax advantages of a 501(c)(9) trust that are not present in benefit plans self-funded from current revenue?

   b. What conditions must be satisfied for a 501(c)(9) trust to meet IRS requirements?

   c. What are the limitation in amounts that may be contributed to a 501(c)(9) trust?

17

Group Insurance Rate Making

■ Describe the process by which manual premium rates are calculated.

■ Explain how manual premium rates are used to determine group term life insurance premiums, both for large groups and for small groups.

■ Identify the ways in which the manual rating process for other types of group insurance differs from the process for group term life insurance.

■ Explain the rationale for experience rating.

■ Describe the process of using experience rating to calculate dividends.

■ Explain how experience rating for determining prospective premiums differs from experience rating for calculating dividends.

| CHAPTER OUTLINE

Manual Rating
   Rating Basis
   Calculation of Manual Rates
   Calculation of Premiums

Experience Rating
   Rationale for Experience Rating
   Dividend Calculation
   Renewal Rating

One of the least understood aspects of group insurance is the pricing process. In the simplest sense, group insurance pricing is no different from pricing in other industries. The insurance company must generate enough revenue to cover its costs (claims and expenses) and to contribute to the net worth of the company. However, this similarity is often overlooked because of the unique terminology that is associated with insurance pricing and because the price of a group insurance product is initially determined on the basis of expected, but uncertain, future events rather than on current tangible cost estimates. In addition, a group insurance plan may be subject to experience rating so that the final price to the consumer can be determined only after the coverage period has ended.

The purpose of this chapter is not to make readers experts in the actuarial intricacies of group insurance pricing, commonly referred to as **rate making,** but rather to provide an understanding of basic principles and concepts. Rate making consists of two distinct steps:

1. The determination of a unit price, referred to as a **rate** or **premium rate,** for each unit of benefit (such as each $1,000 of life insurance)

2. The determination of the total price, or **premium,** that the policyowner will pay for the entire amount of coverage purchased

The mechanics of rate making differ, depending on whether a particular group is subject to manual rating or experience rating. When **manual rating** is used, the premium rate is determined independently of a particular group's claims; when **experience rating** is used, the past claims experience of a group is considered in determining future premiums for the group and/or in adjusting past premiums after a policy period has ended.

The major objective of rate making for all types of group insurance is to develop premium rates that are both adequate and equitable. **Adequate rates** must be sufficient to cover both incurred claims and expenses and to generate the desired profit or contribution to the insurance company's surplus. Obviously, the success and solvency of any group insurance operation is contingent on the long-term adequacy of premium rates. Therefore, several states, concerned about the solvency of insurance companies, have laws and regulations regarding the adequacy of rates. The most significant of these is the New York law that prohibits any insurance company doing business in that state from issuing in any state a group health insurance contract (either medical expense or disability income) that does not appear to be self-supporting on the basis of reasonable assumptions concerning expected claims and expenses.

Equitable rates require that each group pay a premium that reflects the expected cost of providing coverage to that group. Again, practical considerations and state regulations act to encourage equity. Overpricing group coverage for some segments of the market results in lost business; underpricing for other segments attracts unprofitable business. Most states also have laws and regulations that try to encourage equity by prohibiting unfair discrimination in insurance rates. The objective of equity has resulted in group insurance rates that differ because of such factors as the age and gender, as well as income distribution, of a group's members and the size of a group, its geographic location, its occupational hazards, and its claims experience. As discussed later, the factors that are considered vary with the type of group insurance coverage.

The role of competition in the rate making process should not be overlooked. If there is little or no competition, an insurer may develop rates to generate a higher-than-usual profit. In a very competitive market, rates may need to be lower than justified to obtain and retain business.

■ MANUAL RATING

In the manual-rating process, premium rates are established only for broad classes of group insurance business, and the insurance company does not consider the past claims experience of a particular group when determining that group's rates. However, claims experience is not entirely ignored because the aggregate claims experience for a class of business is used to determine the premium rates for that class.

Manual rating is used with small groups for which no credible individual loss experience is available. This lack of credibility exists because the group's size makes it impossible to determine whether other-than-average loss experience is due to random chance or is truly reflective of the group. Manual rating is also frequently used to determine the initial premiums for groups that are subject to experience rating, particularly when a group's past experience is unobtainable or when a group is being written for the first time. In addition, experience rating typically uses a weighting of manual rates and the actual experience of a group to determine the premium. (Rates for very large groups may be based solely on a group's own experience.)

TABLE 17.1	Benefit Units
Type of Group Insurance	**Benefit Unit**
Term Life (including accidental death and dismemberment)	Each $1,000 of death benefit
Short-Term Disability Income	Each $10 of weekly income
Long-Term Disability Income	Each $100 of monthly income
Medical Expense (including dental)	Each employee and each category of dependents

Rating Basis

Prior to the actual calculation of manual premium rates, insurers develop a basis on which the rates are determined. This **rating basis** involves a decision regarding (1) what benefit unit to use, (2) the extent to which rates are refined by factors affecting claims, and (3) the frequency with which premiums are paid.

Benefit Unit.   Subject to certain adjustments, the premium for a group is calculated by multiplying the premium rate by the number of benefit units provided. Although variations do occasionally exist, the benefit units predominantly used for the most common types of group insurance are shown in Table 17.1.

Factors Affecting Claims.   Rates reflect those factors that result in different claims experience for different groups. Although there are variations among insurance companies, the following discussion indicates the factors used by most insurance companies to determine rates for life, disability income, medical expense, and dental insurance. The reasons for considering these factors are discussed in the section on underwriting in Chapter 5.

Gender.   Gender of insured persons is taken into account for determining rates for all the types of insurance mentioned in the previous paragraph.

Age.   Age is also used as a rating factor for life insurance, disability income, and medical expense insurance. Dental insurance rates usually do not take age into consideration.

Geographic Location.   At one time, geographic location was a rating factor for medical expense insurance and dental insurance only. However, an increasing number of insurance companies use geographic variations for determining life insurance and disability income insurance rates. For these latter types of insurance, rates may not be determined separately for a wide variety of locations. Instead, the insurance company may have only two or three rate schedules, with each schedule applying to several different geographic locations on the basis of past experience.

Occupation.   Occupation is virtually always reflected in both group term insurance rates and accidental death and dismemberment rates. It may also be reflected in disability income, medical expense, and dental insurance rates. Some companies ignore it as a rating factor but may not write coverage when certain occupations are involved.

Income.   At one time, the income level of group members was commonly used as a factor in establishing disability income, medical expense, and dental insurance rates. Currently, income level is still a factor in determining dental insurance premiums, but it is more likely to be an underwriting consideration only in disability income and medical expense insurance.

Size.   The size of a group also affects rates because the proportion of the premium needed for expenses decreases as the size of a group increases. All manual premium rates are based on an assumption that the size of a group falls within a certain range. If the size of a group varies from this range, an appropriate rate adjustment is made to reflect this differential. In addition, many insurers reserve the right to rerate a group during the period of the contract or cancel the contract at renewal if the group changes in size by a certain percentage. This is particularly important in an era of downsizing and mergers.

Time.   A final factor considered in the calculation of rates is the length of time for which the rates will be used. This is a concern primarily for coverages that involve medical and dental claims, which over time are expected to increase in severity because of inflation. In inflationary times, monthly rates that are guaranteed for three months can be lower than those guaranteed for one year.

Frequency of Premium Payment Period.   Because group insurance premiums are usually paid monthly, this is the period for which rates are generally determined. When premiums can be paid less frequently (such as annually), they are usually slightly lower than the sum of the monthly premiums for the same period of coverage. The decrease results from the extra investment earnings the insurer can get by collecting premiums earlier. In addition, the annual expense of processing premiums is lower if they are paid less frequently.

Calculation of Manual Rates

Manual rating involves the calculation of the **manual premium rate** (also called **tabular rate**), which is quoted in an insurance company's rate book. The manual rate is applied to a specific group insurance case to determine a **final premium rate** (sometimes called an **average premium rate**) that is then multiplied by the number of benefit units to obtain a premium for the group.

There are three manual-rating methods. However, if identical assumptions are used, each method should result in approximately the same premium for any given group. The first method determines separate manual rates for groups with certain characteristics that an insurance company feels affect claims experience. A second approach establishes a single "standard manual rate" that is adjusted in the premium-calculation process to compensate for any characteristics that deviate from those of the standard group. A third method merely combines the first two approaches and considers some factors in determining the manual rate and other factors in determining the final premium rate.

The first step in the calculation of manual premium rates is the determination of the **net premium rate**, which is the amount necessary to support the cost of expected claims. For any given classification, the net premium rate is calculated by multiplying the probability (frequency) of a claim's occurring by the expected amount (severity) of the claim. For example, if the probability that an employee aged 50 will die in the next month is .0005, then the net monthly premium for each $1,000 of coverage is .0005 × $1,000, or $.50. Because premiums are collected before claims are paid, the insurance company adjusts this figure downward for anticipated interest earnings on these funds.

In general, insurance companies that write a large volume of any given type of group insurance rely on their own experience in determining the frequency and severity of future claims. Insurance companies that do not have enough past data for reliable future projections can turn to many sources for useful statistics. Probably the major source is the Society of Actuaries (Web site: *www.soa.org*), which regularly collects and publishes aggregate data on the group insurance business that is written by a number of large group insurance companies. Other sources of information are industry trade organizations and various agencies of the federal government.

The second and final step in the calculation of manual premium rates is the adjustment of the net premium rates for expenses, a risk charge, and a contribution to surplus. Expenses include commissions, premium taxes, claims settlement costs, and other costs associated with the acquisition and servicing of group insurance business. The **risk charge** represents a contribution to the insurance company's contingency reserve as a cushion against unanticipated and catastrophic amounts of claims. The contribution to surplus or net worth represents the profit margin of the insurance company. Although mutual companies are legally nonprofit, they, like stock insurance companies, require a contribution to net worth that is a source of financing for future growth.

From the standpoint of equity, the adjustment of the net premium rate is complex. Some factors, such as premium taxes and commissions, vary with the premium charge. However, the premium tax rate is not affected by the size of a group, whereas the commission rate generally decreases as the size of a group increases. To a large degree, the expenses of settling claims vary with the number, and not the size, of claims. It costs just as much administratively to pay a $10,000 claim under a group life insurance plan as it does to pay a $100,000 claim. Certain other costs also tend to be fixed regardless of the size of a group. For simplicity, some insurance companies adjust or load their net premium rates by a constant percentage. Other insurance companies consider the different patterns of expenses by using a percentage plus a constant charge. For example, if the net premium rate is $.60, this might be increased by 20 percent plus $.10 to arrive at a manual premium rate of $.82 (that is, $.60 × 1.2 + $.10). Because neither approach adequately accounts for the difference in expenses as a result of a group's size, another adjustment based on the size of the group is made in the calculation of the final premium rate.

Calculation of Premiums

Probably the best way to explain the actual calculation of group insurance premiums is through examples. The following analysis begins with group term life insurance, then

TABLE 17.2 Term Insurance Rates		
Age at Nearest Birthday	**Male Rate**	**Female Rate**
20	$0.16	$0.10
25	0.18	0.11
30	0.21	0.12
35	0.24	0.15
40	0.37	0.21
45	0.48	0.30
50	0.81	0.48
55	1.24	0.75
60	1.87	1.12
65	2.83	1.70
70	4.35	2.52

discusses how the structure of manual premium rates and the premium calculation process differ for certain other types of group insurance.

Group Term Life Insurance. The mechanics of calculating a final premium rate and the premium for a particular group vary among insurance companies because of the differences in methods of preparing manual premium rates and the process by which adjustments are made to these rates.

The following example begins with Table 17.2, which is an abbreviated version of a set of rates on a monthly basis per $1,000 of coverage at selected ages. As with most rate tables, the ages are those at a person's attained age (nearest birthday).

These rates are loaded for expenses, and they assume that the coverage contains a waiver-of-premium provision on disabled lives, accidental death and dismemberment coverage, and a conversion privilege. Consequently, rates are higher than if none of these additional benefits were included. When an employee converts coverage to an individual policy, a charge is assessed against the group insurance business of an insurance company to reflect the increased death claims that result from adverse selection on conversions. The amount of this assessment (commonly $50 to $75 per $1,000 of converted insurance) is transferred to the individual insurance department of the company to compensate it for having to write the converted business at too low a rate.

TABLE 17.3 Age Distribution		
Age	**Males**	**Females**
25	20	30
30	0	30
35	10	30
40	30	10
45	30	10
50	20	10

TABLE 17.4	Calculation of Unadjusted Cost					
Age	Gender	Number of Employees	Amount of Coverage (in Thousands)		Unadjusted Rate (per Thousand)	Unadjusted Cost
25	M	20	× 25	×	$0.18	= $90.00
35	M	10	× 25	×	0.24	= 60.00
40	M	30	× 25	×	0.37	= 277.50
45	M	30	× 25	×	0.48	= 360.00
50	M	20	× 25	×	0.81	= 405.00
25	F	30	× 25	×	0.11	= 82.50
30	F	30	× 25	×	0.12	= 90.00
35	F	30	× 25	×	0.15	= 112.50
40	F	10	× 25	×	0.21	= 52.50
45	F	10	× 25	×	0.30	= 75.00
50	F	10	× 25	×	0.48	= 120.00
					Total unadjusted cost =	$1,725.00

The premium-calculation process starts with the determination of an "unadjusted cost," based on a census of the covered employees and the manual rates. For example, assume a firm has 230 employees. For the sake of simplicity, also assume that each of these employees has $25,000 of life insurance and that the group has the age distribution shown in Table 17.3. The unadjusted cost is then calculated as shown in Table 17.4.

The second step is to reduce the sum of the unadjusted cost by a percentage based on the volume of a group insurance plan as determined by its monthly premium. This reduction results from the fact that the expenses associated with a group insurance plan decrease on a percentage basis as the size (premium volume) of the plan increases. The reductions used in this example are shown in Table 17.5 (for selected premiums).

Thus, the initial monthly premium for the group in this example is calculated as follows:

Unadjusted cost	$1,725.00
Minus expense reduction (7 percent)	− 120.75
Adjusted monthly premium	$1,604.25

The initial monthly premium is also used to calculate the final monthly premium rate per $1,000 of protection for the group:

$$\text{Monthly premium rate per thousand} = \frac{\text{Adjusted monthly premium}}{\text{Total volume (in thousands)}}$$

$$= \frac{\$1,604.25}{(230 \times \$25,000)/\$1,000}$$

$$= \frac{\$1,604.26}{5,750}$$

$$= \$0.28$$

This final monthly premium rate (usually rounded to either the nearest cent or one-tenth of a cent) is used throughout the first policy year and is multiplied each month by the amount of insurance in force to calculate the monthly premium due. Adjustments to the final monthly premium rate as a result of changes in the makeup of employees by age or gender are not made until the beginning of the next policy year as part of the renewal process. The initial rate is guaranteed for at least one year, assuming that there is no change in the benefit structure of the plan. However, two-and three-year rate guarantees are not unusual.

Manual rates are designed so that policies for businesses in most industries can be written at those rates. However, employers in industries that are considered hazardous may be charged higher rates. These increased rates are usually in the form of a surcharge per $1,000 of coverage that is added to the unadjusted cost before the expense reduction percentage is applied. For example, an industry that would be expected to have about one death claim per year per 1,000 employees in excess of those assumed in the manual rates might be charged for this excess mortality with a surcharge of $.06 per $1,000 of coverage per month.

Therefore, the adjusted monthly premium would be calculated as shown below:

Unadjusted cost	$1,604.25
Plus industry surcharge	+345.00
Total cost before expense reduction	$1,949.25
Minus expense reduction (7 percent)	−136.45
Adjusted monthly premium	$1,812.80

Similarly, the expectation of two extra death claims per year would result in an added premium of $.12 per $1,000 per month, or $690.

TABLE 17.5	Premium Reductions

Monthly Premium before Reduction	Percentage Expense Reduction
Under $200	0%
200–249	1
250–299	2
.	.
.	.
.	.
1,000–1,499	6
1,500–1,999	7
2,000–3,999	8
.	.
.	.
.	.
60,000–79,999	19
80,000 and over	20

TABLE 17.6	Premium Adjustments	
Monthly Premium before Adjustment		**Percentage Adjustment**
Under $200		+25%
200–249		+22
.		.
.		.
.		.
700–799		+1
800–999		0
1,000–1,099		−1
.		.
.		.
.		.
50,000–74,999		−14
75,000 and over		−15

Variations for Large Groups. Insurance companies use the premium-calculation process discussed on the previous page for most groups over a certain size, usually from 10 or more to 50 or more lives, but variations do exist. For example, some insurance companies do not incorporate a charge for a waiver of premium or accidental death and dismemberment coverage into their manual rates. Rather, an extra charge, which usually differs by industry, is added for this coverage. Also, some companies use (and are required to use in a few states) manual rates that vary by age but not gender. These unisex rate tables are based on assumptions about the ratio of males to females in the group. However, an adjustment is usually made in the premium-calculation process if the actual group ratio differs from this assumption.

Some companies incorporate a level of expenses into their manual rate so that there is no expense reduction for a certain-size group. In the final premium-calculation process, an adjustment is made; larger groups receive an expense reduction and smaller groups receive an expense surcharge. Table 17.6 is one such table of adjustments.

Variations for Small Groups. The manual-rating process for small groups, including those written by multiple-employer trusts, differs from that of large groups in several ways. In general, the manual rates are banded by age, typically in five-year intervals. Table 17.7 is an example of one such monthly rate table for each $1,000 of coverage.

An unadjusted cost is developed based on a census of the employees by age and by gender unless unisex rates are used. Because the manual rates are loaded for most expenses, and because the groups written tend to be reasonably close in size, typically no adjustment for size is made. However, to compensate for the expenses of periodic billings, most insurance companies apply a flat fee to all groups, commonly between $10 and $20 per billing. Some companies do not levy this charge if the premium is paid annually. To reflect the administrative costs associated with record keeping, some insurance companies also levy a modest one-time expense charge when coverage is added for a new employee.

TABLE 17.7	Banded Rates	
Age at Nearest Birthday	Male Rate	Female Rate
Under 30	$0.24	$0.10
30–34	0.24	0.13
35–39	0.25	0.15
40–44	0.36	0.20
45–49	0.58	0.36
50–54	0.91	0.54
55–59	1.55	0.79
60–64	1.93	1.02
65–69	3.30	1.81
70 and over	6.80	3.23

For large groups, the initial monthly premium is used to determine a monthly premium rate that applies for a specified period of time. In contrast, the monthly premium rate for small groups may be recalculated each month based not only on the volume of insurance but also on changes in the makeup of employees by age and gender (unless unisex rates are used), just as if the group were being newly written. However, most insurance companies do guarantee that the manual rates used when the group was initially written (and any future manual rates applicable to the group) will remain applicable for some period of time, with 12 months being common.

Accidental Death and Dismemberment Insurance. Accidental death and dismemberment insurance is usually not written as a separate coverage unless coverage is voluntary. Rather, it is added by an endorsement to a group term insurance contract. A single manual rate typically applies to all employees regardless of age or gender, but it varies depending on whether coverage is written (1) for nonoccupational accidents only or (2) on a 24-hour basis for both nonoccupational and occupational accidents. The rate for nonoccupational coverage generally does not vary by industry and ranges from $.02 to $.05 per $1,000 of principal sum per month. However, the rate for coverage on a 24-hour basis does vary by industry, and although it falls within this same range for low-risk industries, it may be several times higher for hazardous ones. Some companies calculate a separate cost for the accidental death and dismemberment coverage and add it to the charge for the group term life insurance. However, most employers purchase accidental death and dismemberment coverage. As a result, other insurance companies incorporate the cost into the manual rates for group term life insurance, making the principal sum equal to the amount of life insurance protection purchased, and an additional charge is levied only if a higher level of accidental death and dismemberment coverage is desired.

Dependent Life Insurance. Dependent life insurance may be added as additional coverage to a group life insurance contract that provides protection for employees. Because dependent life insurance coverage is usually a modest fixed amount (such as

$2,000 on the spouse and $1,000 on each child) that generates a relatively small additional premium, a very simplified rate structure tends to be used. However, several variations do exist. Some insurance companies have a single flat rate, independent of the type or number of dependents, for each employee who has dependent coverage. Other companies have two separate flat rates: one for the spouse's coverage and the other for children's coverage. The rate for the children's coverage is a family rate regardless of the number of children, and it is based upon an average-sized family.

Flat rates are based on the assumption that the group has an average age mix of employees. If the group of employees is older than average, the flat rate for dependent coverage may be adjusted (particularly when it applies to spouses) to reflect the likelihood that the dependents are also above average in age when compared to the dependents of most other groups. A flat rate is commonly used when the cost of dependent coverage is paid entirely by the employees. The uniform charge is easy to communicate to employees, and it simplifies the payroll-deduction process for the employer.

Some insurance companies also use a rate for dependent coverage that varies with the employee's age, thereby assuming that older employees have older dependents. Basing the rate on the employee's age may seem illogical, but it is administratively simpler and less expensive than having to determine the ages of dependents. A single variable rate may apply to the total family coverage for the spouse and all children, or it may apply only to the spouse. In this latter case, a flat rate is generally used if coverage for children is also provided.

It is becoming less common to see dependent life insurance added to the basic group life coverage for an employee. Instead, this coverage is more frequently being written as an employee-pay-all voluntary benefit, with higher amounts of coverage available.

Short-Term Disability Income Insurance. In addition to varying by age, by gender, and possibly by geographic location, manual rates for short-term disability income insurance also differ according to (1) the maximum benefit period, (2) the length of the waiting period, and (3) the writing of coverage either on a 24-hour basis or only for nonoccupational disabilities.

Some insurance companies (particularly those for small groups) have only a single standard short-term disability income plan that they sell, and therefore they only need a single manual rate table. On the other hand, some companies allow the employer to exercise a degree of flexibility in designing the plan that will be purchased. Rather than make adjustments to a single rate table, these companies usually have several rate tables. These tables vary by such factors as maximum benefit period (such as 13 or 26 weeks) and waiting period (such as seven days for all disabilities or seven days for illnesses and no waiting period for injuries). If any other variations are allowed, appropriate adjustments are made.

An adjustment may be made for the nature of the industry the group represents. Ignoring the occupational injuries and diseases that are covered under workers' compensation, a few occupations are still characterized by higher-than-average disability income claims. As an alternative to a rate adjustment, some insurance companies have underwriting standards that prohibit the writing of coverage for these groups.

Until the passage of the Pregnancy Discrimination Act and various state laws, it was common for insurance companies to have one manual rate for plans that did not provide benefits for pregnancy-related disabilities and another for plans that did provide such benefits. Because most employers can no longer exclude pregnancy as a cause of disability, rates for coverage without this benefit are usually not published, except for the employers of small groups that still have an option regarding this benefit in many states.

In contrast to group life insurance rates, which are lower for females than for males, disability income rates are higher for females. Ignoring pregnancy-related disabilities, the claims of females at younger ages still somewhat exceed those of males. However, because male and female claims are comparable at older ages, the rates for later years seldom vary. Table 17.8, which illustrates one insurance company's monthly manual rates per $10 of weekly benefit for 26 weeks following a 7-day waiting period, shows how this rate differential is even more pronounced at younger ages if maternity coverage is included.

In the past, it was common for short-term disability income rates to be expressed on the basis of each $10 of weekly benefit. This is probably still the norm, but some insurance companies are now expressing their rates in terms of a higher weekly benefit, such as $50 or $100.

Long-Term Disability Income Insurance.   Like short-term disability income rates, the manual rates for long-term coverage vary by age, gender, the length of the benefit period, the length of the waiting period, and possibly geographic location. In addition, the manual rates reflect the fact that benefits are coordinated with Social Security and certain other disability income benefits for which an employee might be eligible. To the extent that variations are allowed in the coordination provision that was assumed in developing the manual rates, an adjustment is made in the premium-calculation process. As is also the case with short-term rates, an adjustment might be made for certain occupations.

Unlike short-term disability income rates, which are commonly expressed on the basis of a weekly benefit, long-term rates are typically expressed on the basis of a

TABLE 17.8 Disability Income Rates		
Age	**Male**	**Female**
Under 30	$0.48	$1.25
30–34	0.52	1.25
35–39	0.56	1.25
40–44	0.72	1.21
45–49	0.81	1.21
50–54	1.01	1.31
55–59	1.21	1.53
60–64	1.61	1.61
65–69	2.01	2.01
70 and over	2.16	2.16

monthly benefit, usually per $100. Unlike the coverages previously discussed, long-term disability claims fluctuate with general economic conditions. Consequently, insurance companies review and possibly revise their manual rates (and/or their underwriting standards) as economic conditions change.

The period of time for which rates are guaranteed may vary from one to three years, depending on the industry in which the employees work.

Medical Expense Insurance.   In many ways, the manual rates for medical expense insurance (and also for dental insurance) are similar to those for disability income insurance because variations exist by age, gender, and the provisions of the plan, including the size of the deductible, the coinsurance percentage, and the level of benefits. Most providers of medical expense coverage have manual rates for the few standard plans that are sold, and only large employers are given the flexibility to deviate from these plans. Any such deviation is then reflected in adjustments to the manual rates. Adjustments may also be made to the manual rates if the employer is in an industry that is characterized by higher-than-average claims.

One other factor, geographic location, is always a variable in the manual rates because of the significant differences in medical costs across the country. Depending on group size, an adjustment for location may be made in one of two ways. For large groups, the rating process usually starts with a manual rate that does not consider the location of employees. Each county (or other geographic subdivision) where coverage is written is then assigned a factor that is based on the cost of health care in that location compared with the "average" cost that is assumed in the manual rates. For example, if Seattle were 20 percent higher than average, it would have a factor of 1.2. If all of a firm's employees were there, the manual rates for that group would be multiplied by a location factor of 1.2 in the process of determining the group's premium. If employees were in several locations, a composite factor would be calculated as shown in Table 17.9. Consequently, the manual rate for this group would be increased by 5.5 percent because of the employees' locations.

A slightly different approach is used for small groups. Because employees are usually in one location, many companies have manual rate tables for between 10 and 20 rating territories, and each geographic area in which employees are located is assigned a specific territorial rating. The following territorial classifications are from the rating

TABLE 17.9   Calculation of Location Factor

Location	Number of Employees		Location Factor		Product
Seattle	100	×	1.2	=	120
Kansas City	70	×	1.0	=	70
Brimingham	30	×	0.7	=	21
	200				211

$$\text{Location Factor} = \frac{\text{Total product}}{\text{Total number of employees}} = \frac{211}{200} = 1.055$$

manual of one insurance company for some areas in four of the states where it writes business. The first three digits of the zip code identify these areas.

Georgia
301–302, 311	8
303–304, 308–310, 312–319	7
all others	6

Michigan
482	10
480, 483	8
481	6
484–485, 488–489	3
all others	2

Tennessee
370–372	4
all others	3

Utah
entire state	1

Table 17.10, an excerpt from the manual rate tables of another company, shows how the monthly cost for coverage under one of its PPO plans varies by geographic area within a single state.

This excerpt lists manual rates for dependent coverage that are applied regardless of the number of children or the ages of the dependents. For any size group, this is one of several possible methods for pricing dependent coverage. Another method uses rates that vary by the number of children. Some rating structures also take the ages of dependents into consideration.

TABLE 17.10 Medical Expense Rates

Employee's Age	Class of Coverage	Area 1	Area 2	Area 3	Area 4
30–39	Employee	$198	$244	$268	$ 367
30–39	Employee and spouse	323	396	441	634
30–39	Employee and children	349	428	461	633
30–39	Family	566	685	752	1,065
50–59	Employee	358	420	418	552
50–59	Employee and spouse	623	732	747	982
50–59	Employee and children	485	574	594	792
50–59	Family	774	911	964	1,322

Because medical expense claims are continually increasing as a result of inflation, a trend factor must be applied to past claims experience when manual rates are developed. This is often difficult for employers to understand. It is also a complex and often perplexing task for most providers of medical expense coverage. Not only has the overall cost of medical care increased faster than the general cost of living (as measured by the consumer price index), but the increases have been erratic from year to year and are virtually impossible to predict with any degree of accuracy. To further complicate matters, these increases vary significantly for each category of medical expenses; therefore, different trend factors must be applied to different categories of claims.

At one time, group insurance premium rates were guaranteed for at least 12 months and possibly for as long as two or three years. However, to protect themselves against unexpected increases in claims due to increases in the cost of medical care, some insurance companies now guarantee medical expense rates for no more than six months. In fact, a number of multiple-employer trusts have only three-month guarantees, or they contain provisions whereby rates can be increased at any time, provided notice of the rate increase is given 30 or 60 days in advance. Some companies allow an employer to select the length of the rate guarantee, such as six months or one year. However, the longer the rate guarantee, the higher the rate.

Dental Insurance.   Although the rating of dental insurance is similar in many ways to the rating of medical expense insurance, there are some significant differences. Most insurance companies do not vary their manual rates by the ages of group members. Instead, an adjustment is often made for the income levels of employees, because higher-paid persons are much more likely to obtain dental care. This adjustment is usually in the form of a percentage based on the extent to which the portion of employees with incomes higher than some figure (such as $30,000) exceeds the proportion of such employees that is assumed in the manual rates. An adjustment is also made for certain occupations (such as salespeople or teachers) that use dental services more frequently than average. Finally, the manual rates are usually increased when a plan is new (or expands benefits) if the employees have been informed beforehand. Under these circumstances, there is a tendency to postpone needed dental care until the plan is installed.

■ EXPERIENCE RATING

With experience rating, an insurance company considers a group's claims experience, either at the issue date or at the end of a policy period, when determining the premium rate for that group. When applied prospectively (that is, to future periods), experience rating is used to determine (1) adjustments in renewal premiums (either upward or downward) for those groups whose claims experience has deviated from what was expected and (2) initial premiums for large groups that change insurance carriers.

In addition to determining the premium rate for the next policy period (usually 12 months), experience rating is also used to compute the refund payable to the policyowner (usually the employer) for those groups that had better claims experience than anticipated. Mutual insurance companies refer to this refund as a **dividend**, and stock insurance companies call it a **retrospective rate credit** or **premium refund**. (The term *dividend* is used in the remainder of this chapter.) Under some experience-rating arrangements, the premium at the end of a policy period may also be retroactively adjusted upward if a group's claims experience has been worse than anticipated, and an additional premium is charged. These arrangements are not very common and are discussed in Chapter 16.

Rationale for Experience Rating

One argument in favor of experience rating is that it achieves the ultimate degree of premium equity among policyowners. Even though manual rating also results in equity because it considers the obvious factors that affect claims, it is impossible to measure and make adjustments in the manual rates for such factors as lifestyle, working conditions, and morale, all of which contribute to the level of claims experience. Experience rating is also the most cost-effective way to reflect the general health of a group in the premium that is charged.

Probably the major reason for using experience rating is the competition that exists in the group insurance marketplace. If an insurance company were to use identical rates for all groups regardless of their experience, the employers with good experience would soon seek out insurance companies that offered lower rates, or they would turn to self-funding as a way to reduce costs. The insurance company that did not consider claims experience would therefore be left with only the poor risks. This is exactly the situation that led most of the Blues to abandon community rating for group insurance cases above a certain size. Experience rating allows an insurance company to acquire and retain the better cases (from a claims-experience standpoint) and to determine an appropriate premium for the groups that have worse-than-average claims experience.

Dividend Calculation

At first glance, the process of using experience rating to determine dividends appears complex. However, the actual mechanics are relatively simple, and much of the confusion stems from the fact that the process is lengthy. In addition, both the format and the terminology vary somewhat among insurance companies. This discussion focuses on the illustration in Table 17.11 and explains the steps used to calculate the dividend for a group medical expense insurance case of about 450 lives. Although this illustration can be considered a typical example of a dividend calculation, variations could have been (and often are) used.

Premiums Paid. Step 1 shows the total amount of premiums that the policyowner actually paid during the experience-rating period (usually one year) before any adjustment was made to reflect the actual experience of the group. In most instances, this is the sum of 12 monthly premiums. The premiums paid may have been based on manual rates or on the group's past experience.

Stop-Loss Limit. Step 2 specifies the **stop-loss limit**—the maximum amount of any claim that is charged to the group in the experience-rating calculation. Its purpose is to minimize the effect of any chance fluctuations that might occur from year to year because of catastrophic losses within the group. These chance fluctuations tend to

TABLE 17.11	Illustrative Dividend Calculation		
1.	Premiums paid		$1,950,000
2.	Stop-loss limit (per claim)		$250,000
3.	Incurred claims [a + (c − b)]		$1,620,000
a.	Paid claims (below stop-loss limit)	$1,590,000	
b.	Beginning reserve for claims	$400,000	
c.	Ending reserve for claims	$430,000	
4.	Expected claims		$1,700,000
5.	Credibility factor		0.8
6.	Claims charge [(0.8 × 3) + (0.2 × 4)]		$1,636,000
7.	Retention charge (d + e + f + g + h − i)		$225,000
d.	Charge for stop-loss coverage	$40,000	
e.	Commissions	$80,000	
f.	Premium taxes	$40,000	
g.	Administration	$30,000	
h.	Contingency reserve (risk charge) and surplus contribution	$60,000	
i.	Interest on reserves	$25,000	
8.	Dividend earned [1 − (6 + 7)]		$89,000
9.	Deficit carried forward from prior periods		$42,000
10.	Deficit to be carried forward to future periods (8 − 9) if less than 0		−
	OR		$47,000
	Dividend payable (8 − 9) if greater than 0		

become relatively smaller as the size of a group increases, and a stop-loss limit may not be used for very large groups.

The stop-loss limit in medical expense insurance is usually expressed as a dollar amount per claim, and the actual figure is subject to negotiation between the policyowner and the insurance company. In this illustration, $250,000 is used. Therefore, if a claim of $400,000 is incurred because of a premature birth, only the first $250,000 of the claim will be used in the experience-rating calculation.

Obviously, a charge must be made somewhere for incorporating a stop-loss provision into an experience-rating contract, because the insurance company is obligated to pay any excess amount over the stop-loss limit. The charge in this illustration is shown in step 7. In effect, this charge for stop-loss coverage can be viewed as a manual-rate charge for losses in excess of some limit, with only those losses below the limit subject to experience rating.

Incurred Claims. Step 3 involves the determination of incurred claims, which are those claims attributable to the recently ended period of coverage that was subject to experience rating (that is, the **experience period**). It may seem as if the incurred claims are those claims that were paid during the experience period. Unfortunately, it is not that simple. Some of the claims that were paid during the experience period may actually be attributable to previous periods and must be subtracted from the incurred claims. In addition, other claims that are attributable to the experience period may not have been reported or may be in the course of settlement. However, their value must be estimated. Therefore, an appropriate determination of **incurred claims** is as follows:

incurred claims = claims paid during the experience period
 – claims paid during the experience period but incurred during previous periods
 + estimate of claims incurred during the experience period but to be paid in future periods

In actual practice, incurred claims are usually expressed as follows:

incurred claims = paid claims
 + ending claim reserve
 – beginning claim reserve
 or
incurred claims = paid claims
 + change in claim reserve

This **claim reserve**, which is often referred to as the *open-and-unreported claim reserve,* represents an estimate by the insurance company for (1) claims that have been approved but not yet paid, (2) claims that are in the course of settlement, and (3) claims that have been incurred but not yet reported (often referred to as *IBNR*). In addition, when disability income coverage or medical expense coverage is experience rated, an additional amount must be added to this estimate for any claims that have been incurred, reported, and approved but are not yet payable. Essentially, these claims arise from disabilities or current medical claims that will continue beyond the experience period.

Based on past experience, most insurance companies can closely estimate the percentage of claims that are paid after the close of the experience period for a given type of coverage. Although this estimate reflects companywide experience and may not reflect the experience of a particular policyowner, it is usually applied to each group insurance case rather than determining the claim reserve on a case-by-case basis. In general, the claim reserve is based either on a percentage of the annual premium (before experience rating) or on a percentage of claims paid. The first approach is most common for small groups, and the latter approach tends to be used for large groups. This percentage varies considerably by type of coverage, with the claim reserve for group term life insurance usually ranging between 10 percent and 15 percent of the annual premium (and up to 25 percent if a waiver of premium for disability is included), and the claim reserve for medical expense coverage often ranging from 20 percent to 65 percent, depending on what benefits are involved.

Expected Claims. The amount of **expected claims** in step 4 represents the portion of the premiums paid that the insurance company has anticipated would be necessary to pay claims during the experience period. This amount may have been derived either from average experience as in manual rating or from the past experience of the particular group.

Credibility.   The **credibility** factor (step 5), which can vary from zero to one, is a statistical measure of the reliability of the group's past experience. In other words, it is a measure of the probability that the group's actual experience is a true reflection of the group and is not the result of chance occurrences. The credibility factor varies by the size of the group and the type of coverage. In general, the larger the group is, the greater the reliability of estimates is (because of the law of large numbers). In addition, actual experience tends to deviate less from the estimates of expected claims (on a relative basis) as the frequency of claims rises. Therefore, a greater degree of credibility can be attributed to a group's medical expense claims than to its life insurance claims.

In actual practice, credibility factors are usually based on the size of a group as determined by the number of persons (lives) who are insured. However, some insurance companies base their credibility factors on the annual premium of a group. The factors vary somewhat among insurance companies, but the excerpt in Table 17.12 from the rate manual of one insurance company that is used for this illustration is a typical example of the first approach.

Adjustments in these factors may be made to reflect any characteristics of either the group or the insurance contract that deviate from the norm. For example, an older group of employees might be assigned a higher credibility factor than a younger group whose claims are more likely to be due to random fluctuations. In addition, the level of any stop-loss limit may have an effect. As the stop-loss charge is increased (meaning the stop-loss limit is lowered), the credibility that can be assigned to the remaining claims below the stop-loss limit also increases.

Similarly, the size of the credibility factor may be influenced by the amount of the risk charge levied on the group for establishing a contingency reserve. If an insurance company has an adequate contingency reserve for a group insurance case, it is more likely to allow the use of a higher credibility factor than can be statistically justified. This practice results in reduced claims charges for years when the employer has good experience and increased claims charges for years when it has bad experience. Although employers with a history of better-than-average claims experience desire it, a higher-than-justified credibility factor leads to a larger-than-usual deficit for a group with bad

TABLE 17.12   Credibility Factors

Size of Group (Lives)	Long-Term Disability Income Insurance and Life Insurance	Medical Expense Insurance and Short-Term Disability Income Insurance
100	0.0	0.2
200	0.2	0.5
400	0.4	0.8
600	0.7	1.0
800	0.9	1.0
1,000 or more	1.0	1.0

experience. It also increases the probability that the employer will terminate the contract before the deficit is eliminated. A larger contingency reserve can balance the financial consequences of this possibility.

Claims Charge. Once the credibility factor is determined, the process of calculating the **claims charge**, or what claims will be charged against the group in the experience period, is relatively simple and can be expressed by the following formula:

claims charge $= (z)$ (incurred claims subject to experience rating)
               $+ (1 - z)$ (expected claims)

where z is the credibility factor.

In effect, the claims charge is a weighted average of (1) the incurred claims that are subject to experience rating and (2) the expected claims, with the incurred claims being assigned a weight equal to the credibility factor and the expected claims being assigned a weight equal to 1 minus the credibility factor. In step 6 of Table 17.11, the claims charge is calculated as follows:

claims charge $= 0.8\ (\$1,620,000) + (1 - 0.8)\ (\$1,700,000)$
               $= 0.8\ (\$1,620,000) + 0.2\ (\$1,700,000)$
               $= \$1,296,000 + \$340,000$
               $= \$1,636,000$

If a credibility factor of 1.0 is used, the claims charge is equal to the incurred claims that are subject to experience rating, and the expected claims are not taken into consideration.

Retention. The **retention** (step 7) in a group insurance contract is usually defined as the excess of premiums paid over claims payments and dividends. It consists of charges for (1) the stop-loss coverage, (2) expenses (commissions, premium taxes, and administrative expenses), (3) a risk charge, and (4) a contribution to the insurance company's surplus. In this particular illustration, the sum of these charges is reduced by the interest that is credited to certain reserves—the claim reserve and any contingency reserves—that the insurance company holds to pay future claims attributable to this contract. However, some insurance companies do not subtract this interest when determining retention; rather, they treat it as an additional premium paid.

For large groups, each item in the retention is calculated separately, based on the group's actual experience. For small groups, a formula based on insurance company averages is usually applied. This formula varies according to the size of a group and the type of coverage involved; most often it is either a percentage of the claims charge or a flat charge plus a percentage of the claims charge.

Dividend Earned. The **dividend earned** (step 8) is computed by adding the retention to the claims charge and then subtracting this sum from the premiums paid. This is the dividend amount attributable to the group insurance case for the current experience period.

Previous Deficits. Under most experience-rated group insurance plans, any deficits from past periods must be made up before any future dividends are paid. Whenever the sum of the claims charge and the retention charge for any experience period exceeds the premiums paid and results in a negative dividend earned, there is a deficit. In step 9 of Table 17.11, a $42,000 deficit from previous periods exists. Interestingly, the insurance company has no opportunity to recover this deficit if the insurance contract is not renewed. The fact that there is always a chance of nonrenewal is one of the reasons why a risk charge is levied.

As additional protection against the nonrenewal of insurance contracts that have a deficit, some insurance companies require that part of any dividend earned be placed in a **claims fluctuation reserve** when experience is favorable. Monies are drawn from the reserve to indemnify the insurance company for the years in which there is a deficit. Because this reserve lessens the possibility that the insurance company will lose money on a group insurance case, it is usually accompanied by a lower risk charge.

Dividend Payable. The final step in the dividend-calculation process (step 10) is to establish whether there is a **dividend payable**. This is determined by subtracting any deficit that has been carried forward (or placed in a claims fluctuation reserve) from the dividend earned for the experience period. If this figure is positive, it is the amount of the dividend; if the figure is negative, it is the amount of the cumulative deficit that is to be carried forward.

In this illustration, only one type of coverage is experience rated. However, when an employer has more than one type of coverage that is experience rated with the same insurance company, a single dividend is usually determined for the combined package. This typically involves the determination of a separate claims charge for each coverage and a single retention charge for the entire package. Because "losses" for one type of coverage are often offset by "gains" for other types of coverage, the relative fluctuation in the overall experience tends to be less than the fluctuations in the experience of some or all of the individual coverages. Therefore, the overall premium can often be reduced (or the dividend increased) because the insurance company will levy a lower risk charge and/or require a lower contingency reserve.

Variations for Other Types of Coverage

In some types of group insurance, particularly group term life insurance, there is considerable disparity in the amounts of coverage, and top executives often have much greater coverage than do the lowest-paid employees. Claims that arise from the deaths of employees who have large amounts of coverage can have a significant effect on a group's experience for the years in which they occur. Consequently, several methods have been used to exclude these claims (or at least a portion of them) from the process of determining the claims charge in experience rating. One of these methods is the stop-loss limit that was previously mentioned. However, its primary purpose is to limit the claims charge because of a higher-than-anticipated frequency of claims, rather than because of a few high-severity claims. Some of the other methods used to handle these large claims are

■ excess-amounts pooling. This approach limits the amount of insurance that is subject to experience rating on any one person. Amounts over the limit are not experience rated but are subject to manual rates based on the ages of the individuals involved. This results in a "pooling" or an "insurance" charge that is added to either the claims charge or the retention charge, depending on the insurance company's practice. These excess amounts may also be subject to evidence of insurability.

■ a lower credibility factor. Under this method, the credibility factor normally used for a certain-size group is reduced if there is a significant difference between the smallest and largest amounts of coverage. This results in more weight being placed on the group's expected claims than on their incurred claims.

■ an extra contingency reserve. Under this approach, the excess of claims above a certain limit is ignored in the experience-rating process for dividend purposes but is charged against a contingency reserve that has been established (with an appropriate annual charge) for this reason.

Two other factors enter into the incurred claims amount for group term life insurance: disability claims and conversion charges. In addition to death claims, there may be disability claims if a group insurance contract contains a waiver-of-premium provision or another type of disability provision. Once a waiver-of-premium claim has been approved, a charge is made for future death claims, because no future premiums will be received for the disabled employee. This charge is based on the probability that the disabled employee will die prior to recovery or termination of coverage (for example, at age 65). On average, the charge is about $750 for each $1,000 of coverage. If the insurance contract continues, an additional $250 per $1,000 is charged if a death claim is paid. If the employee recovers or coverage terminates prior to death, the $750 charge is credited back to the policyowner.

As mentioned earlier in this chapter, a conversion charge is levied against the group insurance department of an insurance company to reflect the increased mortality on converted coverage. In the experience-rating procedure, this charge (commonly $50 to $75 per $1,000 of coverage converted) is transferred to the group policyowner.

Renewal Rating

Experience rating is also often used to develop future premiums for group insurance cases based on the past experience of the group. For the most part, the procedure is similar to that for determining dividends, and in fact the two procedures are usually done at the same time. However, there are some differences. In most cases, the experience-rating period is three to five years instead of a single year, and thus cumulative premiums and charges for this period are used. In addition, a more conservative (that is, lower) credibility factor is normally applied. For example, an insurance company that uses a credibility factor of 0.8 for dividend purposes for a particular case might use a factor of 0.6 for renewal-rating purposes. Furthermore, because a premium is being developed for the future, it is also necessary to adjust past claims and the retention, not only to reflect current cost levels but also to include expected trends for the next year. Adjustments must also be made to account for any changes in the coverage. Once a renewal premium expected to be sufficient to cover claims and retention is calculated, an additional amount is added for future dividends. This amount in effect becomes a safety margin for the insurance company should both claims and retention be higher than anticipated; otherwise it is returned as an experience dividend to the policyowner.

Experience rating may also be used to develop the initial premiums for any transferred business, requiring that the insurance company obtain past data from the policyowner regarding its experience with the previous carrier. A policyowner may be reluctant to provide this information because poor experience (and the resulting rate increase) is often the reason for changing insurance companies. However, the existence of the poor claims experience is exactly the information the insurance company needs. In fact, some insurance companies actually refuse to write transferred coverage, particularly for large groups, unless verifiable prior claims experience is provided.

If possible, the past data are used to determine what the premiums and charges would have been if the new carrier had written the new contract in previous years. If this can be accomplished, the procedure is a simplified application of the principles previously described. If it cannot be accomplished, manual rating may be used for small groups, but judgment may play a large role in determining the premiums for large groups.

■ KEY TERMS

adequate rates	experience period	rate (premium rate)
claim reserve	experience rating	rate making
claims charge	final premium rate	rating basis
claims fluctuation reserve	(average premium rate)	retention
credibility	incurred claims	retrospective rate credit (premium refund)
dividend	manual premium rate (tabular rate)	risk charge
dividend earned	manual rating	stop-loss limit
dividend payable	net premium rate	
equitable rates	premium	
expected claims		

■ STUDY QUESTIONS

1. The major objective of rate making is to develop rates that are adequate and equitable. What is meant by adequate and equitable?

2. In addition to determining the benefit unit, what decisions must be made in developing a basis on which manual premium rates can be established?

3. Describe the steps in the calculation of manual premium rates.

4. What characteristics of a group are usually considered in determining disability income rates that are not likely to be considered in determining term life insurance rates?

5. How do insurance companies protect themselves against increases in medical expense claims costs due to inflation?

6. a. What is the rationale for the use of experience rating?

 b. Identify the situations in which experience rating may be used.

7. What is the purpose of a stop-loss limit?

8. Explain why paid claims differ from incurred claims.

9. Given the following information for a group insurance contract, calculate its claims charge:

Premiums paid	$250,000
Claims paid	$190,000
Beginning claim reserve	$ 25,000
Ending claim reserve	$ 35,000
Stop-loss limit	120% of premiums paid
Expected claims	$160,000
Credibility factor	0.7

10. How does the credibility factor for a group vary by the size of the group and the type of insurance coverage?

11. Why might the full amount of a dividend earned not be paid to a group insurance policyholder?

12. How does experience rating for determining renewal rates differ from experience rating for calculating dividends?

PART FOUR

Other Nonretirement Benefits and Cafeteria Plans

18 Other Nonretirement Benefits

- Explain why employers often provide fringe benefits.
- Identify the types of payments that employers may make to employees for time not worked and explain the tax consequences of each benefit.
- Describe the types of extra cash payments that employers may provide to employees and explain the tax consequences of each.
- Describe the types of services employers often provide to employees and explain the tax consequences of each.

CHAPTER OUTLINE

Meaning of Highly Compensated Employee

Payments or other Benefits for Time Not Worked
Vacations
Holidays
Personal Time Off with Pay
Personal Time Off Without Pay
   (Family Leave)
Supplemental Unemployment Benefit
   Plans

Extra Payments to Employees
Educational Assistance
Moving-Expense Reimbursement
Suggestion Awards
Service Awards
Productivity and Safety Achievement
   Awards
Holiday Bonuses and Gifts

Services to Employees
No-Additional-Cost Services
Employee Discounts
Dependent-Care Assistance
Adoption Assistance
Wellness Programs
Employee-Assistance Programs
Financial Planning Programs for
   Executives
Preretirement-Counseling Programs
Transportation/Free Parking
Personal Use of Company Cars
Subsidized Eating Facilities

In Chapter 1, employee benefits were divided into five categories:

1. Legally required social insurance payments
2. Payments for private insurance and retirement plans
3. Payments or other benefits for time not worked
4. Extra payments to employees
5. Services to employees

There are variations among employers, but typically about one-quarter of the sum spent on employee benefits is devoted to payments for legally required social insurance programs. More than one-third is spent on employee benefits devoted to payments for retirement plans and group insurance. Often overlooked is the significance of all the remaining types of benefits that may be provided to employees, which as a group account for between one-quarter and one-third of the employee benefit dollars employers spend. Because the list is extensive, not every possible benefit is described. Rather, the discussion is devoted to the following list of more commonly provided "other" benefits:

- Vacations
- Holidays
- Personal time off with pay
- Personal time off without pay (family leave)
- Supplemental unemployment benefit plans
- Educational assistance
- Moving-expense reimbursement
- Suggestion awards
- Service awards
- Productivity and safety achievement awards
- Holiday bonuses and gifts
- No-additional-cost services
- Employee discounts
- Dependent-care assistance
- Adoption assistance
- Wellness programs
- Employee-assistance programs
- Financial planning programs for executives
- Preretirement-counseling programs
- Transportation/free parking
- Personal use of company cars
- Subsidized eating facilities

Most employers provide some of these benefits, such as holidays and vacations. Relatively few employers provide other benefits, such as financial planning. There are many reasons one employer may provide a certain array of benefits: to satisfy specific needs of its employees, for competitive reasons, or because of traditions within its locality or industry. Collective bargaining, the personal whims of the employer, and federal and state laws may also play a role.

These benefits are almost always self-funded from the current revenue of an employer. With rare exceptions, the cost of providing the benefits is tax deductible to the employer. However, the tax treatment of employees receiving benefits varies, and the treatment of each benefit is described separately.

MEANING OF HIGHLY COMPENSATED EMPLOYEE

Several of the benefits discussed in this chapter are subject to nondiscrimination rules. Specifically, these benefits are educational assistance, service awards, safety achievement and productivity awards, no-additional-cost services, employee discounts, dependent-care assistance, adoption assistance, and employee-assistance programs. In each case, there are rules designed to prevent or discourage the benefit plan from discriminating in favor of highly compensated employees.

The consequences of a plan being discriminatory vary. In some cases, the consequences are that no employees can receive benefits on a tax-favored basis; in other cases, this penalty applies to highly compensated employees only.

As used in this chapter, a highly compensated employee is one who meets the definition in Section 414(q) of the Internal Revenue Code. This definition is also used for the nondiscrimination rules that apply to qualified retirement plans. A **highly compensated employee** is an employee who meets one of the following criteria:

■ Is a 5 percent owner of the firm during the current year or was a 5 percent owner during the previous year.

■ Had compensation from the employer in excess of $90,000 during the previous year. However, the employer can elect to define this category of employees as only those whose compensation puts them in the top 20 percent of the organization's employees. The $90,000 figure is subject to periodic indexing.

This definition of highly compensated employee is not the same as the one used with the nondiscrimination rules for self-insured medical reimbursement plans (Chapter 14) or the one used for cafeteria plans (Chapter 19).

PAYMENTS OR OTHER BENEFITS FOR TIME NOT WORKED

Vacations

In terms of employer cost, the most significant benefit mentioned in this chapter is paid vacations. In 2003, the U.S. Chamber of Commerce reported that the cost to employers of providing vacations to employees was equal to more than 4 percent of payroll.[1] The number of vacation days given to employees increased steadily from World War II until the adverse economic times of the late 1970s. During the last few years, this trend has leveled off, and few companies have increased the number of vacation days provided. Unlike many other countries, the United States has no laws that mandate vacation benefits.

Although the specifics of vacation plans vary widely, most plans are based on the employee's length of service, and the number of vacation days given to any particular employee normally increases over time. There is usually a short waiting period (three to six months) during which employees are ineligible for vacations, but for competitive

TABLE 18.1

Length of Service	Vacation Days
First 6 Months	0
After 6 Months	1 for each month in the remaining calendar year (max. of 10)
1–5 Years	10
6–15 Years	15
16 Years or More	20

reasons there is often no waiting period for management employees. Table 18.1 is one employer's benefit schedule for its vacation plan.

Some firms have different schedules for different classes of employees, with higher-paid employees tending to have more vacation time, particularly in the earlier years of service. In contrast to many types of benefits, vacation benefits are often given to part-time employees.

In recent years, many employers have adopted cafeteria plans (Chapter 19) in which employees have some choice in designing their own benefit plans. Although most companies with cafeteria plans have a basic vacation schedule that is outside the cafeteria plan, employees may have the option of using their benefit dollars to purchase extra vacation days, often subject to approval of their supervisor and usually subject to a maximum additional number of days.

Several major issues must be addressed in properly designing a vacation plan. One is the treatment of unused vacation days. Some employers require that any unused vacation days be forfeited, although a few states require payment for the forfeited days; other employers allow them to be carried over to the next year, subject to certain limitations. A few businesses compensate employees for unused vacation days. Another issue is the question of when employees can take their vacations. In general, supervisory approval is necessary, and vacations may not be allowed during busy work times. Junior employees may also have to schedule their vacations around those of senior employees so that the number of people away from work at the same time is minimized. Other issues that must be addressed are those of how unused vacation days are treated upon termination of employment if a state does not require payment for these days and whether sicknesses and holidays occurring during vacation periods are treated as vacation days.

The compensation employees receive during periods of vacation is treated the same as compensation for time worked and is taxed accordingly.

Holidays

Employers normally pay employees for certain holidays. At a minimum, employees in the United States usually receive pay for

- New Year's Day,
- Memorial Day,

- the Fourth of July,
- Labor Day,
- Thanksgiving, and
- Christmas.

Most employees receive at least 6 and often as many as 11 or 12 additional holidays, which may include

- Martin Luther King's Birthday,
- Washington's Birthday,
- Lincoln's Birthday,
- Presidents' Day,
- Cesar Chavez Day,
- Good Friday,
- Columbus Day,
- the Friday after Thanksgiving,
- Veterans Day,
- Christmas Eve,
- New Year's Eve,
- the employee's birthday,
- other religious holidays, or
- various state holidays.

Holidays are prescribed by law for some institutions, such as banks. However, for most companies, management decides which holidays to give, subject to collective bargaining if applicable.

When a scheduled holiday falls on a Saturday, employees who normally do not work on that day are given the preceding Friday off. When a holiday falls on Sunday, it is normally observed on Monday. Restaurants and retail establishments are increasingly open for business on holidays. When this occurs, employees who work are usually paid at least time and a half and sometimes as much as triple time.

Some companies, realizing that not all employees want to take the same holidays, try to satisfy these needs by adopting holiday plans that include a minimum number of scheduled holidays coupled with a specific number (often two or three) of **floating holidays** to be taken at an employee's option. Usually, there is no requirement that the days taken actually be holidays, so in effect they become additional vacation days in lieu of holidays. Floating holidays are usually granted on an annual basis and cannot be carried over to the next year.

Like vacation pay, holiday pay is taxed as regular income.

Personal Time Off with Pay

Because personal situations that require that an employee be away from work occasionally arise, many employers allow employees to take time off with pay for certain reasons, the more common of which are the following:

■ **Reserve/National Guard duty.** Laws sometimes require that employees get time off for reserve or National Guard duty, but there is no stipulation that pay continue during this period. However, many employers pay their employees the difference between their regular pay and any compensation received for reserve or National Guard duty of short duration.

■ **Jury duty.** Most employers grant (and may be required to grant) time off for jury duty. Because employees are usually compensated for jury duty, some employers pay only the difference between this amount and an employee's regular pay. However, the amount paid for jury duty is small; typically, it just barely covers an employee's extra expenses. Therefore, many employers continue regular compensation with no deduction.

■ **Funeral (bereavement) leave.** Employers often allow up to five days off with pay for the death of an immediate family member. At a minimum, this usually includes the death of a parent, child, spouse, or other relative residing in the household. Some employers allow a shorter period of time, such as a day or a half day, to attend funerals of other relatives and sometimes even persons other than relatives.

■ **Sabbatical leave.** Sabbatical leaves are well established as employee benefits at educational institutions. Typically, faculty members are permitted an extended leave of a semester or a year after a specified period of service, such as seven years. During the sabbatical leave, the faculty member receives full or partial pay while performing no services for the employer. However, the faculty member is often required to complete a research project or some similar activity as a condition of the sabbatical. Non-educational employers, particularly those having employees with professional degrees, sometimes provide similar benefits to professional employees to give them an opportunity to engage in research or study that is not directly job related.

■ **Observation of religious holidays.** Although most businesses in the United States treat Christmas and Easter as holidays, not all employees are Christians. Therefore, employees of other faiths may be allowed time off to observe certain major religious days associated with their faith.

Some less common reasons that employers may allow time off with pay include the employee's marriage and serving as a witness in a court proceeding. Because other personal reasons for needing time off may also arise, employers may grant two or three days of personal leave that can be taken at an employee's discretion.

Personal Time Off Without Pay (Family Leave)

For many years, most industrialized countries have had legislation that enables employees to be away from work for extended periods without jeopardizing their jobs.

The reasons for such **family leave** vary among countries, as does the extent to which the employer must continue to provide pay and benefits to an employee on leave.

Over the last two decades, an increasing number of American employers have voluntarily begun to allow employees to take time off without pay. Reasons for such leave may include active military duty, extended vacations, honeymoons, education, the birth or adoption of a child, and the illness of a family member. Usually, such time off has been subject to the approval of the employer. Family leave is becoming more and more common as many states and the federal government adopt family-leave legislation.

Federal Family and Medical Leave Act. In 1993, the first federal family-leave legislation—the **Family and Medical Leave Act**—became effective. Unlike some federal legislation, it applies not only to private employers but also to nonprofit organizations and government entities, including Congress. The provisions of this legislation cover only a small percentage of the nation's employers but approximately two-thirds of all employees.

Despite concerns by employers that the act would increase costs and lower productivity, the actual effect seems to have been minimal, partly because many large employers already had leave policies similar to the act's provisions. A report issued to Congress in 1996 reported the following[2]:

- Approximately 90 percent of employers reported that there was no noticeable effect on productivity, profitability, and growth as a result of the act.

- Only about 16 percent of the persons eligible for leave actually took it. The vast majority of persons who did not take leave for which they were eligible said they could not afford the resulting wage loss.

- The median length of leave time is ten days.

- The group most likely to take leave is employees between the ages of 25 and 34.

The legislation applies only to employers who have more than 50 employees within a 75-mile radius. To comply with the 50-employee requirement, an employer needs only to have that many employees during each workday of 20 or more calendar weeks during the current or preceding calendar year. Part-time employees and employees on unpaid leaves of absence are included in the calculation. The 50-employee requirement is based on "joint employment," which means that two or more related companies can be treated as a single employer on the basis of such factors as common management, interrelations between operations, centralized control of labor relations, and the degree of common ownership or management. The 75-mile radius is based on the shortest route that can be taken on either public roads or public transportation.

With some exceptions, a worker must be allowed to take up to 12 weeks of unpaid leave in any 12-month period under the following circumstances:

- For the birth or adoption of a child
- To care for a child, spouse, or parent with a serious health condition
- For the worker's own serious health condition

An employer may use any one of the following four methods to determine the 12-month period to which the family leave applies:

1. The calendar year
2. Any fixed 12-month period
3. The 12-month period beginning with any employee's first leave
4. A rolling 12-month period measured backward from the date leave is used

With one exception, the method chosen must apply uniformly to all employees. The exception occurs if a multistate employer operates in one or more states that have family leave legislation that mandates a method different from the one chosen. In that case, the employer is permitted to comply with the state's requirement for employees located in that state but must use the chosen method for employees in other states.

A *serious health condition* is defined as one that requires continuing treatment from a health care provider. The regulations implementing the act generally define this as meaning that the condition will require absence from work, school, or regular daily activities for more than three calendar days. However, the regulations also include treatment for pregnancy and certain chronic conditions, such as diabetes and asthma, as being serious health conditions even though treatment at any time may last less than three days. In addition, the definition includes health problems that are not ordinarily incapacitating on a day-to-day basis, but for which a person is undergoing a series of multiple treatments. Examples in the regulations include chemotherapy or radiation for cancer, kidney dialysis, and physical therapy for severe arthritis. The regulations specifically exclude the following from the definition of a serious health condition: common colds, upset stomach, and routine dental problems. Stress is also excluded, but mental illness arising from stress can qualify.

The act applies to both full-time and part-time employees. The latter must be allowed to take leave on a basis that is proportional to that given to full-time employees. However, leave can be denied to anyone who has not worked for the employer for at least one year and worked at least 1,250 hours during that period.

In most cases, the rules allow employees to take leave intermittently or by working a reduced week, but only with the employer's approval. The exception is that leave because of a person's or family member's serious health condition may be taken whenever medically necessary.

An employer is allowed to substitute an employee's accrued paid leave for any part of the 12-week period of family leave. In addition, an employer can deny leave to a salaried employee within the highest-paid 10 percent of its workforce if the leave would create a substantial and grievous injury to the organization's operations.

An employee is required to provide 30 days' notice for foreseeable leaves for birth, adoption, or planned medical treatment. The employer can require that an employee provide a doctor's certification of a serious illness. An employer can also require a second opinion but must pay for the cost.

During the period of leave, an employer has no obligation to continue an employee's pay or most benefits, and the employee is ineligible for unemployment compensation. However, an employer must continue to provide medical and dental benefits during the leave as if the worker were still employed. The employee must continue to pay any required plan contributions and must be given a 30-day grace period for such payments. The employer is also required to send the employee a notice no later than 15 days before the grace period expires stating that coverage terminates if the premium is not paid. The employer is allowed to recover the cost of premiums paid by the employer during the leave if the employee does not return to work for reasons other than (1) the continuance, recurrence, or onset of a serious health condition (as previously defined) affecting the employee or the employee's spouse, parent, or child or (2) other circumstances beyond the employee's control.

Upon returning from leave, an employee must generally be given his or her former job or one that is equivalent. The employee must also be permitted to regain any benefits that he or she enjoyed prior to the leave without having to meet any requalification requirements. With respect to retirement plans, any period of leave must be treated as continued service for purposes of vesting and eligibility to participate. There is an exception to this requirement for restoration of employment that applies to employees who are among the highest-paid 10 percent of the employees employed by the employer within a 75-mile radius of the facility at which the employee works. Restoration of employment can be denied (1) if it is necessary to prevent substantial and grievous economic injury to the operations of the employer and (2) if the employer notifies the employee of the fact at the time the employer determines that such injury would occur.

An employer should have a clear, written family-leave policy that is consistently enforced. In establishing this policy, the employer should address such issues as the following:

- Eligibility requirements
- Employee certification of need for leave
- Employee rights on returning from leave
- Employer rights if employee terminates at end of leave

The federal law requires that an employer post a notice explaining the Family and Medical Leave Act, a sample of which is contained in material from the U.S. Department of Labor, which administers the law. In addition, if an employer does not provide employees with guidance about their rights and obligations under the act in employee manuals or handbooks, this information must be provided to an employee at the time he or she requests leave.

More detailed information about the act and compliance with it can be found by accessing the index on the department's Web site: *www.dol.gov.*

State Laws.   In recent years, the legislatures of almost every state have considered family-leave legislation, and more than half the states have enacted such legislation. As a general rule, these laws allow an employee to take an unpaid leave of absence for such reasons as the birth or adoption of a child and the illness of a family member. The length of leave allowed varies considerably among states but usually ranges from three to six months. When the family leave is completed, the employer is required to allow the employee to return to the same or a comparable job.

Almost all family-leave laws apply to public employers, and about half of the laws apply to private employers with more than a minimum number of employees, usually in the range of 25 to 100. In all states, employers are allowed to limit family leave to employees who have met certain eligibility requirements. Although these requirements vary, the most common requirement is at least one year of full-time employment. At a minimum, most family-leave laws allow an employee to continue medical expense coverage at his or her own cost. Some laws require that all employee benefits be made available.

Employers must comply with any applicable state law as well as with the federal Family and Medical Leave Act. Because most existing state laws have at least one provision that is broader than the federal legislation, an employer must have a broad understanding of both laws.

Uniformed Services Employment and Reemployment Rights Act. Under the **Uniformed Services Employment and Reemployment Rights Act (USERRA)**, an employee who leaves a civilian job for active military duty is entitled to return to that job, with accrued seniority, provided he or she meets the law's eligibility criteria. USERRA applies to voluntary as well as involuntary service in either peacetime or wartime. It also applies to virtually all private and government employers, regardless of size.

To have reemployment rights upon leaving military service, the former employee must meet all the following criteria:

- Have informed the employer that he or she was leaving the job for service in the uniformed services.
- Have, with some exceptions, been in the service for five years or less.
- Have been released from the service under honorable conditions.
- Have reported back to the civilian employer in a timely manner or submitted a timely application for reemployment. The precise meaning of timely varies by the time of military service and whether the former employee is recovering from a disability caused or aggravated by military service.

Even if the above criteria are satisfied, there are circumstances under which an employer is not required to reemploy a former employee. These include the following:

- The employer's circumstances have so changed as to make such reemployment impossible or unreasonable.
- The reemployment would cause an undue hardship on the employer.
- The prior employment was for a brief, nonrecurrent period and there was no reasonable expectation that such employment would have continued indefinitely or for a significant period.

USERRA also provides for the continuation of an employee's and dependents' medical expense coverage under COBRA-like rules. These rules are discussed in Chapter 14.

More detailed information can be found by accessing the index on the U.S. Department of Labor's Web site: *www.dol.gov.*

Supplemental Unemployment Benefit Plans

Collective-bargaining agreements may require that employers contribute to a **supplemental unemployment benefit (SUB) plan** that is designed to supplement state unemployment insurance benefits for workers who are unemployed. These plans rarely exist for nonunion employees. Benefits are often payable for at least a year and with regular unemployment benefits may be as high as 95 percent of what the worker was earning while employed.

SUB plans typically require that employers contribute to a SUB fund on the basis of the compensation of currently active employees; employee contributions may also be required. Trustees selected by the collective bargaining agent usually maintain the fund, and it is frequently a common fund maintained for several employers. Employer contributions to the fund are income tax deductible, and if the fund is properly designed, earnings on fund assets may also be exempt from income taxation. Benefit payments to employees are fully taxable.

■ EXTRA PAYMENTS TO EMPLOYEES

Educational Assistance

The Internal Revenue Code provides favorable tax treatment to employees for the first $5,250 of annual education assistance received from their employers. For benefits to be tax free, the employer's plan cannot discriminate with respect to eligibility in favor of officers, shareholders, highly compensated employees, or their dependents. In addition, no more than 5 percent of the benefits may be paid to shareholders or owners (or their dependents) who are more-than-5-percent owners of the firm.

Eligible benefits include tuition, fees, and books. The costs of supplies and equipment are also included as long as they are not retained after completion of the course. Note that educational assistance can now be provided for graduate courses as a result of the Economic Growth and Tax Relief Reconciliation Act of 2001. Reimbursements for meals, lodging, and transportation associated with educational expenses cannot be received tax free. In addition, courses involving sports, games, or hobbies are ineligible for favorable tax treatment. Although an employer's plan can pay for any of these types of courses, an employee is taxed on the value of the employer's contribution to his or her cost.

Many employers provide reimbursement for certain educational expenses that do not qualify for favorable tax treatment under the Code. Although such reimbursements result in taxable compensation for an employee, the employee may be eligible for a federal income tax deduction (subject to the 2 percent-of-adjusted-gross-income floor on miscellaneous itemized deductions) if he or she itemizes deductions. The deduction is allowed for educational expenses that are incurred (1) to maintain or improve a skill required in employment or (2) to meet the express requirements of the employer as a condition for retaining employment. Other types of educational expenses, such as costs incurred to qualify the employee for a new trade or business, are not deductible.

Moving-Expense Reimbursement

To attract new employees and to encourage current employees to move to suit the employer's needs, many businesses provide reimbursement for moving expenses. Such reimbursement is includible in an employee's income, but the employee is allowed certain offsetting income tax deductions if specified rules are satisfied. To receive the deductions, the employee must have moved because of a change in job location. In addition, the employee must satisfy both a distance test and a time test. The distance test requires that the employee's new workplace be at least 50 miles farther from the employee's old residence than the employee's old workplace (or old residence if the employee was previously unemployed). The time test requires that the employee work full time in the general location of the new residence for at least 39 weeks during the 12 months following the move. An employee may take the applicable deductions in anticipation of satisfying the time test, but additional taxes are payable if the time test is not ultimately met.

If all the preceding rules are satisfied, an employee may deduct the following expenses:

- Transportation expenses in moving household goods and personal effects
- Travel and lodging expenses (but not meal expenses) in moving to the new residence

An employer may pay for other expenses, such as expenses to sell an old residence, premove travel to find a new residence, or temporary living costs at the new location. Because these reimbursements are taxable income without a corresponding deduction, the employer may give the employee a bonus to offset the increased tax.

Suggestion Awards

Some employers, particularly those in manufacturing industries, give awards to employees who make suggestions for improving the operating efficiency of the firm. The awards are often a percentage of the firm's estimated savings over some specified future period of time but may be subject to a maximum dollar amount. If a suggestion plan is properly administered, the benefits of the plan may far exceed its costs while at the same time increasing the motivation and involvement of employees.

Suggestion awards are included in an employee's gross income for tax purposes.

Service Awards

Many employers provide awards to employees for length of service. These awards are often nominal for short periods of service (five or ten years) and may consist of such items as key chains, flowers, or pens. Awards typically increase in value for longer periods of service, and employees may actually be given some choice in the award received.

If the value of a service award is **de minimis**, it is not included in an employee's income. To be *de minimis,* the value of the benefit must be so minimal that accounting for the cost of the benefit would be unreasonable or administratively impractical. Service awards of higher value may also be excludable from an employee's income if they are considered *qualified plan awards.* However, the total amount excludable from an employee's income for qualified plan awards (which also include awards for safety) cannot exceed $1,600 per year. Qualified plan awards must be provided under a permanent written program that does not discriminate in favor of officers, shareholders, or highly compensated employees. In addition, the average annual cost of all awards under the plan cannot exceed $400.

Productivity and Safety Achievement Awards

Some employers provide awards for productivity and safety achievement. Productivity awards are fully treated as compensation. However, although awards for safety achievement given to professional, administrative, managerial, or clerical employees are fully taxable, such awards are treated as qualified plan awards for other employees and are included in the $1,600 figure mentioned previously under service awards.

Holiday Bonuses and Gifts

Many employers, particularly at Christmastime, give gifts or bonuses to employees. Because the value of such gifts is typically small, some employees tend to resent gifts of money. Therefore, such gifts as liquor or a ham are often given.

As with service awards, a holiday gift does not result in taxation for an employee as long as the market value of the gift is small.

■ SERVICES TO EMPLOYEES

No-Additional-Cost Services

Employers in many service industries provide their employees with free or discounted services, often referred to as **no-additional-cost services**. Examples include telephone service to employees of phone companies and airline tickets to employees of airlines. As long as the following rules are satisfied, the cost of these services is not includible in an employee's gross income for tax purposes:

■ The services cannot be provided on a basis that discriminates in favor of highly compensated employees.

■ The employer must not incur any significant additional cost or lost revenue in providing the services. For example, giving a standby ticket to an airline employee if there are unsold seats on a flight satisfies this requirement, but giving an airline ticket to an employee when potential paying customers are denied seats does not.

■ The services must be those that are provided in the employer's line of business in which the employee actually works. Therefore, if a business owns both an airline and a chain of hotels, an employee of the hotels can be given a room as a tax-free benefit but not an airline ticket. However, unrelated employers in the same line of business, such as airlines, may enter into reciprocal arrangements under which employees of any party to the arrangement may obtain services from the other parties.

Employee Discounts

Just as no-additional-cost services are an important employee benefit in certain service industries, discounts on the merchandise sold by manufacturers and retailers are an important benefit to employees in these industries. Discounts may also be provided on services sold by other types of businesses, such as the commission charged by a brokerage house or insurance company.

Rules similar to those discussed for no-additional-cost services apply to discounts. Employees have no taxable income as long as the discounts are made available on a nondiscriminatory basis and are provided on goods or services ordinarily sold to non-employees in the employer's line of business in which the employee works. However, there are some additional rules. Discounts received on real estate or on personal property normally held as an investment (for example, gold coins or securities) are not received tax free. Furthermore, there is a limit on the size of a discount that can be received tax free. The discount for merchandise cannot exceed the gross profit percentage of the price at which the merchandise is offered for sale to customers. For example, if an employer has a gross profit margin of 40 percent on a particular product and an employee purchases the merchandise at a 50 percent discount, the extra 10 percent is taxable income to the employee. In the case of services, including insurance policies, the tax-free discount cannot exceed 20 percent of the price at which the service is offered to nonemployee customers in the normal course of the employer's business. The type of service that cannot be received tax free involves loans that financial institutions give to employees at a discounted rate of interest.

Dependent-Care Assistance

Changes in society and the workforce often create changing needs for both employers and employees. When the workforce was largely male and most families had two parents, caring for children and older parents frequently was the female spouse's responsibility. As the number of families headed by two wage earners or by single parents has increased, so has the need for dependent care. This change in demographics has also created problems for employers. Caring for family members can lead to increased absenteeism, tardiness, turnover, and time taken as family leave. Workplace morale can also suffer if the employer is viewed as insensitive to employee responsibilities.

The nature of employee benefit plans has changed as employers have increasingly responded to the need for dependent care and many employers have established a **dependent-care assistance plan (DCAP)**. Child-care benefits are increasingly common, and a small but growing number of firms also make elder-care benefits available. Firms that have dependent-care assistance plans generally feel that such plans alleviate the problems cited in the previous paragraph. Furthermore, the availability of the benefit often makes it easier to hire new employees.

In addition to a formal dependent-care assistance plan, there are other ways in which employers can respond to employee needs to care for family members. These include flexible work schedules, part-time employment, job sharing, salary reduction options under cafeteria plans, and family-leave policies that are more liberal than those required by federal and state laws.

Child-Care Plans. Several alternative types of benefits can be provided under a **child-care plan**. A few employers maintain on-site day-care centers, and the number is growing. On the other hand, some employers have closed on-site centers and provide alternative forms of assistance because of the following problems encountered with on-site centers:

■ Difficulty in obtaining qualified child-care providers.

■ Difficulty in obtaining liability insurance.

■ Difficulty, time, and expense associated with obtaining necessary zoning variances and child-care licenses.

■ Distractions caused by parents and children being so close together.

■ Underutilization. Although this type of facility would be expected to be popular, many employees prefer other alternatives. A site close to home is often more appealing than a location that may involve a long commute for parent and child. An on-site location may be less convenient if both parents share in child-care activities. Employees may also prefer a different type of child-care arrangement.

Some employers provide benefits by supporting a limited number of off-site child-care centers. The employer may make arrangements to reserve spaces for employees' children at these centers and/or arrange for corporate discounts for employees.

Probably the most common approach is to provide reimbursements to employees who make their own arrangements for child care, either at child-care centers or in their own home or the home of a caregiver. Reimbursement is sometimes tied to pay levels, with lower-paid workers receiving higher reimbursements.

When employees are required to make their own arrangements under a child-care plan, employers may provide information and referral services—often through a contract with community or private referral services. In addition to providing assistance in locating a quality child-care center, these services can provide help in finding drop-in facilities when the usual child-care arrangement has fallen through or when school is closed for a day. They may also maintain a list of persons who care for temporarily ill children at home or for children after school hours. Such services may also be a source of information about facilities that can be used during summer and other school vacations.

Elder-Care Benefits.   Benefits to care for elderly dependents are much less prevalent than benefits for child care, but the need for them continues to grow as parents live longer. In addition, as many couples have delayed having children until later in life, they have become part of what is often referred to as the *sandwich generation*. They must care for elderly parents at the same time they are raising their own children.

Although an **elder-care benefit** may take a variety of forms, frequently it is much like the benefit provided under a child-care plan. Within limits, the employer may pay for costs associated with home care for elderly dependents or care at day-care facilities for the elderly. One interesting development in this area is the establishment of centers that care for both children and the elderly, with the elderly assisting in such activities as the feeding and teaching of the children. Studies have shown that the two groups are very compatible. Children, particularly those without grandparents nearby, can benefit from the attention and knowledge they receive from the elderly, while the elderly can have a feeling of usefulness.

Other employer activities involving elder care may include the following:

- Seminars on issues affecting the elderly

- Information on services available to provide elder care and how to use the services

- Employer-sponsored support groups in which employees can share experiences and learn from others

- Expansion of employee-assistance plans to include elder care

- Making long-term care insurance available to employees, and including parents as an eligible group for coverage

Tax Treatment of Benefits.   Under the Internal Revenue Code, dependent care is a tax-free benefit to employees up to statutory limits as long as certain requirements are met. The amount of benefits that can be received tax free is limited to $5,000 for single persons and married persons who file jointly and to $2,500 for married persons who file separately. The benefits must be for care to a qualifying individual—a child under age 13 for whom the employee is allowed a dependency deduction on his or her income tax return or a taxpayer's spouse or other dependent who is mentally or physically incapable of caring for himself or herself. Although benefits must generally be for custodial care only, educational expenses at the kindergarten or preschool level can also be paid.

Dependent-care benefits are subject to a series of rules. If the rules are not met, highly compensated employees are taxed on the amount of benefits received. However, the benefits for other employees still retain their tax-free status. The following rules must be met:

- Eligibility, contributions, and benefits under the plan cannot discriminate in favor of highly compensated employees or their dependents.

- No more than 25 percent of the benefits may be provided to the class composed of persons who own more than a 5 percent interest in the firm.

- Reasonable notification of the availability of benefits and the terms of the plan must be provided to eligible employees.

■ By January 31 of the following year, each employee must receive an annual statement that indicates the amounts paid or expenses incurred by the employer to provide benefits.

■ The average benefit provided to non–highly compensated employees must be at least 55 percent of the average benefit provided to highly compensated employees.

In meeting the 55 percent benefit test, an employer can exclude employees earning under $25,000 if benefits are provided through a salary reduction agreement. For both the 55 percent benefit test and the nondiscrimination rule for eligibility, an employer can exclude employees who (1) are under age 21, (2) have not completed one year of service, or (3) are covered under a collective bargaining unit that has bargained over dependent-care benefits.

Even if an employer does not provide assistance for dependent care, other tax-saving options may be available to employees. Under the Code, a tax credit (subject to limits) is available for child-care expenses. In addition, the employer may have the opportunity to make before-tax contributions to a cafeteria plan that includes dependent care as an option.

Adoption Assistance

Although many types of benefits have long been available to natural parents because of the birth of a child, comparable benefits historically have not been available to adoptive parents. Over the last few years, this disparity has begun to change as some employers have instituted an **adoption assistance plan.** Even before the passage of family-leave legislation, many employers had established comparable leave policies for natural parents and adoptive parents. For example, if an employer allowed maternity leave (either paid or unpaid) for a new mother, no distinction was made between natural mothers and adoptive mothers. Leave may also be available for time involved in qualifying for the adoption and taking possession of the child.

A smaller number of employers provide reimbursement for some or all of the following expenses associated with adoption:

■ Legal fees

■ Adoption agencies' fees

■ The birth mother's medical expenses

■ The adoptive parents' medical expenses for physical examinations required by the adoption source

■ The child's uninsured medical expenses

■ Foster care charges for the child prior to placement with the adoptive family

■ Transportation expenses associated with taking custody of the child

■ Extra expenses associated with foreign adoptions

Reimbursements are generally available only to employees who have satisfied some minimum service requirement, most commonly one year. Amounts typically range from

$1,000 to $3,000 per adoption, but higher amounts may be paid for adoptions involving handicapped children or children from a foreign country. There may also be a lifetime cap, such as $6,000.

As a result of changes resulting from the Economic Growth and Tax Relief Reconciliation Act of 2001, employer payments of up to $10,390 per child (in 2004) for qualified adoption expenses are now excludible from an employee's gross income if an employer has an adoption-assistance program that satisfies IRS requirements. This amount is subject to annual cost-of-living adjustments.

Employer payments to an employee who adopts a child with special needs can then be provided up to the specified dollar limit whether or not there are qualified adoption expenses. Note that any payments in excess of actual adoption expenses are tax free only if the child is a citizen or resident of the United States and meets a state's definition of a child with special needs.

The adoption-assistance program must be a separate written plan, and employees must have reasonable notification of the availability of the program and its benefits. The program cannot discriminate in favor of highly compensated employees or their dependents, and no more than 5 percent of the benefits under the plan can be paid to shareholders or owners (or their dependents) who are more-than-5-percent owners of the firm.

Qualified adoption expenses include reasonable and necessary adoption fees, court costs, attorney's fees, travel expenses, and other expenses directly related to the legal adoption of an eligible child, defined as a child who is under age 18 or who is incapable of caring for himself or herself. Expenses incurred in adopting a spouse's child or carrying out a surrogate parenting arrangement are not qualified adoption expenses, nor are expenses that are reimbursed from other sources. In addition, expenses to adopt a child with special needs are not qualified adoption expenses unless the adoption becomes final.

The full $10,390 exclusion from gross income is available to employees with an adjusted gross income of $155,860 or less, and married couples must file joint returns to obtain the exclusion. For employees with higher adjusted gross incomes, the exclusion is gradually phased out until it is eliminated when adjusted gross income reaches $195,860. These phase-out amounts are also subject to annual cost-of-living adjustments.

There is a similar tax credit available to all taxpayers for adoption expenses, but the credit is not available for expenses that were paid by employer-provided adoption assistance regardless of whether the employer paid the expenses through an adoption-assistance program. However, the credit can be used for expenses not reimbursed by an employer's plan.

Wellness Programs

Traditional benefit programs have been designed to provide benefits (1) to employees for their medical expenses and disabilities or (2) to their dependents if the employee should die prematurely. In the last few years, it has become more common for an employer, particularly a large corporation, to initiate a wellness program that is designed to promote the well-being of employees (and possibly their dependents). Some wellness programs have been aimed at the discovery and treatment of medical conditions before they become severe and result in large medical expenses, disabilities, or death. Other programs have focused on changing employees' lifestyles to eliminate the possible causes of future medical problems. A few programs, such as making flu shots available to employees, actually provide medical treatment. Recent studies have shown that the costs of establishing and maintaining many of these programs are more than offset by the lower amounts paid for medical expense, disability, and death benefits. In addition, if long-term disabilities and premature deaths can be eliminated, the expenses associated with training new employees can be minimized. Many firms also feel these programs increase productivity by improving the employees' sense of well-being, their work attitudes, and their family relationships.

Many employers undertake wellness programs directly. In addition, they are often integral parts of managed care plans.

Medical Screening Programs.   The use of a **medical screening program** to discover existing medical conditions is not new, but it has often covered the costs (frequently up to some dollar limit) of routine physical examinations only for selected groups of management employees. Although this benefit may be highly valued by these employees, and its use as an executive benefit has been increasing somewhat, there are doubts—even among the medical profession—as to its cost effectiveness, particularly when it is provided on an annual basis. Certain medical conditions undoubtedly are discovered during a complete physical, but most of them are also diagnosed by less frequent and less costly forms of medical examinations.

In recent years, there has been a significant increase in the number of employers that sponsor periodic medical screening programs that detect specific medical problems, such as hypertension (high blood pressure), high cholesterol levels, breast cancer, prostate cancer, and colorectal cancer. Generally, such screenings are conducted at the employment site during regular working hours. A physician sometimes conducts a screening, but lower-paid medical professionals usually perform it. In addition, screenings can sometimes be obtained at little or no cost through such organizations as the American Red Cross, the American Heart Association, or the American Cancer Society.

Lifestyle-Management Programs.   A **lifestyle-management program** is primarily designed to encourage employees and often their dependents to modify their behavior so that they lead healthier lives. Most of these programs strive to discover and eliminate conditions that increase the likelihood of cardiovascular problems (the source of a significant percentage of medical expenses and premature deaths). Some of these conditions (such as obesity and smoking) are obvious, but medical screening can also detect less obvious conditions like hypertension, high cholesterol levels, and the degree of an employee's physical fitness. The types of programs often instituted to promote cardiovascular health include the following:

- Smoking-cessation programs.
- Fitness programs. They may consist of formal exercise programs or exercise facilities (such as swimming pools, exercise rooms, or jogging tracks). Some employee benefit consultants question whether facilities for competitive sports (such as rac-

quetball courts) are cost-justified because their availability is limited, and their use often causes injuries.

■ Weight-reduction programs.

■ Nutrition programs. These are often established in conjunction with weight-reduction programs, but they can also teach methods of cholesterol reduction even if there is no weight problem.

■ Stress-management programs.

These programs may be available to any employees who express an interest in them, or they may be limited only to those employees who have been evaluated and found to be in a high-risk category for cardiovascular disease. This evaluation may consist of questionnaires regarding health history, blood pressure reading, blood chemistry analyses, and fitness tests. Generally, these evaluations and meetings to describe the programs and their value are conducted during regular working hours. However, the programs themselves are usually conducted during nonworking hours, possibly at lunchtime or just after work.

Many wellness programs are designed to include employees, their spouses, and sometimes other family members. In many instances, it is not possible to change an employee's lifestyle unless the lifestyle of his or her entire family also changes. For example, it is not very probable that an employee will stop smoking if his or her spouse also smokes and is making no attempt to stop. Similarly, a weight-reduction or nutrition program is probably more effective if all family members alter their eating habits.

Programs designed to eliminate alcohol or drug abuse are another example of lifestyle management. Participation may be voluntary or it can be mandatory for employees who are known to have alcohol or drug problems and who want to keep their jobs. When these programs have been successful, many employers have found a decrease in employee absenteeism.

Some employers have also instituted programs that seek to minimize back problems—the reason for a large percentage of employee absenteeism and disability claims. These programs are generally intended for employees who have a history of back trouble, and they consist of exercises as well as education in how to modify or avoid activities that can aggravate existing back conditions.

More recently, many employers have become concerned with the spread of AIDS and its effect on the cost of benefit plans. As a result, they have instituted educational programs aimed at encouraging employees to avoid activities that may result in the transmission of AIDS.

The employer may either conduct these wellness activities on the premises or use the resources of other organizations. For example, overweight employees might be sent to Weight Watchers, employees with alcohol problems might be encouraged to attend Alcoholics Anonymous, and employees with back problems might be enrolled in programs at a local YMCA.

Employers in increasing numbers are subscribing to wellness newsletters and distributing them to employees. To encourage wellness for the entire family, these newsletters are often mailed to employees' homes.

Effect of HIPAA. Provisions of the Health Insurance Portability and Accountability Act (HIPAA) affect wellness programs that provide rewards for adherence to health promotion and disease prevention programs. These rewards might be in the form of discounts, rebates, or modification of deductibles or copayments. With an exception mentioned later, HIPAA does not permit such rewards unless a wellness program is considered bona fide.

A bona fide wellness program must meet four requirements:

1. The rewards for the wellness programs, together with rewards from any other wellness programs, cannot exceed a specified percentage of the cost of employee-only coverage under a medical expenses plan. Current regulations, which are relatively new, do not yet specify a final percentage, but 10, 15, and 20 percent are being considered.

2. The program must be reasonably designed to promote good health or prevent disease. The regulations specifically indicate that such a program is not reasonably designed unless it gives employees the opportunity to qualify for the reward at least once a year.

3. The reward must be available to all similarly situated individuals. The program must have a reasonable alternative standard to obtain the reward for persons who cannot satisfy the otherwise applicable standard because meeting the standard is unreasonably difficult or not medically advisable. For example, if a premium discount were allowed for nonsmokers, a person with an addiction to nicotine would need to have an alternative standard to receive the reward. The standard might be to participate in a smoking cessation course. However, the reward could be conditioned on participation only, not whether the course was successful.

4. The availability of a reasonable alternative standard previously mentioned must be disclosed in all plan materials describing the wellness programs.

The HIPAA regulations provide an exception to the requirements for a bona fide wellness program if a reward is based solely on an individual's participation in a wellness program. HIPAA uses the following as examples of programs that are acceptable:

- Reimbursing employees, without regard to health factors, for the cost of health club memberships
- Voluntary testing for specific health problems and making recommendations for their treatment
- Waiving copayments and deductibles for well-baby visits
- Reeimbursing employees for the costs of smoking cessation programs without regard to whether a participant quits smoking

Tax Treatment of Benefits. Because medical screening programs are treated as medical expenses for tax purposes, employees have no taxable income as a result of participating in these programs. Unless the cost of providing lifestyle-management programs is *de minimis,* participation probably results in taxation to employees. The costs of programs that promote general health, such as smoking cessation or weight control, are not considered medical expenses. Although the cost of providing these programs to employees is deductible by the employer, an employee incurs taxable income unless the purpose of the program is to alleviate a specific medical problem. However, there is one exception to this general rule. Employees incur no taxable income as a result of being provided with or using athletic facilities that are located on the employer's premises.

Employee-Assistance Programs

As the trend toward fostering wellness in the workplace continues, it is increasingly common for an employer to establish an **employee-assistance program**. These programs are designed to help employees with certain personal problems through a plan that provides

- treatment for alcohol or drug abuse;
- counseling for mental problems and stress;
- counseling for family and marital problems;
- financial, legal, and tax advice;
- referrals for child care or elder care; and
- crisis intervention.

Numerous studies have shown that proper treatment of these problems is very cost effective and leads to reduced sick days, hospital costs, disability, and absenteeism. It is also argued that employee morale and productivity are increased as a result of the concern shown for employees' personal problems.

Traditionally, employee-assistance programs have used job performance as the basis for employer concern. Essentially, an employee is told that his or her work is substandard and asked if a problem exists that he or she would like to discuss with someone. If the employee says yes, referral is made to an appropriate counselor or agency. No attempt is made by the employee's supervisor to diagnose the specific problem. Newer employee-assistance programs go beyond this approach by allowing employees who have problems to go directly to the program and seek help. Dependents can usually use the employee assistance program and can often seek help without the employee's knowledge.

Another recent trend in employee-assistance programs is to coordinate them more closely with the employer's medical expense plan. For example, several employee-assistance programs act as the gatekeeper for mental health and substance abuse services. An employee must go through the employee-assistance program before benefits can be received under his or her medical expense coverage. The objective of this approach is to establish a course of treatment that has maximum effectiveness for the costs incurred.

Access to an employee-assistance program is through a counselor who may be a company employee, but most often an employer establishes the plan through a professional organization that specializes in such programs. Information provided to the counselor by the employee is kept confidential. Many problems can be solved by discussion between the counselor and the employee, and most plans have 24-hour counseling available, through either a telephone hot line or on-duty personnel. If the counselor cannot solve an employee's problem, it is the counselor's responsibility to make a preliminary determination about the type of professional help the employee should receive. In many cases, this treatment can be provided under existing medical expense or legal expense plans or through community agencies. The employer usually pays the costs of other types of treatment totally or in part. As long as the treatment is for the purpose of alleviating medical conditions, including mental illness, an employee has no taxable income. If the treatment is for a nonmedical condition, the employee has taxable income as the result of employer payments.

Financial Planning Programs for Executives

Employers are increasingly providing financial planning as a benefit to employees. Although traditionally this benefit was limited to a small number of top executives, many firms are now expanding their programs to include members of middle management. In addition, financial planning education and advice are now offered to many employees as part of a broader preretirement-counseling program. Any program in overall financial planning must take into consideration the benefits that are provided or that are potentially available under group insurance plans, under social insurance programs, and through the individual efforts of employees.

The concept of providing financial planning for a limited number of top executives has been widely practiced for many years, particularly in large corporations. However, within the last few years, a significant number of corporations have expanded these programs to include middle management employees in the $50,000 to $100,000 annual salary range. Businesses have deemed this financial planning benefit as necessary for top executives, who have limited time for their own financial affairs, so that they can be free to devote their full talents to important business decisions. A company may also find it easier to attract and retain executives who look on the financial planning program as a way to make existing compensation more valuable (for example, by providing a larger spendable income through tax planning or a greater accumulation of wealth through investment planning).

Although group meetings are sometimes used (for example, to explain certain types of investments or changes in the tax laws), most financial planning programs provide for individual counseling of employees to suit each employee's own particular circumstances and needs.

Types of Planning. Financial planning is composed of many separate but interrelated segments:

- Compensation planning, including the explanation of employee benefits and an analysis of any available compensation options
- Preparation of tax returns
- Estate planning, including the preparation of wills and planning to both minimize estate taxes and maintain proper estate liquidity

■ Investment planning, including both investment advice and investment management

■ Insurance planning, including information on how to meet life insurance, medical expense, disability, and property and liability needs

A financial planning program may be designed to provide either selected services from the list above or a comprehensive array of services. **Comprehensive financial planning** can be thought of as a series of interrelated and continuing activities that begin with the collection and analysis of personal and financial information, including the risk attitudes of an employee. This information is used (1) to establish the priorities and time horizons for attaining personal objectives and (2) to develop the financial plan that meets these objectives. Once the plan is formulated, the next critical step is the actual implementation of the plan. A proper financial planning program should also include a process for measuring the performance of any plan so that, if it is unacceptable, either the plan can be changed or the employee's objectives can be revised.

Sources of Financial Planning. A few firms provide financial planning services using the organization's own employees. Most firms purchase the services either from outside specialists (such as lawyers, accountants, insurance agents, or stockbrokers) or from companies or individuals that do comprehensive financial planning.

Significant differences exist among financial planning firms. Some operate solely on a fee basis and give only advice and counseling, in which case it is the employee's responsibility to have his or her own attorney, insurance agent, or other financial professional implement any decisions. These financial planning firms often work closely with the other professionals in handling the employee's affairs. The cost of using a fee-only financial planning firm varies, depending upon what services it provides, but initial fees of $5,000 per employee and annual charges of $1,000 to $2,000 are not uncommon.

Other financial planning firms operate on a product-oriented basis and sell products (usually insurance or investments) in addition to other financial planning services. The fact that these firms receive commissions from the products they sell may eliminate or reduce any fees paid by the employer. Unfortunately, the insurance or investment advice of these firms may be slanted in favor of the products they sell. Therefore, employers must make sure that the advice of outside specialists is unbiased and presented in a professional manner.

Tax Treatment. Fees paid for financial planning are tax deductible by the employer as long as the total compensation paid to an employee is reasonable. The amount of any fees paid to a financial planning firm or other professional on behalf of an individual employee becomes taxable income to the employee. However, an employee may be able to take miscellaneous itemized deductions for certain services relating to tax matters and investment advice. Services the employer provides to executives on an individual basis also result in taxable income.

Preretirement-Counseling Programs

Businesses, aware of the pitfalls that await unprepared retired employees, have increasingly begun to offer preretirement counseling. It has been estimated that this benefit is offered by approximately 75 percent of companies with 20,000 or more employees. For companies with fewer than 1,000 employees, the figure is closer to 15 or 20 percent. Most of these companies have made this benefit available to all employees over a specific age (such as 50 or 55), but an increasing number of organizations allow employees of any age to participate. Retired employees may also be invited to take advantage of any program benefits that are of interest to them.

A **preretirement-counseling program** differs from a financial planning program for executives in that there is very little individual counseling. Rather, employees meet in groups to listen to media presentations and speakers, and they are given the opportunity to ask questions and discuss their concerns. This counseling may take place during nonwork hours, but there is an increasing trend to have it provided during work hours, often in a concentrated one-day or two-day period. Most companies encourage spouses to participate. Often, one program is developed for all employees, although some organizations vary their programs for different classifications of employees (such as management employees and blue-collar workers).

When these programs are successful, the fears that many employees have about retirement can be alleviated. They learn that with proper planning retirement can be not only financially comfortable but also a meaningful period in their lives.

Financial Planning.   Some preretirement-counseling programs devote at least half their time to the financial aspects of retirement. Because proper financial planning for retirement must begin many years prior to actual retirement, the amount of time devoted to this subject is greatest in programs that encourage employees to begin participation at younger ages.

Some financial planning meetings help employees identify and determine what their financial needs are after retirement and what resources are available to meet those needs from the company's benefit plans and from Social Security. If retirement needs are not met by these sources, employees are informed about how their individual efforts can supplement retirement income through savings or investments. They are also told about the specific advantages and risks associated with each method of saving or investment. In addition, such issues as the need for wills and estate planning may be discussed. Such preretirement financial planning is conducted on a group basis; the programs are unlikely to provide investment advice on an individual basis or through an investment management service, as described in the previous section on financial planning programs for executives. However, some employers do give employees financial planning reports that are prepared through a computerized financial planning system. These reports, which may vary in length from 20 to 60 pages, are generated from the data on a questionnaire completed by the employee. They may offer advice on such topics as the additional amount of money that should be saved for retirement or compare the cost of working with the cost of retiring.

Many employers now make computer software available to employees so they can enter basic personal and financial data for varying scenarios related to retirement, education funding, and the like. The major advantage of these computer programs is that an employee can quickly evaluate alternative assumptions about such factors as retirement dates and savings rates. One potential drawback to the use of computer programs is the lack of employee understanding about the assumptions and reasoning that lie behind the input into the program and about the output that results. Therefore, it is important that computer programs be accompanied by proper training in their purpose, use, and interpretation.

Other Aspects of Preretirement Counseling.   Preretirement counseling focuses on other aspects of retirement besides financial needs. The following are some of the questions that must also be faced by most retired workers and that are often addressed in preretirement-counseling programs:

■ Living arrangements. What are the pros and cons of selling a house and moving into an apartment or condominium? Is relocation in the Sunbelt away from family members and friends advisable?

■ Health. Can changes in lifestyle lead to healthier retirement years?

■ Free time. How can the time that was previously devoted to work be used? Are there opportunities for volunteer work, part-time employment, or continuing education? What leisure activities or community activities can be adopted that continue into retirement? (Studies have shown that alcoholism, divorce, and suicide tend to increase among the retired. Much of this increase has been attributed to the lack of activities to fill free time and to the problems encountered by husbands and wives who are constantly together for the first time in their lives.)

Sources of Preretirement Counseling.   An organization may establish and maintain its own program of preretirement counseling. However, many organizations (such as benefit-counseling firms and the American Association of Retired Persons) have developed packaged programs that are sold to other organizations. These programs typically consist of media presentations and information regarding the types of speakers that should be used in counseling sessions. Generally, these packaged programs are flexible enough to be used with almost any type of employee group. Most firms actually conduct preretirement-counseling programs with a combination of their own employees and outside speakers or organizations. It is becoming common to see the use of an organization's own retirees in the counseling process.

Tax Treatment.   As long as no specific services are provided to employees on an individual basis, they do not have taxable income to report as a result of participating in preretirement counseling programs.

Transportation/Free Parking

Some employers have long provided transportation benefits to employees as a fringe benefit. These benefits are in the form of various types of reimbursement for commuting expenses, the use of company-owned vehicles for vanpooling, and free parking. However, except for free parking, employees have usually had taxable income as a result of these benefits. To increase the use of public transportation and decrease the reliance on the use of private passenger automobiles, the Comprehensive National Energy Policy Act of 1992 changed the tax rules governing transportation benefits. As a result of the act, the Internal Revenue Code provides favorable tax treatment to transportation benefits that meet the definition of a **qualified transportation fringe**, which includes the following:

■ Transportation in a commuter highway vehicle if such transportation is in connection with travel between the employee's residence and place of employment. The commuter vehicle must have a capacity of at least six adults other than the driver. At least 80 percent of the mileage use of the vehicle must reasonably be expected to be for transporting employees to and from work and occur when at least one-half of the vehicle's seating capacity is filled. Traditional vanpools, in which one employee usually has possession of an employer-provided vehicle to drive other employees to work, come under this definition as long as these criteria are satisfied.

■ Transit passes. These include any pass, token, fare card, voucher, or similar item entitling a person to transportation as long as it is on a mass transit system or in a commuter highway vehicle as previously described.

■ Qualified parking. This includes parking provided on or near the business premises of the employer or near a location from which the employee commutes to work by using a mass transit facility or a commuter highway vehicle. Qualified parking does not include parking on or near a premises used by the employee for residential purposes.

The value of the benefit under a qualified transportation fringe is excluded from gross compensation up to specified amounts, which are subject to cost-of-living adjustments. The 2004 figures are

■ $100 per month in the aggregate for any transit passes and transportation in a commuter highway vehicle;

■ $195 per month for qualified parking.

Amounts in excess of the above and the value of employer transportation benefits that do not meet the definition of a qualified transportation fringe are fully taxable to employees. Three additional points should be made about qualified transportation benefits. First, they can be provided on a discriminatory basis. Second, the employer can either provide the benefits directly or give a cash reimbursement to the employee, with one exception: Cash reimbursement for a transit pass is not acceptable if such a pass is readily available for direct distribution by the employer to the employee. Third, when an employer does not wish to assume the cost of the benefits, they can still be provided under an arrangement that allows an employee to enter into a salary-reduction agreement up to the applicable limits. However, such an agreement is irrevocable during its specified term even if the employee is no longer eligible for the transportation benefits. The major advantage of such a salary reduction is that an employee's income is reduced for federal income tax purposes.

Personal Use of Company Cars

Employers often provide employees with company cars (or other types of vehicles). In addition to using a vehicle for business purposes, an employee may also be allowed to use the car for commuting to and from work and for other personal purposes. However, an employee who drives a company car for personal use must include the value of this use in his or her taxable income.

The method for valuing the use of a car is determined by the employer, and several choices are available. The most common method for valuing the car is for the employer to report an annual cost that is a percentage of the car's annual lease value. This value is determined by a table prepared by the IRS and is based on a car's fair market value unless an employer can clearly justify a lower value. Under this table, a car with a fair market value of $20,000 to $20,999 has an annual lease value of $5,600. This figure is then multiplied by the ratio of personal-use miles to total miles. For example, if 20 percent of the miles driven are personal miles, the employer must report $1,120 of income for the employee. Additional income must also be reported if the employer pays for gas.

A second method is for the employer to annually report the entire lease value of the car as taxable income. If the employer uses this alternative, the employee can claim an income tax deduction for any business use of the vehicle if the employee itemizes his or her deduction. However, the deduction is subject to the 2 percent floor requirement for miscellaneous deductions. This alternative is less favorable to the employee but administratively less burdensome to the employer.

A third alternative is to report a value that is based solely on the employee's use of the vehicle. Under IRS regulations, a flat mileage rate may be used for each personal mile driven. The mileage rate, which is adjusted annually, is 36.0 cents in 2003. This alternative is available only if a car's fair market value does not exceed a specified value ($15,300 in 2003) and one of the following criteria is satisfied: (1) more than 50 percent of the car's use is for business, (2) the car is used each day in an employer-sponsored commuting pool, or (3) the car is driven at least 10,000 miles per year and is used primarily by employees. The 2004 figures were not available at the time this book was being revised.

The final alternative is available if the employer has a written policy that the employee must commute in the vehicle and cannot use the vehicle for other than minimal personal use. In this case, the value of the car's use is $1.50 times the number of one-way commutes or $3 times the number of round-trip commutes.

Subsidized Eating Facilities

Employers often provide fully or partially subsidized eating facilities for employees. Lunch is the most commonly served meal, but breakfast and dinner may also be served. Such facilities offer a place for employees to discuss common issues and may minimize the chance that employees will take prolonged lunch periods at off-site restaurants. The popularity of these facilities tends to vary with the price of meals, the convenience of alternative places to eat, and the quality of the food served.

The subsidized value of meals served to employees is excluded from taxable income as long as the meals are (1) provided on the business premises and (2) furnished for the convenience of the employer. In general, meals are considered to be furnished for the employer's convenience if there are inadequate facilities in the area for employees to obtain meals within a reasonable period of time. If the requirements regarding the business premises and/or the convenience of the employer are not satisfied, the subsidized value of any meals consumed by employees is included in taxable income.

Employees are not allowed to deduct any portion of the cost they pay for individual meals. However, if an employee is required to have a fixed periodic charge for meals deducted from wages or salary (such as $15 per week), this amount is excluded from taxable income.

■ KEY TERMS

Adoption assistance plan

child-care plan

comprehensive financial planning

de minimis

dependent-care assistance plan (DCAP)

elder care benefit

employee-assistance program

Family and Medical Leave Act

family leave

floating holidays

funeral (bereavement) leave

highly compensated employee

lifestyle-management program

medical screening program

no-additional-cost services

preretirement-counseling program

qualified transportation fringe

sabbatical leave

supplemental unemployment benefit (SUB) plan

Uniformed Services Employment and Reemployment Rights Act (USERRA)

■ STUDY QUESTIONS

1. What design features are usually found in paid vacation plans?

2. What factors other than employee benefit decisions determine the holidays on which a business is closed?

3. Under what circumstances might an employer allow employees to have time off with pay?

4. Describe the family-leave legislation that exists at both the state and federal levels.

5. With respect to an educational assistance plan that meets the requirements of Code Section 127, explain

   a. the amount of benefits that may be received tax free.

   b. the types of benefits that may be received.

   c. the nondiscrimination rules that apply.

6. Under what circumstances may each of the following employer-provided services be received tax free by employees?
   a. No-additional-cost services
   b. Employee discounts
   c. Adoption assistance
   d. Employee-assistance programs
   e. Financial planning programs
   f. Transportation
   g. Free parking
   h. Subsidized eating facilities
7. What types of benefits may be available under each of the following types of programs?
   a. Child-care
   b. Elder-care
   c. Adoption assistance
8. What are the advantages that may offset the cost of wellness programs?
9. Why are many wellness programs designed to include family members of employees?
10. a. What is the purpose of employee-assistance plans?
    b. How do employee-assistance plans operate?
11. Explain how financial planning programs for executives differ from the financial planning that is available under preretirement counseling programs.
12. In addition to financial planning, what are the other aspects of preretirement counseling programs?

■ NOTES

1. United States Chamber of Commerce, *The 2003 Employee Benefits Study.*
2. U.S. Department of Labor and Commission on Family and Medical Leave, *A Workable Balance: Report to Congress on Family and Medical Leave,* 1996.

For many years, some organizations have had benefit plans that give a limited number of key executives some choice in the selection of types and levels of employee benefits that are provided with employer contributions. Although many organizations have benefit programs in which all or many employees may elect optional or supplemental benefits, the cost of these benefits is normally borne by the employees on an after-tax, payroll-deduction basis. With the possible exception of an HMO option, employees have no choice about how employer dollars are spent.

Many organizations have benefit programs in which all (or almost all) of the employees can design their own benefit packages by purchasing benefits with a pre-specified amount of employer dollars from a number of available options. Generally, such a **cafeteria plan** (often referred to as a *flexible benefit plan, cafeteria compensation plan,* or *Section 125 plan*) also allows additional benefits to be purchased on a payroll-deduction basis. Today, more than one-third of employers with more than 500 employees have a full-fledged cafeteria plan.[1] Most of these employers and many smaller employers offer premium-conversion plans and/or flexible spending accounts.

Despite the popularity of cafeteria plans, there are major obstacles that must be overcome and issues that must be addressed in order to implement and maintain them.

■ RATIONALE FOR CAFETERIA PLANS

The growth in employee benefits has caused two problems. First, some employers feel that many employees do not recognize and appreciate the magnitude of their employee benefits because, as benefits increase, employee appreciation often seems to decrease. Advocates of cafeteria plans argue that by giving employees a stated dollar amount with which they must select their own benefits (from a list of options), employees become more aware of the actual cost of these benefits and are more likely to appreciate the benefits they choose.

A second problem is that the inflexible benefit structure of conventional employee benefit plans does not adequately meet the various benefit needs of all employees, often leading to employee dissatisfaction. For example, single employees often resent the medical coverage that married employees receive for their families because the single employees receive no benefit of corresponding value. Similarly, employees who have no dependents often see little value in life insurance and would prefer other benefits. Those who favor the concept of cafeteria plans feel that such dissatisfaction can be minimized if employees have the option to select their own benefits. Advocates of cafeteria plans argue that this increased employee satisfaction will result in a better employee-retention record and in greater ability to attract new employees.

Some employers see the cafeteria approach to benefit planning as an opportunity to control escalating benefit costs. Because a cafeteria plan is essentially a defined-contribution plan rather than a defined-benefit plan, it provides a number of opportunities for controlling increases in costs. For example, it may encourage employees to choose medical expense options that have larger deductibles or a greater degree of managed care so they can more efficiently use the fixed number of dollars allotted to them under the plan. A cafeteria plan may also enable the employer to pass on to the employees any increased benefit costs that result from having to comply with legislation that mandates additional benefits. In addition, because increases in employer contributions for optional benefits are not directly related to increases in benefit costs, the employer can grant percentage increases in the amounts available for benefits that are less than the actual overall increase in employee benefit costs.

It should be noted that early cafeteria plans were designed primarily to meet the varying needs of employees. In contrast, newer plans are much more likely to be instituted as a cost-saving technique.

■ NATURE OF CAFETERIA PLANS

In its purest sense, a cafeteria plan can be defined as any employee benefit plan that allows an employee to have some choice in designing his or her own benefit package by selecting different types or levels of benefits that are funded with employer dollars. At this extreme, a benefit plan that allows an employee to select an HMO as an option to an insured medical expense plan can be classified as a cafeteria plan. However, the more common use of the term *cafeteria plan* denotes something much broader—a plan in which choices can be made among several different types of benefits and possibly cash.

Prior to the addition of Section 125 to the Internal Revenue Code, the use of cafeteria plans had potentially adverse tax consequences for an employee. If an employee had a choice among benefits that were normally nontaxable (such as medical expense insurance or disability income insurance) and benefits that were normally taxable (such as life insurance in excess of $50,000 or cash), then the doctrine of **constructive receipt** would apply. This would result in an employee's being taxed as if he or she had elected the maximum taxable benefits that could have been obtained under the plan. Therefore, if an employee could elect cash in lieu of being covered under the employer's medical expense plan, an employee who elected to remain in the medical expense plan would have taxable income merely because cash could have been elected. Obviously, this tax environment was not conducive to the use of cafeteria plans unless the only benefits they offered were normally of a nontaxable nature.

Permissible Benefits

Section 125 of the Code defines a cafeteria plan as a written plan under which all participants are employees and under which all participants may choose between two or more benefits consisting of (1) qualified benefits and (2) cash. A **qualified benefit** essentially includes any welfare benefits excluded from taxation under the Internal Revenue Code except scholarships and fellowships, transportation benefits, educational assistance, no-additional-cost services, employee discounts, and *de minimis* fringe benefits. The latter include dependent life insurance coverage in amounts of $2,000 or less. The Health Insurance Portability and Accountability Act (HIPAA) expanded this list of exceptions to include medical savings accounts (MSAs) and any product that is advertised, marketed, or offered as long-term care insurance. Thus, medical expense benefits (other than MSAs and long-term care insurance), disability benefits, accidental death and dismemberment benefits, vacations, and dependent-care assistance (such as day-care centers) can be included in a cafeteria plan as tax-favored benefits. Recent legislation allows health savings accounts (HSAs) to be offered under cafeteria plans. The Code also permits group term life insurance to be included, even in amounts exceeding $50,000. In general, a cafeteria plan cannot include benefits that defer compensation, except for a qualified Section 401(k) or similar plan.

The prohibition of benefits that defer compensation has an important effect on vacation benefits. If an employee elects vacation benefits for the plan year of a cafeteria plan, the vacation days cannot be carried over into the following plan year because this would be a deferral of compensation. (Note: Regular vacation days are considered to have been taken before the additional days elected under the cafeteria plan.) However, an employee can elect to exchange these days for cash as long as the election is made and the cash is actually received prior to the end of the plan year. If this is not done, the days are forfeited and their value is lost.

The term *cash* is actually broader than it would otherwise appear. In addition to the actual receipt of dollars, a benefit is treated as cash as long as (1) it is not a benefit specifically prohibited by Section 125 as cash and (2) it is provided on a taxable basis. This latter provision means that either (1) the cost of the benefit is paid by the employee with after-tax dollars on a payroll-deduction basis or (2) employer dollars are used to obtain the benefit, but the employer reports the cost of the benefit as taxable income for the employee. This rule allows the inclusion of group automobile insurance or long-term care insurance in a cafeteria plan but not on a tax-favored basis. It also allows long-term disability coverage to be provided on an after-tax basis so that disability income benefits can be received tax free.

The list of benefits that Section 125 specifically prohibits from being treated as cash includes any benefits provided under Section 117 (scholarships and tuition expenses) and Section 132 (various fringe benefits, such as discounts and transportation benefits) of the Internal Revenue Code.

As long as a benefit plan offering choice meets the definition of a cafeteria plan, the issue of constructive receipt does not apply. Employees have taxable income only to the extent that normally taxable benefits—group term life insurance in excess of $50,000 and cash—are elected. An employer can have a benefit plan that offers choice but does not meet the statutory definition of a cafeteria plan. In such a case, the issue of constructive receipt comes into play if the plan contains any benefits that normally result in taxable income.

Choice of Medical Expense Plans. Employers often allow employees a choice of medical expense plans for themselves and their dependents. However, there is often confusion over whether this choice constitutes a cafeteria plan. If it does, the employer needs to comply with the rules of Section 125 and ERISA or be subject to the statutory penalties for noncompliance.

Assume an employer has a noncontributory medical expense plan that allows employees to elect among two or more managed care plans. If this is the only choice offered to employees, it is not a cafeteria plan because there is no cash option. It is only a choice among qualified benefits.

Now assume that an employer gives employees the option of electing either a noncontributory managed care plan or an indemnity plan for which the employee must make a monetary contribution on an after-tax basis. Again, by itself this is not a cafeteria plan because there is no option of electing cash. However, if employees are allowed to pay their share of the premiums for the indemnity plan on a before-tax basis through a premium-conversion plan (discussed later in this chapter), a cafeteria plan has been created under Section 125. Because salary reductions technically become employer dollars, the employees who elect salary reductions are considered to be choosing between cash and a qualified benefit.

Some employers allow an employee to elect out of medical expense coverage and receive cash. For example, some employees may feel that they do not need coverage under the employer's plan because they are adequately covered under their spouse's plans. If the cost to provide coverage to employees is $2,000 per year, the employer might feel financially justified in offering these employees $1,000 to waive coverage. Because these employees have a choice between the medical expense coverage and cash, a cafeteria plan has been created.

Benefit Election

Section 125 requires that benefit elections under a cafeteria plan be made prior to the beginning of a plan year. These elections cannot be changed for that plan year except under certain specified circumstances and if the plan allows such changes. Although there is no requirement that any changes be allowed in a cafeteria plan, most plans permit changes under some or all of the specified circumstances. Note, however, that new benefit elections can always be made for subsequent plan years during specified election periods prior to each plan year.

The IRS regulations regarding election changes during a plan year remained unchanged through most of the 1990s. However, revised regulations were finalized in 2001. The regulations, which are generally more liberal but also more complex, allow new cafeteria plan elections for specified *changes in status*. The acceptable changes in status include the following:

- A change in legal marital status. This includes marriage, death of a spouse, divorce, legal separation, or annulment.

- A change in the number of dependents. This can result from birth, adoption, commencement or termination of an adoption proceeding, or death.

- A change in the employment status of the employee, the employee's spouse, or the employee's dependents. This includes the termination or commencement of employment, a strike or lockout, the commencement or return from unpaid leave of absence, or a change in worksite. In addition, a change in employment (such as number of hours worked) is also a change in employment status if the change affects the eligibility of an employee, spouse, or dependent under a cafeteria plan or other qualified benefit plan.

- A change in dependent status. This includes the satisfaction of or ceasing to satisfy dependent status as a result of age, student status, or any similar circumstance.

- A change in residence of the employee, spouse, or dependent.

- The commencement or termination of an adoption agreement if adoption assistance is provided through a cafeteria plan.

The regulations specify that any new cafeteria plan election as a result of a change in status is allowed only if any employee, spouse, or dependent gains or loses eligibility for coverage, and the cafeteria plan election change must correspond with that gain or loss in coverage. For example, if a spouse dies, an employee could delete medical expense coverage for the spouse but could not change coverage for other dependents. As a general rule, the loss of eligibility for coverage for a cafeteria plan benefit would allow an employee only to decrease the amount of an election. However, there is one exception to this rule. If an election results from the loss of medical expense coverage, an increase in the amount of an election to pay for the COBRA coverage for the individual who lost coverage is permissible.

The regulations also allow affected participants in cafeteria plans to make election changes because of specified changes in the cost or coverage of benefits under the cafeteria plan. However, election changes for these reasons are not allowed for health benefits under flexible spending accounts (FSAs). Note that the need for election changes during the plan year of a cafeteria plan is minimized if an employer's plan years for its benefit plans correspond to the plan year for its cafeteria plan.

Election changes can be made if the cost of a benefit plan increases or decreases and, under the terms of the plan, employees are required to make a corresponding change in their payments. In addition, it is permissible for employees to make election changes because of significant cost increases or decreases of a benefit plan. In the case of significant cost increases, an employee can do one of the following: increase payments, change to another benefit package providing similar coverage, or revoke the benefit election and drop coverage if no similar coverage is available. In the case of significant cost decreases, employees currently with coverage and those who elected a different benefit option can revoke their current elections and elect the cost-reduced coverage. Employees who previously elected not to participate in the plan are also permitted to elect coverage. There is one exception to the rules that apply to cost changes: A new benefit election is not allowed because of a change in the cost of dependent care expenses if the dependent care provider is a relative of the employee.

Similarly, election changes by employees are permissible if there are certain changes in coverage. If there is a significant curtailment, but no loss, of coverage (such as significantly increased deductibles and copayments), a cafeteria plan may permit the employee to revoke an election change and make a new election for coverage under another benefit package option providing similar coverage. If the curtailment involves a loss of coverage (such as an HMO ceasing to be available), a new election can be made for a similar option, or the benefit election can be revoked if no similar coverage is available. If a plan adds or improves a benefit, the plan may allow an employee to revoke an existing option and elect an option with the new or improved benefits. In addition, benefit changes are allowed if there is a loss of coverage for an employee, spouse, or dependent under a group health plan sponsored by a government or educational institution. Lastly, a benefit election is permitted if it corresponds with changes in another employer plan (such as that of a spouse or dependent) (1) if the change in the other plan is permitted by any of the rules mentioned previously or (2) if the cafeteria plan allows participants to make an election for a period of coverage different from that under the other employer plan.

Even if none of the above rules are met, election changes are permitted in cafeteria plans as a result of changes in coverage or premiums because of any of the following:

- Special enrollment rights under HIPAA
- COBRA
- Entitlement to Medicare or Medicaid
- Family and Medical Leave Act requirements
- Legal judgments, decrees, or orders that result from divorce, legal separation, annulment, or change in legal custody

Payroll Deductions and Salary Reductions

Under some cafeteria plans, employees are allowed to allocate only a predetermined employer contribution for benefits. Other cafeteria plans are designed so that employees can obtain additional benefits with optional payroll deductions or salary reductions.

Many cafeteria plans that provide a wide array of benefits allow an employee to elect an after-tax payroll deduction to obtain additional benefits. For example, under a cafeteria plan an employee might be given $300 per month with which to select varying types and levels of benefits. If the benefits the employee chooses cost $340, the employee has two options—either to decrease the benefits selected or to authorize a $40 payroll deduction. Even though the payroll deduction is on an after-tax basis, the employee gains to the extent that the additional benefits are selected at a lower cost through a group arrangement than in the individual marketplace.

Section 125 also allows employees to purchase certain benefits on a before-tax basis through the use of a premium-conversion plan or an FSA. Premium-conversion plans or FSAs, both of which are technically cafeteria plans, can be used by themselves or incorporated into a more comprehensive cafeteria plan. They are most commonly used alone by small employers who are unwilling to establish a broader plan, primarily for cost reasons. The cafeteria plans of most large employers contain one or both of these arrangements as an integral part of the plan.

Before-tax salary reductions reduce taxable income for federal income tax purposes. In most (but not all) states, they also reduce income subject to state tax. An example of the effect of a before-tax salary reduction is shown later in this chapter.

Premium-Conversion Plans.   A **premium-conversion plan** (also called a *premium-only plan*, or *POP*) allows an employee to elect a before-tax salary reduction to pay his or her premium contribution to any employer-sponsored health or other welfare benefit plan. For example, an employer might provide medical expense coverage to employees at no cost but make a monthly charge for dependent coverage. Under a premium-conversion plan, the employee can pay for the dependent coverage with a before-tax salary reduction.

As a rule, premium-conversion plans are established for medical and dental expenses only. If such plans are used for group term life insurance, the cost of coverage in excess of $50,000 must be reported as income, defeating the purpose of the salary reduction. If these plans are used for disability income coverage, benefits are taxable as noncontributory employer-provided coverage because the amount of any salary reduction is considered to be the employer's money.

Flexible Spending Accounts.   A **flexible spending account (FSA)** allows an employee to fund certain benefits on a before-tax basis by electing to take a salary reduction, which can then be used to fund the cost of any qualified benefits included in the plan. However, FSAs are used almost exclusively for health expenses not covered by the employer's plan and for dependent-care expenses. A health FSA under Section 125 includes benefits for both medical and dental expenses.

The amount of any salary reduction is, in effect, credited to an employee's reimbursement account, and benefits are paid from this account when an employee properly files for such reimbursement. Reimbursements are typically made on a monthly or quarterly basis. The amount of the salary reduction must be determined prior to the beginning of the plan year. Once the amount is set, changes are allowed only under the specified circumstances previously mentioned for benefit elections. A separate election must be made for each benefit, and the funds are accounted for separately. Monies from a salary reduction for one type of expense (such as medical and dental bills) cannot be used as reimbursement for another type of expense (such as dependent care).

If the monies in the FSA are not used during the plan year, they are forfeited. Because forfeited funds are considered plan assets, they can be used only for the payment of benefits and reasonable administrative expenses. Under ERISA rules, forfeitures may be used to

- defray the administrative costs of the plan.
- protect the underwriting integrity of the plan. This includes the use of these funds to reimburse the plan for benefits paid that exceed a terminated employee's contributions. For example, an employee who contributed $100 per month for medical expenses might be eligible to collect a full annual reimbursement of $1,200 in the first month of participation. If the employee terminated employment at that time, the plan would have paid out $1,100 more than it had taken in.
- reallocate contributions to the following plan year. Such reallocations must be on a per capita basis for all participants and cannot be based on amounts each employee originally contributed.

The ERISA rules specifically prohibit the donating of forfeitures to charity or the reversion of such amounts to the employer for general business expenses.

An election to participate in an FSA program not only reduces salary for federal income tax purposes but also lowers the wages on which Social Security and Medicare taxes are levied. As a result, those employees who are below the wage-base limit after the reduction pay less in Social Security taxes, and their future income benefits under Social Security may also be smaller. However, the reduction in benefits is small in most cases, unless the salary reduction is large. It should be noted that the employer's share of Social Security and Medicare tax payments also decreases. In some cases, the employer's savings are actually large enough to fully offset the cost of administering the FSA program.

Most health FSAs limit benefits to unreimbursed medical and dental expenses that would be deductible under Section 213 of the Internal Revenue Code if an employee were eligible to itemize these expenses for income tax purposes. An employer, however, can have a more restricted list of eligible expenses for purposes of FSA reimbursement. As a result of a 2003 ruling by the IRS, an employer can now also allow FSA reimbursements for over-the-counter medications. (Note that this ruling applies only to FSAs and not to deductible medical expenses in general or to reimbursements under Archer MSAs, HSAs, or HRAs.) These medications must be used to treat personal injuries or to alleviate sickness, and acceptable medications specifically mentioned in the ruling include antacids, allergy medicines, pain relievers, and cold medicines. Reimbursement is not allowed for dietary supplements, vitamins, or other items used for general good health. Even though an employer may allow reimbursement for over-the counter medications, the employer is not required to do so. In fact, many employers have decided to disallow such reimbursements because of the problems associated with required documentation of these purchases.

As the result of another 2003 ruling, the IRS specifically allows the use of electronic payment cards to make health FSA reimbursements as long as certain criteria are satisfied. Such cards, which can be in the form of debit or credit cards, allow an employee to get immediate reimbursement rather than having to submit FSA claims. They also reduce paper administration for the employer. The required criteria for the use of these cards include annual employee certification that the card will be used only for eligible expenses and that it will be used at certain vendors that have health-related merchant codes.

A health FSA is subject to COBRA rules as long as the FSA provides any of the benefits of a group health plan. (It would be very rare for a health FSA not to provide such benefits.) However, it is not necessary for the FSA to make coverage available beyond the current plan year as long as the maximum amount paid by an employee for a full plan year of coverage equals or exceeds the maximum benefit available under the FSA for the plan year. For almost all FSAs, this will be the case. For the remainder of the current plan year, COBRA coverage needs to be offered only if the maximum benefit available for the remainder of the plan year exceeds the amount that could be charged for COBRA coverage during the remainder of the plan year.

EXAMPLE
Assume that an employee contributes $50 per month to a health FSA. If the employee terminates employment after six months, the potential FSA premium for the remainder of the plan year is $306 (that is, $50 per month for six months plus the 2 percent administrative fee). If the employee has received less than $294 in benefits from the FSA during the six months of employment in the plan year, COBRA continuation must be offered.

One issue employers have faced over the years has been whether to limit benefit payments to the amount of an account balance or to allow an employee at any time during the year to receive benefits equal to his or her annual salary reduction. For example, an employee might contribute $100 per month to an FSA to provide benefits for the cost of unreimbursed medical expenses. During the first month of the plan, the employee makes only $100 of the $1,200 annual contribution. If the employee incurs $300 of unreimbursed medical expenses during the month, should he or she be allowed to withdraw $100 or the full $300? The objection to allowing a $300 withdrawal is that the employer loses $200 if the employee terminates employment before making any further contribution. IRS regulations do not give the employer any choice with respect to health benefits. FSAs must allow an amount equal to the full annual contribution to be taken as benefits any time during the year. Therefore, the employee is entitled to a benefit of $300 after the first month. However, the IRS regulations do allow a choice in reimbursement policies for other types of benefits, such as dependent-care expenses.

For these benefits, most plans limit aggregate benefits to the total contributions made until the time benefits are received.

Effect of Salary Reductions. The use of salary reductions under a cafeteria plan can have a significant effect on an employee's spendable income by lowering taxes paid.

EXAMPLE

Charlie is a single employee with an annual income of $75,000. He pays $1,000 per year toward the cost of his employer-provided medical expense coverage. He expects to have $2,000 in unreimbursed medical and dental expenses for the year. Charlie's marginal federal income tax bracket is 27 percent. This percentage is increased to 30 because of state income taxes. Charlie's standard deduction and exemptions for income tax purposes are $15,000.

Without a cafeteria plan, Charlie's federal and state taxes are calculated as follows:

Annual income	$75,000
Minus standard deduction and exemptions	−15,000
Taxable income	$60,000
Income taxes (.30 × $60,000)	$18,000
Social Security and Medicare taxes	
(.0765 × $75,000)	5,738
Total taxes	$23,738

If Charlie participates in his employer's premium conversion plan and FSA, Charlie's taxes are calculated as follows:

Annual income	$75,000
Minus contribution for premium-	
conversion plan	−1,000
Minus FSA contribution	−2,000
Minus standard deduction and exemptions	−15,000
Taxable income	$57,000
Income taxes (.30 × $57,000)	$17,100
Social Security and Medicare taxes	
[.0765 × ($75,000 − $3,000)]	5,508
Total taxes	$22,608

■ TYPES OF PLANS

Core-Plus Plans

Probably the most common type of full-fledged cafeteria plan is a **core-plus plan**, which offers a basic core of benefits to all employees, plus a second layer of optional benefits that permits an employee to choose which benefits he or she will add to the basic benefits. These optional benefits can be "purchased" with dollars, or credits, that are given to the employee as part of the benefit package. If these credits are inadequate to purchase the desired benefits, an employee can make additional purchases with after-tax contributions or with before-tax salary reductions under a premium-conversion plan and/or an FSA.

Perhaps the best way to demonstrate how cafeteria plans operate is to include a brief description of some existing plans.

EXAMPLE

The first example is the core-plus plan of an educational organization with 3,000 employees. Although this type of plan is common, the list of optional benefits in this example is more extensive than what is found in most cafeteria plans.

All employees receive a minimum level of benefits, called *basic benefits,* as follows:

■ Term life insurance equal to one-half of salary

■ Travel accident insurance (when on the employer's business)

■ Disability income insurance

■ Two to four weeks' vacation

Employees are also given *flexible credits,* equal to between 3 and 6 percent of salary (depending on length of service, with the maximum reached after ten years), which can be used to purchase additional or "optional" benefits. There is a new election of benefits each year, and no carryover of any unused credits is allowed. The optional benefits are the following:

■ An array of medical expense options. Although there is no charge for HMO coverage, a charge is made for coverage under an indemnity plan, and additional flexible credits are given if a person elects no medical expense coverage.

■ Additional life insurance, up to 4½ times salary.

■ Accidental death insurance when the basic travel accident insurance does not apply.

■ Dental insurance for the employee and dependents.

■ Up to 2 weeks' additional vacation time.

■ Cash.

If an employee does not have enough flexible credits to purchase the desired optional benefits, additional amounts may be contributed on a payroll-deduction basis for all but more vacation time. In addition, a salary reduction may be elected for contributions to an FSA that provides dependent-care-assistance benefits.

A variation of the core-plus approach is to have the core plan be an "average" plan for which the employee makes no contribution. If certain benefits are reduced, the employee may then receive credits that can be used either to increase other benefits or, if the plan allows, to increase cash compensation. Additional benefits can typically be obtained through employee payroll deductions.

EXAMPLE

This plan covers 15,000 nonunion employees in one division of a major industrial conglomerate. Employees may elect to reduce certain benefits and receive credits that can be either used to purchase additional benefits, taken in cash, or contributed to the company's 401(k) plan. Additional benefits may be purchased on a payroll-deduction basis.

The plan applies to four types of benefits:

1. Medical expense insurance

2. Employee life insurance

3. Accidental death and dismemberment insurance

4. Dependent life insurance

Several medical expense insurance options are available. The standard coverage, for which there is neither a charge nor a credit, is a point-of-service plan. Employees may elect a traditional indemnity plan, but this option results in a charge. Several HMO options are also available, all of which result in credits.

There are several employee life insurance options that range from ½ to 5 times salary. The standard coverage, for which there is no credit or charge, is 1½ times salary.

Although several supplemental accidental death and dismemberment options and a single dependent life insurance option are available, they result in a charge to the employee. So, in effect, there is no basic benefit in these areas.

Modular Plans

Another type of cafeteria plan is a **modular plan** in which an employee has a choice among several predesigned benefit packages. Typically, at least one of the packages can be selected without any employee cost. If an employee selects a more expensive package, he or she is required to contribute to the cost of the package. Some employers may also include a bare-bones benefit package, which results in cash being paid to an employee who selects it.

Under some cafeteria plans using this approach, the predesigned packages may have significant differences. A comparison of two packages may show one to be better than others in certain cases but inferior in other cases. Other employers using this approach have virtually identical packages, with the major difference being in the option selected for the medical expense coverage. For example, the plan of one large bank offers a traditional insured plan, two HMOs, and a PPO.

Modular plans are popular with employers for two reasons. First, adverse selection can be more easily controlled under modular plans than under core-plus plans. Second, modular plans are easier to administer and communicate. For both these reasons, small employers who have full-fledged cafeteria plans are most likely to take a modular approach.

EXAMPLE

The third example is a large financial institution's cafeteria plan that covers almost 20,000 employees. There are seven predesigned benefit packages that can be chosen, with each package designed for a specific segment of the employee population. Each package has one of three medical expense plans and varying amounts of group term life insurance. The packages contain differing combinations of dental insurance, vision coverage, and dependent care benefits. All offer the same level of disability income coverage.

A "cost" is associated with each package. Some packages cost an employee nothing, others require an employee contribution, and at least one option has a negative cost, meaning that an employee who selects it gets additional cash compensation. The cost of each package can vary for two reasons. First, an employee can elect whether to have medical expense coverage for dependents. Second, HMO and PPO choices are available in many of the employee locations.

Salary-Reduction-Only Plans

The final example is a **salary-reduction-only plan**, which consists solely of the two types of salary reductions that can be used in a cafeteria plan: a premium-conversion option and an FSA.

EXAMPLE

The final example is a small nonprofit organization's plan. Employees are allowed to elect salary reductions for each of the following:

■ The employee's share of the cost of medical and dental insurance premiums for dependents. (Under this plan, the employer pays the full cost of the employee's coverage.)

■ Qualifying medical care expenses. These are any medical and dental expenses normally deductible on an employee's federal income tax return (without regard to any gross income limitations). Note that these deductible expenses must not have been reimbursed by insurance.

■ Eligible dependent-care expenses. These are expenses for the types of benefits that could be provided in a qualified dependent-care-assistance program. The maximum annual salary reduction for this category of benefits is limited to $5,000 to prevent the plan from being discriminatory because too large a portion of the benefits would be provided to highly compensated employees.

Employees can request reimbursements for medical care and dependent-care expenses at the end of each month and must file an appropriate form with supporting documentation (bills and receipts). For administrative purposes, reimbursement requests must be for at least $50 except in the last quarter of the year.

The maximum reimbursement at any time for dependent-care expenses is the accumulated amount in an employee's account.

■ OBSTACLES TO CAFETERIA PLANS

Certain obstacles must be overcome before a cafeteria plan can be successfully implemented. Proper plan design would seem sufficient to overcome many of these obstacles. However, it must be realized that any organization that adopts a cafeteria plan other than a simple FSA or premium-conversion plan faces a complex, costly, and time-consuming project.

Legislative Environment

Undoubtedly, the largest obstacle to cafeteria plans for many years was the unsettled federal income tax picture. The passage of the Tax Reform Act in 1984 and the IRS issuance of regulations governing cafeteria plans finally clarified this issue significantly. Since then the number of cafeteria plans has grown significantly, particularly among large firms. However, almost every year, a federal tax bill alters Section 125 in some way, new IRS regulations are issued, or proposals for change are made by elected officials. The benefits that can be included in a cafeteria plan are changed, the nondiscrimination rules are altered, or the rules for FSAs are "clarified." This continuing uncertainty has caused many employers to continue to shy away from cafeteria plans.

Meeting Nondiscrimination Rules

Section 125 imposes complex nondiscrimination tests on cafeteria plans, causing many employees to view cafeteria plans unfavorably. If these tests are not met, adverse tax consequences for key employees and/or highly compensated employees may actually result in higher taxable income for these employees than if no cafeteria plan existed. From a practical standpoint, the test is usually met if an employer has a full-fledged cafeteria plan that applies to all employees. However, care must be exercised in designing a plan that either covers only a segment of the employees or has only a small percentage of employees participating. The latter situation often occurs with FSAs.

As is often the case, the nondiscrimination tests are not applicable if a plan is maintained under provisions of a collective-bargaining agreement.

Concentration Test.   Under the concentration test, no more than 25 percent of the tax-favored benefits provided under the plan can go to *key employees* (as defined for the Section 79 nondiscrimination rules). This test is a particular problem if an employer has a large percentage of key employees and if key employees, being higher paid, contribute large amounts to an FSA.

If a plan fails the concentration test, key employees must include in gross income the maximum taxable benefits that could have been elected under the plan. In effect, these employees are subject to the doctrine of constructive receipt.

Eligibility Test.   Cafeteria plans are subject to a two-part eligibility test, both parts of which must be satisfied. The first part of the test stipulates that no employee be required to complete more than three years of employment as a condition for participation and that the employment requirement for each employee be the same. In addition, any employee who satisfies the employment requirement and is otherwise entitled to partic-ipate must do so no later than the first day of the plan year following completion of the employment requirement unless the employee has separated from service in the interim.

The second part of the test requires that eligibility for participation must not be discriminatory in favor of **highly compensated employees,** who are defined as any of the following:

■ Officers

■ Shareholders who own more than 5 percent of the voting power or value of all classes of the firm's stock

■ Employees who are highly compensated based on all facts and circumstances

■ Spouses or dependents of any of the above

The eligibility test uses Table 19.1, which is found in IRS regulations and can best be explained with the following example.

Assume an employer has 1,000 employees—800 non–highly compensated and 200 highly compensated. The percentage of non–highly compensated employees is 80 per-cent (800/1,000), for which the table shows a safe harbor percentage of 35. This means that if the percentage of non–highly compensated employees eligible for the plan is equal to at least 35 percent of the percentage of highly compensated employees eligible, the plan satisfies the eligibility test. Assume that 160 people, or 80 percent of the highly compensated employees, are eligible. Then at least 28 percent, or 224, of the non–highly compensated employees must be eligible for the plan (calculations: .80 × .35 = .28 and .28 × 800 = 224).

The table also shows an unsafe harbor percentage of 25 percent. Using this figure instead of 35 percent yields 160 employees. If fewer than this number of non–highly compensated employees are eligible, the eligibility test is failed.

If the number of eligible non–highly compensated employees falls between the numbers determined by the two percentages (from 160 to 223 employees in this exam-ple), IRS regulations impose a facts-and-circumstances test to determine whether the eligibility test is passed or failed. According to the regulations, the following factors are considered:

■ The underlying business reason for the eligibility classification

■ The percentage of employees eligible

■ The percentage of eligible employees in each salary range

■ The extent to which the eligibility classification is close to satisfying the safe harbor rule

However, the regulations also state that none of these factors alone is determinative, and other facts and circumstances may be relevant.

If a plan fails this test, highly compensated employees must include in gross income the maximum taxable benefits they could have elected under the plan.

TABLE 19.1	Factors for Eligibility Test	
Non–Highly Compensated Employee Concentration Percentage	**Safe Harbor Percentage**	**Unsafe Harbor Percentage**
0–60	50.00	40.00
61	49.25	39.25
62	48.50	38.50
63	47.75	37.75
64	47.00	37.00
65	46.25	36.25
66	45.50	35.50
67	44.75	34.75
68	44.00	34.00
69	43.25	33.25
70	42.50	32.50
71	41.75	31.75
72	41.00	31.00
73	40.25	30.25
74	39.50	29.50
75	38.75	28.75
76	38.00	28.00
77	37.25	27.25
78	36.50	26.50
79	35.75	25.75
80	35.00	25.00
81	34.25	24.25
82	33.50	23.50
83	32.75	22.75
84	32.00	22.00
85	31.25	21.25
86	30.50	20.50
87	29.75	20.00
88	29.00	20.00
89	28.25	20.00
90	27.50	20.00
91	26.75	20.00
92	26.00	20.00
93	25.25	20.00
94	24.50	20.00
95	23.75	20.00
96	23.00	20.00
97	22.25	20.00
98	21.50	20.00
99	20.75	20.00

Nondiscriminatory Contributions and Benefits. Cafeteria plans cannot discriminate in favor of highly compensated participants with respect to contributions or benefits. Section 125 states that a cafeteria plan is not discriminatory if the plan's nontaxable benefits and total benefits (or the employer contributions allocable to each) do not discriminate in favor of highly compensated employees. In addition, a cafeteria plan providing health benefits is not discriminatory if contributions under the plan for each participant include an amount equal to one of the following:

■ 100 percent of the health benefit cost for the majority of similarly situated (that is, family or single coverage) highly compensated employees

■ At least 75 percent of the health benefit cost for the similarly situated participant with the best health benefit coverage

Contributions exceeding either of these amounts are nondiscriminatory if they bear a uniform relationship to an employee's compensation.

Employer's Obligation

Under the most liberal cafeteria plan, each employee has an unrestricted choice of the benefits his or her employer provides. Some critics of this concept argue that both the motivational and the security aspects of a cafeteria plan may be damaged by unwise employee selection because many employees may not have the expertise to select the proper benefits. In addition, there is concern about the organization's moral and perhaps legal obligation to prevent employees from financial injury through faulty decisions. These concerns have been incorporated into the design of most plans presently in existence. Employees are given both certain basic benefits that provide a minimum level of security and a series of optional benefits on top of the basic ones.

Negative Attitudes

Employees, insurers, and unions have expressed some negative attitudes toward cafeteria plans. No cafeteria plan can be truly successful without the support of the employees involved. To win the employees' initial support and to overcome any potential negative attitudes, companies that contemplate the development of such programs must spend a considerable amount of time and resources in making sure that employees are adequately informed about (1) the reasons for the proposed program, (2) its advantages and disadvantages, and (3) its future implications. For best results, the opinions of employees should be solicited and weighed, and employees should be involved in various aspects of the decision-making process.

Some insurers have been reluctant to participate in cafeteria plans. A few seem unwilling to try anything new; others are concerned about the problem of adverse selection as a result of employee choice. However, as explained below, the problem of adverse selection can be minimized.

Unions have also had a negative attitude. Union management often feels that bargaining for a cafeteria plan is contrary to the practice of bargaining for the best benefit program for all employees. There is also a concern that a cafeteria plan will be used primarily as a cost-containment technique to pass on the cost of future benefit increases to union members. Consequently, the existing programs often apply only to nonunion employees.

Adverse Selection

When employees are allowed a choice in selecting benefits, the problem of adverse selection arises. This means that employees who are likely to have claims tend to pick the benefits that minimize their out-of-pocket costs. For example, an employee who previously selected a medical expense option with a high deductible might switch to a plan with a lower deductible if medical expenses are ongoing. An employee who previously rejected dental insurance is likely to elect this benefit if dental care is anticipated in the near future.

Adverse selection is a problem whether a plan is insured or self-funded. The problem even exists outside cafeteria plans if choice is allowed. However, the degree of choice within a cafeteria plan tends to increase the potential costs unless actions are taken to combat the problem.

Several techniques are used to control adverse selection in cafeteria plans. Benefit limitations and restrictions on coverage can be included if a person wishes to add or change coverage at a date later than initial eligibility. This technique has been common in contributory benefit plans for many years. Another technique is to price the options accordingly. If an option is likely to encourage adverse selection, the cost to the employee for that option should be higher than what would have been charged if the option had been the only one available. Such pricing has been difficult in the past, but it is becoming easier and more accurate as more experience with cafeteria plans develops. The control of adverse selection is also one reason for the use of predesigned package plans. If, for example, the medical expense plan in one option is likely to encourage adverse selection, the option may not include other benefits for which adverse selection is also a concern (such as dental benefits). To further counter increased costs from the medical expense plan, the option may also offer minimal coverage for other types of benefits.

Cost

An organization that adopts a cafeteria plan will incur initial development and administrative costs that are over and above those of a more traditional benefit program. Some of this extra cost is the value of the employee hours that must be spent in preparing the program for implementation. Another sizable portion must be paid for the reprogramming of the organization's computer system to include necessary information and to accept the employees' benefit elections. ERISA also requires the annual filing of Form 5500.

Until recently, the cost of a cafeteria plan was beyond the means of all but large employers. However, package plans developed by many insurers now make it a viable option for employers with only a few hundred employees.

Continuing costs depend on such factors as the benefits included in the plan, the number of options available with each benefit, the frequency with which employees may change benefit elections, and the number of employees covered by the plan. The firms with cafeteria plans have incurred increased costs because of the need for additional employees to administer the program and additional computer time to process employee choices. However, the costs have been regarded as small in relation to the total cost of providing employee benefits. In addition, as cafeteria plans have grown in popularity, many vendors have developed software packages that can be used by employees to enroll and make benefit changes and to provide other administrative functions more cost effectively.

Selection among benefits, particularly a wide variety of benefits, is often daunting for many employees. As a result, an employer may also need to incur additional costs to provide employee counseling, either with their own employees or from outside financial planning specialists.

■ ISSUES IN PLAN DESIGN

Before establishing a cafeteria program, an employer must be sure a valid reason exists for converting the company's traditional benefit program to a cafeteria approach. For example, if there is strong employee dissatisfaction with the current benefit program, the solution may lie in clearly identifying the sources of dissatisfaction and making appropriate adjustments in the existing benefit program, rather than making a shift to a cafeteria plan. However, if employee dissatisfaction arises from widely differing benefit needs, conversion to a cafeteria plan may be quite appropriate. Beyond having a clearly defined purpose for converting from a traditional benefit program to a cafeteria program and being willing to bear the additional administrative costs associated with a cafeteria approach, the employer must face a number of considerations in designing the plan.

Type and Amount of Benefits to Include

Probably the most fundamental decision that must be made in designing a cafeteria plan is determining what benefits should be included. An employer who wants the plan to be viewed as meeting the differing needs of employees must receive employee input concerning the types of benefits perceived as most desirable. An open dialogue with employees will undoubtedly lead to suggestions that every possible employee benefit be made available. The enthusiasm of many employees for a cafeteria plan will then be dampened when the employer rejects some—and possibly many—of these suggestions for cost, administrative, or psychological reasons. Consequently, it is important that certain ground rules be established regarding the benefits that are acceptable to the employer.

The employer must decide whether the plan should be limited to the types of benefits provided through traditional group insurance arrangements or be expanded to include other benefits. At a minimum, it is important to ensure that an overall employee benefit program provides employees with protection against all major areas of personal risk. This suggests a benefit program with at least *some* provision for life insurance, disability income protection, medical expense protection, and retirement benefits, but it is not necessary that *all* these benefits be included in a cafeteria plan. For example, most employers have a retirement plan separate from their cafeteria plan because of Section 125 requirements. Other employers make a 401(k) plan one of the available cafeteria options.

In some respects, a cafeteria plan may be an ideal vehicle for providing less traditional types of benefits. Two examples are extra vacation time and child care. Some plans allow an employee to use flexible credits to purchase additional days of vacation. When available, this option has proven a popular benefit, particularly among single employees. A problem may arise, however, if nonvacationing employees must assume the work of vacationing employees in addition to their own regularly assigned work. Those not electing extra vacation time may resent doing the work of someone else who is away longer than the normal vacation period. In recent years, employers have been under increasing pressure to provide care for employees' children, which represents an additional cost if added to a traditional benefit program. Employees who include child-care benefits in a cafeteria plan can pay for the cost of such benefits, possibly with dollars from an FSA. However, lower-paid employees may be better off financially by paying for child care with out-of-pocket dollars and electing the income tax credit available for dependent-care expenses.

One question that may arise is whether dependent life insurance should be included in a cafeteria plan. As mentioned before, amounts of $2,000 or less do not fit the definition of a qualified benefit and cannot be included. If the amount of coverage available exceeds $2,000, the benefit can be provided if it is treated as a cash benefit. An employee electing coverage with employer-provided dollars has taxable income as determined by Uniform Premium Table I (described in Chapter 6). Because this amount exceeds the actual cost of coverage in some cases, dependent life insurance is often made available outside a cafeteria plan. When it is included in a cafeteria plan, there is frequently a requirement that it be purchased with after-tax salary reductions.

The greater the number of benefits, particularly optional benefits, the greater the administrative costs. A wide array of options may also be confusing to many employees and require extra personnel to counsel employees or to answer their questions.

Level of Employer Contributions

An employer has considerable latitude in determining the amount of dollars that are available to employees to purchase benefits under a cafeteria plan. These dollars may be a function of one or more of the following factors: salary, age, family status, and length of service.

The major difficulty arises in situations in which the installation of a cafeteria plan is not accompanied by an overall increase in the amount of the employer's contributions to the employee benefit plan. Each employee should be provided with enough dollars so that he or she can purchase optional benefits that, together with basic benefits, are at least equivalent to the benefits provided by the older plan.

Offering Premium-Conversion and FSA Options

Premium-conversion and FSA options, either by themselves or as part of a broader cafeteria plan, enable employees to lower taxes and therefore increase spendable income. Ignoring administrative costs, there is probably no reason not to offer employees these options for such benefits as dependent care or for health insurance premiums. However, salary reductions for unreimbursed medical expenses pose a dilemma. Although such deductions save taxes for an employee, they may also result in nearly 100 percent reimbursement for medical expenses, which may negate many cost-containment features in the employer's medical expense plan.

Offering an FSA for unreimbursed medical expenses also means that employees will need to submit medical information for reimbursement. Employees may be reluctant to do this if they fear that the employer will know about their medical conditions. For this reason, and because of HIPAA privacy provisions, many employers use an external administrator to process FSA claims.

Change of Benefits

Because employees' needs change over time, a provision regarding their ability to change their benefit options must be incorporated in a cafeteria plan. As a rule, changes are allowed prior to the beginning of the plan year. Additional changes may be allowed as long as they are permissible under Section 125 regulations.

Two situations may complicate the issue of the frequency with which benefits may be changed. First, the charges to employees for optional benefits must be adjusted periodically to reflect experience under the plan. If the charges for benefits rise between dates on which employees may change benefit selections, the employer must either absorb these charges or pass them on to the employees, probably through increased payroll deductions. Consequently, most cafeteria plans allow benefit changes on annual dates that are the same as the dates when charges for benefits are recalculated as well as the date on which any insurance contracts providing benefits under the plan are renewed.

The second situation arises when the amount of the employer's contribution is based on compensation. If an employee receives a pay increase between selection periods, should he or she be granted more dollars to purchase additional benefits at that time? Under most cafeteria plans, the dollars available to all employees are calculated only once a year, usually before the date by which any annual benefit changes must be made. Any changes in the employee's status during the year have no effect on the employer's contribution until the date on which a recalculation is made in the following year.

■ KEY TERMS

cafeteria plan	highly compensated employees	premium-conversion plan
constructive receipt		qualified benefit
core-plus plan	modular plan	salary-reduction-only plan
flexible spending account (FSA)		

■ STUDY QUESTIONS

1. Explain the advantages claimed for cafeteria plans.

2. a. What types of welfare benefits can be provided under a cafeteria plan?

   b. What types of retirement benefits can be provided?

   c. What is meant by a cash benefit?

3. A benefit plan may offer employees choices among benefits but not satisfy the statutory definition of a cafeteria plan. What are the implications of such a situation?

4. a. When must benefit elections be made under a cafeteria plan?

   b. To what extent can a cafeteria plan permit changes in benefit elections?

5. a. What is the advantage of funding employee benefits through a premium-conversion plan or an FSA?

   b. What types of benefits are usually funded through premium-conversion plans and FSAs?

   c. What happens to balances in an FSA if they are not used for expenses incurred during the election period?

6. What is the difference between a core-plus cafeteria plan and a modular plan?

7. Other than meeting nondiscrimination rules and adverse selection, what are the obstacles to establishing cafeteria plans?

8. What types of nondiscrimination rules apply to cafeteria plans?

9. What techniques can be used to control adverse selection in a cafeteria plan?

10. Briefly discuss the issues that must be addressed in designing a cafeteria plan.

■ NOTE

1. LIMRA International, Inc., *The Changing Group and Health Care Marketplace, 2003.*

PART FIVE

Retirement Plans

20

Introduction to Qualified Plans

Retirement plans are among the most common employee benefits offered by employers. Nearly half of all benefit spending by employers goes to retirement benefits,[1] and employees rate retirement benefits as the second most important employee benefit, after health insurance.[2] Moreover, retirement plans are probably the most complicated benefit—in terms of design, administration, and taxation—commonly provided by employers. The purpose of this chapter is to explain the reasons for this importance and complexity and to provide an introduction to pension plan design and government regulation of pension plans.

■ MANAGEMENT OBJECTIVES IN RETIREMENT PLAN DESIGN

Generally, a primary management objective in designing and maintaining an employer-sponsored retirement plan is to maximize those factors by which the plan improves employee productivity. In other words, to maximize the extent to which the costs of the plan represent investment rather than pure expense. A retirement plan improves productivity by attracting and keeping a better work force and providing incentives for good work performance. Although the quantitative evidence for the productivity relationship for specific plan features is relatively scanty at this time, there has been much qualitative experience in this area.

Benefit managers and retirement planners must begin with an overall idea of what employer objectives can be promoted by a retirement plan. While not every potential objective can be met with a single plan—in fact, some are conflicting—it's useful to begin this chapter by noting broadly what retirement plans can do. Here are the basic objectives:

- ■ *Help employees with retirement saving.* This is the most fundamental reason for employer-sponsored retirement plans and it shouldn't be overlooked. Most employees, even highly compensated employees, find personal savings difficult. It is difficult not merely for psychological reasons but also because our tax system and economy are oriented toward consumption rather than savings.

    For example, the federal income tax system imposes tax on income from savings (even if it is not used for consumption) with only three major exceptions: (1) deferral of tax on capital gains until realized, (2) benefits for investment in a personal residence, and (3) deferral of tax and other benefits for qualified retirement plans, IRAs, and similar arrangements. In other words, a qualified retirement plan is one of only three ways our government encourages savings through the tax system—but it is available only if an employer adopts the plan. (IRA benefits are very limited.)

- ■ *Tax benefits for owners and highly compensated employees.* While many employees in all compensation categories can benefit from retirement plans, owners and other key employees have more money available for saving, have higher compensation, have longer service with the employer, and often are older than regular employees; thus they can benefit more from the plan. When designing a plan for a business owner, a typical objective is to maximize the benefits for the owner (or, in some cases, to minimize the discrimination *against* the highly compensated employee that is built into some of the qualified plan rules).

■ *Help recruit, retain, and retire employees.* These "three Rs" of compensation policy are important in designing retirement plans. The plan can help *recruit* employees by matching or bettering pension benefit packages offered by competing employers; it can help *retain* employees by tying maximum benefits to long service; and it can help *retire* employees by allowing them to retire with dignity—without a drastic drop in living standard—when their productivity has begun to decline and the organization needs new members.

■ *Encourage productivity directly.* Certain types of plan design can act as employee incentives; this is particularly true of plans whose contributions are profit-based or those providing employee accounts invested in stock of the employee.

■ *Discourage collective bargaining.* An attractive retirement package—as good as or better than labor union-sponsored plans in the area—can help keep employees from organizing into a collective bargaining unit. Collective bargaining often poses major business problems for some employers.

■ THE GOVERNMENT'S ROLE—PENSION POLICY ISSUES

Management objectives are one major factor in retirement plan design; the other is the government regulatory structure. This section discusses the development of the government's role in this area.

Qualified plan–nonqualified plan distinction. Most employees covered under an employer-sponsored retirement plan are covered under what is known as a **qualified retirement plan**. A qualified plan is one that receives certain valuable federal tax benefits, but its design, funding, and administration must meet an extraordinarily complex set of federal statutory and regulatory requirements. Most federal regulation in this area specifically preempts state and local regulation. The tax benefits from such plans to both employer and employee are generally (though not always) adequate to justify the inconvenience of this severe regulatory regime. A *nonqualified* plan is any other retirement or deferred compensation plan. Nonqualified plans are subject to much simpler federal regulation, along with less favorable tax treatment. Nonqualified plans are used primarily for executive compensation arrangements that replace or supplement qualified plan coverage for a selected group of highly compensated executives. These are discussed in Chapter 29.

The government's role in the retirement income area has been dictated primarily by historical factors. Beginning in the late nineteenth century, the economy of the United States changed fairly rapidly from predominantly agricultural to predominantly industrial and service oriented. Coinciding with this change—and probably in response to it—the large, supportive extended family of the agricultural economy was largely replaced by smaller, more fragmented family units. The shift away from agriculture reduced the amount of economically useful work available to older people, and family structural changes reduced the amount of family support for the aged.

Because of these economic and social trends, people generally must make specific plans for their retirement. This is a difficult matter for most individual employees to do alone and, consequently, employer-sponsored retirement plans have become increasingly important.

In the 20th century, federal government involvement in retirement plans for the aged also greatly expanded. The federal government's involvement is twofold. For most people, the most obvious federal government program in this area is the Social Security system adopted in the 1930s to provide direct benefit payments to the aged. But even before the Social Security system was adopted, the federal government became involved in a more traditional way by measures designed to encourage the private pension system.

Governments tend to be reluctant to adopt direct payment arrangements for dependent individuals, particularly in the United States—a reflection of the generally conservative social values of the American public. Historically, governments have tended to look first at private organizations to act in this area. This is one reason why charitable institutions, such as orphanages and hospitals, have for centuries been granted various forms of tax exemption.

In the tradition of encouraging private initiatives, in the 1920s the federal government began encouraging private, employer-sponsored retirement plans by providing two kinds of tax benefits. First, pension funds were made tax exempt under the Revenue Acts of 1921 and 1926. Then, in the Revenue Act of 1928, employer contributions to plan funds were made currently deductible by the employer, even though benefits were not paid to employees until later years. These basic provisions still apply and form the basis for today's vast federal regulatory scheme for qualified plans.

The embryonic private pension system of the 1920s declined significantly during the Great Depression of the 1930s. This was one reason for the adoption of the Social Security system. However, since the 1940s, private retirement plans have revived to an enormous degree. Assets in tax-favored retirement arrangements now amount to about $10 trillion,[3] which constitutes a very substantial portion of the nation's entire capital.

Because of the large sums involved, any tax benefits provided to qualified plans cost the government a great deal in lost tax revenues; the government estimate is well over $270 billion annually.[4] This large "tax expenditure" is often given as a primary justification for the exhaustive scheme of government regulation that now applies to qualified retirement plans. Fundamentally, the argument is that the large tax expenditure is designed to help prevent individuals from becoming dependent on the government in retirement. Consequently, the government attempts to make sure that plan benefits go where they are most needed so that this tax expenditure is cost effective. Much of the regulation is aimed at discouraging plans that primarily benefit **highly compensated employees** who have other sources of retirement income. Other rules are intended to ensure that the large sums set aside for plan benefits are managed in the exclusive interest of plan participants and beneficiaries.

In practice, the government frequently adopts new or modified statutes and regulations relating to retirement plans without clear or articulated long-range policy objectives. The absence of a coherent federal retirement policy is currently a critical federal policy issue. Current issues in retirement plan regulation include those covered in the following sections.

Tax Revenue Loss

At times, revenue-raising needs outweigh retirement policy issues in Congress. The tax benefits for qualified plans cause a substantial apparent decrease in tax revenues. The criticism is also frequently made that too much of the tax benefit goes to high-income individuals who don't need government help. Whatever the merits of this argument, it is indisputable that "fine tuning" the rules to reduce tax benefits for certain plan participants can increase tax revenues in the short run, without the political pain of visibly "raising taxes." The need to raise revenue has motivated many recent changes in the qualified plan law, and it probably will be a factor in future legislation. Changes of this type are often enormously complex as a result of the need to carefully target the group whose benefits are to be reduced, typically the owner-employees of closely held businesses. Revenue-motivated changes are often criticized as resulting in bad retirement policy.

Discrimination in Favor of Highly Compensated Employees

Although a major thrust of virtually all qualified plan legislation since the 1940s has been to discourage employers from discriminating in their plans in favor of highly compensated employees, a considerable amount of such discrimination is still possible, as discussed throughout this text. Because of this, much qualified plan legislation has been designed to reduce the "tax shelter" aspects of qualified plans, particularly those for smaller businesses whose owner-employees receive substantial benefits. Many of the most complex and awkward provisions of the law, such as the top-heavy rules discussed in Chapter 26, were designed in this vein.

Seemingly, it would be easy to eliminate the discrimination problem by simple, appropriate benefit or contribution limits. However, there is a countervailing policy consideration. Small businesses, collectively, employ a large and increasing segment of the work force. Owners of these businesses may not be interested in maintaining a qualified plan for their employees unless the plan provides substantial, and possibly disproportionate, benefits for the owners themselves. This policy issue, therefore, involves tension between tax-benefit equity and efficiency on the one hand, and the need to encourage small business retirement plans on the other. No simple resolution of this is likely in the near future, and complex legislative compromises on this issue will probably continue to emerge from Congress.

Encouraging Private Saving

Surprisingly, in view of the trillions invested in retirement plans, relatively little policy emphasis has been given to the role of the qualified plan rules in encouraging private savings. One problem is that policy makers agree neither on the appropriate level for private savings nor on whether government policy should encourage savings rather than allowing the free market to set the level. Another factor is that economists are divided about the efficacy of the qualified plan provisions in encouraging savings. Some economists argue that these plans merely displace private saving that would take place in any event. Nevertheless, the savings issue is an ongoing factor in the policy debate.

Interest-Group Pressures

As the foregoing discussion indicates, retirement policy poses difficult problems even if viewed from a neutral intellectual viewpoint. The actual political climate, of course, is not neutral. The qualified plan business is large and involves many firms and individuals. Most of these organizations eagerly and frequently convey their views to Congress in great technical detail. This complicates the resolution of issues and makes change more difficult.

Mandatory Retirement Plan Coverage

A presidential commission formed in the late 1970s to study pension policy recommended the establishment of a Minimum Universal Pension System (MUPS) for all workers, to be funded by employers at an initial rate of at least 3 percent of payroll.[5] The MUPS benefit would be completely portable from job to job. In general, the MUPS approach is not popular with employers and benefit plan designers, who prefer the flexibility of current rules; at the present time, Congress is not considering it seriously.

Age and Sex Discrimination

Age and sex discrimination have not been addressed by Congress specifically as retirement plan issues. However, recent federal legislative and regulatory activity related to employment discrimination in general has affected retirement plans, as discussed later in this text.

■ QUALIFIED PLAN CHARACTERISTICS

A qualified plan, in general, is one that receives special tax benefits (described below) in return for compliance with complex rules that will take all of Part Five of this text to describe. It is helpful at the outset to take a brief overall look at the most significant requirements before getting into the details. These requirements are discussed in appropriate detail in subsequent chapters.

Eligibility and Plan Coverage

The plan can have almost any kind of initial eligibility provision, except for specific restrictions based on age or service. Generally, no minimum age over 21 can be required, nor can more than one year of service be required for eligibility. In addition, the plan *in operation* must generally cover at least 70 percent of all non–highly compensated employees. These rules have many complex exceptions and limitations, as discussed in Chapter 21.

Nondiscrimination in Benefits and Contributions

Generally speaking, a qualified plan may not discriminate, either in plan benefits or employer contributions to the plan, in favor of highly compensated employees. The law includes a detailed definition of *highly compensated* for this purpose. However, the plan contribution or benefit can be based on the employee's compensation or years of service, which often will provide a higher benefit for certain highly compensated employees. In addition, the qualified plan can be integrated with Social Security so that a greater contribution or benefit is available for higher-paid employees whose compensation is greater than an amount based on the Social Security taxable wage base. Because of the possibilities for abuse in these areas, the rules for Social Security integration, discussed in Chapter 22, are complex.

Funding Requirements

Generally, a qualified plan must be funded in advance of the employee's retirement. This can be done either through contributions to an irrevocable trust fund for the employee's benefit or under an insurance contract. There are strict limits on the extent to which the employer can exercise control over the plan fund. The fund must be under the control of a **fiduciary**—the legal designation for a person who holds funds of another— and must be managed solely for the benefit of plan participants and beneficiaries.

Vesting Requirements

Under the vesting rules, an employee must be given a nonforfeitable or **vested benefit** at the normal retirement date specified in the plan and, in case of termination of employment prior to retirement, after a specified period of service. For example, one common vesting provision grants a fully vested benefit after the employee has attained five years of service, with no vesting until then. If the plan has this vesting provision, an employee who leaves after, say, four years of service with the employer will receive no plan benefit even though the employer has put money into the plan on his behalf over the four-year period. However, an employee who leaves after five or more years of service will receive the entire plan benefit earned up until that time.

The vesting rules are discussed more fully in Chapter 21. These rules are designed to make it more difficult for employers to deny benefits to employees by selectively discharging or turning over employees.

Limitations on Benefits and Contributions

To limit the use of a qualified plan as a tax shelter for highly compensated employees, Section 415 of the Internal Revenue Code contains a limitation on the plan benefit or employer contributions, depending on the type of plan. Under these limitations, a plan cannot generally provide an annual pension of more than $165,000 (as indexed for inflation) or annual employer and employee contributions of more than $41,000 (these are the indexed 2004 figures). The limitations are discussed further in Chapter 26. Practically speaking, these limits are high enough so that only highly compensated participants are likely to encounter them.

Benefits for highly compensated employees are further limited by a requirement that only the first $205,000 (as indexed for 2004) of a participant's compensation can be taken into account in a plan's contribution or benefit formula.

Payout Restrictions

To ensure that qualified plan benefits are used for their intended purposes, there are various restrictions on benefit payouts. Certain plans (pension plans in particular; see discussion below) do not allow withdrawals of funds before termination of employment. In addition, there is a 10 percent penalty on withdrawal of funds from any qualified plan before early retirement, age 59½, death, or disability, with certain exceptions. Funds cannot be kept in the plan indefinitely; generally, the payout must begin by April 1 of the year after the participant's attainment of age 70½, in specified minimum annual amounts. Loans from the plan to participants are restricted.

Top-Heavy Rules

To reduce the possibility of excessive discrimination in favor of business owners covered under a qualified plan, special rules are provided for **top-heavy plans**. Basically, a top-heavy plan is one that provides more than 60 percent of its aggregate accumulated benefits or account balances to **key employees** (as defined in Chapter 25; not the same as the "highly compensated" group). A plan that is top-heavy must meet a special rapid vesting requirement and provide minimum benefits for non–key employees.

■ TAX BENEFITS OF QUALIFIED PLANS

The most important tax advantage of a qualified plan is tax deferral. This is best understood by comparison with the rules applicable to a nonqualified deferred compensation plan. In a nonqualified plan, the timing of the employer's income tax deduction for compensation of employees depends on when the compensation is included in the employee's income. If the employer puts no money aside in advance to fund the plan, there is no deduction to the employer until the retirement income is paid to the employee, at which time the employee also reports the compensation as taxable income. If the employer puts money aside into an irrevocable trust fund, insurance contract, or similar fund for the benefit of the employee, the employer can get an immediate tax deduction, but then the employee is taxed immediately; there is no tax deferral for the employee.

These rules do *not* apply to a qualified plan. In a qualified plan, the employer obtains a tax deduction for contributions to the plan fund (within specified limits) for the year the contribution is made. Employees pay taxes on benefits when they are received. The combination of an immediate employer tax deduction plus tax deferral for the employee can be obtained only with a qualified plan.

In detail, four advantages are usually identified:

1. The employer gets an immediate deduction, within certain limits, for amounts paid into the plan fund to finance future retirement benefits for employees.
2. The employee is not taxed at the time the employer makes contributions for that employee to the plan fund.
3. The employee is taxed only when plan benefits are received.
4. Earnings on money put aside by the employer to fund the plan are not subject to federal income tax while in the plan fund; thus the earnings accumulate tax free.

■ CLASSIFICATION OF QUALIFIED PLANS

There are two broad classifications of qualified plans, as well as a number of specific plan types. The first classification differentiates between *pension plans* and *profit-sharing plans* and the second between *defined-benefit* and *defined-contribution plans*. The classifications overlap each other, as indicated in the following descriptions. These broad classifications are useful in identifying plans that meet broad overall goals of the employee. Once detailed employer objectives have been determined, a specific qualified plan program can be developed for the employer using one or more of the types of plans from a menu of specific plan types. The specific plan types contain a lot of flexibility in design to meet employer needs, and one or more different plans or plan types can be designed covering the same or overlapping groups of employees to provide the exact type of benefits that the employer desires.

Pension and Profit-Sharing Plans

A **pension plan** is a plan designed primarily to provide income at retirement. These plans have the following characteristics:

■ Benefits are generally not available from a pension plan until the employee reaches a specified age, referred to as the *normal retirement age.* Some plans also provide an optional benefit at an earlier age (the *early retirement age*).

■ The employee's benefit is reasonably predictable in advance. (The rule is that the plan must provide *definitely determinable benefits.*)

■ Because the object of a pension plan is to provide retirement security, the employer must keep the fund at an adequate level. Pension plans are subject to the *minimum funding* rules of the Code, and these generally require that the employer make regular deposits to avoid a penalty.

By contrast, a *profit-sharing plan* is designed to allow a relatively short-term deferral of income; it is a somewhat more speculative benefit to the employee because the employer's contribution can be (but does not have to be) based on profits. Furthermore, a profit-sharing plan can provide for a totally discretionary employer contribution so that even if the employer has profits in a given year, the employer need not make a contribution for that year. The minimum funding rules do not apply. However, there must be substantial and recurring contributions or the plan will be deemed to be terminated.

In a profit-sharing plan, it is difficult to determine the employee's benefit in advance, and the plan is considered more an incentive to employees than a predictable source of retirement income. Because it is not exclusively designed for retirement income, employees may be permitted to withdraw funds from the plan before retirement. The plan may allow amounts to be withdrawn as early as two years after the employer has contributed them to the plan. However, as with any qualified plan, preretirement withdrawals may be subject to a 10 percent penalty.

Defined-Benefit and Defined-Contribution Plans

A **defined-contribution plan** has the following characteristics:

- There is an *individual account* for each employee; defined-contribution plans are, therefore, sometimes referred to as *individual-account plans*.

- The plan document describes the amount the employer will contribute to the plan, but it does not promise any particular benefit. Employee contributions are also common.

- When the plan participant retires or otherwise becomes eligible for benefits under the plan, the benefit will be the total amount in the participant's account, including past investment earnings on the amounts put into the account. The participant can look only to his or her own account to recover benefits; he or she is not entitled to amounts in any other account.

- Because of these characteristics, the plan participant (not the company) bears the risk of bad plan investments.

In a **defined-benefit plan,** by contrast:

- The plan document specifies the amount of benefit promised to the employee at normal retirement age.

- The plan itself does not specify the amount the employer must contribute annually to the plan. The plan's actuary will determine the annual contribution required so that the plan fund will be sufficient to pay the promised benefit as each participant retires. If the fund is inadequate, the employer is responsible for making additional contributions. There are no individual participant accounts, and each participant has a claim on the entire fund for the defined benefit.

- As a result of these characteristics, employers bear the investment risk under the plan.

- Plan benefits are insured by the federal government through the Pension Benefit Guaranty Corporation (PBGC), which is funded by insurance premiums paid by employers who sponsor plans.

- Because of the actuarial aspects, defined-benefit plans tend to be more complicated and expensive to administer than defined-contribution plans.

| FIGURE 20.1 | Types of Qualified Plans |

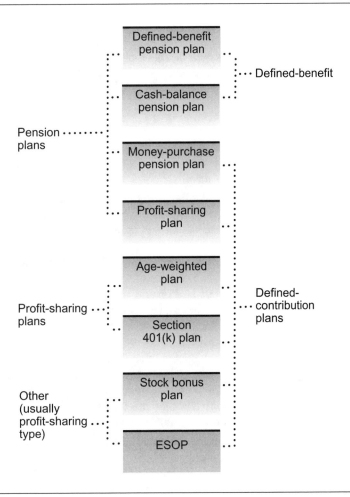

Specific Types of Qualified Plans

As Figure 20.1 indicates, within the broad categories (pension, profit-sharing, defined-benefit, defined-contribution), there are specific types of plans available to meet various retirement-planning objectives.

Defined-Benefit Pension Plan (Traditional Formula). All defined-benefit plans are pension plans; they are designed primarily to provide income at retirement. A traditional defined-benefit plan specifies the benefit in terms of a formula, usually based on compensation and years of service, of which there are many different types.

> **EXAMPLE**
> A defined-benefit plan might promise a monthly retirement benefit equal to 50 percent of the employee's average monthly earnings over the five years prior to retirement. Or instead of a flat 50 percent, the plan might provide something like 1.5 percent for each of the employee's years of service, with the resulting percentage applied to the employee's earnings averaged over a stated period.

Employer contributions to the plan are determined actuarially. Thus, for a given benefit, a defined-benefit plan will tend to result in a larger employer contribution on behalf of employees who enter the plan at older ages, because there is less time to fund the benefit for them.

Cash-Balance Pension Plan. A **cash-balance plan** (also called a *guaranteed account plan* and various other titles), is a type of defined-benefit plan under which each participant has an "account" that increases annually as a result of two types of credits: a compensation credit, based on the participant's compensation, and an interest credit equal to a guaranteed rate of interest. As a result of the guarantee, the participant does not bear the investment risk. Unlike traditional defined-benefit formulas, the plan deposits are not based on age, and younger employees receive the same benefit accrual as those hired at older ages. The plan is funded by the employer on an actuarial basis; the plan fund's actual rate of investment return may be more or less than the guaranteed rate, and employer deposits are adjusted accordingly. Because of the guaranteed minimum benefit, the plan is treated as a defined-benefit plan. From the participant's viewpoint, however, the plan appears very similar to a money-purchase plan, described below. However, a cash-balance plan is not a true individual account plan because the employee's benefit is guaranteed by the employer and the fund is a pooled or unallocated trust fund with no actual segregation of assets for the employee.

Money-Purchase Pension Plan. A **money-purchase pension plan** is a defined-contribution plan that is in some ways the simplest form of qualified plan. The plan simply specifies a level of contribution to each participant's individual account. For example, the plan might specify that the employer will contribute each year to each participant's account an amount equal to 10 percent of that participant's compensation for the year. The participant's retirement benefit is equal to the amount in the account at retirement. Thus, the account reflects not only the initial contribution level but also any subsequent favorable or unfavorable investment results obtained by the plan fund. The term *money purchase* arose because in many such plans, the amount in the participant's account at retirement is not distributed in a lump sum but rather is used to purchase a single or joint life annuity for the participant.

Profit-Sharing Plan. As described earlier, the significant features of a profit-sharing plan are that employer contributions are, within limits, discretionary on the part of the employer and that employee withdrawals before retirement may be permitted. Under current law, employer contributions to the plan do not have to have any connection with actual profits, although a formula based on profits can be used. Profit-sharing plans that are designed to allow employee contributions are sometimes referred to as *savings* or *thrift plans.*

Age-Weighted Plan.   An **age-weighted plan** is a profit-sharing type of plan in which the allocation of employer contributions to an employee's account is based on the age of the employee at the time the employee enters the plan. This has the effect of providing a more adequate benefit for older employees, who in particular may be owners or key employees in the business. There are a number of types of such plans. If the plan is structured to provide the maximum amount of age-weighting, it is referred to as a *cross-tested plan.* A money-purchase pension plan structured with an age-weighted contribution formula is called a *target plan.*

Section 401(k) Plan.   A **Section 401(k) plan,** also called a **cash or deferred plan,** is a plan allowing employees to choose (within limits) to receive compensation either as current cash or as a contribution to a qualified profit-sharing plan. The amount contributed to the plan is not currently taxable to the employee. Such plans have become popular because of their flexibility and tax advantages. However, such plans must include restrictions that may be burdensome to the employer or the employees. The most significant restrictions are a requirement of immediate vesting for amounts contributed under the employee election and restrictions on distribution of these amounts to employees prior to age 59½.

Stock Bonus Plan.   The **stock bonus plan** resembles a profit-sharing plan, except that employer contributions are in the form of employer stock rather than cash, and the plan fund consists primarily of employer stock.

The fiduciary requirements of the pension law forbid an employer to invest more than 10 percent of a pension plan fund in stock of the employer company. This prevents the employer from utilizing pension plan funds primarily for financing the business rather than providing retirement security for employees. However, the 10 percent restriction does not apply to profit-sharing or stock bonus plans.

Stock bonus plans are intended specifically to give employees an ownership interest in the company at relatively low cost to the company. Stock bonus plans are also used by closely held companies to help create a market for stock of the employer.

ESOP.   Employee stock ownership plans **(ESOPs)** are similar to stock bonus plans in that most or all of the plan fund consists of employer stock: employee accounts are stated in shares of employer stock. However, ESOPs are designed to offer a further benefit to the employer. The employer can use an ESOP as a mechanism for financing the business through borrowing or "leveraging." Various tax incentives exist to encourage this.

■ PLANS FOR SPECIAL TYPES OF ORGANIZATIONS

Plans Covering Partners and Proprietors

Under federal tax law, partners and proprietors (sole owners) are not considered employees of their unincorporated business, even if they perform substantial services for the business. By comparison, shareholders of a corporate business who are employed by the business are considered employees for retirement planning and other employee benefit purposes. For many years, there were restrictions on the benefits available from a qualified plan to partners or proprietors. Special plans called **Keogh** or **HR-10** plans were used if partners or proprietors were covered. Since 1983, most of these restrictions no longer apply, and qualified plans can cover partners and proprietors on virtually the same terms as regular employees of the business.

S Corporations

An **S corporation** is a corporation that has made an election to be treated substantially like a partnership for federal income tax purposes. Certain shareholder employees of S corporations were once subject to qualified plan restrictions similar to those for partners and proprietors; today, after 1983, most of these restrictions do not apply. Thus, as with partners and proprietors, S corporation shareholder-employees are now treated basically like regular employees for qualified plan purposes. However, an S corporation employee who owns more than 2 percent of the corporation's stock is treated as a partner for *other* employee benefit purposes, such as group life and health plans.

Multiple-Employer, Collectively Bargained, and Multiemployer Plans

In this text, if not stated otherwise, it is assumed that any qualified plans referred to are maintained by a single employer or by a group of related employers. It is possible, however, for more than one employer or related group to participate in a single qualified plan. If such a plan is established under a collective bargaining agreement (as is usually the case), it is referred to as a **collectively bargained plan**. With a collectively bargained plan, the plan is usually designed and maintained by a labor union, and employers who recognize the union as a bargaining agent for their employees agree to contribute to the plan on a basis specified in the collective bargaining agreement. If the plan is not the result of a collective bargaining agreement, it is referred to as a **multiple-employer plan**. Such plans might, for example, be maintained by trade associations of employers in a certain line of business. There are special rules for applying the participation and other requirements to these plans.

There are also provisions for a special type of collectively bargained plan known as a **multiemployer plan** (Code Section 414(f)). A multiemployer plan is a plan to which more than one employer is required to contribute and that is maintained under a collective bargaining agreement covering more than one employer; the Department of Labor can also impose other requirements by regulation. Presumably, most large collectively bargained plans will qualify as multiemployer plans. Because of the nature of the multiemployer plan, the funding requirements are somewhat more favorable than for other plans. However, the employer may incur a special liability on withdrawing from the plan.

■ GOVERNMENT REGULATION OF QUALIFIED PLANS

It was noted earlier in this chapter that a qualified retirement plan receives special federal tax benefits in return for being designed in accordance with rules imposed by the federal government. This section of the chapter will discuss how the federal government imposes these rules. The federal rules are the most important because federal law generally preempts state and local laws in the qualified plan area.

The rules applicable to a qualified plan start with a private contract between employer and employees—the written plan document itself. However, there is an extensive federal regulatory scheme that prescribes what can be in the document and how it is to be interpreted if it is to receive the benefits available to a qualified plan. Benefit planners need a basic understanding of this federal regulatory scheme to interpret the significance of various official rules and interact with government organizations. Planners must understand these government rules and organizations to be effective in plan design and administration.

Government regulation is expressed through the following, in the order of their importance: (1) statutory law, (2) the law as expressed in court cases, (3) regulations of government agencies, and (4) rulings and other information issued by government agencies.

Statutory Law

Theoretically, the highest level of regulatory law is the U.S. Constitution because all regulation must meet constitutional requirements, such as due process of law and equal protection for persons under the law. However, relatively few issues of federal regulation are actually resolved under constitutional law. For practical purposes, the "law" as expressed by statutes passed by the U.S. Congress is the highest level of authority and is the basis of all regulation; court cases, rulings, and regulations are simply interpretations of statutes passed by Congress. If the statute was detailed enough to cover every possible case, there theoretically wouldn't be any need for anything else. But despite the best efforts of Congressional drafting staffs, the statutes can't cover every situation.

Benefit planners should become as familiar as possible with statutory law because it is the basis for all other rules, regulations, and court cases. One of the main causes for confusion among nonexperts is a lack of understanding of the relative status of sources of information. That is, while a rule found in the **Internal Revenue Code** is fundamental, a statement in a ruling by the **Internal Revenue Service** (the IRS, an administrative agency charged with administering the provisions of the Internal Revenue Code) or in the instructions to IRS forms may be merely a matter of interpretation that is relatively easy to "plan around."

In the benefits area, the following are the sources of statutory law:

■ *Internal Revenue Code (the Code).* The tax laws governing the deductibility and taxation of pension and employee benefit programs are fundamental. These are found primarily in Sections 401–425, with important provisions also in Sections 72, 83, and other sections.

- *ERISA (Employee Retirement Income Security Act of 1974), as amended, and other labor law provisions.* Labor law provisions such as ERISA govern the nontax aspects of federal regulation. These involve plan participation requirements, notice to participants, reporting to the federal government, and a variety of rules designed to safeguard any funds that are set aside to pay benefits in the future. There is some overlap between ERISA and the Code in the area of plan participation, vesting, and prohibited transactions.

- **Pension Benefit Guaranty Corporation (PBGC).** The PBGC is a government corporation set up under ERISA in 1974 to provide termination insurance for participants in qualified defined-benefit plans up to certain limits. In carrying out this responsibility, the PBGC regulates plan terminations and imposes certain reporting requirements on covered plans that are in financial difficulty or in a state of contraction.

- *Securities laws.* The federal securities laws are designed to protect investors. Benefit plans may involve an element of investing the employees' money. While qualified plans are generally exempt from the full impact of the securities laws, if the plan holds employer stock, a federal registration statement may be required and certain securities regulations may apply.

- *Civil rights laws.* Benefit plans are part of an employer's compensation policies; these plans are subject to the Civil Rights Act of 1964, which prohibits employment discrimination on the basis of race, religion, sex, or national origin.

- *Age discrimination.* The Age Discrimination Act of 1978, as amended, has specific provisions aimed at benefit plans, as discussed throughout this book.

- *State legislation.* ERISA contains a broad "preemption" provision under which any state law in conflict with ERISA is preempted—has no effect. If ERISA does not deal with a particular issue, however, there may be room for state legislation. For example, there is considerable state legislation and regulation governing the types of group term life insurance contracts that can be offered as part of an employer plan. There are also certain areas where states continue to assert authority even though ERISA also has an impact, as in the area of creditors' rights to pension fund assets.

Court Cases

The courts enter the picture when a taxpayer decides to appeal a tax assessment made by the IRS. The courts don't act on their own to resolve tax or other legal issues. Consequently, the law as expressed in court cases is a crazy-quilt affair that offers some answers but often raises more questions than it answers. However, after statutes, court cases are the most authoritative source of law. Courts can and do overturn regulations and rulings of the IRS and other regulatory agencies.

A taxpayer wishing to contest a tax assessment has three choices: (1) the Federal District Court in the taxpayer's district, (2) the United States Tax Court, or (3) the United States Claims Court. Tax law can be found in the decisions of any of these three courts.

All three courts are equally authoritative. Most tax cases, however, are resolved by the U.S. Tax Court, because it offers a powerful advantage: The taxpayer can bring the case before the Tax Court without paying the disputed tax. All the other courts require payment of the tax followed by a suit for refund.

Decisions of these three courts can be appealed to the Federal Court of Appeals for the applicable federal "judicial circuit"—the United States is divided into 11 judicial circuits. The circuit courts sometimes differ on certain points of tax law; as a result, tax and benefit planning may depend on what judicial circuit the taxpayer is located in. Where these differences exist, one or more taxpayers will eventually appeal a decision by the Court of Appeals to the United States Supreme Court to resolve differences of interpretation among various judicial circuits; however, this process takes many years and the Supreme Court may ultimately choose not to hear the case. Congress also sometimes amends the Code or other statute to resolve these interpretive differences.

Regulations

Regulations are interpretations of statutory law that are published by a government agency; in the benefits area, the most significant regulations are published by the Treasury Department (the parent of the IRS), the Labor Department, and the PBGC.

Regulations are structured as abstract rules, like the statutory law itself. They are not related to a particular factual situation, although they often contain useful examples that illustrate the application of the rules. Currently, Treasury regulations are often issued in question-and-answer form.

The numbering system for regulations is supposed to make them more accessible by including an internal reference to the underlying statutory provision. For example, Treasury Regulation Section 1.401(k)-2 is a regulation relating to Section 401(k) of the Internal Revenue Code. Labor Regulation Section 2550.408b-3 relates to Section 408b of ERISA.

Issuance of regulations follows a prescribed procedure involving an initial issuance of *proposed regulations,* followed by hearings and public comment, then *final regulations.* The process often takes years. Where taxpayers have an urgent need to know answers, the agency may issue *temporary regulations* instead of proposed regulations. Technically, temporary regulations are binding, while proposed regulations are not. However, if a taxpayer takes a position contrary to a proposed regulation, the taxpayer is taking the risk that the regulation will ultimately be finalized and be enforced against him.

Rulings and Other Information

IRS Rulings. **IRS rulings** are responses by the IRS to requests by taxpayers to interpret the law in light of their particular fact situations. A *General Counsel Memorandum (GCM)* is similar to a ruling, except that the request for clarification and guidance is initiated from an IRS agent in the field during a taxpayer audit, rather than directly from the taxpayer.

There are two types of IRS rulings—*Revenue Rulings,* which are published by the IRS as general guidance to all taxpayers, and *Private Letter Rulings (PLRs),* which are addressed only to the specific taxpayers who requested the rulings. The IRS publishes its Revenue Rulings in IRS Bulletins (collected in Cumulative Bulletins [CB] each year). Revenue rulings are binding on IRS personnel on the issues covered in them, but often IRS agents will try to make a distinction between a taxpayer's factual situation and a similar one covered in a ruling if the ruling appears to favor the taxpayer.

PLRs are not published by the IRS, but are available to the public with taxpayer identification deleted. These "anonymous" PLRs are published for tax professionals by various private publishers. They are not binding interpretations of tax law except for the taxpayer who requested the ruling, and even then they apply only to the exact situation described in the ruling request and do not apply to even a slightly different fact pattern involving the same taxpayer. Nevertheless, PLRs are very important in research because they are often the only source of information about the IRS position on various issues, and they may contain language that is helpful in drafting plan documents.

Other Rulings.   The Department of Labor and the PBGC issue some rulings in areas of employee benefit regulation under their jurisdiction. DOL rulings include the **prohibited transaction exemptions (PTEs),** which rule on types of transactions that can avoid the prohibited transaction penalties—for example, sale of life insurance contracts to qualified plans.

Other Information.   Because of frequent changes in the tax law, the IRS has been unable to promulgate regulations and rulings on a timely basis, and has increasingly used less formal approaches to inform taxpayers of its position. These include various types of published *Notices* and even speeches by IRS personnel. Finally, many important IRS positions are found only in *IRS Publications* (pamphlets available free to taxpayers) and *instructions* for filling out IRS forms. The IRS also maintains telephone question-answering services, but the value of these for information on complicated issues is minimal.

■ KEY TERMS

Age-weighted plan	Internal Revenue Code	Pension plan
Cash-balance plan	Internal Revenue Service (IRS)	Profit-sharing plan
Cash or deferred plan		Prohibited transaction exemption (PTE)
Collectively bargained plan	IRS ruling	
Defined-contribution plan	Keogh plan	Qualified retirement plan
Defined-benefit plan	Key employee	Regulation
ESOP	Money-purchase pension plan	S corporation
Fiduciary		Section 401(k) plan
Highly compensated employee	Multiple-employer plan	Stock bonus plan
HR-10 plan	Multiemployer plan	Top-heavy plan
	Pension Benefit Guaranty Corporation (PBGC)	Vested benefit

■ STUDY QUESTIONS

1. List four major management objectives for a retirement plan and explain how the plan helps achieve these objectives.
2. What are the underlying social and historical reasons for the federal government's involvement in regulating private retirement plans?
3. List some of the general features required for qualified retirement plans.
4. Identify the tax benefits available to the employer and the employees from a qualified plan.
5. Explain the difference between a pension plan and a profit-sharing plan.
6. Compare defined-benefit plans with defined-contribution plans with respect to
   a. administrative costs.
   b. individual account balances for participants.
   c. risk of bad plan investments.
   d. need for an actuary.
7. Identify the types of defined-contribution plans and their primary features.
8. Discuss the coverage available to partners and sole proprietors under qualified plans.
9. How are shareholder-employees treated under an S corporation for purposes of qualified plans?
10. Distinguish between multiple-employer plans, collectively bargained plans, and multiemployer plans.
11. Explain the role of the courts in interpreting the tax laws pertaining to qualified plans.
12. What are the respective regulatory roles of Treasury Regulations, IRS Revenue Rulings, and IRS Private Letter Rulings?

■ NOTES

1. Employee Benefit Research Institute, Facts from EBRI, *www.ebri.org/facts/*, Oct. 2002.
2. Employee Benefit Research Institute, EBRI Notes, Washington, D.C. March 2002.
3. Includes IRAs and similar arrangement. Plans of private employers account for about half of this total. Employee Benefit Research Institute, Facts from EBRI, December 2003 (figures as of end of 2002), *www.ebri.com.*
4. Employee Benefit Research Institute, Facts from EBRI, (Fiscal Year 2005 budget), *www.ebri.com.* Employee benefit-related tax expenditures are estimated to total about $312 billion for fiscal year 2005.
5. *Coming of Age: Toward a National Retirement Income Policy,* President's Commission on Pension Policy, 1981.

Plan Qualification Requirements

- Explain the eligibility and participation requirements that must be met by qualified retirement plans with respect to
    1. age and service requirements.
    2. maximum age limits.
    3. years of service.
    4. breaks in service.
    5. overall coverage tests.
- Explain the coverage rules when an employer has
    1. a group of employees in a collective bargaining unit.
    2. separate lines of business.
    3. affiliated or commonly controlled related employers.
- Explain the vesting requirements for qualified plans.
- Explain why most pension plans are noncontributory.
- Discuss the importance of normal, early, and late retirement ages in a qualified plan.
- Describe the rules for nondiscrimination in contributions and benefits and the exception for permitted disparity (Social Security integration)
- Describe the federal nontax antidiscrimination provisions that apply to qualified plans.

CHAPTER OUTLINE

There are many types of qualified plans, but there is a structure of underlying rules that apply to most or all types of plan. This chapter, therefore, covers the basic rules before getting into the specific types of plan.

In designing a qualified plan, there is a continuing interaction between the employer's objectives and the limits imposed by the qualified plan rules under the Internal Revenue Code and other provisions of the law. In this discussion, the approach will be to discuss both aspects of plan design in an integrated way. Plan design topics will be discussed from the standpoint of employer objectives and how these objectives can be accomplished within the rules.

■ STRUCTURE AND DESIGN OF A QUALIFIED PLAN

A qualified plan is a labyrinth of concepts and terminology. One way to thread the labyrinth is to follow an employee covered under a typical defined-benefit pension plan. This may help to introduce the process of qualified plan design discussed in these chapters.

EXAMPLE

Suppose Clutch Company has a qualified defined-benefit plan. When employee Tom Bill is hired, he does not automatically become a participant because he must first meet the plan's eligibility requirements, basically consisting of a definition of the covered group and a waiting period. When Tom enters the plan and becomes a plan *participant,* Clutch Company must begin to put money into a fund designed to accept, invest, accumulate, and pay out money belonging to the plan. Also, when Tom enters, he begins to *accrue benefits* under the plan. In the Clutch Plan, as in many plans, the amount of benefit accrued each year is determined by estimating the benefit Tom will receive at retirement and allocating that amount in a specified manner over each of Tom's anticipated years of employment prior to his expected retirement date.

Because the Clutch Plan does not allow loans to participants or provide incidental insurance coverage (although it could do these things), Tom will receive no benefit from the plan until he terminates employment with Clutch. If he terminates before retirement and before he has served Clutch long enough to be vested, he will receive nothing, even though he has accrued a benefit under the plan. If he terminates after vesting, he will receive all or a portion of his benefit accrued to that date. This benefit will begin immediately if he has reached either the plan's specified early retirement age or normal retirement age. These ages are 62 and 65 in the Clutch Plan, a typical choice of ages that is within the limits of the qualified plan law. If Tom has not reached either of these ages, the Clutch Plan will not pay benefits until he reaches age 65. If the benefit is very small, Tom will be paid his benefit immediately in a cash lump sum. Except for this, the plan gives Tom a choice of various forms of benefit at retirement; all of these are of equal value to the plan—a life annuity, an annuity for the joint lives of Tom and his wife, or several others.

This little scenario illustrates the major planning decisions. These are, as discussed in this and the next several chapters:

- What group of employees should be covered under the plan? (Chapter 21)
- Should there be a waiting period for plan entry by new employees? (Chapter 21)
- Should the plan be funded solely by the employer or should employees contribute? (Chapter 21)
- What is the plan's normal retirement age and how are earlier and later retirement treated? (Chapter 21)
- What is the plan benefit at retirement? (Chapters 22–24)
- How fast do benefits accrue to employees? (Chapters 22–24)
- What do employees receive on termination of employment before retirement (what is the vesting schedule)? (Chapters 22–24)
- What provisions should the plan have for employees who terminate employment because of death or disability? (Chapter 24)
- Who should hold the plan funds and on what terms? (Chapter 24)
- What will the plan cost the employer each year? (Chapter 24)
- In what form are benefits paid? (Chapter 25)

ELIGIBILITY AND PARTICIPATION

The employer must decide what group is to be covered by the qualified plan. In a closely held business, the employer will often want to provide a large portion of the plan's benefits to controlling and key employees and minimize benefits for rank-and-file employees. In larger plans, employers will often want to provide a different qualified plan (or no plan) for different groups of employees for various reasons; for example, the existence of collective bargaining units with separate plans, a desire for different benefit structures for hourly and salaried employees, or differences in benefit policy for employees at different geographic locations.

In reviewing the many limitations imposed on the plan designer by the qualified plan rules, note that the overriding purpose for most of these rules is to prevent discrimination by the employer in favor of highly compensated employees. A secondary purpose, related to the first, is to provide and maintain some security of benefits for participants, particularly participants who are not highly compensated. Most of the qualified plan rules can be explained by these rationales; most questions about the meaning of particular rules and how they apply in a particular situation can be resolved by referring to these basic purposes of the law.

The Code imposes two types of limitations on the employer's freedom to designate the group of employees to be covered under the plan. The first limitation applies to the plan as it exists on paper—the eligibility provisions written into the plan. The second type of limitation applies to the plan in operation and provides minimum coverage requirements in the form of three alternative coverage tests. Both limitations are contained in Code Section 410 and its accompanying regulations and rulings.

First of all, as to plan coverage in the document itself, the designer has a good deal of freedom. The plan may cover only employees at a certain geographic location, employees in a certain work unit, salaried employees only, hourly employees only, or almost any other variation. However, when eligibility is restricted on the basis of age or service with the employer, there are specific limits.

■ AGE AND SERVICE REQUIREMENTS

Although not all plans have age or service conditions for entry, many employers prefer such conditions because they help avoid the cost of carrying an employee on the records as a plan participant when the employee quits after a short period of service. Generally, a plan cannot require more than one year of service before eligibility, and an employee who has attained the age of 21 must be permitted to participate in the plan if the employee has met the other participation requirements of the plan. Both **age and service requirements** can be imposed.

> **EXAMPLE**
> For an employee hired at age 19, the plan can require that employee to wait until age 21 to participate in the plan. However, an employee hired at age 27 cannot be required to wait more than one year before participating in the plan.

As an alternative to the one-year waiting period, a plan may provide for a waiting period of up to two years if the plan provides immediate 100 percent vesting upon entry. (In most other cases, graduated vesting is allowed—see the discussion in Chapter 20.) The two-year provision is often used by employers with very few employees and a high turnover rate.

> **EXAMPLE**
> A self-employed physician has one or two clerical or technical employees who have high mobility in their labor market. With a two-year waiting period provision, few of the employees may ever be covered under the plan. The two-year/100 percent vesting provision may be appropriate.

One problem with these age and service requirements is that it is often desirable for a plan to have *entry dates*—that is, specific dates during the year in which plan participation is deemed to begin—to simplify recordkeeping. The regulations provide that no employee may be required to wait for participation more than six months after the plan's age and service requirements are met.[1] Thus, a plan having entry dates must adjust its eligibility provisions accordingly.

EXAMPLE

The Blarp, Inc., pension plan wishes to have a one-year, age-21 entry requirement and to use an entry date or dates. Any of the following options will meet the requirement in the regulations:

- Two entry dates in the year, six months apart, with participants entering on the next entry date after they satisfy the one-year, age-21 condition
- One entry date, but a minimum entry age of no more than 20½ and a maximum waiting period of six months
- One entry date, with participants entering the plan on the date nearest (before or after) the date on which the one-year, age-21 requirement is satisfied

All qualified plans are subject to the age 21 requirement, except for a plan maintained exclusively by a tax-exempt educational institution as defined in Code Section 170(b)(1)(a)(ii). To avoid coverage of temporary employees such as graduate teaching assistants, such a plan may provide a minimum age of 26, but the plan must have 100 percent vesting after one year of service.

Maximum Age Limits and Coverage of Older Employees

Coverage of employees who enter a defined-benefit or age-weighted plan when they are close to the plan's retirement age can present a funding problem because there are relatively few years available to fund the benefit. If the participant enters the plan within a few years of retirement, the employer contribution may be burdensome.

EXAMPLE

Using a given set of actuarial assumptions, the annual cost to fund the same benefit of $1,000 per month at age 65 varies with age at entry as shown in the table.

Age at Plan Entry	Annual Cost
30	$ 537
50	3,410
55	6,391
60	15,783
62	28,521
64	92,592

The age discrimination law prohibits exclusion of employees who enter at later ages. However, as discussed later under "Retirement Age," a plan can define **normal retirement age** as the fifth anniversary of plan entry for a participant entering within five years of normal retirement age. This provides at least five years for funding. Alternatively, the time for funding the benefit can be extended simply by having the plan delay the beginning of benefit payments beyond retirement age, but payments cannot be delayed beyond the tenth anniversary of plan participation, and benefit payments must begin no later than April 1 of the year after attainment of age 70½ or at retirement, if later; see Chapter 24.

Definition of Year of Service

The term *year of service* is used in different ways in the qualified plan rules. It is used to define the age and service rules for eligibility that were just discussed, and is also used in connection with the vesting and benefit accrual rules discussed in Chapter 20. Because it plays such an important part in these rules, it has a specific definition under the law.

Generally, a year of service is a 12-month period during which the employee has at least 1,000 hours of service.[2] For purposes of determining eligibility, the *initial* 12-month period must be measured beginning with the date the employee begins work for the employer. For other purposes, the 12-month accounting period used by the plan (the *plan year*) can generally be used.

> **EXAMPLE**
> Suppose the plan uses the calendar year as the plan year. If an employee began work on June 1, 2005, the initial 12-month period for determining whether the 1,000-hour requirement had been met would be June 1, 2005, through May 31, 2006. If the employee did not perform 1,000 hours of service during that period, the plan could begin the next measuring period on January 1, 2006, with subsequent years being determined similarly on the basis of the plan year.

The employer may determine hours of service using payroll records or any other type of records that accurately reflect the hours worked. Alternatively, the regulations allow a plan to use "equivalency" methods for computing hours of service. These equivalencies allow employees to be credited with hours worked based on completion of some other unit of service, such as a shift, week, or month of service, without actual counting of hours worked.

Breaks in Service

A larger employer may reduce the cost of a plan somewhat by including a **break-in-service provision** in the plan's eligibility requirements. Under such a provision, an employee whose continuous service for the same employer is interrupted loses credit (upon returning to work) for service prior to the break and must again meet the plan's waiting period for eligibility. For a smaller employer, breaks in service followed by reemployment are relatively rare, and such a provision may have no substantial cost impact other than possibly to complicate plan administration.

The rules under which a plan may interrupt service credits for breaks in service are somewhat complicated. The rules are set out in Code Section 410(a)(5) and regulations thereunder, as well as Labor Regulations Section 2530.200b. A one-year break in service for this purpose is defined as a 12-month period during which the participant has 500 or fewer hours of service. Service prior to a break cannot be disregarded until there is a one-year break in service. If the employee then returns to work, prebreak service may be disregarded (and the participant regarded as a new employee for participation purposes) within the following three limitations:

1. Service prior to the one-year break in service does not have to be counted unless the returned employee completes a year of service. Participation is then effective as of the first day of the plan year in which eligibility was reestablished.

2. If the plan has a two-year, 100 percent vesting eligibility provision, prebreak service need not be counted if the employee did not complete two years of service before the break.

3. If the participant had no vested benefits at the time of the break, prebreak service need not be counted if the number of consecutive one-year breaks in service equals or exceeds the greater of five or the participant's years of service before the break. For example, suppose that participant Arlen works for Maple Corporation for eight months, quits, and then returns seven years later. For purposes of determining eligibility in the Maple Corporation Plan, Arlen's eight months of prebreak service do not have to be counted.

Other Eligibility Criteria Related to Age and Service

Because the age and service limitations must be met by the plan document as drafted, the IRS will scrutinize the plan to ascertain whether there are eligibility criteria that indirectly base eligibility on age and service. For example, the employer may wish to exclude part-time employees. The IRS views an exclusion of part-timers as a service-based eligibility provision. If the plan has a one-year service requirement for entry, it will exclude all employees who never work 1,000 hours or more in any year. However, the plan cannot exclude part-timers who work 1,000 hours or more in a year, but less than a full year, because such a requirement would be seen as a service requirement that violated the one-year, 1,000-hour rule. On the other hand, even if some part-timers must be included, the plan is allowed to have a benefit formula that provides smaller benefits for them because of their lesser compensation, or because part-time service is given less credit for benefit purposes than full-time service.

The IRS will also look at how a plan is actually operated to make sure that the age and service limitations are not violated.

> **EXAMPLE**
> Suppose an employer has a plan for Division B of the business, and employment in Division B requires five years of service in Division A. Division B has a qualified plan and Division A does not. This service requirement, although outside the plan itself, could be seen as an attempt to circumvent the service limitation for the plan maintained by Division B.

■ OVERALL COVERAGE TESTS

In addition to the specific rules relating to age and service eligibility provisions, the second major limitation on the employer's freedom to exclude employees from a qualified plan is a set of two alternative statutory tests (Code Section 410) to be applied to the plan in actual operation to determine if coverage is discriminatory. A qualified plan must satisfy one of two coverage tests:

1. The *ratio percentage test:* The plan must cover a percentage of non–highly compensated employees, that is, at least 70 percent of the percentage of highly compensated employees covered.
2. The *average benefit test:* The plan must benefit a nondiscriminatory classification of employees, and the average benefit, as a percentage of compensation, for all non–highly compensated employees of the employer, must be at least 70 percent of that for highly compensated employees.

In addition, no defined-benefit plan can be qualified unless it covers, on each day of the plan year, the lesser of (1) 50 employees of the employer or (2) 40 percent or more of all employees of the employer [Code Section 401(a)(26)].

Employees Excluded

In applying these tests, certain employees are not taken into account:

■ Employees who have not satisfied the plan's minimum age and service requirements, if any

■ Employees included in a collective bargaining unit, if there is evidence that retirement benefits were the subject of good-faith bargaining under a collective bargaining agreement

■ Employees excluded under a collective bargaining agreement between air pilots and employers under Title II of the Railway Labor Act

■ Employees who are nonresident aliens and who receive no earned income from sources within the United States

The coverage tests apply not only at the plan's inception but on an ongoing basis. Generally, all of the nondiscrimination requirements must be met by a plan on at least one day of each quarter of the plan's taxable year [Code Section 401(a)(6)]. Although the IRS does not perpetually monitor a plan's compliance with the percentage coverage requirements, these requirements give the IRS an ongoing weapon to challenge a plan that may have become discriminatory.

Highly Compensated

For purposes of the coverage tests just described (and for many other employee benefit purposes as well), Code Section 414(q) provides a specific definition of a *highly compensated employee.* A highly compensated employee is any employee who during the preceding year met either of the following tests:

- Was at any time an owner of a more than 5 percent interest in the employer
- Received compensation from the employer in excess of $80,000 (this nominal $80,000 amount is indexed annually for inflation; the 2004 amount is $90,000)

Features of the Average Benefit Test

In some respects, the average benefit test is the least stringent of the two coverage tests, and many types of plan design will be able to qualify only under this test. For example, a common plan design provides separate plans for salaried and hourly employees. In many cases, neither plan individually—the salaried plan in particular—can meet the ratio percentage test and thus meets the average benefit test.

The average benefit test is two-pronged. First, the plan must cover a *nondiscriminatory classification* of employees. Because of this aspect of the test, the IRS has a degree of discretion in the determination of whether a classification is nondiscriminatory. The IRS has issued detailed regulations as guidance in interpreting whether there is a nondiscriminatory classification.

The second requirement of the average benefit test is that the *average benefit,* as a percentage of compensation for non–highly compensated employees, must be at least 70 percent of that for highly compensated employees. In making this determination, all employees, whether covered or not under the plan in question, are counted and benefits from all qualified plans are taken into account.

Examples of Plan Coverage Meeting Various Tests

- Acme Trucking Company has ten employees, three of whom are highly compensated. A qualified plan covers the three highly compensated employees and five of the seven non–highly compensated employees. This plan meets the ratio percentage test because it covers at least 70 percent of non–highly compensated employees.
- Barpt Products, Inc., has 20 employees, 5 of whom are highly compensated. If a qualified plan covers four of the highly compensated employees (80 percent), then the plan meets the ratio percentage test if it covers at least 56 percent of non–highly

compensated employees—70 percent of 80 percent—or, in this case, nine non–highly compensated employees.

■ Flim Company, Inc., has 500 employees, 100 of whom are salaried. Flim has a plan for salaried employees that covers 50 employees. Flim has received a determination from the IRS that the 50 salaried employees covered do not form a discriminatory classification, presumably because some low-paid salaried employees are covered as well as highly paid employees. The Flim Company Plan will qualify, as long as benefits are provided for non–highly compensated employees as a group that are at least 70 percent of those for highly compensated employees as a group. Thus, some kind of retirement plan coverage for the hourly employees would be necessary.

Plans for Separate Lines of Business

If an employer has separate lines of business, the participation tests can be applied separately to employees in each line of business [Code Section 414(r)]. A separate line of business must be operated for bona fide business reasons and must have at least 50 employees. If highly compensated employees constitute more than a specified percentage of the employees in the separate line of business, special guidelines apply or IRS approval may be required to use the separate line of business provision.

The separate line of business provision may allow a larger employer, or a controlled group of employers, to design separate plans—with separate coverage provisions—for its various operations. This increases the flexibility available in plan design to some extent.

■ SERVICE FOR PREDECESSORS AND OTHER EMPLOYERS

A plan of one employer generally does not need to give an employee credit for service with another employer. There are some situations, however, in which this is required. Under collectively bargained, multi-employer, or multiple employer plans, service with more than one employer may have to be taken into consideration. Also, if the employer has chosen to take over or maintain the plan of a predecessor employer, service for the predecessor must be given credit. The IRS has not yet made clear what is meant by "predecessor employer," leaving some doubt as to the rules in this area. A common situation is the incorporation of a partnership and the continuation of the qualified plan of that partnership by the new corporation. The IRS once took the position that corporate employees who were partners in the prior partnership may not be given credit for prior service as partners. However, the IRS currently will probably permit this so long as regular employees receive full credit for service under the partnership.

Finally, service credit must be given for service with all employers under **common control**. The definition of *common control,* an important concept in the qualified plan area, is discussed in general terms on the following page.

■ COMMONLY CONTROLLED EMPLOYERS

Often an employer organization (incorporated or unincorporated) is owned or controlled in common with other such organizations. The qualified plan designer often must coordinate plan coverage for the first employer with plan coverage for employees of other members of the commonly controlled group of employers.

The Code has several provisions relating to this issue; their basic objective is to prevent a business owner from getting around the coverage and nondiscrimination requirements for qualified plans by artificially segregating employees to be benefited from the plan into one organization with the remainder being employed by subsidiaries or organizations with lesser plan benefits or no plan at all. While this is still technically possible, the **controlled group rules** restrict this practice considerably.

Controlled Group Rules in General

Because the forms of business ownership can be tangled and complex, the common control rules for qualified plans are appropriately complicated. There are three sets of these rules.

1. Under Code Section 414(b), all employees of all corporations in a *controlled group* of corporations are treated as employed by a single employer for purposes of Sections 401, 408(k), 410, 411, 415, and 416. The major impact of this comes from the participation rules of Section 410, which require that the participation and coverage tests be applied to the entire controlled group rather than to any single corporation in the group. Code Section 414(c) provides similar rules for commonly controlled partnerships and proprietorships.

2. Code Section 414(m) provides that employees of an *affiliated service group* are treated as employed by a single employer. This requirement similarly has its major impact in determining participation in a qualified plan; however, it applies to other employee benefit requirements as well.

3. A *leased employee* is treated as an employee of the lessor corporation under certain circumstances, under Code Section 414(n).

Some examples will give a general idea of the impact of these provisions on plan design; a detailed discussion is beyond the scope of this book. Note that the common thread of these examples is that the related organization's employees must be *taken into account* in applying the participation rules. This does not mean that these employees must necessarily be covered.

■ Alpha Corporation owns 80 percent of the stock of Beta Corporation. Alpha and Beta are members of a parent subsidiary controlled group of corporations. In applying the participation and coverage rules of Code Section 410, Alpha and Beta must be considered as a single employer.

■ Bert and Harry own stock as shown in the chart.

Owner	Corporation A	Corporation B
Bert	60%	60%
Harry	30	30
	90%	90%

Corporations A and B are a brother-sister controlled group. Thus, A and B must be considered as a single employer for purposes of Code Section 410 and most other qualified plan rules.

■ Medical Services, Inc., provides administrative and laboratory services for Dr. Sam and Dr. Joe, each of whom is an incorporated sole practitioner. Dr. Sam and Dr. Joe each own 50 percent of Medical Services, Inc. If either Dr. Sam or Dr. Joe adopts a qualified plan, employees of Medical Services, Inc., will have to be taken into account in determining if plan coverage is nondiscriminatory.

■ Calculators Incorporated, an actuarial firm, contracts with Temporary Services, Inc., an employee-leasing firm, to lease employees on a substantially full-time basis. The leased employees will have to be taken into account in determining non-discrimination in any qualified plan of Calculators, unless Temporary maintains a minimum (10 percent nonintegrated) money-purchase pension plan for the leased employees.

■ VESTING

A qualified plan must provide a minimum nonforfeitable, or vested, benefit for participants who attain certain service requirements. Once vested, the participant cannot forfeit this minimum vested benefit.

> **EXAMPLE**
> The plan cannot require that an employee forfeit part or all of the vested benefit required by the Code even if the employee commits an act of misconduct, such as embezzlement or going to work for a competitor. The strictness of the vesting rules was designed to provide additional benefit security and to protect employees against arbitrary acts of the employer.

Vesting at Normal Retirement Age and Termination of Employment

The plan must provide a fully vested benefit at the normal retirement age. The plan must also provide that benefits are vested under a specified **vesting schedule** during the participant's employment, so that if the participant terminates employment prior to retirement age, he or she is entitled to a vested benefit with some stated minimum amount of service. The vested benefit can be payable immediately on termination or deferred to the plan's normal retirement age.

If the plan provides for employee contributions, the participant's accrued benefit is divided between the part attributable to employee contributions and the part attributable to employer contributions. The part attributable to employee contributions must at all times be 100 percent vested. The part attributable to employer contributions must be vested in accordance with a vesting schedule set out in the plan.

There is some flexibility in designing a vesting schedule in order to meet various employer objectives. However, the vesting schedule must be at least as favorable as one of two alternative minimum standards, five-year vesting or three- to seven-year vesting.

Five-Year Vesting

The vesting schedule satisfies this minimum requirement if an employee with at least five years of service is 100 percent vested in the employer-provided portion of the accrued benefit. This rule is satisfied even if there is no vesting at all before five years of service. This rule is sometimes referred to as **cliff vesting**.

Three- to Seven-Year Vesting

A vesting schedule satisfies this minimum standard if the vesting is at least as fast as in the table.

Years of Service	Vested Percentage
3	20
4	40
5	60
6	80
7 or more	100

In applying the vesting rules, all of a participant's years of service for the employer must be taken into account, even years prior to plan participation, except that years of service prior to age 18 may be excluded. The plan's vesting schedule may also ignore service prior to a break in continuous service with the employer; however, there are elaborate restrictions on how this may be done [Code Section 411(a)(6)].

Probably the most common vesting provision in defined-benefit plans is the five-year provision, because of its simplicity and because it is generally the most favorable to the employee. Defined-contribution plans are often designed with a more generous (to the employee) vesting schedule using the three- to seven-year schedule or one that is even faster.

Top-Heavy Vesting

To complete this discussion, it should be mentioned that plans that are top-heavy, as defined in the Code, are required to provide faster vesting than under most of the schedules previously mentioned.

The top-heavy minimum vesting schedule is shown in the table on page 540.

Years of Service	Vested Percentage
2	20
3	40
4	60
5	80
6 or more	100

A 100 percent vesting provision with two years' eligibility also meets the top-heavy minimum vesting requirement. Top-heavy plans are discussed in detail in Chapter 25. As discussed below, the top-heavy requirements have a significant impact in designing a vesting schedule for plans of smaller employers.

Choosing a Vesting Schedule

Choosing an appropriate vesting schedule is an important plan design decision. When a pension plan participant terminates employment, invested funds contributed to the plan for that participant in excess of any benefits paid to the participant on termination (forfeitures) are generally used to reduce future employer costs for the pension plan. Strict vesting, therefore, can reduce a pension plan's cost to the employer. In a defined-contribution plan, forfeitures also can be reallocated to remaining participants' accounts. Thus, there should be a reason for adopting more than a strict minimum vesting schedule. Some reasons for using liberal vesting include the need to provide employee incentive and involvement in situations where a five-year vesting schedule might appear too remote and therefore of no value to employees. Also, a simplified liberal vesting schedule may reduce administrative costs.

Vesting on Plan Termination

The final vesting rule relates to a plan that has terminated. The IRS will regard a plan as having terminated either if it is formally terminated or if the employer permanently ceases to make contributions to the plan (see Chapter 27). When a plan is terminated, all benefits must be fully vested to the extent funded. Therefore, when a defined-contribution plan terminates, all participants are immediately 100 percent vested in their account balances. When a defined-benefit plan terminates, participants are 100 percent vested in their accrued benefits; however, if the plan funds are insufficient, they are vested only to the extent that the plan is funded. Many terminated qualified defined-benefit plans are insured by the Pension Benefit Guaranty Corporation (PBGC). The provisions that come into operation on plan termination under the PBGC rules will be discussed in Chapter 27.

■ WHO WILL PAY FOR THE PLAN?

Most qualified pension plans are funded entirely by the employer. Pension plans requiring contributions by employees, referred to as **contributory plans**, were once popular but are currently of diminishing importance. There are two reasons for this.

First, employee contributions to a qualified plan other than "salary reductions" (see below) are *after-tax* contributions—the employee receives no tax deduction or exclusion for the contribution. Also, employee contributions involve administrative complications discussed in Chapter 23.

Many employers believe that retirement plan benefits are appreciated more by employees if the employees themselves contribute (or feel that they are contributing) toward their cost. In most cases, of course, most of an employee's income comes in the form of compensation from the employer, so there is some degree of illusion in this approach. Some employers may also believe that a contributory approach lowers plan costs, but this is not actually true. To the extent that a contributory approach results in the loss of tax benefits (in effect, losing a contribution to the plan by the U.S. Treasury), a contributory plan actually costs the employer more for the same level of benefits. A better justification for contributory plans is that they give the employee some degree of choice in allocating his or her compensation between cash and deferred benefits.

Currently, the most favorable contributory plan design is to use **salary reductions** in a plan that is permitted to use salary reductions—a Section 401(k) plan, a Section 403(b) plan, a Section 457 plan, or a SIMPLE plan (discussed in later chapters). Qualified pension plans cannot use salary reductions, except for some older plans that were "grandfathered" (permitted to use older law) when current law was enacted. Salary reductions are subject to FICA and FUTA (Social Security and federal unemployment) taxes but not to federal income tax. Thus, the tax benefits of qualified plans are not completely lost to the employee if the salary reduction approach is used.

■ RETIREMENT AGE

A plan's *normal retirement age* is the age at which a participant can retire and receive the full specified retirement benefit. A defined-benefit plan must specify a normal retirement age to fully define the benefit. Defined-contribution plans do not need a normal retirement age for this purpose, but they may have a normal retirement age in order to specify an age at which participants can retire and begin to receive benefits or, as discussed below, an age beyond which no further employer contributions will be made.

Under Code Section 411(a)(8), a plan's normal retirement age can be no greater than the latest of

- age 65 or
- the fifth anniversary of plan entry if a participant entered within five years of normal retirement age.

Thus, for example, a plan having a normal retirement age of 65 could provide normal retirement at age 67 for a participant entering at age 62.

Although most plans use 65 as the normal retirement age, the plan may specify an earlier normal retirement age. The use of an earlier normal retirement age in a defined-benefit plan requires that funding be accelerated—larger amounts must be contributed to the plan each year to fund each employee's benefit because the benefit will become payable at an earlier date. For plans in which tax sheltering is a primary consideration, such as plans oriented toward key employees in a closely held business, the use of the earliest possible normal retirement age can provide significant additional tax benefits by increasing the deductible plan contributions each year. However, if the normal retirement age is less than the Social Security retirement age, the Section 415 limitations are reduced, as discussed in Chapter 26. This tends to provide some limit on the use of unrealistically low normal retirement ages.

The IRS considers a plan's retirement age to be an actuarial assumption. Therefore, the IRS requirement of "reasonableness" for actuarial assumptions also puts some limit on the use of unrealistically low normal retirement ages.

Early Retirement

A qualified plan may designate an **early retirement age** at which an employee may retire and receive an immediate benefit. The early retirement benefit is usually reduced below that payable at normal retirement. The plan may have some service requirement for early retirement, such as ten years of service, or it may permit early retirement simply upon attainment of the early retirement age.

Under most defined-benefit plans, the monthly early retirement benefit is reduced below the monthly normal retirement benefit payable at age 65 because of two factors. First, the early retirement benefit will usually be limited to the participant's accrued benefit, and the participant will often have not accrued the full benefit at early retirement. Second, most plans require an **actuarial reduction**. The actuarial reduction is a mathematical adjustment based on (1) longer life expectancy at early retirement, (2) loss of investment earnings to the plan fund due to payments beginning earlier, and (3) loss of the possibility that the participant might die before payments begin—mortality.

Most plans do not require employer consent for early retirement. If employer consent is required, the IRS limits the early retirement benefit to the vested accrued benefit that would be payable if the employee terminated employment unilaterally, to avoid the possibility that the employer will favor highly compensated employees in granting early retirement benefits.

For defined-contribution plans, early retirement is usually treated the same as a termination of employment, and the benefit payable at early retirement is simply the amount of the participant's account balance as of that date. Thus, many defined-contribution plans do not specify an early retirement age.

Some employers offer a "subsidized" early retirement benefit—one that is reduced by less than the full amount dictated by the three factors discussed above—as an incentive for retirement. The subsidized benefit is often offered during a limited *window period*, during which the employee must either choose the benefit or lose the opportunity to receive it forever (or at least until the employer decides to offer another window benefit). There are specific legal protections under the Age Discrimination Act for employees in this situation.

Late Retirement

A qualified plan design should also cover the possibility of **late retirement**—retirement after the normal retirement age. Under the age discrimination rules discussed below, the plan must continue benefit accruals for employees who continue working after the normal retirement age unless the plan's benefit formula stops benefit accruals after a specified number of years and the employee has enough years of service to cease accruals for that reason. Benefit formulas must be designed carefully to ensure appropriate treatment of older employees. In smaller businesses, older participants are often owners or key employees who will want the plan to provide substantial benefits. On the other hand, many larger employers want to encourage earlier retirement and will want to provide only the minimum late retirement benefit required under the law.

■ NONDISCRIMINATION IN CONTRIBUTIONS AND BENEFITS

A broad general rule applying to qualified plans is that plan benefits and contributions must not discriminate in favor of highly compensated employees. The purpose of this nondiscrimination rule is to ensure that the tax benefits provided for qualified plans are cost-effective for the government and actually serve to provide retirement income to a wide base of the population, thus lessening the pressure on Social Security and other government-provided benefits.

If plan contributions in a defined-contribution plan, or benefits in a defined-benefit plan, are the same percentage of compensation for all employees covered under the plan, the plan generally meets the nondiscrimination requirement. In addition, the law also permits three types of departures from the "same percentage" approach.

- A plan can be integrated with Social Security contributions or benefits, allowing a **permitted disparity** in contributions or benefits. These **Social Security integration** rules are discussed further below.

- In a 401(k) plan (Chapter 23), the highly compensated group can contribute a higher percentage of salary to the plan within the limits of the ADP rules. Similarly, **employer matching contributions** can follow this pattern within the limits of the ACP rules.

- Defined-contribution formulas can be varied by age-weighting (discussed in Chapter 22).

Purpose and Effect of Social Security Integration

Qualified plan formulas can be designed to reflect, or integrate with, the participants' Social Security benefits. Integration of a plan with Social Security avoids duplication of plan benefits by those of Social Security and also tends to lower the employer's cost for the plan, for a given level of total benefits. More than half of all private qualified plans are integrated with Social Security, and the percentage is even higher among defined-benefit plans considered separately. The reason for this is the obvious overlap between private retirement benefits and the Social Security benefit. Although this is a complication, it provides advantages in private plan design.

The existence of Social Security benefits is relevant to a number of objectives in designing a qualified plan.

■ The objective of providing an appropriate income replacement ratio must take into account the fact that the employee will receive Social Security benefits as well as benefits from the plan. If plan benefits alone are considered for this purpose, the actual replacement ratio will often be very different from what was intended.

■ The objective of plan efficiency can be met only if retirement benefits from Social Security are considered in designing the plan. Otherwise, private plan benefits for some employees may duplicate benefits they already receive from Social Security.

■ For a small business owner who is interested in maximizing the tax-sheltering benefits from the qualified plan, an integrated plan provides a method by which the plan benefit or contribution formula can, to a considerable extent, discriminate in favor of higher-paid employees. In fact, in the tax law, the Social Security integration rules are referred to as the *permitted disparity* rules, referring to the maximum extent to which the plan's benefit or contribution formula can deviate from a uniform percentage of compensation. Therefore, the objective of maximizing the tax-sheltering benefits of the qualified plan will generally lead to a consideration of integrating the plan with Social Security.

■ Finally, with regard to the employer's cost objectives, an integrated plan may provide a satisfactory level of retirement benefits to all employees at the lowest possible employer cost.

The integration rules are based on the way the old age, survivors, and disability insurance (OASDI) Social Security benefit is calculated. For simplicity, this benefit will be referred to in this chapter as OASDI.

OASDI uses a unit-benefit type of formula based on the employee's past years of work experience and the employee's compensation income in each of those years. More credit is given for the "first dollars" of compensation than for larger amounts; for compensation in a given year that exceeds the taxable wage base for that year, there is no benefit credit. The OASDI calculation was covered in detail in Chapter 3.

The integration rules are designed to allow a private qualified plan to provide a benefit that is a mirror image of OASDI so that the two sources of retirement income together form a retirement program that is nondiscriminatory. Because of the nature of the OASDI calculation, Social Security alone provides a higher percentage of income replacement for lower-paid employees than for higher-paid employees. Thus, the private plan may correspondingly provide a proportionately greater benefit for the higher paid. Figures 21.1 and 21.2 illustrate this qualitatively. In all cases, note how OASDI integration allows the private plan, considered alone, to discriminate substantially in favor of the highly compensated, both in terms of benefit amounts and percentages of compensation.

An employer has much less freedom in integrating a qualified plan with OASDI than in integrating other types of benefit plans such as disability income plans. Because

| FIGURE 21.1 | Integrated Plan—Portion of Replacement Income (50% of Final Average Compensation [FAC]) Provided by OASDI and Private Plan |

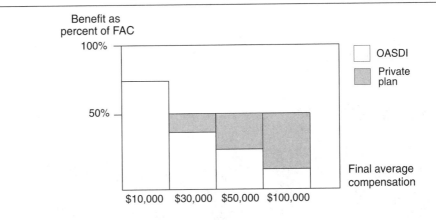

of the potential for discrimination, Code Section 401(a)(5) and 401(1) and associated regulations and IRS rulings impose detailed limitations on integrating qualified plans.

Under the principles of Code Section 401(1), there are two basic approaches by which a qualified plan can be integrated with OASDI—the **offset approach** and the **integration-level approach** (sometimes called the *excess approach*). Under the offset approach, a specified fraction of the benefit is subtracted from the benefit otherwise payable under the plan. The offset approach can be used only with a defined-benefit plan. Under the integration-level approach, the plan specifies a level of compensation called the *integration level*. Benefits or contributions below this integration level are provided at a lower rate than benefits or contributions for compensation above the integration level. An integration-level approach can be used with both defined-benefit and defined-contribution plans. The rules will be discussed in detail next, beginning with the integration of defined-benefit plans. These rules may be more readily understood after consideration of the types of benefit formulas used in qualified plans, which are discussed in the next three chapters; the reader may wish to refer back to the discussion here after reviewing those chapters.

Integration of Defined-Benefit Plans

Offset Approach.   As indicated above, a defined-benefit plan can be integrated with OASDI using either the offset approach or the integration-level approach. Because the offset approach is simpler, it will be discussed first.

With the offset method, the private plan benefit is initially structured to provide the replacement ratio desired, without taking OASDI into account. Then the benefit formula is modified to subtract a specified amount to reflect the employee's OASDI benefit. For example, an offset formula might read as follows:

| FIGURE 21.2 | Integrated Plan—Sources of Total Retirement Benefit Qualitative Diagram for Illustration, Nor for Calculation) |

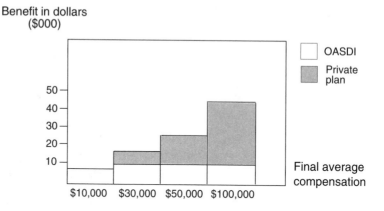

Upon retirement, the participant shall be entitled to a monthly retirement benefit equal to 60 percent of the participant's final average monthly compensation, less ½ percent of the participant's monthly final average compensation for each year of service. If the participant retired with 20 years of service and monthly final average compensation of $10,000, the benefit would be $6,000 less $1,000 (10% of $10,000) or $5,000.

An offset approach cannot result in a complete elimination of the private plan benefit. The plan benefit may not be reduced by more than the **maximum offset allowance,** which is

■ for any year of service, 4 percent of the participant's final average compensation;

■ for total benefits, ¾ percent of the participant's final average compensation multiplied by the participant's years of service with the employer, not in excess of 35.

Furthermore, in no event can the maximum offset allowance be more than 50 percent of the plan benefit that would have accrued without the offset.

The ¾ percent fraction is reduced if the participant's final average compensation exceeds an amount referred to as covered compensation. (See Table 21.1 on page 549 and the explanation that follows.) The IRS is scheduled to publish annually a table with the appropriate offset factors for brackets of final average compensation that exceed covered compensation.

An offset plan must base benefits on average annual compensation for at least a three-year period, or the total number of the participant's years of service, if less. The ¾ percent factor in the maximum excess allowance is actuarially reduced for early retirement benefits. For this purpose, an early retirement benefit is any unreduced benefit other than disability benefits beginning before the Social Security retirement age. The ¾ percent factor is to be reduced by ¹⁄₁₅ for each of the first five years that the benefit's commencement date precedes Social Security retirement age, and by an additional $\frac{1}{30}$ for each of the next five years that the benefit commencement date precedes the Social Security retirement age, with actuarial reductions for additional years (more than ten) of commencement prior to the Social Security retirement date.

OASDI is currently subject to indexing to reflect increases in the cost of living. However, the benefit paid by a private integrated plan cannot be reduced to reflect postretirement increases in OASDI, even if an offset formula is used. In other words, the amount of benefit payable to a participant from the plan itself generally will be fixed when the participant retires, regardless of changes in OASDI paid thereafter to the participant.

As will be evident after reviewing the rules for Social Security integration using the integration-level approach, the principal advantage of an offset formula is its simplicity, both in designing the plan and in communicating the plan effectively to employees.

Integration-Level Approach. Under the integration-level approach in a defined-benefit plan, a specified level of compensation, called the *integration level,* is defined by the plan. The plan then provides the participant with a higher rate of benefits for compensation above the integration level than for compensation below the integration level. This clearly is a mirror image to the OASDI benefit structure, which provides a lower (zero) rate of benefits above a specified compensation level (the taxable wage base) than it does for compensation below the taxable wage base.

An example of a formula using an integration-level approach:

> Upon retirement, a participant will be entitled to an annual retirement benefit equal to 30 percent of the participant's final average annual compensation up to $7,000, plus 56 percent of the participant's final average annual compensation in excess of $7,000.

Another way of drafting the same formula:

> Upon retirement, a participant will be entitled to an annual retirement benefit equal to 30 percent of the participant's full final average annual compensation, plus 26 percent of the participant's final average compensation in excess of $7,000.

The integration level in both plans is $7,000.

Under the Code, two percentages are defined. The excess-benefit percentage is the benefit as a percentage of compensation above the integration level. The base-benefit percentage is the percentage provided for compensation up to and including the integration level. The difference between these two percentages cannot exceed the maximum excess allowance. The maximum excess allowance is $\frac{3}{4}$ percent for any year of service, or in total, $\frac{3}{4}$ percent multiplied by the participant's years of service up to 35.

For example, if the plan provides a benefit of 1 percent of compensation below the integration level for each year of service, then it can provide no more than 1.75 percent of compensation above the integration level for each year of service. Or, for a participant with 35 years of service, if the plan provides a benefit of 30 percent of final average compensation below the integration level, it cannot provide more than 56.25 percent of compensation above the integration level. (The spread of 26.25 percent is $\frac{3}{4}$ of 1 percentage point multiplied by 35 years of service.)

Furthermore, the maximum excess allowance can be no greater than the base percentage. Thus, if a plan provides 10 percent of final average compensation below the integration level, it can provide no more than 20 percent of compensation above the integration level.

The maximum permitted integration level is the appropriate amount from the IRS table of covered compensation (see Table 21.1). This table essentially gives the average of the taxable wage base over the 35-year period prior to an employee's retirement, as explained further below. Covered compensation can be taken from either the exact or the rounded figures in Table 21.1. Because this amount varies with each participant's age, some planners may prefer to use a uniform dollar amount as the integration level for all participants to make the plan simpler and easier to communicate to participants. It should be permissible to use any uniform dollar amount that does not exceed the covered compensation from Table 21.1 for the oldest possible prospective employee of the employer.

The Covered Compensation Table. In specifying the maximum integration levels and the maximum percentages that may be used in integration-level plans, IRS actuaries have made a computation based on the value of OASDI benefits. Because the integrated private plan is designed to be a mirror image of the OASDI benefit, the maximum integration level in private plans should correspond generally to the maximum compensation taken into account in determining the OASDI benefit. For this purpose, the IRS has promulgated the *covered compensation table.* Covered compensation represents an averaging of the taxable wage base that has been in effect over each employee's working career. As shown in Table 21.1, the covered compensation figure will, therefore, vary, depending on the year in which the employee reaches age 65 and becomes eligible for full OASDI retirement benefits. The relevance of the table of covered compensation is that, as described above, it specifies the maximum integration level permitted for most types of defined benefit plans.

Integration of Defined-Contribution Plans

Because the benefits in a defined-contribution plan are based on the participant's account balance, the integration rules for defined-contribution plans apply to the amounts allocated to participants' accounts rather than to the benefits. Only an integration-level, not an offset, approach can be used.

The integration level for a defined-contribution plan is generally the taxable wage base for the year. While other integration levels may be used, under IRS regulations, this generally reduces the excess contribution percentage allowable. Table 21.2 gives the taxable wage base for recent years. The integration rules for defined-contribution plans are further stated in terms of two defined quantities: the **base contribution percentage** is the plan's contribution level for compensation below the integration level, while the **excess contribution percentage** is the contribution level for compensation above the integration level. The difference between the excess contribution percentage and the base contribution percentage cannot be more than

■ the base contribution percentage or
■ the greater of (a) 5.7 percent or (b) the old-age Social Security tax rate.

TABLE 21.1	2004 Covered Compensation Table			
Calendar Year of Birth	Calendar Year of Social Security Retirement Age	2004 Covered Compensation	Year of Birth	2004 Rounded Covered Compensation
1907	1972	$4,488		
1908	1973	4,704		
1909	1974	5,004		
1910	1975	5,316		
1911	1976	5,664		
1912	1977	6,060		
1913	1978	6,480		
1914	1979	7,044		
1915	1980	7,692		
1916	1981	8,460		
1917	1982	9,300		
1918	1983	10,236		
1919	1984	11,232		
1920	1985	12,276		
1921	1986	13,368		
1922	1987	14,520		
1923	1988	15,708		
1924	1989	16,968		
1925	1990	18,312		
1926	1991	19,728		
1927	1992	21,192		
1928	1993	22,716		
1929	1994	24,312		
1930	1995	25,920		
1931	1996	27,576		
1932	1997	29,304		
1933	1998	31,128		
1934	1999	33,060		
1935	2000	35,100		
1936	2001	37,212		
1937	2002	39,444	1937	39,000
1938	2004	43,992	1938–1939	45,000
1939	2005	46,284		
1940	2006	48,576	1940	48,000
1941	2007	50,832	1941	51,000
1942	2008	53,028	1942–1943	54,000
1943	2009	55,164		
1944	2010	57,276	1944	57,000
1945	2011	59,352	1945–1946	60,000
1946	2012	61,392		
1947	2013	63,396	1947	63,000
1948	2014	65,256	1948–1949	66,000
1949	2015	67,020		

| TABLE 21.1 | 2004 Covered Compensation Table (continued) |

Calendar Year of Birth	Calendar Year of Social Security Retirement Age	2004 Covered Compensation	Year of Birth	2004 Rounded Covered Compensation
1950	2016	68,688	1950–1951	69,000
1951	2017	70,272		
1952	2018	71,760	1952–1953	72,000
1953	2019	73,200		
1954	2020	74,580	1954	75,000
1955	2022	77,148	1955–1956	78,000
1956	2023	78,372		
1957	2024	79,512	1957–1960	81,000
1958	2025	80,556		
1959	2026	81,540		
1960	2027	82,464		
1961	2028	83,340	1961–1963	84,000
1962	2029	84,120		
1963	2030	84,876		
1964	2031	85,596	1964–1967	87,000
1965	2032	86,244		
1966	2033	86,796		
1967	2034	87,240		
1968	2035	87,564	1968 and later	87,900
1969	2036	87,780		
1970	2037	87,864		
1971 and later	2038	87,900		

Under this rule, a plan having a zero base-contribution percentage would also have to have a zero excess-contribution percentage. Therefore, it is not possible to have a plan that provides no contribution at all for participants at compensation levels below the integration level.

Some examples of the application of the rules are as follows:

■ A plan providing a 4 percent base-contribution percentage could provide no more than 8 percent excess-contribution percentage.

■ A plan providing a 6 percent base-contribution percentage could provide no more than an 11.7 percent excess-contribution percentage, assuming the old-age Social Security tax rate is less than 5.7 percent.

Multiple Plans

If the employer has more than one plan covering the same employee, both plans cannot be fully integrated. The degree of integration must be cut back in one or both. The most common approach is to fully integrate one plan (typically a defined-benefit plan) and not to integrate the other (typically a defined-contribution plan).

EXAMPLE

Summary of Integration Rules

Qualified plan benefit or contribution formulas can be integrated with OASDI to reflect the value of the employer's OASDI contribution for the employee. This reduces plan costs by avoiding duplication of benefits provided by OASDI. It also tends to provide relatively higher plan benefits for highly compensated employees.

Defined-Benefit Plans

A defined-benefit plan can be integrated using either the offset or the integration level method:

■ The maximum offset allowance is ¾ percent of final average compensation for any year of service, or a total of ¾ percent multiplied by years of service up to 35; total offset cannot exceed 50 percent of benefit otherwise payable.

■ The maximum integration level is covered compensation. Maximum excess allowance is ¾ percent for any year of service, or, in total, ¾ percent multiplied by years of service up to 35.

Defined-Contribution Plans

A defined-contribution plan may use only the integration level approach. The maximum integration level is the taxable wage base for the year. The difference between the base-contribution percentage and the excess-contribution percentage cannot exceed the lesser of the base-contribution percentage or the non-Medicare OASDI tax rate.

TABLE 21.2	Social Security Taxable Wage Base		
Year	Taxable Wage Base (Annual)	Year	Taxable Wage Base (Annual)
1972	$ 9,600	1989	48,000
1973	10,800	1990	51,300
1974	13,200	1991	53,400
1975	14,100	1992	55,500
1976	15,300	1993	57,600
1977	16,500	1994	60,600
1978	17,700	1995	61,200
1979	22,900	1996	62,700
1980	25,900	1997	65,400
1981	29,700	1998	68,400
1982	32,400	1999	72,600
1983	35,700	2000	76,200
1984	37,800	2001	80,400
1985	39,600	2002	84,900
1986	42,000	2003	87,000
1987	43,800	2004	87,900
1988	45,000		

■ NONTAX FEDERAL REGULATION AFFECTING QUALIFIED PLANS

As discussed in this chapter, the tax-law requirements for qualified plans include numerous provisions to prevent discrimination in favor of highly compensated employees. Other federal statutes also have some impact on qualified plan benefit and contribution formulas:

■ The Civil Rights Act of 1964 prohibits employers from discriminating on the basis of race, color, religion, sex, or national origin. Sex discrimination, as discussed below, is the only issue under this law that has a significant practical impact on pension benefit design.

■ The Age Discrimination in Employment Act (Title 29 USC) prohibits discrimination by employers on the basis of age; the major implications of these provisions are also discussed below.

■ The Americans with Disabilities Act (Title 42 USC) prohibits discrimination against disabled employees. This would prohibit special pension provisions applicable only to disabled employees and might also require general pension provisions to be changed to accommodate disabled employees. The law is broadly written and its full implications, including its effect on retirement plans, are not yet entirely apparent.

■ The Family and Medical Leave Act of 1993 (Title 29 USC Secs. 2601 et seq.) generally requires employers with 50 or more employees to provide 12 weeks per year of unpaid leave for childbirth, adoption, health condition, or care for a sick family member. When the employee returns, all accrued pension and other employee benefits must be restored, but the employer is not required to provide accrual of benefits during the period of the leave.

Sex Discrimination

Of the issues arising under these nontax federal statutes, **sex (gender) discrimination** is the one issue that has the most direct relevance to pension plan design.

Sex discrimination as it relates to qualified plans, annuities, and life insurance is a subject that is not yet completely resolved, but some clear rules for qualified plan design have emerged. The issue arises from the statistical fact that women, as a group, live longer than men. This means that if actuaries make separate calculations for men and women, the same periodic annuity costs more for women than for men of the same age. Or, for a given annuity premium, the periodic annuity amount is lower for women than for men.

The Civil Rights Act of 1964, like its predecessor, the Equal Pay Act of 1963, provides that it is an unlawful employment practice for an employer

> . . . to discriminate against any individual with respect to his compensation, terms, conditions or privileges of employment, because of such individual's race, color, religion, sex or national origin [Section 2000e-2(a), Civil Rights Act of 1964].

It is clear that qualified plan benefits are part of an employee's compensation; it was not originally clear, however, what constituted sex discrimination in a qualified plan.

■ Must the plan provide the same periodic benefit for both men and women employees?

■ Must the plan provide only the same employer contribution to the plan?

Early federal administrative guidelines under the Equal Pay Act of 1963 indicated that an employer satisfied the nondiscrimination requirement if it provided either equal periodic benefits or equal contributions. However, in 1972, the Equal Employment Opportunity Commission (EEOC) issued a revised sex discrimination guideline under the Civil Rights Act of 1964: To avoid sex discrimination in retirement plans, the employer must provide equal periodic benefits to men and women employees in all circumstances. Employers originally resisted this guideline, but recent court cases clearly point in this direction. The first significant case went to the United States Supreme Court, *Los Angeles Department of Water and Power v. Manhart*, 435 US 702 (1978). That case involved a contributory pension plan of a municipality. The Supreme Court held that the plan could not require women to pay higher contributions than men to receive equal periodic benefits upon retirement. Subsequently, the Supreme Court held in *Arizona Governing Committee v. Norris*, 103 S.Ct. 3492 (1983), that a municipal retirement plan could not provide sex-based annuity choices at retirement. No employer contributions were involved—only employee contributions.

Although technically the *Manhart* and *Norris* cases did not completely establish that the Civil Rights Act requires equal periodic benefits for men and women in an employer-provided retirement plan under all circumstances, the trend of the cases favors an equal-benefit approach and virtually all planners assume this to be the law.

Most qualified plans already avoid obvious sex discrimination problems. Most defined-benefit plans provide the same normal retirement benefit for men and women employees; most defined-contribution plans provide the same employer contribution for men and women employees. Discrimination problems arise when a qualified plan (either defined-benefit or defined-contribution) offers participants a choice of benefits including a retirement annuity. Most plan designers advise using only unisex annuities (those providing the same annuity rate for both men and women) for this purpose. Similarly, if a qualified plan offers life insurance as an incidental benefit (see Chapter 24), the life insurance cost to the employee must be determined on a unisex basis. However, in determining the annual deposit to a defined benefit plan, the sex of covered employees may be taken into account, because it affects only the employer's costs and not the ultimate benefit that the employee will receive.

The sex discrimination issue is complicated by the fact that the Civil Rights Act does not govern the pricing of insurance products; private insurance companies, therefore, currently are allowed to use sex as a factor in determining life insurance and annuity rates. The argument has been made that when a qualified plan uses a group pension contract for funding, sex-based annuity options should be allowed under the group contract. However, it is the employer, not the insurance company, that provides the pension as part of an employee's compensation. In view of this and the trend of the court cases, insurance companies no longer offer sex-based annuities as part of a group pension contract.

Even if employers remove any conceivable sex discrimination from qualified plan documents, if the plan is designed so that participants can withdraw their benefits at retirement, effective sex discrimination will still be possible so long as sex-based annuities are available from insurance companies. In that situation, men can withdraw their benefits and purchase an annuity from an insurance company providing greater periodic payments than women would be able to purchase for the same amount (or payments greater than those available under the plan if the plan provides a unisex annuity). Because of this and other related problems, the law may at some point reconsider the question of whether insurance companies should be allowed to determine annuity and life insurance premiums on the basis of sex.

There is no doubt that sex is a relevant actuarial classification, as is any ascertainable factor affecting life expectancy, which could conceivably include such things as race, religion, or national origin. Insurance companies do not commonly use race or other potentially offensive actuarial factors, regardless of their relevance as predictors of life expectancy. However, they are strongly attached to the use of sex classifications and have vigorously opposed restrictions proposed in Congress.

Both sides of the controversy view the issue as one of fairness. Advocates of sex classification argue that unisex annuity rates are unfair to men, who should be allowed to purchase annuities reflecting their group's life expectancy. Opponents argue that it is unfair to attribute to an individual the characteristics of a group to which that individual belongs, regardless of whether the individual actually possesses those characteristics. Ultimately, Congress may have to determine the appropriate social policy in connection with insurance company practices.

Age Discrimination

The federal Age Discrimination in Employment Act,[3] as amended in 1978, 1986, and 1989, has an impact on qualified plans. The Age Discrimination Act applies to workers and managers of any business that engages in interstate transactions (a very broad category) and employs at least 20 persons during the year. Certain hazardous occupations are excluded as well as executive employees who would be entitled, upon retirement, to an annual pension of $44,000 or more over and above Social Security benefits.

The main provision of the Age Discrimination Act that affects qualified plans is that which prohibits involuntary retirement at any age. A qualified plan must not in any way require mandatory retirement.

In addition, Code Sections 411(b)(1)(H) and 411(b)(2) deal specifically with benefits for older workers. In general, older workers must be treated the same as younger workers with regard to plan contributions (for a defined-contribution plan) and benefit accruals (for a defined-benefit plan). However, for a defined-benefit plan, the benefit formula can provide that benefits are fully accrued not at a specified age but after a specified number of years of service, such as 25. This will cut off further benefit accrual for many older employees, but it is permitted. If a plan provides for normal retirement at 65 with actuarial increases for later retirement, the actuarial increases are credited toward any requirement of benefit accrual that applies.

> **EXAMPLE**
> If a plan provides a benefit of $1,000 per month beginning at age 65 or an actuarially adjusted $1,100 per month beginning at age 66, the extra $100 is counted as an additional benefit accrual for purposes of meeting any age discrimination requirements.

■ KEY TERMS

actuarial reduction

age and service requirements

base contribution percentage

break-in-service provision

cliff vesting

common control

controlled group rules

contributory plans

covered compensation

early retirement age

employer matching contributions

excess contribution percentage

integration-level approach

late retirement

maximum offset allowance

normal retirement age

offset approach

permitted disparity

salary reductions

sex (gender) discrimination

Social Security integration

vesting schedule

■ STUDY QUESTIONS

1. Describe the coverage of employees who enter into a defined-benefit or a target plan when they are close to the plan's normal retirement age.

2. For purposes of a qualified plan, explain what requirements an employee must satisfy to earn credit for a year of service.

3. Jane Chaney worked two years for BIGGO and acquired two years of service under BIGGO's defined-benefit plan. The BIGGO Company has a vesting schedule that grants a fully vested benefit after the employee has attained five years of service with no vesting until then. Jane left after two years, but returned to work after a four-year absence. Will Jane's break in service cause her to lose her prebreak service? Explain.

4. Which of the following employees of the Kelvin Company are considered highly compensated employees for nondiscrimination purposes?

	Salary
Kathy Kelvin (100 percent stock owner/president)	$400,000
Lou Jane (vice president/treasurer)	180,000
Manny Martin	47,000
Nancy Norris	40,000
Oprah Oliver	22,000
Peter Peaquin	20,000

5. a. The Alpha Company has 20 employees, six of whom are highly compensated. The Alpha Plan covers the six highly compensated employees and 11 of the 14 employees who are not highly compensated. Does the Alpha Plan pass the ratio percentage test?

   b. The Beta Company has ten employees, two of whom are highly compensated. The Beta Plan covers the two highly compensated employees and covers seven of the eight employees who are not highly compensated. Does the Beta Plan pass the ratio percentage test?

6. For qualified plan purposes, what is the significance of treating more than one business as a controlled group of corporations?

7. Explain whether the following vesting schedules comply with the vesting rules.

a.

Years of Service	**Percentage Vested**
0–9	0%
10	100

b.

Years of Service	**Percentage Vested**
1	50%
2	60
3	70
4	80
5	90
6	100

c.

Years of Service	**Percentage Vested**
0–4	0%
5	50
6	100

8. Explain whether the following vesting schedule meets the vesting schedule rules for top-heavy plans.

Years of Service	Percentage Vested
0–1	0%
2	20
3	40
4	60
5	80
6 or more	100

9. a. Under what conditions would you recommend that an employer choose a restrictive vesting schedule for the plan?

   b. Under what conditions would you recommend that an employer choose a liberal vesting schedule for the plan?

10. The president of The New England Cannery (250 employees) is undecided about whether her company's qualified pension plan should provide for employee contributions.

   a. Explain the advantages and disadvantages of including mandatory employee contributions in the plan.

   b. What type of plan eliminates the problem of lost tax benefits arising from employee contributions?

11. a. Why do defined-benefit plans use a normal retirement age requirement?

   b. What is the latest normal retirement age that a qualified plan may use?

   c. What are the advantages and disadvantages of using a pre-65 normal retirement age in a closely held business?

12. Why are early retirement benefits typically reduced below the monthly normal retirement benefit payable at age 65?

13. What is the purpose of the rules for integrating qualified plans with Social Security?

14. Briefly describe the integration rules for

   a. offset plans.

   b. integration-level plans.

   c. defined-contribution plans.

15. Explain how sex discrimination in retirement benefits is still possible even if there is no explicit discrimination in the pension plan documents.

■ NOTES

1. Regulations Section 1.410(a)–4(b)(1).

2. See Code Sections 410(a)(3) (eligibility) and 411(a)(5) (vesting), and regulations thereunder.

3. Employee Benefit Research Institute, Facts from EBRI, January 2003, *www.ebri.org/facts/*. Data gathered by Department of Labor from Form 5500, filed annually by plan sponsors.

22 Defined-Contribution Plans I: Money-Purchase, Profit-Sharing, and Similar Plans

OBJECTIVES

■ Explain current trends in employer-sponsored retirement plans.

■ Describe money-purchase plans and their advantages and disadvantages.

■ Describe the characteristics of profit-sharing plans with respect to the following factors:

1. Eligibility
2. Vesting
3. Contribution provisions
4. Allocations to employee accounts
5. Forfeitures
6. Integration with Social Security
7. Deductibility of employer contributions
8. Section 415 limits
9. Investment earnings and account balances
10. Incidental benefits

■ Describe the characteristics of age-weighted plans.

■ Describe the characteristics of stock plans.

CHAPTER OUTLINE

Current Qualified Plan Trends

Money-Purchase Defined-Contribution Pension Plans

Qualified Profit-Sharing Plans
Eligibility and Vesting
Employer Contribution Provision
Allocations to Employee Accounts
Forfeitures
Integration with Social Security
Section 415 Limits
Investment Earnings and Account Balances
Participant-Directed Investments
Withdrawals during Employment and Loan Provisions
Incidental Benefits

Age-Weighted Plans

Using Employer Stock in Qualified Plans
Advantages of Investing in Employer Stock
Stock Bonus Plan
Employee Stock Ownership Plan (ESOP)
Creating a Market for Closely Held Stock

■ CURRENT QUALIFIED PLAN TRENDS

Trends in management, the economy, and the workforce have produced a gradual erosion in qualified defined benefit plan coverage and a movement toward "nonretirement" plans—that is, defined-contribution plans that provide a form of savings and incentive benefits for employees without a specific funding commitment by the employer. As a percentage of all private pension plans, defined-contribution plans increased from 66.8 percent in 1975 to 92.3 percent in 1998.[1] Defined-benefit plans tend to have more employee participants per plan, so this statistic exaggerates the importance of defined-contribution plans somewhat, but the trend is clear. The reasons for this trend include the following:

■ Increasing competition and cost pressures to minimize wage and benefit costs.

■ Increasing acquisition, dissolution, and reorganization of business enterprises that discourage employer long-term commitment to employees.

■ Decline in collective bargaining; labor unions have traditionally favored the defined-benefit plan.

■ Employers are using more part-time employees, leased employees, and independent contractors who would generally receive little benefit from a traditional pension plan.

■ Increase in families with two wage earners; traditional pension plans tend to duplicate benefits in such cases.

■ Defined-contribution plans with their individual, periodically reported, and valued employee accounts are easier for the employee to understand and appreciate as a valuable benefit.

■ Administration and government regulations are generally simpler for defined-contribution plans. For example, Pension Benefit Guaranty Corporation (PBGC) coverage and reporting requirements do not apply to defined-contribution plans (see Chapter 27) and ongoing actuarial services are not generally required for defined-contribution plans.

■ Defined-contribution plans fit the nature of today's workforce, which experiences frequent job-changing, thereby putting a premium on a portable benefit that increases steadily from the first day of employment. Few employees enjoy the luxury of a 40-year career with the same employer, which typically provides the best result for defined-benefit plan participants.

This chapter will discuss the following:

■ Money-purchase pension plans
■ Qualified profit-sharing plans
■ Age-weighted plans
■ Employer stock plans (stock bonus plans and ESOPs)

TABLE 22.1	Defined-Contribution Plan Accumulations
Age at Plan Entry	**Account Balance at Retirement**
25	$213,609
30	147,913
40	67,676
50	26,888
55	14,783
60	6,153

Assumptions: Annual employer contributions: $1,000 per employee; retirement age: 65; average investment return: 7%.

Increasingly, the trend in qualified planning is toward salary savings (thrift savings) plans such as 401(k) plans, which are primarily funded through employee salary reductions that are contributed to the plan. These plans are typically combined with the traditional employer-funded profit-sharing plans, or with those in which employer contributions match the employee salary reductions. Salary savings plans are discussed in the next chapter.

■ MONEY-PURCHASE DEFINED-CONTRIBUTION PENSION PLANS

In some ways, a money-purchase plan is the simplest of all qualified plans. As in all defined-contribution plans, there is an individual account for each employee. The plan document requires that the employer make a specific contribution each year to each employee's account. Typically, this is a percentage of compensation—for example, 6 percent of compensation. Percentages up to 25 percent are typically used; the limiting factor is the limitation of the employer's annual deduction to 25 percent of covered payroll (see Chapter 24). The amount of the benefit at retirement is equal to the employee's account balance at the retirement date or at a valuation date near the time of the retirement date. The plan may provide for payment of the benefit in a lump sum; a variety of payment options, including annuity benefits, may also be made available. The accounts of all employees are usually commingled for investment purposes; each account is kept separate administratively, so that the account increases and decreases in accordance with the investment performance of the fund. Thus, the benefit available at retirement cannot be predicted exactly. Investment risk lies with the employee. If the employee's account is less than anticipated, the employer is not required to make additional contributions.

As Table 22.1 shows, money-purchase plans tend to provide a better benefit for employees who enter the plan at younger ages because a longer period of time is available to accumulate plan contributions and compound these contributions with investment earnings. If the employer has employees with a wide range of ages at the inception of the plan, this feature of a money-purchase plan makes it impossible to provide older employees with retirement income that is comparable—as a percentage of their preretirement income—to that of the younger employees.

To avoid discrimination in favor of the highly compensated, the contribution formula for a money-purchase plan must provide a uniform percentage of each employee's compensation, with two exceptions. First, the money-purchase formula can be integrated with Social Security under the rules described in Chapter 21. Also, the formula can be weighted according to the age of entering participants, so that older entrants receive a higher percentage of compensation than younger entrants. An age-weighted money-purchase-type formula is referred to as a *target plan*. Age-weighted plans in general are discussed later in this chapter.

EXAMPLE

Integrated Money-Purchase Formula

Suppose that the plan has an integration level of $87,900, and the plan provides that the employer contributes 6 percent of all compensation plus 5.7 percent of compensation above the integration level. (Another way of describing this formula is that it provides 6 percent of compensation below the integration level and 11.7 percent of compensation above the integration level.) Employee Bob earns $97,900. The employer's contribution to his account for the year will be $6,444 (6 percent of $97,900, or $5,874, plus $570 [5.7 percent of $10,000, the amount of Bob's compensation above the integration level]).

Money-purchase and target plans are considered pension plans, because their focus is on providing retirement benefits with some degree of security to the employee, with the only uncertainty being the rate of investment return. The employer is obligated to make the prescribed contributions each year; there is no discretion permitted, unlike a profit-sharing plan. This requirement of annual employer contributions meets the **definitely determinable benefit** requirement applicable to qualified pension plans. From the employer viewpoint, a money-purchase plan is therefore less flexible with regard to annual cost than a profit-sharing plan.

■ QUALIFIED PROFIT-SHARING PLANS

The term profit-sharing plan originated at a time when qualified profit-sharing plans typically based employer contribution levels on company profits. This is no longer true; most qualified profit-sharing plans do not use profits as a measuring stick for contribution levels, although some do. There is, however, no requirement for the employer to have profits in order to contribute to the plan. Even a nonprofit organization may have a "profit-sharing" plan. The general characteristics are as follows:

■ The employer contribution may be specified as a percentage of annual profits each year or, for even more flexibility, the plan may provide that the employer determines the amount to be contributed on an annual basis, with the option of contributing nothing even in years in which there are profits or, conversely, making contributions in unprofitable years.

■ The plan must have a nondiscriminatory formula for allocating the employer contribution to the accounts of employees.

■ Because the plan is a defined-contribution plan, the benefit from it consists of the amount in each employee's account, usually distributed as a lump sum at retirement or termination of employment.

■ The plan may permit employee withdrawals or loans during employment.

■ Eligibility and vesting are usually liberal because of the incentive nature of the plan.

■ Forfeitures from employees who terminate employment are usually reallocated to the accounts of remaining participants, thus making the plan particularly attractive to long-service employees.

Eligibility and Vesting

Profit-sharing plans are typically designed with relatively liberal eligibility and vesting provisions, compared with pension plans. This is because the employer generally wishes the incentive objective of the plans to operate for short-term as well as long-term employees, and also because the simplicity of administering a profit-sharing plan makes it less necessary to exclude short-term employees to reduce plan administrative costs. Thus, many profit-sharing plans permit employees to enter the plan immediately on becoming employed, or after a short waiting period—for example, until the next date on which the plan assets are valued. A great variety of vesting provisions are used, and they are typically tailored to the employer's specific needs.

As a qualified plan, a profit-sharing plan is subject to the restrictions on eligibility and vesting provisions discussed in detail in earlier chapters. In summary, a minimum age requirement greater than 21 is not permitted, nor can a waiting period for entry be longer than one year, or up to 1½ years if entry is based on plan entry dates. Under the age discrimination law, no maximum age for entry can be prescribed (and contributions must continue for as long as the employee continues to work). The coverage tests discussed in Chapter 21 apply to a profit-sharing plan as they do to all qualified plans.

The vesting requirements discussed in Chapter 21 are also applicable to profit-sharing plans. A profit-sharing plan is more likely to discriminate in favor of highly compensated employees as a result of high employee turnover and the use of forfeitures, as discussed below. Therefore, the IRS may require the more stringent three- to seven-year vesting schedule in new profit-sharing plans. Most profit-sharing plans use a vesting schedule that is at least as generous as this schedule. Even more stringent vesting is required if the plan is top-heavy (Chapter 26).

Employer Contribution Provision

There is great flexibility in designing an employer contribution provision for a profit-sharing plan. The contribution provision can be either a **discretionary contribution provision** or a **contribution formula.**

With the discretionary provision, the company's board of directors determines each year what amount will be contributed. It is not necessary for the company actually to have current or accumulated profits. Many employers will wish to contribute the maximum deductible amount each year, but a lesser amount can be contributed.

Although employers are permitted to omit contributions under a discretionary provision, the IRS requires that contributions be **substantial and recurring**. If too many years go by without contributions, the IRS is likely to find that the plan has been terminated, with the consequences discussed in Chapter 27 (basically 100 percent vesting for all plan participants and distribution under a specified payment schedule). No specific guidelines are given by the IRS as to how many years of omitted contributions are permitted, so the decision to skip a profit-sharing contribution must always be made with some caution.

With a formula contribution provision. a specified amount must be contributed to the plan whenever there are profits. Typically, the amount is expressed as a percentage of profits determined under generally accepted accounting principles. There are no specific IRS restrictions on the type of formula, so flexibility is possible. For example, the plan might provide for a contribution of 7 percent of all current profits in excess of $50,000, possibly with a limitation on the amount deductible for the year. There is also considerable freedom in defining the term *profit* in the plan. For example, profit before taxes or after taxes can be used, with before-tax profits being the most common. Profit as defined in the plan can also include capital gains and losses or accumulated profits from prior years. Even an employer that is organized under state law as a "nonprofit" corporation can have a profit-sharing plan funded from a suitably defined surplus account.

The advantage of the formula approach is that it is more attractive to employees than the discretionary approach and more definitely serves the incentive purpose of the plan. However, if a formula approach is adopted, the employer must remember that the formula amount must always be contributed to the plan; the formula constitutes a continuing legal and financial obligation for the business as long as the plan remains in effect. It is possible to draft formulas that take into account possible adverse financial contingencies. Without such provisions, the formula may have to be amended in the future in the event of financial difficulty.

Allocations to Employee Accounts

The plan's contribution provision determines the total amount contributed to the plan for all employees. The plan must also have a formula under which appropriate portions of this total contribution are allocated to the individual accounts of employees. Here there is less flexibility because the allocation provision must meet nondiscrimination requirements. The law provides that contributions must be allocated under a definite formula that does not discriminate in favor of highly compensated employees. Any formula that meets these requirements can be acceptable, but most formulas allocate to participants on the basis of their compensation, compared with the compensation of all participants. That is, after the total employer contribution is determined, the amount allocable to a given participant is

$$\text{Total employer contribution} \times \frac{\text{Participant's compensation}}{\text{Compensation of all participants}}$$

If compensation is used in the allocation formula, the plan must define compensation in a way that does not discriminate. Compensation might include only base pay or might be total compensation including bonuses or overtime. Only the first $200,000 (as indexed for inflation; the figure for 2004 is $205,000) of each employee's compensation can be taken into account in the plan formula.

Service is another factor often used in the formula for allocating employer contributions. However, since highly compensated employees are likely to have long service, the IRS will probably require a showing that any service-based formula will not produce discrimination.

Forfeitures

A **forfeiture** is an unvested amount remaining in a participant's account when the participant terminates employment without being fully vested under the plan's vesting schedule. Thus, forfeitures can occur in any defined-contribution plan that does not have 100 percent immediate vesting. Forfeitures can be reallocated to accounts of other participants or used to reduce future employer contributions. In a profit-sharing plan, forfeitures are usually reallocated to participants to provide an additional incentive for continuing service.

Forfeitures must be allocated in a nondiscriminatory manner. In most plans, forfeiture allocations are made in the same manner as allocations of employer contributions—on the basis of compensation or a combination of compensation and service. The IRS usually will not accept a forfeiture allocation provision based on account balances of remaining participants because such a provision may provide substantial discrimination.

Analysis of profit-sharing plans of smaller employers that have existed for a number of years generally shows that by far the largest account balances are those for highly compensated participants. This is because the combination of higher compensation, longer service (and therefore more years in the plan), and low turnover among the highly compensated group eventually produces a great disparity in account balances. This phenomenon is, in fact, one of the reasons why closely held businesses adopt profit-sharing plans. As such, they are not deemed to be discriminatory. However, if a plan contains any features designed to multiply this inherent discrimination (such as forfeiture allocation based on account balance), the IRS generally will not approve it.

Integration with Social Security

The allocation formula of a profit-sharing plan may be integrated with Social Security to avoid duplication of benefits and reduce plan costs to the employer. Under those rules, as discussed earlier, the integration level is generally equal to the taxable wage base for the year, although other levels are used in some cases. The difference between the plan's excess contribution percentage (contribution percentage for compensation above the integration level) and its base contribution percentage (contribution percentage for compensation up to the integration level) cannot be more than the lesser of

- the base contribution percentage or
- the greater of (a) 5.7 percent or (b) the old-age Social Security tax rate.

The integrated plan gives credit to the employer for contributions made to Social Security as if they had been made to the plan, thus overall providing a nondiscriminatory allocation formula.

As an example of integrated formulas, if the plan uses an integration level of $87,900, it could provide a base allocation percentage of 10 percent of compensation below $87,900, plus an allocation of 5.7 percent of compensation above $87,900, assuming the old-age Social Security tax rate is less than 5.7 percent. Or if the plan provided 4 percent of compensation below the integration level, it could provide no more than 4 percent of compensation above the integration level.

Plan allocations counted toward the 5.7 percent limitation must include not only employer contributions for the year but also any forfeitures allocated to the participant's account. For example, suppose that for the year 2004 a plan has two participants with compensation as shown below. For 2004, the employer contributes $5,000 to the plan, and a forfeiture of $8,000 is available for allocation to participants' accounts. The plan's integration level is $87,900. Under the plan's allocation formula, each participant's account is to receive the maximum permitted percent of plan contributions plus forfeitures for compensation above $87,900 (up to 5.7 percent). The remaining amount of the plan contributions plus forfeitures are allocated in proportion to total compensation. Plan allocations, shown below, show that the amount in the sixth column is arrived at by subtracting the excess allocation (total of column five) from the $13,000 of contributions plus forfeitures; this remaining amount of $12,430 is multiplied by a fraction, the numerator of which is the participant's total compensation and the denominator of which is the total payroll. This allocation meets the integration rules because the amount allocated to compensation below $87,900 is more than 5.7 percent.

Employee		2004 Compensation	Compensation above $87,900	5.7% of Excess	Allocation of Remainder	Total Allocation
A		$97,900	$10,000	$570	$10,779	$11,349
B		15,000	0	0	1,651	1,651
	Payroll	$112,900				$13,000

Section 415 Limits

The **Section 415 limits** (discussed in more detail in Chapter 26) that apply to profit-sharing plans are those applicable to all defined-contribution plans. The annual addition to any participant's account cannot exceed the lesser of 100 percent of the participant's compensation or $40,000 (as indexed for inflation; $41,000 for 2004). For a profit-sharing plan, the annual addition includes the participant's share of any forfeitures as well as employer and employee contributions. This means that when forfeitures are allocated to a participant's account, the amount of employer contributions that can be allocated may be reduced. The Section 415 limits usually affect only highly compensated employees covered under the plan.

Investment Earnings and Account Balances

As a defined-contribution plan, a profit-sharing plan must provide separate accounts for each participant. However, unless the plan contains a provision permitting participants to direct investments (discussed below), the plan trustee or other funding agents will generally pool all participants' accounts for investment purposes. The plan must then provide a mechanism for allocating investment gains or losses to each participant. Most methods for doing this effectively allocate such gains and losses in proportion to the participant's account balance.

IRS revenue rulings require that accounts of all participants be valued in a uniform and consistent manner at least once each year, unless all plan assets are immediately invested in individual annuity or retirement contracts meeting certain requirements. The plan usually will specify a **valuation date** or dates on which valuation occurs. Investment earnings, gains, and losses are allocated to participants' accounts as of this date.

Participant-Directed Investments

Under ERISA Section 404c, any "individual account" plan (such as a profit-sharing, stock bonus, or money-purchase pension plan) can include a **participant-directed investment** provision allowing the participant to direct the trustee or other funding agent as to the investment of the participant's account.

If the plan administrator provides a broad range of investment choices—so that the participant's choice has real meaning—then the trustee and other plan fiduciaries are not subject to fiduciary responsibility for the investment decision.[2] A plan can technically allow unlimited choice of investments, but this increases the plan's administrative burdens. Often, a family of mutual funds is offered as an investment option to increase the administrative feasibility of participant direction. At least three investment alternatives must be included.

Investment direction gives the participant a considerable degree of control over the funds in his or her account. It is frequently used in profit-sharing plans, particularly those for closely held businesses where the controlling employees have by far the largest accounts. On the other hand, to the extent that participant direction of investments removes the security provided by the fiduciary rules, such a provision is at odds with a plan objective of providing retirement security, and it would not be appropriate if this were a major objective of the plan for a particular employee group.

To prevent certain abuses associated with participant-directed investments, the Code provides that an investment by a participant-directed qualified plan account in a **collectible** will be treated as if the amount invested were distributed to the participant as taxable income to the participant. A collectible is defined in Code Section 408(m) as a work of art, rug or antique, metal or gem, stamp or coin (excluding certain federal and state-issued coins), alcoholic beverage, or any other tangible personal property designated as a collectible by the IRS.

Withdrawals During Employment and Loan Provisions

The incentive (rather than retirement security) focus of profit-sharing plans tends to dictate that participants be given the opportunity to control or benefit from their accounts even before retirement or termination of employment. There are various ways to do this. One such provision is a participant-directed account, as discussed above. Another is a special feature permitted in profit-sharing plans but not in pension plans— a provision for account withdrawals from the plan during employment.

The regulations require that employer contributions under a profit-sharing plan must be accumulated for at least two years before they can be withdrawn by participants.[3] However, in some revenue rulings, the IRS has permitted a plan provision allowing employees with at least 60 months of participation to withdraw employer contributions, including those made within the previous two years. Also, revenue rulings have permitted a plan provision for **hardship withdrawal,** including contributions made within the previous two years. *Hardship* must be sufficiently defined in the plan and the definitions must be consistently applied.[4] All these limitations apply only to amounts attributable to employer contributions to the plan. If the plan permits employee contributions, the employee contributions can be withdrawn at any time without restriction.

In considering the design of withdrawal provisions, it is important to keep in mind that the taxation and early-withdrawal penalty rules act as disincentives for participants to withdraw plan funds. These rules (discussed in Chapter 25) indirectly reduce the advantages of using a qualified plan as a medium for preretirement savings.

Many plan designers prefer to have a prohibition or at least restrictions on withdrawals from the employer-contributed portion of the account. This is because favorable investment results sometimes depend on having a pool of investment money that is relatively large and not subject to the additional liquidity requirements imposed by the possibility of participant withdrawals. Some typical restrictions found in profit-sharing plans include a requirement that the participant demonstrate a need for the money coming within a list of authorized needs either set out in the plan or promulgated by the plan administrator and applied consistently. Such needs might include educational expenses for children, home purchase or remodeling, sickness or disability, and so forth. Another method of restricting plan withdrawals is to provide a penalty on a participant who withdraws amounts from the plan (in addition to the 10 percent federal penalty tax, which also applies). A plan penalty might include suspension of participation for a period of time, such as six months after the withdrawal. The plan penalty cannot, however, deprive a participant of any previously vested benefit.

Loan provisions are appropriate for profit-sharing plans. Again, however, a generous loan provision in a plan may have the effect of reducing the amount of funds available for other plan investments.

Incidental Benefits

The regulations permit profit-sharing plans to provide as an **incidental benefit** life, accident, or health insurance for the participant and the participant's family. Incidental life insurance is the only one that is commonly provided. If employer contributions are used to provide insurance, the following incidental benefit limitations must be met.

If the plan provides incidental whole life insurance, the usual test is that aggregate premiums for each participant must be less than 50 percent of the aggregate of employer contributions allocated to the participant's account. If the plan purchases term insurance or accident and health insurance, the aggregate premiums must be less than 25 percent of the employer contributions allocated to the participant's account. The current IRS position is that universal life premiums also must meet the 25 percent limit. Note that these tests apply to the *aggregate*—that is, the total contributions made for all years at any given time. If either of these limits is exceeded, the plan could be disqualified. However, insurance premiums paid with employer-contributed funds that have accumulated for at least two years are not subject to these limitations.

If the employee dies before normal retirement age, the plan can provide that the face amount of the policies plus the balance credited to the participant's account in the profit-sharing plan can be distributed to the survivors without the life insurance violating the incidental benefit requirement. This can be done even though the amount of life insurance might be more than 100 times the account balance expressed as an expected monthly pension.

If life insurance is provided by the plan, the term insurance cost is currently taxable to the employee under IRS Table 2001, as discussed in Chapter 6. Accident and health insurance provided by an employer under the plan might not be taxable because of the exclusion provided for employer-provided health insurance. However, there usually is no particular benefit in providing accident and health insurance under a profit-sharing plan. It is usually provided in a separate plan not connected with the profit-sharing plan.

■ AGE-WEIGHTED PLANS

In general, qualified plan benefits and contributions must not discriminate in favor of highly compensated employees. The purpose of this nondiscrimination rule is to ensure that the tax benefits provided for qualified plans actually serve to provide retirement income to a wide base of the population, thus lessening the pressure on Social Security and other government-provided benefits.

It might seem that the nondiscrimination rule as applied to defined-contribution plans would require that all employees covered under the plan receive an employer contribution that is a uniform percentage of compensation. However, as discussed earlier, there are three general exceptions to this rule:

1. In a plan integrated with Social Security, the plan can provide a higher percentage of compensation, within limits, for compensation above the plan's integration level (generally the taxable wage base for the year).

2. In a 401(k) plan (next chapter), the highly compensated group can contribute a higher percentage of salary to the plan within the limits of the ADP rules. Similarly, employer matching contributions can follow this pattern within the limits of the ACP rules.

3. Age-weighting, as discussed here.

This third major exception to the "uniform percentage" standard for nondiscrimination relates to age-weighted formulas under the "cross testing" regulations of Code Section 401(a)(4). These regulations permit a plan to provide a higher percentage of compensation as an employer contribution for employees as a function of age at plan inception or date of hire. For example, the plan might provide an annual contribution of 20 percent of compensation for an employee who is aged 53 at the plan's inception, while providing only 5 percent of compensation for an employee hired at age 30. This type of design tends to provide greater benefits for key employees or business owners, because they tend to be the older employees when a plan is instituted.

This type of plan might appear inequitable on the surface, but if you look to the total benefit to the employee at retirement, this is not necessarily the case. For the employee aged 53, there are only 12 years of employer contributions remaining to the employee's age 65, while for the 30-year-old, there are 35 years of potential employer contributions. If you look at the total accumulation at age 65, the retirement income available to the employees, as a percentage of final compensation levels, will be much closer.

The cross-testing regulations formalize this type of analysis to provide a set of rules by which qualified defined-contribution plans can be designed with an age-weighted formula. The age-weighted formula is tested for discrimination by projecting the retirement benefits to each participant's retirement age and subjecting them to specific mathematical tests. The fact that the plan might not in fact last long enough for the younger employees to reach retirement is not taken into account in the cross-testing regulations, although if the employer's clear intent was to terminate the plan in the near future, the IRS probably would not permit the use of the cross-testing regulations.

The regulations are general in nature and permit a wide range of design possibilities, but three distinct approaches to plan design can be identified:

1. **Cross-tested/new comparability plan.** The most common approach is to design the plan to provide maximized benefits to highly compensated employees, and benefits for other employees are designed to provide whatever is required by the nondiscrimination regulations under Code Section 401(a)(4). For example, a plan covering 13 employees might provide for a $41,000 annual contribution for each of the three highly compensated employees, and for the remaining 10 employees the

plan would provide a flat percentage of compensation that meets certain tests under the nondiscrimination regulations. A minimum of 5 percent of compensation for the non–highly compensated participants is generally required.

2. **(Fail-safe) age-weighted profit-sharing plan.** A plan can also be designed using a fixed formula based on each participant's age and compensation. An age-weighted profit-sharing plan is a profit sharing plan in which the allocation formula contains an actuarial age-weighting factor (i.e., providing a higher allocation for older plan entrants). If this fixed formula meets the cross-testing requirements as discussed below, it will be subject to annual testing in theory but in general it will automatically meet the requirements each year.

3. **Target plan.** A target plan is a pension plan with an age-weighted contribution formula. A target plan, unlike an age-weighted profit-sharing plan, requires annual employer contributions meeting the Code's minimum funding standards. Otherwise, it does not differ much from a fail-safe age-weighted profit-sharing plan.

Currently, the cross-tested approach is the most common type of age-weighted plan. It has a number of advantages. First, it generally provides the most favorable benefits to older plan entrants. In addition, most employers consider it easier to explain to employees than fixed formula approaches. Employees have difficulty understanding why the contribution level varies from employee to employee based on age, as it does in a fail-safe age-weighted profit sharing plan or target plan. In most cross-tested plans, most of the non–highly compensated employees receive the same percentage of compensation, usually the 5% minimum.

If the objective of the plan is to minimize costs for non–highly compensated employees, the age-weighting approach tends to be most effective if most of the highly compensated employees are older at the plan's inception. If a significant number of non–highly compensated employees are also in the older age group, the age-weighted plan costs could be considerable for these employees. Finally, the major disadvantage of age-weighted plans is that their complexity increases the cost of plan design and administration.

The cross-testing regulations are designed to carry out the nondiscrimination requirements of the regulations under Code Section 401(a)(4). In general, the underlying approach of the cross-testing regulations is to test the plan's ultimate benefits for nondiscrimination, even though the plan is a defined contribution plan rather than a defined-benefit plan (hence the term cross-testing). This is done by projecting the year's contribution for each employee to that employee's retirement age (at an assumed rate of interest) and analyzing the benefit provided by the projected amount as a percentage of the employee's compensation. If these projected benefits, as a percentage of compensation, do not discriminate in favor of highly compensated employees, then the plan is considered nondiscriminatory.

To use cross-testing, the regulations have a "gateway" requirement. For most small-business plans, this gateway generally requires a minimum allocation of 5 percent of compensation for non–highly compensated employees.[5] Note that this is higher than the 3 percent-of-compensation minimum required under the top-heavy rules described in Chapter 26.

In a typical cross-tested plan, highly compensated employees are provided with a large annual allocation, generally the maximum amount permitted under the Section 415 annual addition limit (the lesser of $41,000 [as indexed for 2004] or 100 percent of compensation). Then, the remaining employees are provided with an allocation that meets the requirements of the cross-testing regulations. Often, the 5 percent minimum gateway allocation is enough to satisfy the cross-testing regulations.

While the cross-testing rules are complex, a simple example showing their application will illustrate how they work and also will show the characteristics and advantages of the cross-tested plan. (See the example on the following page.)

If there is more than one highly compensated employee in the plan, the test may be more complicated. In that case, the plan must be broken into "rate groups" consisting of each highly compensated participant and all the employees who have projected benefits equal to or greater than the highly compensated participant. The Section 410 coverage tests are then applied to the rate groups.

■ USING EMPLOYER STOCK IN QUALIFIED PLANS

For a number of years, the Internal Revenue Code has included special provisions for qualified plans that invest primarily in employer securities. Congress wants to encourage these plans on the premise that it is desirable to give employees some ownership interest in the company for which they work. The most important special benefit is the leveraging technique for ESOPs, described below, that allows the employer to use the ESOP as a means of financing corporate growth. There are also provisions that encourage the use of a stock plan to help create a market for employer stock.

There are two types of qualified plans that invest primarily in employer securities, the traditional *stock bonus plan* and the *employee stock ownership plan* (ESOP). In addition, a regular profit-sharing plan may invest in employer stock without limit, and profit-sharing plans are sometimes used, formally or informally, for this purpose. Qualified pension plans may not invest more than 10 percent of their assets in employer stock, so pension plans are not very useful as employer stock plans.

Advantages of Investing in Employer Stock

There are certain employer and employee advantages to any plan that invests in employer stock, including a regular profit-sharing plan, a stock bonus plan, or an ESOP.

- ■ A market can be created for employer stock. This has many planning implications and is discussed in detail below.
- ■ The employer can obtain a deduction for noncash (that is, employer stock) contributions to the plan.
- ■ Employees receive an ownership interest in the company, which may act as a performance incentive.
- ■ As described below, unrealized appreciation of stock is not taxed to the employee at the time of distribution.

EXAMPLE

Dr. Shoal, a solo medical practitioner, has an incorporated medical practice employing him and four other employees. Dr. Shoal is highly compensated and the others are non–highly compensated within the meaning of the qualified plan rules (see Chapter 26). A cross-tested plan is proposed with the following characteristics:[6]

Participant	Age	Compensation	Plan Contribution	% of Compensation
Dr. Shoal	53	$205,000	$41,000	20
A	55	50,000	2,500	5
B	30	30,000	1,500	5
C	25	30,000	1,500	5
D	25	30,000	1,500	5

The proposed plan provides a contribution of 5 percent of pay to meet the gateway required for the use of cross testing.

The next step is to project the contribution to each participant's age 65, at an assumed rate of 8½ percent interest (a rate between 7½ percent and 8½ percent must be used;[7] choosing the maximum of 8½ percent provides the best result for the highly compensated employees). For example, for Dr. Shoal, his $41,000 contribution accumulates to $85,438 at age 65 at an 8½ percent rate. The accumulated contribution is then expressed as a life annuity and the annuity as a percentage of compensation is determined.[8] For example, for Dr. Shoal, the $85,438 accumulation equates to a $9,160 annuity, which is 4.47 percent of his compensation of $205,000.

Participant	Compensation	Plan Contribution	Plan Contribution Projected to Age 65	Projected Benefit	Projected Benefit as % of Compensation
Dr. Shoal	$205,000	$41,000	$85,438	$9,160	4.47
A	50,000	2,500	4,425	474	.95
B	30,000	1,500	20,410	2,188	7.29
C	30,000	1,500	30,690	3,291	10.97
D	30,000	1,500	30,690	3,291	10.97

The final step under the cross-testing regulations is to test the projected benefit under the coverage tests of Section 410(b). These benefits must satisfy either the ratio percentage test or the average benefit test of that section (see Chapter 21 for a general discussion of the overall coverage tests of Section 410). The ratio percentage test is applied to a hypothetical "plan" consisting of the highly compensated participant (Dr. Shoal) and all non–highly compensated participants whose projected benefits are equal to or greater than those of Dr. Shoal. In this case, this consists of Dr Shoal and participants B, C, and D. Under the ratio percentage test, at least 70% of the non–highly compensated employees must be covered. The ratio percentage test is met because the percentage of non–highly compensated participants who are covered is 75 percent (3 of 4). Therefore, this plan meets the requirements of the cross-testing regulations.

Stock Bonus Plan

The stock bonus plan is the older of the two types of qualified plans that invest primarily in employer securities. Under the regulations, a stock bonus plan is a qualified defined-contribution plan similar to a profit-sharing plan, except that the employer's contributions are not necessarily dependent on profits; benefits are distributable in the stock of the employer company.

Typically, the plan contribution formula is based on employee compensation. Employer contributions to the plan may be made in cash or directly in the form of employer securities, newly issued or otherwise. Shares of stock are allocated to participants' accounts under a formula that must meet the same nondiscrimination requirements as the allocation formula in a profit-sharing plan. Some stock bonus plans also provide for after-tax employee contributions or salary reductions. (A salary reduction stock plan is sometimes referred to as a *KSOP*.)

The value of each participant's account in a stock bonus plan is stated in terms of a certain number of shares of employer stock. The value of the account varies with the value of the underlying employer stock. Dividends on the shares can be used to increase participants' accounts, or cash dividends can be paid through the plan directly to participants as currently taxable income, in which case the employer gets a tax deduction.

Plan Distributions. Distributions from both stock bonus plans and ESOPs are generally subject to the same restrictions applicable to distributions from any qualified plan. Thus, distributions prior to age 59½, death, disability, or retirement are subject to a 10 percent penalty, with some exceptions (Chapter 25). However, for a stock bonus plan or ESOP, there is no requirement of providing a joint and survivor annuity or other spousal death benefit.

Because an employee retains the investment risk in the employer company until the stock is distributed, a deferred distribution to a terminated employee would not be appropriate, so payouts from stock bonus plans or ESOPs have a special earlier beginning date than those for other qualified plans. Distributions from a stock bonus plan or ESOP must occur no later than one year after the end of the fifth plan year after the employee's separation from service or no later than one year after retirement, disability, or death.

In general, the plan must distribute benefits in the form of employer stock. However, the participant can be given the option of receiving cash of equal value, subject to a right to receive employer stock. If the participant receives stock that is not traded on an established market, the participant has a right to require that the employer repurchase the securities under a fair valuation formula. This is referred to as the **put requirement**. If an employee exercises the put option on distribution—that is, sells the securities back to the plan—the participant must be paid over no more than five years, and during that time the plan must provide adequate security for the payment. An employer that adopts a stock plan must be aware of future liabilities and cash requirements to comply with the put requirement, and must plan its finances accordingly.

Voting Rights. If the employer company is closely held, plan participants must be given the right to vote with respect to stock held for them in the plan on corporate issues requiring more than a majority of the outstanding common shares. If the employer stock is publicly traded, participants must be permitted to vote on all issues.

Taxation of Employees.   In addition to the usual tax advantages for qualified plans, an additional employee tax benefit provided by the Code for a plan holding employer stock is the deferral of taxation of **unrealized appreciation**. When the plan makes a lump-sum distribution including employer stock, the unrealized appreciation of the stock—that is, the difference between the value of the stock when contributed to or purchased by the trust and its value when distributed to the employee—is not taxable to the employee at the time of the distribution to the extent that it (1) represents nondeductible employee contributions or (2) represents employer contributions, and the participant's entire account is distributed within one taxable year as a result of death, the attainment of age 59½, or the employee's separation from the service of the employer.

This means that the taxable amount of a lump-sum distribution from a stock bonus plan does not include unrealized appreciation of employer securities if the recipient is entitled to the special tax treatment for lump-sum distributions in general. The unrealized appreciation is taxable only when the employee or other recipient sells the securities at a later date. The unrealized appreciation amount is taxable as a capital gain when the stock is sold.

Deductibility of Contributions.   As indicated above, the employer can deduct a contribution to a stock bonus plan in the form of employer securities as well as cash. Deductions for contributions can be taken even if there are no current or accumulated profits. The deduction limit is the same as that for a profit-sharing plan—25 percent of covered payroll.

Employee Stock Ownership Plan (ESOP)

The ESOP is a stock bonus plan with an important additional feature: If certain requirements are met, the plan can be used by the employer company as a means of raising funds on a tax-favored basis. The funds can be used for any corporate purposes, which can include acquiring the assets or stock of another company.

In effect, an ESOP allows an employer to indirectly borrow money from a bank and repay the loan with fully deductible repayment amounts. The repayment amounts are deductible in full because they are structured as contributions to an ESOP; normally, only the interest portion of a loan repayment would be tax-deductible.

This bit of tax magic (see Figure 22.1) is accomplished by first having the plan trustee borrow money from a bank or other lender. The borrowed money is then used to purchase a block of employer stock from the employer. Shares of this stock also will subsequently be allocated to participants' accounts in the ESOP as plan contributions are made. The employer makes periodic plan contributions to the ESOP and obtains a tax deduction for them. These plan contributions are designed to be enough to enable the plan trustee to gradually repay the loan to the bank. The net result is that the employer immediately receives the full proceeds of the bank loan and in effect pays off the loan through tax-deductible contributions to the plan on behalf of plan participants.

Because the ESOP normally has no financial status independent of the employer, the employer usually must guarantee the loan to the bank. If the plan gives collateral for the loan, the collateral may consist only of qualifying employer securities.

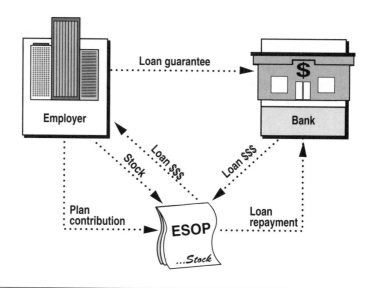

FIGURE 22.1 How an ESOP is Used by an Employer To Obtain Financing with Tax-Deductible Loan Repayments

Contribution Formulas and Accounts. An ESOP's contribution allocation formula may not be integrated with Social Security because plan allocations must be based on total compensation. In other respects, contribution formulas and participants' accounts are handled in the same manner as for the stock bonus plan described earlier.

Deductibility of Contributions. The rules for contribution deductibility for an ESOP are somewhat different from those for a stock bonus plan or profit-sharing plan. If employer contributions to the ESOP are applied to the repayment of a loan, amounts applied by the plan to repay the loan principal are deductible by the employer up to a limit of 25 percent of compensation of employees covered under the plan. Amounts used to repay interest are deductible without any percentage limit.

Plan Distributions. The distribution rules, voting rights, and taxation considerations regarding ESOP distributions are the same as those discussed earlier in connection with stock bonus plans.

Diversification Requirement. To reduce investment risks, participants in ESOPs who have reached age 55 with ten years of service are entitled to an annual election requiring that the employer diversify investment in the participant's account. The plan must offer at least three investment options, other than employer stock, to the participant for diversification purposes.

Creating a Market for Closely Held Stock

In small companies, it is often important for shareholders to find a market for their stock for financial and estate planning purposes. Many types of plans have been designed to enable the use of company funds for purchasing stock, such as stock redemption and corporate-owned life insurance plans. An ESOP or stock bonus plan can also be helpful for this purpose. The shareholder can sell stock to the plan during lifetime or at death, generally with favorable tax results. These techniques involve various complexities and must be designed with some care.

A special ESOP provision enhances the ability of closely held business owners to sell their company stock to an ESOP. Under certain circumstances, such owners can elect nonrecognition of gain on such sales. To take advantage of this provision, the ESOP must own at least a 30 percent interest in the company after the sale.

■ KEY TERMS

collectible

contribution formula

cross-tested/new comparability plan

definitely determinable benefit

discretionary contribution provision

(fail-safe) age-weighted profit-sharing plan

forfeiture

hardship withdrawal

incidental benefit

participant-directed investment

put requirement

substantial and recurring

target plan

unrealized appreciation

Section 415 limits

valuation date

■ STUDY QUESTIONS

1. a. How are employer contributions usually determined under a money-purchase plan?
   b. What determines the amount of an employee's retirement benefit under a money-purchase plan?
2. a. What is a profit-sharing plan?
   b. Explain how the eligibility and vesting requirements of profit-sharing plans differ from the eligibility and vesting requirements of pension plans.
3. a. Describe the two types of contribution formulas that can be used for a profit-sharing plan.
   b. Why is a formula approach more attractive to employees?
4. a. Explain the importance of the allocation formula in a profit-sharing plan.
   b. What is the usual allocation formula?
5. Explain how the allocation formula of a profit-sharing plan may be integrated with Social Security.
6. a. What is the maximum amount that an employer can deduct for contributions to a profit-sharing plan?

b. What is the maximum annual addition to any participant's account in a profit-sharing plan?

7. Explain the ramifications of participant-directed investments.

8. a. To what extent are preretirement withdrawals allowed from profit-sharing plans?

b. Describe the restrictions on withdrawals of employer contributions from profit-sharing plans.

9. a. What incidental benefits are allowed in profit-sharing plans?

b. What limitations are placed on incidental life insurance benefits?

10. a. What is an age-weighted plan?

b. What are the three major types of age-weighted plans and what are their advantages and disadvantages?

11. a. Describe the characteristics of a stock bonus plan.

b. How do ESOPs differ from stock bonus plans?

■ NOTES

1. Employee Benefit Research Institute, Facts from EBRI, January 2003, *www.ebri.org.facts/.* Data gathered by Department of Labor from Form 5500, filed annually by plan sponsors.

2. Labor Regulation Section 2550.404c-1.

3. Revenue Ruling 73-55, 1973-2 CB 130; Rev. Rul. 71-295, 1971-1 CB 184; Rev. Rul. 80-155, 1980-1 CB 84.

4. Rev. Rul. 68-24, 1968-1 CB 150.

5. Reg. Sec. 1.401(a)(4)-8(b)(1)(vi).

6. This example is based on an example used by Bruce Temkin, MSPA, EA, at an ALI-ABA course, "Representing the Professional and Closely Held Business," Scottsdale, Arizona, February 13–15, 2003.

7. See definition of "standard interest rate," Reg. Sec. 1.401(a)(4)-12.

8. A standard interest rate and mortality table, with no mortality prior to retirement, is used. Reg Sec.1.401(a)(4)-8(b)(2)(ii). Standard interest rate and mortality tables are defined in Reg. Sec. 1.401(a)(4)-12. The interest rate is not less than 7.5 percent and not greater than 8.5 percent. A list of permissable mortality tables is provided in the Regulation.

Defined-Contribution Plans II: 401(k) and Other Salary Savings Plans

11 Nonqualified plans	12a See instructions for box 12 C o d e
13 Statutory employee ☐ Retirement plan ☐ Third-party sick pay ☐	12b C o d e
14 Other	12c C o d e
	12d C o d e

tax	18 Local wages, tips, etc.	19 Local income tax	20 Locality name

- Describe the purpose of salary savings plans.
- Describe the characteristics of a 401(k) plan.
- Explain the actual deferral percentage test.
- Describe SIMPLE/IRAs and contrast them with 401(k) plans.
- Describe the role of Section 403(b) plans.
- Explain how the maximum annual 403(b) contribution is determined.
- Describe Section 457 plans and their applications.

CHAPTER OUTLINE

Salary Savings Plans in General

Section 401(k) Plans (Cash or Deferred Plans)
Eligible Employers
Advantages and Disadvantages
Salary Reductions in 401(k) Plans
Employer Matching Contributions
Employer Profit-Sharing Contributions
Employee After-Tax Contributions
Coverage Requirements
Vesting of Employee Accounts
Actual Deferral Percentage (ADP) Tests
Designing a Plan To Meet the ADP Tests
Distribution Restrictions
Social Security and Employment Taxes

SIMPLEs
Eligible Employers
Advantages and Disadvantages
Design Features of SIMPLEs
Installation of a SIMPLE

Section 403(b) Tax-Deferred Annuity Plans
Eligible Employers
Coverage and Participation Tests
The Limits on the Employee's Annual Contributions
Types of Investments for 403(b) Plans
Distributions and Loans from Section 403(b) Plans
Loans
Taxation of Section 403(b) Plans
Regulatory and Administrative Aspects

Section 457 Plans
Eligible Employers
Limit on Amount
Other Rules

■ SALARY SAVINGS PLANS IN GENERAL

A **salary savings plan**, as it is called here (there is no single accepted term for these plans), is a plan under which employees are given a choice, or election, to receive a part of their compensation in cash or to contribute it to a qualified plan or similar arrangement under which the amount contributed to the plan is not subject to income taxation in the year in which it is contributed. Instead, income tax on the contributions and investment earnings on those contributions is deferred until actual withdrawals are made by the employee. Amounts contributed by the employee under such an arrangement are sometimes referred to as *elective deferrals.*

In the last decade, such plans have become extremely popular with employers and employees as a result of the trends discussed at the beginning of the preceding chapter, as well as specific advantages of the salary savings approach such as the following:

- No annual funding commitment for the employer except to the extent that the plan requires a matching or formula contribution
- Initial cost to the employer is minimized because elective deferral amounts come out of existing cash payroll
- No long-term liability for employer
- Benefits have high portability to employee—fast vesting, annual or more frequent account valuation, easy for employee to understand how much has accumulated
- Employee has option to save at desired level (or not to save at all)
- Apparent administrative simplicity (although complex plans with directed investment may be as costly to administer as a defined-benefit plan)

Many salary savings plans make use of directed investment provisions (where the employee chooses the investments for his or her account, usually among a family of mutual funds), so that the employee's choices regarding savings programs are further enhanced.

The trend toward this type of qualified benefit is not without its disadvantages. Overall, the movement from the traditional pension plan to profit-sharing and salary savings approaches, however inevitable, probably results in a reduction in potential retirement income for employees, although employees who change jobs frequently (an increasing category of employees) may do better with the newer types of arrangements, as long as they do not dissipate their account accumulations before retirement. Many mobile workers, however, tend to spend distributions from profit-sharing or salary savings plans when they change jobs, particularly if the distribution is relatively small. Another emerging problem, in the case of plans using directed investment provisions, is that employees tend not to make good investment allocations in their plan accounts and, overall, may earn less on their money than if the employer chose the investments. Employees who do well with salary savings plans tend to be people who would save wisely and well for retirement even without the plan, thus raising questions as to the social utility of these plans. These problems, along with already well-known demographic problems with Social Security, threaten to haunt American society in the early 21st century as the baby boomers retire. Some time soon, we will have to better address, both individually and as a society, the issue of retirement income adequacy.

Among the general public, the best-known salary savings plan is the 401(k) plan, which is basically a qualified profit-sharing plan with an elective deferral feature. In addition, there are several other plan types (**SIMPLE**s, **403(b) tax-deferred annuity plans**, and **Section 457 plans**) that, although not qualified plans, provide elective deferrals and have much the same income tax and other consequences for the participants. These plans are discussed together in this chapter because of their practical similarity, but the student must be careful to note that they all have different rules and all are different from qualified plans.

■ SECTION 401(k) PLANS (CASH OR DEFERRED PLANS)

A qualified cash or deferred profit-sharing plan, usually referred to as a *401(k) plan* because the special rules for these plans are found in Code Section 401(k), is a qualified profit-sharing or stock bonus plan that incorporates an option for participants to put money into the plan or receive it as taxable cash compensation. In other words, a 401(k) plan differs from a regular profit-sharing plan in that employees can participate in deciding how much of their compensation is deferred. Amounts contributed to the plan are not federal income–taxable to participants until they are withdrawn; this is a significant advantage over contributions to a savings plan, which are taxable to the employee before contribution to the plan. However, 401(k) amounts for which the employee can elect to receive either cash or a plan contribution—elective deferrals—are subject to an annual dollar limit of $9,500, indexed for inflation (2004 figure is $13,000).

A 401(k) plan can be an independent plan or the 401(k) feature can be included with a regular profit-sharing, savings, or stock bonus plan of the employer. The plan can be designed in a number of ways to combine both employer and employee contributions, or the entire plan can be funded through salary reductions by employees.

Eligible Employers

Section 401(k) plans can be adopted only by private employers, including tax-exempt organizations. They are not available to government employers. As discussed later in this chapter, government employers may be eligible to adopt Section 403(b) or Section 457 plans to provide results somewhat similar to 401(k) plans.

Advantages and Disadvantages

Section 401(k) plans are currently very attractive to employees. First, they have the basic attraction of all qualified plans—they provide a tax-deferred savings medium. But 401(k) plans have an additional advantage: They give employees an opportunity to choose the amount of deferral according to their individual need for savings. From the employee's viewpoint, a 401(k) plan appears much like an individual IRA, but with additional advantages: The 401(k) plan has higher contribution limits than an IRA, in certain cases it provides special averaging on qualifying lump-sum withdrawals, and the withdrawal provisions during employment are slightly less restrictive.

From the employer's viewpoint, 401(k) plans are favorable because the entire plan can be funded through salary reductions by employees. Thus, the plan provides no direct additional compensation costs to the employer. Because of the popularity of the plan with employees, partly due to good publicity for these plans in the media, the employer can obtain employee goodwill with this type of plan at a relatively low cost. There are also some actual dollar savings in using the 401(k) type of design, because salary reductions by employees may reduce employer expense for workers' compensation and unemployment compensation insurance by reducing the payroll subject to those taxes.

The 401(k) type of design has some disadvantages, but in reviewing these it is important always to ask: disadvantages to whom and disadvantages compared with what? First of all, the dollar limit (see below) on elective deferrals is lower than that for other types of qualified plan contributions. However, as a practical matter, this limit primarily affects highly compensated employees. Another disadvantage is that a 401(k) plan is a qualified plan and as such is much more complicated than simply leaving savings up to individual employees, either through individual IRAs or otherwise. Generally speaking, integration of a 401(k) salary-reduction formula with Social Security is not possible, but the 401(k) nondiscrimination rules nevertheless permit significant discrimination in favor of higher-paid employees. Section 401(k) plans are more difficult to administer than regular qualified plans because of the additional rules (discussed later) that must be satisfied. Deferral amounts must be 100 percent vested; thus, there is no opportunity for the employer to save on plan costs by making use of employee forfeitures on Section 401(k) deferral amounts. Finally, distributions to employees prior to termination of employment are more restrictive than for a regular qualified plan. However, these restrictions are more liberal than those for an IRA.

Salary Reductions in 401(k) Plans

Section 401(k) plans are generally based on salary reduction contributions elected by employees. Alternatively, the employer can provide an annual "bonus" to employees that the employees can either receive in cash or contribute to the plan. "Negative election" provisions are also permitted; these are plan provisions whereby the employer automatically contributes a specified portion of each employee's salary to the 401(k) plan, unless the employee specifically requests to receive the amount in cash.[1]

Salary reductions must be elected by employees before compensation is earned—that is, before they render the services for which compensation is paid. Salary reductions elected after compensation is earned are ineffective as a result of the tax doctrine of **constructive receipt**.

Generally, plan participants are provided with a salary reduction election form that they must complete before the end of each calendar year. The election specifies how much will be contributed to the plan from each paycheck received for the forthcoming year. Usually the plan will permit the employee to reduce or entirely withdraw the election for pay not yet earned, if circumstances dictate. The plan must restrict each participant's salary reductions to no more than the annual limits set forth in the Code (see below).

The participant is always 100 percent vested in any salary reductions contributed to the plan and any plan earnings on those salary reductions. The purpose of this vesting provision is to provide maximum portability of this part of the benefit; even if a participant leaves employment after a short time, his portion of his plan account attributable to salary reductions cannot be forfeited.

Salary reductions, as well as any other plan contribution that the employee has the option to receive in cash (referred to as elective deferrals), are subject to an annual limit. The limit is a "per employee" rather than a "per plan" limit. The employee must add together each year all elective deferrals from (1) Section 401(k) plans, (2) salary reduction *SEPs* (available if established before 1997—see Chapter 28), (3) SIMPLE/IRAs, and (4) Section 403(b) tax deferred annuity plans (covered later in this chapter). The total must not exceed the following limits:

Year	Amount
2003	$12,000
2004	13,000
2005	14,000
2006 and thereafter	15,000

In addition to the foregoing salary reductions, employees who have reached age 50 during the plan year can make **catch-up contributions**. For regular 401(k) plans, the elective deferral limit is increased by the following catch-up amounts:

Year	Amount
2003	$2,000
2004	3,000
2005	4,000
2006 and thereafter	5,000

It is possible for a 401(k) plan to be funded entirely through employee elections to reduce salary by a specified amount and contribute the reduced amount to the plan. The major appeal of this approach is that the plan can be funded based on existing salary scales without any specific additional costs to the employer. Also, the plan can be described to employees as being somewhat like an IRA.

Employer Matching Contributions

The benefits of a 401(k) plan can be increased by adding employer **matching contributions** to the plan. Under this approach, the employer makes a contribution to the plan for every employee who elects a salary reduction. This employer matching contribution can be either dollar-for-dollar or some specified fraction of the employee's contribution. Matching can be limited to a specified percentage of each employee's compensation.

> **EXAMPLE**
> A plan might provide that an employee can elect salary reductions up to 6 percent of compensation, with the employer contributing an additional 1 percent of compensation for each 2 percent of employee salary reduction.

A significant advantage of this approach is that employer matching encourages plan participation by lower-paid employees. This helps to meet the qualification tests for 401(k) plans—the actual deferral percentage tests discussed later.

Employer Profit-Sharing Contributions

The plan also may provide for additional employer contributions not related to salary reductions by employees. These contributions can be completely discretionary or subject to a formula, as in the case of a regular profit-sharing plan. These contributions can be allocated in any manner permitted in a profit-sharing plan, including a simple uniform percentage of the participant's compensation as well as integration with Social Security or an age-weighted or cross-tested approach.

Employee After-Tax Contributions

The plan may permit employees to make additional **after-tax contributions** to the plan—that is, contributions not subject to the elective deferral rules and subject to income tax. These contributions are immediately fully vested to the employee. The earnings on these contributions build up on a tax-free basis just like other contributions to the 401(k) plan. The only difference is that they come out of the employee's taxable income.

Coverage Requirements

A 401(k) plan is considered to be a qualified profit-sharing plan, so it must meet all the eligibility and coverage requirements discussed earlier for qualified plans in general. However, substantial additional participation by lower-paid employees may indirectly be required to meet the actual deferral percentage requirements applicable under Section 401(k) as discussed below.

Vesting of Employee Accounts

As already indicated in this discussion, vesting requirements in a 401(k) plan may depend on the source or identity of the plan contributions. To summarize, the rules are as follows:

- Nontaxable employee salary reductions or elective deferrals made under a Section 401(k) cash or deferral option must be immediately 100 percent vested.
- Any after-tax employee contributions must be 100 percent immediately vested.
- Employer contributions to the plan must meet the usual vesting rules for qualified plans, discussed in Chapter 21. That is, the plan must have a vesting schedule for employer contributions that meets at least one of the ERISA minimum vesting standards (five-year vesting or three- to seven-year vesting).

Actual Deferral Percentage (ADP) Tests

It has long been recognized that because higher-paid employees have more discretionary income and, in particular, more income to save, any qualified plan that allows employees to choose deferral or cash will be used disproportionately by higher-paid employees. The concept of cash or deferral plans has existed for a long time, but until Congress enacted Section 401(k) in 1978, these plans were not permitted by statute because of this potential discrimination problem. The most important provision of Section 401(k) is a series of tests designed to prevent disproportionate use of these plans by higher-paid employees. These are the **actual deferral percentage (ADP) tests**.

These tests are in the nature of an additional nondiscrimination rule that must be met by 401(k) plans in addition to the usual rules for qualified plans. A qualified 401(k) plan must meet one of the following two tests in actual operation:

1. The ADP for eligible highly compensated employees must not be more than the ADP of all other eligible employees multiplied by 1.25 (i.e., it must not exceed this percentage by more than 25 percent).

2. The ADP for eligible highly compensated employees must not exceed the lesser of (a) 200 percent of the ADP of all eligible non–highly compensated employees or (b) the ADP for all eligible non–highly compensated employees plus 2 percentage points.

The ADP for a given year is

$$\frac{\text{Employer contribution to plan for employee (or salary reduction)}}{\text{Employee's compensation}}$$

This amount is computed for each employee and averaged for each of the two groups (highly compensated, non–highly compensated). Employer matching contributions and other employer contributions, as well as salary reductions (elective deferrals) of the employee can be included in the numerator of this fraction.

A few examples will illustrate the operation of the ADP tests better than any extended explanation.

EXAMPLE 1
Ten percent of compensation bonus, which the employee can take as cash or as a contribution (deferral) to the 401(k) plan; only employee A is highly compensated.

Employee	Compensation	Cash	Deferral	ADP
A	$30,000	$1,350	$1,650	5.5%
B	15,000	750	750	5
C	10,000	600	400	4

Test 1 is satisfied; ADP for highly compensated (A only) is 5.5%; ADP for non–highly compensated is 4.5% (average of 4% and 5%); 1.25 times 4.5% is 5.625%.

These examples are simplified for illustrative purposes. In actual practice, the ADP for non–highly compensated employees is generally determined for the preceding year to simplify administration, although the employer can elect a "current year" computation method. There are also **safe harbor 401(k) plan** approaches to plan design that can provide simplified administration and compliance with nondiscrimination tests.

EXAMPLE 2

Six percent of compensation bonus; D, E, and F are highly compensated.

Employee	Compensation	Cash	Deferral	ADP
D	$100,000	0	$6,000	6%
E	80,000	0	4,800	6
F	60,000	0	3,600	6
G	40,000	800	1,600	4
H	30,000	600	1,200	4
I	20,000	400	800	4

Plan fails test 1 (1.25 × 4% is less than 6%) but passes test 2 (ADP for highly compensated is no more than two percentage points greater and less that two times 4%).

Designing a Plan To Meet the ADP Tests

Obviously, it is critical to design the 401(k) plan so that the ADP tests are met; otherwise the plan will fail to qualify and all tax benefits will be lost. Fortunately, it is not as difficult as plan designers once believed and disqualifications are rare. Some of the methods used to ensure compliance are as follows:

■ *Mandatory deferral.* For example, an employer contributes 5 percent of compensation for all employees that must be deferred and allows an additional 2 percent under a cash or deferral option. This plan will always meet the second ADP test.

■ *Safe-harbor* design approaches, as discussed earlier.

■ *Limiting deferral by the higher paid.* This approach involves administrative problems. The highly compensated group must be identified and deferral must be monitored, with a mechanism to stop deferrals at an appropriate point during the year if necessary. Alternatively, excess deferrals for highly compensated employees can be computed at the end of the year and corrective distributions, including interest earnings, can be made to affected employees. Such corrective distributions are income-taxable to the recipients and must be made within 2½ months after the end of the plan year to avoid an additional penalty tax. Instead of cash distributions if the plan permits after-tax contributions, these excess amounts can be retained in the plan and recharacterized as after-tax contributions within 2½ months after the plan year. Related matching contributions can be forfeited and generally cannot be distributed.

■ *Counting on the popularity of the 401(k) approach.* In actual practice, many companies find that participation by lower-paid employees is substantial. It is not unusual for 75 percent of all employees of an organization to participate in the plan. This may eliminate the problem without any special mechanisms coming into effect.

■ *Employer matching and other contributions.* These generally result in easier compliance with ADP tests.

Because of the ADP tests, not every employer is suitable for a 401(k) plan. Because substantial participation by lower-paid employees is necessary, pay levels must be reasonably high in the organization, at least high enough so that some amount of retirement saving is possible by most of the employees.

Distribution Restrictions

Account balances attributable to amounts subject to the cash or deferral election—the 401(k) amounts—are subject to special distribution restrictions. These amounts may not be distributed earlier than on retirement, death, disability, separation from service, hardship, age 59½, or termination of the plan. Also, as with any qualified plan distribution, the 10 percent early withdrawal penalty applies (see Chapter 25). Amounts attributable to matching and profit-sharing contributions can generally be withdrawn according to the rules for profit-sharing plans discussed earlier.

The income taxation of distributions from 401(k) plans, including both 401(k) and non-40l(k) amounts in the plan, follows the usual rules for qualified plan distributions. The qualified plan rules relating to loans and plan distributions are discussed in detail in Chapter 25.

Social Security and Employment Taxes

Section 401(k) plans are an exception to the general rule that contributions by an employer to a qualified plan are free of federal employment taxes (Social Security [FICA] and unemployment tax [FUTA]). The popularity of 401(k) plans when first introduced caused such a noticeable reduction in federal employment tax revenues that Congress made special rules for 401(k) plans. Under current law, 401(k) amounts subject to an employee election to defer instead of receiving cash (elective deferrals) are subject to FICA and FUTA, whether these are contributed through salary reduction or employer bonuses. FICA and FUTA do not apply to non-40l(k) amounts—matching or profit-sharing contributions made by the employer to the plan that are not subject to elective deferrals.

In general, state unemployment compensation and workers' compensation payments are not required for either employer contributions or salary reductions in a 401(k) plan.

■ SIMPLEs

In an attempt to increase coverage of employer-sponsored plans, Congress has provided certain simplified arrangements that are not qualified plans but provide employers and employees with some of the same benefits as qualified plans. One such arrangement, structured as a salary savings plan somewhat similar to a 401(k) plan, is the SIMPLEs (savings incentive match plans for employees). SIMPLE are employer-sponsored plans under which plan contributions are made to the participating employees' IRAs. SIMPLEs also can be part of a 401(k) plan, but this arrangement is somewhat more complicated than a SIMPLE/IRA. Tax-deferred contribution levels are generally significantly higher than the deductible limit for individual IRAs (Chapter 28). SIMPLEs feature employee salary reduction contributions (elective deferrals) coupled with employer matching contributions.

SIMPLEs are easy to adopt and generally simple to administer, while providing employees with the tax-deferred retirement savings benefits of a qualified plan. However, qualified plans potentially can provide higher contribution levels. An employee's salary reduction under a SIMPLE can be no greater than a specified annual dollar limit.

Eligible Employers

Any employer may adopt a SIMPLE if it meets the following requirements:

- The employer has 100 or fewer employees.
- The employer does not maintain a qualified plan, 403(b) plan, or SEP except for a collectively bargained plan.

Advantages and Disadvantages

SIMPLEs can be adopted by completing a simple IRS form (Form 5304-SIMPLE or 5305-SIMPLE) rather than by the complex procedure required for qualified plans. Benefits of a SIMPLE/IRA are totally portable by employees because funding consists entirely of IRAs for each employee, and employees are always 100 percent vested in their benefits. Employees own and control their accounts, even after they terminate employment with the original employer. Individual IRA accounts allow participants to benefit from good investment results, as well as run the risk of bad results. As with a 401(k) plan, a SIMPLE can be funded in part through salary reductions by employees.

However, SIMPLEs have some disadvantages. As with profit-sharing or salary savings plans in general, employees cannot rely on a SIMPLE to provide an adequate retirement benefit. First, benefits are not significant unless the employee makes significant regular salary reduction contributions. Such regular contributions are not a requirement of the plan. Furthermore, employees who enter the plan at older ages have only a limited number of years remaining prior to retirement to build up their SIMPLE accounts. Also, annual contributions generally are restricted to lesser amounts than would be available in a qualified plan. SIMPLE contributions are limited to a maximum dollar limit that is less than that for 401(k) or 403(b) plans.

Design Features of SIMPLEs

The following are the most significant Internal Revenue Code requirements for SIMPLEs (Section 408(p)):

- The employer must have 100 or fewer employees (only employees with at least $5,000 in compensation for the prior year are counted) on any day in the year.
- The employer may not sponsor another qualified plan, 403(b) plan, or SEP under which service is accrued or contributions made for the same year the SIMPLE is in effect, except for a plan covering exclusively collective bargaining employees.

■ Contributions may be made to each employee's IRA or to the employee's 401(k) account. In effect, there are thus two types of SIMPLEs—those that include the 401(k) requirements and those funded through IRAs. SIMPLEs meeting the 401(k) requirements are rarely adopted and will not be discussed further here.

■ Employees who earned at least $5,000 from the employer in the preceding two years and are reasonably expected to earn at least $5,000 in the current year can contribute (through salary reductions) up to the following dollar limit:

2003	$8,000
2004	9,000
2005	10,000
After 2005	10,000 indexed for cost-of-living increases in $500 increments[2]

SIMPLEs also have a provision for additional deferrals for participants who are aged 50 or over:

Taxable Year Beginning In	50-or-Over Additional Deferral Permitted (SIMPLE)
2003	$1,000
2004	1,500
2005	2,000
2006	2,500
After 2006	2,500 indexed for cost-of-living increases in $500 increments[3]

■ The employer is required to make a contribution equal to either

  a. a dollar-for-dollar matching contribution up to 3 percent of the employee's contribution (the employer can elect a lower percentage, not less than 1 percent, in not more than two out of the past five years) or

  b. 2 percent of compensation for all eligible employees earning at least $5,000 (whether or not they elect salary reductions).

In a SIMPLE/IRA plan, each participating employee maintains an IRA. Employer contributions are made directly to the employee's IRA, as are any employee salary reduction contributions. Employer contributions and employee salary reductions, with the limits discussed above, are not included in the employee's taxable income.

Direct employer contributions to a SIMPLE are not subject to FICA or FUTA taxes. However, as with 401(k) plans, employee salary reduction contributions are subject to FICA and FUTA. The impact of state payroll taxes depends on the particular state's laws. Both salary reductions and employer contributions may be exempt from state payroll taxes in some states.

Distributions to employees from a SIMPLE/IRA plan are treated as distributions from an IRA. All the restrictions on IRA distributions apply and the distributions are taxed the same. The taxation of IRA distributions is discussed in Chapter 28.

Installation of a SIMPLE

Installation of a SIMPLE can be very easy. The employer merely completes IRS Form 5304-SIMPLE or Form 5305-SIMPLE. Form 5305-SIMPLE provides for a "designated financial institution" for participant investments, while Form 5304-SIMPLE does not have this provision, which some plan sponsors and participants may find restrictive. Under a SIMPLE, salary reduction elections must be made by employees during a 60-day period prior to January 1 of the year for which the elections are made. The form does not have to be sent to the IRS or other government agency.

The reporting and disclosure requirements for SIMPLEs are simplified if the employer uses Form 5304-SIMPLE or 5305-SIMPLE. The annual report Form 5500 need not be filed if these forms are used. In other cases, reporting and disclosure requirements are similar to those for a qualified profit-sharing plan.

■ SECTION 403(b) TAX-DEFERRED ANNUITY PLANS

The 403(b) plan is another specialized plan that is available to some employers as an alternative or supplement to a qualified plan. The 403(b) plan was provided as a result of Congress's concern that employees of tax-exempt organizations might not have adequate qualified plan coverage. Tax-exempt employers may have relatively little money available for employee benefits, and the tax deductibility of a qualified plan does not act as an incentive because the tax-exempt employer pays no federal income taxes. As a result, Congress enacted Code Section 403(b), which, within limits, allows employees of certain tax-exempt organizations to have money set aside for them by salary reductions or direct employer contributions in a tax-deferred plan somewhat similar to a qualified plan.

Section 403(b) plans are an important consideration in designing the benefit program for any tax-exempt employer. However, today many tax-exempt employers have regular qualified plans for their employees, with the Section 403(b) plan being made available as a supplemental retirement or savings program. Tax-exempt, but not government, employers can adopt 401(k) plans as well as 403(b) plans, so such employers may be in a position to choose between the two approaches for salary savings. For most tax-exempts, the 403(b) plan is somewhat more advantageous than a 401(k) plan.

Section 403(b) plans are sometimes referred to as **tax-deferred annuity (TDA) plans** or **tax-sheltered annuities**, but because these terms also can refer to annuities not covered under Section 403(b), the term *Section 403(b) plans* will be used here to avoid confusion.

Eligible Employers

Employees of the following two types of organizations are eligible to adopt Section 403(b) plans:

1. A **501(c)(3) organization**—that is, a tax-exempt employer described in Code Section 501(c)(3)—an employer "organized and operated exclusively for religious, charitable, scientific, testing for public safety, literary or educational purposes, or to foster national or international amateur sport competition . . . or for the prevention of

cruelty to children or animals." Section 501(c)(3) also requires that the organization benefit the public rather than a private shareholder or individual and that the organization refrain from political campaigning or propaganda to influence legislation.

2. An educational organization with a regular faculty and curriculum and a resident student body that is operated by a state or municipal agency—in other words, a public school or college. This is the only type of government employer that can adopt a 403(b) plan.

Thus, Section 403(b) plans are available to a wide range of familiar nonprofit institutions such as churches, private and public schools and colleges, hospitals, and charitable organizations.

To participate in a Section 403(b) plan of an eligible employer, the participant must be a full-time or part-time employee. This requirement is significant because tax-exempt organizations often have ties with persons who are independent contractors rather than employees. For example, many physicians on a hospital staff technically are not employees but rather independent contractors. A person is an employee when the employer exercises control or has the right to control the person's activities as to what is done and when, where, and how it is done. The question of employee status also affects federal income tax withholding, employment taxes (Social Security and federal unemployment), and participation in other fringe benefit plans of the employer. If the employer wishes to cover a person under a Section 403(b) plan, it must at least treat that person consistently as an employee for all these purposes.

To be eligible for a Section 403(b) plan, a public school employee must perform services related directly to the educational mission. The employee can be a clerical or custodial employee, as well as a teacher or principal; a political officeholder is eligible only if he or she has educational training or experience.

Coverage and Participation Tests

Section 403(b) plans to which the employer makes contributions are subject to relatively complicated nondiscrimination requirements. Employer matching contributions are also subject to the tests described in the discussion of savings and thrift plans. However, if the plan is funded entirely through employee salary reductions, as many plans are, these requirements do not apply. There is a simpler nondiscrimination requirement for salary reductions, however: If the plan permits salary reductions for any employee, then it must permit salary reductions of more than $200 for any other employee, except for those covered under a Section 457 plan or Section 401(k) plan or under another 403(b) plan. Certain part-time and student employees can be excluded.

A Section 403(b) plan (except for a church-related, public school, or public college plan) is covered under the age and service provisions of ERISA Section 202, which are the same as the analogous age and service code provisions for qualified plans. Thus, if a Section 403(b) plan uses age or service eligibility, these can be no greater than age 21 and one year of service. However, age and service requirements are rarely used in Section 403(b) plans.

The Limits on the Employee's Annual Contributions

The maximum contribution that can be made to a 403(b) plan for an employee cannot exceed the Section 415 *annual additions limit* for that employee. As discussed in Chapter 26, this limit is the lesser of (a) 100 percent of the employee's compensation or (b) an indexed dollar limit ($41,000 for 2004).

> **EXAMPLE**
> Employee A's compensation for 2004 is $30,000. The maximum annual addition to his account for 2004 is $30,000. Employee B's compensation for 2004 is $90,000. The maximum annual addition to B's account for 2004 is $41,000.

The annual addition to a participant's account for the year is the total of employer and employee contributions to the account, including salary reductions. However, in determining compensation for purposes of the 100 percent limit, salary reductions are not counted.

> **EXAMPLE**
> Employee A has a stated salary of $30,000 for the year. A elects to reduce salary by $12,000 and contribute this amount to his 403(b) plan. His annual additions limit for the year is $30,000 (not $30,000 less $12,000, or $18,000). Thus, the employer could contribute up to an additional $18,000 to the plan (making the total annual addition equal to $30,000—the employer's contribution of $18,000 plus the employee's contribution of $12,000.)

Only highly compensated employees are generally in a position to have the full Section 415 maximum limit contributed to their 403(b) accounts. Generally, the contribution is much less for most employees.

Salary reduction contributions to a 403(b) plan are limited to the same dollar amount that applies to Section 401(k) plans, as discussed above. The 50-or-over catch-up limit is also the same. The salary reduction limit is a per-individual limit rather than a per-plan limit.

> **EXAMPLE**
> Alex, aged 40, works for Mercy Hospital and has another job at Wize Consultants. Mercy has a 403(b) plan and Wize has a 401(k) plan, and Alex is eligible for both. For 2004, Alex elects to contribute $8,000 to the 403(b) plan through a salary reduction. He can contribute no more than $5,000 for 2004 to the 401(k) plan (i.e., $13,000 in total, the dollar limit for 2004).

A unique feature of 403(b) plans, applicable to no other type of plan, is a "catch-up" salary reduction based on years of service. If the employee has at least 15 years of service, the catch-up limit allows additional salary reductions above the regular dollar limit equal to the least of

- $3,000;
- $15,000 less prior catch-up contributions; or
- $5,000 times the employee's years of service with the employer, less all prior salary reductions with that employer.

Types of Investments for 403(b) Plans

Section 403(b) plan funds must be invested in either

- annuity contracts purchased by the employer from an insurance company or
- mutual fund shares held in custodial accounts [referred to as *403(b)(7) accounts*].

Many different types of annuities may be used for Section 403(b) plans. Thus, the annuities can be individual or group contracts, level or flexible premium annuities, and fixed dollar or variable annuities. Face-amount certificates providing a fixed maturity value and a schedule of redemptions are also permitted. In addition, the annuity contract may provide incidental amounts of life insurance for the employee; however, the value of such insurance is taxable to the employee each year under **IRS Table 2001**. The annuity contracts can provide the employee with a choice of broad types of investment strategies— for example, a choice between investment in a fixed-income fund and an equity-type fund. However, if the contract gives the employee specific powers to direct the investments of the fund, the IRS will regard the employee as in control of the account for tax purposes and the employee will be currently taxed on the fund's investment income.

Annuity contracts used in Section 403(b) plans must be nontransferable. This means that they cannot be sold or assigned as collateral to any person other than the insurance company issuing the contract. However, the employee is permitted to designate a beneficiary for death benefits or survivorship annuities. Because similar restrictions apply to annuities transferred to participants from qualified plans, most insurance companies use the same standard provisions for both types of annuity contracts.

Mutual fund accounts [403(b)(7) accounts] are used in 403(b) plans much as they are in 401(k) plans, and can give participants the opportunity to allocate their accounts according to their own investment strategies by providing a family of funds with different investment approaches.

Distributions and Loans from Section 403(b) Plans

Distributions from Section 403(b) plans are subject to rules similar to those applicable to qualified 401(k) plans; however, there are differences in detail. Withdrawal restrictions are quite complicated. In general, withdrawals are not permitted from 403(b)(7) custodial accounts (mutual funds) or from any salary-reduction 403(b) account except for withdrawals after age 59½, or on death, disability, separation from service, or financial hardship. These withdrawal restrictions technically do not apply to annuity-type 403(b) accounts funded by direct employer contributions rather than salary reductions. However, this "loophole" is of limited usefulness because all early withdrawals are subject to the 10 percent early distribution penalty of Code Section 72(t). As discussed in Chapter 25, this penalty applies to most distributions prior to age 59½ from qualified plans, IRAs, and Section 403(b) plans. The penalty applies even to distributions that are permitted; for example, many hardship distributions from Section 403(b) plans will be subject to the penalty.

Other qualified plan distribution rules also apply to Section 403(b) plans. Distributions must begin by April 1 of the calendar year following the attainment of age 70½ or actual retirement, if later. The minimum annual distribution thereafter is a level amount spread over the participant's life expectancy or over the joint life expectancies of the participant and beneficiary, as discussed in Chapter 25.

Loans

Section 403(b) plans with either annuity or mutual-fund accounts may permit loans on the same basis as regular qualified plans. Plan loans are discussed in Chapter 25. Because of the restrictions on Section 403(b) distributions, plan loan provisions are particularly important to employees and should be considered in any Section 403(b) plan.

Taxation of Section 403(b) Plans

A Section 403(b) plan provides the same general tax advantages as a qualified plan. Thus, plan contributions within the limits discussed above are not currently taxable to the employee. Investment earnings on plan funds are also not currently taxable.

The full amount of any distribution from a Section 403(b) plan, whether during employment or at termination of service, is fully taxable as ordinary income to the participant, except for any **cost basis** the participant has in the distribution. A cost basis could result if the employee paid tax previously on any amount contributed to the plan or reported Table 2001 costs if the plan provides incidental life insurance. There are no averaging or capital-gain provisions for the taxable amount of a distribution from a Section 403(b) plan. The bad tax effect of having all of the income taxable in a single year can be alleviated only by having a periodic form of payout from the plan or by rolling the distribution over to an IRA. A periodic distribution from a Section 403(b) plan is taxed under the annuity rules the same as an annuity from a qualified plan.

Death benefits are subject to tax treatment similar to that applicable to death benefits from qualified plans. Death benefits are subject to income tax to the beneficiary except to the extent of the pure death benefit paid out as life insurance from the plan. Section 403(b) death benefits are included in the gross estate of the deceased participant for **federal estate tax** purposes. However, if they are paid to a spouse, they escape federal estate taxation under the unlimited marital deduction. In other cases, there may be no estate tax because the tax applies only to relatively large estates (the exemption increases to $1 million by 2007).

Regulatory and Administrative Aspects

A Section 403(b) plan is considered a pension plan, rather than a **welfare benefit plan**, for purposes of the reporting and disclosure provisions. The applicable reporting and disclosure requirements are similar to those applicable to qualified plans, as discussed in Chapter 27. However, as with qualified plans, Section 403(b) plans of government units and churches that have not elected to come under ERISA are exempt from these requirements, unless mutual funds rather than annuity contracts are used for funding. If a Section 403(b) plan is purely of the salary reduction type and does not include any direct employer contributions, the reporting and disclosure and other regulatory requirements are greatly reduced.

■ SECTION 457 PLANS

These plans are primarily used by government employers. Government employers may have qualified plans for employees, except that they are not eligible to adopt 401(k) plans, and only a very limited category of government employers (public schools) can adopt 403(b) plans. Thus, for a government employer the opportunity to offer employees a plan of the salary savings type is limited. Section 457 provides the only alternative in designing a salary savings arrangement for most government employers. Plans designed under this Code provision are not qualified plans; moreover, the rules are in many cases very different from those discussed previously in this chapter. The rules were enacted by Congress primarily to forestall perceived abuses in retirement plans of government employers rather than to benefit government employees, so they are somewhat lacking in flexibility or generosity, although they have been recently improved.

Eligible Employers

Section 457 applies to government employers and to employers that are exempt from federal income tax. However, these plans are not much used by private tax-exempt organizations because they have better alternatives such as 401(k) plans.

Limit on Amount

The dollar limit on annual salary reductions by a participant in a Section 457 plan is the same as that for 401(k) plans (see the tables on page 585). For example, for 2004 a participant under 50 can elect to contribute up to $13,000 to the plan by salary reductions. The 50-or-over catch-up also applies. The rules regarding timing of 401(k) elections and other rules for salary reductions are similar to those for 401(k) plans.

Other Rules

- Elections to defer compensation under Section 457 are made monthly, under an agreement entered into before the beginning of the month.

- For government employers, employee salary deferrals must be placed in a trust fund or custodial account. However, for private tax-exempt employers, the plan cannot be funded—all deferred compensation and income therefrom remains the property of the employer.

- Plan distributions cannot be made before separation from service or "unforeseeable emergency."

- Plan distributions must meet the minimum distribution rules of Section 401(a)(9) regarding beginning date (April 1 after age 70½ or retirement—see Chapter 25).

- A special incidental death benefit provision applies—the participant must expect to receive at least two-thirds of the total payout where there is a survivor annuity.

- Plan distributions are taxable in full when received. They are not eligible for averaging or capital-gain treatment. However, they can be rolled over to an IRA and escape taxation until withdrawn from the IRA.

- There are no specific coverage requirements—the plan can be offered to all employees, or any group of employees, even a single employee. However, for a tax-exempt organization (but not for a government organization) the participation, fiduciary, and other ERISA rules may apply.

If the state or local government employer or tax-exempt employer has a nonqualified deferred-compensation plan that does not comply with Section 457—for example, one that exceeds the limits—then it is treated for tax purposes as a funded plan, whether or not it is actually funded. This means that the deferred amount is includable in the participant's income when there is no substantial risk of forfeiture. This does, however, provide some opportunity for governments and tax-exempts to design plans for top executives above the salary-reduction dollar limit by including forfeiture provisions.

■ KEY TERMS

actual deferral percentage (ADP) tests

after-tax contributions

catch-up contributions

constructive receipt

cost-basis

federal estate tax

IRS Table 2001

matching contributions

salary savings plan

safe harbor 401(k) plan

SIMPLEs

Section 457 plans

tax-deferred annuity (TDA) plans

tax-sheltered annuities

welfare benefit plan

403(b) tax-deferred annuity plans

501(c)(3) organization

STUDY QUESTIONS

1. Describe a qualified Section 401(k) plan. Include the following points in your description:

   a. What are the advantages and disadvantages of a 401(k) plan?

   b. What are the vesting requirements in a 401(k) plan?

   c. What is the limit on elective deferrals under a 401(k) plan?

2. Fixemup, P.C., is a professional corporation for a group of four doctors, two nurses, and one receptionist. The census data for the current year is as follows:

	Salary/Percentage of Stock Ownership	401(k) Contributions
Dr. Able	$90,000 / 50%	8%
Dr. Baker	85,000 / 30	8
Dr. Resident	44,000 / 20	8
Dr. Intern	35,000 / 0	8
Nurse Marmer	25,000 / 0	5
Nurse Devries	25,000 / 0	5
Receptionist Smith	15,000 / 0	0

   Does the Fixemup, P.C., 401(k) plan meet the ADP test? Explain.

3. What are the major similarities and differences between a SIMPLE/IRA and a qualified 401(k) plan?

4. Explain the rules for SIMPLE matching contributions.

5. What types of organizations may adopt a 403(b) plan for employees?

6. Ed Greave's salary in his first year of employment with a nonprofit charitable organization is $50,000. He elects a salary reduction under a Section 403(b) plan. What is the maximum salary reduction possible for Ed Greave?

7. Describe the major differences between a salary-reduction type Section 403(b) plan and a qualified Section 401(k) plan.

8. What types of organizations are subject to Code Section 457?

9. Compare a 457 plan for a government employer with a qualified Section 401(k) plan.

NOTES

1. Rev. Rul. 2000-35, 2000-31 IRB.

2. Code Sec. 408(p)(2)(E)(ii).

3. Code Sec. 414(v)(2)(c).

CHAPTER
24
Defined-Benefit Plans

■ Describe the types of retirement benefit formulas that can be included in defined-benefit plans, including cash balance plans.

■ Explain how pension plans can provide inflation protection.

■ Describe the purpose for the accrued-benefit rules.

■ Explain how benefits are paid on nonretirement terminations of employment.

■ Describe the preretirement and postretirement survivorship benefits that must be provided by qualified plans.

■ Explain the extent to which incidental death benefits and disability benefits may be included in qualified plans.

■ Describe the general features of the following pension funding instruments:

   1. Trusts

   2. Insurance contracts

■ Describe fully insured plans and when they are advantageous.

■ Explain what is meant by an actuarial method and actuarial assumptions.

■ Explain the minimum funding standards of the Internal Revenue Code.

■ Explain the rules for deductibility of employer contributions to qualified pension plans.

CHAPTER OUTLINE

Defined-Benefit Formulas
General Characteristics of Defined-Benefit Formulas
Replacement Ratio Approach
Types of Formulas
The Cash-Balance Plan Formula
Definition of Compensation

Inflation Protection
Preretirement Inflation
Postretirement Inflation

The Accrued Benefit
Benefit Accrual Rules

Benefits at Termination of Employment

Death and Disability Benefits
Qualified Joint and Survivor Annuity
Preretirement Survivor Annuity
Subsidizing Survivor Annuities
Incidental Death Benefits

Planning Considerations
Disability Benefits from Qualified Plans

Funding of Qualified Plans
Trusts
Insurance Contracts
Individual Life Insurance and Annuity Contracts
Fully Insured Plans

Actuarial Methods and Assumptions
Choosing an Actuarial Cost Method
Ongoing Actuarial Valuations

Minimum Funding Standards
Exemptions from the Minimum Funding Standard

Deductibility of Pension Plan Contributions

■ DEFINED-BENEFIT FORMULAS

In a defined-benefit plan, the plan formula specifies the benefit that will be paid to the employee rather than the amount of the contribution. There are no individual accounts for employees and, consequently, the employee does not bear the risk of bad investment results. Payment of the promised benefit is an obligation of the employer, and the employer is required to fund the plan in advance so that sufficient funds will be available. Within certain limits, benefits in a defined-benefit plan are insured by the federal government through the Pension Benefit Guaranty Corporation (PBGC).

Defined-benefit plans are the most complex of all qualified plans. The benefit formulas themselves tend to be complex because of the variety of employer objectives sought. The actuarial funding approach requires additional administrative costs for the plan. Hence, the law dealing with defined-benefit plans is appropriately complex, and only a summary of the applicable rules and techniques is appropriate for this book.

General Characteristics of Defined-Benefit Formulas

Defined-benefit formulas have two basic characteristics that determine their use in pension plan design. First, the amount of an employee's benefit is not necessarily directly related to total compensation from the employer during the period the employee is covered under the plan. This means that the employer can design the plan with reference to a desired retirement income level for an employee, even if the employee had relatively low compensation in certain years or participated in the plan for a relatively short time.

The second basic characteristic is that defined-benefit formulas can favor those employees who enter the plan at later ages. This is because the benefit for such employees is a stated amount—often the same amount payable to employees who entered the plan at earlier ages—even though the employer's annual cost for funding the benefit is greater for employees entering the plan at later ages. As an example, consider three employees having the same compensation of $50,000 annually and a plan providing a benefit of 50 percent of this compensation at age 65. If these employees entered the plan at ages 30, 40, and 50, the employer's level annual cost to provide the same retirement benefit for each is illustrated in Table 24.1.

TABLE 24.1	Entry Age and Defined-Benefit Contribution	
Age at Entry	**Employer Contribution Each Year to Retirement**
30	$ 1,971
40	4,309
50	10,847

These basic characteristics relate to the two principal types of employer objectives that can be met with a defined-benefit plan. One objective is to provide a reasonable income **replacement ratio** for all covered employees. The flexibility of defined-benefit formulas permits this. The other type of objective is philosophically quite different—the objective of providing the maximum tax shelter under the plan for key employees. In a closely held business where this objective is often dominant, key employees are typically older at the plan's inception. Thus, the second basic defined-benefit plan characteristic illustrated in Table 24.1 is significant, as is the flexibility of defined-benefit formula design.

Replacement Ratio Approach

In adopting an income replacement ratio approach to benefit formula design, the starting point is to examine the census of the employees to be covered and determine an appropriate level of retirement income. For all but the lowest-paid employees, a retiree's standard of living can usually be maintained with less than 100 percent of preretirement income. Some reasons for this are that there are no work-related expenses after retirement, that the need to save after retirement is reduced, and that living expenses of older persons tend to be less than those of working persons. Certain expenses of older persons that tend to go up, such as medical care, are often covered under Medicare or other health insurance. Replacement ratios for lower income employees should be higher because an individual closer to the subsistence level tends to spend most of his or her income for basic items such as food and shelter, and these expenses at a basic level are not likely to decline after retirement. Qualified plans that use this approach typically aim at providing about 50 percent to 75 percent of preretirement gross (before-tax) income from the plan plus Social Security retirement benefits.

An appropriate benefit formula is designed to provide the desired replacement ratio, using the design rules discussed in the rest of this chapter. The annual cost of the plan is then determined. If this exceeds the employer's cost objectives, the plan must be redesigned until the cost comes within the appropriate range. It is also possible to vary the annual cost by varying the actuarial methods and assumptions used, as discussed below.

Types of Formulas

Many different benefit formulas have been developed to meet various plan design objectives. A large degree of variation is possible, within the limits of the benefit accrual rules and rules for integration with Social Security, discussed later, and the general nondiscrimination requirements for qualified plans covered in Chapter 21. The possible benefit formulas can be divided into specific types. The IRS distinguishes two types of benefit formulas, the **flat-benefit formula** and the **unit-benefit formula**.

Flat-Benefit Formula.   This type of formula does not take an employee's service into account. Such a benefit formula might be either a **flat-amount formula,** such as a formula providing a benefit of $100 per month at retirement for each employee, or a **flat-percentage formula**—for example, a benefit of 40 percent of compensation at retirement.

The flat-amount approach is usually suitable only for a group of employees having almost the same compensation levels because most pension planners would want to take differing compensation levels into account in determining the retirement income level. However, the flat-amount formula has the advantage of simplicity. The flat-percentage approach takes differing compensation into account and is frequently used. The plan's definition of compensation, as discussed below, is an important element of this formula.

All flat-benefit formulas raise the problem of fairness among employees with differing lengths of service with the employer. Many employers would prefer not to give the same benefit to short- and long-service employees, even though they have the same compensation levels. This objection often can be resolved by having a minimum period of service required to receive the full stated dollar amount or percentage, with reductions for lesser amounts of service. A more definite solution is to use a unit-benefit formula, discussed next.

Unit-Benefit Formula.   A unit-benefit formula is based on the employee's service. Some unit-benefit formulas take only service, not compensation, into account—for example, a benefit of $10 per month for each year of service. As with the flat benefit formula, such a formula is usually only suitable for a group having a fairly narrow range of compensation. Such formulas are sometimes used in collectively bargained plans. A unit-benefit formula may also take compensation into account—for example, a formula providing a benefit of 1 percent of compensation for each year of service (or to state it another way, 1 percent of compensation times the employee's years of service). Under this formula, an employee who retired with 15 years of service would receive a retirement benefit equal to 15 percent of compensation.

Past Service.   When a unit-benefit plan is installed for an existing, rather than new, employee group, the employer must decide whether to give service credit only for prospective or future service or to give some credit for existing employees' prior service for the employer. In small, closely held businesses, the owners and key employees often have considerable **past service** compared with other employees; it is particularly common to have past-service provisions in such plans. Past-service credit can be provided in many ways, so long as there is no discrimination in favor of highly compensated employees. Past service can be treated the same as future service, or the formula can provide lesser credit for past service.

The ability to utilize past service is one of the major advantages of a defined-benefit plan over a defined-contribution plan. For example, suppose a plan is adopted by an employer with two employees, one age 30 with 5 years of prior service and the other age 50 with 25 years of prior service. If a defined-contribution plan is adopted, the younger employee will have at age 65 a plan account representing 35 years of employer contributions, while the older employee will have only 15 years of contributions at retirement. However, a unit-benefit plan providing an annual benefit of 1 percent of compensation for each year of past and future service would allow each employee to retire at age 65 with an annual benefit of 40 percent of compensation.

The Cash-Balance Formula

The cash-balance formula—sometimes referred to as a **guaranteed-account formula,** as well as other names—is a type of hybrid between defined-benefit and defined-contribution approaches that is in a sense the opposite of the other hybrid, the target formula. In the target formula, employer contributions are based on age at entry, but ultimate benefits are not guaranteed. With a cash-balance formula, employer contributions are based on compensation, not on age at entry; the ultimate benefit (account balance) is subject to a guaranteed rate of return.

In a cash-balance plan, accounts are set up for each participant. Unlike the accounts in a defined-contribution plan, there is no investment risk—the accounts are merely a computational formality. The accounts are credited at least annually with two types of credits, a **pay credit** and an **interest credit.**

The pay credit is generally a percentage of compensation. The pay credit formula may be integrated with Social Security; for example, the plan might provide a pay credit each year of 2 percent of each participant's total earnings plus 3 percent of the participant's earnings above an integration level related to the Social Security taxable wage base. An integrated cash-balance formula must meet the rules for integrating a defined-benefit plan (see discussion in Chapter 21). The actuary typically will do this by showing that the "worst case"—the most discriminated-against participant—will receive at least as much as under the defined-benefit integration rules.

The interest credit is an amount representing earnings on the participant's account balance. To meet the definitely determinable rule applicable to pension formulas, the interest credit must be an amount that is defined in the plan and not subject to the employer's discretion. For example, the interest credit each year might be defined as the lesser of the change in the consumer price index (CPI) for the preceding year or the one-year rate for Treasury securities. However, the employer can have the option of crediting actual plan earnings, if these are higher.

Because there are no true individual accounts—participants have a guaranteed minimum benefit that can be legally satisfied out of the entire plan fund—the plan does not meet the definition of a defined-contribution plan and is thus technically a defined-benefit plan. Consequently, the plan is subject to a more complex legal environment; it is subject to PBGC reporting and termination requirements and the requirement of actuarial certification.

The employer's cost for the plan is determined actuarially because of the guarantee features. Costs can be controlled to some extent by choosing appropriate factors for the interest credits. However, if interest credits do not keep pace with actual plan earnings, participants are likely to be dissatisfied with the plan.

Despite the plan's technical status as a defined-benefit plan, a cash-balance plan looks to participants very much like a money-purchase plan and serves some of the same objectives. Typically, the cash-balance plan will be attractive to younger employees because benefits (and employer costs) build up faster in the employee's earlier years than in a traditional defined-benefit plan (see Figure 24.1). Thus, it is attractive to employers wishing to retain younger employees or allocate pension costs in a way that does not

FIGURE 24.1	Comparison of Cash-Balance and Traditional Defined-Benefits (DB) Plans

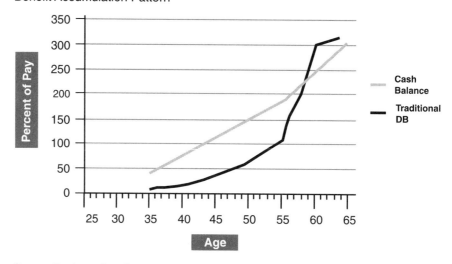

Traditional Defined-Benefits versus
Cash-Balance Plan Employee Hired at Age 30

Source: *Employee Benefits Journal,* June 1999.

discriminate against younger employees. At the same time, the guarantee features help to meet some of the retirement security objectives of the traditional defined-benefit plan.

Cash-balance plans have attracted current interest because some large companies have announced that they are converting their regular defined-benefit plans to the cash-balance variety. Some employers that have a traditional defined-benefit plan have become dissatisfied with the plan because of the rising costs for employees nearing retirement and the belief that younger employees do not find traditional defined-benefit plans attractive. Termination of the defined-benefit plan and substitution of a defined-contribution plan, if any, is costly to the employer because most or all of existing plan assets have to be immediately credited to participants. A less costly alternative is to revise the existing plan's formula into a cash-balance formula. Generally, the new formula provides a benefit equal to the greater of the cash-balance formula applied over all years of service or the amount earned under the old defined-benefit formula up to the date of the conversion. Existing benefits earned by employees are not lost, but some older employees may not receive much additional benefit under the cash-balance formula. Some plans provide a phase-in period to ease this adjustment.

There are a number of recent court cases that have raised questions about cash balance plans, and within a few years new legislation is expected that will resolve these issues.

Definition of Compensation

For formulas that are based on compensation, the definition of compensation provides some flexibility in planning. Definitions of compensation can be classified into two categories: **career average** and **final average.** With a career-average formula, the employee's compensation over the entire working period is averaged. Another way of putting this is that the benefit earned in a given year of service is based on the compensation for that year. Any defined-contribution formula is effectively a career-average formula, but defined-benefit plans can also use the career-average approach. In a final-average formula, the compensation used is averaged over a specified period of years, usually chosen to produce a relatively high benefit. For example, the compensation used in the benefit formula could be defined as compensation over the employee's five final years of service. To guard against the possibility of a salary decrease in the final years of service due to partial disability or other cause, many plans define compensation as the compensation over a specified consecutive period during which the average compensation is the highest.

In defining compensation for plan purposes, a decision must be made whether to use total compensation (salary or wages plus bonuses, overtime, and so forth) or some lesser amount, such as base salary only. Flexibility is permitted here, but if anything other than total compensation is used, the method chosen must not produce discrimination. For example, excluding overtime pay in the benefit formula may be discriminatory if lower-paid workers typically receive substantial overtime pay while prohibited group employees do not.

■ INFLATION PROTECTION

Inflation has been a persistent feature of the U.S. economy, at least since World War II. Although the rate of inflation has gone up and down during that period, many economists believe that some degree of inflation is a permanent structural feature of our economy. A qualified plan, particularly a defined-benefit pension plan, is a theoretically long-range program; levels are often determined for a 25-year-old employee's benefits that will not be paid until 40 years later. Thus, inflation is a serious problem in the design of pension plans.

Although no really satisfactory solution to the problem of inflation in private pension plans has yet been devised, there are some planning approaches that can help with this problem. A distinction can be made between approaches that are applied in the preretirement period while the employee is still at work and in the postretirement period, when the employee is least able to protect against inflation.

Preretirement Inflation

Some types of benefit design are inherently better able to cope with preretirement inflation than others. If the plan benefit depends on employee compensation, the final-average definition of compensation usually does a better job of protecting the employee against inflation than the career-average definition because the final-average definition bases benefits on the employee's highest compensation level. Much of the increase in an employee's compensation level over a working career merely reflects inflation. Other reasons for compensation increases are increases in general employee productivity and increases in the individual employee's merit, and both are also appropriately reflected in the retirement benefit. If the plan does not use a final-average formula, the employer should consider periodically reviewing the plan's benefit level in light of inflation and amending the plan to increase benefits as appropriate. It is also possible to include an automatic mechanism in the plan under which future benefit levels for current employees are increased in accordance with some kind of formula based on the inflation rate; however, this is rarely done.

Defined-contribution plans provide some inflation protection not available under defined-benefit plans because the benefit in the defined-contribution plan depends on the value of the investments in each participant's account. In the long run, a reasonably diversified investment portfolio tends to increase in value to keep pace with inflation. This is not necessarily true for short periods; in the 1970s, for example, common stocks often declined even as inflation reached new heights. However, most economists believe that the long-range linkage between asset values and inflation will continue, so defined-contribution plans can be useful in dealing with inflation. Naturally, for this to occur the investment portfolio has to be chosen to emphasize the types of assets—common stocks, for example—that typically show inflation-related growth.

A defined-contribution plan, however, has a disadvantage similar to that of a career-average benefit formula: contributions to the participant's account in the early years are based on then-current compensation, which typically is at a low level compared with later years. This disadvantage tends to reduce the advantage of possible investment-related growth.

Postretirement Inflation

In the postretirement period, one approach to inflation protection in defined benefit plans is indexing of retirement benefits. With an indexed formula, the plan provides that the benefit is to be increased after retirement in accordance with some formula contained in the plan. The design problem here is the choice of a formula that is affordable by the employer and that accurately reflects the impact of inflation on retirees.

One approach is to use the **consumer price index (CPI),** a price index provided by the government. The CPI is a measure of the relative rise from month to month of a "market basket" of consumer products purchased by a hypothetical average consumer. There is some debate as to whether the CPI accurately reflects the impact of inflation, particularly on retirees, because it may emphasize rising prices of items not normally purchased by retirees or, conversely, may understate the impact of rising prices for items particularly important to retirees. At one time, for example, the CPI had a large component reflecting the cost of new housing, which typically is not a significant item in retirees' budgets.

The government also provides various types of wage indexes indicating the increase in wages in specific portions of the work force. Theoretically, it is possible to index retirement benefits in accordance with a wage index. Based on past experience, this would produce a larger increase in retirement benefits than a price index because wage indexes reflect increases in productivity that have historically outdistanced inflationary price increases. However, in short-term periods, wage indexes can fall behind cost indexes such as the CPI. A theoretical advantage of wage indexing is that retirees will obtain the same protection against inflation as people currently in the work force (but no better). Whatever the merits of this argument, however, wage indexes are rarely used.

A third approach to indexing is to use a formula for increasing benefits that is included in the plan itself and is not dependent on external price or wage indexes. Such a formula makes it easier for the employer to anticipate the cost of the benefit increases. The risk of possibly running ahead of the CPI can be minimized by providing that the formula increase will not exceed an amount determined by reference to the CPI or other chosen economic indexes.

Indexed pension benefits are obviously attractive to participants, but currently they are not extensively used in the private pension system. This is because even a small annual or periodic percentage increase in pension benefits can result in a very large increase in the ultimate cost of the benefit. Private employers, therefore, often avoid indexing because of the possibility of incurring an uncontrollable future liability. However, indexing is quite common in pension programs of federal, state, and local government units. Elected officials often grant indexed pensions to government employees with the implicit expectation that taxpayers in the future (after current officials' terms have expired) will accept tax increases to fund the increased pension costs.

In the private sector, probably the most common mechanism for dealing with postretirement inflation is to increase pension benefits through ad hoc "supplemental payments" to retirees. At one time, there was some concern that a program of supplemental payments might be deemed a separate pension plan involving various federal regulatory complexities. However, to encourage employers to make such supplemental payments, the Labor Department has issued relatively permissive regulations concerning these payments. Under these regulations [Labor Regulations Section 2510.32(g)], a supplemental payment plan will not be treated as a separate pension plan but rather as a welfare plan, which is subject to much simpler regulatory requirements if the amount paid is limited by a formula that effectively restricts it to the cost-of-living increases that have occurred since the retirees' pension payments commenced. The supplemental payments can be made out of the employer's general assets or from a separate trust fund established for them. In addition, there are special provisions [Code Section 415(k)(2)] allowing employees to contribute additional amounts to a defined-benefit plan to provide cost-of-living adjustments to benefits.

■ THE ACCRUED BENEFIT

Under the vesting rules for qualified plans, many employees will be entitled to a benefit from their qualified plan if they terminate employment before retirement. Also, if an employer terminates a plan before all employees have retired, plan participants generally receive the benefits they have earned at that point. Therefore, the plan must provide a means of determining the amount of benefits payable to employees with a given termination date. To do this, the qualified plan benefit is treated as having been earned over the employee's entire period of employment. The amount of benefit earned as of a given date is referred to as the **accrued benefit** at that date. The concept of the accrued benefit is also important in determining annual plan costs under the plan's actuarial method, as discussed below.

Every qualified plan must include a means for determining the participant's accrued benefit. Furthermore, to prevent discrimination, Code Section 411(b) and extensive IRS regulations under Code Section 401(a)(4) require that benefits accrue at minimum specified rates. The purpose of the Section 411(b) benefit accrual rules is to prevent the plan from having an excessive amount of what is known as **backloading.** An extreme example of a backloaded plan would be one that had a normal retirement age of 65 with a provision that no employee who terminated employment prior to age 63 would receive any benefit under this plan. In effect, all of the benefits under this plan would accrue during the two years between ages 63 and 65. This much backloading is not permitted under current rules. Obviously, the purpose of the accrual rules is to prevent employers from favoring highly compensated employees who are the ones most likely to continue employment to later ages.

Benefit Accrual Rules

In a defined-contribution plan, a participant's accrued benefit is simply equal to the balance in that participant's account under the plan. The account balance includes employer and employee contributions, forfeitures from accounts of other employees, and investment earnings on the account, less any distributions from the account. If a defined-contribution plan has a nondiscriminatory contribution formula, there normally is no problem of backloading. Consequently, there are no specific rates of accrual required for defined-contribution plans.

For defined-benefit plans, however, benefits must accrue at a rate specified in Code Section 411(b). The plan's accrual rate must be at least as fast as one of three alternative minimum rules:

1. *Three Percent Rule.* Under this rule, the benefit accrued by a participant during each year of participation must be at least 3 percent of the maximum benefit that a hypothetical participant can accrue by entering at the plan's earliest entry age and participating until normal retirement.

2. *133⅓ Percent Rule.* Under this rule, the rate of benefits accrued in any given plan year cannot be more than 133⅓ percent of the rate of benefit accrual during any prior year.

3. *Fractional Rule.* Under this rule, the benefit the employee has accrued at the date of termination must be proportionate to the normal retirement benefit. The following requirement must be satisfied:

$$\text{Benefit on termination} = \begin{array}{c}\text{Normal retirement}\\ \text{benefit if participant}\\ \text{continued to normal}\\ \text{retirement age}\end{array} \times \begin{array}{c}\text{Years of actual participation}\\ \hline \text{Years of participation if}\\ \text{terminated at normal retirement}\end{array}$$

EXAMPLE

Suppose that an employee has participated in the plan for 20 years and terminates at age 55. The plan's normal retirement age is 65. If the employee had continued working to age 65, the plan would have provided an annuity of $12,000 per year beginning at age 65. The fractional rule would require a termination benefit of at least two-thirds of this, or $8,000 annually beginning at age 65. If the plan does not provide at least this amount, it must meet one of the other two benefit accrual rules or it will be disqualified.

The tendency is for most plans to provide a termination benefit based on the fractional rule, because it is simpler to design and explain to participants.

Fully insured plans are plans that are funded exclusively by the purchase of insurance contracts providing level annual premium payments to retirement and providing benefits guaranteed by an insurance company. These plans are not specifically subject to the preceding three accrual rules if the accrued benefit meets the following tests:

- The accrued benefit is not less than the cash surrender value of the participant's insurance contracts at any time.

- The insurance premiums are paid up, the insurance contracts are not subject to a security interest, and there are no policy loans outstanding.

The assumption is that if all these conditions are satisfied, plans funded with insurance contracts will automatically meet or exceed the benefit accrual test. Note that this exception applies only to fully insured plans, not to all plans that use an insurance contract or contracts for funding. The use of insurance contracts in plan funding is discussed later in this chapter.

■ BENEFITS AT TERMINATION OF EMPLOYMENT

The vesting provisions of a plan determine the amount of benefit that a participant is entitled to receive on terminating employment prior to retirement.

In a defined-contribution plan, the termination benefit is the vested portion of the participant's account balance. In defined-contribution plans, particularly profit-sharing plans, the account balance usually is distributed to the participant in full at termination of employment. It is technically possible to defer the distribution to the participant's normal retirement date, but this is rarely done in defined-contribution plans because it causes additional expense to the plan with little or no corresponding benefit to the employer or the plan. However, the plan may give the participant the option to leave the funds on deposit in the plan for withdrawal at a later date, to allow the participant to take advantage of the tax-deferred investment medium afforded by the plan, with a possible loss of favorable income tax treatment on the later plan distribution (see Chapter 25).

For a defined-benefit plan, the benefit on termination of employment is more complicated. The benefit will be the vested accrued benefit as of the date of termination, determined under the vesting and the accrual rules already described. Use the same example as in the discussion of the fractional accrued-benefit rule, again supposing that an employee terminates employment at age 55 after 20 years of service and the plan's normal retirement age is 65. If the participant is fully vested and the accrued benefit is $8,000 as discussed in the earlier example, an annuity of $8,000 per year will be payable beginning at age 65.

To make sure that terminated participants actually receive deferred vested benefits at retirement, which may be many years after termination, the employer must report all deferred vested benefits of terminated participants to the Social Security Administration, which then can inform retirees of their rights to benefits from plans of former employers.

In some cases, the deferred vested benefit may be such a small amount that keeping track of it until the participant's retirement is merely a nuisance for both employer and employee. The employer can treat the benefit as a **cashout**—that is, pay cash to the employee in lieu of the deferred vested benefit—without the employee's consent, so long as the entire benefit is distributed and the employer portion of the benefit so distributed does not exceed $5,000. The involuntary cashout must be within one year of termination of participation in the plan; the plan must have a provision permitting the employee to repay the cashout to the plan if the employee was not fully vested at the time of termination, in case the employee should resume participation in the plan. A cashout of a benefit that exceeds the $5,000 limit can be made, but only with the consent of the employee.

■ DEATH AND DISABILITY BENEFITS

Qualified plans are intended primarily to provide retirement benefits or, in the case of profit-sharing and similar plans, deferred-compensation benefits. However, the regulations indicate that a plan may provide for the payment of incidental death benefits through insurance or otherwise, and also that the plan may provide for the payment of a pension due to disability. Moreover, a qualified plan must in certain circumstances provide a survivorship pension to the participant's spouse.

Currently under Code Section 401(a)(11), two types of survivorship benefits are required: the **qualified joint and survivor annuity** and the **qualified preretirement survivor annuity**. All pension plans must provide these, but profit-sharing plans need not provide them if the participant's vested account balance is payable as a death benefit to the spouse. ESOPs and stock bonus plans generally do not have to provide spousal survivorship benefits.

Qualified Joint and Survivor Annuity

The qualified joint and survivor annuity is a postretirement death benefit for the spouse. Plans subject to this requirement must provide, as an automatic form of benefit, an annuity for the life of the participant with a survivor annuity for the life of the participant's spouse. The survivor annuity must be not less than 50 percent of nor greater than the annuity payable during the joint lives of participant and spouse. The spouse annuity must be continued even if the spouse remarries. The joint and survivor annuity must be at least the actuarial equivalent of the plan's normal form of benefit or any optional form of benefit offered under the plan. Optional benefit forms are discussed further in Chapter 25.

The qualified joint and survivor form must be offered automatically to a married participant at retirement. The participant may elect to receive another form of benefit if the plan so provides; however, the spouse must consent in writing to the election and the consent form must be notarized or witnessed by a plan representative. An election to waive the joint and survivor form must be made during a 90-day period ending on the annuity starting date. A waiver of the joint and survivor annuity can be revoked—the participant can change the election during the 90-day period. The plan administrator must provide the participant with a notice of the election period and an explanation of the consequences of the election within a reasonable period before the annuity starting date.

Preretirement Survivor Annuity

Code Section 401(a)(11) mandates a preretirement death benefit for the spouse of a vested plan participant. The survivor annuity payable if the participant dies before retirement is the amount that would have been paid under a qualified joint and survivor annuity, computed as if the participant had either (1) retired on the day before his or her death or (2) separated from service on the date of death and survived to the plan's earliest retirement age, then retired with an immediate joint and survivor annuity. For a defined-contribution plan, a qualified preretirement survivor annuity is an annuity for the life of the surviving spouse actuarially equivalent to at least 50 percent of the participant's vested account balance as of the date of death.

As with the qualified joint and survivor annuity, a participant can elect to receive an alternative form of preretirement survivorship benefit, including a benefit that does not provide for the spouse. However, written consent by the spouse is required for such an election. The right to make such an election must be communicated to all participants with a vested benefit who have attained age 32, and the participant can elect to waive the preretirement survivor annuity at any time after age 35.

Subsidizing Survivor Annuities

A plan can provide that a participant who receives either the qualified joint and survivor annuity or the preretirement survivor annuity will receive an annuity payment lower than the amount that would be paid under a straight-life annuity; the reduction reflects the extra cost to the plan of the survivorship feature. For example, the normal form of benefit might be a straight-life annuity of $1,000 per month, but the joint and survivor annuity might pay only $800 per month while both spouses survived, then $400 per month to the survivor. However, a plan is permitted to subsidize all or part of the cost of the survivorship feature. If the survivorship feature is fully subsidized, the plan does not have to allow the participant to elect an alternative form of benefit.

Incidental Death Benefits

A qualified plan may provide a death benefit over and above the survivorship benefits required by law. In a defined-contribution plan, probably the most common form of death benefit is a provision that the participant's vested account balance will be paid to the participant's designated beneficiary in the event of the participant's death before retirement or termination of service. Defined-benefit plans, unless they use insurance as discussed later, usually do not provide an additional death benefit; in such cases, the survivors receive no death benefit except for whatever survivor annuity the plan provides.

To provide any substantial preretirement death benefit, it is usually necessary for the plan to purchase life insurance. This provides the plan with significant funds at a participant's death; it is particularly important in the early years of a participant's employment, when the participant's accrued benefit is still relatively small. An insured preretirement death benefit can be provided in either a defined-benefit or defined-contribution plan. Contributions to the plan by the employer may be used to pay life insurance premiums, as long as the amount qualifies under the tests for incidental benefits.

In general, the IRS considers that nonretirement benefits such as life, medical, or disability insurance in a qualified plan will be incidental and therefore permissible, as long as the cost of providing these benefits is less than 25 percent of the cost of providing all the benefits under the plan. In applying this approach to life insurance benefits, the 25 percent rule is applied to the portion of any life insurance premium that is used to provide current life insurance protection. Any portion of the premium used to increase the cash value of the policy is considered a contribution to the plan fund available to pay retirement benefits and is not considered in the 25 percent limitation.

The IRS has ruled, using its general 25 percent test, that if a qualified plan provides death benefits using ordinary life insurance (life insurance with a cash value), the death benefit will be considered incidental if either (1) less than 50 percent of the total cumulative employer contribution credited to each participant's account has been used to purchase ordinary life insurance or (2) the face amount of the policies does not exceed 100 times the anticipated monthly normal retirement benefit or the accumulated reserve under the life insurance policy, whichever is greater. In practice, defined-benefit plans using ordinary life insurance are usually designed to take advantage of the 100-times rule, while defined-contribution plans, including profit-sharing plans, that use ordinary life contracts generally make use of the 50 percent test.

If term insurance contracts are used to provide the death benefit, the 25 percent test will be applied to the entire premium, and the aggregate premiums paid for insurance on each participant should be less than 25 percent of aggregate additions to the employee's account. Term insurance is sometimes used to fund death benefits in defined-contribution plans but rarely in defined-benefit plans.

The discussion so far is somewhat simplified because insurance can be used in qualified plans in many ways, and the IRS has issued many rulings, both revenue rulings and letter rulings, applying the basic 25 percent test to a variety of different fact situations. Thus, there is considerable room for creative design of life insurance-funded death benefits within qualified plans.

If life insurance is provided for a participant through a qualified plan (i.e., by using employer contributions to the plan to pay premiums for the insurance), part or all of the cost of the insurance is currently taxable to the participant. Life insurance provided by the plan is not considered part of a Section 79 group term plan, and consequently the $50,000 exclusion under Section 79 does not apply.

If cash value life insurance is used and if all of the death proceeds are payable to the participant's estate or beneficiary, the **term cost,** or cost of the **pure amount at risk,** is taxable income to the employee. The term cost is the difference between the face amount of insurance and the cash surrender value of the policy at the end of the policy year. In other words, the cost of the policy's cash value is not currently taxable to the employee because the cash value is considered part of the plan fund to be used to provide the retirement benefit. The term cost is calculated using a table of rates (Table 24.2) provided by the IRS, known as Table 2001.

If the plan uses term insurance rather than cash-value insurance to provide an insured death benefit, the cost of the entire face amount of insurance is taxable to the employee. Similarly, if the plan provides medical or disability insurance for participants, the entire cost of the insurance is taxable to the employee, unless the insurance can be excluded under Code Section 106 as part of the employer's medical or disability plan.

Planning Considerations

It is relatively uncommon for a qualified plan to provide medical, disability, or term life insurance to participants because the tax treatment provides no advantage to the employee in so doing. It is more common, however, to use cash-value life insurance as funding for the plan because the cost to the employee using Table 2001 may prove to be a relatively favorable way to provide life insurance. The use of life insurance for funding qualified plans will be discussed further below.

The decision whether to include life insurance in a qualified plan relates to the employee benefit design objective of efficiency. The employer must first decide whether and to what extent it will provide death benefits to employees. Death benefits can be provided for employees under group term plans and other plans as well as providing them as an incidental benefit in qualified plans. The death benefit should be designed to produce the lowest employer and employee cost for the benefit level desired. A death benefit should be included in the qualified plan only to the extent it is consistent with this objective.

TABLE 24.2	One-Year Term Premiums For $1,000 of Life Insurance Protection—One Life				
Age	Premium	Age	Premium	Age	Premium
0	$0.70	35	$ .99	70	$20.62
1	0.41	36	1.01	71	22.72
2	0.27	37	1.04	72	25.07
3	0.19	38	1.06	73	27.57
4	0.13	39	1.07	74	30.18
5	0.13	40	1.10	75	33.05
6	0.14	41	1.13	76	36.33
7	0.15	42	1.20	77	40.17
8	0.16	43	1.29	78	44.33
9	0.16	44	1.40	79	49.23
10	0.16	45	1.53	80	54.56
11	0.19	46	1.67	81	60.51
12	0.24	47	1.83	82	66.74
13	0.28	48	1.98	83	73.07
14	0.33	49	2.13	84	80.35
15	0.38	50	2.30	85	88.76
16	0.52	51	2.52	86	99.16
17	0.57	52	2.81	87	110.40
18	0.59	53	3.20	88	121.85
19	0.61	54	3.65	89	133.40
20	0.62	55	4.15	90	144.30
21	0.62	56	4.68	91	155.80
22	0.64	57	5.20	92	168.75
23	0.66	58	5.66	93	186.44
24	0.68	59	6.06	94	206.70
25	0.71	60	6.51	95	228.35
26	0.73	61	7.11	96	250.01
27	0.76	62	7.96	97	265.09
28	0.80	63	9.08	98	270.11
29	0.83	64	10.41	99	281.05
30	0.87	65	11.90		
31	0.90	66	13.51		
32	0.93	67	15.20		
33	0.96	68	16.92		
34	0.98	69	18.70		

Disability Benefits from Qualified Plans

A qualified plan may provide as an incidental benefit a pension payable upon disability. The plan must provide a specific definition of disability. Usually some minimum service or age requirements are imposed to appropriately restrict the class of participants entitled to the disability pension. The disability benefit may be the participant's accrued benefit actuarially reduced because of a commencement date earlier than normal retirement, or the plan may provide some subsidy of the disability benefit to be sure that it is adequate for the participant's needs.

It is becoming increasingly common for companies to cover disability through separate benefit programs, often insured. These were discussed in Chapter 8. Such programs tend to be fairer and more efficient than providing disability coverage as an incidental benefit under a qualified plan. In all events, the planner should be sure that there is no duplication of disability coverage between the qualified plan and a separate short-term or long-term disability plan of the employer.

Qualified plans that do not provide immediate disability coverage prior to normal retirement age should, however, include some provision for the treatment of the employee's retirement benefit if the employee becomes disabled. Separate long-term disability programs usually cease paying benefits when the participant reaches age 65 or other normal retirement age. After this age, the company's retirement plan must provide whatever income the participant will receive from the employer. Therefore, from an employee's standpoint, the plan should be designed so that the retirement benefit will be adequate when long-term disability benefits cease. For example, the plan might provide that a participant who is disabled as defined in the plan will continue to receive service credit for purposes of vesting or benefit accrual, or both. The definition of disability in the plan should be coordinated with the definition in the employer's long-term disability plan. The plan also should indicate what definition of compensation will be used to determine retirement benefits if the participant becomes disabled before retirement.

■ FUNDING OF QUALIFIED PLANS

The assets of a qualified plan must be held either by a trustee or by an insurance company. It is also possible to hold plan funds in a bank custodial account that is not technically a trust, but under Code Section 401(f), such an account is treated the same as a trust for all practical purposes. The trustee or insurance company is referred to as the plan's **funding agency**.

Plan assets are held by a funding agency under a legal document called a **funding instrument**—either a **trust agreement** or an **insurance contract**, depending on the funding agency. There are many legal requirements applicable to a funding instrument; these are discussed in this chapter and in Chapter 27. Within these requirements, however, there is opportunity for flexibility in plan design, funding procedures, and investment policy. The employer's choices in these areas are an important part of qualified plan design.

Trusts

The trust is the leading funding agency for qualified plans, in terms of both the number of employees covered and aggregate plan assets. A trust used for qualified plan funding is based on the same general principles of trust law as trusts used for other purposes, such as estate planning and administering the affairs of minors or incompetent persons. A trust is an arrangement involving three parties—the grantor of the trust, the trustee, and the beneficiaries. In qualified plan funding, the grantor is the employer and the beneficiaries are the employees. The trustee is a party holding funds contributed by the employer for the benefit of employees.

Legally speaking, a trustee is a *fiduciary*. A fiduciary is a person or organization that holds money on behalf of someone else (here, the plan participants and beneficiaries) and that must administer that money solely in the interest of those other persons. The trustee's compensation is a fee for services rendered; the trustee is prohibited from personally profiting as a result of investing the trust funds.

The duties of a qualified plan trustee, like those of any other trustee, are set out in a formal trust agreement. Usually, the duties of a plan trustee are to accept employer contributions, invest those contributions, accumulate the earnings, and pay benefits to plan participants and beneficiaries out of the plan fund. The trustee performs these acts only at the direction of the plan administrator and not at the trustee's own discretion. However, in some cases, a trustee is given direct responsibility for choosing plan investments or choosing an investment adviser. The trustee must account periodically to the plan administrator or the employer for all investments, receipts, and disbursements. The trustee does not guarantee the payment of benefits or the adequacy of the trust fund to pay benefits. That remains the obligation of the employer.

A trustee may be an individual or group of individuals or a commercial entity such as a bank or trust company. Often employers name individual trustees, such as the company president or a major shareholder, to obtain an extra measure of control over plan assets. This is permissible under the law; however, when acting as trustee, such an individual is legally obligated to act solely in the interests of the plan participants and beneficiaries and not in the interests of the employer or shareholders.

Although a qualified plan trust is created and exists under the laws of the state in which it is established, the most significant provisions of trust law affecting qualified plan trusts have been codified in federal statutes that supersede state law whenever they apply. The area of trust investments and related issues is treated in more detail in Chapter 27.

Insurance Contracts

Because insurance companies are regulated by the states to ensure their financial soundness, the law permits qualified plans to be funded through contracts issued by insurance companies. Insurance contracts used in funding qualified plans can be divided into *allocated* and *unallocated* types. When funding is allocated under an insurance contract, this means that the insurer has assumed the employer's obligation to pay specific benefits to specific participants. The employer is still primarily responsible, but under the terms of the insurance contract, participants and the employer can look to the insurance company for payment of specific amounts. An example of allocated funding would be a plan that is funded exclusively with life insurance and annuity contracts (a *fully insured* plan under Code Section 412(i)—see page 620). With unallocated funding, the insurance company acts as a holder of the funds, much like a bank trustee. With unallocated funding, the insurance company is, of course, obligated to deal prudently with the funds, but it makes no guarantee that the funds will be adequate to pay any specific benefits under the plan. An insurance contract used in a qualified plan can be either purely allocated or purely unallocated, or it can offer a mixture of both.

Individual Life Insurance and Annuity Contracts

For qualified plans of employers with few employees, particularly defined-benefit plans, one of the most common funding methods traditionally has been the use of individual life insurance or annuity contracts. These contracts are typically level premium contracts. Once a benefit level for a given employee has been determined, the benefit is funded using life insurance or annuity contracts with equal annual premiums paid by the employer until the employee's retirement.

Insurance contracts can be divided into two types—those providing only term insurance and those with a cash value. Term insurance contracts are not suitable as funding instruments for qualified plans, although they can be used by the plan to provide incidental insurance. Cash value contracts, on the other hand, can be used in a qualified plan to provide both retirement benefits and death benefits because they are designed to accumulate a reserve that, if the insured lives long enough, grows to a size sufficient to pay the entire face amount of the contract's death benefit. The purpose for the accumulation of this reserve is to allow the policy to be offered to the insured with the assurance of a level premium for a long period of time—the excess cost in early years is used to provide insurance in later years. Term insurance, by comparison, increases in cost each year as the insured grows older; there is no reserve for any period longer than one year. The reserve feature of cash value contracts means that such a contract is an investment medium that can be used in funding a qualified plan.

The most familiar cash value insurance contract, usually referred to as the **whole life contract**, provides increasing cash values up to an advanced age, such as 90 or more. Until that age, the scheduled cash value is usually less than the face amount of the death benefit, although many policies provide dividends that accelerate the cash value increase considerably. As discussed later in this chapter, the death benefit in a qualified plan cannot be increased to an amount greater than 100 times the expected monthly pension, and a whole life policy with this level of death benefit cannot be used to provide the sole funding for the retirement benefit in a qualified plan with a normal retirement age of 65, because its cash value at age 65 is usually insufficient. If whole life contracts are used in funding a qualified plan, it is also necessary to include an additional trust called a **side fund** or **conversion fund** to hold the additional investment assets that are necessary. Another approach, rarely used currently because of its high costs, is to use life insurance contracts with rapidly rising cash values called **retirement income contracts**. These contracts provide a cash value at the participant's retirement age that is sufficient to fund the retirement benefit.

> **EXAMPLE**
> If the plan provides a monthly pension of $100 per month, no more than $10,000 of whole life insurance can be provided, and the cash value of a $10,000 policy at age 65 is usually insufficient to provide a pension of $100 per month. If whole life policies are used to fund a qualified plan, the plan fund must be supplemented with a side fund or conversion fund.

Fully Insured Plans

A *fully insured plan* is a defined benefit plan that is funded exclusively by the purchase of individual insurance or annuity contracts that meets the following requirements:

- The contracts provide for the payment of premiums in equal annual amounts over a period no longer than the preretirement period of employment.
- The plan benefits are equal to those guaranteed by the insurance carrier under the contracts.
- The premiums on the contracts have been paid when due or, if there has been a lapse, the policy has been reinstated.
- No rights under the insurance contract have been subject to a security interest at any time during the plan year.
- No policy loans are outstanding at any time during the plan year.

A fully insured plan has a number of advantages. First, the benefits are generally more secure than with any other type of funding, because of the insurance company benefit guarantees and the regulation of insurance companies. Also, insurance companies typically provide relatively low-cost plan design and administrative services in connection with these plans. Another advantage derives from the funding pattern for fully insured plans. Fully insured plans tend to use level annual funding, by comparison to regular trust-fund plans, which have a pattern of increasing annual funding. This "upfront" pattern of deductible contributions to fully insured plans maximizes the tax benefits from the plan by allowing tax deductions earlier than in a regular plan. This feature may be attractive to businesses that want to maximize tax benefits, typically smaller, closely held businesses where the owners benefit significantly from the plan.

Plans that are fully insured are exempt from the minimum funding standards discussed below, as long as the contracts meet the above conditions. This is an additional advantage because it simplifies plan administration.

■ ACTUARIAL METHODS AND ASSUMPTIONS

The final or ultimate cost of a qualified plan cannot be determined until the last benefit dollar has been paid to the last surviving plan participant. However, the ultimate cost is not of immediate concern to the employer. Rather, the employer wants to know what the annual cost burden of the plan will be, particularly over the first several years of the plan. For a defined-contribution plan, this is not difficult to determine; the plan document itself specifies the amount of annual contribution that is required, usually in terms of some parameter of business operations, such as payroll or profits. Thus, it is not difficult to get an idea of the kind of burden the business will be assuming if it adopts this kind of plan. For a defined-benefit plan, however, actuarial methods and assumptions determine the annual cost, because the plan itself specifies only the benefits that will be paid.

Under current law, all qualified defined-benefit plans subject to the funding provisions of ERISA must provide advance funding over the working lives of the participants, using an actuarial cost method and assumptions. The ERISA funding requirements apply basically to all qualified defined-benefit plans of private employers. Certain government and church plans are exempted from coverage, as well as certain types of plans having no employer contributions. Also, fully insured plans are treated under special rules described ealier in this chapter.

An **actuarial cost method** is a method of determining an annual employer contribution for a given set of plan benefits and group of employees. The method produces a schedule of annual contributions aimed at providing a plan fund sufficient to make all benefit payments when they come due without any further contributions by the employer. There are a number of permitted actuarial cost methods, and these provide a range of annual deductible contributions for the employer for a given plan and group of employees.

EXAMPLE

Actuarial methods is a complex topic beyond the scope of this book. However, as a simplified illustration, just to give some idea of the range of possibilities, a level-funding method aims at equalizing the amount of annual deposits over the period to a participant's retirement. An accrued-benefit method, by contrast, aims at funding each year only the amount actually earned as a retirement benefit during that year. Generally, for a given benefit formula for a given participant, the level-funding method would produce a higher annual deposit in the earlier years of the plan. So an employer might choose the level-funding method if it had enough funds available and wanted to maximize tax-deductible contributions in the early years.

Actuarial assumptions refer to assumptions about future investment return and the character of the employee group that are made to determine the annual contribution.

Choosing an Actuarial Cost Method

The initial choice of an actuarial cost method may be affected by the employer's concerns as to how plan costs will be spread over future years. Certain methods will often produce a lower initial cost than other methods and might be chosen if the employer wishes to minimize costs at the plan's inception with the expectation of increased funding

EXAMPLE
Actuarial assumptions include, among others, investment return and mortality. An investment return assumption of 10 percent is an assumption that current amounts deposited into the plan will earn 10 percent annually. For a given amount needed in the future, a 10 percent assumption therefore will require a lower annual deposit than a 5 percent assumption. Similarly, a high mortality assumption assumes that a larger than average number of employees will die before receiving benefits. The higher this mortality assumption, the lower the amount of the annual deposits to the plan.

in later years. Sometimes this deferral of funding can lead to underfunding of plans in declining industries.

Some employers might prefer to *maximize* initial contributions. This is often the case when a plan benefits mostly key employees and the employer wishes to maximize tax-sheltering effects. An example of such an approach is the fully insured pension plan, discussed on page 620.

Sometimes, employers wish to match pension costs as closely as possible to payroll costs. In that situation, an actuarial approach known as the *aggregate* method is typically used because it expresses normal cost as a percentage of participants' compensation and thus rises automatically with payroll costs. The aggregate method is typically used with larger employee groups for this reason, although it produces the same results with a smaller group of employees as well.

Methods that spread costs over too many years can produce problems of underfunding. If a plan's initial funding method proves unacceptable in practice, the plan administrator can change the actuarial assumptions or method.

Ongoing Actuarial Valuations

A qualified plan's funding experience is likely to deviate somewhat from the assumptions made in determining first-year cost. If the deviations are significant enough, one response may be to change the actuarial methods or assumptions. There are, however, other ways to deal with variations from the initial assumptions.

The assets of all qualified plans are valued periodically by the actuary. Under ERISA, the valuation must be made at least once every three years. If the plan assets are found to be insufficient, there is an actuarial deficiency (or **experience loss**), which is made up with increased contributions that are usually deposited (**amortized**) over a period of years. Similarly, if there is an actuarial surplus (or **experience gain**), contributions are decreased over future years. The minimum funding standards, discussed below, determine how rapidly these experience gains and losses must be amortized.

The valuation of the plan's assets may be made on the basis of any reasonable valuation method, as long as the method takes into account the fair market value of the assets—rather than using cost or some other purely formal method of valuation. The regulations under Section 412 specify rules that must be used in valuation. For example, debt instruments may be valued by amortizing the difference between initial cost and maturity value over the life of the bond, because it may not be possible to determine current fair market value by market quotations. Also, because valuations are relatively infrequent, the plan can use any reasonable and consistent procedure for averaging actual market value over a period of years or smoothing out the fluctuations in the market value of assets.

■ MINIMUM FUNDING STANDARDS

The *minimum funding standards* of Code Section 412 and corresponding ERISA provisions provide the legal structure for enforcing the advance funding requirement that applies to qualified pension plans. A plan to which the minimum funding standard applies must maintain a **funding standard account**. The funding standard account is annually charged with the plan's normal cost and certain other costs and credited with certain items that benefit the plan. At the end of the year, if the charges exceed the credits, there may be an **accumulated funding deficiency**. In that case, there is a penalty tax and other enforcement provisions. The penalty tax consists of an initial tax of 5 percent of the deficiency, with an additional 100 percent tax if the deficiency is not corrected after notification by the IRS.

Obviously, the employer's objective is to *balance* the funding standard account for each year. If the employer is unable to make sufficient contributions to do this, the employer can request a waiver from the IRS of the minimum funding standard for the plan year or request an extended amortization period for certain plan liabilities.

The employer is not required to contribute annually any more to the plan than an amount referred to as the **full funding limitation**, even if the funding standard account would then be left with a deficit for the plan year. This important limitation is generally defined as the difference between the accrued actuarial liability of the plan computed under the plan's funding method (or if this is not possible, under the entry-age normal method) and the value of the plan assets. Finally, certain plans are allowed to establish an **alternative minimum funding standard account** and can then avoid a funding deficiency by avoiding a deficit in either the funding standard account or the alternative minimum funding standard account, whichever is lesser. The alternative minimum funding standard account is somewhat simpler than the funding standard account and it is usually possible to avoid a deficit with a lower employer contribution.

Exemptions from the Minimum Funding Standard

The minimum funding standard rules basically apply to all qualified pension plans. However, government plans, church plans that have not elected to be treated as qualified plans, and various types of plans having no employer contributions are exempted in Code Section 412.

More significantly, the minimum funding standards do not apply to profit-sharing or stock bonus plans. Technically, the standards apply to defined-contribution pension plans as well as defined-benefit pension plans. However, for defined-contribution pension plans (money-purchase and target plans), the minimum funding standard will be met, so long as the employer contributes the amount required under the plan's contribution formula each year.

As discussed earlier, fully insured plans are exempt from the minimum funding standards.

■ DEDUCTIBILITY OF PENSION PLAN CONTRIBUTIONS

Excessive contributions to a pension plan fund, if they are allowed to be deducted, will accelerate the employer's tax deduction and thereby increase the tax benefit of the qualified plan beyond what is considered appropriate. To prevent this, there are specific limits on the amount of pension plan contributions that an employer can deduct in a given plan year.

Unlike the deduction limit for defined-contribution plans, which is 25 percent of payroll (see Chapter 22), the deduction limit for defined-benefit plans is based on actuarial considerations. For a given plan year, an employer can deduct contributions to a defined-benefit plan up to a limit determined by the largest of three amounts [Code Section 404(a)(1)].

1. The amount necessary to satisfy the minimum funding standard for the year.

2. The amount necessary to fund benefits based on past and current service on a level funding basis over the years remaining to retirement for each employee. However, if the remaining unfunded cost for any three individuals is more than 50 percent of the total of the unfunded costs, fundings for those three individuals must be distributed over a period of at least five taxable years.

3. An amount equal to the normal cost of the plan plus, if there is a supplemental liability, an amount necessary to amortize the supplemental liability in equal annual payments over a ten-year period.

In determining the applicable limitation, the funding methods and the actuarial assumptions used must be the same as those used for purposes of the minimum funding standards. Furthermore. the tax deduction for a given plan year cannot exceed the full funding limitation that was discussed earlier. Thus, there is little incentive for the employer to contribute beyond the full funding limitation.

Although these limits are expressed in actuarial language, the implications are relatively easy to understand. First of all, if the plan is funded on the basis of individual insurance contracts, the second limit will generally be the one applicable to the plan because most such contracts have premiums determined on the basis of level funding for the years remaining until retirement for each employee. On the other hand, plans funded with group contracts and trust funds using a variety of actuarial methods and assumptions will generally be governed by the third alternative limit.

Note that this limit specifies the *maximum* deductible amount. The amount required to be contributed under the minimum funding standard as applied to the plan may be somewhat less than this limit. Therefore, in a given plan year, the employer's actual contribution and deduction may be less than the maximum limit that applies. This is one of the reasons why a defined-benefit plan with a group pension contract or trust fund can be relatively flexible for the employer. Between the minimum limit required by the minimum funding standards and the maximum deductible limit discussed earlier, there may be a relatively comfortable range of contributions that can be adjusted according to the employer's specific financial situation.

Technically, the rules previously stated apply to both defined-benefit and defined-contribution pension plans. However, for defined-contribution plans, the minimum funding standards are satisfied whenever the employer makes the annual contributions specified by the plan document. In other words, the limit on the amount deductible under a defined-contribution pension plan is simply the amount specified in the plan document. For example, the plan document in a money-purchase plan might require that each year the employer must contribute an amount equal to 6 percent of each employee's compensation to that employee's account. The total of such contributions would then be both the amount required by the minimum funding standard and the maximum amount deductible.

If an employer has a combination of defined-benefit and defined-contribution plans covering the same employee or employees, a percentage deduction limit applies. The deduction for a given year cannot exceed the greater of 25 percent of the common payroll (compensation of employees covered under both plans) or the amount required to meet the minimum funding standard for the defined-benefit plan alone. As discussed in Chapter 26, this provision has its greatest impact on highly compensated employees.

Penalty for Nondeductible Contributions

Generally, there is no advantage in contributing more to a plan than is deductible, because not only is the deduction for the excess unavailable but under Code Section 4972, a 10 percent penalty is imposed on the nondeductible portion of the contribution, with some exceptions. However, if nondeductible contributions are made, they can be carried over and deducted in future years. The deduction limit for future years, however, applies to the combination of carried-over and current contributions.

Timing of Deductions

The rules for timing of contributions and deductions for qualified plans are relatively favorable. Contributions will be deemed to be made by the employer for a given taxable year of the employer, and will be deductible for that year, if they are made by the time prescribed for filing the employer's tax return for that year, including extensions. For example, a corporation using a calendar year could contribute to the plan for 2004 as late as September 15, 2005 (the basic tax filing date of March 15, plus the maximum six-month extension). The rules for timing of contributions and deductions are the same for both cash and accrual-method taxpayers; there is no advantage for this purpose in using the accrual method.

■ KEY TERMS

accrued benefit	final average	pay credit
accumulated funding deficiency	flat-benefit formula	pure amount at risk
	flat-amount formula	replacement ratio
actuarial cost method	flat-percentage formula	retirement income contracts
alternative minimum funding standard account	full funding limitation	qualified joint and survivor annuity
	fully insured plans	
amortized	funding agency	qualified preretirement survivor annuity
backloading	funding instrument	
career average	funding standard account	side fund
cashout	guaranteed-account formula	term cost
		trust agreement
consumer price index (CPI)	insurance contract	unit-benefit formula
conversion fund	interest credit	whole life contract
experience gain	past service	
experience loss		

■ STUDY QUESTIONS

1. Explain how a defined-benefit plan tends to favor employees who enter the plan at a later age.

2. Describe the replacement ratio approach to benefit formula design.

3. a. What is a flat-benefit formula?

   b. Explain how a flat-benefit formula may create a problem of fairness among employees.

   c. How can this problem be resolved?

4. A firm has two long-time devoted employees. A retirement plan is about to be adopted and the employer desires to provide these two older employees with an adequate retirement benefit at retirement.

   a. What type of plan should the employer adopt?

   b. What special provision should be included in the plan to achieve the employer's objective?

5. What is a cash-balance plan and how does it operate?

6. Distinguish between a career-average formula and a final-average formula in a defined-benefit plan.

7. What kinds of qualified plans are inherently better able to cope with preretirement inflation?

8. For defined-benefit plans, benefits must accrue at an accrual rate that must be at least as rapid as one of the three alternative minimum rules. What are these rules?

9. a. What is a qualified joint and survivor annuity?

   b. What rules affect the amount of the joint and survivor annuity?

   c. What requirements apply to a joint and survivor annuity that must be offered to married participants as part of a qualified plan?

10. a. What is a preretirement survivor annuity?

    b. How is the amount of a preretirement survivor annuity determined?

11. Explain the rules that determine whether a death benefit that is funded with life insurance is considered incidental in a qualified plan.

12. Explain how the taxable income to an employee is determined when employer-provided life insurance is included in a qualified plan.

13. Why might you recommend that an employer include life insurance in a qualified plan?

14. a. What is a trust?

    b. What is the role of a trustee?

15. What is the difference between allocated and unallocated insurance contracts used in funding qualified pension plans?

16. Define

    a. Actuarial method

    b. Actuarial assumption

17. What types of plans are subject to the minimum funding requirements?

25

Qualified Plan Distributions and Loans

- Review the management issues in designing plan distribution provisions.
- Describe the normal and optional forms of benefit payments that are available for distributions from qualified plans and explain the restrictions imposed on distributions.
- Describe the federal taxation of distributions from a qualified plan that occurs at the following:
  1. Over more than one taxable year
  2. In one taxable year
  3. At death
- Explain the rules applying to loans from qualified plans.

CHAPTER OUTLINE

MANAGEMENT ISSUES IN DESIGN OF DISTRIBUTION PROVISIONS

Employee interests are best served by maximum flexibility in plan distribution provisions. However, plan designers may find it necessary to reduce this flexibility somewhat to meet the employer's management objectives.

First of all, flexibility increases administrative complexity and costs. In addition, flexibility can potentially cause cash-flow and liquidity problems to the plan fund. Finally, flexibility can create extremely complex federal income tax problems, due to the inordinately complex rules in this area. The rules are merely summarized in this chapter, but the reader will undoubtedly note that even this summary is startlingly complicated. The complexity is probably due more to congressional inattention to this issue rather than to any clear policy rationale. Simplification is on the congressional agenda.

The complex distribution rules are management's problem as well as the participant's because employees often ask employers about the tax treatment of a plan distribution. An employer's wrong answer likely will subject the employer to liability to reimburse the employee for any excess tax payments that result. And management cannot simply "stonewall" on this issue by refusing to advise employees on tax treatment of distributions because employee resentment as well as legal liability may result that can negate the value of the plan as an employee incentive.

The planner's objective in designing plan distribution provisions is to provide employees with the maximum amount of distribution flexibility that is consistent with management's needs as outlined above. In a small business with limited personnel management resources, this may dictate only very limited distribution flexibility. For example, some smaller plans provide for distributions only in the form of a lump sum at retirement or termination of employment.

Normal Form of Benefit

A qualified plan must specify not only the amount of the benefit but the form of the benefit. In a defined-benefit plan, the **normal form of benefit** is the basic "defined benefit," the form that quantifies the benefit due and provides a standard for calculating equivalent alternative benefits. At one time, the normal form was the form a participant received if he or she did not choose an alternative form, but this is not necessarily true because of joint and survivor provisions.

The normal form in a defined-benefit plan is usually either a **straight-life annuity** or a **life annuity with period certain**. A straight-life annuity simply provides periodic (usually monthly) payments for the participant's life. A life annuity with period certain provides periodic payments for the participant's life, but additionally provides that if the participant dies before the end of a specified period of years, payments will be continued until the end of that period to the participant's designated beneficiary. Specified periods of 10, 15, and 20 years are commonly used.

In comparing defined-benefit plans, it must be remembered that straight-life annuities and life annuities with periods certain are not equivalent; a plan providing an annuity of $100 per month for life with period certain as the normal form of benefit provides a significantly larger benefit than a plan providing $100 per month as a straight-life annuity. Period-certain annuities as the normal form of benefit are most commonly found in plans using insurance contracts for funding.

As discussed in Chapter 24, a pension plan must automatically provide a qualified joint and survivor annuity for the participant and spouse to a married participant (unless the participant elects otherwise). To avoid discrimination against single participants, most plans provide that the qualified joint and survivor annuity is "actuarially equivalent" to the normal form. For example, if the normal retirement benefit would be $1,000 per month as a straight-life annuity, the qualified joint and survivor annuity might be something like $800 per month to the participant for life, then $400 per month to the spouse for life. However, the plan can partially or fully subsidize the joint and survivor annuity; for example, it might provide a straight-life annuity of $1,000 per month or a

$1,000/$500 joint and survivor annuity. This might be desirable to the employer even though it would discriminate against unmarried participants.

Defined-contribution pension plans (such as money-purchase plans) can provide an annuity as the normal benefit form. This is particularly common if an insurance contract is used for funding. The amount of the annuity depends on the participant's account balance at retirement, with annuity purchase rates specified in the insurance contract, if any. Optional forms of benefit, particularly a lump sum, are usually provided in defined-contribution plans. Profit-sharing and other types of defined-contribution plans generally do not provide annuity forms of benefit because they can avoid the joint and survivor benefit rules if they do not include an annuity form of benefit.

Optional Alternative Forms of Benefit

Participants generally benefit from having a choice of benefit forms as an alternative to the normal form. Participants can then choose a benefit that is structured in accordance with their individual financial needs, family situations, and retirement activities. In defined-benefit plans, the most common alternative forms (assuming a straight-life annuity as the normal form) are, in addition to the qualified joint and survivor annuity that must be offered, (1) joint and survivor annuities for the participant and spouse or other beneficiary, with varying survivorship annuity percentages such as 50 percent, 75 percent, and 100 percent, and (2) annuities for the participant and beneficiary, with varying periods certain, such as 5, 10, 15, or 20 years. The plan also can allow payouts over a fixed period of years without a life contingency. All these options are subject to the limitations described below.

To avoid undesirable or prohibited discrimination among employees in different situations, the plan should provide that any optional benefit is actuarially equivalent to the normal form of benefit. Under Code Section 401(a)(25), the actuarial assumptions used for this purpose must be specified in the plan, either by stating the actuarial interest and other factors or by specifying an equivalency table for the various benefits, to avoid employer discretion in favor of highly compensated employees.

Lump-Sum Option.   A lump-sum distribution can provide planning flexibility for participants. Lump-sum distribution provisions are most common in defined-contribution plans; in fact, in a profit-sharing plan, the lump sum is often the only distribution option. However, even a defined-benefit plan can offer a lump-sum option. The Code provides in Section 417(e) that the lump sum must be at least that determined on the basis of interest and mortality factors specified in the Code.

Higher-income participants often would like a lump sum because they have other sources for retirement income and wish to invest their plan funds in riskier, high-return investment vehicles. A defined-contribution plan can be designed to accommodate this need to some extent within the plan, however, by providing participant investment direction. Also, investment results within the plan are enhanced by the tax deferral on plan income and may provide an effective rate of return that the participant cannot match outside the plan. However, funds cannot be left in the plan indefinitely; distributions must generally begin at age 70½ or retirement, if later.

In some defined-benefit plans, particularly insured plans, the assumptions used for funding are too conservative. For example, a plan may have accumulated $140,000 to fund a benefit of $12,000 per year to a retiree. In many cases, however, it might be possible for a retiree to individually invest $140,000 and receive a better return than $12,000 per year for life. Thus, the retiree might rather have a $140,000 lump sum from the plan fund than the plan's annuity benefit. In some cases, this situation results from bad plan design, while in others it is done deliberately to increase the benefit for key employees. The Code limits the extent to which this can be done by prescribing minimum interest and mortality assumptions.

Distribution Restrictions

Plan distributions can be designed to provide considerable flexibility, but they must be designed within a rather complex network of rules that have been accumulating in the law over many years. These rules are aimed at protecting the financial interests of participants and, more significantly, they are designed to limit the use of qualified plans merely as a tax-sheltered investment medium for key employees. The significant rules are as follows:

- Distinctions between the types of distributions permitted in pension plans as opposed to profit-sharing plans
- Rules preventing employers from unjustly delaying benefit payments
- Minimum distribution requirements
- Early distribution penalties
- Incidental benefit requirements
- Nonalienation rules

Pension versus Profit-Sharing Plans.   The IRS generally will not allow a pension plan to pay benefits prior to retirement, early retirement, death, or disability, although some limited cashout provisions may be allowed in the event of termination of employment prior to these events, as previously discussed. With a profit-sharing plan, there is much more flexibility, and the plan may allow in-service distributions, as discussed in Chapter 22. However, the 10 percent penalty described below may deter employees from making certain withdrawals.

Delaying Benefit Payments.   Under Code Section 401(a)(14), all qualified plans must provide for payment not later than the 60th day after the latest of the following three dates:

1. The earlier of age 65 or the plan's normal retirement date
2. The tenth anniversary of the participant's entry into the plan
3. The participant's termination of service with the employer

The plan may allow the participant to elect a payout that begins at a date later than this maximum limit. However, the extent to which a participant can stretch out payments is limited by the rules discussed in the next section.

Minimum Distribution Rules. Congress does not like qualified plans to be used as tax shelters for funds that are not actually needed by participants for retirement income. Therefore, Code Section 401(a)(9) requires that plan distributions begin no later than April 1 of the calendar year following the later of the year in which the employee attains age 70½ or the year of actual retirement. If the employee owns more than 5 percent of the employer, deferral to the actual retirement date is not permitted.

If the annual distribution is less than the minimum amount required, there is a penalty of 50 percent of the amount not distributed that should have been.[1] But a participant can always take out more than the required minimum.

The required minimum distribution each year is generally determined by dividing the account balance (determined for the last valuation date in the preceding year) by the appropriate number in an IRS table (see Table 25.1).

> **EXAMPLE**
> Frank is aged 73 on the last day of 2004. His qualified account balance at the end of 2003 is $400,000. Frank's required distribution for 2004 is $16,194.34 ($400,000 divided by 24.7, the Table 25.1 factor for a 73-year old).

The factors in the table are based on the life-expectancy factors that would apply to a distribution over the joint life expectancy of the participant and a joint annuitant who is 10 years younger than the participant. However (except for the young-spouse exception described below), the factors in Table 25.1 are used regardless of who the beneficiary is (including a nonindividual beneficiary) or even if the participant does not name a beneficiary (i.e., where in effect the participant's beneficiary is his estate).

A more favorable minimum distribution (lower required annual amount) is available for a plan participant whose beneficiary is a spouse who is more than 10 years younger than the participant. In this case, a minimum distribution can be determined using the actual joint life expectancy of the participant and the spouse.[2]

At the participant's death, the minimum distribution to the participant's designated beneficiary is generally based on the beneficiary's remaining life expectancy. Under the current minimum distribution rules, there is likely to be a significant remaining account balance at the owner's death, so the minimum distribution rules for survivors are significant in retirement and estate planning. The designated beneficiary is determined as of September 30 of the year following the year of the participant's death.

Early Distribution Penalty. Code Section 72(t) provides a tax penalty for **early distributions (premature distributions)** from qualified plans. This penalty provision was added by Congress to encourage plan participants to use qualified plans primarily for retirement and not merely for deferral of compensation. The 10 percent penalty tax applies to distributions from a broad range of tax-advantaged retirement plans. As

TABLE 25.1		IRS Table for Determining Distribution Period for Lifetime Distributions to an Employee		
Age of Participant	**Distribution Period**	**Age of Participant**	**Distribution Period**
70	27.4	93	9.6
71	26.5	94	9.1
72	25.6	95	8.6
73	24.7	96	8.1
74	23.8	97	7.6
75	22.9	98	7.1
76	22.0	99	6.7
77	21.2	100	6.3
78	20.3	101	5.9
79	19.5	102	5.5
80	18.7	103	5.2
81	17.9	104	4.9
82	17.1	105	4.5
83	16.3	106	4.2
84	15.5	107	3.9
85	14.8	108	3.7
86	14.1	109	3.4
87	13.4	110	3.1
88	12.7	111	2.9
89	12.0	112	2.6
90	11.4	113	2.4
91	10.8	114	2.1
92	10.2	115 and older	1.9

applied to regular qualified plans and 403(b) plans, the penalty applies to all distributions, *except* distributions

- made on or after attainment of age 59½;
- made to a beneficiary or employee's estate on or after the employee's death;
- attributable to disability;
- that are part of a series of substantially equal periodic payments made at least annually over the life or life expectancy of the employee, or the joint lives or life expectancies of the employee and beneficiary (separation from service is required);
- made after a separation from service after age 55;
- related to certain tax credit ESOP dividend payments;
- to the extent of medical expenses deductible for the year under Code Section 213, whether or not actually deducted.

The penalty also applies to IRAs and IRA-funded plans (SEPs and SIMPLE/IRAs), with a somewhat different list of exceptions—see Chapter 28.

Note that a plan may be permitted to make a distribution to an employee without disqualifying the plan, but the distribution may nevertheless be subject to penalty. For example, many hardship distributions from 401(k) plans or 403(b) tax-deferred annuity plans, though permissible, will be subject to the penalty tax.

Despite the penalty, withdrawals from qualified plans may still be important to participants in many situations—to obtain emergency funds, for example. Therefore, plan designers may wish to provide withdrawals in plans, where permitted, despite the existence of the 10 percent penalty.

Nonalienation Rules.   A qualified plan must provide that plan benefits may not be assigned or alienated [Code Section 401(a)(13)]. This means, for example, that a plan participant can't pledge future anticipated qualified plan payments as security for a bank loan. For divorce, child support, and similar domestic disputes, there are special provisions discussed later in this chapter.

■ FEDERAL TAXATION OF DISTRIBUTIONS

Plan distributions generally are taxed in accordance with the rules for taxing annuity payments found in Code Section 72. A lump sum distribution from a plan is generally taxed in full on receipt unless it is rolled over to an IRA, as discussed below. This section deals with *federal* income and estate taxation. Some states apply similar tax treatment, but there is some variation. Federal taxes are usually the dominant factor in the overall tax burden on plan distributions.

The initial step in determining the taxation of a qualified plan distribution is determining the **taxable amount** of the distribution. For a distribution upon retirement, disability, or termination of employment, the taxable amount consists of the total amount of the distribution less the following amounts, sometimes referred to as the employee's *cost basis* in the plan:

■ The total nondeductible contributions made by the employee (in the case of a contributory plan)

■ The total cost of life insurance reported as taxable income by the participant, assuming that the plan distribution is received under the same contract that provided the life insurance protection

■ Any employer contributions previously taxed to the employee (for example, where a nonqualified plan later became qualified)

■ Certain employer contributions attributable to foreign services performed before 1963

■ Amounts paid by the employee in repayment of loans that were treated as distributions

■ In the case of a stock bonus plan or other stock plan, the net unrealized appreciation, as discussed in Chapter 22

The first two items in the list are the ones most frequently encountered. If the employee is self-employed or was self-employed in the past, the items excludable from the taxable amount are slightly different from the above list. The most important difference is that for a self-employed person who is an owner/employee (a more-than-10-percent owner of an unincorporated business), the insurance costs (the second item above) are not part of the cost basis.

The simplest way to describe the taxation of qualified plan distributions is to distinguish between those benefits that are paid out fully in a single taxable year of the participant and those that are spread out over more than one taxable year. The latter are discussed first.

Payment over More than One Taxable Year

If the plan distribution is made over more than one taxable year of the employee, the usual annuity rules apply to taxation of the distribution. The distribution will be taxable to the participant or beneficiary in the year received, except to the extent that there is a cost basis to be recovered.

In general, basis is recovered using a table specified in Section 72 of the Code. The total basis is to be divided by a number from the table, and the resultant amount is the amount of each monthly payment that is nontaxable. The table for a payout based on a single life is as follows:

Age on Annuity Starting Date	Number of Anticipated Payments
Not more than 55	360
More than 55–60	310
More than 60–65	260
More than 65–70	210
More than 70	160

There is an additional table for annuities paid over the life of more than one individual:

Combined Age of Annuitants	Number of Payments
Not more than 110	410
More than 110 but not more than 120	360
More than 120 but not more than 130	310
More than 130 but not more than 140	260
More than 140	210

Payment in One Taxable Year

If the qualified plan distribution is paid to the participant in a single taxable year, the taxable amount (the amount in excess of the participant's cost basis as described above) potentially is all taxable to the participant as ordinary income in the year received.

> **EXAMPLE**
> Employee Green retires at age 65 and is entitled to a pension of $1,000 per month, based on his single life expectancy. Green's cost basis in the plan is $26,000. Green pays taxes on $900 per month; the remaining $100 of his monthly pension is excluded from tax ($26,000 divided by the factor from the table, 260).
> If the recipient receives payments long enough for the entire basis to be recovered, subsequent payments are taxable in full. Correspondingly, if the recipient dies before the entire basis is recovered, there is an income deduction allowable to the beneficiary for the unrecovered basis.

Because this can increase the participant's effective tax rate by pushing up the marginal tax bracket in that year, a special one-time relief provision applies if the distribution qualifies as a **lump-sum distribution** and is received after age 59½. A lump-sum distribution must meet all of the following requirements:

- It is made in one taxable year of the recipient.
- It represents the entire amount of the employee's benefit in the plan.
- It is payable on account of the participant's death, attainment of age 59½, separation from service (non–self-employed person only), or disability (self-employed person only).
- It is from a qualified plan.
- Except for death benefits, the employee must have participated in the plan for at least five years prior to the distribution.

In determining whether the entire amount of the employee's benefit has been distributed, all pension plans maintained by the employer are treated as a single plan, all profit-sharing plans are treated as one plan, and all stock bonus plans are treated as one plan.

If the distribution qualifies as a lump-sum distribution, the taxable amount of the distribution (the amount remaining after the cost basis is subtracted) is eligible for special tax treatment in certain cases, owing to expiring tax provisions that are retained ("grandfathered") for long-term plan participants. For participants who attained age 50 before 1986, there is a "ten-year averaging" computation. For amounts accumulated before 1974, a special capital-gain treatment is available. All other distributions are treated as ordinary income, to the extent of the taxable amount. Note that the number of plan participants affected by these provisions is rapidly diminishing as eligible participants are past retirement or soon will be.

Taxation of Death Benefits from Qualified Plans

The income tax treatment described above also applies in general to plan death benefits paid to beneficiaries of participants. That is, if the death benefit is paid as periodic payments, the annuity rules described above generally apply; if the death benefit qualifies as a lump-sum distribution, the special favorable tax treatment is available to the beneficiary. However, if the death benefit is payable under a life insurance contract held by the plan, the pure insurance amount paid—the difference between the policy's face amount and its cash value—is excluded from tax.

EXAMPLE

Employee Haines dies before retirement and his beneficiary receives a lump-sum death benefit from the plan consisting of $100,000 of the proceeds of a cash-value life insurance contract, the cash value of which was $50,000. The plan was non-contributory, and Haines reported a total of $8,000 of insurance costs on his income tax return during his lifetime as a result of the plan's insurance coverage. The taxable amount of this distribution to the beneficiary is the total distribution of $100,000 less the following:

■ The pure insurance amount ($100,000 minus the cash value of $50,000) and
■ Haines's cost basis—in this case, only the $8,000 of insurance cost reported during his lifetime.

The taxable amount is therefore $42,000. This amount is taxable income to the beneficiary, subject to the special averaging provisions described above, if applicable.

Federal Estate Tax

The **federal estate tax** on qualified plan death benefits affects only highly compensated participants (those with a gross estate of at least $950,000 [2005 figure]) and is discussed further in Chapter 26.

■ QUALIFIED DOMESTIC RELATIONS ORDERS

The prohibition against nonalienation of benefits does not apply to an assignment of a benefit under a **qualified domestic relations order (QDRO).** Under Code Section 414(p), a QDRO is a decree, order, or property settlement under state law relating to child support, alimony, or marital property rights that assigns a participant's plan benefits to a spouse, former spouse, child, or other dependent of the participant. Currently, therefore, a participant's plan benefits generally become the subject of negotiation in domestic disputes. The pension law itself does not indicate how such benefits are to be divided; this is still a matter of state domestic relations law. The QDRO provision simply provides a means by which state court orders in domestic relations issues can be enforced against plan trustees.

To protect plan administrators and trustees from conflicting claims, a QDRO cannot assign a benefit that the plan does not provide. Also, a QDRO cannot assign a benefit that is already assigned under a previous order. If, under the plan, a participant has no right to an immediate cash payment from the plan, a QDRO cannot require that the trustees make such a cash payment. If a cash settlement is desired, the parties will generally agree to allow one participant to keep the entire plan benefit and pay compensating cash to the other.

■ LOANS FROM QUALIFIED PLANS

The qualified plan law permits loans, within limits, to participants in regular qualified plans and Section 403(b) tax-deferred annuity plans. However, a participant cannot borrow from a plan unless the plan document specifically permits loans, and as discussed below, loan provisions may not be appropriate for all plans. Loans from IRAs, SEPs, and SIMPLE/IRAs are effectively prohibited; they are treated as taxable distributions and may be subject to penalties for early distribution.

Limits on Loan Amount

Under Code Section 72(p), loans will be recognized as loans (rather than taxable current distributions) only to the extent that the loan, together with all other outstanding loans, does not exceed the lesser of

- $50,000 reduced by the highest outstanding loan balance during the preceding one-year period or
- one-half of the present value of the vested accrued benefit of the employee under the plan.

A loan up to $10,000 may be made even if this is more than one-half of the present value of the employee's vested accrued benefit. Some examples are shown in the table.

Vested Accrued Benefit	Maximum Aggregate Loans
$120,000	$50,000
40,000	20,000
5,000	10,000

Terms of Loans

To obtain loan treatment, the loan must be repayable by its terms within five years. The rule noted above for reducing the $50,000 limit by the loan balance in the preceding year was designed to prevent avoidance of the five-year limit by simply repaying and then immediately reborrowing the same amount every five years. The five-year requirement does not apply to any loan used to acquire a principal residence of the participant.

Transactions with an effect similar to that of loans (for example, the pledging of an interest in a qualified plan or a loan made against an insurance contract purchased by a qualified plan) are also covered by the loan limitations and rules.

If the plan permits loans, they must be made available on a nondiscriminatory basis. Also, the loans must be adequately secured and bear a reasonable rate of interest. Usually, the security for a plan loan is simply the participant's vested accrued plan benefit. Interest on the loan is generally consumer interest that is not deductible as an itemized deduction unless secured by a home mortgage. However, if the loan is to a key employee as defined in the top-heavy rules or is secured by 401(k) or 403(b) elective deferrals, interest is not deductible in any event.

Any loan that does not meet these requirements will be treated as a current distribution and may be currently taxable to the employee when received.

Should the Plan Permit Loans?

Whether the plan should permit loans depends on the employer's objectives for the plan. Plan loan provisions are often desired by the controlling employees of closely held businesses because a plan loan provides the advantage of tax sheltering the plan funds without losing control of the cash. However, the same considerations may make plan loans desirable for regular employees as well. A disadvantage of plan loans is that if they are too extensively utilized, they deplete the plan funds available for investment. More fundamentally, however, plan loan provisions are inconsistent with a primary plan objective of providing retirement security. Thus, they are less common in pension plans than in profit-sharing plans. Plan loan provisions are particularly uncommon in defined-benefit plans because such plans have no individual participant accounts; it is complicated to convert a participant's vested accrued benefit to a cash equivalent at a given time to determine the amount of loan that can be allowed. Plan loans also add significant administrative costs to the plan.

■ KEY TERMS

early distributions
    (premature
    distributions)
federal estate tax
life annuity with period
    certain

lump-sum distribution
normal form of benefit
qualified domestic
    relations order
    (QDRO)

straight-life annuity
taxable amount

■ STUDY QUESTIONS

1. a. What is meant by the "normal form of benefit" in a defined-benefit plan?

   b. What optional forms of benefit are commonly made available to participants?

2. What is the distinction between types of preretirement distributions allowable in a pension plan and types allowable in a profit-sharing plan?

3. a. What is the latest date on which a qualified plan may allow retirement benefits to commence?

   b. What is the latest age at which a participant of a qualified plan must begin to receive benefits?

4. Explain the minimum distribution rules applicable to a beneficiary if

   a. the employee dies before the entire plan interest is distributed.

   b. the employee dies before distributions have begun.

5. Which of the following plan distributions is not subject to the 10 percent Section 72(t) penalty?

   a. A lump-sum distribution to a participant age 55

   b. A death benefit payable to a beneficiary upon the death of an employee age 52

   c. A lump-sum benefit payable to a disabled employee age 57

   d. A life annuity payable beginning immediately upon separation from service to an employee age 45

   e. A distribution of $30,000 to Employee Slick who plans to use the money to build a swimming pool prescribed by his doctor for arthritis treatments

   f. A distribution from a 401(k) plan to an employee age 52 who qualifies under the plan's "extreme hardship" distribution provision

6. Joe Smith retired at age 65 with a pension of $400 per month. His life expectancy is 20 years. To what extent is his pension benefit taxable if Smith's cost basis is $16,400?

7. a. What requirements must a lump-sum distribution meet to qualify for special tax treatment?

   b. What is the special tax treatment that is available?

8. Explain how death benefits from a qualified plan are taxed.

9. The ABC Company (an S corporation) has a qualified money-purchase plan that allows employees to take loans up to the maximum legal limit. What is the maximum loan that can be taken by the following employees?

Employee	Vested Account Balance	Percentage of Corporate Ownership
a. Don Taich	$ 17,000	0%
b. Peter Demunney	160,000	0
c. Dana N. Runn	200,000	50

10. What are the advantages and disadvantages of designing a plan that includes a loan provision?

■ NOTES

1. Code Section 4974.

2. Table VI, Ordinary Joint Life and Last Survivor Annuities; Two Lives—Expected Return Multiples, from Reg. Sec. 1.72-9, may be used.

26

Plan Restrictions Aimed at Highly Compensated Employees

CHAPTER OUTLINE

Congress and the IRS have long been aware of the possibility that the tax advantages of qualified plans will be abused by plan provisions or practices that confer most of the plan's benefits on highly paid key employees, typically employees who are stockholders or partners in a closely held business. This is arguably inconsistent with the social policy behind the qualified plan provisions. Therefore, the law contains a variety of rules aimed at this type of abuse. The provisions discussed in this chapter will have little actual effect on plans typically designed for larger employers. However, these rules technically apply to *all* plans, and thus they must be considered at least in drafting every plan.

There is a large community of pension planners who specialize in designing plans to avoid the provisions discussed in this chapter, so from time to time Congress and the IRS add new rules to close various "loopholes" that plan designers have found. Thus, the provisions discussed here have become the most complex in the entire pension law.

■ CEILING ON COMPENSATION

The most fundamental limit of this type is the rule [Code Section 401(a)(17)] that only the first $200,000 of each employee's compensation (as indexed for inflation: $205,000 in 2004) can be taken into account in a qualified plan's contribution or benefit formula.

> **EXAMPLE**
> If an employee earns $300,000 in 2004 and is covered under a money-purchase pension plan with a 10 percent of compensation contribution formula, the contribution for that employee in 2004 is limited to $20,500 (10 percent of $205,000, rather than 10 percent of $300,000).

■ LIMITATIONS ON INDIVIDUAL BENEFITS OR ANNUAL ADDITIONS (SECTION 415 LIMITS)

Section 415 of the Internal Revenue Code contains limitations on the amount of benefit or annual account additions that any participant can receive under a qualified plan. These limitations are intended to prevent the qualified plan from being used as an individual tax-sheltering device beyond any reasonable need for retirement savings. They have their greatest impact on small businesses where one or more of the business owners are plan participants. However, the limitations also can have an impact on larger plans that cover high-salaried executives. There are two types of **Section 415 limits**—one for defined-benefit plans and one for defined-contribution plans.

Defined-Benefit Plans

For defined-benefit plans, the applicable limitation restricts the amount of *benefit* that any individual can receive. Basically, the plan cannot permit a benefit at age 65 (or the Social Security retirement age, if later) that exceeds the lesser of 100 percent of the participant's compensation averaged over the three years of highest compensation or $160,000 (as indexed for inflation: $165,000 in 2004) annually. A pension of up to $10,000 annually can be paid even if it exceeds the 100 percent limit, but this $10,000 floor applies only if the participant has never been covered by a defined-*contribution* plan.

The benefit limit of Section 415 applies to employer-provided benefits only. If the plan provides for employee contributions (which is relatively rare in defined-benefit plans), these employee contributions can be used to increase benefits above the Section 415 limit.

The $160,000 limit, as indexed, is adjusted in $5,000 increments under a cost-of-living formula. The limit is also adjusted actuarially—it is reduced for retirement ages earlier than age 62 and increased for retirement later than age 65.

The Section 415 benefit limitation must be part of every qualified plan document. The plan language must, therefore, prohibit the accrual of any benefit in excess of the limit. For any given employee, however, except an employee who is contemplating retirement in the current plan year, it is impossible to know what the applicable dollar limitation under Section 415 will be in the year of retirement. Nevertheless, the IRS does not allow benefits to be accrued in excess of the Section 415 limits based on current compensation and the current dollar limit, even for a participant far from retirement.

Defined-Contribution Plans

For a defined-contribution plan, the Section 415 limitation is a restriction not on the benefit but on the **annual addition** to each participant's account. The annual addition cannot exceed the lesser of 100 percent of the participant's annual compensation or $40,000 as indexed (2004 figure: $41,000).

The annual addition to each participant's account includes three elements:

1. Employer contributions including employee salary reductions
2. Reallocated forfeitures from other participants' accounts
3. Nondeductible (after tax) employee contributions

It is important to note that both of the Section 415 limitations apply to individual participants, not to the plan as a whole. Also, it should be noted that the annual-additions limit is not a limit on the amount that the employer can deduct for income tax purposes. The deduction limits are a separate set of rules from the Section 415 limits, and the two items should not be confused. However, no deduction can ever be taken for an employer contribution that causes an employee's benefit or account to exceed the Section 415 limit.

Combined Deduction Limit

A combined deduction limit [Code Section 404(a)(7)] has the effect of restricting the benefits of many combination plans. If an employer maintains both defined-contribution and defined-benefit plans covering the same employer or employees, the employer's annual tax deduction for the plans cannot exceed 25 percent of the compensation of the employees covered under both plans. The 25 percent deduction limit can be exceeded only to meet the minimum funding requirements for the defined-benefit plan. For older plan entrants, the defined-benefit funding level will often exceed 25 percent of compensation, thus (depending on the overall nature of the employee group) potentially eliminating the possibility of adding a defined-contribution plan. For example, if there is only one participant, or only one highly paid participant and a few others (such as the typical plan for a doctor or dentist), this will be the case.

EXAMPLE
Dr. X, age 55, adopts a plan providing a pension of $75,000 a year (50 percent of compensation) at retirement age 65. Annual cost is $44,428 (8 percent interest assumption) which is 30 percent of Dr. X's compensation. Thus, if Dr. X is the only employee, under the limits of Section 404(a)(7) there is no room for additional deductible contributions to a defined-contribution plan.

■ TOP-HEAVY PLANS

The *top-heavy* rules are another addition to the arsenal of weapons Congress has provided against the use of qualified plans by small businesses primarily as tax shelters for owners and highly compensated employees. The rules (Code Section 416) provide additional requirements that must be met by all qualified plans that meet the definition of top-heavy. To summarize, the top-heavy requirements do the following:

■ Provide faster vesting of benefits for plan participants who are not key employees

■ Provide minimum unintegrated benefit or contribution levels for plan participants who are not key employees

The top-heavy restrictions must be written into the plan document itself, even a plan for a large employer that is unlikely ever to be top-heavy. The plan document must provide that if the plan meets the definition of top-heavy on a given determination date, all of the top-heavy restrictions automatically become part of the plan. So long as the plan is not top-heavy, the top-heavy restrictions need not necessarily apply, although, of course, the planner is free to add these restrictions to the plan even if it is not top-heavy.

Definition of Top-Heavy

A defined-benefit plan is a top-heavy plan for a given plan year if, as of the determination date (see below), the present value of the accumulated accrued benefits for participants who are key employees is more than 60 percent of the present value of all accumulated accrued benefits in the plan. A defined-contribution plan is considered top-heavy if, as of the determination date, the sum of the account balances of participants who are key employees exceeds 60 percent of the aggregate value of the accounts of all employees. Benefits and account balances attributable to both employer and employee contributions are to be taken into account, except for accumulated voluntary deductible employee contributions or rollovers from other plans. The present value of a participant's accrued benefit or the value of the participant's account balance is to be increased by any aggregate distributions made with respect to the participant during the five-year period ending on the determination date. Plans of related groups can be lumped together, and if the contributions or benefits of the overall group are top-heavy, each plan in the group will be considered top-heavy.

Determination Date

The *determination date* for any given plan year is the last day of the preceding plan year. For the first year of the new plan, the determination date is the last day of the first plan year. The IRS also has the authority to apply the top-heavy provisions on the basis of years other than plan years.

Definition of Key Employee

A *key employee* is any participant in the plan, including a self-employed person, who at any time in the four preceding years was an officer earning more than $130,000 (2004 figure as indexed), a more-than-5-percent owner, or a more-than-1-percent owner earning more than $150,000. Because the term *officer* is not clearly defined, there is a limit on the number of employees that can be treated as officers. No more than 50 employees can be treated as officers in general, while for small employers the limit on the number of officers is the greater of three individuals or 10 percent of the employees (presumably the highest paid). For example, suppose a small company has 25 employees. In determining who are key employees, the IRS cannot designate more than three of these employees (the greater of three individuals or 10 percent of the employees) as officers.

Note that *key employee* is defined differently from *highly compensated employee* used in all other nondiscrimination provisions of the law.

In determining ownership in the business for purposes of identifying key employees, the top-heavy provisions have rules for attributing stock ownership from related persons, and there are special rules for aggregating commonly controlled groups of employers and affiliated service groups.

An illustration of what constitutes a top-heavy plan might be helpful in defining the concept of top-heavy.

EXAMPLE

Suppose that a corporation with ten employees has a defined-contribution money-purchase pension plan. The employees include Wolfe (president and sole shareholder), Hare (vice-president), and Flynn (foreman), all three of whom earn more than $130,000. All of the other employees are clerical or production workers paid by the hour. The IRS would most likely identify the three named employees as the plan's key employees. As of the end of the 2004 plan year, aggregate account balances of all participants in the plan total $200,000. The account balances for Wolfe, Hare, and Flynn total $100,000. On these facts, the plan is not top-heavy for the plan year 2005 because the aggregate account balances for the three key employees total less than 60 percent of the total account balances as of the determination date, the end of 2004. However, suppose that in 2003 Wolfe received a distribution of $100,000 from the plan. In this case, the account balances as of the end of 2004 would have to be increased by the amount of this distribution, so they would total $300,000. The account balances for the key employees would then be $200,000, because the $100,000 distribution to Wolfe would have to be included for this purpose. Now the plan would be deemed to be top-heavy for the plan year 2005 because the account balances for key employees would be more than 60 percent of the total.

Although the example above involved a plan of a small employer that fell on the line between being top-heavy and avoiding that status, planners find that virtually all plans of employers with fewer than ten employees will be top-heavy at all times. Key employees in such businesses usually have not only higher salaries but also much longer service than regular employees, so their account balances or accrued benefits are much higher as a percentage of the total. Therefore, the top-heavy rules become an additional set of qualification requirements that must be met by all small plans.

Additional Vesting Requirements for Top-Heavy Plans

If a plan meets the definition of top-heavy, the plan provisions must meet one of two special vesting schedules applicable during years in which the plan is top-heavy. One alternative is 100 percent after two years of service. The other alternative is six-year graded vesting, as shown in the table.

Years of Service	Vesting Percentage
2	20
3	40
4	60
5	80
6 or more	100

Minimum Benefit Requirements

A qualified plan must provide minimum benefits or contributions for top-heavy years. For defined-benefit plans, the benefit for each nonkey employee must be at least a minimum percentage of average compensation. The applicable minimum percentage of compensation for a given employee is two multiplied by the number of the employee's years of service, with a maximum percentage of 20 percent (i.e., ten years of service or more). The average compensation used for this test will generally be based on the highest five years of compensation.

For a defined-contribution plan, employer contributions during a year of topheaviness must be not less than 3 percent of each nonkey employee's compensation.

A top-heavy plan can consider only nonintegrated benefits in meeting the vesting and minimum benefit requirements. That is, these requirements must be met based on benefits from the plan itself. Benefits received by the participant from Social Security cannot be taken into account.

■ QUALIFIED PLANS FOR OWNERS OF UNINCORPORATED BUSINESSES

The owner of an unincorporated business often works full time or performs substantial services for the business as its proprietor or one of its partners. However, under the law such a person is not technically an employee of the business, but is referred to instead as a *self-employed person*. For many years, partners and proprietors were not eligible to be covered under qualified plans adopted by their unincorporated businesses. Beginning in 1962, qualified plan coverage was allowed, but only under very restricted conditions. In particular, there was a relatively low limit on the amount that could be contributed to the plan (or on the benefit provided by the plan) for partners and proprietors. The special plans designed under these restrictions were known as *Keogh* or *HR-10* plans. These restrictions were enough to induce many unincorporated businesses to incorporate, simply so that the partner or proprietor could become a legally recognized *employee* of the business and be eligible for full qualified plan coverage. However, for plan years beginning after 1983, most of these previous restrictions were eliminated and partners and proprietors were able to participate fully in qualified plans adopted by their unincorporated businesses. There are, however, a few differences in the treatment of unincorporated businesses, most of them related to basic differences in the form of business.

Earned Income

An unincorporated business is not treated for federal income tax purposes as a taxable entity but rather as a conduit for passing the business's taxable income or loss through to the partners or proprietor. By comparison, a corporation is a tax-paying entity, and income can be passed through to owners only in the form of salaries representing reasonable compensation for services rendered or as dividends. Because of this difference, plan benefits or contributions for partners and proprietors are based on a defined amount referred to as *earned income,* which is intended to be comparable to the *compensation* that employees receive.

Earned income is the partner's or proprietor's share of the net earnings of the business after taking all appropriate business deductions, and without including nontaxable income. However, earned income includes only earnings with respect to the trade or business in which the personal services of the partner or proprietor are a material income-producing factor. For example, the net profits of an investment type business could not be treated like compensation in order to provide a benefit under a qualified plan for a partner who provided no personal services to the business.

The fact that earned income is determined after all business deductions creates a computational complication. Business deductions include the plan contribution itself, as well as one-half the Social Security self-employment tax that is based on net income [Code Section 164(f)]. An illustration will show this without getting into the details of the algebra.

EXAMPLE

Dot Matrix is a self-employed computer consultant with no regular employees. She earned $100,000 of net income in 2004, not counting her Keogh plan contribution and the deduction for self-employment tax. Her deduction for self-employment tax is $6,788.88. The Keogh plan is a money-purchase plan calling for an annual contribution of 25 percent of earned income. How much can Dot contribute? The answer is $18,642.23. This amount is 25 percent of Dot's earned income. Her earned income is equal to

Initial net income		$100,000.00
Less	Self-employment tax deduction	6,788.88
Keogh contribution		18,642.23
Earned income		$ 74,568.89

Insurance

Another group of special rules applies to a qualified plan providing insurance for a partner or proprietor. No deduction can be taken by the business for plan contributions that are allocatable to the purchase of incidental life, health, or accident insurance for the partner or proprietor. If cash-value life insurance is used, the deduction is denied for the portion of the premium allocatable to pure insurance protection, but the remainder of the premium is deductible as a plan contribution. The amounts not deducted are taxable income to the business owners, because all taxable income of a partnership or proprietorship flows through to the individual owners. Therefore, there are no Table 2001 costs to include in the owner's income if insurance has been purchased, because the full cost of the insurance has already been included in the owner's income. However, unlike regular employees, the owners do not obtain a cost basis for the cost of the insurance to apply to any distribution from the qualified plan.

■ EARLY TERMINATION RULE FOR 25 HIGHEST-PAID EMPLOYEES

Potentially, a qualified defined-benefit plan can be used as a one-time tax shelter for key employees if it is designed with the expectation that most of the key employees will retire within a few years, taking most of the plan assets out for their retirement, thus terminating the plan. For many years, the Regulations [Section 1.401–4(c)] have contained a provision designed to limit this abuse by requiring defined-benefit plans to limit benefits for the 25 highest-paid employees if they are paid out within ten years of the plan's establishment or the plan terminates within ten years.

In such cases, benefits to the 25 highest-paid employees are limited by limiting the total employer contributions used to fund such benefits. The employer contributions for each such employee cannot exceed the greater of $20,000 or 20 percent of the first $50,000 of employee compensation multiplied by the number of years the plan was in effect prior to the benefit payment or plan termination. Often, this will produce a lower limit on benefits than the Section 415 benefit limit.

■ FEDERAL ESTATE TAX TREATMENT OF QUALIFIED PLAN BENEFITS

The federal estate tax is a tax separate from the income tax that is imposed on the value of a decedent's property at the time of death. The estate tax is payable out of the decedent's estate and, therefore, reduces the amount available to the beneficiaries. Only a small percentage of decedents—less than 5 percent—have enough wealth to be concerned about the estate tax because of a high initial minimum tax credit applicable to the estate tax. No estate tax return need be filed for a decedent whose gross estate is less than an amount scheduled to rise incrementally to $1 million in 2006. Also, there is an unlimited marital deduction for federal estate tax purposes—that is, there is no federal estate tax imposed on property transferred at death to a spouse, regardless of the amount.

As a general rule, a lump-sum death benefit, or the present value of an annuity payable to a beneficiary from a qualified plan, is includable in the estate of a deceased participant for federal estate tax purposes. For some high-income participants, avoiding federal estate taxes on the plan benefit will be important. Their estates may be large enough to be subject to federal estate tax. The marital deduction may not be significant, because they may not wish to pay the plan benefit to a spouse—they may be widowed or divorced or may wish to provide for another beneficiary. Also, even if the benefit is payable to a spouse, a spouse is often about the same age as the decedent, and thus within relatively few years most of the property transferred to the spouse is potentially subject to federal estate tax again at the spouse's death. As a result, it is often useful to design a qualified plan death benefit that can be excluded from the participant's estate.

The general rule of the federal estate tax is that all items of property are includable unless a specific code provision excludes them. Thus, qualified plan death benefits are generally includable because there is no specific exclusion. However, the estate tax law does have a specific provision dealing with life insurance, Section 2042. Under Section 2042, life insurance proceeds are includable in a decedent's estate if the decedent has "incidents of ownership" in the insurance policies. Incidents of ownership are various rights under the policy, particularly the right to designate the beneficiary. If a qualified plan death benefit is provided through a life insurance policy, in most cases this provision would require inclusion because the participant retains the right to name the beneficiary. Noninsured death benefits presumably would not be excludable in any event.

■ KEY TERMS

annual addition   Section 415 limits

■ STUDY QUESTIONS

1. a. Why are so many provisions of the qualified plan law aimed primarily at the closely held business?

   b. How do Congress and the IRS often react to aggressive design by pension planners?

2. What is the purpose of the Section 415 limitations on qualified plan benefits and contributions?

3. a. What is the basic Section 415 limitation on benefits from a defined-benefit plan?

   b. Under what circumstances might this basic limit be adjusted?

4. a. What is the basic Section 415 limitation on annual additions to a defined-contribution plan?

   b. What elements are included in annual additions?

5. a. Describe the reasons for the combined limit under Section 415 when an employee is a participant in a defined-benefit and a defined-contribution plan with the same employer.

   b. Briefly describe the rule that applies to benefits and contributions when such dual participation exists.

6. Assume a corporation has 15 employees and that three employees, Tom, Ed, and Jim, individually earn more than $130,000 annually. They are the only officers of the corporation. The remaining employees are hourly paid and clerical workers. Assume that the aggregate account balances of all participants in the firm's defined-contribution plan are equal to $200,000, and for Tom, Ed, and Jim the total is $100,000.

   a. Who are the plan's key employees? Explain.

   b. Is the plan top-heavy? Explain.

7. Explain how each of the following is affected if a qualified plan is top-heavy:

   a. Vesting

   b. Minimum benefits

   c. Section 415 limits

8. Explain how the rules applying to qualified plans of unincorporated businesses differ from those applying to the qualified plans of corporations.

9. Explain the early termination rule for the 25 highest-paid employees of a qualified plan.

10. What is the federal estate tax treatment of qualified plan benefits?

CHAPTER

27

Plan Installation and Administration; Investments; Plan Termination

OBJECTIVES

- Describe the basic steps that must be taken to install a qualified plan and explain the significance of an advance-determination letter.
- Explain the reporting and disclosure requirements that apply to qualified plans.
- Describe the impact of the ERISA fiduciary requirements and other investment restrictions on qualified plans.
- Explain the procedures for terminating a qualified plan and describe the general coverage of plan termination insurance provided by the Pension Benefit Guaranty Corporation (PBGC).

CHAPTER OUTLINE

Plan Installation
Adoption of the Plan
Plan Year
Advance Determination Letters
Master and Prototype Plans

Plan Administration
Employee Benefit Plans Other than Qualified Plans
Plan Administrator
Claims Procedure
Tax Withholding
Reporting and Disclosure

Investment Issues
Fiduciary Requirements of ERISA and the Internal Code
Prohibited Transactions
Unrelated Business Income
Investment Policy

Plan Termination
When Should a Plan Be Terminated?
Consequences of Termination

The Pension Benefit Guaranty Corporation and Its Plan Insurance
Plans Covered
Benefits Insured
PBGC Funding and Premiums
Plan Termination Procedures

◼ PLAN INSTALLATION

Installing a qualified plan can be fairly complex, particularly if the plan is complicated and the employer wishes to maximize the tax benefits by having the plan effective at the earliest possible date. The best way to discuss the installation process is to use as a framework for reference the checklist for the installation of a hypothetical qualified plan provided in Table 27.1. This checklist should be used for general discussion only; IRS guidelines for plan installation are frequently revised, and procedures may even vary from one Internal Revenue district to another.

TABLE 27.1	Checklist for Installation of Quicktime Construction Company, Inc. (calendar-year taxpayer), Employees' Profit Sharing Plan *(effective January 1, 2005)*

BEFORE DECEMBER 31, 2005

1. Board must pass resolution adopting the plan. It is sufficient for the board to adopt either a preliminary draft of the plan or a simple resolution listing the major provisions of the plan.
2. Trust instrument must be executed. (Under state law, a nominal contribution to the trust corpus may also be necessary in order to establish the existence of the trust.) If there is a separate group pension contract, the contract need not be in final form before December 31, 2005, but application must have been accepted by insurer and partial payment made.
3. Plan should be communicated to employees. (There is no specific statutory deadline for this, but communication before the end of the year is recommended.) Communication can be oral (e.g., at employee meetings) or written. Alternatively, the Summary Plan Description (SPD) can be used for this purpose.

BEFORE EMPLOYER'S TAX-FILING DATE (March 15, 2006; extension to September 15, 2006, is possible)

1. Execute plan in final form. (Plan may be adopted subject to right to rescind if determination letter is not obtained.)
2. Make 2005 contribution to trust. (Plan may allow contribution to be returned if plan does not qualify.)

WITHIN 120 DAYS AFTER PLAN IS ADOPTED BY BOARD OF DIRECTORS (e.g., if resolution adopted December 31, 2005, by April 30, 2006)

Furnish SPD to participants. (See "Reporting and Disclosure" in this chapter.)

BEFORE FILING APPLICATION FOR DETERMINATION WITH IRS

Time

No statutory deadline. However, should be filed before employer's tax-filing date (March 15, 2006, plus extensions). Filing of letter will extend the retroactive amendment date to give time to amend plan to meet IRS objections, if any.

What to file

Form (5300 series)

Other schedules as required under Form 5300 instructions and IRS procedures

Plan—executed

Trust Agreement—executed (or Insurance Contract)

Other items (e.g., Power of Attorney)—depending on circumstances

ON OR BEFORE JULY 31, 2006 (AND EACH JULY 31 THEREAFTER)

File Annual Report (Form 5500) with IRS (see "Reporting and Disclosure")

Adoption of the Plan

To be effective during a particular year, the plan must be adopted by the employer during that year. For a corporation, the corporate board should pass a resolution adopting the plan before the end of its year for the plan to become effective during that year. It is not proper to backdate documents for this purpose—the board must actually act legally before the end of the year. It may not be necessary to draft the final form of the plan at this time; however, the board usually can adopt a resolution merely outlining the basic provisions of the plan. If the plan uses a trust, the trust must be established before the end of the year in which the plan is to be effective. This means that a trust agreement must be executed between the employer and the trustee, and at least a nominal principal contribution may be necessary to establish the existence of the trust. If the plan uses an insurance contract as a funding instrument, the insurer must have accepted the terms of the agreement before the end of the year, although the contract may not be put into final form until sometime later. The plan and insurance contract should be finalized prior to the time the employer makes its first plan contribution other than a nominal contribution required to establish the trust or insurance contract; this usually means the employer's tax filing date, because the plan contribution for a given year can be deferred to the tax filing date for that year.

Plan Year

It is possible to establish a plan with a plan year that is different from the employer's taxable year. In that case, one plan year will end and another will begin in the same taxable year of the employer. The employer can then take a deduction that taxable year for a contribution on behalf of either plan year or for partial contributions for both taxable years; however, the employer must follow a consistent procedure so there is no undue tax benefit. For simplicity, unless otherwise indicated in this chapter, it will be assumed that the plan year is the same as the employer's taxable year.

Advance Determination Letters

A central feature of the plan installation process is usually an application to the IRS District Director for an **advance determination letter** stating that the plan as designed is a qualified plan eligible for the accompanying tax benefits. It is not necessary for the plan to have such a letter to be qualified; any plan that complies with the applicable Code provisions is a qualified plan. However, if there is no advance determination by the IRS, the IRS will not examine the plan until the time comes for an audit of the employer's tax returns. If the IRS finds at that time that the plan is not qualified, the possible tax consequences can be disastrous: the loss of the employer's tax deductions for plan contributions, the taxation of all plan contributions to participants, and the loss of the trust's tax-exempt status. To avoid this, most employers consider it desirable to have the IRS review the plan in advance and issue a determination letter. There are some other advantages to the determination letter procedure. The process of IRS review will often reveal drafting problems that might otherwise have gone unnoticed. During the review procedure, the IRS usually suggests any changes in the plan that are necessary to make it qualify.

There is a **retroactive amendment procedure** that allows the employer to make amendments to the plan effective for a prior year if the amendments are necessary to make the plan qualify. In general, retroactive plan amendments may be made up to the employer's tax filing date for the year in question, plus extensions. For example, if a corporate employer uses a calendar year, the tax filing date for the year 2005 is March 15, 2006, with possible extensions to September 15, 2006. Thus, an employer could install a qualified plan effective January 1, 2005, and could amend the plan retroactively to January 1, 2005, as late as September 15, 2006. The filing of a determination letter prior to this deadline extends the retroactive amendment procedure while the determination letter request is pending—this is another advantage of requesting an IRS determination letter.

Generally, the employer wishes to make the plan effective as early as possible to obtain the maximum tax deduction at the outset. This can present a problem if, on filing the application for determination, the IRS finds the plan not qualified and retroactive amendments are unavailable or the employer does not wish to make the amendments the IRS suggests. The employer's prior contributions to the plan then might not be retrievable because the trust generally must be an irrevocable trust. To avoid this problem, the plan can be drafted making the plan's existence and the employer's contribution contingent on obtaining a determination letter.

The IRS provides various forms for purposes of making an application for determination. Some of these are described in the checklist (Table 27.1). IRS publishes an annually revised Revenue Procedure that prescribes the requirements for an Application for Determination.

One final point should be made concerning IRS determination letters. Determination letters indicate that the IRS has approved the plan on the basis of the plan documents and the facts submitted to it. They are no guarantee that the plan qualifies and will continue to qualify if these facts are not accurate or if the facts change at a subsequent date. Therefore, the continuing qualification of the plan must always be a concern of the employer and its employee benefit advisers.

Master and Prototype Plans

A qualified plan must be evidenced by a formal written document. Because of the many complex provisions that must be included, it is not unusual for such documents to run to 50 pages or more. If all of the plan language is custom designed, the drafting expense alone can be considerable.

Various methods have been devised to simplify plan drafting for smaller employers. One of the most common is the use of master and prototype plans offered by financial institutions and other types of plan advisers. A **prototype plan** is a standardized plan form, such as a prototype profit-sharing plan or a prototype money-purchase pension plan, usually offering some choice of provisions in the important features. For example, the plan might allow the employer to specify the contribution rate or choose the vesting schedule. A master plan is similar to a prototype plan, but the term **master plan** usually refers to a plan form designed by a financial organization and adopted only by employers that wish to use that financial organization for plan funding. Also, most qualified plan consultants use standardized plan language of one kind or another to a considerable extent to reduce drafting costs, even if they do not provide formal master or prototype plans.

■ PLAN ADMINISTRATION

Plan administration encompasses a host of clerical and managerial functions related to a plan, including record keeping, receipt and disbursement of funds, claim administration, and investments. The discussion of plan administration in this chapter will focus on specific obligations imposed by ERISA and the Internal Revenue Code affecting plan administration.

Many of the administrative requirements of the law involve penalties for noncompliance, so it is important to impose these duties on specific individuals or groups of individuals to limit the scope of this liability to a known group. Otherwise, persons involved with the plan might find themselves held responsible for actions over which they may think they have no control. This problem is greatest in the area of investment decisions; therefore, it is important to be as specific as possible in the plan and trust agreement as to who has responsibility for making investment decisions and how these persons are chosen.

Employee Benefit Plans Other than Qualified Plans

As discussed in Chapter 5, many of the requirements of ERISA apply to a broad range of employee benefit plans as well as to qualified plans. In general, all of the rules discussed in the sections of this chapter beginning with "Plan Administration" through the section on "Unrelated Business Income" apply to all employee benefit plans, with the exceptions noted in the next paragraph. The rules are discussed in detail here because they typically have a much greater impact on qualified plans than on other plans, particularly the fiduciary rules.

The following employee benefit plans (retirement and other) are exempt from the fiduciary and reporting and disclosure requirements of ERISA:

- Government plans
- Church plans (unless they elect to be covered)
- Plans maintained solely to comply with workers' compensation, unemployment compensation, or disability insurance laws

In addition, through regulations issued by the secretary of labor, certain types of plans have been declared not to be employee welfare benefit plans and are thus exempt from the regulations of ERISA. Among these are the following:

- Compensation for work performed under other than normal circumstances, including overtime pay and shift, holiday, or weekend premiums

- Compensation for absences from work due to sickness, vacation, holidays, military duty, jury duty, or sabbatical leave and training programs to the extent such compensation is paid out of the general assets of the employer

- Group insurance programs under which (1) no contributions are made by the employer; (2) participation is completely voluntary for employees; (3) the sole function served by the employer, without endorsing the program, is to collect premiums through payroll deduction and remit the amount collected to the insurer; and (4) no consideration is paid to the employer in excess of reasonable compensation for administrative services actually performed. (Most of the mass-marketed plans described in Chapter 13 fall into this category.)

Plan Administrator

Any employee benefit plan subject to ERISA is required to name a **plan administrator** in the plan document. If none is named, the employer is assumed to be the plan administrator. Some employers prefer to designate a plan committee to be the plan administrator. This committee is usually made up of a group of management and sometimes rank-and-file employees responsible for administering the plan. If this is done, the plan should spell out how committee members are to be named, so that there can be no doubt who has the responsibility of plan administrator. Many employers prefer to simply designate the employer as plan administrator, with administration duties delegated to specific employees, usually in the personnel department, in the same manner as other management functions are carried out. Where the plan is funded through an insurance contract, some administrative duties may be carried out by the insurance company for a fee; this is particularly likely for smaller employers where the amount of administrative work involved does not justify the employment of a qualified plan specialist. Often, plan administrators also rely on outside benefit consultants for assistance with various administrative duties.

Claims Procedure

One of the plan administrator's duties is to evaluate employee claims for benefits and to direct the trustee or other fund holder to make payments as appropriate. If the plan is properly drafted, there should be little ambiguity about whether a particular participant or beneficiary is entitled to a plan benefit. However, due to the complexity of many plan provisions, disputes sometimes arise.

Every plan must include a written **claims procedure** under which a claimant can appeal the denial of a plan benefit to the plan administrator. There are specific time limits, 60 to 120 days generally, within which the plan administrator must make a decision on the appeal. The purpose for the claims procedure requirement is to require that plans develop internal procedures for evaluating claims so that participants will not always be compelled to bring a lawsuit against the plan if a claim is denied. If a claim dispute cannot be satisfactorily resolved internally, however, claimants have the right to sue and many will do so.

Tax Withholding

Distributions from a qualified retirement plan are subject to federal income tax withholding in a manner similar to payments of wages or other compensation. However, a recipient can elect not to have tax withholding on the qualified plan distribution, without providing any reason. (This, of course, will not relieve the recipient of any obligation to pay whatever income taxes are due.) The payer of the plan distribution must notify the recipient of the right not to have taxes withheld.

The withholding requirement applies to both lump-sum distributions and periodic payments. The liability for withholding is imposed on the payer of the distribution, but the plan administrator will be held liable unless the plan administrator directs the payer to withhold the tax and provides the payer with the information necessary to make the withholding. If the payer is a different person from the plan administrator, a trustee for example, it is important that there is a clear understanding between the parties about the responsibilities for withholding.

Reporting and Disclosure

The reporting and disclosure provisions, enacted as part of ERISA in 1974, impose a variety of duties on employee benefit plans to report or disclose various plan information to the government and plan participants. The purpose of the **reporting and disclosure provisions** is to indirectly discourage various plan abuses on the theory that wrongdoers will be deterred by knowing that their wrongdoing may be exposed to public view. This approach to federal regulation is based on the success of the securities laws of the 1930s and is common in other areas of federal regulation. The statutory format in ERISA for reporting and disclosure is extremely complex and confusing, and many modifications of the original statutory procedure have since been made by regulation, although the underlying statutes remain the same.

The reporting and disclosure requirements currently consist of this series of reports, some annual and some not, that must be provided to the participant or filed with the government or both:

- *Summary Plan Description (SPD).* The SPD is a document intended to describe the plan to its participants in plain language. Whether they ask for it or not, it must be furnished to participants within 120 days after the plan is established or 90 days after a new participant enters the plan. There is no government form for the SPD; it can be designed according to the employer's specifications. However, the contents of the SPD are specified in minute detail by Department of Labor regulations. These regulations require, among other things, clear identification of the plan sponsor and funding entities, the plan's eligibility requirements, any possibilities of losses or forfeiture of benefits, procedures for making claims for benefits under the plan, and a prescribed statement of the participant's rights under the law.

  There is also a plain language requirement, and this can be extremely important in practice. If a participant or beneficiary claims a benefit and is disappointed to find that the benefit was not provided under the plan, it is quite likely that the disappointed claimant will find a lawyer who will look closely at the SPD for any ambiguities that might provide grounds for a lawsuit. Such lawsuits sometimes prove successful.

- *Annual Report (Form 5500).* This form is the centerpiece of the reporting requirements. The form is filed only with the IRS, but it is made available to both the IRS and the Department of Labor. The form includes detailed financial information about the plan, including a signed report by an independent qualified public accountant, along with any separate financial statements forming the basis of the independent accountant's report. If a qualified plan is subject to the minimum funding requirements, a signed report by the plan's enrolled actuary must be included, along with a certified actuarial valuation.

  Plans covering fewer than 100 participants are subject to simpler reporting requirements designed to reduce the cost of compliance for these plans. To get a better idea of the scope of the reporting requirements, it is useful to obtain from the IRS copies of Form 5500 and accompanying instructions and review them. These are available on the IRS Web site, *www.irs.gov.*

  Form 5500 also includes Schedule SSA, a schedule identifying participants who have separated from service during the year with deferred vested benefits under the plan. It is provided by the IRS to the Social Security Administration so that at retirement any former participant may be notified of a deferred vested benefit from the plan.

- *Report on Termination, Merger, or Other Changes (Forms 5310 and 5310A).* The plan administrator of a plan covered under the Pension Benefit Guaranty Corporation (PBGC) plan termination insurance discussed later in this chapter must notify the PBGC in advance of the termination. The Code and ERISA also contain a number of other reporting requirements in the event of a plan termination, merger, split up, transfer of assets, and various other similar events. These are generally reported on Form 5310 or 5310A.

■ *Individual Benefit Statement.* On written request, the plan administrator must furnish an individual participant or beneficiary with a prescribed statement of his or her vested and unvested current plan benefits. This need not be furnished more than once a year. Some plan administrators provide these individual statements annually, even without a request from participants or beneficiaries.

The Health Insurance Portability and Accountability Act (HIPAA) imposes some additional requirements for information that must be included in summary plan descriptions for group health plans. (See the definition in Chapter 9.) These include the following:

■ Whether a plan is self-funded or whether an insurer (including a health maintenance organization) is responsible for the administration or financing of a plan

■ The name and address of any insurer responsible for administration or financing of a plan, the extent to which benefits under the plan are guaranteed by a contract or policy issued by the insurer, and the nature of any administrative services provided by the insurer

■ The office of the Department of Labor from which a participant may obtain information about HIPAA

ERISA does not require that a summary plan description be provided on a specific form, only that certain information be provided. Some employers use a single document; other employers incorporate much of the required information into the employee benefits handbook provided to their employees. Electronic transmissions of summary plan descriptions and other required information for participants are acceptable as long as certain conditions are met:

■ Electronic documents may be used only for participants who can access the documents at work and convert them to paper form.

■ The plan administrator must take appropriate measures to ensure that documents are actually received, such as the use of return receipt electronic mail features.

■ The electronic documents must be prepared in accordance with style, format, and content requirements of Department of Labor regulations.

■ Each participant must be notified, electronically or in writing, about which documents will be furnished electronically, the significance of such documents, and that paper copies of the documents can be received free of charge.

■ The plan administrator must furnish a paper copy of any electronically submitted documents free of charge on request of a participant.

The reporting requirements are enforced by various types of penalties, including criminal penalties for willful violations or false statements.

In addition to the specific forms that must be filed or distributed, the reporting and disclosure requirements include a variety of sunshine provisions that give government agencies and participants rights to inspect and copy various documents and records relevant to the plan and its operation. Also, to obtain an advance determination letter or other IRS ruling, the plan documents usually must be submitted to the IRS.

■ INVESTMENT ISSUES

Investment issues are among the most complex and significant issues relating to employee benefit plans, involving the fiduciary relationship of plan sponsors to participants and beneficiaries, as well as larger issues of public policy. In this section, some basic rules and some of the more frequently occurring investment issues are discussed.

Fiduciary Requirements of ERISA and the Internal Revenue Code

A relationship in which one person holds and administers money or property belonging to another is legally described as a *fiduciary* relationship. A funded employee benefit plan, therefore, involves fiduciary relationships—plan assets are held by a trustee or insurance company, under the direction of the employer, on behalf of plan participants and beneficiaries. The rules governing fiduciary relationships are generally a subject of state law; however, in the case of qualified plans and other employee benefit plans, federal law (primarily ERISA) has superimposed specific federal fiduciary requirements that supersede state law where applicable. The federal requirements are usually stricter than the superseded state law requirements. While these rules are applicable to most employee benefit plans, they have their greatest impact on qualified pension and profit-sharing plans because welfare-benefit plans are typically insured or unfunded, although the use of funded welfare-benefit plans is increasing.

The fiduciary requirements were not intended as a helpful guide for employers and trustees in administering qualified plans. They do not spell out the specific responsibilities of each person involved in designing and maintaining the plan. Rather, the rules are intended to spread a net of liability over various persons involved with the plan, aimed at maximizing the protection of participants and beneficiaries. Thus, there are not always simple rules explaining how employers, trustees, and other persons should act with regard to qualified plans; rather, they must be aware of their fiduciary responsibilities and do their best to comply with them or avoid them.

The definition of *fiduciary* is broad enough to include the employer, the plan administrator, and the trustee. It also includes a wide variety of other possible targets. However, the government has stated that an attorney, accountant, actuary, or consultant who renders legal, accounting, actuarial, or consulting services to the plan will not be considered a fiduciary solely as a result of performing those services. Also, labor regulations exclude broker/dealers, banks, and reporting dealers from being treated as fiduciaries simply as a result of receiving and executing buy-sell instructions from the plan. Furthermore, a person giving investment advice will be considered a fiduciary only with respect to the assets covered by that investment advice.

Every plan must specify a **named fiduciary** in the plan document. The purpose of this requirement is not to limit liability to named persons, but rather to provide participants and the government with an easy target in case they decide to take legal action against the plan. Of course, other unnamed fiduciaries can also be included in the legal action.

The duties of fiduciaries specified in the law are primarily of an investment nature. According to ERISA Section 404, a fiduciary must do the following:

- Discharge duties with respect to a plan solely in the interest of the participants and the beneficiaries
- Act for the exclusive purpose of providing benefits to participants and their beneficiaries and defraying the reasonable expenses of administering the plan
- Act with the care, skill, prudence, and diligence under the prevailing circumstances that a prudent man acting in a like capacity and familiar with such matters would use in the conduct of an enterprise of a like character and with like aims
- Diversify the investments of the plan to minimize the risk of large losses, unless under the circumstances it is clearly prudent not to do so
- Follow the provisions of the documents and instruments governing the plan, unless inconsistent with ERISA provisions

In interpreting the **prudent-man requirement**, labor regulations indicate that the fiduciary must, in making an investment, determine that the particular investment is reasonably designed as part of the plan's portfolio to further the purposes of the plan. The fiduciary must consider (1) the composition of the portfolio with regard to diversification, (2) the liquidity and current return of the portfolio relative to the anticipated cash flow requirements of the plan, and (3) the projected return of the portfolio relative to the funding objectives of the plan.

A major exception to the **diversification requirement** applies to holdings of employer securities and employer real property. An eligible individual account plan (a profit-sharing, stock bonus, or employee stock ownership plan that specifically permits the holding of employer real property or qualifying employer securities) may hold such property in any amount, and may even hold such property as the exclusive assets of the plan. Other plans can hold such property only up to the extent of 10 percent of the fair market value of the plan assets. The purpose of this exception is, of course, to encourage the adoption of employer stock plans of the type discussed in Chapter 22. A qualifying employer security means employer stock or marketable debt obligations meeting the various requirements of ERISA Section 407. Employer real property is real property owned by the plan and leased to the employer, again under limitations set out in ERISA Section 407.

Fiduciaries can delegate fiduciary responsibilities and, therefore, avoid direct responsibility for performing the duty delegated. For example, the employer can delegate duties relating to the handling and investment of plan assets to a trustee, and investment management duties can be delegated to an appointed investment manager. The plan must provide a definite procedure for delegating these duties. The delegation of a fiduciary duty does not remove all fiduciary responsibility. A fiduciary will be liable for a breach of fiduciary responsibility of any other fiduciary under certain circumstances.

The broad scope of the fiduciary liabilities indicates that, in addition to careful delegation of fiduciary duties to well-chosen trustees and advisers, the employer should take care that its liability insurance coverage adequately covers any liabilities that might arise out of the fiduciary responsibility provisions. ERISA specifically prohibits a plan from excusing or exculpating any person from fiduciary liability, but individuals and employers are permitted to have appropriate insurance and employers can indemnify plan fiduciaries.

Prohibited Transactions

In addition to the general fiduciary requirements already described, both Code Section 4975 and ERISA Section 406 include a specific list of **prohibited transactions** or "don'ts" for employee benefit plans, including qualified plans. Under these rules, a **party-in-interest** is forbidden to do any of the following, with a number of exceptions described later:

- Sale or exchange, or leasing, of any property between the plan and a party-in-interest
- Lending of money or other extension of credit between the plan and a party-in-interest
- Furnishing of goods, services, or facilities between the plan and a party-in-interest
- Transfer to, or use by or for the benefit of, a party-in-interest of any assets of the plan
- Acquisition, on behalf of the plan, of any employer security or employer real property in excess of the limits described previously in this chapter

A *party-in-interest*—the Code uses instead the term **disqualified person**—is defined very broadly, again to bring the largest possible number of persons into the net to provide the maximum protection for plan participants. A party-in-interest includes the following:

- Any fiduciary, counsel, or employee of the plan
- A person providing services to the plan
- An employer, if any of its employees are covered by the plan
- An employee organization, any of whose members are covered by the plan
- An owner, direct or indirect, of a 50 percent or more interest in an employer or employee organization
- Various individuals and organizations related to those on this list, under specific rules given in Code Section 4975 and ERISA Section 406

Because of the breadth of the prohibited transaction rules, certain specific exclusions are provided in the law, and the IRS and Department of Labor are also given the authority to waive the prohibited transaction rules in certain circumstances.

First, the specific statutory exemptions: Loans to participants or beneficiaries are permitted under the rules discussed in Chapter 25. A loan to an ESOP by a party-in-interest is also permitted under certain circumstances to permit the ESOP to function as described in Chapter 22. Similar provisions permit such a plan to acquire employer securities or real property without violating the prohibited transaction rules. Also, the plan is allowed to pay a reasonable fee for legal, accounting, or other services performed by a party-in-interest. There are provisions permitting various financial services to the plan by a bank or insurance company that is a party-in-interest. Other provisions exempt normal benefit distributions from any possible conflict with the prohibited transaction rules.

In addition to the specific statutory exemptions, the Department of Labor has broad authority to grant an exemption to the prohibited transaction rules for a transaction or a class of transactions after finding that the exemption is administratively feasible, in the interest of the plan and its participants and beneficiaries, and protective of their rights. There are specific administrative procedures for obtaining such exemptions. Pursuant to this authority, the Department of Labor has granted, among others, a class exemption permitting the sale of life insurance policies by participants to the plan or by the plan to participants. Another exemption, PTE84–14, permits a wide variety of transactions by qualified plan asset managers (QPAMs) such as banks and insurance companies. Individual exemptions have been granted for a variety of transactions, usually involving a sale to the plan by a party-in-interest of property that represents a particularly favorable investment opportunity for the plan.

Penalties. A violation of the prohibited transaction rules can result in a two-step penalty under the Internal Revenue Code, with the initial penalty equal to 15 percent of the amount involved, and an additional 100 percent penalty if the transaction is not corrected within a certain period of time. A violation of the prohibited transaction rules can also result in penalties for breach of fiduciary liability.

Unrelated Business Income

The trust fund under a qualified plan and trust funds used in some other self-insured employee benefit plans, such as Section 501(c)(9) trusts, are given a broad exemption from federal income tax similar to that granted to a variety of other institutions and organizations, such as churches, schools, and charities. Nevertheless, such tax-exempt organizations are subject to federal income tax on **unrelated business taxable income** according to Code Sections 511–514. Unrelated business taxable income is income of a tax-exempt organization from a trade or business that is not related to the function that is the basis for the tax exemption. For example, if a charitable organization operates a full-time shoe store in a shopping center, the shoe store income would be taxable to the charity. However, the charity's tax exemption for its other income probably would not be jeopardized unless the effect of operating the shoe store was to shift the focus of the organization totally away from its exempt function.

The basic function of an employee benefit plan trust is to receive, invest, and distribute plan funds to participants and beneficiaries. Thus, passive investment income of the plan trust is usually not unrelated business income unless the investment is debt-financed, as described in the next paragraph. Problems sometimes arise in distinguishing passive investments from activities that might be considered a trade or business. The law specifically exempts dividends, interest, annuities, and royalties, as well as rents from real property and from personal property leased with real property. Despite this, the wide variety of possible leasing arrangements indicates that each rental arrangement must be looked at on the basis of its own facts and circumstances. For example, a number of revenue rulings have held that investments in manufacturing or railroad equipment for leasing constituted an unrelated trade or business, even though these leasing arrangements are usually looked on by investors as strictly investment activities. Another revenue ruling, however, allows a qualified plan trust to hold shares in a real estate investment trust without incurring unrelated business taxable income. In short, the possible impact of unrelated business taxable income is an additional factor that must be taken into account by the investment advisers of a benefit plan trust.

Code Section 514 specifies that income from *debt-financed property* is to be treated by a tax-exempt organization as unrelated business taxable income. However, there is an exception in Section 514(c)(9) for qualified plans holding certain real estate investments that typically are highly leveraged or debt-financed. Therefore, such investments may still be advantageous to a qualified plan, particularly if they provide long-term growth or other benefits.

Investment Policy

The policy baseline for the investment of qualified plan funds is set by the rules previously discussed—the exclusive-benefit rule, the prudent-expert rule, the diversification requirement, liquidity requirements, the plan document itself, and the additional limitations imposed by the prohibited transaction and unrelated business income provisions. Within these constraints, however, a broad range of investment strategies is possible.

Growth-Oriented Strategies. Trustees governed by fiduciary rules aimed primarily at the preservation of principal generally do not follow aggressive, growth-oriented investment strategies, and pension trustees are no exception. However, qualified plan design offers a number of opportunities for incorporating growth-oriented investment strategies without running into fiduciary problems.

Defined-contribution plans can provide that part or all of each participant's account be put in a participant-directed account, with the participant then choosing the investment strategy. This relieves the trustee of liability for that choice if the plan meets requirements of Department of Labor regulations under ERISA Section 404c. Also, defined-contribution plan funds can be invested in pooled accounts of a bank or insurance company that offer participants choices of investment strategies—an equity fund, a fixed-income fund, and so on.

For defined-benefit plans, there is no provision for participant direction of investment; however, as discussed in Chapter 24, defined-benefit plan funds can be invested in insurance company funds utilizing separate account funding, with a choice by the employer of investment strategies such as equity or fixed income. It is also possible to structure the trust agreement to allow the employer to recommend investments, and the employer can pursue a growth-oriented strategy. In such a case, of course, the employer is still responsible for the adequacy of the pension fund and is subject to full fiduciary liability for its investment recommendations. Finally, there is the possibility of designing a plan to invest primarily in employer securities, which can be viewed as a type of growth-oriented investment strategy.

Risk. Most of the ERISA investment rules can be seen as prescriptions for avoiding risk, particularly the risk of large losses; for example, the requirement for diversification of investments. Within the ERISA limits, however, the qualified plan investment manager, like any investor, must balance risk and return.

Social Effects.   According to the Employee Benefit Research Institute,[1] at the end of 2002, private pension funds (trusteed and insured) in the United States totaled about $4.8 trillion, with government-employee funds comprising an additional $2.8 trillion. This is a sizable portion of the nation's capital. If there is any pattern to the investment strategies of qualified plan investment managers, such a pattern is likely to have an effect on the economy and on society. Because so much pension money is held and invested by large institutions such as banks and insurance companies, current pension investment policies largely reflect the views of these organizations. In general, such organizations will tend to invest in conventional ways that support the status quo. The question is often raised whether there is a role in pension investing for active attempts to support a particular social result not dictated merely by market conditions.

Existing legislation and other laws relating to qualified plan investments focus primarily on fiduciary aspects of the relationship between plan managers and participants; they do not address issues of social policy. That is, they encourage investment managers to invest so as to prevent direct losses to participants and beneficiaries, but they do not deal with possible indirect losses that may accrue to participants and beneficiaries as a result of trends in overall pension investment policy that may be contrary to the social and economic interests of plan participants.

Social Investing.   In recent years, objections to prevailing pension investment policies have been raised, particularly on behalf of unionized employees in large manufacturing industries. Although these objections are not always clearly stated, four types of arguments can be distinguished. First, it is stated that the usual pension investment policies contribute to the disinvestment in basic manufacturing industries that has been occurring, particularly in certain geographic areas such as the Midwest. This results in the loss of jobs for persons covered under the pension plans, with the attendant economic and social costs, and also in disinvestment in housing and other facilities in communities where plan participants live. Second, it is stated that pension investors can undercut the union movement by investing in nonunionized corporations. Third, pension investment policies allegedly can affect the welfare of workers adversely by investing in corporations that violate health, safety, or nondiscrimination principles. Finally, some object to investing in certain corporations on moral or political grounds (not directly related to the interests of plan participants), such as environmental pollution or weapons production. Although advocates of social investment for union pension funds sometimes make common cause with religious and academic groups who advocate social investment policies for church or university endowment funds, it is clear that on this issue the interests of unionized employees are quite distinct.

A decision by a pension investment manager to pursue a **social investment strategy** that attempts to avoid one or more of these objections raises a number of issues. The first relates to fiduciary responsibility. Does a social investment strategy result in a lower return on the fund? There are some studies indicating that an investment portfolio of "good guy" investments has a lower return. However, such studies usually choose the "good" investments using a broad range of criteria, so they do not indicate the effects of narrower targeting such as simply excluding nonunion employers. The "efficient markets" theory proposed by some economists would suggest that in the long run an investment strategy based on social investing should have no effect on investment return, so long as investments are sufficiently diversified and the market includes other investors who do not use the same social criteria.

Some social investment advocates suggest that even if the return is lower, the indirect social and economic benefits to plan participants are a compensating factor. However, under current fiduciary law, both state and federal, this argument probably could not protect an investment manager in the event of a lawsuit by a plan participant injured directly by a low return on the fund. Suggestions have been made in Congress to amend federal legislation to permit social investment of various types, but no such provision has yet been enacted. The Department of Labor is reportedly studying the issue, but no regulations or rulings in this area have been issued.

A second problem, assuming a social investment strategy has been chosen, is how does the investment manager evaluate possible investments to determine their compliance with the chosen social criteria? It is currently difficult to identify corporations that meet even such simple criteria as compliance with health and safety legislation. There are various social investment indices available, but these are generally inadequate as guidance in any specific program of social investing. Because of these difficulties, social investing usually involves additional administrative costs.

The pension investment community has generally reacted with some hostility to social investing, with most pension advisers taking the view that any considerations other than the traditional ones of risk and return have no part in pension investment decisions, and that it would be a violation of fiduciary responsibility to use other criteria.

■ PLAN TERMINATION

Qualified plans are subject to a **permanence requirement.** By this it is meant only that the employer must not have an *initial* intention of operating the plan for a few years to obtain tax benefits and then terminating it. Thus, despite the permanence requirement, qualified plans can be terminated and often are.

A plan can be terminated unilaterally by the employer, unless a collective bargaining agreement or other employment contract prohibits it. If an employer does not formally terminate a plan, but merely discontinues contributions to it, the IRS may find that the plan has been terminated, with the same consequences as if a formal termination had been made by the employer. It is also possible to have a **partial termination** of a plan, which usually means that the plan is terminated for an identifiable group of employees, such as employees at a given geographic location, while it is continued for other employees.

When Should a Plan Be Terminated?

If a qualified plan ceases to be an effective method of compensating employees, or becomes too expensive for the employer, it should be terminated. However, under the rules discussed in this chapter, a proposed termination may have such undesirable consequences that the employer will decide to continue the plan, possibly in amended form. As discussed below, the substitution of a different plan or plans may avoid some of the undesirable consequences of simply terminating the old plan.

Asset-Reversion Terminations. Defined-benefit plans are sometimes terminated not because they are too costly or ineffective but because the employer wants to take out some of the plan's assets. If the plan is fully funded, excess plan assets will revert to the employer, if the plan so provides. The assets that revert are taxable income to the employer.

For some time, commentators have expressed concern that the applicable law in this area favors stripping of assets from qualified plans, with a possible detriment to the retirement security of employees. Congress initially responded to this concern by imposing a 10 percent tax on asset reversions, in addition to the income tax payable on the reversion amount. This tax was criticized as merely penalizing employers slightly without any direct benefit to employees. Consequently, the law was changed; the penalty is now set at 50 percent of the reversion amount unless (1) the employer adopts a replacement plan, (2) the employer provides pro rata increases in the benefits of participants in the terminated plan totaling at least 20 percent of the reversion, or (3) the employer is in bankruptcy. If any of these three conditions is met, the excise tax is 20 percent rather than 50 percent (Code Section 4980).

Consequences of Termination

If an employer terminates a plan within a few years after its inception, the employer must usually show that the termination resulted from *business necessity* or the IRS will infer that the permanence requirement for qualification never existed. The plan will thus be treated as a nonqualified deferred compensation arrangement, resulting in a loss of tax benefits for both employer and employees. If the plan is terminated after many years of operation, the IRS will not raise a presumption of impermanence so long as the plan is properly funded and termination does not result in prohibited discrimination.

Plan termination results in immediate 100 percent vesting for some or all employees. With a defined-benefit plan, 100 percent vesting means that the accrued benefits of affected participants become 100 percent vested at the time of termination, to the extent the plan is funded. Most defined-benefit plans are insured by the PBGC, and the further complications involved are discussed below. At termination, with a defined-contribution plan, participants become 100 percent vested in their account balances derived from employer contributions, regardless of where they stand otherwise on the vesting schedule. This precludes the possibility of any future forfeitures (and therefore, in a profit-sharing plan, any future reallocation of forfeitures). Obviously, the purpose of the vesting remedy is to limit the possibility of any discrimination resulting from termination of the plan.

■ THE PENSION BENEFIT GUARANTY CORPORATION AND ITS PLAN INSURANCE

If an employer encounters financial difficulty and is forced to terminate or curtail a qualified defined-benefit plan, the ultimate payment of plan benefits is often jeopardized. If the plan uses an insurance company contract as the funding medium, the employee's benefit is usually to some extent guaranteed by the insurance company. However, the use of trust funds predominates in defined-benefit plans, and these funds usually involve no insurance company guarantees. Actuarial funding methods assume that plans will be in existence indefinitely. As a result, the plan fund in many cases is, at a given moment, inadequate to fund all of the benefits accrued under the plan if the plan terminates at that moment.

Recognizing this problem, Congress established a scheme of mandatory plan insurance for certain defined-benefit plans as part of ERISA (Title 4) in 1974. The insurance is administered by a quasi-governmental corporation called the Pension Benefit Guaranty Corporation, or PBGC. Defined-contribution plans do not involve the same benefit security problems as defined-benefit plans because the participant's accrued benefit is always equal to the participant's account balance. Therefore, the PBGC plan insurance scheme does not apply to defined-contribution ("individual account") plans.

Plans Covered

PBGC coverage can be summarized by stating that, in general, all qualified defined-benefit plans are covered, while individual account (defined-contribution) plans are not covered. With respect to defined-benefit plans, the usual exclusions applicable to ERISA provisions apply: There is no PBGC coverage for federal, state, and local government plans; church plans (unless the plan elects coverage); plans with no employer contributions; plans for highly compensated individuals or substantial owners; plans frozen prior to ERISA; and various other exclusions.

Benefits Insured

The PBGC does not insure or guarantee all benefits provided under a qualified defined-benefit plan covered by PBGC insurance. A distinction is made between *basic* and *nonbasic* benefits. The PBGC is required under the terms of its federal charter to insure basic benefits. PBGC is allowed to extend coverage to nonbasic benefits, but it has not yet done so.

There are numerous conditions and limitations on what qualifies as a guaranteed basic benefit, set out in Part 2613 of the PBGC regulations. The most significant limitations are as follows:

■ The benefit must be nonforfeitable or vested. This refers to vesting that existed under the terms of the plan immediately prior to plan termination, not to benefits that became vested solely on account of plan termination.

■ The benefit must be a "pension benefit"—a benefit payable as an annuity to a retiring or terminating participant or surviving beneficiary, providing a substantially level retirement income to the recipient. Consequently, the PBGC generally does not insure a lump-sum benefit.

■ There is a dollar limitation on the amount of monthly payment the PBGC will guarantee. Regardless of the plan provisions, the insured monthly benefit is limited to one-twelfth of the participant's average annual gross income from the employer during the highest paid five consecutive calendar years or lesser number of years of active participation. Furthermore, in no event will the insured benefit exceed a dollar limit, originally $750 monthly in 1974, which is subject to an indexation procedure. For plans terminated in 2004, the limit was $3,698.86 monthly. The dollar limitation applies to a benefit in the form of a straight-life annuity beginning at age 65 and payable monthly. The limit is adjusted actuarially for other forms of benefits.

■ The participant must be "entitled" to the benefit as of the date of plan termination. Generally, this means that the recipient must have satisfied the conditions of the plan necessary to establish the right to receive the benefit (other than mere application for it or satisfying a waiting period) prior to the plan termination date. Also, the benefit must be payable to or for the benefit of a natural person (not, for example, a corporation).

PBGC Funding and Premiums

The PBGC has established several funds to provide benefit guarantees. It has the power to borrow up to $100 million from the U.S. Treasury if necessary. However, the PBGC is expected to be self-supporting and is therefore required to charge insurance premiums for its guarantees. For single employer plans, the basic annual premium for 2004 is $19 per participant. For certain underfunded plans, an additional annual premium may be required, depending on the amount of the plan's unfunded vested benefits. Congress has the authority through a joint resolution procedure to review and change PBGC rates from time to time, based on various factors set out in the law. Payment of the premiums is mandatory, and is enforced by various penalties.

Plan Termination Procedures

Reportable Events. The PBGC becomes involved with a plan that is terminating or encountering various difficulties in somewhat complex ways. First of all, the plan administrator is obligated to report to the PBGC certain events that could potentially cause financial difficulty. There is a long list of these *reportable events;* some significant ones are these:

■ An IRS or Department of Labor disqualification of the plan

■ A plan amendment decreasing retirement benefits

■ A decrease in the number of active participants to less than 80 percent of the number at the beginning of the plan year or 75 percent of the number at the beginning of the previous plan year

■ A determination by the IRS that there has been a termination or partial termination of the plan

■ A failure to meet the minimum funding standards

■ An inability by the plan to pay benefits when due

■ Certain large distributions to a substantial owner

■ A plan merger, consolidation, or transfer of its assets

■ The occurrence of another event indicative of a need to terminate the plan—the regulations refer to such items as insolvency of the employer or a related employer and certain breakups of commonly controlled groups of employers

If the consequences of these reportable events are significant enough, the plan can be *involuntarily terminated* by the PBGC. Also, of course, a *voluntary termination* can be carried out by the plan administrator under one of the two procedures described below. In any event, the actual termination of a plan covered by PBGC guarantees is carried out under detailed procedures set out in the law.

Allocation of Plan Assets on Termination.   The PBGC termination procedures revolve around the rules for allocation of the assets of a terminated defined-benefit plan under ERISA Section 4044. On termination, such plan assets must be allocated in descending order to the following categories:

■   Benefits attributable to voluntary employee contributions.

■   Benefits attributable to mandatory employee contributions.

■   Annuity benefits attributable to employer contributions that were, or could have been, in "pay status" as of three years prior to termination. A benefit in "pay status" means a benefit being paid to a retired (nonactive) employee. The high priority reflects the fact that such employees are least able to protect themselves against a failure of the plan fund.

■   All other PBGC guaranteed benefits.

■   All other vested benefits.

■   All other plan benefits.

Any amount remaining after these categories may revert to the employer, if the plan so provides.

Voluntary Plan Termination.   ERISA Section 4041(a) provides for two types of voluntary termination procedures, the *standard termination* and the *distress termination*. A plan is eligible for the standard termination only if assets at the termination date are sufficient to provide for all *benefit commitments* as of the termination date. A benefit commitment to a participant or beneficiary means all benefits guaranteed by the PBGC as described earlier, but determined without certain limitations, such as the maximum dollar limit or the restriction on benefits in effect for less than 60 months before plan termination. Certain early retirement supplements and plant closing benefits also come within the definition of benefit commitments. If benefit commitments are not met, a voluntary termination must follow the distress termination procedures.

With a standard termination, the plan administrator must provide 60 days' advance notice of intent to terminate to participants, beneficiaries, and other affected parties.

The plan administrator must begin distributing plan assets at the end of the 60-day determination period if the PBGC has not issued a notice of noncompliance and if the plan assets are sufficient to meet benefit commitments. The assets are distributed in accordance with the priorities of ERISA Section 4044 described above. Assets must be distributed either through the purchase of annuities from an insurance company to provide plan benefits or in some other manner providing adequate benefit security.

A distress termination is available only if one of three distress criteria is met:

1. Each contributing sponsor of the plan or substantial member of a controlled group sponsoring the plan must be in a liquidation proceeding under federal bankruptcy law or similar state law; or

2. The sponsor must be involved in a reorganization in bankruptcy or an insolvency proceeding; or

3. The plan administrator must demonstrate to the PBGC that unless the termination occurs, the sponsor will not be able to pay its debts and will be unable to continue in business, or the cost of providing benefits under the pension plan has become unreasonably burdensome (for example, because of a declining workforce).

On a distress termination, the plan administrator must submit to the PBGC information similar to that required under a standard termination, plus information related to the distress criteria. If the PBGC determines that there are sufficient plan assets to fulfill benefit commitments, the plan administrator may begin to distribute the assets in accordance with ERISA Section 4044.

Contingent Liability of Employer.   In the event of a plan termination covered by PBGC insurance, the employer must reimburse the PBGC for the PBGC's liability for guaranteed benefits in excess of the plan's assets. However, under ERISA Section 4062, any amount of the employer's liability that exceeds 30 percent of the employer's net worth can be deferred under "commercially reasonable" terms. This PBGC remedy may be of limited value for large bankrupt employers with no net worth or financial resources.

Multiemployer Plans.   The previous discussion of termination procedures applies primarily to single employer plans or plans of controlled groups of employers. The termination problems are somewhat different where contributions to the plan are made by a number of unrelated employers—that is, a multiemployer plan such as a plan adopted under industrywide collective bargaining agreements. For such plans, there are different asset allocation provisions and somewhat different provisions for involuntary termination by the PBGC.

The most significant difference from single employer plans involves the *withdrawal liability* of an employer that completely or partially withdraws from a multiemployer plan. A sale of the employer's assets in an arm's-length transaction will not be treated as a withdrawal as long as the purchaser of the business continues the plan, the purchaser provides an acceptable surety bond or escrow deposit for five years after the sale, and the seller of the business remains secondarily liable for five years. If an employer withdraws from the plan, the employer's withdrawal liability is an amount based on the withdrawing employer's share of unfunded vested benefits under the plan. The withdrawing employer must pay all or a substantial portion of the withdrawal liability to the plan on a periodic basis over a number of years. The law provides for the PBGC to establish a supplemental fund to reimburse multiemployer plans for any uncollectible employer withdrawal liabilities.

■ KEY TERMS

advance determination letter

claims procedure

disqualified person

diversification requirement

master plan

named fiduciary

partial termination

party-in-interest

permanence requirement

plan administrator

prohibited transactions

prototype plan

prudent-man requirement

reporting and disclosure provisions

retroactive amendment procedure

social investment strategy

unrelated business taxable income

■ STUDY QUESTIONS

1. What are the steps necessary for an employer to adopt a qualified plan for a given year?

2. a. Why is it desirable to obtain an advance determination letter for a qualified plan?

   b. What recourse might be available to an employer if the IRS finds a plan is not qualified?

3. What types of employee benefit plans are exempt from the fiduciary, reporting, and disclosure requirements of ERISA?

4. a. What is the purpose of the reporting and disclosure provisions of ERISA?

   b. Briefly describe the reports ERISA requires qualified plans to provide to participants or to the federal government.

5. What objectives were the fiduciary requirements of ERISA enacted to accomplish?

6. What are the investment responsibilities of a fiduciary under ERISA?

7. Explain why each of the following is or is not a prohibited transaction.

   a. The sale of real estate owned by the ABC Plan to the wife of the treasurer of the ABC Company.

   b. Loaning money from the plan to an officer of the corporation. The plan contains a loan provision that permits loans on a nondiscriminatory basis.

   c. The acquisition of 25 percent of employer stock by a defined-benefit plan.

   d. The acquisition of real estate from the plan for less than its market value by the plan's trustee.

8. What is unrelated business taxable income and what is the effect of having it?

9. The Faulty Corporation installed a pension plan five years ago and because of declining profits, the firm is considering terminating the plan to help prevent insolvency.

   a. What will be the IRS's likely reaction to this termination? Explain.

   b. What alternatives are available to the corporation other than terminating the plan?

10. What qualified plan benefits are insured by the Pension Benefit Guaranty Corporation?

■ NOTE

1. *Facts from EBRI, www.ebri.com* (December 2003).

28 Individual Retirement Plans and Simplified Employee Pensions

- Describe individual retirement plans with respect to
    1. Eligibility
    2. Deduction limit
    3. Spousal IRAs
    4. Nondeductible IRAs
    5. Timing of contributions
    6. Distributions
    7. Funding
- Describe Roth IRAs and how they are used.
- Explain the rollover rules.
- Describe simplified employee pensions (SEPs) with regard to
    1. Eligibility and coverage
    2. Contributions and deductions

Certain tax-favored arrangements that are not technically qualified plans can offer employees the same tax deferral advantages as the qualified plans discussed in previous chapters. These nonqualified but tax-favored arrangements are individual retirement accounts and simplified employee pensions. Where these plans are available, they can be a useful supplement or alternative to a qualified plan adopted by an employer.

INDIVIDUAL RETIREMENT PLANS

Complete retirement planning, at least from the employee's viewpoint, requires consideration of individual retirement accounts or annuities (IRAs), which allow individuals to adopt a plan that provides tax deferral benefits somewhat similar to those available from an employer plan. The role of IRAs is a limited one, however. Individuals who are participants in qualified plans and whose income exceeds specified limits are limited or excluded altogether from eligibility for IRA deductions. And no employee can contribute more than a specified annual deduction limit (see below) that is generally less than can be contributed to a qualified plan.

IRAs can be used by employers as part of their employee plan design, either through simply sponsoring an IRA plan or adopting an arrangement known as a **simplified employee pension (SEP),** under which employer contributions are made systematically to employees' IRAs. SEPs permit a contribution level similar to that for a qualified plan and are viewed as an alternative to a qualified plan.

Eligibility for IRAs

To be eligible for an IRA, an employee or self-employed person must have compensation or earned income.[1] Compensation or earned income means income received from services actually performed by the individual. This includes compensation from self-employment as well as from an employer. The definition has been extended to also include taxable alimony received by a divorced spouse. It does not include investment income, any amount received as a pension or annuity, or any amount received as deferred compensation. The deductible contribution must not exceed 100% of compensation or earned income.

Deduction Limit

The annual IRA deduction limit for an individual is as follows:

Taxable year beginning in	Deductible amount
2001	$2,000
2002 through 2004	3,000
2005 through 2007	4,000
2008 and thereafter	5,000

For individuals who have attained age 50 before the close of the tax year, an additional deductible amount is allowable for IRA contributions—the resulting total deductible amount is as follows:

Year	Total deductible amount
2001	$2,000
2002 through 2004	3,500
2005	4,500
2006 and 2007	5,000
2008 and thereafter	6,000

After 2008, the deductible amount is scheduled to be adjusted for cost-of-living increases.

The deductible limit is reduced by contributions made by the taxpayer to a Roth IRA for the year (see below). Deductible IRA contributions are restricted to the following:

- Individuals who are not active participants in an employer-maintained retirement plan for any part of the retirement plan year ending with or within the individual's taxable year.

- Any other individual, as long as the individual has adjusted gross income (AGI) below a specified limit. If the adjusted gross income exceeds this limit, the annual deductible IRA limit is reduced under a formula that eventually permits no deduction.

The *active participant* restriction applies if the individual is an active participant in any of the following:

- A regular qualified plan

- A Section 403(b) tax-deferred annuity plan

- A SEP

- A federal, state, or local government plan, not including a Section 457 nonqualified deferred-compensation plan

If an otherwise eligible person is subject to the active participant restriction, the available IRA deduction is reduced below the dollar amount for the year (e.g., below $4,000 for 2005–2007) if the AGI of the taxpayer is within the phaseout ranges indicated below, with the deduction eliminated entirely if the AGI is above the upper limit of the phaseout range.

IRA Active Participant AGI phaseout ranges

Year	Single	Married filing jointly	Married filing separately
2003	$40,000–$50,000	$60,000–$70,000	$0–$10,000
2004	45,000–55,000	65,000–75,000	0–10,000
2005	50,000–60,000	70,000–80,000	0–10,000
2006	50,000–60,000	75,000–85,000	0–10,000
2007 and later	50,000–60,000	80,000–100,000	0–10,000

The reduction in the applicable dollar limit in the phaseout AGI region is proportional to the amount by which the AGI exceeds the lower limit.

EXAMPLE

Suppose that in 2005 a single (age 40) taxpayer's AGI is $54,000. The taxpayer is $4,000 into the phaseout region of $10,000, so his annual IRA deduction is reduced by $4,000/$10,000 or 40%. This is a reduction of $1,600 (40% of $4,000), so the maximum IRA deduction for 2005 is $2,400 ($4,000 less $1,600).

There is a $200 "floor" under the reduction formula. That is, as long as the taxpayer is below the upper AGI cutoff level, at least $200 can be contributed and deducted. For example, if the taxpayer in the preceding example had AGI of $59,900, he could contribute and deduct up to $200.

An individual is not subject to the "active participant" restrictions just because his or her spouse is an active participant in a tax-favored retirement plan. However, the benefit of this provision phases out for joint adjusted gross incomes from $150,000 to $160,000.

> **EXAMPLE**
> Les and Pat, both aged 31, are married and file jointly. Both are working and Les,
> but not Pat, actively participates in an employer-sponsored qualified plan. Les and
> Pat each earn $75,000 in 2005. Pat may contribute and deduct up to $4,000 to an
> IRA. Les may not make any deductible contributions to an IRA. However, if Les
> and Pat together earned a total of $160,000 or more in 2005, neither one could
> make a deductible IRA contribution since this "no-spousal-attribution-of-active-par-
> ticipation" rule would be fully phased out at their joint AGI level of $160,000. If joint
> AGI was between $150,000 and $160,000, Pat's deduction limit would be reduced
> ratably below $4,000 as in the preceding example.

Spousal IRAs

The spousal IRA provision permits married couples who file a joint return to make
a higher level of deductible IRA contributions in some cases by permitting an additional
deduction for the nonworking spouse. If one spouse is nonworking or earns less than
the other spouse, the maximum amount deductible for the lower-earning spouse is the
lesser of (1) the annual deduction limit or (2) 100 percent of the lower earner's compensation, plus 100 percent of the higher earner's compensation minus the amount taken
as an IRA deduction by the higher earner.

> **EXAMPLE**
> Individual Pat earns $30,000 and Pat's spouse, Chris, is not working. The couple
> may contribute and deduct up to $4,000 in 2005 to an IRA for Chris. If Pat is eligi-
> ble for an IRA, the couple may also contribute and deduct up to $4,000 in 2005 for
> Pat's IRA.

Nondeductible IRAs

Individuals not permitted to make deductible IRA contributions may, nevertheless,
make such contributions on a nondeductible basis, up to the annual dollar limit (for
example, $4,000 for 2005). The total of any individual's annual IRA contributions both
deductible and nondeductible, together with Roth IRA contributions (see below), cannot
exceed the annual dollar limit. Nondeductible contributions (but not income on those
contributions) are tax free when ultimately distributed to the individual. If nondeductible
contributions to an IRA are made, any amounts withdrawn are treated as partly tax free
and partly taxable under rules similar to the exclusion ratio calculation for annuities
under Code Section 72.

Other Restrictions on IRAs

Because the IRA is designed primarily for retirement savings, no IRA deduction is
allowed to an individual for the taxable year in which the individual attains age 70½
or any later year.

Contributions to an IRA must be made in cash; contributions of property such as an insurance policy are not permitted.

Excess Contributions

A contribution in excess of the deductible limits described above is an *excess contribution* subject to an annual nondeductible 6 percent excise tax (Code Section 4973). The excise tax continues to be applied each year until the contribution is withdrawn from the IRA. Many complex rules apply to excess contributions; their complexity seems out of proportion to the actual issue involved.

Timing of Contributions

An IRA for any given year may be established up to the time for filing the tax return for the given year, not including extensions. Deductible contributions for a given year may be made within the same time limit. This "last minute" feature of IRAs helps to explain a lot of their popularity. For example, suppose Frank Filer works out a draft of his 2004 tax return on April 1, 2005, and discovers that he owes the government $600. His local savings bank is running an advertising campaign touting its IRAs and offering to lend money to contribute to an IRA. Frank does some quick figuring and discovers that if he borrows $2,000 from the bank and contributes it to an IRA, it will wipe out his tax liability and he will be entitled to a $160 tax refund, enough to make the first monthly payment on the loan. This may be a more attractive deal to Frank than borrowing $600 to pay taxes.

Limitations on IRA Distributions

To limit any benefits for nonretirement distributions from IRAs, there is a penalty under Code Section 72(t) for certain early IRA distributions similar to the early distribution penalty applicable to qualified plans. The IRA early distribution penalty is 10 percent of the taxable amount of any distribution except for the following:

- Distributions made on or after attainment of age 59½
- Distributions made to a beneficiary or employee's estate on or after the employee's death
- Distributions attributable to disability
- Distributions that are part of a series of substantially equal periodic payments made at least annually over the life or life expectancy of the participant, or the joint lives or life expectancies of the participant and beneficiary
- Certain distributions to unemployed individuals for health insurance premiums
- Distributions to the extent they are eligible for an itemized medical expense
- Distributions to pay for certain higher education expenses for the taxpayer, spouse, child, or grandchild
- Distributions up to $10,000 for first-home purchases

Loans from IRAs are treated as distributions and, therefore, are not available for practical purposes. This is another aspect of IRAs that makes them less flexible than regular qualified plans, which allow loans.

There is an *upper limit* on the length of time amounts may be maintained in an IRA. IRAs are subject to the same minimum distribution requirements as those applicable to qualified plans, as discussed in Chapter 25. For IRAs (and for SEPs and SIMPLE/IRAs as well), however, distributions must begin at age 70½; there is no extension of time to the retirement date.

Taxation of Distributions

The amount distributed from an IRA is taxable as ordinary income in the year of receipt. Lump-sum distributions are taxable when received and do not qualify for the special capital-gain or averaging provisions applicable to lump-sum distributions from qualified plans. An IRA annuity is taxed under the Section 72 annuity rules—payments based on deductible contributions and all investment earnings are ordinary income and are taxable in full as received. Nondeductible IRA contributions, if any, are recovered tax free through an exclusion ratio applied to each payment.

The value of an annuity or lump sum received by any beneficiary of a participant in an IRA is included in the deceased participant's gross estate for federal estate tax purposes. However, if the beneficiary is a spouse, there is no estate tax because of the unlimited marital deduction under the estate tax. Even for a nonspouse beneficiary, there may be no estate tax if the estate is relatively small—less than $850,000 for 2004 (scheduled to rise to $1 million in 2007).

Funding of IRAs

The code provides two funding vehicles for IRAs: individual retirement accounts and individual retirement annuities.

Individual Retirement Accounts. An individual retirement account must be a plan established under a written trust created or organized in the United States for the exclusive benefit of the individual creating the IRA. A written custodial agreement can also be used. The written instrument must include the following provisions:

- The contributions must be in cash and not exceed the applicable deduction limit on behalf of any individual.
- The trustee must be a bank or "other person" approved by the IRS.
- No part of the trust fund will be invested in life insurance contracts. Annuities, however, can be purchased.
- An individual's account is nonforfeitable.
- The assets of the trust will not be commingled with other property except in a common trust fund or common investment fund.
- The individual's account must be distributed in accordance with certain distribution requirements, such as the age 70½ provision and the minimum distribution requirement.

Many banks and other savings institutions are actively marketing trusteed IRAs. Brokerage houses and mutual funds also market trusteed IRAs. These technically use a bank as trustee but the bank's role is purely formal and the investor views the broker or fund as the sponsor of the IRA.

A bank or institution acting as trustee or custodian may prepare its own prototype trust agreement and submit the agreement to the IRS for approval on Form 5306. Alternatively, the IRS has issued prototype trust and custodial agreements (Forms 5305 and 5305A), which, if used, are automatically qualified. An individual who deposits funds in an IRA that uses an approved form of trust agreement does not have to submit the IRA to the IRS for approval.

Individual Retirement Annuities.   An individual may fund an IRA by purchasing an *individual retirement annuity.* An individual retirement annuity is a contract that is issued by an insurance company and that meets requirements parallel to those listed above for individual retirement accounts. The premium for the annuity may not be fixed, so the only insurance product that can be used is a flexible premium annuity. Both fixed-dollar and variable annuities can be used.

Insurance companies that wish to market individual retirement annuities may apply for IRS approval of their own prototype contracts. As with trusteed plans, an individual who purchases an approved prototype individual retirement annuity contract does not apply separately for IRS approval of the individual IRA plan.

Rollovers

To increase the amount of investment flexibility available to participants in IRAs and qualified plans, the Code contains a number of provisions relating to the use of IRAs as vehicles for investment *rollovers*. Three types of tax-favored rollovers are possible.

Rollover from One IRA to Another.   There is no current taxation if an individual withdraws an amount out of an IRA trust fund, IRA annuity, or retirement bond plan and invests part or all of it in another IRA plan. To receive this treatment, the amount to be rolled over must be paid into another IRA plan not later than the 60th day after the withdrawal. If such a rollover is made, no additional tax-free rollover of this type is permitted for a period of one year thereafter.

A direct transfer of an account from one IRA trustee to another (with the participant never receiving the money) is not treated as a rollover for purposes of these rules. Thus, a direct transfer can be used as a way of avoiding the one-year rule.

Rollover of Distribution from Qualified Plan or Annuity.   An IRA may be used as a vehicle for receiving the proceeds of a distribution from a qualified plan or a Section 403(b) plan, thereby avoiding immediate taxation on the distribution. If the rollover amount is transferred to the participant, however, tax must be withheld. To avoid this, the rollover should be a direct transfer from the plan trustee to the IRA trustee. All or any portion of the amount received can be rolled over. The annual deductible dollar limit does not apply to a rollover contribution. If the rollover is made by the participant (rather than as a direct transfer), the rollover contribution must be made on or before the 60th day after receipt of the distribution. An existing IRA can be used, or a new one may be set up.

The part of the distribution that is rolled over into the IRA will not be currently taxable to the recipient. The usual rules for taxation of IRA distributions will apply when this amount is subsequently withdrawn. Any part of the distribution from the qualified plan or Section 403(b) plan that is not rolled over into the IRA will be taxable at the time of receipt under the usual rules for taxation of distributions, except that the averaging provisions may not be used.

In deciding whether to roll over all or part of the proceeds of a distribution from a qualified plan to an IRA, the alternatives must be considered. A lump-sum distribution from a qualified plan may qualify for the special averaging provisions of the Code. Thus, even though a distribution that is not rolled over is taxable immediately, it is taxable under advantageous provisions if it qualifies as a lump-sum distribution. A distribution that is rolled over will not be taxed immediately; taxation will be deferred to the time when it is withdrawn from the IRA. However, this subsequent distribution, like any IRA distribution, is not eligible for the averaging provisions; rather, the taxable amount is taxed as ordinary income.

Despite the possible loss of averaging, however, the mere deferral of taxes resulting from a rollover may be advantageous. Furthermore, taxes on investment earnings of the IRA are also deferred until the rollover amount is distributed. Although it is somewhat complex, the tax consequences of the two alternatives can be calculated (under appropriate assumptions) and compared; some financial planners provide such advice to their clients. Computer software for this purpose is now widely available.

IRA as Conduit for Transfer from One Plan to Another. Finally, an IRA may be used as a conduit to carry out a tax-free transfer of cash or property from one corporate qualified plan to another. Basically, if the amount received from the qualified plan is transferred within 60 days to an IRA, the transfer is tax free, as described earlier. In addition, if the IRA plan contains no assets other than those attributable to the distribution from the qualified plan, then the amount in the IRA may subsequently be transferred tax free to another qualified plan. Similar provisions allow an IRA to be used as a conduit between two Section 403(b) annuity plans.

Employer-Sponsored IRAs

Although the IRA is viewed primarily as a device for facilitating individual retirement savings, an employer may sponsor an IRA for some or all employees. A labor union may also sponsor an IRA plan for its members. There is no requirement that employer-sponsored IRAs be available to all employees or be nondiscriminatory in coverage.

The contributions to the employer-sponsored IRA may be made as additional compensation or as a salary reduction. Any amount contributed by the employer to the IRA is taxable to the employee as additional compensation income. The employee is then eligible for the IRA tax deduction up to the applicable limitation for the year. Because the amounts contributed are additional compensation, they are subject to FICA and FUTA taxes, therefore adding to employer costs. No federal income tax withholding is required if the employer believes that the employee will be entitled to the offsetting IRA tax deduction.

■ ROTH IRAS

A Roth IRA is a specialized form of nondeductible IRA. Contributions to a Roth IRA are nondeductible, but distributions (including earnings on accumulated contributions) are tax free as long as certain requirements are satisfied. Roth IRAs are not limited or prohibited if the individual is an active participant in a qualified plan, as with deductible IRAs. Many individuals will have a choice between using the traditional IRA or contributing to the new Roth IRA. As indicated above, total contributions for the year (to either type of IRA) cannot exceed the annual dollar limit (the same figure as the regular IRA deduction limit). Generally the annual dollar limit for Roth IRA contributions is as follows:

Taxable year beginning in	Dollar limit
2001	$2,000
2002 through 2004	3,000
2005 through 2007	4,000
2008 and thereafter	5,000

For individuals who have attained age 50 before the close of the tax year, an additional dollar amount is allowable—the resulting total amount is as follows:

Year	Total dollar limit
2001	$2,000
2002 through 2004	3,500
2005	4,500
2006 and 2007	5,000
2008 and thereafter	6,000

After 2008, the dollar limit is scheduled to be adjusted for cost-of-living increases.

The maximum contribution to a Roth IRA is phased out for individuals with AGIs between $95,000 and $110,000 (pro rata reduction over $15,000 income spread). For joint filers the phaseout occurs for AGIs between $150,000 and $160,000 (pro rata reduction over $10,000 income spread). Unlike traditional IRAs, contributions can even be made after attainment of age 70½.

> **EXAMPLE**
> Alex and Barbara are married and file jointly. Alex's AGI is $85,000 and Barbara's AGI is $90,000. Neither Alex nor Barbara can make a Roth IRA contribution, because their joint AGI exceeds $160,000.

For distributions to be tax free they generally have to be made after the participant attains age 59½, although exceptions are made if payments are made on account of death or disability or used for qualifying first-time homebuyer expenses. An otherwise eligible distribution won't be qualified if made within the five-tax-year period beginning with the first tax year for which a contribution was made to an individual's Roth IRA. If a nonqualifying distribution is made, amounts representing earnings are subject to both income tax and the 10 percent penalty tax that currently applies to early distributions from regular IRAs and other qualified retirement plans. However, Roth IRA contributions can be withdrawn first, before earnings are taxed.

There are no minimum distribution requirements for Roth IRA accounts during the account owner's lifetime. However, minimum distribution requirements apply to the beneficiary of a Roth IRA account after the owner's death.

■ SIMPLIFIED EMPLOYEE PENSIONS

The SEP is an expanded version of the employer-sponsored IRA, designed by Congress to make it easy and attractive for employers to adopt a retirement plan which, although not a qualified plan as such, has similar features. A SEP is designed much like an employer-sponsored IRA, but the deduction limits are much higher—instead of the dollar limit for IRAs described above, the limit on deductible contributions for each employee is the lesser of $41,000 (as indexed for 2004) or 25 percent of the employee's compensation. The price for this expanded deduction limit is that the employer loses discretion as to who must be covered; there is a coverage requirement that in some ways is more stringent than that for regular qualified plans.

Eligibility and Coverage

If the employer has a SEP plan, it must cover all employees who are at least 21 years of age and who have worked for the employer during three out of the preceding five calendar years. Part-time employment counts in determining this; there is no 1,000-hour definition of a year of service. However, contributions need not be made on behalf of employees whose compensation for the calendar year was less than $300 (as indexed for inflation: 2004, $450). The plan can exclude employees who are members of collective bargaining units if retirement benefits have been the subject of good-faith bargaining, and it can also exclude nonresident aliens. Employer contributions to a SEP can be made for employees over age 70½; these employees are not eligible for regular IRAs, as discussed earlier.

Contributions and Deductions

An employer need not contribute any particular amount to a SEP in a given year or even make any contribution at all. In this respect, a SEP is more flexible than any type of qualified plan, even a profit-sharing plan, which requires substantial and recurring employer contributions. However, any employer contribution that is made must be allocated to employees under a definite written formula. The formula may not discriminate in favor of highly compensated employees. In general, the formula must provide allocations as a uniform percentage of total compensation of each employee, taking only the first $200,000 (as indexed for inflation: 2004, $205,000) of compensation into account. The SEP allocation formula can be integrated with Social Security under the usual integration rules for qualified defined-contribution plans.

Each individual in a SEP maintains an IRA, and employer contributions to the SEP are channeled to each employee's IRA. For tax purposes, the employer contributions are treated as if they are paid to the employee in cash and included in income and then contributed to the IRA. The Code provides a deduction to both the employer and to the employee for these amounts.

If the employer maintaining a SEP also has a regular qualified plan, contributions to the SEP may reduce the amount that can be deducted for contributions to the regular plan.

Other Requirements

Except for the contribution, allocation, and deduction provisions, the IRAs maintained as part of a SEP are the same as other IRAs and the rules discussed in the previous sections apply to them as well. For example, the rules for taxation of distributions from SEP-IRAs are the same as those for other IRAs. As with regular IRAs, loans to participants from SEP-IRAs are not permitted.

Labor and IRS regulations contain certain reporting and disclosure provisions for SEPs. These are simplified if the employer uses the IRS prototype SEP contained on Form 5305-SEP. This form was designed to simplify the adoption of SEPs by employers; however, it uses a nonintegrated formula.

When Should an Employer Use a SEP?

The term *simplified* in the name of these plans is somewhat misleading; a SEP is not really much simpler than a regular qualified profit-sharing plan, especially where a qualified master or prototype plan is used. However, installation costs are minimal where the government Form 5305-SEP is used; administration costs are low because the annual report form (5500) need not be filed. Thus, SEPs are attractive for cases where administrative costs must be absolutely minimized, such as a one-person plan. In other specific situations, the special coverage rules for SEPs may be more attractive than the regular coverage rules. From an employee viewpoint, the complete portability of the SEP benefit is attractive.

■ KEY TERM

simplified employee pension (SEP)

■ STUDY QUESTIONS

1. Who is eligible to make deductible IRA contributions?
2. George and Mary Barke (marrieds filing jointly) have an adjusted gross income of $56,317. What is the amount of the deductible IRA contribution that they can make if they do not contribute toward a spousal IRA?
3. What are the advantages of Roth IRAs?
4. How are IRA distributions taxed?
5. What are the financial planning advantages associated with IRA rollovers?
6. What are the major similarities and differences between a SEP and a qualified profit-sharing plan?

■ NOTE

1. Most of the IRA rules are found in Code Sections 219 and 408 and related regulations; these references will not be repeated in this chapter.

Executive Benefits and Nonqualified Deferred-Compensation Plans

- Review the types and objectives of benefits typically provided to select groups of executives.
- Explain why supplemental nonqualified deferred-compensation plans are often provided for executives.
- Explain the distinction between funded and unfunded nonqualified deferred-compensation plans.
- Describe the types of benefits available and the employer's tax treatment with respect to nonqualified deferred-compensation plans.
- Describe the distinction among nonqualified deferred-compensation plans that are funded with restricted property, stock options, or incentive stock options.
- Describe the uses of life insurance in deferred-compensation plans.

CHAPTER OUTLINE

Executive Benefit Checklist

Nonqualified Deferred-Compensation Plans
Objectives for the Plan
Funded and Unfunded Plans
Form of Benefits
Employer's Tax Treatment
Impact of ERISA and Other Regulatory Provisions

Compensation with Restricted Property

Stock Option Plans for Executives (nonstatutory)

Incentive Stock Options

Life Insurance for Executives

The employee benefit plans discussed so far in this text usually are designed for relatively broad groups of employees. Some of the more tax-favored plans, such as qualified retirement plans, actually include specific nondiscriminatory coverage provisions. However, employers often wish to provide special or additional employee benefits to key employees.

In designing plans for executives and key employees, the first step is to identify the employer and employee objectives that the plan is to meet. Then, the plan must be designed to prevent—as far as possible—any undesirable tax or other legal consequences. Employer objectives for executive benefit plans usually include the attraction of appropriate key employees and the retention of such employees once they are hired. In particular, the employer may wish to prevent the employee from going to work for a competing organization. Key employees themselves are usually concerned about their high marginal income tax brackets and their need for savings and estate planning. They therefore favor benefit plans that provide them with tax-favored current compensation or a tax-favored savings medium. There are many types of plans that can be designed to meet employer or employee objectives of this type. In smaller organizations, key employees are often the owners of the business, so there is no difference between employer and employee objectives.

An important basic consideration for an employer in designing executive compensation is whether the amount paid is deductible by the employer as a business expense. Generally, the amount must constitute **reasonable compensation** to be deducted. There is much tax litigation over the issue of reasonableness in this context. In addition, there is a specific annual deduction limit of $1 million on compensation for an employee. However, this $1 million limit applies only to publicly held companies—those whose securities are traded on a securities exchange. Also, it applies only to the company's chief executive officer and the four highest-paid officers. In addition, there are exceptions for "performance-based" compensation.

Some common types of executive benefit plans will be listed here at the beginning of the chapter. In the rest of the chapter, some of these benefits will be discussed in more detail, particularly those involving design features that must be coordinated with tax and other laws.

■ EXECUTIVE BENEFIT CHECKLIST

1. **Nonqualifed deferred-compensation** *or* **supplemental retirement plans.** A nonqualified deferred-compensation plan provides additional retirement or deferred-compensation benefits to key employees in addition to, or in place of, the amounts received under the employer's qualified plan, if any. There is a great deal of flexibility in the design of such plans, and many approaches have been used. (See later discussion.)

2. **Restricted stock** *or Other Property.* Restricted property plans provide compensation to executives in the form of property, usually stock of the employer company, that is restricted in such a way as to help retain the services of the executives or provide an incentive for good executive performance. (See later discussion.)

3. **Stock options.** Stock option plans are used for purposes similar to restricted stock plans; however, with an option plan, the employee is given an option to buy the stock at a stated price rather than an outright grant of the stock subject to restrictions. (See later discussion.)

4. *Life insurance.* Life insurance is a valuable benefit for key employees. As discussed later, it can be provided in a variety of ways.

5. *Severance pay.* Most employers have some form of severance pay policy for employees, often at a minimal level for rank-and-file employees. Executives, however, often negotiate favorable severance pay provisions as part of their compensation package. One particular type of contract regarded by Congress as abusive is the "golden parachute" contract, under which a company agrees to pay an executive large amounts of severance pay if the company changes ownership. Under Code Section 280G, tax deductions for golden parachute payments can be denied to the employer if the amount is excessive—generally, if it is at least three times the executive's average annual salary.

6. *Cash bonus and incentive plans.* Executive compensation plans often include plans for cash bonuses paid currently or deferred for a relatively short period of time that are tied to company or executive performance. Most of these programs are based in some manner on growth in company earnings during the executive's tenure in office. Often the bonus or incentive award depends on the attainment of specified target earnings objectives. There are many design considerations for such plans, including eligibility for the plan, the amount of the award and the benefit formula, and the period of time over which executive performance will be assessed. All these design features must be tailored to the employer's specific situation. There are no special tax complications for these plans; generally, the compensation is taxable to the executive when received and deductible to the employer at the same time.

7. *Additional Medical Expense Benefits.* Additional health insurance is an attractive executive benefit, particularly where the company's basic plan has gaps in coverage.

8. *Disability Income Plans.* As with health insurance, the company may wish to provide a disability income (salary continuation) plan for executive employees to cover any gaps in or to supplement the company's broad-based disability income plan. If the additional coverage is provided through insurance owned by the company, the premium is fully deductible to the employer but benefits are taxable to the employee when paid, subject to a disability income tax credit that disappears for higher income employees. If instead of relying on a company-provided plan, the executive purchases his or her own disability income insurance, the premium payments by the employee are nondeductible, but disability income payments are nontaxable. Because of this, many companies may prefer simply to provide extra compensation income to executives with the understanding that the executive will have the option of obtaining personally owned disability income insurance coverage.

9. *Loans to executives.* A plan providing loans from company funds to executives on favorable terms may be attractive to executives. If the executives are owners of the company, such a program also provides a means of withdrawing corporate funds on a favorable basis, that is, without being taxed on the receipt of a dividend. While interest-free and bargain loans were once used for this purpose, Code Section 7872 now prescribes a minimum interest rate for such loans, which is basically the interest rate applicable during the same period for federal marketable securities of similar term. If the employee loan has a lower interest rate, the bargain element is taxed as if the employee had received that amount as cash compensation. The purpose of this Code provision is to treat as nearly as possible a bargain-rate loan as if it were a market-rate loan, in order to discourage bargain-rate loans.

   Any employee loan should be a bona fide loan and should be evidenced by a formal written note with a fixed maturity date or a repayment schedule. The employee could be required to provide security for the loan, such as a home mortgage. Loan plans can be relatively unrestricted or can restrict executive loans to specific purposes, such as the purchase of a home or children's educational expenses.

   Interest on the loan will generally be consumer interest that is nondeductible to the employee unless secured by a home mortgage. Interest could also be deductible as investment interest if the loan proceeds are used for investments.

10. *Other fringe benefits.* An infinite variety of perquisites and fringe benefits for executives is possible; for example, executive dining rooms, favorable expense account provisions, financial counseling and estate planning for executives, additional moving expense reimbursements, payment of professional association dues, and trips to professional seminars. The usefulness of these benefits depends entirely on individual facts and circumstances.

The decision whether to provide any of these benefits is often affected by their federal income tax treatment because executives tend to be in high marginal income tax brackets and prefer to receive extra compensation in tax-free form.

■ NONQUALIFIED DEFERRED-COMPENSATION PLANS

For qualified plans, Code Section 415, as discussed in Chapter 26, imposes limits on the benefits or contributions that can be provided to any one individual. Annual additions to a qualified defined-contribution plan are limited to the lesser of 100 percent of the employee's compensation or $41,000 (as indexed for 2004). Correspondingly, for a defined-benefit plan, the maximum projected annual benefit is the lesser of 100 percent of the employee's compensation or $165,000. For very highly paid executives, it may be desirable to provide additional retirement income in excess of these limits. Also, in some cases, an employer does not have a qualified plan because the employer does not want to provide the kind of broad retirement plan coverage required by the nondiscriminatory coverage requirements. Thus, a common form of executive benefit is the provision of retirement income or deferred compensation outside a qualified plan. Plans that do this are generally referred to as *nonqualified deferred-compensation plans.* Many names have been coined by consulting firms and insurance companies to describe specific plans of this type—for example, *supplemental retirement plans, top-hat plans,* and the like. The design of nonqualified deferred-compensation plans is open-ended and almost any combination of features can be provided in one way or another.

Objectives for the Plan

The design of a nonqualified deferred-compensation plan will reflect the objectives of the person establishing it. A broad distinction can usually be made between plans designed to meet employer objectives and those designed primarily to meet employee objectives. The employer's objectives in instituting the plan are usually to provide an inducement for hiring key employees and then to provide additional inducements to the key employees to continue working for the employer—especially so that employees do not leave and go to work for a competitor. Employee objectives are usually to obtain an additional form of compensation at retirement or termination of employment, with tax on the additional amounts deferred, if possible, until the money is actually received.

Employer-Instituted Plan. Eligibility in an employer-instituted plan is usually confined to key executives or technical employees who are difficult to recruit and keep. The plan does not have to specify the class of employees to be covered; it can simply be adopted for specific individuals as the need arises. However, the need for fairness among a similarly situated group of executives often dictates that the plan cover a specified class of employees rather than individuals.

A plan instituted for employer objectives usually has some kind of forfeiture provision to discourage key employees from leaving. The plan may require that the employee forfeit all rights under the nonqualified deferred-compensation plan in the event of termination of employment prior to normal retirement age without the employer's consent. The employer might wish to soften this forfeiture provision somewhat by including graduated vesting similar to that required under a qualified plan. However, as long as the plan avoids the applicability of the ERISA vesting provisions discussed later, no particular vesting schedule is required and complete forfeiture can be provided for any reason. The plan might include additional forfeiture provisions, such as a forfeiture of any unpaid benefits, if the employee enters into competition with the employer or goes to work for a competitor. The courts have held that such covenants not to compete can be enforced by the employer, so long as the scope of the prohibited competition is reasonable in terms of the geographic area over which it applies and the period of time during which it is in effect.

Nonqualified deferred-compensation plans often require that the employee remain available for consulting services to the employer after retirement, with possible forfeiture of benefits if the employee does not comply. Actually, consulting services provisions can be beneficial to the employee, as they often provide a means for the employee to receive additional amounts from the employer after retirement in return for relatively nominal consulting services.

Employee-Option Nonqualified Deferred Compensation.   Different objectives for a nonqualified deferred-compensation plan come from the employee's side. Employees with enough income to have substantial savings programs often seek tax-favored methods of saving. Additional amounts of tax-favored savings can be provided beyond the limits of a qualified plan through a salary-reduction arrangement, with the amount of the salary reduction paid to the employee after retirement instead of currently. This provides tax savings because income tax on the salary reduction is paid in the future instead of currently, a valuable benefit because of the time value of money. It is also possible that the employee may be in a lower marginal tax bracket after retirement.

The initial problem in designing a plan for this objective is to ensure that the employee is not taxed currently on the salary reduction that goes into the plan. The salary-reduction arrangement must avoid the constructive receipt doctrine, under which income is taxable to a taxpayer if it is credited to the taxpayer's account, set apart, or otherwise made available, even though it is not actually received. To avoid this doctrine, the amount set aside must be subject to substantial limitations. This can generally be accomplished if the salary-reduction agreement is made prior to the time the income is earned by the employee and if the employee's receipt of it is deferred for a period of time, such as to termination of employment or retirement, which constitutes a substantial limitation.

Plans designed to meet employee objectives generally will have generous provisions and, in particular, there will be few forfeiture provisions—usually 100 percent immediate vesting—unless the plan is formally funded.

Funded and Unfunded Plans

A nonqualified deferred-compensation plan can be either funded by the employer or unfunded. With a funded plan, the employer sets aside money or property to the employee's account in an irrevocable trust or through some other means that restricts access by the employer and the employer's creditors to the fund. With an unfunded plan, either there is no fund at all or the fund that is set up is accessible to the employer and its creditors at all times, so that it provides no particular security to the employee other than the knowledge that the fund exists.

It might appear desirable from the employee's point of view to have a funded plan. However, there are significant disadvantages: The amounts put into a funded plan generally are taxable to the employee at the time the employee's rights to the fund become nonforfeitable, or substantially vested, a concept to be discussed under "Compensation with Restricted Property." This may occur well in advance of the time these funds are actually received by the employee, thus producing a tax disadvantage. Also, funded plans are subject to the ERISA vesting and fiduciary requirements, as discussed later, and this is usually undesirable from the employer's point of view.

As a result of these disadvantages, nonqualified deferred-compensation plans generally are unfunded. The employee relies only on the employer's unsecured contractual obligation to pay the deferred compensation. Because such plans provide no real security to the employee, their value as an inducement may be minimal if the company is risky; employees will then probably opt for greater benefits in current cash or property rather than deferred compensation.

Informal Funding. To provide some assurance, the employer can informally fund the plan by setting money aside in some kind of separate account, with this arrangement known to the employee but with no formal legal rights on the part of the employee and with the amount in the fund therefore available to the employer's creditors. Life insurance policies on the employee's life (owned by and payable to the employer) are often used to provide this kind of informal funding. Life insurance is particularly useful for this purpose if the deferred-compensation plan provides a death benefit to the employee's designated beneficiary, because if the employee dies after only a few years of employment, the life insurance will make sufficient funds available immediately to pay the death benefit. Sometimes a trust is set up by the employer to finance the plan. If the trust assets are available to the employer's creditors, the arrangement is deemed unfunded by the IRS. This type of arrangement is sometimes referred to as a *rabbi trust* because an early IRS ruling on this issue involved a rabbi.

Form of Benefits

Most nonqualified deferred-compensation plans provide for benefit payments in installments beginning at retirement or termination of employment. The averaging provision available for qualified plan lump-sum benefits does not apply to nonqualified plans; benefits are taxable as ordinary income when received at the taxpayer's regular tax rates, assuming that the taxpayer has not already paid taxes on the amounts in prior years.

Nonqualified deferred-compensation plans often provide a death benefit, usually in the form of a benefit to a designated beneficiary in the amount the employee would have received if he or she had lived. If the plan uses life insurance as an informal funding medium, it usually also provides a flat-amount death benefit—usually related to the face amount of the life insurance policies—that is payable regardless of how much deferred compensation has accrued to the date of death. Death benefits are taxable as ordinary income to the beneficiary.

Employer's Tax Treatment

In a nonqualified deferred-compensation plan, the employer does not receive a tax deduction for deferred compensation until the year in which the employee must include the compensation in taxable income. This is the case even if the employer has put money aside through formal or informal funding of the plan in an earlier year. For an unfunded plan, the year of inclusion for the employee is the year in which the compensation is actually or constructively received. If the plan is formally funded, the employee includes the compensation in income in the year in which it becomes substantially vested.

Impact of ERISA and Other Regulatory Provisions

To retain design flexibility and keep administrative costs down, most deferred compensation plans are designed to avoid the fiduciary, vesting, and reporting and disclosure requirements of ERISA to the maximum extent possible. Generally, if the plan is unfunded and is maintained by an employer primarily for the purpose of providing deferred compensation for a select group of management or highly compensated employees, the plan will be exempt from all provisions of ERISA. However, if the plan does not come within this exemption, most of the provisions of ERISA become applicable, and the plan must comply with almost all of the ERISA provisions that apply to a qualified plan. The nonqualified plan could discriminate in participation, benefits, or contributions, but for all other purposes—vesting, fiduciary, and reporting and disclosure—the plan would have to be designed like a qualified plan without the tax benefits of qualified plans. Consequently, most nonqualified deferred-compensation plans are designed to be unfunded and are limited to management or highly compensated employees.

■ COMPENSATION WITH RESTRICTED PROPERTY

An employee's compensation can be paid in either cash or noncash property. It is common for an executive's compensation to include payment in property, usually employer stock or securities, that is subject to some form of restriction at the time it is paid. The restriction on the property is usually designed to serve an employer goal, such as retaining a valued employee, and the restriction also can be designed to postpone taxability of the compensation to the employee and correspondingly postpone the employer's tax deduction.

Restricted stock or other restricted property is not an attractive benefit to an executive if the executive must pay income tax on the property when it is received, even though it is subject to restrictions. Therefore, most restricted property plans are designed around Code Section 83 that allows deferral of taxation to the employee if the restrictions meet certain requirements. Basically, the rules provide that an employee is not subject to tax on the value of restricted property until the year in which the property becomes *substantially vested.* Property is not considered substantially vested if it is subject to a *substantial risk of forfeiture* and not transferable by the employee free of the risk of forfeiture. As with most types of nonqualified compensation plans, the employer does not get a tax deduction until the year in which the property becomes substantially vested and includable in the employee's income.

The question whether there is a substantial risk of forfeiture depends on the facts and circumstances of each case. However, a substantial risk of forfeiture usually exists when the employee must return the property if a specified period of service for the employer is not completed—for example, five years of service. A forfeiture that results only from an unlikely event, such as the commission of a crime by the executive, probably would not constitute a substantial risk of forfeiture. Forfeitures as a result of failing to meet certain sales targets or going to work for a competitor could constitute substantial risks, depending on the facts and circumstances. If the employee is an owner of the company, the IRS is likely to be skeptical of any forfeiture provision in the plan, no matter how rigid it may appear on paper.

The nontransferability provision—the second half of the test—can be complied with in the case of the company stock by inscribing a statement on the share certificate to the effect that the shares are part of a restricted property plan. Thus, any prospective transferee is aware that the employee is not free to sell the shares to an outsider without restriction.

EXAMPLE

Suppose that executive Rita Bill is permitted to buy 500 shares of company stock at $10 per share in 2000, while the current market value is $100 per share. Rita must resell the shares to the company for $10 per share if she terminates employment with the company at any time during the next five years. The share certificates are also stamped with an appropriate statement to meet the nontransferability requirement. Rita pays no taxes on this arrangement until the restriction expires in 2005. If the unrestricted shares in 2005 have a market value of $200 per share, Rita will have additional taxable compensation income for 2005 of $100,000, the market value of the shares, less $5,000, the amount Rita paid, or a net additional compensation income of $95,000. The company will get a tax deduction of $95,000 in 2005, but gets no deduction for 2000. Also, the allowance of the tax deduction to the company is, like all tax deductions for compensation paid, subject to the requirement that the total compensation package for the employee constitutes reasonable compensation for services rendered.

Many variations are possible in the design of restricted stock plans. The plan, for example, may provide that dividends on the restricted stock are payable to the executive during the restriction period; if so, these dividends are taxable currently to the executive as compensation income. The plan also might provide graduated vesting over a period of years, rather than full vesting at the end of a specified period such as five years; this would mean that the executive would be taxed each year on the value of the property that became substantially vested that year.

In some plans, there are no forfeiture provisions; instead the stock is subject to other restrictions. For example, the employee may have a fully vested interest in the stock but may not be permitted to resell the stock without first offering it back to the company at a specified price. In that case, the value of stock to the executive would not be its market value, but would be a reduced value reflecting the restriction. Under the Internal Revenue Code, a restriction will be taken into account in valuing the property for tax purposes only if it is a *nonlapse restriction*—a restriction which by its terms will never lapse. The restriction in the example with a requirement of resale to the company at a fixed price would qualify as a nonlapse restriction. Other types of restrictions must be assessed on their own facts and circumstances, and the IRS tends to take a very limited view of what constitutes a nonlapse restriction.

Once an executive has become substantially vested in the restricted property and paid any tax on the compensation element involved, gain on a subsequent sale of the property is usually taxed as capital gain just as in the case of the sale of such property acquired by other means.

■ STOCK OPTION PLANS FOR EXECUTIVES (NONSTATUTORY)

A stock option is an offer to sell stock at a specified price at some time in the future or over a limited period of time with a specific termination date. Stock options have long been used for executive compensation to accomplish some of the same purposes as compensation with restricted stock. Over the years, Congress has designed special tax incentives to make certain types of stock option plans attractive. The type of tax-favored plan currently in effect is known as an **incentive stock option (ISO) plan**, which will be discussed separately. In this section, stock options in general—sometimes referred to as **nonstatutory stock options** or **nonqualified stock options**—will be discussed first.

Options to buy stock in the employer company are typically granted to executives as additional compensation at a favorable price, with the hope that the value of the stock will rise and make the option price a considerable bargain for the executive. If the stock price declines, the executive simply declines to exercise the option to buy the stock. This gives the executive a benefit whose potential value is tied to the fate of the company, but with no downside risk. This valuable incentive to the executive appears to cost the company very little, although this is somewhat misleading, as discussed below.

Stock options other than ISOs can be designed in any manner the employer and employee desire. Typically, a stock option runs for a period such as ten years, and is granted at a price equal to the fair market value of the stock on the date that it is granted.

EXAMPLE

Bill Kate is given an option in Year 1 to purchase up to 1,000 shares of stock at $50 per share, which is the current market price, with the option to be exercised over the next ten years. The plan may provide a waiting period before the option may be exercised, or it may provide that the option can be exercised only in successive installments—i.e., only 20 percent of the option can be exercised during the first two years, 40 percent over the first four years, and so on. The option has no value to Bill at the date of the grant because the option price was the same as the market price. Therefore, as of Year 1, there was no taxable income to Bill. Under the general tax rules in this situation, Bill will not be taxed until shares are actually purchased.

Suppose Bill purchases 400 shares in Year 4 for a total of $20,000. If the fair market value of the shares in Year 4 has risen to $40,000, the executive has $20,000 of ordinary income in Year 4. The company will get a tax deduction of $20,000 in Year 4, the same as the amount of Bill's compensation income, again assuming that Bill's compensation meets the reasonable compensation test for deductible compensation. However, the company gets no further deduction if Bill resells the stock and realizes a capital gain.

Options with an immediate value to the executive are sometimes used in executive compensation.

EXAMPLE

Suppose that the option had been granted at $40 per share, a bargain over the prevailing market price of $50 at the time of the grant. If the option has a determinable value and the option could be traded on an established market, the value of the option is taxable as ordinary income to Bill at the time of the grant, with a corresponding deduction to the employer. If tax is payable at the grant of the option, there is no further taxable compensation income when the option is exercised later. This can be an advantageous approach if the stock is expected to appreciate substantially in value, because the taxable compensation income at the time of the grant is relatively small, while the remainder of the gain on the overall deal will be taxed as capital gain only when the stock is sold.

Suppose that Bill is granted an option for 500 shares of company stock at $40 per share in Year 1, the current market price being $50 per share. Bill has $5,000 of ordinary compensation income in Year 1, the year of the grant. In Year 4, Bill exercises the option and buys 400 shares for $16,000. There is no ordinary income tax to Bill at the time of the exercise in Year 4.

The stock option appears to be an almost ideal method of compensating executives, providing a valuable incentive-based compensation arrangement at practically no cost to the company. However, the company's cost is comparable to the cost of cash compensation. While it costs the company almost nothing to grant options and print stock certificates to provide shares when the options are exercised, the executive will exercise the option only when the stock has a substantial market value. If this is the case, the company could itself have sold the stock used in the option arrangement on the open market and received the full proceeds. However, the grant of an option does not result in a charge to the company's income statement, so this form of compensation can be attractive from an accounting point of view.

The tax rules applicable to nonstatutory stock options do not provide any particular tax advantage to the employer company in using stock option plans. Therefore, in designing a stock option plan the company must look for benefits to itself just as in the case of any other kind of executive compensation. Typically, stock option plans would be used where the executive has a strong desire to obtain an interest in the business, or where the executive has a direct impact on the company's profits and, therefore, its stock value.

■ INCENTIVE STOCK OPTIONS

The incentive stock option (ISO) is the current form of stock option plan eligible for special tax benefits, which are provided by Code Section 422. Under an ISO plan, the usual tax rules previously discussed do not apply. Instead, for stock purchased under an ISO plan, there is no taxation to the employee until the stock is sold. Employees do not realize any taxable income when they receive the option, even if the option has an ascertainable fair market value and, furthermore, there is no taxable income when the option is exercised. However, the difference between the option price and the fair market value at the time of exercise is a tax preference item that may be subject to the alternative minimum tax. Because there is no regular taxable income to the employee at either the grant or the exercise of the option, the corporation gets no deduction at any time.

Options under an ISO plan must generally be granted to employees within ten years of the plan's adoption or approval by the shareholders, and an option must be exercised by the employee within ten years after it is granted. The option price must equal or exceed the stock's fair market value at the time the option is granted. Any good-faith attempt to value stock will be acceptable if there is no readily established market.

ISO plans increase the tax benefit of stock options as a form of compensation by providing increased tax deferral and, therefore, represent an attractive executive benefit. However, they are most likely to be used in large corporations. If an option holder has stock with more than 10 percent of the total combined voting power of the employer corporation, taking certain stock attribution rules into account, there are additional restrictions on ISO plans that may make them unattractive for closely held corporations. In such cases, the option price must be at least 110 percent of the stock's fair market value at the time it is granted and the option must be exercised within five years after it is granted rather than ten. Also, an employee receives the maximum tax benefit from an ISO plan only when the stock is sold, and there may be no ready market for a stock of a closely held corporation. Furthermore, it may be undesirable to pass ownership of stock in a closely held corporation to outsiders. However, the plan may permit the employee to exercise an option and pay for the shares of stock with other stock of the employer.

The aggregate fair market value of stock for which an employee can be granted an option under an ISO plan during a single calendar year cannot exceed $100,000. There are carryover provisions if the employee does not use the full limit in any year.

■ LIFE INSURANCE FOR EXECUTIVES

Life insurance can be an important executive benefit. Life insurance is important to high income employees as a means of providing income security to their families during the early part of their careers. In later years, it can provide or augment the executive's estate to be left to family and other heirs, or it can help provide liquidity to the estate to meet estate taxes and other expenses. A number of methods with favorable tax consequences have been devised to provide life insurance to executives. Generally, the aim is to provide insurance in a way that minimizes the current year-to-year income tax cost of the plan to the employee, and also keeps the life insurance out of the employee's estate for federal estate tax purposes. Some of the methods used include the following:

■ *Split-dollar plans.* In a split-dollar plan, cash-value life insurance is used, with the death benefit divided or split between the employer and the employee's designated beneficiary. The premium can be paid entirely by the employer or premium costs can be shared between employer and employee. The employer does not receive a tax deduction for its share of the premium payments. However, the plan is designed so that the employer is reimbursed for its premium payments by its share of the death benefit, which is received by the employer tax-free. Thus, the employer's cost for a split-dollar plan is the loss of the use of its share of the premium payments during the time in which the plan is in effect.

Under current tax regulations, if the employer owns the life insurance policy in a split-dollar plan, the arrangement is treated as a loan by the employer to the employee. If the employee pays no interest or a bargain rate of interest, the employee is taxed under the provisions of Code Section 7872 mentioned above in connection with direct loan programs to executives. If the employee or the employee's beneficiary owns the life insurance policy, the arrangement is treated as consisting of the annual provision of a term insurance benefit to the employee, and the employee pays tax on the term insurance cost of the portion of the death benefit payable to the employee's beneficiary, using Table 2001 (set out in Chapter 24). From this is subtracted any amount paid by the employee toward the premium.

Many variations on the basic split-dollar approach are possible. For example, to avoid federal estate taxes, the plan is often designed so that the employee has no incidents of ownership in the policy. This can be done, for example, by having the policy applied for by a beneficiary such as a spouse or a family trust, with a split-dollar arrangement between the employer company and the policyholder. Although this arrangement may eliminate the federal estate tax in the employee's estate, it is still considered by the IRS to result in compensation income to the employee.

- **Death benefit only (DBO) plans**. A DBO plan is a form of deferred-compensation plan in which the benefits are paid only to a designated beneficiary upon the death of the employee. The purpose of this arrangement is to avoid federal estate taxes on the death benefit.

  Under the federal estate tax law, a death benefit from a deferred-compensation plan is included in the employee's estate if the employee had a nonforfeitable right to receive benefits while living, even if the employee never actually received such benefits while alive. Thus, the DBO benefit is designed to be paid only at death. If there is a DBO plan, the employer's fringe benefit arrangements for the employee must also be designed carefully to make sure the DBO plan will accomplish its intended purpose. The IRS will lump other deferred-compensation plans—not including qualified plans—together with the DBO plan to determine if the company provides a lifetime benefit to the employee.

  To provide a substantial death benefit even during the early years of the plan, DBO plans are usually funded informally with life insurance. That is, the employer owns insurance on the life of the employee, with the employer itself as beneficiary. At the death of the employee, the policy provides funds enabling the employer to pay the death benefit to the employee's beneficiary.

  For income tax purposes, a DBO plan is treated the same as any other deferred-compensation plan—death benefits are taxable in full to the beneficiary as ordinary income when received.

- *Group term life insurance plan.* Under Section 79, a group term life insurance plan can have a special class for executives and provide them with amounts of group term insurance relatively greater than the amounts provided for other employees. However, if the plan provides amounts of insurance that are higher multiples of compensation for key employees, it probably will be deemed discriminatory and, therefore, the tax exclusion for the value of the first $50,000 of insurance will be lost by key employees.

■ KEY TERMS

death benefit only (DBO) plans	nonqualified stock options	supplemental retirement plans
incentive stock option (ISO) plan	nonstatutory stock options	
	reasonable compensation	
nonqualified deferred-compensation	restricted stock	
	stock options	

■ STUDY QUESTIONS

1. Briefly describe the present rules for interest-free and bargain loans made by a company to its executives.
2. What management objectives can be accomplished by using a nonqualified deferred-compensation plan for a selected group of executives?

3. What features does an executive typically want in his or her nonqualified deferred-compensation plan?

4. a. What is the usual form of benefit payments from a nonqualified deferred-compensation plan?

   b. How are these payments taxed?

5. When does the employer receive a tax deduction for nonqualified deferred-compensation payments made under an unfunded plan?

6. Why are nonqualified plans generally unfunded in the tax sense?

7. How can a nonqualified plan be informally funded (while remaining unfunded in the tax sense) to provide covered executives with some degree of benefit security?

8. Jim Franco purchased 100 shares of company stock at $5 per share. At the time of purchase, the market price for the shares was $50 per share. Jim must resell the shares back to the company for $5 per share if he terminates employment within three years of the purchase. The stock is nontransferable.

   a. Is there a tax impact on Jim when the shares are purchased? Explain.

   b. Will there be a tax impact on Jim if the stock is worth $100 per share when the restriction expires in three years? Explain.

   c. When will the company be allowed a tax deduction for the additional compensation to Jim?

   d. What amount will be deductible by the corporation?

9. In what ways does an incentive stock option differ from a nonstatutory stock option?

10. Describe a split-dollar plan by explaining the roles played by the employer and employee in order to achieve the intended benefits from the arrangement.

11. Explain DBO plans with respect to

    a. the primary purpose of the arrangement;
    b. how the plan is funded;
    c. the income tax impact to the beneficiary.

A Additional Resources

■ WEB SITES

Web sites on the Internet continue to come into existence and change locations. As a result, there is no substitute for searching the World Wide Web whenever information is needed about a specific topic. The general Web sites below contain information on many topics as well as numerous links to other Web sites. The other Web sites focus on more specific topics.

■ GENERAL WEB SITES

International Foundation of Employee Benefit Plans
http://www.lifebp.org

Benefits Link
http://www.benefitslink.com

■ OTHER WEB SITES

Academy for Health Services Research and Health Policy
http://www.academyhealth.org

American Association of Health Plans
http://www.aahp.org

American Association of Preferred Provider Organizations
http://www.aappo.org

American Society of Pension Actuaries
http://www.aspa.org

America's Health Insurance Plans
http://www.aahp.org

Association of Health Insurance Advisors
http://ahia.net

Blue Cross and Blue Shield Association
http://www.bluecares.com

Bureau of Labor Statistics
http://www.bls.gov

Centers for Medicare & Medicaid Services (formerly the Health Care Financing Administration)
http://www.cms.gov

Council for Affordable Health Insurance
http://www.cahi.org

Department of Labor Pension and Welfare Benefits Administration
http://www.dol.gov/dol/pwba

Economic and Social Research Institute
http://esresearch.org

Employee Benefit Research Institute
http://www.ebri.org

Employee Benefits Institute of America
http://www.ebia.com

Equal Employment Opportunity Commission
http://www.eeoc.gov

Focus on Benefits/Willis—National Benefits Resource
http://www.focusonbenefits.com

Health Care Financing Administration
http://www.hcfa.gov

Henry J. Kaiser Family Foundation
http://www.kff.org

Internal Revenue Service
http://www.irs.gov

Joint Commission on Accreditation of Healthcare Organizations
http://www.jcaho.org

LIMRA International
http://www.limra.com

Medicare
http://www.medicare.gov

Milliman USA
http://www.milliman.com

National Association of Dental Plans
http://www.nadp.org

National Association of Health Underwriters
http://www.nahu.org

National Association of Insurance Commissioners
http://www.naic.org

National Committee for Quality Assurance
http://www.ncqa.org

Pension Benefit Guaranty Corporation
http://www.pbgc.gov

Profit Sharing 401(k) Council of America
http://www.psca.org

Robert Wood Johnson Family Foundation
http://www.rwjf.org

Self-Insurance Institute of America
http://www.siia.org

Social Security Administration
http://www.socialsecurity.gov

The Urban Institute
http://www.urban.org

Thomas (Library of Congress site for legislative information)
http://thomas.loc.gov

URAC
http://www.urac.org

U.S. Chamber of Commerce
http://www.uschamber.com

■ PERIODICALS

Benefit Facts. Brookfield, Wis.: International Foundation of Employee Benefits Plans. (annual)

Benefits Quarterly. Brookfield, Wis.: International Foundation of Employee Benefits Plans. (quarterly)

Best's Review. Oldwick, N.J.: A.M. Best Company, Inc. (monthly)

Business Insurance. Chicago: Crain Communications, Inc. (weekly)

Employee Benefit Plan Review. Chicago: Charles D. Spencer & Assocs. (monthly)

Employee Benefits Journal. Brookfield, Wis.: International Foundation of Employee Benefits Plans. (quarterly)

Health Plan and Provider. Washington, D.C.: Bureau of National Affairs

Inside Consumer-Directred Care. Washington, D.C.: Atlantic Information Services (biweekly)

Journal of Financial Service Professionals. Bryn Mawr, Pa.: Society of Financial Service Professionals. (bimonthly)

Journal of Pension Planning and Compliance. New York: Aspen Publishers. (quarterly)

Life Insurance Fact Book. Washington, D.C.: American Council of Life Insurance. (annual)

Managed Care Week. Washington, D.C.: Atlantic Information Services. (weekly)

Medical Benefits. New York: Panel Publishers. (semimonthly)

National Underwriter (Property Casualty/Employee Benefits Edition). Chicago: National Underwriter Co. (weekly)

Pension and Benefits Reporter. Washington, D.C.: Bureau of National Affairs. (weekly)

Pension and Benefits Week. New York: Thomson RIA.
Pensions & Investments. Chicago: Crain Communications, Inc. (biweekly)
Personnel Administration. Alexandria, Va.: American Society for Personnel Administrators. (monthly)
Personnel Journal. Costa Mesa, Calif.: A. C. Craft, Inc. (monthly)
Social Security Bulletin. Washington, D.C.: U.S. Dept. of Health and Human Services. (monthly)
Social Security Manual. Cincinnati: The National Underwriter Company. (annual)
Source Book of Health Insurance Data. Washington, D.C.: Health Insurance Association of America. (annual)
Tax Facts on Life Insurance. Cincinnati: The National Underwriter Company. (annual)
WorldatWork Journal. Scottsdale, Ariz.: American Compensation Association. (quarterly)

■ LOOSE LEAF/ONLINE SERVICES

Benefits Coordinator. New York: Thomson RIA.
Cafeteria Plans. Seattle, Wa.: Employee Benefits Institute of America.
COBRA: The Developing Law. Seattle, Wa.: Employee Benefits Institute of America.
Consumer-Driven Health Care. Seattle, Wa.: Employee Benefits Institute of America.
Employee Benefit Handbook. Jeffrey D. Marmorsky, ed. Boston: Warren, Gorham & Lamont.
Employers Guide to Self-Insuring Health Benefits. Washington, D.C.: Thompson Publishing Group.
ERISA Compliance for Health and Welfare Plans. Seattle, Wa.: Employee Benefits Institute of America.
401(k) Plans. Seattle, Wa.: Employee Benefits Institute of America.
Group Health Plans: Federal Mandates Other Than COBRA and HIPAA. Seattle, Wa.: Employee Benefits Institute of America.
HIPAA Portability and Privacy. Seattle, Wa.: Employee Benefits Institute of America.
Pension Coordinator. New York: Thomson RIA.
Pension and Profit-Sharing Service. Englewood Cliffs, N.J.: Prentice-Hall.
Pension Plan Guide. Chicago: Commerce Clearing House.
Pension Plan Service. Indianapolis, Ind.: Longman/R & R Newkirk.

■ BOOKS

Allen, Everett T., Jr.; Melone, Joseph J.; Rosenbloom, Jerry S.; and Van Derhei, Jack L. *Pension Planning.* New York: McGraw-Hill.
Beam, Burton T., Jr. *Group Benefits: Basic Concepts and Alternatives.* 10th ed. Bryn Mawr, Pa.: The American College, 2004.
Beam, Burton T., Jr; and O'Hare, Thomas P. *Meeting the Financial Need for Long-Term Care.* Bryn Mawr, Pa.: The American College, 2003.
Black, Ann. *New Era of Benefits Communication.* 2d ed. Brookfield, Wis.: International Foundation of Employee Benefit Plans, 1997.
Canan, Michael J. *Qualified Retirement.* St. Paul: West Publishing Co., 2004.

Canan, Michael J. and Mitchell, William D. *Employee Fringe and Welfare Benefit Plans.* St. Paul: West Publishing Co., 2004.

Chandler, Darlene K. *The Group Life Insurance Handbook.* Cincinnati: The National Underwriter Co., 1997.

Douglas, Janet. *Integrated Disability Management.* Brookfield, Wis.: International Foundation of Employee Benefit Plans, 2000.

Garner, John C. *Health Insurance Answer Book,* 6th ed. Frederick, Md.: Aspen Publishers, 2001. (Annual update also available).

Golub, I. M; Chevlowe, Roberta; De Scherer, Dorinda; and Myers, Terrance M. *2000 COBRA Handbook.* Frederick, Md.: Aspen Publishers, 2004.

Harker, Carlton. *Self-Funding of Health Care Benefits.* 5th ed. Brookfield, Wis.: International Foundation of Employee Benefit Plans, 1998.

Humo, Terry. *ERISA Health and Welfare Handbook.* 2d ed. Washington, D.C.: Thompson Publishing Group, 1999.

Johnson, Richard E. *Flexible Benefits—A How-To Guide,* 6th ed. Brookfield, Wis.: International Foundation of Employee Benefit Plans, 2002.

Kongstved, Peter R. *Managed Care: What It Is and How It Works,* 2d ed. Frederick, Md.: Aspen Publishers, 2002.

Krass, Stephen J. *The Pension Answer Book.* Frederick, Md.: Aspen Publishers, 2004.

Leimberg, Stephan R., and McFadden, John J. *Tools and Techniques of Employee Benefit and Retirement Planning.* 8th ed. Cincinnati: The National Underwriter Co., 2003.

Life Office Management Association. *Intro to Managed Care.* Atlanta: Life Office Management Association, 1998.

McGill, Dan M. *Fundamentals of Private Pensions.* 7th ed. Philadelphia: University of Pennsylvania Press, 1996.

Martocchio, Joseph J. *Employee Benefits.* New York: McGraw-Hill/Irwin, 2003.

Oher, James M. *The Employee Assistance Handbook.* New York: John Wiley & Sons, Inc., 1999.

Podgurski, Walter B. *From Worksite Marketing to Website Marketing,* 4th ed. Cincinnati: The National Underwriter Co., 2000.

Purdue, Pamela. *Qualified Pension and Profit Sharing Plans,* 2d ed. Warren Gorham & Lamont, 2004.

Rosenbloom, Jerry S. Ed. *The Handbook of Employee Benefits,* 5th ed. New York: McGraw Hill, 2001.

Tacchino, Kenn Beam, and Littell, David A. *Planning for Retirement Needs.* 6th ed. Bryn Mawr, Pa.: The American College, 2003.

24-hour coverage   A single benefit plan that responds to injuries whether they occur on or off the job. In effect, this arrangement combines medical expense coverage, disability income coverage, and workers' compensation benefits into a single plan.

401(k) plan   *See* section 401(k) plan.

403(b) plan   *See* section 403(b) plan.

457 plan   *See* section 457 plan.

501(c)(3) organization   An organization exempt from federal income taxes that engages only in certain specified charitable, educational, and other activities.

501(c)(9) trust (VEBA)   A funding arrangement under which an employer can establish a trust to provide a benefit to employees because of death, medical expenses, disability, and unemployment. If the trust is properly designed in light of stringent IRS rules, the employer, within limits, can deduct contributions to the trust at the time they are made.

accelerated-benefits provision   A provision in a group life insurance contract that allows an insured to receive a portion of his or her death benefit while still living if one or more of the following events occur: a terminal illness that is expected to result in death within 6 to 12 months; a specified catastrophic illness; and the incurring of nursing home and possibly other long-term care expenses.

accidental death and dismemberment (AD&D) insurance   Insurance that gives additional benefits if an employee dies accidentally or suffers certain types of injuries. Coverage is commonly provided as a rider to a group life insurance contract but may also be provided through a separate group insurance contract.

accreditation   A process that provides consumers with information about a health plan and compares it with benchmark standards of quality care.

accrued benefit   In a qualified retirement plan, the portion of the total retirement benefit earned by the participant in a given year.

accumulated funding deficiency   The result if charges exceed credits in a funding standard account.

accumulation period   The time period within which expenses used to satisfy a per-cause deductible must be incurred for each illness or accident.

actively-at-work provision   An eligibility provision for group benefit coverage whereby an employee is not eligible for coverage if absent from work because of sickness, injury, or other reasons on the otherwise effective date of his or her coverage.

activities of daily living (ADLs)   Generally defined to include eating, bathing, dressing, transferring from bed to chair, using the toilet, and maintaining continence. The inability to perform a certain number of ADLs triggers long-term care insurance benefits.

actual deferral percentage (ADP) tests   Tests designed to prevent excessively disproportionate salary reduction contributions by highly compensated employees to Section 401(k) plans.

actuarial cost method   A method of determining an employer's annual contribution to fund a qualified defined benefit plan, based on the characteristics of the employee group and certain assumptions about future experience.

actuarial reduction   A reduction in an amount payable in a specific year as a result of payment of that amount in an earlier year; the reduction is based on the time value of money, mortality, or other factors.

AD&D   *See* accidental death and dismemberment insurance.

ADA   *See* Americans with Disabilities Act.

adequate rates   Rates that are sufficient to cover both incurred claims and expenses and to generate the insurer's desired profit or contribution to surplus.

ADLs   *See* activities of daily living.

administrative-services-only contract   *See* ASO contract.

adoption assistance plan   A benefit plan designed to provide benefits for legal, medical, and other expenses associated with the adoption of a child.

adult day care   Day care at centers specifically designed for the elderly who live at home, but whose spouses or families cannot stay home to care for them during the day.

advance determination letter   A determination by the IRS that a qualified plan, as drafted, meets the qualified plan requirements.

adverse selection The tendency of those who are most likely to have claims to also be those who are the most likely to seek insurance.

after-tax contributions Employee contributions to a qualified plan or similar plan that are made out of income that has been subjected to federal income tax before they are made.

age and service requirements Waiting-period requirements often used in qualified plans; the maximum permitted is age 21 and one year of service.

Age Discrimination in Employment Act (ADEA) A federal law that prohibits age discrimination for most working persons. The act, which applies only to employers with 20 or more employees, prohibits discrimination with respect to employee benefits for employees aged 40 and older.

agent An employee of an insurance company who acts as a representative of the insurance company in the sale of the company's products, including employee benefits.

age-weighted plan A qualified defined contribution plan in which employer contributions to a participant's account are based on the participant's age when the participant entered the plan; the objective is to provide an increased annual contribution for older entrants (who have relatively few years to retirement age) so that their ultimate benefit at retirement will be adequate.

aggregate stop-loss coverage Stop-loss coverage under which the insurance company is responsible if total claims under a self-funded plan exceed some specified dollar limit during a set time period.

AHP *See* association health plan.

all-causes deductible A deductible that must be satisfied only once during any given time period, regardless of the number of causes from which medical expenses arise.

allowable charge The amount paid to which a managed care plan may apply a coinsurance percentage if care is received outside the plan's network. In most cases, this is the amount paid to network providers for the same procedure.

allowable expenses For purposes of a coordination-of-benefits provision, any items of expense, all or a portion of which are covered under at least one of the plans that provides benefits to the person for whom a claim is made.

alternative medicine *See* complementary and alternative medicine.

alternative minimum funding standard account An alternative method for an employer to avoid a deficit in the funding standard account.

alternative plan of care A plan of long-term care that is an alternative to what is covered under the policy. Many policies will pay for the alternative if it is appropriate and cost-effective.

ambulatory surgical center A facility, separate from a hospital, that is operated primarily to perform surgical procedures. It has continuous physicians' services and professional nursing services but does not provide overnight accommodations for patients.

Americans with Disabilities Act (ADA) A federal law designed to make it possible for disabled persons to join the mainstream of everyday life. Among other provisions, the act makes it unlawful to discriminate on the basis of disability against a qualified individual with respect to any term, condition, or privilege of employment. This includes payments for private insurance and retirement plans, legally required payments for such government programs as Social Security and Medicare, payments for time not worked, extra cash payments to employees, and the cost of services to employees, such as wellness programs and retirement counseling.

amortized Spread over a period of years, as in the case of gains and losses in a pension fund.

annual addition For purposes of the Section 415 limitations, the amount added to a participant's account in a qualified defined-contribution plan, including employer and employee contributions and forfeitures, but not including investment earnings on the account.

annual return/report (Form 5500) An annual report that ERISA requires that plan administrators file with the Internal Revenue Service within 210 days after the end of the plan year. The return includes financial information about the plan and must be given to plan participants upon written request.

antigag-clause legislation Legislation that prevents managed care organizations from including provisions in contracts with doctors that prevent them from discussing with patients treatment options that may not be covered under their plans or from referring extremely ill patients for specialized care outside their plans.

any-willing-provider law A state law requiring HMOs and other networks of medical care providers to accept any provider who is willing to agree to the medical expense plan's basic terms and fees.

Archer MSA A type of personal savings account from which unreimbursed medical expenses can be paid. It can be used for employees of small employers or the self-employed and is established in conjunction with a high-deductible health plan.

ASO contract A contractual arrangement under which an employer purchases specific administrative services from an insurance company or an independent third-party administrator. These services usually include the administration of claims, but they may also include a wide variety of other services.

assignment A provision in a group benefit plan under which a covered person may transfer any or all rights under the contract (including benefit payments) to another party.

assisted-living care Long-term care benefits in facilities that provide care for the frail elderly who are no longer able to care for themselves but who do not need the level of care provided in a nursing home.

association health plan (AHP) A mechanism for allowing small businesses to band together through trade and professional associations to purchase medical expense benefits.

assumption-of-risk doctrine A common-law defense available to employers under which a worker cannot recover damages for an injury if he or she knowingly assumed the risks inherent in the job.

backloading In a qualified defined-benefit pension plan formula, accruing an excessive portion of the participant's total benefit in the later years of the participant's service.

base contribution percentage In a qualified defined contribution plan formula that is integrated with Social Security, the contribution percentage for compensation below the integration level.

bed reservation benefit A benefit under a long-term care insurance policy that continues to pay a long-term care facility for a limited time if a patient must temporarily leave because of hospitalization. Without a continuation of benefits, the bed might be rented to someone else and unavailable upon the patient's release from the hospital.

behavioral health program A program, often a carve-out, that treats behavioral health problems with case management and coordinates treatment plans.

beneficiary A person designated by a group benefit plan participant, or by the terms of the plan, who is or who may be entitled to a benefit under the plan.

benefit bank An account in which coordination-of-benefit savings from a secondary payer accumulate for future claims.

benefit handbook An employee reference book that summarizes the benefit plans available to all employees.

benefit outsourcing *See* outsourcing.

benefit period The period of time benefits will be paid prior to which a new deductible for benefits must be satisfied.

benefit schedule A schedule that classifies employees who are eligible for coverage under a benefit plan and specifies the amount of coverage that is provided to the members of each class.

benefit statement A personalized statement that specifies the benefit plans for which an employee is eligible and that explains what benefits are available to that particular employee and his or her family. It is usually given to employees on an annual basis.

bereavement leave *See* funeral leave.

big-deductible plan *See* specific stop-loss coverage.

birthing center A facility, separate from a hospital, designed to provide a homelike atmosphere for the delivery of babies. Deliveries are performed by nurse-midwives, and mothers and babies are released shortly after birth.

Blue Cross and Blue Shield Association The national organization that sets standards for Blue Cross and Blue Shield plans.

Blue Cross and Blue Shield plans Nonprofit organizations formed for the purpose of prepaying subscribers' medical care expenses. Blue Cross plans provide coverage primarily for hospital expenses, and Blue Shield plans provide coverage primarily for physicians' services.

break-in-service A period between the time a participant leaves employment with a particular employer and returns to employment with that employer.

broker A representative of the buyer of insurance who owes his or her allegiance to the buyer rather than to the organization through which coverage is placed. Brokers have traditionally been compensated on the basis of commissions for the coverages they have placed on behalf of clients, but fees may also be charged.

business associate Under HIPAA, a person or organization, other than a member of a covered entity's workforce, that performs services that involve protected health information.

buy-up plan A benefit plan under which a covered person can purchase additional coverage at his or her own expense.

cafeteria plan A benefit program in which employees can design their own benefit packages by purchasing benefits with a prescribed amount of employer dollars from a number of available options.

calendar-year deductible An all-causes deductible that applies to medical expenses incurred within a calendar year. A new deductible must be satisfied in a subsequent calendar year.

capitation A managed care payment system under which physicians receive a fixed payment per month for each member without regard to the services a member actually receives.

care coordination The services of a care coordinator who works with an insured, family members, and medical care practitioners to assess a person's condition, evaluate care options, and develop an individualized plan of long-term care.

care manager *See* gatekeeper.

career average A defined-benefit pension formula based on compensation in all years of service.

carryover provision A provision in a medical expense plan that allows any expenses applied to the deductible and incurred during the last three months of the year to be applied to the deductible for the following year.

carve-out (1) The practice of excluding certain classes or employees from a benefit plan and providing benefits to them under an alternative arrangement. Carve-outs are generally used to contain employee costs or provide broader or tax-favored benefits to key employees and executives. (2) Coverage under a medical expense plan for a service that has been singled out for individual management by a third-party. (3) *See also* Medicare carve-out.

case management The coordination of medical care, usually involving a single episode of inpatient care.

cash-balance plan a qualified defined benefit plan in which the benefit is based on a hypothetical account that is credited each year with a percentage of the employee's compensation (or similar formula amount) and with a guaranteed rate of investment return.

cash or deferred plan *See* Section 401(k) plan.

cashout Payment of the participant's benefit at termination of employment in a cash sum at the employer's discretion, a practice generally permitted only for total benefits valued at $5,000 or less.

catastrophic benefits rider A rider to a disability insurance contact that provides additional benefits if the insured suffers a severe disability. The benefit triggers are the same criteria that trigger benefits in long-term care policies.

catch-up contributions A term referring to certain contributions above the usual salary reduction limitations in salary savings plans that are available to individuals meeting specific criteria such as age or service with the employer.

Centers for Medicare & Medicaid Services The part of the federal Department of Health and Human Resources that administers the Medicare and Medicaid programs.

centers of excellence Hospitals that have excellent outcomes and reputations for certain types of medical procedures.

certificate of insurance A description of the coverage provided to employees. Although it is given to the employees, it is not part of the master contract.

child-care plan A dependent-care assistance plan that provides benefits for child care.

chronically ill individual A person, for purposes of a qualified long-term care insurance contract, who expects to be unable to perform at least two activities of daily living for at least 90 days *or* needs substantial supervision to protect him or her from threats to health and safety because of a severe cognitive impairment.

claim reserve An estimate by the insurance company for claims that have been approved but not yet paid, claims that are in the course of settlement, and claims that have been incurred but not yet reported.

claims charge The amount included in the experience rating formula for claims that will be charged against a group. It is equal to the incurred claims subject to experience rating multiplied by the credibility factor *plus* expected claims multiplied by 1 minus the credibility factor.

claims fluctuation reserve A reserve into which insurance companies require that part of a dividend earned be placed. Monies are drawn from the reserve to indemnify the insurance company for the years in which a group insurance case has a deficit.

claims procedure A written procedure for making claims under an employee benefit plan that is mandated by ERISA.

cliff vesting A vesting schedule under which there is no vesting of benefits until a specified period of years of employment has been attained (under ERISA this generally must be five years or less), at which time the participant becomes 100% vested.

closed-panel plan A benefit plan under which covered persons must obtain services from practitioners selected by the provider of benefits.

CMS *See* Centers for Medicare & Medicaid Services.

coalition A group of employers, unions, providers of health care, insurance companies, and regulators whose purpose is to control costs and improve the quality of health care. They may act as a catalyst for health care legislation or as a purchasing group to negotiate lower-cost coverage for members.

COBRA A provision of the Consolidated Omnibus Budget Reconciliation Act of 1985 that requires group health plans to allow employees and certain beneficiaries to elect that their current health insurance coverage be extended at group rates for up to 36 months following a qualifying event that results in the loss of coverage. The provision applies only to employers with 20 or more employees. In addition, a person electing COBRA continuation can be required to pay a premium equal to as much as 102 percent of the cost to the employee benefit plan for the period of coverage for a similarly situated active employee to whom a qualifying event has not occurred.

coinsurance The percentage of covered expenses under a major medical plan that will be paid once a deductible is satisfied.

COLA *See* cost-of-living adjustment.

collectible For purposes of the prohibition on participant-directed investments in collectibles under Internal Revenue Code Section 408(m), a work of art, rug or antique, metal or gem, stamp or coin (excluding certain federal and state-issued coins), alcoholic beverage, or any other tangible personal property designated as a collectible by the IRS.

collectively bargained plan A qualified plan established as part of a collective bargaining agreement.

common accident provision A provision in a major medical expense contract whereby if two or more members of the same family are injured in the same accident, the covered medical expenses for all family members will at most be subject to a single deductible, usually equal to the individual deductible amount.

common control Ownership or control of two or more corporations or business entities by the same owners or group of owners.

common deductible The term used for a medical expense plan deductible if there is a single deductible that applies to the aggregate expenses of each family member. There is no separate deductible for individual family members.

community rating The practice of using the same rate structure for all subscribers to a medical expense plan, regardless of their past or potential loss experience and regardless of whether coverage is written on an individual or a group basis.

competitive bidding The process of preparing specifications for a benefit plan and inviting several providers of coverage or third-party administrators to present a document detailing the cost at which they are willing to provide desired benefits or services.

complementary and alternative medicine (CAM) Types of medical care that are alternatives or complementary to conventional treatments covered under medical expense plans. Examples include acupuncture, hypnosis, herbal medicine, yoga, and chiropractic treatment.

comprehensive financial planning A series of financial planning activities that begins with collecting and analyzing personal financial data. It also includes designing, implementing, and monitoring a financial plan.

comprehensive long-term care insurance policy A policy that combines benefits for facility care and home health care into a single contract.

comprehensive major medical coverage A major medical plan that is designed to stand alone without any accompanying basic medical expense coverages.

concurrent management The process of monitoring the length of a hospital stay and determining whether other alternatives to hospitals can be used. The process is usually carried out by a registered nurse and typically begins with precertification of a hospital stay.

constructive receipt (1) The principle under which an employee who is given a choice of benefits is taxed as if he or she had elected the maximum taxable benefit that could have been obtained under the plan even if the actual election had been a benefit that is normally nontaxable.

The issue of constructive receipt when choice is given can be overcome by using a cafeteria plan. (2) A tax doctrine under which amounts such as compensation are treated as received when they are available to the taxpayer without substantial restriction or limitation, even if the taxpayer has not actually received them.

consultant A representative of a buyer of insurance and employee benefits who owes allegiance to the buyers rather than to the organizations through which the clients' coverage is placed. Consultants traditionally have been compensated on the basis of fees charged to clients.

consumer-choice plan *See* consumer-directed medical expense plan.

consumer-directed medical expense plan A medical expense plan that gives the employee increased choices and responsibilities with the selection of his or her own medical expense coverage.

consumer price index (CPI) An index computed by the government to show the change each year in the price of a "market basket" of consumer goods, as a measurement of inflation.

continued stay review *See* concurrent management.

continuing care retirement community (CCRC) A facility that offers a full continuum of supportive living arrangements and is obligated to provide access to housing and defined long-term care service at each level of care for the life of the resident. Also known as a *life-care facility*.

contribution formula In a qualified plan, the plan provision that determines the amount, if any, that the employer must contribute each year.

contributory negligence doctrine A common-law defense available to employers, under which a worker cannot collect if his or her negligence contributed in any way to an injury.

contributory plan An employee benefit plan under which participants pay a portion, or possibly all, of the cost of their own coverage.

controlled group rules Rules by which organizations under common control are considered as a single employer for purposes of applying the participation rules of the qualified plan law.

conversion charge A charge levied against a group term life insurance plan in the experience rating process that reflects the increased mortality associated with coverage that has been converted to an individual policy.

conversion fund *See* side fund.

conversion provision A provision in a group benefit plan that gives an employee whose coverage ceases the right to convert to an individual insurance policy without providing evidence of insurability. The conversion policy may or may not be identical to the previous group coverage.

coordination-of-benefits (COB) provision A provision in most group medical expense plans under which priorities are established for the payment of benefits if an individual is covered under more than one plan. Coverage as an employee is generally primary to coverage as a dependent. When parents are divorced, the plan of the parent with custody is primary, the plan of the spouse of the parent with custody is secondary, and the plan of the parent without custody pays last. Other rules apply to specific situations.

copayment A fixed-dollar amount that an insured must pay for a covered service under a medical expense plan.

core-plus plan A cafeteria plan with a basic core of benefits for all employees and a second layer of optional benefits that an employee can choose with employer-provided monies. An employee can typically purchase further benefits with after-tax contributions or with before-tax reductions under a premium-conversion plan and/or a flexible spending account.

corridor deductible A deductible in a major medical plan under which an individual will receive no benefits until he or she has incurred a specific amount of covered expenses above those paid by his or her basic coverages.

cost basis The cost to a taxpayer of property, including an employee benefit distribution; the cost can generally be received tax-free.

cost containment The attempt to control benefit costs by reducing the size of claims or minimizing administrative costs associated with benefit plans. This approach is in contrast to cost shifting, which transfers costs to employees.

cost-of-living adjustment (COLA) An increase in benefit levels because of changes in some index, such as the CPI. The increase applies to Social Security income benefits and sometimes to benefits under private insurance and retirement programs.

cost-plus arrangement An alternative funding arrangement frequently used by large employers to provide life insurance benefits. Under this arrangement, the employer's monthly premium is based on the claims paid by the insurance company during the preceding month, plus a specified retention charge that is uniform throughout the policy period.

cost shifting   The attempt by employers to control benefit costs by shifting these costs to employees. Examples include requiring larger employee contributions and increased deductibles.

covered classification   One of the classifications in a group benefit schedule. To have coverage, an employee must fall into one of the covered classifications. No employee may be in more than one classification, and it is the employer's responsibility to determine the appropriate classification for each employee.

covered compensation   In a qualified defined benefit plan formula that is integrated with Social Security, the level of compensation above which benefits are higher (the integration level). Covered compensation is determined from an IRS table that is revised annually.

credentials   Qualifications that providers must have and maintain to participate in a managed care network.

credibility   A statistical measure of the reliability of a group's past claims experience.

creditable coverage   Coverage under a medical expense plan for purposes of HIPAA. The coverage must have existed within the last prior 63 days.

creditor-debtor group   An eligible group for purposes of providing insurance. The debtors are the insureds, but the creditor is the policyowner and beneficiary of the coverage.

cross-tested plan   An age-weighted defined contribution plan that generally is designed to provide the maximum permitted difference in contributions between older and younger plan entrants.

currently insured   An insured status under Social Security that requires a person to have credit for at least 6 quarters of coverage out of the 13-quarter period ending with the quarter in which death occurs.

current revenue funding   The practice of funding benefits out of a firm's current revenue. This is in contrast to prefunding certain benefits, such as retirement income or postretirement life insurance.

custodial care   Care given to help with personal needs, such as walking, bathing, dressing, eating, or taking medicine. Such care can usually be provided by someone without professional medical skills or training.

DBO plan   *See* death benefit only plan.

DCAP   *See* dependent care assistance plan.

death benefit only plan   (1) A type of employee benefit plan providing only a death benefit to the employee's beneficiary and no benefit during the employee's lifetime. (2) A benefit plan under which the employer agrees to pay a death benefit to the employee's beneficiary out of corporate assets. The employee has no taxable income, but death benefits result in taxable income to the beneficiary.

deductible   The initial amount of medical expenses an individual must pay before he or she will receive benefits under a medical expense plan.

defined-benefit plan   A qualified plan in which the participant's benefit is guaranteed by the employer, with the employer assuming the risk of investments in the plan fund.

defined-contribution medical expense plan   A consumer-directed medical expense plan under which an employer makes a fixed contribution with which an employee can purchase his or her own coverage. The employee has increased responsibility for the selection of his or her own coverage, and some plans minimize employer involvement in health plan choice. There may also be greater accountability for health plans and providers.

defined-contribution plan   a qualified plan that provides individual accounts for each participating employee. The benefit from the plan is the participant's account balance, and investment risk is assumed by the employee.

definitely determinable benefit   A requirement for qualified pension plans; either the plan's benefit or the total of employer contributions must be determinable in advance of retirement.

Delta Dental Plans   Service plans sponsored by state dental associations for the purpose of providing dental benefits. They are also called *Delta Plans*.

demand management   A category of utilization management that guides medical expense plan members with respect to their personal health conditions. Examples are wellness programs and health risk assessments.

de minimis   The value of a benefit that is so minimal that accounting for its cost would be unreasonable or administratively impractical. Some employee benefits that would otherwise be taxable can be given to employees on a tax-free basis for this reason.

dental health maintenance organization (DHMO)   An HMO that provides dental care only.

dental insurance A specialized form of health insurance designed to pay for normal dental care as well as care needed as a result of accidents.

dependent Most commonly defined under a group medical expense plan to include an employee's spouse who is not legally separated from the employee and any other unmarried dependent children (including stepchildren and adopted children) under age 19 or, if full-time students, age 23.

dependent-care assistance plan (DCAP) Employer-provided benefits, often in the form of reimbursements of day-care expenses for children. However, dependent-care assistance can be provided for elderly parents and may also include flexible work schedules, part-time job sharing, and family leave policies.

dependent life insurance Group life insurance on the lives of eligible dependents of persons covered under the plan. Amounts of coverage are usually limited, and the employee is automatically the beneficiary.

diagnosis-related group *See* per-case rate.

direct-access HMO An HMO that allows members to see network specialists without going through a gatekeeper.

direct reimbursement A self-funded dental insurance plan under which the employee selects the provider of dental services, pays any charges incurred, and submits the bills to the employer for reimbursement.

disability-based policy A long-term care insurance policy with a per diem basis of payment that provides benefits even if no care is being received as long as the insured satisfies the policy's benefit trigger.

disability income benefits Insurance or self-funded benefits to partially or totally replace the income of employees who are unable to work because of sickness or accident.

disability insured The insured status under Social Security necessary to receive disability benefits. It requires that a worker be fully insured and have had a minimum amount of work under Social Security within a recent period.

discount plan A dental or other benefit plan that provides members with a discount on the purchase of professional services.

discretionary contribution provision A provision in a qualified plan under which the employer's contribution

can vary from year to year, or be omitted in some years, within the employer's discretion.

disease management The coordination of medical care, usually for a selected condition that is chronic, severe, and expensive to treat.

disqualified person The term for *party-in-interest* used in the Internal Revenue Code.

diversification requirement A traditional investment requirement for fiduciaries not to concentrate investments excessively that under ERISA also applies to fiduciaries of employee benefit plans.

dividend The refund given by mutual insurance companies to groups that are experience rated and have had better claims experience than anticipated.

dividend earned The dividend attributable to a group insurance case for the current experience period. It is computed by adding the retention to the claims charge and then subtracting this sum from the premiums paid.

dividend payable The dividend earned for an experience period reduced by any deficit that has been carried forward or placed in a claims fluctuation reserve.

doctrine of comity The practice by which states recognize within their own territory the laws of other states. Under this doctrine, it is generally accepted that the state in which a group insurance contract is delivered has governing jurisdiction.

domestic partners Usually defined to mean unmarried couples as long as they live together, show financial interdependence and joint responsibility for each other's common welfare, and consider themselves life partners.

early distributions Generally, distributions from a qualified plan, IRA, or tax-deferred annuity before the plan participant attains age 59½.

early retirement age An age specified in a qualified plan (generally age 55 or later) at or after which an employee can retire and begin receiving benefits immediately instead of having to wait for the normal retirement age.

earnings schedule A benefit schedule under which benefits are a function of each employee's earnings.

earnings test The process for determining whether income benefits of Social Security beneficiaries under age 65 should be reduced because of wages that exceed a specified level. The earnings threshold at which benefits are reduced changes annually on the basis of changes in national wage levels.

educational assistance A benefit plan designed to compensate employees for costs associated with education. If provided in accordance with specific IRS rules, benefits can be received on a tax-free basis.

elder care benefits Dependent-care assistance for elderly dependents. It may include costs associated with home care for elderly dependents or care at day-care facilities for the elderly. Other employer activities related to elder care may include seminars on issues affecting the elderly, referral services for information, employer-sponsored support groups, and making parents an eligible group for coverage under the employer's long-term care insurance plan.

eligibility provision A provision in an employee benefit plan that determines who will be eligible for coverage under the plan and when coverage will begin.

elimination period *See* waiting period.

employee-assistance program An employer-provided program to help employees with certain personal problems. Benefits may include treatment for alcohol or drug abuse, counseling for mental or marital problems, referrals for child care or elder care, and crisis intervention.

employee benefit planning The process of establishing, reviewing, and modifying an overall benefit plan. Steps include determining needs, analyzing costs, implementing the plan, communicating the plan to employees, and monitoring the plan's performance.

employee benefits All benefits and services, other than wages for time worked, that employers provide to employees in whole or in part. Narrower definitions include only employer-provided benefits for situations involving death, accident, sickness, retirement, or unemployment.

Employee Retirement Income Security Act *See* ERISA.

employee welfare benefit plan Those group benefits, other than retirement benefits, to which ERISA applies. While most employee benefits fall under the definition, there are some exceptions. Specifically excluded are government plans, church plans, and plans to comply with workers' compensation, unemployment compensation, and disability insurance laws. Compensation for absences from work because of sickness, vacation, holidays, etc., are also excluded to the extent that such compensation is paid out of the employer's general assets. Payroll-deduction plans are also generally excluded as long as no contri-

bution is made by the employer and participation is completely voluntary for employees.

employer mandate An approach to national health insurance that requires virtually all employers to make medical expense coverage available to employees and their dependents and to pay a portion of the cost.

employer matching contributions In a qualified plan formula, contributions required to be made by the employer to a participant's account if the participant contributes to the account for the year, through salary reductions (elective deferrals) or otherwise.

enrollee *See* member.

enrollment The signing up of participants for coverage in an employee benefit plan.

entire contract clause A provision in a group insurance contract stating that the insurance policy, the policyowner's application that is attached to the policy, and any individual applications of any insured person constitute the entire insurance contract. The insurance company cannot use any other statements made by the policyowner or by any insured as the basis for contesting coverage.

equitable rates Rates that require that each group pay a premium that reflects the expected cost of providing coverage to that group.

ERISA A federal act to protect the interests of participants in employee benefit plans and participants' beneficiaries. Sections of the act affecting all types of group benefits are those dealing with fiduciary responsibility and reporting and disclosure.

ESOP Employer stock ownership plan, a variation on the stock bonus plan under which the plan borrows money to buy stock from the employer, thus providing a vehicle for the employer to help finance its business.

evidence of insurability The requirement that an applicant meet the underwriting standards of an insurance company before coverage is issued.

excess-amounts pooling The process by which the amount of insurance that is subject to experience rating on any one person is limited. Amounts in excess of the limit are not experience rated but are subject to manual rates based on the ages of the individuals involved.

excess contribution percentage In a qualified defined contribution plan formula that is integrated with Social Security, the contribution percentage for compensation above the integration level.

exclusion   A provision in an insurance contract that indicates situations that the insurer does not intend to cover.

exclusive-provider organization (EPO)   A variation of a preferred-provider organization in which coverage is not provided outside the preferred-provider network, except in those infrequent cases where the network does not have an appropriate specialist.

expected claims   The portion of premiums paid that the insurance company anticipates will be necessary to pay claims during the experience period.

experience gain   A gain in the value of qualified plan assets that may permit reduced contributions to the fund in future years.

experience loss   A loss in the value of qualified plan assets that may require additional contributions to the fund in future years.

experience period   The period subject to experience rating.

experience rating   The practice by which the actual experience of a particular group is a factor in determining the premium the policyowner is charged.

extended care facility   A health care facility for a person who no longer requires the full level of medical care provided by a hospital but does need a period of convalescence under supervised medical care.

extension of benefits   A provision in a medical expense plan under which benefits are extended for any covered employee or dependent who is totally disabled at the time coverage would otherwise terminate. The disability must have resulted from an injury or illness that occurred while the person was covered under the group contract. The length of the extension generally ranges from 3 to 12 months.

facility-only policy   A long-term care policy that provides benefits for care in a nursing home and other settings such as an assisted-living facility or hospice.

fail-safe age-weighted profit sharing plan   An age-weighted profit sharing plan with a fixed actuarial formula for allocating employer contributions that is designed to meet the requirements of the age-weighting regulations in all cases.

Family and Medical Leave Act   A federal law that requires that employers with more than 50 employees within a 75-mile radius allow employees to take up to 12 weeks of unpaid leave in any 12-month period, for the birth or adoption of a child; to care for a child, spouse, or parent with a serious health condition; or for the worker's own serious health condition that makes it impossible to perform a job. The employee must be allowed to return to an equivalent job, and health care benefits, but not pay or other employee benefits, must be continued during the period of the leave.

family deductible   A provision in a major medical plan that waives future deductibles for all family members once a specified aggregate dollar amount of medical expenses has been incurred or after a specified number of family members have satisfied their individual deductibles.

family leave   An employer practice under which employees, within limits, may take personal time off without pay for such reasons as active military duty, extended vacations, honeymoons, education, the birth or adoption of a child, and the illness of the employee or a family member.

Federal Employees Compensation Act   Federal law that provides workers' compensation benefits to employees of the federal government and the District of Columbia.

Federal Employer's Liability Act   Federal law that provides workers' compensation benefits to railroad employees and employees aboard ships.

federal estate tax   A federal tax on the estate of a decedent based on transfers of property to estate beneficiaries.

federally qualified HMO   An HMO that meets the requirements of the Health Maintenance Organization Act.

fee-for-service plan   *See* traditional medical expense plan.

fee schedule   A list of covered benefits and the maximum fee that will be paid to the provider of benefits. Such a schedule is found in many surgical expense policies, dental policies, vision care plans, and group legal expense plans.

fellow-servant doctrine   A common-law defense available to employers under which a worker cannot collect if an injury resulted from a fellow worker's negligence.

fictitious group insurance statute   A state regulation that prohibits the grouping of individual property and liability insurance risks in order to give them favorable treatment in underwriting, coverage, or rates.

fiduciary   Generally, an individual or organization that handles funds of another person and is obligated under law to act in the interests of the actual owner of the funds, and not in the fiduciary's own interest. Under ERISA, a person who exercises discretionary authority or control over an employee benefit plan's management and provides investment advice to the plan for compensation or has discretionary authority or responsibility in the plan's administration is a fiduciary. ERISA requires that a fiduciary discharge his or her duties regarding the plan solely in the interest of the participants and their beneficiaries.

final average A defined-benefit pension formula based on compensation for a limited period of years, typically the participant's last three or five years, or a specified number of years of highest compensation.

final premium rate A manual rate after it has been applied to a specific group insurance case. It is then multiplied by the number of benefit units to obtain a premium for the group.

financial planning program An employer-provided plan, traditionally limited to a small number of topics, to offer financial planning as a benefit to employees. Some firms provide benefits to members of middle management. Benefits include services or reimbursement for preparation of tax returns, estate planning, investment planning, and insurance planning.

Financial Services Modernization Act A federal act that allows affiliations and mergers between securities firms, banks, and insurance companies and allows banks and securities firms to offer insurance products. The act also has provisions for the protection of personal financial information. Also called the *Gramm-Leach-Bliley Act.*

first-dollar coverage Coverage for benefits without a deductible or percentage participation.

flat-amount formula A defined-benefit pension formula that provides a specified dollar amount of pension without regard to the participant's compensation or years of service.

flat-benefit formula A defined-benefit pension formula that does not take years of service into account.

flat-benefit schedule A benefit schedule under which the same amount of coverage is provided for all employees regardless of salary or position.

flat-percentage formula A defined-benefit pension formula that provides a benefit equal to a percentage of the participant's compensation without taking the participant's years of service into account.

flexible benefit plan *See* cafeteria plan.

flexible funding *See* cost-plus arrangement.

flexible spending account (FSA) A provision in a cafeteria plan that allows an employee to fund certain benefits on a before-tax basis by electing to take a salary reduction, which can then be used to fund the cost of any qualified benefits included in the plan. Benefits are paid from an employee's account as expenses are incurred, but monies in the account are forfeited if they are not used by the end of the plan year.

floating holiday A holiday that can be taken at an employee's option. It is usually more like an additional vacation day because there is usually no requirement that it be taken on an actual holiday.

forfeiture In a benefit plan, an employee's loss of an accrued benefit or some portion of an accrued benefit because the employee leaves employment before he or she has enough years of service to be fully vested.

Form 5500 *See* annual return/report.

formulary A list of preferred medicines for a specific medical condition.

FSA *See* flexible spending account.

full funding limitation A definition of full funding under the minimum funding standards, a situation in which the employer may not make additional deductible contributions to a qualified pension plan fund.

full retirement age The age at which nonreduced Social Security retirement benefits are paid.

full-time employee An employee who works no fewer than the number of hours in a normal work week. For insurance purposes, the employee generally must work at least 30 hours.

fully insured An insured status under Social Security. This status requires one of the following: 40 quarters of coverage *or* credit for at least as many quarters (but a minimum of six) of coverage as there are years elapsing after 1950 (or after the year in which a person dies, becomes disabled, or reaches age 62, whichever occurs first.)

fully insured plan A plan that is funded exclusively by insurance and annuity contracts.

funding agency An entity such as a trust that holds funds of a qualified retirement plan.

funding instrument A legal document that specifies the terms under which a **funding agency** holds funds of a qualified retirement plan.

funding standard account An account required by ERISA for all qualified pension plans that is charged and credited with the plan's gains and losses and serves as a standard to determine the minimum funding amount required each year.

funeral (bereavement) leave   Paid time off because of the death of an immediate family member or sometimes to attend funerals of other persons.

gatekeeper   A physician who serves as a managed care member's initial contact for medical care and who authorizes the use of specialty physicians.

gatekeeper PPO   A point-of-service plan that requires a participant to select a primary care physician in the manner of an HMO subscriber. However, at the time medical service is needed, the participant can elect to go outside the PPO network.

grace period   A period specified in a group insurance contract (usually 31 days) during which a policyowner may pay any overdue premium without interest.

Gramm-Leach-Bliley Act   *See* Financial Services Modernization Act.

group benefits   A broad term that refers to retirement plans and welfare benefits.

group insurance   A method of providing employee benefits, characterized by a group contract, experience rating of large groups, and group underwriting.

group-model HMO   A closed-panel HMO under which physicians and other medical personnel are employees of another legal entity that has a contractual relationship with the HMO to provide medical services for its subscribers.

group representative   An employee of an insurance company who specializes in the selling and servicing of his or her company's group insurance products.

group term carve-out   A practice by which coverage for certain employees under a group term life insurance plan is limited to the $50,000 that can be provided income tax free. Coverage in excess of $50,000 is then provided under some alternative arrangement, often a form of cash value life insurance.

group universal life insurance   A flexible-premium group life insurance policy that divides the pure protection and cash value accumulation into separate and distinct components. The interest rate credited to cash value accumulations can vary, but there is a minimum guarantee.

group variable universal life insurance   A group universal life insurance contract under which certificate holders can allocate net premiums to one or more of several

investment accounts. The investment risk is borne by the certificate holders.

guaranteed-account formula   Another term for *cash balance pension plan*.

guaranteed issue   Group insurance coverage issued without an employee's having to provide evidence of insurability.

hardship withdrawal   A withdrawal by a 401(k) plan or 403(b) plan participant from his or her plan account for a specific reason defined by the plan that constitutes a hardship.

health insurance   Protection against the financial consequences of poor health. It includes disability income insurance, medical expense insurance, and long-term care insurance.

Health Insurance Portability and Accountability Act (HIPAA)   Federal legislation, passed in 1996, that reforms the health care system through numerous provisions. One of the act's primary purposes is to make insurance more available, particularly when an employed person changes jobs or becomes unemployed.

health insurance purchasing cooperative (HIPC)   An entity that acts as a broker between the purchasers and the providers of medical expense coverage.

health maintenance organization (HMO)   A managed system of health care that provides a comprehensive array of medical services on a prepaid basis to voluntarily enrolled persons living within a specific geographic region. HMOs both finance health care and deliver health services. There is an emphasis on preventive care as well as cost control.

Health Maintenance Organization Act   A 1973 federal act that introduced the concept of the federally qualified HMO. The act establishes plan standards, mandates open-enrollment periods, and establishes nondiscrimination requirements with respect to employer contributions.

Health Plan Employer and Data Information Set (HEDIS)   Performance measures developed by the NCQA that enable purchasers and consumers to obtain information to reliably compare the performance of managed care plans.

health reimbursement arrangement (HRA)   A type of personal savings account from which unreimbursed medical expenses can be paid. An HRA can be established by any employer for its employees.

health risk assessment An evaluation of plan member's health status using self-reported information.

health savings account (HSA) A type of personal savings account from which unreimbursed medical expenses can be paid. It can be used by employees or the self-employed and is established in conjunction with a high-deductible medical expense plan.

HEDIS *See* Health Plan Employer and Data Information Set.

high-deductible health plan A medical expense plan that uses insurance policies with high deductibles, often as much as $5,000 or more. They are commonly used with consumer-directed medical expense plans.

highly compensated employee A class of employee in whose favor discrimination is prohibited if an employee benefit plan is to receive the most favorable income tax treatment. The term is defined differently in sections of the Internal Revenue Code that apply to different types of employee benefits. One definition (referred to as a *highly compensated individual*) applies to self-insured medical reimbursement plans, another definition applies to cafeteria plans, and a third definition in Internal Revenue Code Section 414 applies to qualified retirement plans and numerous other types of benefits, such as dependent-care assistance, no-additional-cost services, and educational assistance. *See* references in the index to specific definitions.

highly compensated individual An individual who will incur taxable income if benefits are received under a self-insured medical reimbursement plan unless the benefits are also received by other employees.

HIPAA *See* Health Insurance Portability and Accountability Act.

HIPC *See* health insurance purchasing cooperative.

HMO *See* health maintenance organization.

home health care Care that is received at home and includes part-time skilled nursing care, speech therapy, physical or occupational therapy, part-time services from home health aides, and help from homemakers or chore workers.

home health care coverage Benefits provided in a patient's home following hospitalization when a physician has ordered necessary part-time nursing care. Benefits are often provided for nursing care; physical, occupational, and speech therapy; and medical supplies and equipment.

home health care only policy A long-term care insurance policy designed to provide benefits only for care outside an institutionalized setting, although some policies may provide for care in assisted-living facilities.

hospice care Care that emphasizes the easing of the physical and psychological pain associated with death rather than on curing a medical condition. It can be provided in a separate facility or a dying person's home.

hospital expense coverage Benefits provided under a medical expense plan for hospital charges incurred. Benefits are for room and board and other charges for certain services and supplies ordered by a physician during a person's hospital confinement.

hospital precertification A requirement under many medical expense plans that a covered person or his or her physician obtain prior authorization for any nonemergency hospitalization.

HR-10 plan *See* Keogh plan.

HRA *See* health reimbursement arrangement.

HSA *See* health savings account.

identifier standards Under HIPAA, the requirement for a uniform identifier for health care organizations for the purpose of reducing errors, uncertainty, and duplication.

incentive payment program A system under managed care that rewards physicians who meet budgeted cost and utilization levels.

incentive stock option A type of stock option plan with special tax benefits (and special restrictions) used to compensate employees.

incidental benefit A benefit such as life insurance or health insurance in a qualified plan that is incidental to the plan's primary purpose of providing retirement income.

incontestability provision A provision in a group insurance contract stating that, except for the nonpayment of premiums, the validity of the contract cannot be contested after it has been in force for a specified period, usually either one or two years.

incurred claims Those claims attributable to the recently ended period of coverage that was subject to experience rating equal to claims paid during the experience period, *minus* claims paid during the experience period but incurred during the previous period, *plus* an estimate of claims incurred during the experience period but to be paid in future periods.

indemnity concept   Benefits expressed in terms of reimbursement of actual expenses up to dollar maximums.

indemnity medical expense plan   *See* traditional medical expense plan.

individual employer group   The most common type of eligible group for group insurance purposes. The employer is the policyowner and may be a corporation, a partnership, or a sole proprietorship.

individual equity   The principle under which benefits for any individual are actuarially related to contributions made by that individual.

individual practice association (IPA)   An HMO under which participating physicians practice individually or in small groups in their own offices. In many cases these physicians also accept non-HMO patients on a traditional fee-for-service basis.

initial deductible   A deductible that must be satisfied before any benefits are paid under a medical expense plan.

insurance contract   An insurance policy or similar contract issued by an insurance company.

integrated disability management   A single program to manage all of an employer's disability claims, regardless of whether they are covered under short-term plans, long-term plans, or workers' compensation.

integration-level approach   A method of integrating a qualified plan formula with Social Security by providing greater contributions or benefits above a specified level of compensation known as the *integration level*.

interactive voice-response system   A telephone system for administering employee benefits that allows employees to obtain information about benefit plans and possibly to make benefit changes and elections.

interest credit   In a cash-balance pension plan, the amount of guaranteed earnings credited each year on the participant's benefit account.

intermediate care   Care involving occasional nursing and rehabilitative care that must be based on a doctor's orders and can be performed only by or under the supervision of skilled medical personnel.

internal maximum   A maximum amount that will be paid for a certain type of medical care during the lifetime of a covered person, even though a medical expense contract has a higher lifetime maximum.

Internal Revenue Code   A collection of statutes passed by the U.S. Congress that constitute the basis for the federal tax law.

Internal Revenue Service (IRS)   An administrative agency under the U.S. Treasury Department that is charged with administering the provisions of the Internal Revenue Code.

IPA   *See* individual practice association.

IRS ruling   An interpretation of tax law issued by the IRS, generally in response to a request by a taxpayer.

IRS Table 2001   A table for determining the current annual value of life insurance protection provided to employees as an employee benefit under a qualified plan or other plan.

ISO   *See* incentive stock option.

JCAHO   *See* Joint Commission on Accreditation of Healthcare Organizations.

joinder agreement   A contract between a multiple-employer welfare arrangement and an employer that spells out the relationship between the MEWA and the employer and specifies the coverages to which the employer has subscribed.

Joint Commission on Accreditation of Healthcare Organizations (JCAHO)   The primary organization that accredits hospitals and other types of medical care facilities. JCAHO also accredits certain types of health care networks.

Keogh plan   Also called an HR-10 plan, a qualified plan of an unincorporated business in which one or more participants in the plan are partners or proprietors of the business.

key employee   (1) A participant in an employee benefit plan who, at any time during the plan year containing the discrimination date, is any of the following: an officer of a firm who earns more than $130,000 in annual compensation, 5 percent owner of a firm, *or* a 1 percent owner of a firm who earns over $150,000 per year. (2) An employee who meets a specific definition in Section 416 of the Internal Revenue Code relating to top-heavy plans.

labor union group   An eligible group for purposes of providing benefits to members. The policyowner is the labor union. Because of federal prohibitions, premiums come either solely from union funds or partially from union funds and members' contributions.

late retirement Generally, retirement after the normal retirement age specified in an employment-based arrangement such as a pension plan.

legal expense plan A benefit plan that covers legal expenses incurred by an employee.

legal HMO A term used to describe a legal expense plan that provides a comprehensive array of legal services.

length-of-service schedule A benefit schedule under which the amount of coverage is a function of an employee's length of service.

life annuity with period certain A form of annuity providing equal annual amounts for the participant's life, but if the participant dies before a specified period, such as five or ten years, the remaining payments continue for the specified period to the participant's designated beneficiary.

life-cycle approach An approach to benefit planning that takes into account the fact that different persons have different benefit needs and that these needs will change over the course of a person's life.

life insurance The transfer to an insurance company of part of the financial loss due to the death of an insured person.

lifestyle management program A wellness program primarily designed to encourage employees and often their dependents to modify behavior so that they will lead healthier lives. Examples include programs for smoking cessation, weight reduction, and stress management.

lifetime maximum A specified overall maximum that applies to all benefits paid during the entire period an individual is covered under certain types of health insurance contracts.

limitations Internal limits in a medical expense plan for the maximum benefit that will be paid for certain types of medical expenses.

limited-liability arrangement A reserve-reduction arrangement for long-term disability income insurance. The employer purchases a one-year contract in which the insurer agrees to pay claims for that year only, even for employees who are already disabled.

LIMRA International A membership organization that provides marketing and distribution information and advice to its members. Its Web site is *www.limra.org*.

long-term care insurance An insurance policy designed to provide coverage for at least 12 months to persons who need nonacute care for their health needs, often in the form of personal care services.

long-term disability (LTD) income insurance Disability insurance that provides extended benefits (possibly for life) after an employee has been disabled for a period of time, frequently six months.

LTD *See* long-term disability income insurance.

lump-sum distribution A distribution of a qualified plan participant's entire benefit amount, meeting certain conditions under the Internal Revenue Code.

major medical coverage A medical insurance plan designed to provide substantial protection against catastrophic medical expenses. There are few exclusions and limitations, but deductibles and coinsurance are commonly used.

managed care A process to deliver cost-effective health care without sacrificing quality or access. Common characteristics include controlled access to providers, comprehensive case management, preventive care, risk sharing, and high-quality care.

managed competition A philosophy for national health insurance based on the idea that competition for medical expense insurance should be based on price rather than on the risk characteristics of those needing coverage.

mandated benefits Benefits that states require be included in group insurance contracts issued in the state.

manual premium rate The rate that is quoted in an insurance company's rate book.

manual rating The process of determining a premium rate on the basis of broad classes of group insurance business, rather than on a particular group's claims.

mass-marketed individual insurance *See* voluntary benefits.

master contract A contract issued to someone other than the persons insured that provides benefits to a group of individuals who have a specific relationship to the policyowner.

master plan A standardized form document for a qualified retirement plan promulgated by a financial institution that will hold the funds for plan sponsors who adopt the master plan.

matching contribution An employer contribution in a salary savings plan that is based on the contribution made by the employee; under the plan formula, the amount of the match is generally mandatory for the employer.

maternity management A cost-containment technique that identifies high-risk pregnancies and provides proper medical treatment.

maximum offset allowance In a qualified defined contribution plan formula that is integrated with Social Security, the maximum difference in the contribution percentage for compensation above and below the integration level—the difference between the base contribution percentage and the excess contribution percentage.

McCarran-Ferguson Act (Public Law 15) A federal law that exempts insurance from certain federal regulations to the extent that individual states actually regulate insurance. It also provides that most other federal laws are not applicable to insurance unless they are specifically related to the business of insurance.

Medicaid A federal/state program to provide medical expense benefits for certain classes of low-income individuals and families.

medical child support order A court judgment, decree, or order that provides for child support for the child of a group plan participant or provides benefit coverage to such a child, is ordered under state domestic relations law, and relates to benefits under a plan *or* that enforces a state medical support law enacted under Medicaid rules.

medical expense insurance Protection against financial losses that result from medical expenses because of accident and/or illness.

medical information program A program that manages medical care by providing professional medical information that members can use for self-care of common conditions or to decide when to seek professional care.

medical savings account (MSA) A personal savings account from which unreimbursed medical expenses, including deductibles, percentage participation, and copayments can be made. It is used with a high-deductible medical expense policy. Examples are Archer MSAs, HRAs, and HSAs.

medical screening program A wellness program designed to discover and treat medical conditions before they become severe and result in large medical expense, disability, or death claims. Common examples are screening for cholesterol, high blood pressure, and breast cancer.

Medicare The health insurance program of the federal government that is available to persons who are aged 65 or older and to limited categories of persons who are under age 65.

Medicare Advantage Part C of Medicare, under which beneficiaries can select one of several options to the traditional Medicare program.

Medicare carve-out An employer-provided medical expense plan for persons over age 65 under which benefits are reduced to the extent that they are payable under Medicare for the same expense.

Medicare+Choice *See* Medicare Advantage.

Medicare Part A The hospital insurance portion of Medicare. In addition to benefits for inpatient hospitalizations, it also provides benefits for care in skilled-nursing facilities, home health care, and hospice care.

Medicare Part B The portion of Medicare that provides benefits for many medical expenses not covered under Part A. However, there is little or no coverage for such medical expenses such as prescription drugs, routine physicals, dental care, and long-term care.

Medicare secondary rules Regulations that specify when Medicare will be secondary to an employer's medical expense plan for disabled employees and active employees aged 65 or older.

Medicare supplement An employer-provided medical expense plan for employees aged 65 or older under which benefits are provided for certain specific expenses not covered under Medicare. These may include a portion of expenses not paid by Medicare because of deductibles, coinsurance, or copayments and certain expenses excluded by Medicare, such as prescription drugs.

member A person covered by a managed care plan that uses network providers.

Mental Health Parity Act Federal legislation that requires annual and lifetime dollar limits on mental health benefits to be on par with limits that apply to other medical conditions. The act applies to employers with more than 50 employees.

MET *See* multiple-employer trust.

MEWA *See* multiple-employer welfare arrangement.

minimum-premium plan An alternative funding arrangement under which the employer assumes the financial responsibility for paying claims up to a specified level, such as 90 percent of estimated claims. The actual payment of claims is made with employer funds by the insurance company, which acts as an agent of the employer. When claims exceed the specified level, the balance is paid from the insurance company's own funds.

misstatement-of-age provision A provision in a group life insurance policy stating that the premium will be adjusted to reflect the true age of the individual if the age has been misstated. Unlike individual life insurance, there is no adjustment in the benefits that will be paid.

mixed-model HMO An HMO that has characteristics of two or more of the basic HMO forms. It occurs most often when one HMO purchases a different type of HMO or when an HMO expands its capacity or geographic region by adding additional medical care providers under a different type of arrangement.

model law Sample legislation promulgated by the NAIC that individual states at their discretion can adopt either as written or with changes.

modified fee-for-service payment system A managed care payment system under which providers are paid on a fee-for-service basis, subject to negotiated maximum payments per procedure.

modified guaranteed issue An underwriting category that falls between guaranteed issue and simplified issue. The insurer accepts most applicants but asks a few medically related questions that may result in the declination of a small number of applicants.

modular plan A cafeteria plan in which an employee has a choice among several predesigned benefit packages. However, the employee cannot pick and choose specific benefits.

money-purchase pension plan A qualified defined contribution plan in which the employer makes a mandatory annual contribution to the participating employee's account, under a specific formula generally based on compensation; for example, 10% of each participant's compensation.

morbidity The sickness and disability rates of a group of persons covered under an employee benefit plan.

mortality The death rate of a group of persons covered under a benefit plan.

MSA *See* medical savings account.

multiemployer plan A collectively-bargained plan that covers more than one employer and is usually maintained by a labor union-related group.

multiple employer plan A qualified plan sponsored by a group of employers rather than a single employer.

multiple-employer trust (MET) A fully insured multiple-employer welfare arrangement.

multiple-employer welfare arrangement (MEWA) An eligible group for purposes of providing benefits to participants. It is a legal entity in the form of a trust, which is the policyowner, and may be sponsored by an insurance company or some other person or organization.

multiple-option plan A single medical expense contract that combines two or more of the following: a traditional medical expense plan, an HMO, a PPO, or a POS plan. Such arrangements simplify administration and allow the entire plan to be subject to experience rating.

NAIC *See* National Association of Insurance Commissioners.

named fiduciary A fiduciary required under ERISA to be specified in the documents of an employee benefit plan

National Association of Insurance Commissioners (NAIC) An association composed of state insurance regulatory officials that has as its goal the promotion of uniformity in legislation and administrative rules affecting insurance.

National Committee for Quality Assurance (NCQA) An independent nonprofit organization that accredits managed care organizations and has established a quality measurement program to help consumers evaluate the quality of care provided by managed care plans.

NCQA *See* National Committee for Quality Assurance.

negotiated trusteeship An eligible group for group insurance purposes. It is formed as a result of collective bargaining over benefits between a union and the employers of the union members. The policyowner is a trust with an equal number of trustees from the employers and the union.

net premium rate The amount necessary to support the cost of expected claims.

network-model HMO An HMO that contracts with two or more independent groups of physicians to provide medical services to its subscribers.

new comparability plan *See* cross-tested plan.

Newborns' and Mothers' Health Protection Act Federal legislation that establishes minimum hospital stays for maternity that must be covered by insurance carriers.

no-additional-cost service A service an employer can provide to an employee without any adverse income tax consequences. The service must normally be provided in the employer's line of business in which the employee actually works, and the employer must not incur any significant additional cost or revenue in providing the service.

no-loss no-gain legislation A state law that prohibits a new insurance company from denying (by using a preexisting-conditions clause) the continuing claims of persons who were covered under a previous group insurance plan if these claims would otherwise be covered under the new contract.

noncontributory plan An employee benefit plan under which the employer pays the entire cost of the coverage.

nondiscrimination rules Rules that deny favorable treatment to employee benefit plans that do not provide equitable benefits to a large cross section of employees. Not all plans are subject to nondiscrimination rules, and different rules may apply to different types of benefits.

nonforfeiture benefit A provision in an insurance policy to create a residual value after the policy has been in force for some time, even if premium payments cease.

nonoccupational disability law *See* temporary disability law.

non-qualified deferred compensation A retirement plan for a select group of management or highly compensated employees.

nonqualified stock option Another term for *nonstatutory stock option.*

nonstatutory stock option A stock option that is not an ISO—that is, one that is subject to the normal tax law rules.

normal form of benefit The form of benefit in a qualified defined-benefit plan upon which plan funding is based, usually a life annuity. Most plans allow participants to choose actuarially equivalent alternative forms of benefit as the actual form of plan payments.

normal retirement age An age specified as the retirement date in a qualified plan; the plan cannot require the participant to retire at this age but the plan is funded and administered on the basis of this normal retirement age. *See* also full retirement age.

nursing home care A broad term that encompasses skilled care, intermediate care, and custodial care in a licensed facility.

OASDHI The old age, survivors, disability, and health insurance program of the federal government, commonly referred to as *Social Security* and *Medicare.*

OASDI The old-age, survivors, and disability insurance program of the federal government, commonly referred to as *Social Security.*

offset approach A method of integrating a qualified defined benefit plan formula with Social Security by reducing the benefit otherwise payable under the formula by an amount that reflects the participant's anticipated Social Security benefits.

open-ended HMO A point-of-service plan that allows a subscriber to go outside the HMO network of medical care providers.

open-enrollment period The time during which coverage can be obtained under an employee benefit plan and during which the evidence-of-insurability requirement is lessened or waived.

open-panel plan A benefit plan under which covered persons may obtain services from any practitioner or may have to select one from a limited list of practitioners who have agreed to the plan's terms and conditions.

outsourcing The process of contracting with third parties to perform functions associated with employee benefit administration.

paid time off (PTO) program A benefit program that combines sick-leave and other types of payments for time not worked into a single program.

partial advance funding The method used to fund Social Security and Medicare. Taxes are more than sufficient to pay current benefits and provide some accumulation of assets for the payment of future benefits. Taxes are set at a level lower than that needed to fund all promised future benefits for those persons making current contributions.

partial disability A disability that is neither total or permanent but leaves an employee unable to perform some of the duties of his or her job.

partial termination A change in organizational structure by the sponsor of a qualified plan, such as a closing of a division or sale of a subsidiary, that results in a significant number of employees losing their coverage under the qualified plan.

participant-directed investment An investment that is chosen by the participant for his or her account in a qualified defined contribution plan.

party-in-interest A person who is subject to the prohibited-transactions provisions of ERISA. A party-in-interest includes any plan fiduciary, any counsel or employee of the plan, any person providing services to the plan, any employer of employees covered under the plan, and any relative of a party-in-interest.

past service With respect to defined-benefit pension formulas, years of service for an employer before the participant has entered the pension plan, or before the plan was adopted by the employer.

pay credit In a cash-balance pension plan, the amount credited to the participant's benefit account based on the participant's compensation.

payroll deduction plan *See* voluntary benefits.

Pension Benefit Guaranty Corporation (PBGC) A government corporation set up under ERISA to provide termination insurance for participants in qualified defined-benefit plans.

pension plan Generically, a plan under which an employer provides retirement or deferred income to an employee. With respect to qualified plans, a pension plan is a plan that provides definitely determinable benefits, as contrasted with a profit-sharing plan.

pension schedule A benefit schedule in group life insurance plans under which the amount of coverage is a function of an employee's projected pension at retirement.

pension supplement A provision in a disability income plan that pays benefits to continue the accruing of benefits for disabled employees.

per-case rate A reimbursement method under which hospitals are paid a specified fee for all inpatient costs, regardless of a patient's length of stay.

per-cause deductible A deductible amount that must be satisfied for each separate accident or illness before major medical benefits are paid.

per-cause maximum A maximum benefit in a medical expense plan for all expenses arising from a certain cause.

percentage participation The percentage of covered medical expenses that will not be paid by a medical expense plan and must be paid by a person receiving benefits.

per-day rate A reimbursement method for hospitals under which a hospital is paid a specified amount for each day a patient is hospitalized, regardless of the actual cost of services on any particular day.

per diem basis A method of paying benefits under long-term care insurance policies in which the insured receives a specified daily or weekly benefit regardless of the actual cost of care.

permanence requirement The requirement that a qualified retirement plan must be adopted with an initial intention that the plan be a permanent program of employee benefits.

permitted disparity The maximum variation from a uniform percentage of compensation that can be used in a qualified plan formula that is integrated with Social Security.

persistency The length of time a group insurance contract will remain on the insurance company's books.

pharmacy benefit manager An organization that administers prescription drug plans on behalf of self-funded employers, third-party administrators, HMOs, PPOs, insurance companies, and other providers of prescription drug benefits.

PHO *See* physician-hospital organization.

physician-hospital organization (PHO) A legal entity, formed by one or more physicians' groups and hospitals, that negotiates, markets, and contracts the services of the physicians and hospitals.

physicians' visits expense coverage Benefits for fees of attending physicians other than surgeons. Benefits may be provided for hospital visits only but may also be provided for home and office visits.

PIA *See* primary insurance amount.

plan administrator An organization or individual named in an employee benefit plan document as the legally responsible administrator of the benefit plan.

point-of-service (POS) plan A hybrid arrangement that combines aspects of a traditional medical expense plan with an HMO or a PPO. At the time of medical treatment, a participant can elect whether to receive treatment within the plan's network or outside the network.

pool of money The maximum available benefits under a long-term care insurance policy calculated by multiplying the daily benefit by the benefit period to create a total amount of funds from which benefit payments may continue as long as the funds last.

POP *See* premium-conversion plan.

portability (1) The ability to continue employer-provided or employer-sponsored benefits after termination of employment. (2) Under HIPAA, the concept of allowing an employee to use evidence of prior medical expense coverage to eliminate or reduce the length of any preexisting-conditions provision when the employee moves to another medical expense plan.

position schedule   A benefit schedule under which the amount of coverage is based on an employee's position within a firm.

PPO   *See* preferred-provider organization.

preadmission testing   The practice of performing diagnostic tests and x-rays on an outpatient basis prior to hospitalization.

precertification   *See* hospital precertification.

predetermination-of-benefits provision   A provision in a dental insurance contract under which there is a requirement for a pretreatment review of certain dental services, generally when they exceed some specified dollar amount.

preexisting-conditions provision   A provision that excludes coverage, but possibly only for a limited period of time, for a physical and/or mental condition for which a covered person in a benefit plan received treatment or medical advice within a specified time period before becoming eligible for coverage.

preferred-provider organization (PPO)   (1) A benefit plan that contracts with preferred providers to obtain lower costs for plan members. (2) Groups of health care providers that contract with employers, insurance companies, union trust funds, third-party administrators, or others to provide medical care services at a reduced fee. PPOs may be organized by the providers themselves or by such organizations as insurance companies, the Blues, or groups of employers.

Pregnancy Discrimination Act   A federal law requiring that women affected by pregnancy, childbirth, or related medical conditions be treated the same for employment-related purposes as other persons who are not so affected but who are similar in their ability to work.

premature distributions   *See* early distributions.

premium   The total price that a group insurance policyowner pays for the entire amount of coverage purchased.

premium-conversion plan   A provision in a cafeteria plan under which an employee can elect a before-tax salary reduction to pay his or her premium contribution to an employer-sponsored health or other welfare benefit plan.

premium-delay arrangement   An alternative funding method that allows the employer to defer payment of monthly premiums for some time period beyond the usual 30-day grace period.

premium-only plan (POP)   *See* premium-conversion plan.

premium rate   The price for each unit of group insurance benefit, such as each $1,000 of life insurance.

preretirement-counseling program   An employer-provided benefit to make employees aware of the pitfalls that can result if they are unprepared for retirement. Benefits are usually in the form of group meetings that focus on such issues as financial planning, living arrangements after retirement, health issues for retirees, and use of free time after retirement.

prescription drug plan   A benefit plan that covers the cost of drugs that are required by law to be dispensed by prescription.

primary insurance amount (PIA)   The amount a worker will receive under Social Security if he or she retires at age 65 or becomes disabled. It is also the amount on which all other Social Security income benefits are based.

privacy standards   HIPAA rules that protect the privacy of personal health information.

probationary period   A period of time that must be satisfied before an employee is eligible for coverage under a group benefit plan.

profit-sharing plan   Generically, an employer plan that provides some of the benefits of business success to employees as additional compensation. A qualified profit-sharing plan is a type of plan that provides an undetermined amount of benefit at retirement (as compared with a qualified pension plan which provides definitely determinable benefits). A qualified profit-sharing plan does not actually have to base its benefits on employer profits, and an employer does not need to have profits to make contributions to a qualified profit-sharing plan.

prohibited transaction   An activity specified in ERISA that may not be engaged in by a party-in-interest to a benefit plan. Prohibited transactions include the following: the selling or leasing of property; the lending of money; the furnishing of goods, services, or facilities; and the transfer of any asset to or for the use of a party-in-interest.

prohibited transaction exemption (PTE)   A ruling by the Department of Labor exempting a specific transaction, or type of transaction, from the prohibited transaction rules of ERISA.

proposal   The document given to a client by a provider of employee benefits. It spells out the design of the employee benefit plan and the premium rates that will be charged.

prospecting   The first step in the process of marketing employee benefits. It involves persuading the employer or the employer's representative to accept a proposal from the provider of employee benefit products or services.

prospective management   The process of analyzing a case to see what type of medical treatment is necessary and to authorize the prescribed care.

protected health information (PHI)   Health information to which HIPAA health administrative standards apply.

prototype plan   A standardized form document for a qualified retirement plan, usually incorporating some choices of provisions for adoption by plan sponsors.

provider network   A list of medical care providers that members of a managed care plan are encouraged to use, usually with financial incentives.

prudent-man requirement   A traditional legal standard for investment practices by fiduciaries that has been applied by ERISA to employee benefit plan fiduciaries.

PTE   *See* prohibited transaction exemption.

PTO   *See* paid time off program.

pure amount at risk   *See* term cost.

put requirement   A requirement applicable to qualified plans investing in stock of a closely-held employer under which the participant has a right to demand that the employer purchase stock that is distributed to the participant under the plan.

qualified beneficiary   For purposes of COBRA, any employee, spouse, or dependent child who was covered under the employee's group insurance plan on the day before a qualifying event.

qualified benefit   A benefit (other than cash) that can be provided under a cafeteria plan. It can include any welfare benefits excluded from taxation under the Internal Revenue Code except scholarships and fellowships, transportation benefits, educational assistance, no-additional-cost services, employee discounts, and *de minimis* fringe benefits.

qualified domestic relations order   A court order directing the trustees of a qualified plan to distribute amounts from a qualified plan in accordance with a divorce, child-support, or similar decree.

qualified joint and survivor annuity   A benefit that must be automatically provided by qualified pension plans to married participants in certain cases; it consists of an annuity payable during the joint lives of participant and spouse, with a survivor annuity that is not less than 50 percent of the joint annuity.

qualified long-term care insurance contract   A long-term care contract that meets specified standards and qualifies for favorable tax treatment under the Health Insurance Portability and Accountability Act.

qualified long-term care services   Necessary diagnostic, preventive, therapeutic, curing, treating, and rehabilitative services, and maintenance or personal care services that are required by a chronically ill person and are provided by a plan of care prescribed by a licensed health care practitioner.

qualified plan   *See* qualified retirement plan.

qualified plan award   An award for service, productivity, or safety achievement that can be excludible from an employee's income. However, the total amount excludible cannot exceed $1,600 per year for any employee, and the awards must be provided under a permanent written plan that does not discriminate in favor of officers, shareholders, or highly compensated employees.

qualified preretirement survivor annuity   A benefit for the spouse of a qualified pension plan participant that must be paid if the participant dies before retirement.

qualified retirement plan   An employer-sponsored retirement plan that receives special tax benefits if designed, funded, and administered in accordance with applicable federal statutes, rules and regulations.

qualified transportation fringe   Employer-provided benefit for transportation to work and parking. Employees may receive this benefit tax free, within limits, as long as certain rules are adhered to.

qualifying event   Under COBRA, an event that results in loss of coverage by a qualified beneficiary or an increase a qualified beneficiary must pay for coverage.

quarters of coverage   The basis on which eligibility for benefits under Social Security is determined. Credit for up to four quarters of coverage may be earned in any calendar year.

rate   A unit price for each unit of insurance benefit.

rate making   The process of pricing group insurance and employee benefit products.

rating basis The basis on which group insurance rates are determined, involving decisions on the benefit unit to use, the extent to which rates will be refined by factors affecting claims, and the frequency with which premiums will be paid.

reasonable-and-customary charge A charge that falls within the range of fees normally charged for a given procedure by physicians with similar training and experience in a geographic region. It is usually based on some percentile of the range of charges for specific medical procedures.

reasonable compensation A requirement in the tax law for an employer's deductibility of compensation paid to employees, including amounts paid for employee benefits.

referral An authorization by a gatekeeper for a managed care plan member to receive treatment by a specialist. Without a required referral, benefits will not be paid or will be reduced.

referral and discount plan A legal expense plan under which members are referred to an attorney who provides benefits based on a fee schedule or at a discount from his or her usual fees.

referral management A managed care function that requires members to select a primary care physician who will make referrals to specialists for any care he or she cannot provide.

regulation An interpretation of statutory law published by the a government agency; in the case of tax law, regulations are issued by the Treasury Department.

rehabilitation benefit A benefit under workers' compensation laws or disability income plans that provides rehabilitative services for disabled workers. Benefits may be given for medical rehabilitation and for vocational rehabilitation, including training, counseling, and job placement.

rehabilitation provision A provision in a disability income contract that permits an employee to enter a trial work period during which benefits are reduced by some percentage of the earnings from rehabilitative employment.

reimbursement basis The dominant method of paying benefits under long-term care insurance policies. The covered person is reimbursed for actual expenses incurred up to the specified policy limit.

replacement ratio The ratio of retirement income to the retiree's earnings prior to retirement.

reporting and disclosure provisions ERISA requirements for reporting to the government and disclosure to participants of information about employee benefit plans.

reserve-reduction arrangement An alternative funding method under which the employer is allowed at any given time to retain an amount of the annual premium equal to the claim reserve.

respite care Care provided under a long-term care insurance policy for occasional full-time care at home for a person who is receiving home health care. This care enables family members (or other persons) who are providing much of the home care to take a needed break.

restricted stock Company stock provided by a company to executives as additional compensation, with the stock subject to a forfeiture provision such as a requirement that if the executive does not stay with the company for a specified number of years the executive's rights to the stock will be forfeited.

retention The excess of premiums paid over claims payments and dividends.

retired lives reserve A fund established during employees' working years to pay all or a part of the cost of group term insurance after retirement.

retirement income contract A life insurance contract that, if used to fund a qualified defined benefit plan, is designed with rapidly rising cash values so that the cash value at the insured's retirement age is sufficient to provide the full retirement benefit.

retroactive amendment procedure A procedure whereby if an application for an advance determination letter is timely filed, the plan can be amended retroactively to its effective date in order to meet IRS requirements for granting an advance determination letter.

retrospective management An analysis of the pattern of medical care services after the fact to see if the medical treatment performed was appropriate and to take corrective actions as needed.

retrospective rate credit A refund given by stock insurance companies to groups that are experience rated and have had better claims experience than anticipated.

retrospective-rating arrangement An alternative funding method under which the employer pays an initial premium that is less than what would be justified by the expected claims for the year. However, if claims plus the insurance company's retention exceed the initial premium, the employer will be called upon to pay an additional amount at the end of the policy year. There is a cap put on the employer's additional payment, above which the insurance company assumes the risk.

rider An endorsement to an insurance policy for the purpose of adding, deleting, or classifying coverage.

risk charge A factor in the calculation of rates for group insurance benefits. It represents a contribution to an insurance company's contingency reserve as a cushion against unanticipated and catastrophic amounts of claims.

sabbatical leave An extended leave after a period of full employment at full or partial pay, usually to engage in some type of research or study.

safe harbor 401(k) plan A plan design for Section 401(k) plans under which the ADP tests for nondiscrimination are generally deemed to be met automatically.

salary continuation plan *See* sick-leave plan.

salary reduction An arrangement in an employee benefit plan under which an employee can receive all of his or her stated salary in cash, or can elect each year to contribute a specified portion of salary to the plan, typically on a before-tax basis (the salary reduction amount is not subject to income tax). In the case of a qualified plan, a salary reduction provision is also called a *cash or deferral provision*.

salary-reduction-only plan A cafeteria plan that consists solely of one or both types of before-tax salary reductions that can be used in a cafeteria plan—a premium-conversion plan or a flexible spending account.

salary savings plan An informal term used in this text to refer to qualified plans that are entirely or partially funded through employee salary-reduction (deferral election) contributions or employee after-tax contributions.

S corporation A corporation that has made an election under federal tax law to be taxed as a partnership.

second surgical opinion A cost-containment strategy under which covered persons are encouraged or required to obtain the opinion of another physician after certain categories of surgery have been recommended. If a second opinion is mandatory, benefits are reduced if the second opinion is not obtained. Benefits are usually provided for the cost of a third opinion if the opinions of the first two physicians are in disagreement.

Section 125 plan *See* cafeteria plan.

Section 401(k) plan Also referred to as a *cash or deferred plan*, a qualified defined contribution plan in

which employees are offered an option to reduce their stated salary each year and make an equivalent before-tax contribution to the plan, within specified annual dollar limits.

Section 403(b) plan A salary-savings plan similar to a qualified plan that can be adopted only by certain tax-exempt organizations and public schools.

Section 415 limits Limits provided under the Internal Revenue Code on qualified plan benefits or annual contributions (annual additions) to a participant's account intended to reduce discrimination in favor of highly compensated employees.

Section 457 plan A type of salary savings plan similar to a qualified plan that can be adopted only by governmental organizations and tax-exempt organizations.

Section 79 The section of the Internal Revenue Code that provides favorable tax treatment to employer contributions for life insurance that qualifies as group term insurance.

security standards Under HIPAA, rules that require a covered entity to implement measures to maintain reasonable and appropriate administrative, physical, and technical safeguards for electronic personal health information.

self-funding A method by which an employer can finance the cost of an employee benefit plan. In the method's purest sense, the employer pays benefits from current revenue, administers all aspects of the plan, and bears the risk that benefit payments will exceed those expected.

self-insurance *See* self-funding.

self-insured medical reimbursement plan For federal income tax purposes, a self-funded medical expense plan under which employers either pay medical providers directly or reimburse employees for their medical expenses.

self-referral HMO *See* direct-access HMO.

SEP A Simplified Employee Pension, a plan similar to a qualified profit-sharing plan under which employers make contributions that are allocated in a nondiscriminatory manner to IRAs owned by participants.

service-benefit concept Medical expense benefits expressed in terms of services that will be provided by hospitals or physicians rather than in terms of dollar maximums.

settlement options The methods by which proceeds from a group life insurance contract can be received. In general, proceeds are payable in a lump sum unless the insured or the beneficiary has selected an optional form of settlement.

sex (gender) discrimination In the benefit plan context, unlawful differences in benefits or employer contributions to the plan for male and female employees.

shared benefit A provision in a long-term care insurance policy that allows a husband and wife insured under the same policy to access each other's unused benefits.

shared funding *See* specific stop-loss coverage.

short-term disability (STD) income plans Disability income plans that provide benefits for a limited period of time, usually six months or less.

sick-leave plan An uninsured arrangement to replace lost income for a limited period of time, usually on the first day of disability.

side fund In a qualified defined benefit plan using whole life contracts as part of the funding, a trust fund that provides the benefits not provided through the insurance policy cash values.

SIMPLE An employer-sponsored salary-savings plan similar to a qualified plan under which employees make salary reduction contributions and the employer provides mandatory matching contributions.

simplified employee pension *See* SEP.

simplified issue group insurance Coverage that is issued with satisfactory responses to questions on an abbreviated application form.

single-payer plan An approach to national health insurance under which everyone is automatically covered by a single program run by the government.

skilled care Daily nursing and rehabilitative care that can be performed only by or under the supervision of skilled medical personnel and that must be based on doctors' orders.

skilled-nursing facility *See* extended care facility.

Small Employer Health Insurance Availability Model Act An NAIC model act designed to promote medical expense coverage for small employers. Most states have adopted some form of the act.

social adequacy A basic principle of social insurance programs under which benefits are designed to provide a minimum floor of income to all beneficiaries regardless of their economic status.

social insurance Government-run or government-regulated insurance programs designed primarily to solve major social problems that affect a large portion of society. Distinguishing characteristics are compulsory employment-related coverage, partial or total employer financing, benefits prescribed by law, benefits as a matter of right, and emphasis on social adequacy.

social investment strategy A strategy not to invest in organizations that are thought to engage in socially undesirable activities.

Social Security The term commonly used to identify the old-age, survivors, and disability insurance (OASDI) program of the federal government.

Social Security integration Design of a qualified plan formula to reflect that the participant also receives Social Security benefits paid for by the employer.

Social Security Statement A statement that the Social Security Administration issues that enables an employee to verify his or her contributions to the Social Security and Medicare programs. The statement also contains an estimate of benefits that will be available because of retirement, disability, or death.

SPD *See* summary plan description.

specific stop-loss coverage A stop-loss arrangement under which the insurance company reimburses the employer to the extent that claims for any person exceed a specified dollar amount during a given time period.

stacked deductible A medical expense plan deductible that consists of a deductible for each family member and a separate larger family deductible.

staff-model HMO An HMO that owns its own facilities and hires its own physicians. It may also own hospitals, laboratories, or pharmacies, or it may contract for these services.

STD *See* short-term disability income plans.

step therapy The practice in prescription drug plans under which approval for higher cost medications is contingent on a member first trying lower-cost, often well-established drugs to see if they are effective.

stock bonus plan For purposes of this text, a qualified defined contribution plan similar to a profit-sharing plan, except that the participants' accounts are invested in stock of the employer.

stock option An offer to sell stock at a specified price at a specified future time, often used by companies as an incentive form of compensation for its executives.

stop-loss coverage Protection for employers who self-fund benefits. Under this arrangement, an insurance company provides coverage if claims exceed some specified limit during a set period of time. It may apply to aggregate claims or claims on each individual employee.

stop-loss limit (1) The maximum amount of out-of-pocket expenses that a covered person must bear during a period of time under a medical expense plan. Above the stop loss limit, there is 100 percent coinsurance. Sometimes called *coinsurance limit.* (2) The maximum amount of any claim that is charged to a group in an experience-rating calculation.

straight deductible *See* initial deductible.

straight-life annuity A form of payment providing equal annual amounts, ending at the recipient's death.

subrogation provision A provision in a medical expense plan that allows the plan or organization providing plan benefits the right to recover from a third party who is responsible through negligence or other wrongdoing for a covered person's injuries that result in a claim being paid.

subscriber *See* member.

substantial and recurring A requirement for employer contributions to a qualified profit-sharing plan.

successive beneficiary provision A provision found in group term insurance contracts for the payment of proceeds if no beneficiary has been named or if all the beneficiaries have died before the insured. This provision gives the insurance company the right to pay the proceeds at their option to any one or more of the following survivors of the insured person: spouse, children, parents, brothers and sisters, or executor of the employee's estate.

summary annual report A brief description of a plan's annual return/report (Form 5500) that must be automatically provided to each plan participant within nine months after the end of a plan year.

summary of material modification A document required by ERISA that must be automatically provided to plan participants and the Department of Labor within 210 days after the end of a plan year in which a material change was made to the plan.

summary plan description (SPD) A detailed report about an employee benefit plan that ERISA requires a plan administrator to give plan participants within 120 days after the plan's adoption and the Department of Labor upon request. It must also be given to new participants within 90 days of first becoming eligible to participate and be updated at specified times.

supplemental life insurance Additional life insurance that all or certain classes of employees may purchase. Coverage is generally contributory and either incorporated into a basic group life insurance contract or contained in a separate contract.

supplemental major medical coverage A major medical plan that is coordinated with various basic medical expense coverages.

supplemental retirement plans A term often used to describe a *nonqualified deferred compensation plan* for a specific group of executives.

supplemental unemployment benefit (SUB) plan A plan established in collective bargaining agreements under which employers are required to supplement state unemployment insurance benefits for unemployed workers.

surgical expense coverage Medical expense benefits for physicians' charges associated with surgical procedures.

surgical fee schedule A schedule in some insurance policies that specifies the maximum amount that will be paid for listed surgical procedures.

Table I *See* Uniform Premium Table I.

target plan An age-weighted defined contribution pension plan with a fixed actuarial formula for employer contributions to the plan.

taxable amount The portion of the amount realized or distributed that is taxable, not including the distributee's basis or capital investment.

tax-deferred annuity plan Another term for Section 403(b) plan.

tax-sheltered annuities A term sometimes used to describe a Section 403(b) plan.

telephone access plan A legal expense plan that provides unlimited telephone use for most legal matters. There may be a small amount of consultation time available, with discounts on further services.

temporary disability laws A program in a few states that requires employers to provide short-term disability income benefits to employees for non-work-related disabilities. These laws are often referred to as *nonoccupational disability laws.*

term cost The value of pure life insurance protection (the death benefit from a life insurance policy less its cash value, if any) provided to an employee under an employee benefit plan.

terminal report A report that ERISA requires be filed with the Internal Revenue Service for an employee welfare benefit plan that has been terminated. This report must be given to plan participants upon request.

term insurance Life insurance which provides death benefits for a limited period of time.

therapeutic substitution The substitution of a drug that has a similar therapeutic effect as a prescribed drug. Such substitution requires the approval of a patient's physician.

third-party administrator (TPA) A person or organization hired to provide certain administrative services to employee benefit plans.

top-heavy plan A qualified plan that provides excessive benefits to key employees under Section 416 of the Internal Revenue Code and must therefore provide certain enhanced benefits for non-key employees.

TPA *See* third-party administrator.

trade association An eligible group for group insurance. The association, however, is formed for purposes other than providing benefits to employees. It usually consists of employers in the same industry or type of business. The master contract may be issued directly to the trade association or to a trust that has been established.

traditional medical expense plan A medical expense plan under which patients have considerable freedom to choose providers of medical care, claims are paid on the basis of billed charges, and there are virtually no attempts to control costs.

transaction and code set standards Under HIPAA, a code system established for diagnosis and treatment as well as electronic transmitting of health information.

trust agreement The *funding instrument* for a trust under a qualified plan.

underwriting The process by which an insurance applicant is evaluated, decisions are made on his or her acceptability for insurance, and a rating basis is established.

unemployment insurance Joint federal and state programs to provide income benefits to unemployed workers who meet the specific program requirements. In most states, these programs are financed entirely by employer contributions.

Uniformed Services Employment and Reemployment Rights Act (USERRA) A federal law that entities an employee who leaves a civilian job for active military duty to return to the job with accrued seniority.

Uniform Premium Table I A table incorporated into IRS regulations for Section 79 that is used to determine imputed income for group term insurance in excess of $50,000.

unit-benefit formula A defined-benefit pension formula that provides a specified unit of benefit for each of the participant's years of service.

United States Longshore and Harbor Workers' Act A federal law that provides workers' compensation benefits for stevedores, longshoremen, and workers who repair ships.

universal access The availability of medical expense coverage to all persons, even though they may not actually purchase coverage.

universal coverage Coverage of all Americans under some type of universal health plan.

unrealized appreciation In a qualified plan that invests in employer stock, the increase in value, if any, of stock between the time it is allocated to the participant's account and the time it is distributed to the participant. Such unrealized appreciation is not currently taxed to the participant if stock is distributed in a lump sum distribution.

unrelated business taxable income Income from a business or similar activity that is taxable even though carried on by a nominally tax-exempt organization.

URAC An organization that accredits specific aspects of managed care, such as utilization review.

USERRA *See* Uniformed Services Employment and Reemployment Rights Act.

usual, reasonable, and customary charge *See* reasonable-and-customary charge.

utilization management The process of reviewing the appropriateness and quality of care provided to patients. It consists of demand management, referral management, and management of institutional services.

valuation date A date on which participants' accounts in qualified defined contribution plans are valued.

VEBA *See* 501(c)(9) trust.

vested benefit A benefit in a pension plan or other employee benefit plan that is not forfeitable by the employee.

vesting schedule A schedule in an employee benefit plan specifying when a participant's benefits become non-forfeitable, usually over a period of years of employment.

vision plan An employee benefit plan that provides benefits for vision care expenses that are not usually covered under other medical expense plans. Benefits are provided for the cost of eye examinations and eyeglasses or contact lenses.

voluntary benefit A plan offered to employees under which an employee may purchase individual insurance coverage with the premium paid through payroll deductions by the employee.

voluntary employees' beneficiary association (VEBA) *See* 501(c)(9) trust.

waiting period A period of time that an employee must be disabled (or otherwise wait) before benefits commence under certain employee benefit plans, such as disability income insurance, Social Security, and workers' compensation insurance. Waiting periods for disabilities resulting from accidents may differ from waiting periods for disabilities resulting from sickness. Waiting periods are also used in long-term care insurance.

waiver-of-premium provision A provision in group insurance plans under which coverage is continued without the payment of premiums as long as an employee is totally disabled.

welfare benefits The term used to describe employee benefits other than retirement benefits.

wellness program An employer-provided program to promote the well-being of employees and sometimes their dependents. Such a program may be designed to discover and treat medical conditions before they become severe and/or change employees' lifestyles to eliminate possible causes of future medical problems.

whole life contract A life insurance contract that provides cash values that increase up to an advanced age such as age 90.

withhold arrangement A system under managed care that imposes financial penalties or decreases compensation if physicians fail to meet budgeted cost and utilization levels.

Women's Health and Cancer Rights Act A federal act that requires medical expense plans which provide benefits for mastectomy to also cover breast reconstruction, surgery on the other breast to produce a symmetrical appearance, and prostheses.

workers' compensation laws Social insurance programs in all states under which employers are required to provide benefits to employees for losses resulting from work-related accidents or diseases. Benefits include medical care, disability income, income for survivors, and rehabilitative services.

work/life approach The concept of providing benefits at work so that employees can more fully enjoy their lives outside the office. Examples include flexible work schedules, child-care plans, family leave, and on-site services, such as travel agencies, post offices, and pharmacies.

yearly renewable term insurance Term insurance that is renewed annually with each successive policy period being for one year.